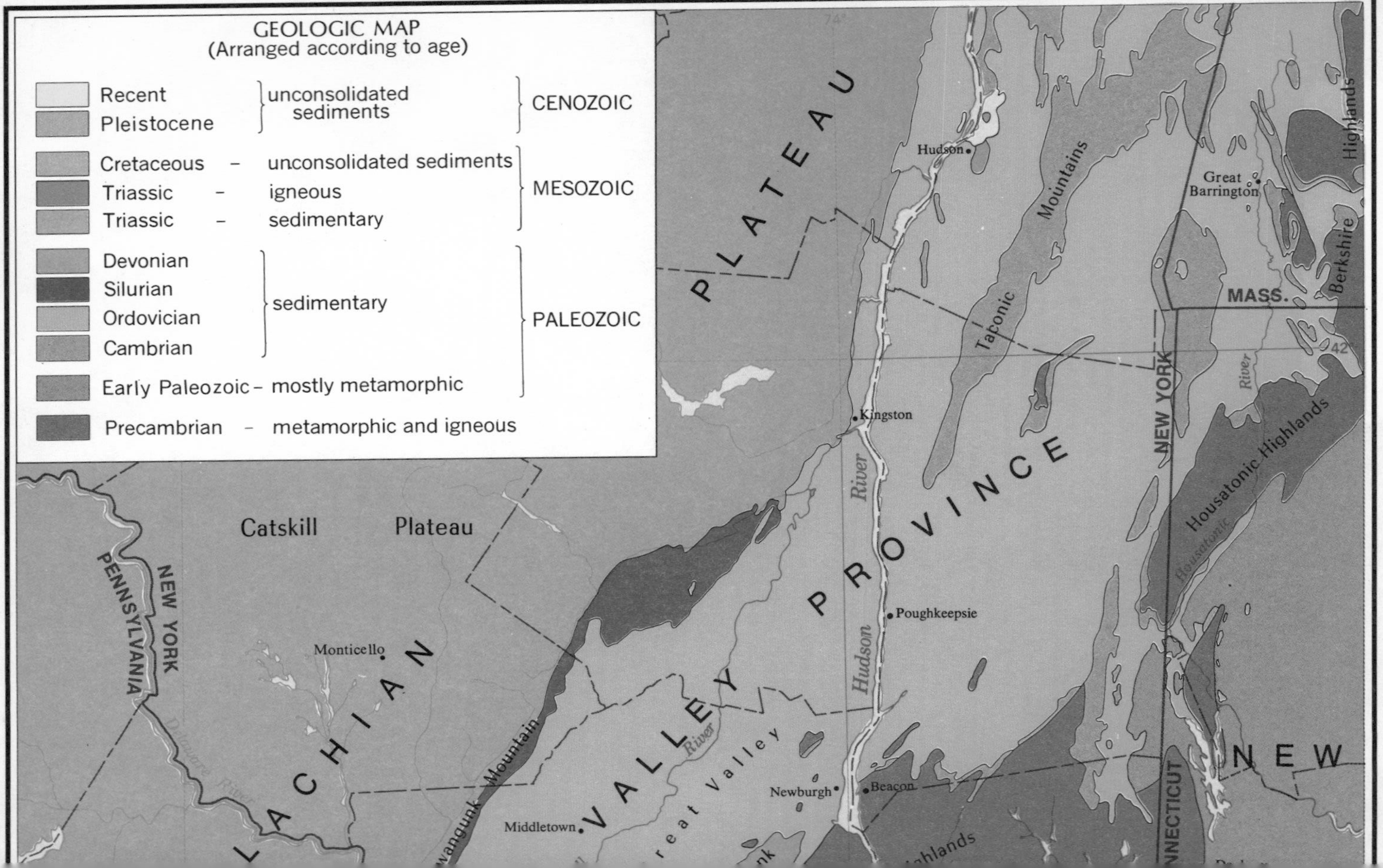
GEOLOGIC MAP
(Arranged according to age)
Recent
Pleistocene
unconsolidated sediments
CENOZOIC
Cretaceous – unconsolidated sediments
Triassic – igneous
Triassic – sedimentary
MESOZOIC
Devonian
Silurian
Ordovician
Cambrian
sedimentary
Early Paleozoic – mostly metamorphic
PALEOZOIC
Precambrian – metamorphic and igneous
PLATEAU
Hudson
Kingston
Poughkeepsie
Newburgh
Beacon
Middletown
Monticello
Great Barrington
Taconic Mountains
Housatonic Highlands
Housatonic
Berkshire
Highlands
MASS.
NEW YORK
NEW
NNECTICUT
Catskill Plateau
PROVINCE
VALLEY
LACHIAN
Hudson River
River
Delaware River
reat Valley
Mountain
NEW YORK
PENNSYLVANIA
74°
42

ENGLAND
UPLAND
RIDGE AND
NEWARK
BASIN
ATLANTIC
COASTAL
PLAIN
Port Jervis
Kittatinny Mountain
Stroudsburg
Newton
Prong
Jersey
Highlands
Ramapo Mountains
Suffern
Hudson
Bear Mountain
Peekskill
Haverstraw
Croton on Hudson
NEW YORK
NEW JERSEY
White Plains
Stamford
Long Island Sound
41°
Paterson
Palisades
Manhattan Prong
Fort Lee
Harbor Hill Moraine
Ronkonkoma Moraine
Long Island
Reading Prong
Morristown
Watchung Mountains
Newark
Phillipsburg
Somerville
NEW JERSEY
PENNA.
New Brunswick
Perth Amboy
Staten Island
Rockaway Beach
Jones Beach
ATLANTIC OCEAN
Sandy Hook
0
10
20
MILES
74°

Geology of the Lower Hudson Valley

NEW YORK WALK BOOK

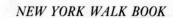

NEW YORK

Pen sketches by Robert L. Dickinson

and Richard Edes Harrison

WALK BOOK

FIFTH EDITION

COMPLETELY REVISED
UNDER THE SPONSORSHIP OF THE
New York–New Jersey Trail Conference

ANCHOR BOOKS
ANCHOR PRESS/DOUBLEDAY
Garden City, New York
1984

Library of Congress Cataloging in Publication Data

Main entry under title:

New York walk book.

Includes index.
1. Hiking—New York Metropolitan Area—Guide-books.
2. Trails—New York Metropolitan Area—Guide-books.
3. New York Metropolitan Area—Description—1981–
—Guide-books. I. New York–New Jersey Trail Conference.
GV199.42.N652N486 1984 917.47'044 82-45115
ISBN 0-385-15584-0

Printed in the United States of America

PREFACE

IN THE early 1920s, New York City, with the boundaries we know today, had been in existence a mere quarter century. Farms dotted the outlying boroughs, and surrounding suburbs measured their populations in hundreds instead of today's hundreds of thousands. The Appalachian Trail and the Palisades Interstate Park Commission were in their infancy. Hikers, or "trampers" as they were sometimes called, had to depend on word-of-mouth or the indulgence of local residents to learn of trails in the New York–New Jersey area.

Then in 1923, three tireless and talented men, Raymond H. Torrey, Frank Place, Jr., and Robert L. Dickinson, produced the first edition of the *New York Walk Book,* under the sponsorship of the American Geographical Society. The volume offered trail descriptions by Mr. Torrey, historical and geological lore by Mr. Place, and Dr. Dickinson's intricate, enchanting sketches. It soon became a fixture in the packs of the region's walkers and was revised and greatly expanded by the three men in 1934.

Eventually the open space around us shrank as our vocabularies expanded to include megalopolis, thruway, and suburbia. Like the grizzly seeking higher ground in the face of encroaching civilization, those who turned to the outdoors for respite found ever-narrower bands of undeveloped land. As old trails disappeared or were rerouted and new paths were blazed, the *Walk*

Book again needed revision. Volunteers under the aegis of the New York–New Jersey Trail Conference accomplished this task in 1951. Just then the postwar boom was beginning to rearrange the landscape to such an extent that the Trail Conference published yet another revision in 1971, this time with additional sketches by Richard Edes Harrison, whose style and eye for detail so perfectly matched that of Dr. Dickinson.

In presenting this, the fifth edition, we hope to preserve the spirit of earlier versions. With more sketches by Mr. Harrison and expanded sections on new hiking areas, we've attempted to present a picture of current hiking routes as best as any fluid, ever-changing situation can be captured in print. At the same time, the edition includes new material on natural history and background information from earlier editions—all designed to provide both enlightening reading and pleasurable walking.

From the rugged terrain of the Hudson Highlands to the gentler countryside closer to New York City, the walks described here vary greatly in length, difficulty, and setting, but each offers a contrast to an increasingly urban and technological environment.

This edition will, we hope, give those who read it the incentive to experience a sunset from a Catskill peak, to wander in the stark beauty of pine-barren country, to stroll around a Westchester pond, to walk a path that Washington's soldiers trod, or to find an endangered flower in the midst of suburbia.

Above all, we hope to encourage you to partake of the special joy that comes from a brisk walk, that sharpening of the senses that makes us all feel more alive. For as we become attuned to the natural rhythms of the world, we begin, as Thoreau said, "to confront only the essential facts of life."

NEW YORK–NEW JERSEY TRAIL CONFERENCE

New York Walk Book Committee:
Janet Gross, co-chairman and editor
Helen Ostrowski, co-chairman and editor
Tom Casey, editor
Ken Lloyd, map coordinator
Tom Millard, map chairman
Michael Sabrio, editor
George Zoebelein, editor

ACKNOWLEDGMENTS

This edition of the *New York Walk Book* could not have been possible without the assistance of many generous people. We would especially like to thank George Harlow, associate curator, New York Museum of Natural History, who assisted with the new geology introduction, contributed several new geological entries, and checked all geological references; John Serrao, naturalist, Greenbrook Sanctuary, who reviewed natural history references and wrote several new sections on flora and fauna; and Miklos Pinther, who played a key role in revising the maps. Valuable information, advice, and general support were also provided by: Warren Balgooyen, Teatown Lake Reservation; Eugene Curry, Mianus River Gorge Conservation Committee; Jack Karnig, forest superintendent, Harvard Black Rock Forest; Peter Keibel, Hudson River Nature Center, The Nature Conservancy; Bruce Keeler, Somerset County Park Commission; Paul Krarup, Essex County Department of Cultural Affairs and Recreation; James Ransom, author of *Vanishing Ironworks of the Ramapos;* Tim Sullivan, chief ranger for the Palisades Interstate Park Commission; and the Hammond Map Store.

In addition, we are particularly indebted to Frank Oliver, who contributed the newest chapter in the book, "The Ramapos of New Jersey," and Robert Redington, who prepared the entire chapter on the Southern Taconics, each of whom also handled fieldwork for the map of his area. We also acknowledge the contributions of Neil Zimmerman, who updated the entire chapter on the Catskills, and Ike Siskind, who organized the members of the Ramapo Chapter of the Adirondack Mountain Club for their field-checking of the trails in Bear Mountain–Harriman State Parks. Maurice Avery and Donna Horn also merit special mention for their work in preparing the Shawangunk and Kittatinny chapters, respectively.

Finally, we would like to express our appreciation to all those members and friends of the New York–New Jersey Trail Conference who donated their time and effort in walking trails, gathering and checking facts, history, and legends, and preparing trail descriptions:

Contributors to the Walk Book

Catherine Allen
Oton Ambroz
Rick Anderson
John Blenninger
Richard Block
Ludwig Bohler
Frank Bouton
Hal and Mimi Cohen
John Cryan
George Delano
William Donnelly
Elizabeth Engels
Albert Field
Ken and Valerie Garrison
James Gartner
Frederick Gerty, Jr.
John Giuffrida
Helen and Lawrence Gross
Marilyn Gross
Richard Grunebaum
Kim Hausner
Don Hendrickson
Rudolf Henkel
Herb Hiller
Louise Kaiser
Bob Katz
Al Kent
Herman Klausen
Paul Leiken
John Linderman
James Lober
George LoCascio
Bob Lommel
Joan McFarland
David Mack
Leonard Magnus
Nancy Manfredonia
Stewart Manville
Alice Maram
Bert May
Jack and Sue Morrison
George Muller
Bill Myles
Lorraine Nicholetti
Dick Nicholson
Vince Obal
Marion Olsen
Peter Ovenburg
Kip Patnode
Larry Paul
Frank Perutz
Howard Pierson
Dick Redfield
Dan Rile
Al Rosen
Jim Ross
Ruth Russell
Charles Sanders
Tom Sanders
George Schelling
George Schmidt
Arthur Schneier
John Schoen
Aaron Schoenberg
Marianne Schubert
Bruce Scofield
Roy and Carolyn Sengstacken
Stephen Sepe
Mary Sive
June and Gene Slade
F. I. Smith
Gilbert Snyder
Marian and Jim Stankard
Tim Sullivan
Harris Tallen
Robert Vogel
Bert Waller
Dick Warner
Richard Weinland
Vic Williams
Paul Wilson
Tom Yoannou

CONTENTS

Part IV: New Jersey

MAPS

TRAIL MAPS *(back of book)*

NEW YORK WALK BOOK

'Send your road is clear before you when the old
Spring-fret comes o'er you
And the Red Gods call for you

Kipling: Feet of the Young Men

THE LOOK-OFF

(from the first edition)

SOIL THAT was ever Indian can never lose all of that impress. Our Island of Islands, borne down at one end by the world's biggest burden of steel and stone and pressure of haste and material gain, still holds, on the primitive sweep of its further free tip, the Redman's cave and the beached canoe, tall trees, steep cliffs, and airs of the Great Spirit. The magic of the moccasin still makes good medicine. Fortunate are we that in civilization lurks the antidote to civilization—that strain in the blood of all of us, of caveman and treeman, of nomad and seaman, of chopper and digger, of fisher and trailer, crying out to this call of the earth, to this tug of freefoot up-and-over, to the clamor for out-and-beyond. Happy are we, in our day, harking back to this call, to be part of an ozone revival toward lucky finds in this wide fair wilderness and toward breakaway into Everyman's Out-of-doors.

The order and fashion of the revival were somewhat in this wise. Our seniors remember the days of swift expansion, when the sole concern was the building site. "Blast the scenery," said the seventies and proceeded to do it. Railroads and roads and money returns from quarries and lumber had full right of way. Into our towns one came, through the ugly suburbs, into uglier urbs. And then, when hope was least, a messenger of the new-old freedom appeared. The bicycle swung us, a generation now white-haired, round a wide radius of country roads, and gave back to us the calves and the leg gear of our patroon saint, Father Knickerbocker, and with the legs two eyes for environs. When the time came for supplanting tandem tired by a rubber quartette, and a touch of the toe leapt past all two legs could do, a motor radius that swept a circle almost infinitely wide gave new concepts of the countrysides. Still attention was focused on the roadway, and the new driver saw even less over wheel than over handlebar. Next golf arose, and the well-to-do strolled upon greenswards, ever watching a ball. Then scout training arrived to set the young generation on its feet and to teach it to see what it saw and to care for itself in the open. With it came nature study to fill the woods and fields with life and growth. And then the fashion for walking was upon us—walking, with its leisure to observe the detail of beauty; walking, organized and planned, imparting impetus to safeguard and preserve the best of the countryside: walking, the only simple exercise, at once democratic, open-air, wide-eyed, year-round.

It has been amusing to watch New York, which is hardly in other ways hesitant, waken by degrees to the idea that as a center for exercise on foot she may claim variety and advantage and adventure surpassed by few cities. You can choose your walk along the sweep of the beaches of the Atlantic, of the deep hill bays of Long Island, or the rocky coves of Connecticut; over ridges showing fair silhouettes of the citadels and cathedrals of commerce—or where beavers build; on the looped, mile-long bridges that span an estuary—or across a canal lock; above precipices overhanging a mighty river and through noble community forests between lonely peaks and little lakes—or just in lovely common country, rolling and wooded, meadowed, and elm-dotted, interlaced with chuckling brooks. To and from these multitudinous footways and campsites transportation is provided with an expedition and diversity possible only to a large city. And, last of all, the chance at this will be under the variegated stimulus of our particular climate and around the only great capital that is within easy reach of the second color wonder of the world—Indian summer in steep-hill country.

Truly with the "Englysche Bybels" that antedate King James's we may say:

Blessed of the LORDE is this land,
for the sweetnesse of heven, and of the scee vnderliende;
for the sprynges;
for the precious thinges off the Sonne;
for the sweetnesse of the toppes of the oold mounteynes,
and for the daynties of the hillis that last foreuer.

Raymond H. Torrey
Frank Place, Jr.
Robert L. Dickinson

Spring 1923

AN INTRODUCTION TO THE GEOLOGY OF THE NEW YORK REGION

You needn't be a geologist to notice that the region within a hundred-mile radius of Manhattan is as diverse a landscape as will be found anywhere in this country. Head for the shore of Long Island or New Jersey and you will traverse sandy coastal plains. Go north from the Battery, staying east of the Hudson through Westchester and on to Connecticut, and you will pick your way over the southern reaches of rocky New England terrain. Journey west past the Palisades and the expanse of the Newark Basin opens before you. Beyond it lie long, sinuous ridges and valleys running northeast into New York State. Still farther west stretches the Appalachian Plateau, taking in the Poconos and their more steeply eroded cousins to the north, the Catskills. Each of these five distinct physiographic provinces, identified on the frontispiece map, has a fascinating origin. Each offers its own rewards for hikers.

Distinct though they are, the provinces share a common heritage in the inexorable processes that continue to change the surface of the earth. At the root of all these forces is the relatively recent but generally accepted model of *plate tectonics,* which depicts the earth as a hot, somewhat plastic ball with a brittle skin. The interior behaves something like a pot of boiling water, convecting in a rolling motion, and the less-dense skin—the continental plates—tends to follow along, "floating" on the mantle beneath. Where all of this material rises, it breaks up; where it falls, it is compressed or pushed down into the mantle. Thus the junctions of colliding plates are often marked by the formation of mountain ridges, island chains, or deep trenches. These movements take place over virtually incomprehensible eons.

In the last 500 million years, the New York region has been subjected to the breakup, collision, and again the breakup of plates, coupled with the unending forces of erosion that make the surface of the earth smoother, in proportion to its size, than an eggshell. The region has also seen volcanism, mountain-building (orogeny), deposition of sediments, heating and compression (metamorphism), and occasional submergence beneath advancing seas. On the surface, immense sheets of ice have periodically bulldozed, scarred, and generally rearranged the land. A detailed account of the order and frequency of these events is best left to a geology text. What follows is an overview of how the land formed and how it looks at this geological moment.

No province offers hikers richer visual evidence of the forces that have shaped the earth than the *New England Uplands.* Two spurs of this complicated, broken terrain extend into a number of areas familiar to readers of the *Walk Book.* One, the Manhattan Prong, underlies Westchester, the Bronx, and Manhattan before ending in the northern tip of Staten Island; the other, the Reading Prong, gives the Hudson and New Jersey Highlands their character as it courses southwest into Pennsylvania. Both prongs present evidence of how glaciers, which receded a "mere" ten thousand years ago, left their traces on the oldest rocks visible in our region.

The Highlands are the roots of mountains formed 1100 to 1200 million years ago largely from sediments deposited by ancient seas. As they accumulated to a thickness of several miles, they compressed and heated until they metamorphosed into gneisses, marbles, and mica-rich schists. These, along with diorite that intruded as magma, are the oldest rocks in the area. Associated with this Highlands Complex is a medium-grained, gray granite which may be, unlike most, metamorphic in origin. This "Canada Hill granite phase" shows clearly on Anthonys Nose, just east of the Bear Mountain Bridge. Another form of granite, the igneous rock of Storm King, is highly resistant to erosion and caps the crests of Bear Mountain, Dunderberg, West Mountain, and most other prominent ridges in the Highlands.

Even as the mountains rose, in a period called the Grenville Orogeny, erosion gnawed at their flanks, limiting their height to about fifteen thousand feet and leaving enormous deposits of sediments to the west. By about 600 million years ago, little was left but a flat land of resistant rock. In another 140 million years, the Taconic Orogeny, interpreted as the result of a collision of continental plates, began another episode of uplifting and folding, leaving the Highlands and Taconics in their present position. What was once an eastern version of the Rocky Mountains had now become a tortuously folded region with summits no higher than thirteen hundred feet.

Stand atop one of these rises and you will look out upon a landscape of rounded knobs and ridges. Much of this is the result of simple weathering, age upon age of wind and water, freeze and thaw, that reduces the mightiest peaks. Still more of this rounding is the work of waves of Pleistocene glaciers whose handiwork is visible everywhere in the Highlands. Moving sheets of ice thousands of feet thick scraped their way across the area as they advanced south-southeast. As they did, they abraded north slopes with debris transported from the north, and pried and plucked rocks from south slopes. Called either *roches moutonnées* or sheepbacks, these smooth outcrops with rugged south sides are common in the Highlands.

The glaciers also transported large boulders, called "erratics" because they are often of a different composition from the ground upon which they now rest. Sandstone erratics brought thirty-five miles from Schunemunk Mountain are common in the Highlands. Likewise, chunks of the Highlands appear on the Palisades, and blocks of the Palisades surface in Brooklyn. Finer debris from all these places and points north color the sands of Coney Island. In Harriman Park, erratics dot Hogencamp Mountain, among others; occasionally, erratics, such as Hippo Rock on Fingerboard Mountain, become propped at odd angles or balanced on smaller rocks and become popular landmarks for hikers.

Frequently, accumulations of glacial debris, or "drift," rode to the valley bottoms on torrents of meltwater and piled up in irregular hillocks, or "kames." The same water settled into shallow glacial lakes throughout the region. Lakes by nature are fleeting phenomena; flowing water tends to downcut their outlets and drain them, turning them into swamps. Patches of valley floor covered in willow are likely the sites of former lakes. Occasionally, the old outlets have been dammed and the lakes recreated, as in the Seven Lakes area of Harriman Park in the 1920s and '30s.

More subtle footprints of the glaciers exist in the striations and gouges that marked many of the region's exposed rocks as drift ground into them. More pronounced pits and furrows, however, are usually the work of weathering forces. One common feature of the Highlands that is partly glacial in origin is exfoliation, the leaf-like flaking of rock as it uplifts. Much of this uplift has its roots in mountain-building forces, but some is the result of the off-loading of the great ice sheet. Bear Mountain's summit is a good place to see this rounding process at work.

As the majestic Hudson River slices through the Highlands, it illustrates yet another effect of the Pleistocene Era. Ice speeding up as it cut through the narrow Hudson Gorge cut the river channel well below sea level. Thus the river here is a fjord, the only one on the east coast south of Maine.

The Manhattan Prong of the New England Uplands is a generally younger and less hilly terrain than the Highlands. The oldest rock in the prong, the tough, crystalline Fordham gneiss, dates anywhere from 575 to 1100 million years ago. Overlying this is the glittery mica schist familiar to anyone who has visited Central Park, and the softer Inwood marble. Both are about 350 million years old. Contact between the two is visible on the Manhattan shore of Spuyten Duyvil. In Westchester and Putnam counties, all three types are complexly folded together.

The Manhattan skyline in the midtown and Wall Street areas reflects in striking profile where the skyscrapers rest on this solid bedrock. In the area in between, which includes Chinatown and Greenwich Village, the bedrock dips too low to anchor the foundations. The tip of the prong continues on to include Clove Lakes Park, La Tourette Park, and other sections traversed by the Staten Island Greenbelt Trail. Prominent here is the greenish serpentinite, visible in Clove Lakes Park and on Forest Avenue. Along with the salt-and-pepper Harrison diorite of the Bronx and the more northerly Hartland schist, they are the product of the collision of continental plates at the time of the Taconic Orogeny. At that time, an island arc of volcanic origin, analogous to the modern Aleutians, slammed into the East Coast, burying the region that is now the Manhattan Prong, creating igneous intrusions, and metamorphosing some formations. Thus a portion of the prong is younger rock welded to older types by tectonic forces. Near the tip of the prong, the serpentinite is buried under the terminal Harbor Hill Moraine, the limit of the last advance of the great Wisconsin Ice Sheet. This glacial dumping ground reaches 410 feet above sea level at Todt Hill, the highest point on the Atlantic seaboard south of Massachusetts.

The *Ridge and Valley Province* constitutes the great Appalachian cordillera that runs northeast to Newfoundland and southwest to Alabama. In our region its two prominent features are the Great Valley, extending from the Hudson and Wallkill watersheds to the Shenandoah Valley, and a long, narrow ridge the Lenape Indians called "Endless Mountain." We now call the latter Shawangunk Mountain in New York, Kittatinny in New Jersey, and Blue and Tuscarora mountains in Pennsylvania.

The Great Valley contains, from the bottom up, layers of sandstone, limestone and dolomite, siltstone, and claystone, all deposited between 550 and 345 million years ago by intruding seas. The bottom layer slightly metamorphosed into quartzite; alongside Kittatinny Mountain, the top layer changed into the largest deposit of gray slate in the country, the Martinsburg formation. Low, steep-sided kames dot the valley.

The rocks of Kittatinny and Shawangunk were deposited atop the valley claystone around the time of the Taconic Orogeny. Their strikingly white quartzite originally consisted of sandstones and conglomerates, which were partially marine sediments and partially the erosional waste of the ancestral Taconics. Called the Queenston Delta, the rubble sloped to the west much in the way the Great Plains now slope to the east from the Rockies, and gradually filled in a shallow western sea that had left limestone deposits. As the mountains wore down, the rivers that ate at them flowed at a shallower angle, and so were able to carry only finer muds and silts, which formed the darker top layer of the deposits. Orogenic forces during the Acadian Orogeny, over 350 million years ago, folded and faulted the Ridge and Valley Province even as the sediments accumulated. Differential erosion between soft limestones and shales and the more resistant layers created the parallel ridges that mark the region.

One of the best places to observe the features of the province is the Delaware Water Gap, one of the narrowest segments of this mountain system. The magnificent gap itself demonstrates the power of the Delaware as it cut through the gradually uplifting terrain. The cleft was made long before the last ice sheets receded through here about seventeen thousand years ago. Large talus blocks of sandstone and conglomerate on Kittatinny's southeast side overlie Martinsburg slate, which is visible in outcrops along Route 46 to the south. East of the gap on Interstate 80, a scenic overlook offers a fine view of the broad valley and the "endless" mountain.

Two peculiarities of the Ridge and Valley Province are Schunemunk and Bellevale mountains, whose resistant caps of sandstone and conglomerate are more related to the Catskills, at least twenty miles distant, than they are to the surrounding ridges. Though their origin is uncertain, they seem likely to be extensions of the plateau country that lies north and west; whether the plateau once reached even beyond these points is a matter of conjecture.

The *Appalachian Plateau* itself presents a somewhat less complicated geological history. It was formed from a combination of sediments eroded out of mountains to the east and others deposited by seas to the west in Devonian time, roughly 350 to 400 million years ago. Although at first glance they may seem to be different, the Poconos, Catskills, and much of Central New York are products of the same deposition. The plateau was gently westward-sloping terrain which rose to as much as four thousand feet above sea level without being radically folded during the ancient mountain-building episodes. Thus the Poconos and Catskills are not mountains in a strict geological sense. What gave the province the relief it now exhibits was the relentless power of streams carving deep, V-shaped valleys into the plateau.

The Poconos, in particular, retain the aspect of plateau country; drive north on Interstate 380 or find any high overlook, and the evenness of the highest elevations becomes apparent. Interspersed with these "mountains" are relatively narrow streambeds. In the Catskills, on the other hand, streams ran their courses through greater thicknesses of sediment; their valleys widened with age and eroded toward the water's source, leaving fractions of the plateau isolated as high peaks. Slide, Thomas Cole, Blackhead, and all the other summits here are what is left of the plateau. A topographical map of the Catskills gives a good "aerial view" that makes it easier to understand the extent and direction of these forces.

Glaciation and weathering have helped shape the Catskills into the fabled land of Rip Van Winkle. There is evidence of this in the rounded summits, the talus slopes, the telltale grooves and gouges. Almost any wooded hillside will tell you that subtle changes still occur: curved tree trunks bending skyward show that in their lifetime the soil has crept downhill, seeking the valley bottom. In ages to come, the plateau will be level again.

After all the orogenic and depositional forces ended, a rifting process—begun when the African continent began to split away from North America to which it had been welded for over a hundred million years—formed the *Newark Basin* between 190 and 150 million years ago. The floor of the basin is a large block of undeformed sandstones and shales that faulted at its eastern and western edges and tilted slightly downward to the west. Similar fault-block basins are found near Gettysburg, Pennsylvania, and Southbury, Connecticut, and in the Connecticut River Valley. Its northwestern boundary runs roughly from Haverstraw southwest through Suffern and Morristown, and on into Pennsylvania. Called the Ramapo-Canopus Fault, the western side formed a scarp a few thousand feet higher than the eastern expanse; as it eroded, the higher block filled the regions below it with sediments.

As the basin widened, molten rock intruded through cracks in the floor parallel to the Ramapo Fault. The Watchungs and Hook Mountain were formed of fine-grained black basalt that poured out upon the surface. The Palisades—the geologic feature best known to residents of the metropolitan area—intruded in thicknesses up to a thousand feet, in a line extending from Haverstraw to Staten Island. Unlike the Watchungs, magma never reached the surface while the Palisades were forming. Instead, a subterranean sill cooled and crystallized more slowly into coarser diabase, the columnar rock so prominent in the cliffs along the Hudson. Uplift and weathering then exposed the sill. The freezing and expansion of water seeping into the cliffs has broken the diabase into large blocks that litter the foot of the Palisades. These slopes resemble giant stairs; deriving its name from "trappa," the Swedish word for stairs, traprock has long been quarried in the Palisades and crushed for industrial uses. The diabase was used extensively in the late nineteenth century as "Belgian bluestone" to pave much of lower Manhattan. The creation of the Palisades Interstate Park Commission helped end quarrying operations that could have left the cliffs extensively scarred. Another basin resource, red sandstone, is still visible in the old brownstone houses of Manhattan and Brooklyn.

Hikers will notice frequent erratics and glacial scarring atop the Palisades. In this province, the Wisconsin Ice Sheet reached as far south as Metuchen and left an arc of terminal moraine that stretched north beyond Morristown before swinging west under what is now Interstate 80. As it receded, the melting ice created Glacial Lake Hackensack, which covered the northern part of the basin west of the Palisades. Today the Meadowlands are its slowly drying vestige.

The *Atlantic Coastal Plain*, extending from Long Island to Florida, is the youngest of the provinces, having formed out of the unconsolidated sediments of flood plains and river deltas over the last 75 million years. Abundant plant fossils indicate these nonmarine origins, while sharks' teeth and fragments of marine reptiles suggest periodic invasions of shallow seas. The plain was greatly reduced in width when the sea level rose at the end of the last glacial period. The pre-Pleistocene sediments remain clearly definable throughout the flat expanse of southern New Jersey, where elevations rarely approach three hundred feet. Commercial sand-and-gravel operations, common on the plain, attest to its deltaic origin, and clay deposits figured in a once-thriving pottery industry in New Jersey.

On Long Island, however, much of the original deposition

from rivers in New England is buried under two terminal moraines—the Ronkonkoma and the younger Harbor Hill—and the outwash plain created when glacial streams carried sands and silts toward the sea. The island's backbone and eastern forks are all morainal, ending spectacularly in the bluffs of Montauk Point, where rising seas inundated the outwash and brought the surf to the base of the glacial rubble. The same seas invaded a shallow depression that is now Long Island Sound. Many erratics sprinkle the moraine, from huge Shelter Rock in Nassau County to small boulders nestled unobtrusively in quiet corners of the Pine Barrens of Suffolk. Isolated ice blocks left water-filled depressions—or kettles—such as Lake Ronkonkoma; smaller, dried-out kettles are much less apparent to the eye but are easy to spot on a topographical map of Suffolk County, which will also reveal subtle traces of channels that once bore the ice's runoff seaward.

The coast's numerous barrier beaches and sandspits are the ever-shifting manifestations of littoral drift, the transportation of sand on prevailing ocean currents. So swift is this action that Colonial maps of the Jersey Shore and Long Island bear little resemblance to modern ones. Fire Island and Sandy Hook, for instance, have been reshaped considerably by tugging currents and buffeting storms. Indeed, some strands have grown at a rate approaching a mile every quarter century, by geological standards an incredibly swift pace.

The rapid changes wrought in the fragile dunes contrast markedly with the seeming stability of Highlands bedrock, yet everywhere we look we see that change governs the landscape. We say "to move at a glacial pace" when we wish to describe a slow procession of events; but in the unfathomable expanses of time involved in shaping the earth, the glaciers were here but yesterday, and their icy breath still chills the hollows and dells they departed ten thousand years ago. To stand braced against the wind atop a Highlands ridge, to let the surf pull at our feet, to ford a rushing brook in spring, to step gingerly over the icy talus of the Palisades—all this is to feel firsthand the great forces still at work around us. We can contemplate with awe the hundreds of millions of years of history beneath our feet as we walk in solitude in this, our speck of time in an ever-old, ever-new world.

Part I

WEST OF THE HUDSON RIVER

Column near Greenbrook above the dock at Lambiers
The Palisades Interstate Park
Dickinson

1 · *THE PALISADES*

(Map 4)

SOME EARLY voyager up the Hudson named the cliffs of the lower river the Palisades, probably from the likeness of the giant pillars of traprock to the palisaded villages of the Indians. There has been much debate as to whether the first European to see the Hudson was Giovanni da Verrazano, a Florentine in the service of the King of France, or Estévan Gomez, a Portuguese in the service of the King of Spain. The controversy hinges on a famous letter which the Verrazano supporters claim he addressed to Francis I of France on July 8, 1524, in which he relates his entry in March 1524 into what, from his description, his opponents as well as his supporters agree could have been none other than the Upper Bay. However, there seems to be no question as to the authenticity of Gomez's voyage along the east coast of North America in 1525 and his entry into New York harbor. The opponents of the Verrazano claim contend that the Verrazano letter, including the date, is pure fiction, whether or not Verrazano wrote it; that there is no official record that Verrazano ever made such an expedition for the King of France; and that the descriptions of the east coast of North America contained in the letter were plagiarized from Gomez's report.

Well-documented events begin only with Henry Hudson in 1609, when the *Half Moon,* on September 13, made its second anchorage of the day opposite the present location of Fort Lee. Hudson ascended the river as far as the site of Albany in search of the Northwest Passage and returned on finding no outlet up the river. He was attacked by the Indians of Inwood on the point now under the George Washington Bridge.

We think of the Palisades as wooded and inaccessible cliffs. But the Hollanders peopled this strip in such numbers that no part of northern New Jersey, except Hackensack, had as many inhabitants as "Under the Mountain" in the days of uniformly bad roads, when the river constituted the highway. Although Indian names rarely remain, the Dutch left many names, some not altogether simple to recognize when given English sounds. The hollows where Greenbrook Pond is located have always been known as the "Kelders"; this is readily seen to mean the "cellars." It requires study, however, to trace "Bombay Hook" to "Boomje," meaning "little tree." "The Miraculous," the name of the glen south of Englewood Landing, is puzzling. It is not derived from its neighbor, St. Peters College, which did not arrive until long after the place was named.

On the terraces "Under the Mountain" one little farm crowded another; several of these lasted until the park bought them out. At the beginning of the twentieth century descendants of the original settlers were still tilling the ground and gathering famous French pears from tall and ancient trees. These families became rich, their prosperity due to the shallows of the river and the rocks on the shore. The river swarmed with shad in season. The swamp-edged island of Manhattan required docks and bulkheads and here by the Palisades were blocks of extreme hardness ready-shaped for wall building, and soft stone for house construction.

In the days when river steamers burned wood, it was cut on top of the Palisades and pitched down where the water was deep inshore; hence High Gutter Point at the state line. When fireplaces heated houses, wealthy New Yorkers bought sections on top of the plateau, each with a convenient "pitching place." The spot chosen for throwing down the wood had to have beneath, not huge rocks where logs would wedge or smash, but a smooth or small-stone slope, or a cliff edge overhanging the river, with a fair landing place below; often a wooden chute was built to slide the timbers to shore. One was at Allison Point; the DePeyster pitching place was north of Clinton Point; another, belonging to the Jeffries and having a stone dock, was north of Greenbrook.

The Revolutionary history of this region is a rich one. In 1776 General Hugh Mercer built Fort Lee to control the river. On top of the cliff a redoubt guarded the sunken ships and chained logs stretching across to Jeffries Hook on the Manhattan side, where the little red lighthouse now stands under the George Washington Bridge. To the north the highest land within Manhattan was crowned by Fort Washington, supposed by some of Washington's officers to be impregnable. Southeast, the location of the battle of Harlem Heights may be seen through the dip at 125th Street to Columbia University; Barnard College stands on the famous buckwheat field. After this fight the Americans marched along the east shore of Manhattan to dig in at White Plains, and the British army marched south over the same road to attack Fort Washington. From the west shore, General Washington watched that disaster and surrender and, as Cornwallis crossed at Alpine with six thousand men, had to order Fort Lee and all its stores of war material abandoned in such haste that the British found kettles on the fires.

The beginning of the Palisades Park dates from the time when New York City was slowly aroused to the devastations of the quarrymen blasting along the cliffs for traprock. About the middle of the nineteenth century much of the loose and easily accessible talus was pushed down to be used as ships' ballast. The real menace to the Palisades came with the demand for more and more concrete to build skyscrapers and roads. Quarries were opened from Weehawken to Verdrietige Hook above Nyack. To check this activity the Palisades Interstate Park Commission was created in 1900 jointly by New York and New Jersey. Enabling legislation was pushed in New Jersey by the New Jersey Federation of Women's Clubs, whose memorial is the charming Women's Federation Park with its "castle" near Alpine. In New York, Andrew H. Green, "Father of Greater New York" and founder of the American Scenic and Historic Preservation Society, worked for the necessary legislation with the cordial support of Governor Theodore Roosevelt and other conservation-minded officials. Land was acquired and developed as parks with all needed facilities.

In the early days most of this development was accomplished with gift money received from the commissioners and interested individuals, but in recent years funds for development projects have been provided by the two states. Of the many individuals who contributed generously of time, talents, and money in creating the system of parks, special recognition must be given to George W. Perkins, Sr., who was the commission's first president and the organizing genius of its development. With the story of his leadership should be coupled the generous action of J. Pierpont Morgan at a critical time, and many notable gifts of land and funds, private and public in about equal proportions. As one result, quarrying of the river faces of many mountains in Rockland County was stopped. Later the Park Commission was also charged with the preservation of the natural beauty of the lands lying in New York State on the west side of the Hudson, including the Ramapo Mountains as well as state park lands in Rockland and Orange counties and those in Sullivan and Ulster counties outside the Catskill Forest Preserve.

In 1933 John D. Rockefeller, Jr., offered to the Park Commission certain parcels of land on top of the Palisades which he had been assembling for some time. He wrote to the commission: "My primary purpose in acquiring this property was to preserve the land lying along the top of the Palisades from any use inconsistent with your ownership and protection of the Palisades themselves. It has also been my hope that a strip of this land of adequate width might ultimately be developed as a parkway . . ." In that year there seemed little likelihood of finding funds for a parkway, but various lines were explored and legislation passed which enabled the commission, in December 1935, to accept the deeds to the land offered. Additional properties were donated by the Twombleys, and by the trustees of the estate of W. O. Allison. The parkway, completed to Bear Mountain in 1958, is an attractive limited-access drive for noncommercial traffic only.

Since 1937 both the New York and New Jersey sections have been administered by a single Palisades Interstate Park Commission under a compact which legally cemented a uniquely successful cooperation between two states.

GEOLOGY

The contrast between the red sandstone, in horizontal strata, at the bottom of the cliffs, and the gray vertical columns above it, may interest the hiker and perhaps puzzle him. By what geological processes was this area built of such contrasting rock types?

The rocks of the Palisades section of the park are almost exclusively of two kinds: sedimentary sandstones and shales, and the igneous intrusive diabase of the Palisades. Both were formed during the Triassic Period, some 190 million years ago. For millions of years, sand and mud had washed down from surrounding highlands and had spread out over wide areas in sedimentary layers thousands of feet thick. Consolidated partly by pressure, but in greater degree by the deposition of mineral matter which penetrated the porous mass and cemented particles together, these deposits are today identified as the Newark Series. They can be seen exposed both beneath the igneous rocks of the Palisades and beneath the Hackensack meadows farther to the west.

After these sedimentary strata were laid down, molten rock was forced upward through rifts and then between sedimentary layers to form a single, prominent sill, the Palisades, about a thousand feet thick for some forty miles along the Hudson. At the contact of the hot magma and the adjoining sandstone and shale layers, some of the thermal metamorphic rock—hard quartzite and baked shale (hornfels)—are visible in many places. As the molten mass cooled underground, contraction fissures broke the sheet into crude vertical columns, often hexagonal or pentagonal in outline. After the diabase became exposed, these contraction joints were lines of weakness and were further affected by frost and rain, causing blocks to be pried off and fall into heavy talus slopes at the base. Since it is much more resistant to weather and water than is sandstone, the crumbling away of the sandstone has left the diabase exposed in the monolith we admire today. This igneous body ends in Rockland County, near Haverstraw, curling westward to two summits, High Tor and Little Tor.

Newark sandstone forms the walls of most of the old Dutch farmhouses in New Jersey, and the brownstone fronts of many of the older private homes in Manhattan. At a number of localities in New Jersey, footprints and other fossils of land animals of the Triassic Period have been found. Huge reptiles wandered over the mud flats then. The oldest inhabitant of the New York region, of whom any authentic relics have been found, curled himself up, lay down to die, and turned into stone in what is today the borough of Fort Lee, along the shore near Du Pont Dock. He was discovered there in 1910, in the sandy shale hardened by the overhanging traprock, about twenty feet below the diabase. As the American Museum of Natural History pictures this first fossil of our region, he looks something like a narrow-nosed, long-legged alligator, twenty-three feet from his slender snout to the tip of his tapering tail. He is a phytosaur, and his name is *Clepsysaurus manhattanensis.* There are also mud cracks and fossils of freshwater fish that testify to the continental origin of the sediments. The reddish ledges of Newark sandstone are exposed in many places along the shore path. The rock occurs chiefly near the river level and is often hidden behind the talus. Not far from the state line, however, it rises as high as 180 feet above the water.

An ice sheet that subsequently covered the New Jersey region, with its tools of sharp rock fragments borne along under the glacier and pressed against the underlying rocks by the enormous weight above, left its indelible imprint on the bedrock surfaces.

Glacial striations are found in great abundance on the top of the Palisades ridge, in places several inches to one foot deep and five feet wide, as at Englewood. The polish produced by fine glacier-borne materials on the hard bedrock surfaces may be seen also all along the top of the diabase ridge, as, for example, north of the administration building at Alpine. Where the ice scoured off loose earth and even rocks of immense size (and differing compositions) west of the Palisades, erratics can be seen scattered all through the park.

NATURAL HISTORY

The fall between precipice and beach in the Palisades is well wooded, except on the talus slopes at the base of the cliffs. Up to 1895, there were 11,000 acres of unbroken forest on the top of the Palisades, providing some of the finest timber in New Jersey.

An attractive addition to the native species there are the princess trees *(Paulownia tomentosa),* more popularly called royal paulownias, imported from China for the old estate gardens along the present route of the Palisades Parkway. Around Memorial Day, they startle the visitor with their exotic masses of bluebells.

Not too long ago, the upland forests of the Palisades were dominated by American chestnut—which has since disappeared due to the blight—and several species of oak. Today there are mixed oak forests. The red oak—the state tree of New Jersey—is the most common and fastest growing species. Other common trees are the black birch, white oak, tulip tree, black oak, chestnut oak, sweet gum, and sugar maple—the state tree of New York. A common understory tree is the flowering dogwood.

Sometimes one sees the cut stumps of red cedar. Valued as fence posts before the turn of the century, their decay-resistant trunks remain rooted in the cliff edge like pieces of driftwood. A tree that thrives in sunny exposures is the *Ailanthus altissima,* or tree-of-heaven, a fast-growing weed tree from China found along the shore.

Actually, along this narrow strip between beach and cliff, where most of the mileage is on edge, there is a surprising variety of trees, shrubs, and flowering plants, some of them reminders of the former estates located here.

TRAILS OF THE PALISADES INTERSTATE PARK

The Palisades Interstate Park covers 2472 acres, of which twenty are in New York. Between cliff top and water, the park width averages less than an eighth of a mile; the maximum elevation at the front, 530 feet, is at two spots west of Forest View. The highest clear cliff is 330 feet.

The two main trails that traverse the length of the Palisades, the Palisades Shore Trail and the Long Path, have been designated National Recreational Trails. The Palisades Shore Trail is mostly a broad and level path with white blazes, about 13.5 miles in length. At Forest View, about 10.5 miles from the start, its character becomes rugged as it weaves up and down among the talus to reach the cliff edge at the state line.

Fishing and crabbing are allowed in the stretch between Ross Dock and Englewood, and from the shore at Alpine. Bathing, for many years a feature of the shore, is now prohibited due to the pollution of the Hudson. Good paths lead at intervals to the top, and at Englewood and Alpine fine driveways descend to the river and the parking areas. These are connected midway by a motor road built in 1909, which is closed to walkers.

On top, the blue-blazed Long Path runs between cliff edge and the parkway. The route is mostly level, providing fine glimpses of the Hudson and its shore beyond. In the region beyond Greenbrook Sanctuary, the presence of the parkway fades as the trail takes advantage of the increased park width.

Palisades Shore Trail

To reach the trail, walk or take any bus across the George Washington Bridge to Bridge Plaza (Fort Lee). From the bus stop walk south to the first cross street, turning left toward the river. To the south was the site of Fort Lee itself.

At the bottom of the incline is Fort Lee Historic Park, where there are fine views of the city, the Statue of Liberty, and Staten Island. The earthworks of 1776 located on the southern tip (Bluff Point) have been recreated. This redoubt guarded the barriers placed in the river to prevent passage by the British. It was here in November of that year that General Washington watched the flag being hauled down at Fort Washington across the river, as the Colonials surrendered to the British.

A fine little museum concerned with these events is located here. Walk around the grounds to see the location of the batteries and get a foreshortened view of the bridge north of the museum, showing curves of cable, a closeup of a tower, and a basalt column in the foreground. Picnic tables are nearby.

Returning to the street, turn left and follow Hudson Terrace downhill to the park entrance. This is the beginning of the Palisades Shore Trail. It is only occasionally marked with white blazes but one can never get lost since it follows the shore.

Descend the steps to the shore and walk north past the remnants of Du Pont (Powder) Dock to the boat launching ramp under the bridge. Passing former beaches at Hazards and Carpenters, note that the absence of talus at the base of the cliff is a consequence of the quarrying done here. About 2 miles from Bridge Plaza, just before reaching the broad expanse of Ross Dock, Carpenters Trail leads to the top. The middle section of the trail presents some of the finest cliff faces on the Palisades.

On the shore, water and refreshments are available seasonally at Ross Dock. Then for more than a mile north, terraces and open groves are arranged as picnic places. Beyond is Englewood Boat Basin.

To reach Route 9W and buses to New York, walk 20 minutes up the approach road from the boat basin. From the sidewalk along the road the grade is easy and the views are fine, but there is little shade. A pleasant alternative is the shaded footpath rising near a cascading stream.

Englewood Boat Basin has an immense parking space, which makes it an ideal starting point for those who come in cars. The path north crosses picnic grounds at Bloomers Dock, passes Franks Rock, a huge boulder hanging between path and shore, and winds picturesquely past Undercliff Dock, with its large well-shaded picnic area on an upper terrace. All this stretch once was a settlement, "Under the Mountain," in the days before the park began. Scattered in between the small farms were quarries, fishing shacks, and manure and bone factories. South of Undercliff, on the upper level, is a cemetery, a relic of this settlement. The point above is High Tom.

Picnic tables fashioned from fallen rock are found along the way at Canoe Beach, a mile and a half north of the boat basin. Just beyond, above Powder Dock, Clinton Point makes a picture between the trees.

Continue on the level path, and after crossing Lost Brook, which loses itself flowing under the talus, arrive at Lambiers Dock. From the tip of the dock there is a fine profile of several headlands as far as Man-in-the-Rock, the northern column of Bombay Hook.

A few minutes later cross Greenbrook Falls, a trickle in August and an ice mass in January, but in spring, after rain, impressive when seen from the riverbank. There is much loosened rock here, but the columnar structure is in evidence south of the brook. All of this section is finely wooded and stately.

From the falls the path follows the river, soon to reach Huyler Dock, about 4 miles from Englewood. This was an important transfer point for goods and passengers between interior New Jersey and the city. The Huyler Landing Trail follows the old road, said to be used by the British, to connect with the Long Path on top.

For the remaining mile to Alpine Boat Basin the path is picturesque. Here the route is full of variety and charm, wandering up and down owing to washouts on the river's edge.

Beyond a fine growth of laurel is a big boulder called Hay-Kee-Pook ("His Body") where legend has it that an Indian lover committed suicide (despite the shallowness of the water). On reaching the grassy level, do not fail to look north to see the slender, curved pinnacle of Bombay Hook. This highest, most isolated, and most conspicuous pillar of rock in the Palisades curves seventy feet high between two mighty slides.

The northern approach road enters here but has no sidewalk. The walker continues past the boat basin to "Cornwallis' Headquarters," once a tavern where the British spent a night. They are said to have also scaled these cliffs by the Revolutionary Trail, which the present path to the top follows in part. The tavern was the first headquarters of the park and is now a museum open in the summer months. The ascent to Closter Dock Road, for buses to New York, takes about half an hour.

At Alpine Boat Basin, there are picnic space, a refreshment stand, and a good-sized parking area for cars.

Northward from Alpine, about 9 miles from the start, follow a wide path behind the former Riverview bathhouse past fine hemlocks, a brook, and some good woods. At the shore is Cape Flyaway, where Indian remains have been found. When a fork is reached, continue on the upland path through a former picnic ground to reach the shore before Bombay Hook.

Bearing right at the fork takes one to Excelsior Dock and the grassy expanse at Twombleys. The name comes from the former owner who gave the grounds to the park. Because of the layers of oyster shells found here, Twombleys is believed to have been the site of Indian camps. A half mile farther beyond a stand of white birch, look up to the two vast bastions called Ruckman Point. Also look north to Indian Head; from here, the best aspect of this face becomes apparent—not the Indian or the patroon—but the Yankee pioneer. Here near the former greensward of Forest View Landing, a path ascends to the top of the cliff. The upper part has steep steps with high risers. At the top, turn left to see a stone castle commemorating the work of the New Jersey

The Giant Stairs north of Forrest View, opposite Hastings, in the Autumn

Federation of Women's Clubs in securing the first lands of the park. Turn west on a footbridge over the parkway to the Scout Camp and the stop for buses to New York.

At Forest View it is 11.5 miles from Fort Lee. The final 2-mile segment of the path includes its most striking scenery. This walk below the five-hundred-foot cliffs of Indian Head and past the rough talus of the Giant Stairs, where the peregrine falcon and bald eagle are again sometimes seen, is preserved in its natural state, accessible only to hikers. Royal paulownia trees dominate the talus here.

From Forest View, head north, either on the level or on the upper path, to observe some of the immense masses the cliffs have cast down—their flat cleavages, their wave lines, their variety of marking. The caves and cavities created by these rock masses are homes for raccoons, foxes, many small rodents, and snakes. The two routes join again at the top of a stone stairway. The route is now a series of traverses over exposed slide and talus. Reenter the shade with fine outlooks, then cross another talus slide and more woods. A mile from Forest View, the expanse of the Giant Stairs is met. Descending the "stairs" to the shore, the trail ultimately passes a slough which marks the state line. Beyond take the left fork up on a well-built trail to the front at High Gutter Point. The path ahead goes to the Italian Garden area, recently donated to the Park Commission. There can be seen the ruins of a pergola at the foot of a waterfall.

Follow the upper path through Skunk Hollow, on the lands of the Lamont Sanctuary, to reach the state line opposite the main entrance to Columbia University's Lamont-Doherty Geological Observatory at Route 9W.

With consummate landscape art this footway has wandered past high monoliths and giant staircases from one view to another on a course that, in Europe, would be justly famous. The vast wall hangs above; the river of wonders is at one's feet. The matchless Palisades offer the grandeur of a bit of an unspoiled, faroff mountain range within sight of one of the biggest cities in the world.

The Long Path: Fort Lee to State Line. Length: 12 miles. Blazes: turquoise.

The Long Path follows the level cliff top of the Palisades northward from the George Washington Bridge. The vistas here are excellent for watching thousands of migrating hawks each fall. The amount of vegetation is a surprise and the outlooks up and down the river are unsurpassed. The Long Path, traversing the high, dry cliff top, offers fine examples of the "mixed oak" forest, where five different species of oak (red, white, black, scarlet, and chestnut) dominate the woods.

The most popular approach, and the most scenic, is on foot across the George Washington Bridge; an alternative is by bus to Bridge Plaza in Fort Lee. From the bridge, a wide, level path swings toward the cliff. View lower New York from the farthest-projecting cliff near the bridge tower. A quarter mile farther along, view one of the best of the southern rock faces; beyond, Carpenters Trail descends to the shore.

The turquoise-blazed route soon passes a mounted cannon, a remnant of Coytesville Park. A little more than a mile from the start, after passing the walls of several former estates, is William O. Allison Park, maintained by the Palisades Interstate Park Commission. It is open most of the year; water and rest rooms are available.

Past the campus of St. Peters College, the path swings to the shoulder of the parkway and enters a small woodland near Allison Park. This was the site of the Palisades Mountain House, built in 1869. At Palisades Avenue, it is 2 miles from the start. Here the shore may be reached by a zigzag path or by the sidewalk along the road.

Continuing northward, the path soon traverses the former Dana estate; note an exotic oriental pine near the parkway. In the woodland beyond, watch for the rock promontory, High Tom, with views north and down to Undercliff Grove and the old cemetery. Next cross Rockefeller Lookout, a level mile from Palisades Avenue. Opposite is Spuyten Duyvil and the northern tip of Manhattan.

After passing the ruins of the Cadgene estate, the path follows undulating terrain through woodland to an ever-decreasing meadow and depression, Devils Hole. The slight rise beyond is Clinton Point, a favorite view point from the time of the first settlers. Few heights along the "mountain" give a more striking effect from above of a prow overhanging the water.

In another mile cross the road into Greenbrook Sanctuary. This is a restricted nature preserve whose purpose is to protect the native species. Information can be obtained from park headquarters at Alpine. There is limited parking near the sanctuary entrance; the bus from New York also stops here.

The route continues north along the fence, with a few short, steep stretches. At the end of the fence, the Huyler Landing Trail joins from the shore below. The Long Path then reaches the Alpine Lookout; the finest view point is from the pinnacle just south of the main area. Reenter the woods and pass a house foundation. Descend slightly to cross Walker Hollow, a long, open swale with views of downtown Yonkers across the river; then ascend past the foundation of the Zabriskie House, whose dry cellar may be used as an emergency shelter.

Pass several other foundations and note the fine views of the Alpine Boat Basin far below. Shortly an underpass under the parkway leads to Closter Dock Road, 7.5 miles from the bridge. To reach the shore, continue on the path for several minutes more and then descend on the fine, broad, and well-shaded path.

Continuing ahead, pass the Administration Building of the Palisades Interstate Park, the former Oltman House. There is limited parking here. Note the tower west of the parkway, the site of the first FM radio station, built by Major Edwin Armstrong, the radio pioneer.

The path reenters woodland, including the former Ringling (circus) estate. One mile from Closter Dock Road, the trail swings to the cliff edge and passes the largest separated section of rock in the Palisades, Grey Crag. It is some three hundred feet long and ten to twenty feet wide, accessible by a bridge now closed to the public. In winter and early spring look for three-hundred-foot ice columns where water plunges over the cliff.

Skirting a quarter-mile-long retreat in the cliff edge, the path then swings past Bombay Hook. Eventually the route leads over broad, flat, embedded rocks, ending at Ruckman Road, now abandoned, at the edge of the cliff, here 520 feet high. No part of the Palisades has better scenery.

Cross Ruckman Road, bearing left at the fork. The wood road to the right leads to a projection overlooking Forest View. On the main wood road, exotic plantings from the former Burnet estate occasionally appear. Upon reaching a well-used wood road, turn toward the cliff edge. The route to the left leads over a bridge to the Scout Camp entrance—a good place to catch the Route 9W bus—10 miles from the start of the hike.

Walking northward, descend and cross the brook coming from a flat called Maisland (Cornlot) Hollow. The stairway on the right continues down to Forest View at the shore. Continue up another stairway and swing right along a park road to State Line Lookout (Point Lookout). Here a small snack bar and rest rooms are available, as well as unlimited parking.

Various circular hikes follow what are now wood roads but initially were bridle paths built in the 1930s. A good wood road begins at a corner of the parking area, a number of yards to the left of the snack bar. Its various branches ultimately lead back to

Ruckmans, where the
cliff is 520 feet above
the river and 280 feet
sheer drop. A solid pillar.
Dobbs Ferry: the coun-
try back of Tarrytown
Sleepy Hollow and
Irving's country. Below
Forest View Basin

the extension of the park road (here closed to autos) and then back to the snack bar. The best route is to generally bear to the right until the road is reached. These wood roads are also used for cross-country skiing.

Beyond the snack bar, the path continues through a picnic area and then along a wide wood road near the cliff. In a half mile a fine forest road comes in on the left and leads to the park road.

Just ahead is the state line, marked by a fence and a six-foot shaft erected in 1882. Descend near the cliff edge, through a gate to High Gutter Point. This name recalls the early wood-burning river steamers which docked at a wooden chute on the bank for their fuel. Here there are good views toward Hook Mountain, the old mile-long pier at Piermont, and Tappan Zee. A staircase of natural stone leads down and west, joining the path from the river, into Skunk Hollow, whose magnificent hemlocks and waterfalls belie its name. Part of this area is the Lamont Sanctuary, and beyond was the site of an early black community, now long since disappeared. When the stream is crossed, the trail on the right leads to the former Italian Garden at the shore. The main trail goes left to Route 9W, where buses stop at the Lamont-Doherty Geological Observatory entrance, 12 miles from the start. Several cars may be parked near the boulders at the state line and Route 9W.

The Long Path (State Line to Piermont). Length: 3 miles. Blazes: turquoise.

Cross the state line at the observatory entrance and follow Route 9W for a few yards around a bend. Then turn downhill on a wood road, at times somewhat steep. This is the last remaining portion of the "boulevard," forerunner of the modern highway. Ultimately the trail rejoins the highway to reach Oak Tree Road, a mile from the state line.

This is Palisades—a hamlet of such old-time charm that it seems hardly credible that it should still exist so close to the metropolis. Houses which Hollanders built, with greenswards and gardens, and former artists' cottages are scattered up and down the parklike hillsides.

The road to the right leads to Snedens Landing, the western end of a ferry route established in 1719, and made famous during the Revolution when Mollie Sneden, whose house still stands under the cliff, rowed the boat across. On this road is the site where the American flag received, by order of Parliament, its first salute from the British in May 1783. The British fleet had been using the anchorage below since 1776.

The trail continues along Route 9W, almost immediately passing an old flagpole and a converted church, now an auction house for antiques, on the left. Opposite is the handsome "Big House," the oldest in the area. A few yards farther along, beyond a gas station, bend right onto a wood road. Here is a parking area for a dozen cars at the southern end of Tallman Mountain State Park.

In a quarter mile the blazed trail makes an abrupt left turn, as a bike path continues ahead. Pass through an area with tall reeds and then follow an unbending, shaded wood road. Here and there are scattered long, elevated mounds of earth at right angles to each other. Originally intended to retain oil seepage from a tank farm that was to be built here, some are now filled with rainwater and, although shallow, make good "birding" sites. This entire area is a haven for frogs and salamanders, which breed in the pools each spring, as well as a veritable wildflower paradise in April and May—spring beauties, anemones, Dutchman's-breeches, Mayflowers, and many others.

At the end of the straight wood road, swing right on an old berm toward the river. When the bike path is recrossed, continue ahead, soon picking up an old farm road near the cliff edge. Farther along is a small picnic area with a comfort station; this is also the start of a bike path which provides an easy walk back to the small parking area. To reach the picnic grove, keep bearing to the right from the main park entrance on Route 9W.

Cross a ravine near a swimming pool, pass the park's traffic circle, and regain the height of land at a larger, more active picnic area. There are fine views of the river and the marsh below. Plunge downhill on a moderately steep path and cross Sparkill Creek, here a tidal brook, to reach Piermont.

Piermont was once the bustling terminus of the Erie Railroad. A mile-long pier was built in the shallow part of the river so that passengers could transfer directly from trains to boats for New York. Today the village-owned pier makes for an interesting diversion, particularly for the views up and down the river. Take the side road immediately north of Sparkill Creek. As you walk out to the end, note the variety of bird life, including herons, ducks, rails, swallows, and wrens. Some of the trees include white mulberries, cottonwoods, and willows. The area is now being preserved as an estuarine sanctuary.

Piermont has several interesting art and craft shops. A stop at one of the restaurants or coffeehouses makes a delightful pause. The hourly bus to New York stops at the small park near the tidal brook.

The Long Path (Piermont to Upper Nyack). Length: 7.5 miles. Blazes: turquoise.

The Long Path in this area hugs the western slope of the Palisades ridge and passes through some of the finest examples of old-growth forests in the area. Between here and Mount Ivy, some route changes are anticipated, but the general direction will remain the same. Additional trails will be developed to permit circular hikes.

From the southern end of Piermont where a railroad spur line crosses the street, head uphill on a side road, up a stairway, past a former railroad station to gain the upper highway. After crossing 9W, follow Highland Avenue (Tweed Boulevard) north. This "boulevard" was built, beginning in 1871, to connect Sparkill and the village of Rockland Lake and was so-named because local politicians tried to emulate the notorious "boss" Tweed and his New York City boulevards. Beyond a bend in the road (1 mile) the path climbs the embankment to a corner of Rockland Cemetery, established as a National Cemetery in 1847 by Eleazer Lord, a founder of the Erie Railroad, and designed by Andrew Downing. Here on a rise nearby is the grave of John C. Frémont, "The Pathfinder," and just to the south that of Henry Honeychurch Gorringe, whose exploits in bringing Cleopatra's Needle to America are depicted on his monument, a replica of the obelisk in Central Park. Here one gets a good view of the Tappan Zee and the old Erie Pier extending far out into the Hudson.

From the cemetery, the trail proceeds north on a wood road along the west side of Mount Nebo. In time access across the summit will also be possible. This Clausland Mountain area is now mostly protected woodland and is one of the few areas in the Palisades where deer still thrive.

The route afterward courses through the woods ultimately to cross a stream. After climbing a little, the trail descends through more mature woods, eventually crossing another brook and a paved road. This is Clausland Mountain Road, 3 miles from the beginning.

Cross the road, pass through the parking area, and swing downhill past a water impoundment, once part of the Blauvelt Rifle Range built in 1911. Designed to replace a facility at Creedmor, Long Island, it was abandoned after three years when it became apparent that the range of firearms could not be safely contained within the facility.

At the other end of the impoundment, cross a brook and enter somewhat dense undergrowth. After passing a huge red oak, one reaches a broad wood road. Here turn right along the Blauvelt State Park boundary. Then, following a series of wide paths through a reforestation project of white pine planted about 1930, cross a park road to an area of flat rocks.

Beyond is a concrete wall. This was the backstop which supported the targets of the former rifle range. A maze of tunnels and walks leads from here. Explore them only with extreme caution.

Continue in a northeasterly direction along various undulating paths. Cross a brook, enter a hemlock forest, and regain Tweed Boulevard. Turn uphill and reach the crest of a ridge, the former site of Balance Rock, a famous erratic, now destroyed, some 5 miles from Piermont. From either side of the road, there are excellent views of both the Hudson and Hackensack valleys. The body of water to the southwest is Lake Tappan.

In a few hundred yards down the road the trail bears right on a gravel route, past a water tank and impressive rubble of talus, to a good view of the Tappan Zee and bridge, then past Nyack Missionary College. At Bradley Hill Road the trail jogs left, climbs over a small wooded knoll, and proceeds along a hard-surfaced road (the continuation of Mountainview Avenue) to reach Route 59, 6.5 miles from Piermont. Note the old stone mile marker across the street.

A pleasant return to Piermont or New York is to walk right along Route 59 to reach the collection of antique shops, restaurants, and interesting architecture which makes Nyack so worth the visit. The bus to New York stops along Broadway in Nyack.

For those continuing on the trail, stride along Mountainview Avenue, over the New York State Thruway. Swing sharply right uphill and gain a plateau at a much higher elevation. Proceed northward skirting the edge of the condominium complex, over a poor track. Descend from this elevation to follow a wood road and follow Christian Herald Road to Route 9W for the New York bus.

The Long Path (Upper Nyack to Long Clove). Length: 6 miles. Blazes: turquoise.

This portion of the Long Path is a summit walk on trails and wood roads over several steep areas. From the bus stop at Route 9W and Christian Herald Road, walk north on Route 9W toward the base of Hook Mountain to pick up the old location of the roadway on the right, now a path at a lower level. The path climbs first the south, then the west side of Hook Mountain. Its summit is the second highest in the Palisades rampart (729 feet) and is the site of a busy hawk flyway each autumn. The site commands a view in a complete circle. Rockland and Congers lakes are in the bowl behind the ridge to the north; the rampart of the Ramapos and the highlands are to the west and north; to the east is the long slope of Westchester County with Tarrytown and other villages along its front; and to the south is the Tappan Zee Bridge and Nyack, with the broad fields of the estates of Upper Nyack in the foreground.

Hook Mountain juts into the river to match Tallman, but it is higher and wilder, with fine views. The name is derived from the Dutch, "Verdrietige Hoogte" (Hook), meaning tedious or troublesome point, because of the contrary winds which navigators encountered off the point. It is literally a hook, however, when viewed from the air or on a map.

In the last quarter of the nineteenth century, the quarrying which started at the Palisades spread upriver, threatening the defacement of Hook Mountain on the Tappan Zee, and the entire riverfront. The landings, such as Snedens, Tappan Slote (Piermont), Rockland Landing, and Waldberg (or Snedekers), where ferries plied across the river or where steamers docked en route to New York, could expect to see a bustle of new activity, and some did.

In 1872 the erection of a stone crusher at Hook Mountain signaled the beginning of large-scale operations. By the turn of the century, this and thirty-one smaller quarries between Piermont and Nyack were in vigorous operation; blasting was going on furiously. Sentiment was growing to stop this defacement, as had been done on the Palisades. George W. Perkins, president of the Park Commission, had the greatest part in stimulating this opinion among philanthropic men and women of wealth. He believed the forested hills of the Highlands of the Hudson, famous for their scenery and their Revolutionary strongholds, would be an outlet for the people of the metropolitan district. In addition to various bond issues, the commission was aided in its plans by generous givers, including members of the Harriman, Perkins, and Rockefeller families, who have been adding to park holdings even up to the present time.

The first of the purchases at Hook Mountain was in 1911, with the acquisition of the large quarry at the south end of the mountain. By 1920 the last of the quarries ceased operations and the public had a six-mile-long park along the river where once such a park seemed only a dream.

The trail slopes down Hook Mountain, then ascends along the ridge close to the edge of an abandoned quarry. On the next summit, the ruins of a chimney are the last traces of the Gerard Cottage. There are fine views across the Hudson to Ossining and Croton Point and beyond to Croton Dam. Downhill, within 0.25 mile, a wood road branches left to the park golf course below, where a good flowing spring is located 200 yards along the fairway. The trail stays on a fine wood road along the ridge, turns uphill to pass the "dark pond" near the summit. Following a somewhat steep gradient downhill, one ultimately reaches a sheer cliff edge, especially dangerous in winter or on slippery days. From the edge of the height of land the trail follows a wood road and then switches back on itself to reach Rockland Landing Road, 3 miles from the start.

Rockland Lake was the hub of another great industry which broke the serenity of the riverfront: the harvesting of Rockland Lake ice from 1831 to 1924. The discoverer of the superiority of ice from spring-fed Rockland Lake is unknown, but its renown became widespread to the point where the better New York restaurants would accept no other. In 1711 John Slaughter purchased land at Rockland Landing, including Trough Hollow, the gap in the ridge where a narrow and precipitous path leads to the river. A dock was built and gradually there was some commercial traffic, but Nyack and Haverstraw had better natural facilities. As ice was harvested it was conveyed to Rockland Landing by a sort of "escalator" and loaded on riverboats. Later the giant Knickerbocker Ice Company was formed, at one time employing four thousand men. Icehouses over 350 feet long and 50 feet high, each with a fifty-ton capacity, were situated at the northeast corner of the lake. In 1860 a cog railway was built through Trough Hollow, connecting lake and dock. A spur line of the West Shore Railway also ran to the icehouses. But the growth of mechanical refrigeration permanently halted ice harvesting operations in 1924. Thereafter Rockland Lake became a popular, privately owned recreation center for summer swimming and picnicking and winter ice-skating.

In 1958 the commission acquired 256-acre Rockland Lake and surrounding upland areas. Later, additional acreage was purchased so as to include the entire "bowl."

The Long Path continues across the Rockland Lake village crossroads, past a family cemetery on the right, and up a somewhat steep slope. The next descent, along the face of an abandoned quarry, is steep and spectacular. At the bottom is Trough Hollow, once the main road from the village to the river landing. Past a stone wall near the refreshment building for the golf course, the trail crosses wooded knolls to the top of a cliff, the site of another former quarry. There are views east across the Hudson and west to Rockland, Swartwout, and Congers lakes. Cement markers indicate the boundary of Hook Mountain State Park, the land between the ridge and the river.

The trail keeps undulating until it climbs to the highest point on the ridge, 5.5 miles from Upper Nyack, to a view of Lake DeForest, a large reservoir on the Hackensack. Then it descends through well-developed hemlock ravines, crosses a power line over a railroad tunnel to reach a large overgrown area and Route 9W. This is Long Clove, a natural cleft in the Palisades ridge.

Return from Long Clove to Upper Nyack via River Path

To return to Upper Nyack, the walk near the river is a pleasant alternative. From Long Clove descend along a wood road which tunnels under the railroad and ultimately reaches the shore path. (To reach Long Clove from the shore path from Nyack, soon after passing a small parking area on the left, a wood road will descend and join in from the left. This is the road which leads to the Long Path along the ridge.)

From the wood road proceed south along the shore path and almost immediately come to a side trail leading to Haverstraw Beach State Park, now unused. Here was once a thriving settlement, known at various times as Waldberg or Snedekers Landing, or as Red Sandstone Dock.

At low tide (about two and a half hours later than at Sandy Hook) a walk along the river's edge is well worth taking for the geological exhibit it provides. Sandstone and shale, overlaid with traprock talus, appear in the cliffs; pebbles and boulders range in age from mostly Precambrian granite and gneiss through red Triassic sandstone and shale to Pleistocene clay sand and gravel, with gravel planing and erosional features for good measure. The low land projecting from the opposite shore almost to the middle of the Hudson is Croton Point; Tellers Point is its southern tip. This was the delta of the old Croton River, formerly at river level but now elevated to a height of eighty feet. The crust of the earth gradually rose with the disappearance of the last glacier and the removal of the tremendous weight of ice. Beyond are the Westchester hills of a more ancient metamorphic terrain; in the distance is Long Island's terminal moraine.

From Haverstraw Beach, the shore path soon passes a watchman's cabin, where there is parking for a few cars. (Reach this spot by auto by taking the road passing under the quarry conveyer seen from Route 9W and continue to its end.) Then the path comes to the first of the abandoned quarries in Hook Moun-

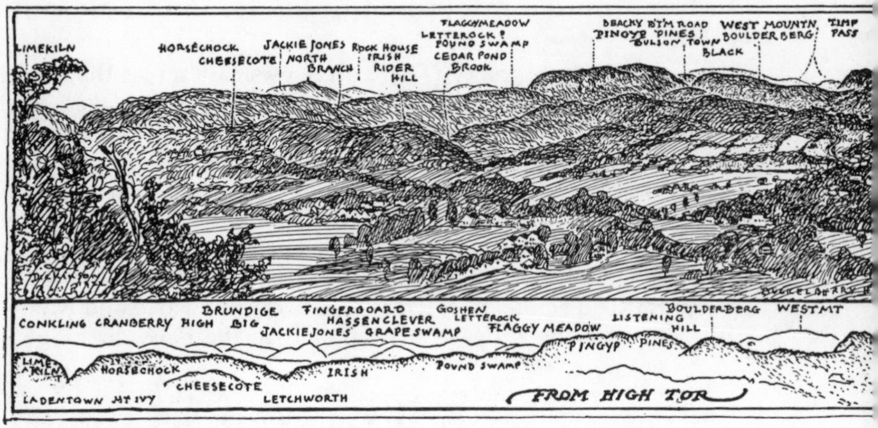

tain State Park and continues along the level which marks the contact between the red sandstone beneath and the traprock which overlays it. The princess tree *(Paulownia tomentosa)* grows here on the diabase talus slopes resulting from old rockslides. The common tree of the upper level is the box elder, and along the path are many hundred-year-old hemlocks and the small, attractive striped maple or moosewood tree, rare this far south. The slopes are covered with a lush growth of evergreen ferns, and wildflowers in the spring. On the terraces above are old Indian oyster-shell middens. At the end of the second quarry, a path bears left to Rockland Landing North (3 miles from Long Clove). Immediately beyond, a wood road bends up the ridge to Trough Hollow. Next is the third quarry, somewhat larger than the others, and once landscaped as part of the park development. The columns of the cliff face reveal Triassic intrusive diabase (traprock). The automatic navigation beacon on a reef in the river is Rockland Light, some 3 miles from Long Clove. This is the remains of Rockland Landing South, where there may still be old hulks of iceboats and remains of the "escalator" by which the ice was once lowered to the river.

The path then turns upward onto a road, which if one follows to the right leads to the top of the ridge and the largest of the quarries. This road may be followed to return to Long Clove over the top, or across the ridge to Rockland Lake and the highway. The cliffs here rise four hundred feet or more, with columnar flutings noticeable at the south end. However, the path almost immediately leaves the road to rejoin the riverbank.

It then runs close to the sandstone cliffs where a park lean-to was built of plentiful talus, then around a headland to the Tap-

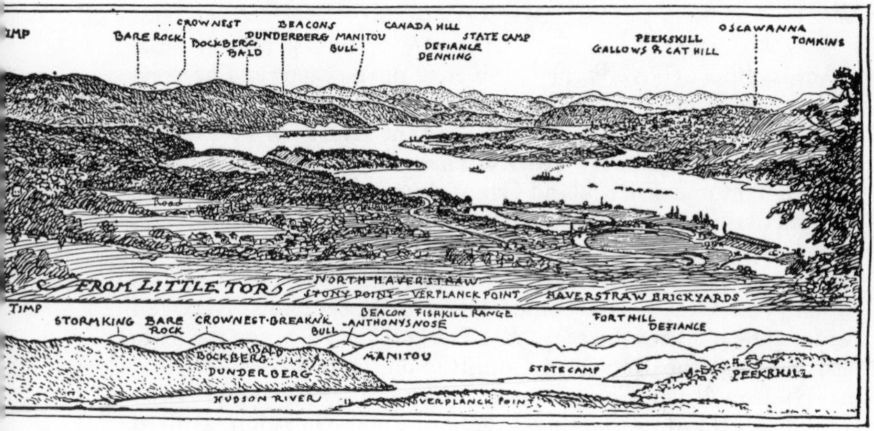

pan Zee. Below the last of the quarries is Nyack Beach State Park, now only a picnic area (5 miles). South of the park's entrance, follow North Broadway, a beautiful street with unusual houses, both old and new, in Upper Nyack for 1 mile. Turn uphill onto old Mountain Road past Rockland County's oldest cemetery and soon reach Route 9W, where the hike from Nyack began. (A few blocks farther south on North Broadway is Old Stone Church, the oldest church building in the county.) The next street is Castle Heights Avenue, with a bus stop for the trip back to New York.

The Long Path (Long Clove to Mount Ivy). Length: 7 miles. Blazes: turquoise.

The Long Path crosses Route 9W at Long Clove and, on little-used back roads, skirts one of the last operating quarries in the area. In a mile, reach Short Clove. Cross the road near the stone crusher and make a short, steep ascent, after which the climb is more moderate. The trail continues northward and climbs the southeast side of High Tor in a series of natural steps in the diabase. Near the base of High Tor, in a shallow hollow, the white-blazed Deer Path leads steeply down to meet Route 9W about a half mile south of the old Haverstraw railroad station. On the summit of High Tor is the foundation of an airplane beacon, now removed, surrounded by the polygonal pattern of the diabase column ends, like a honeycomb in stone. High Tor is the highest point on the Palisades-Tor ridge (827 feet). There is a sweeping view from this lichen-covered, bald peak. The tower on the horizon to the south is at Alpine; the one to the north is Jackie Jones in the Ramapos.

Across Short Clove is the harsh edge of the quarry. The view to the west shows the curving range yet to be traveled. Straight below is the village of Haverstraw and the river. On a clear day, the towers of Manhattan are also visible.

High Tor, one of Rockland County's most striking landmarks, was once used as a signal point by colonists during the Revolution. Long cherished as part of the Van Orden farm on its south side, High Tor was threatened by quarrying for its traprock, as Elmer Van Orden grew older without descendants. Maxwell Anderson's picturesque play *High Tor* and local love for the little peak aroused the Rockland County Conservation Association, the Hudson River Conservation Society, and the New York–New Jersey Trail Conference to action. Their campaign resulted in the purchase of the ridge and its presentation in 1943 to the commission. But the slope facing the Hudson all the way north from Long Clove is still in private hands and in danger of being developed.

From High Tor, a scramble, short but steep, brings the path down to a fire road leading through the woods. It is a good half hour's walk to Little Tor. Just south of Little Tor is a brook that rarely runs dry, 4.5 miles from Long Clove. A path downhill leads to the base of the mountain near the swimming pool; to the right a branch leads for a quarter mile to the north-side ledge and then to the summit of Little Tor (710 feet), a fine view point. Garnerville, West Haverstraw, and some of the clay banks once used in brickmaking lie below. One mile north is Helen Hayes Hospital, built on the site of the Hett Smith house where Arnold and André met on September 21, 1780, to arrange the delivery of West Point to the British. To the right is the Bowline generating plant and above that is Grassy Point, where a town marina has been built; farther north is Stony Point Reservation. Beyond, Dunderberg rises from the river, with Bear Mountain looking over the saddle and the summit of the Timp to the left.

The route along South Mountain, as the ridge from here west to Mount Ivy is named, was a gift to the Park Commission in 1943 by Archer M. Huntington, writer and philanthropist, including the famous and impressive Little Tor, and much of the south slope. Two miles from High Tor and 5 miles from Long Clove is Central Highway, which crosses the ridge. A few cars can be parked at the trail crossing, and a much larger number 100 yards south of the trail.

As you cross the road, avoid the obvious wood road, but seek a higher elevation where the views are better. Soon you will see an antenna and related equipment used to relay television transmissions.

The trail now runs pretty much along the crest through red cedars and scraggly pitch pine. Northward, west of Thiells, the buildings of Letchworth Village, a state institution named in honor of the philanthropist William Pryor Letchworth, are visible. At the end of the ridge is the grassy opening on the summit of Mount Ivy above the long-abandoned Gurnee quarry, now a county preserve, as is the entire ridge from Central Highway. Ahead is a panorama of the Ramapo rampart. In the middle is Cheesecote Mountain, so-named from the original patent for the land; it is now a Haverstraw town park. The troughlike hollow running back into the mountains opposite is File Factory Hollow, with Horse Chock Mountain to the north of it and Limekiln Mountain to the south. Mount Ivy is the end of the Palisades traprock above ground. The trail swings down around the quarry to reach Route 202 and Route 45. This intersection marks the spot where the Palisades dip under the surface, never to reappear, as they swing northward and westward.

At this intersection is also a large commuter parking area which can be used by hikers with club identification on nonbusiness days only. Telephone the Haverstraw town police beforehand, or visit them 2 miles east on Route 202. A visit to an orchard stand less than a mile south on Route 45 makes a delightful respite. Refreshments can also be found near the parking area at Mount Ivy.

The Long Path (Mount Ivy to Calls Hollow). Length: 4 miles. Blazes: turquoise.

From the Mount Ivy parking area at Route 202 go under the parkway and swing right onto the grassy shoulder of the exit ramp. In a few yards, pass Quaker Road, and then, just before the parkway is reached, slip into a grove of evergreens and proceed northward. This is part of the parkway right-of-way, but below and out of sight of traffic. Continue for a mile with stony underfooting through second-growth woodland until the south branch of Minisceongo Creek is crossed on a rude bridge.

Leaving bottomland quickly behind, turn right onto an old wood road. Soon the route turns left up Cheesecote Mountain and after a short, steep climb reaches a knob. From here, a glance to the east reveals the plateau at Thiells and the Hudson River in the distance.

Descend from the knob and turn right onto another wood road

in a small valley heading in a northerly direction. Then intersect a fire road, the Old Letchworth Road, turning left with it but soon doubling back on the wood road as it climbs to a higher elevation. At the top of the mountain is a gem, Cheesecote Pond, 2.5 miles from Mount Ivy. This is part of a town park, and parking is available for local residents only. There are a few picnic tables and rest rooms.

Swing around the south end of the pond and continue on a wood road heading westward, at first level and then downhill, with uncertain underfooting. Calls Hollow itself is seen below in the distance. Crossing the swath of a power line, turn right (north) downhill, past a cemetery without headstones. This is one of the cemeteries of Letchworth Village, a state mental institution to which this whole area once belonged. Continue on a short way and reach paved Calls Hollow Road. A turn to the left for a few yards and then a right into the woodlands of Harriman Park marks the end of this segment of the Long Path. Safe parking in this area is unfortunately scarce.

PARKS IN THE PALISADES AT A GLANCE

Tallman Mountain State Park (687 acres), Route 9W, Sparkill, New York

The park area is mostly a broad wooded plateau, from whose two higher "peaks" there are good views over the Hudson. Most of Tallman is developed as a picnic area with roads and parking areas; in the northwest corner are sports facilities and near the river a swimming pool, and marshes that provide good "birding." The Long Path traverses it, passing some of the abandoned relics of a former oil project.

Blauvelt State Park (590 acres), Route 303, Blauvelt, New York

At present the area is undeveloped as a park. Numerous hiking and bridle trails go in every direction. The western part is quite level, but the northern and eastern areas are rugged.

Hook Mountain State Park (676 acres), Route 9W, Upper Nyack, New York

Hook Mountain Park is still largely undeveloped, but the trails are among the finest for ruggedness and views. At its south end is the tiny Nyack Beach Park, today a picnic area; at the north end is Haverstraw Beach Park, now almost entirely unused.

Rockland Lake State Park (1079 acres), Route 9W, Rockland Lake, New York

This is now one of the most intensively developed and heavily used of the parks, with pools, golf courses, and huge parking areas on the level plain with a sweeping view of the gentle hills around and toward the Hudson. In the northwest corner a nature museum and trail have been set up. Fishermen are welcome, as are skaters when conditions permit.

High Tor State Park (564 acres), South Mountain Road, New City, New York

The commission has built a small swimming pool on the south side of Little Tor and plans to maintain most of this park along the South Mountain ridge as a bird and game sanctuary with facilities for hikers.

Suggested Readings

Bradley, Stanley W.
Crossroads of History—The Story of Alpine, New Jersey
Bicentennial Commission, Alpine, N.J., 1978

Palisades Interstate Park Commission
Sixty Years of Park Cooperation: New York–New Jersey, 1900–1960
Palisades Interstate Park Commission, Bear Mountain, N.Y., 1960
(Available at the Commission Administration Building, Bear Mountain, N.Y. 10911)

2 · *BEAR MOUNTAIN–HARRIMAN STATE PARKS*

(Maps 5 and 6)

THE NAME Harriman Park perpetuates the name of Edward H. Harriman, the railroad builder, who conceived the idea of establishing a park in the Hudson Highlands, and of his widow, Mrs. Mary A. Harriman, who carried out his intention by giving ten thousand acres to the state in 1910. The 54,000 acres of the jointly operated Bear Mountain and Harriman State Parks constitute more than seventy-five percent of the Palisades Interstate Park.

In 1908 the state of New York secured Bear Mountain for the incongruous purpose of erecting Sing Sing prison at that location, and established a stockade between Popolopen Brook and what is now Hessian Lake, where hundreds of convicts were put to clear the timber for the prison site. There was much public objection to this use for an area that possessed not only such scenic and recreational values, but sacred historical associations as well. It was on this natural terrace above the Hudson that Fort Clinton and Fort Montgomery had been built during the Revolution, and the militia of Orange and Putnam counties had fallen in fruitless defense of them in 1777. Mrs. Harriman, however, insisted that in exchange for her gift the Palisades Commission's jurisdiction be extended to Newburgh and that the state discontinue its plan to use Bear Mountain as a prison site.

The immediate years after the Harriman gift saw funds for park extension and development raised by private subscription. On this, Mrs. Harriman worked closely with George W. Perkins, then president of the commission. In a sense, the whole park is a memorial to Mr. Perkins. His interest for twenty years, until his death in 1920, his enthusiasms and his capacity for enlisting men and women of wealth in the support of what he saw as a necessary recreational outlet for the metropolitan district were of vast benefit to the park in its formative years. In the 1930s, the road to the summit of Bear Mountain and the tower were constructed as a special memorial to his service.

In subsequent years, further large gifts were made by nearly all the well-known philanthropists and the extension of both the area and the engineering works was pressed under the able supervision of the late Major William Welch, general manager and chief engineer from 1910 to his retirement in 1940. He may well be remembered by all who use the roads and the lakes which he created. Appropriately, Lake Welch, the newest of the large artificial bodies of water in the park, was named for him in 1947. Since 1922 the Bear Mountain Inn has been open and a Trailside Museum, established by special gifts in 1927, provides information on regional history and wildlife to visitors.

The postwar years saw the construction of convenient, although at times distressing, new parkways to and through Harriman State Park. These replaced the former picturesque roads that could not handle the crowds wishing to use more recent facilities such as those at Anthony Wayne, Lake Welch, Sebago Beach, and Silvermine. In 1963 over three thousand additional acres were joined to Harriman State Park, particularly in the area north of Suffern. Two years later the commission acquired Iona Island, a 118-acre rocky promontory jutting out into the Hudson just south of Bear Mountain. The island has a colorful history—as Indian campground, strategic point in Revolutionary War activities, farmland where the Iona grape (which gave the island its name) was developed, summer resort and excursion playground, and finally, beginning in 1899, as an "off-continental United States" base of the U.S. Navy operated as an ammunition depot. Iona Island is now a federally sponsored wildlife and estuarine sanctuary.

Of chief interest to the walker, however, is the great expanse of wild park property which neither the motorists nor the picnickers who crowd the "developed" areas ever see. In the early years of the park, walkers had at their disposal many dirt roads and miles upon miles of the wood roads built by the ironworkers, or they could choose their own way through the thickening woodland according to topography, taste, and compass. As the park administration began to build roads and enlarge the ponds into lakes, hikers blundered into them to their surprise and disappointment. Many are the amusing stories old-timers can tell of coming out in unexpected spots, perhaps uncomfortably late in the day. With a job that must be reached on Monday morning there are limits to the pleasures of exploration. More unsatisfactory still was the difficulty of getting to the real tops of the wooded slopes or of finding the splendid views from cliff and ledge in which the region abounds. Now the blazed trails through the park have sought out these objectives for the hiker to enjoy but still many other "undiscovered" gems have been left for the experienced to find on their own.

Car parking is noted in specific trail descriptions. Public transportation to Bear Mountain–Harriman State Parks is possible from the New York Port Authority Bus Terminal. Buses to the Bear Mountain Inn also stop if requested along Route 9W at Tompkins Cove and Jones Point, where several trails begin. On the western side of the parks, buses to Suffern, Sloatsburg, Tuxedo, Southfields, and Arden give access to trails that enter the park in these locations.

PLACE NAMES IN THE HUDSON HIGHLANDS

Some place names in the Highlands, especially those of Dutch derivation, may seem quaint but their origins are part of our history. One of these is the name of the hamlet of Doodletown, which, until recently, was located in the valley between Bear Mountain and Dunderberg. A picturesque story connects the name Doodletown with the song "Yankee Doodle," claiming that the town was named after the British passed through it in October 1777, playing that march while on their way to attack the forts on Popolopen. It is disproved by the fact that Governor George Clinton, in his report to General Washington on the loss of the forts, tells of sending, a few hours before the British stormed the American works, a half company out to "the place called Doodletown" to scout the British advance. The name, therefore, was a familiar one before the battle. According to Cornelius C. Vermeule of South Orange, the New Jersey expert on place names, "Doodletown" is derived from two Dutch words, "dood" meaning dead, and "del," meaning dale or valley. He suggests that when the Dutch skippers put into the mouth of Doodletown Brook for wood and water, they noticed some aspect of the hollow—possibly dead trees standing after a forest fire, or perhaps a dark, forbidding look that led them to call it "Dooddel" or Dead Valley. The suffix "town" was added later, probably by English settlers. Another word of Dutch origin is "clove," used in early days to refer to certain valleys in the area. This comes from the word "kloof," meaning a ravine.

Among the quaint names in the area the oddest are "Timp"

and "Pyngyp." The cliffs at the west end of the Dunderberg massif and the pass between it and West Mountain were called "Timp," Mr. Vermeule believes, from an obscure Dutch word, "timpje," a colloquial diminutive, meaning a small cake or bun, although the older form, "timp," is almost forgotten. Perhaps some early Dutch skipper, looking across Haverstraw Bay at Dunderberg and noting the general shape of the Dunderberg-Bockberg-Timp massif from Jones Point to Timp Pass, thought of it as a loaf of bread or cake taken out of the baking pan and laid upside down for frosting, with slightly slanting ends and a flat top. From the Dutch-settled farmlands to the south this appearance would have been even more marked. "Pyngyp" is another colloquial name, and good sailor's slang, according to Mr. Vermeule. "Pijngjip," pronounced "pingyp," is an onomatopoeic marine term in the language of the Zuyder Zee, which means the slatting or cracking sound as the boom of a fore and aft rigged vessel, schooner or sloop, comes around on a tack. Pyngyp is the name of a rocky knob on the Palisades Interstate Parkway at Tiorati Brook Road. Its bare cliffs served as a steering point for Dutch skippers tacking across Haverstraw Bay against a head wind. As they neared Grassy Point on a westerly beat, and came in range of those cliffs up the valley of Tiorati Brook, they were due to "pijngjip" or go about with the usual slatting of sails and booms that sounds like the word. This explanation sounds probable and nothing better has been offered. Another interesting term that appears several times in Hudson Highlands names is "torne," probably a variation of "tor"—as in High Tor—a name of Celtic origin meaning a high craggy hill, a rocky pinnacle or peak. Peaks bearing this name in the Hudson Highlands are Popolopen Torne and Ramapo Torne.

Animal names have been given to many places in the area. There is a Catamount Mountain, a Panther Mountain, and a Wildcat Mountain. Turkey Hill, behind Queensboro Reservoir, is called that because wild turkeys once were plentiful on it. Bear Mountain is thought to have received its name because bears once lived there, and one of the earliest mentions of it, the Richard Bradly Patent of 1743, refers to it as "Bear Hill." So also do maps used by both the Americans and British in the Revolutionary War. However, S. W. Eager in his *An Outline History of Orange County* (1847) writes that it "had its name from its bald crest." If Eager is correct, then perhaps the person who drew up the Bradly Patent, on having the name communicated to him verbally, interpreted it to mean the animal and not the condition of the mountain, and spelled it accordingly. To complicate the situation further, the people across the Hudson in Peekskill knew it by still another name—Bread Tray Mountain.

Orange and Rockland counties were occupied by Indians, who left many relics of their residence in that area, some of which are to be seen in the Bear Mountain Trailside Museum. Place names in this region may have their origin in these pre-Columbian settlements. The word Ramapo is regarded as an Indian name meaning "formed of round ponds" and hence applicable to a river where potholes occur. After the river had been so named, it would be only natural to refer to the adjacent hills as the Ramapo Plateau or more specifically the Ramapo Torne. Mr. Vermeule, however, believes it may be a corruption of a Dutch name. "Tuxedo" is a word that may be of Indian origin. It is said to be derived from *P'tauk-seet-tough,* which means "the place of bears." But it may perhaps come from "Duck Cedar," a name found on old maps of the area.

Scattered all through the Bear Mountain–Harriman State Parks are lakes with Indian names. Many of these lakes are artificial, built between 1910 and 1940. Their names are coined from Indian syllables or taken from the Algonquin names of other lakes. Some of the Indian names replaced earlier Anglo-Saxon names. For example, after Cedar Pond and Little Cedar Pond had been converted by damming into one much larger body of water, it was given the name of Lake Tiorati. Similarly Little Long Pond became Lake Kanawauke and Old Car Pond was renamed Lake Stahahe.

A few of the place names the hiker will encounter, and their meanings, are:

Askoti	One side
Cohasset	Place of pines
Kanawauke	Place of much water
Massawippa	Huron Indian maiden
Menomini (Now Silvermine Lake)	Wild rice
Minsi	Place where stones are gathered together
Nawahunta	Place of trout
Oonotoukwa	Cattails
Sebago	Big water
Skannatati	The other side
Skenonto	Deer
Stahahe	Stones in the water
Te-Ata	The dawn
Tiorati	Sky-like
Wanoksink	Place of sassafras

DUNDERBERG SCENIC RAILWAY

This uncompleted and abandoned scenic venture is one of the curiosities of the Highlands. Walkers over Dunderberg Mountain, on the Ramapo-Dunderberg Trail, or on old roads that climb the sides of the mountain, come upon sections of the grade of a railway that can be followed for stretches as long as a mile. But each section ends abruptly and gives the casual walker little impression of a unified scheme. The whole "railway" can be

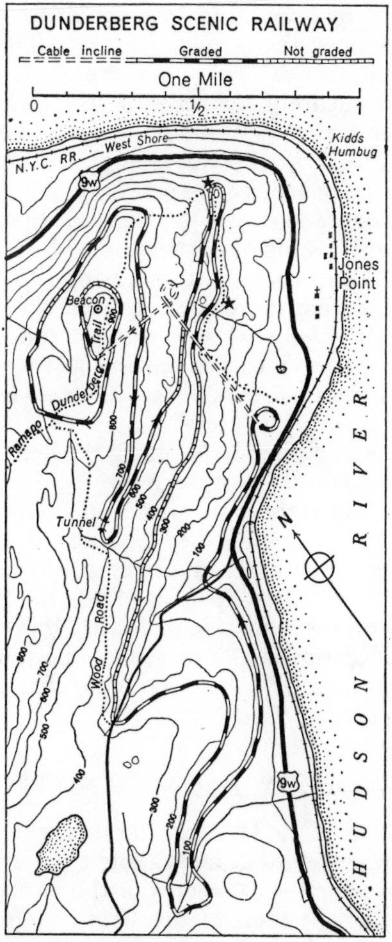

explored in a day by bushwhacking from one section to the next, once the general plan is understood (see the illustration). The "railway" was to have consisted of a cable incline starting from the level of the Hudson River at a point about a half mile south of Jones Point and rising in two stages to the summit (926 feet), where a hotel and summer colony were projected. The descent was to be made by gravity on a winding course with gentle grades over the face of the mountain, some 10 miles in all. The southernmost of these loops approaches the road to the "Mott Farm" west of Tompkins Cove.

William Thompson Howell seems to have been the one who discovered and mapped it for the twentieth century. George Goldthwaite located the original prospectus and description in engineering journals of 1890, when the work started, and Priscilla Chipman filled out the account from other contemporary sources. An enterprising promoter, H. J. Mumford of Mauch Chunk, Pennsylvania, who was doing well operating a similar switchback there, conceived the scheme as another moneymaker, nearer New York, and, to quote his prospectus, "the toiling millions who take an outing in the summer." A company was incorporated in 1889 and work went on during 1890 and part of 1891. But these years were the beginning of a grave depression and money gave out. The work was stopped suddenly. Those who had put their money into the venture lost it. Workmen rioted when payrolls were not met. Thus the "railway" remains as we see it today, grown up to trees.

The map was compiled by plotting the details from Howell's map on the Peekskill sheet of the Army Engineers map, 1:25,000. Note in the upper right-hand corner of the map "Kidds Humbug." This refers to the supposed landing place of Captain Kidd, when he and his men came ashore to bury treasure in the hills to the west. The so-called Spanish Mine near the Ramapo-Dunderberg Trail on the west side of Black Mountain is reputed to have been the location of this treasure. The story continues that it was removed later by a few men who left the bones of one of their number behind them.

GEOLOGY, FAUNA, AND FLORA

The Highlands of the Hudson and their extension southwesterly into the Ramapo Mountains along the New York–New Jersey border, in which 51,000 acres of the park are now located, constitute one of the most picturesque topographic features of the eastern states. The bedrock is among the oldest of geological record, all Precambrian in age, and includes greatly metamorphosed sandstones, shales, and limestones known as the Greenville Series, but is mostly composed of high-grade metamorphic rock, known as the Highlands Complex. Subsequent invasions of granitic magma late in the Precambrian, some 700 to 800 million years ago, have considerably complicated the geology. The banded gneisses display extreme metamorphism of the older sedimentaries, and, in part, flow structures in the invading molten rock. The Highlands probably were once more than ten thousand feet high but most of their mass has since eroded away within the past 600 to 700 million years. The present hills are the remnants of what was a mountain system comparable to the present-day Rockies, and they constitute one of the oldest landmasses in North America.

Among the striking evidences of the most recent episode of continental glaciation in Harriman Park are the abundant glaciated rock surfaces, which are polished, scratched, and grooved, and the many immense erratic boulders transported by ice from the Catskills and elsewhere to the north.

Like the rest of the Hudson Highlands, the Bear Mountain–Harriman State Parks harbor a wide range of plant and animal life. But because of its size, the area offers a more varied habitat —from the brackish Iona Island marsh at sea level to the mountainous interior reaching fourteen hundred feet with its twenty-eight lakes, numerous swamps, open fields, hemlock forests, and hardwood ridges—that has made it an especially popular haunt of amateur students of ornithology, botany, and ecology. Observers can admire any one of the area's roughly forty species of mammals, twenty-five species of reptiles, and more than ninety species of nesting birds.

Among the larger mammals, deer, raccoon, woodchuck, and squirrel probably are the most often seen, although otter, mink, beaver, and bobcat are present in limited numbers. While rare, porcupine and even black bear have been reported. Reptiles that the hiker may encounter include the copperhead and timber rattlesnakes, though they tend to avoid human contact. Visitors to the parks are far more likely to come across garter or water snakes. In rocky, open areas, milk snakes and ring-necked snakes can be found, while hog-nosed snakes are occasionally seen sprawled out on sandy roads, trails, and exposures. Five-lined skinks, who belong to the lizard family, may also scamper across a hiker's path.

With more than 240 species of birds, the birder—and the hiker —has plenty of activity to watch in the sky. Among the more exciting birds are wood duck, goshawk, red-tailed hawk, broad-winged hawk, ruffled grouse, woodcock, screech owl, great horned owl, pileated woodpecker, tree swallow, veery, blue-gray gnatcatcher, hooded warbler, black-throated green warbler, prairie warbler, Louisiana water thrush, and scarlet tanager. Perhaps the two most common and characteristic nesting birds are catbird and towhee, which seem to be everywhere during summer hikes. Iona Island is particularly excellent for birding, with its ducks, herons, bitterns, and marsh wrens in summer and its winter ducks and occasional bald eagle in winter.

A mature forest, the parks' trees are a pleasant blend of evergreen and deciduous varieties. Some of the principal evergreens are red cedar, hemlock, and white pine. The leaf-bearing trees include oak, maple, hickory, ash, tulip, beech, and sour gum. Among the shrubs are rhododendron, laurel, witch hazel, spicebush, wild azalea, sweet pepperbush, alder, blueberry, and sumac, while prickly-pear cactus inundates Iona Island. In addition to the well-known flowers of meadow and forest, the watchful hiker will find many others less known and even rare. Numerous lichens, mosses, and ferns abound in the forest, including evergreen species such as polypody, Christmas and evergreen wood ferns.

IRON MINES IN THE HUDSON HIGHLANDS

The abandoned shafts, pits, and dumps of old iron mines are among the most fascinating features of the Highlands and the Bear Mountain–Harriman State Parks today. There were over twenty mines that were worked at one time or another. The iron is probably of igneous origin, possibly having been a part of an upwelling of molten rock that affected the older rock formations. Mining began in Colonial times, about 1730, and at the height of the industry, at the time of the Civil War, the industry controlled the life of the region and supported a sizable population.

With all the historical emphasis that has been given to the Boston Tea Party and the stamp taxes, it is not always realized that one of the chief reasons for dissatisfaction in the Colonies was the policy of the ministers of King George III, who permitted the mining of iron but refused to allow Americans to manufacture it into articles of common use. The law required that the iron must be shipped to England in pigs as they came from the charcoal furnaces, and there made into bars, cutlery, nails, pots, pans, and so forth, then reshipped to America, with duty being collected both ways. Iron manufactures, therefore, were "bootlegged" in hidden "slitting mills," as they were called, and a source of graft enjoyed by Colonial administrators was to conceal these mills, when properly "fixed," against discovery by agents of the Crown and consequent forced demolition or confiscation.

The largest and by far the most important mine was the Forest of Dean, which was first opened about 1754 by Vincent Mathews. On land now belonging to the U.S. Military Academy, and with the opening filled in, the mine can no longer be located. It was last worked in November 1931.

Another mine, with a name going back to the operations of one of the most remarkable characters of our Colonial history, is the Hasenclever, south of Lake Tiorati on the wood road leading south toward Lake Welch. It is named for "Baron" Peter Hasenclever, a German industrial adventurer whose modest start in the New Jersey Ramapos (see chapter 13) initiated a thriving industry that played a critical role in the history of the area.

A third mine is the Bradley Mine, whose great dark chamber on the south face of Bradley Mountain about 6 miles east of the Arden railway station or 2 miles west of Lake Tiorati, is impressive both in summer, when it is filled with black water in its lower shafts and hung with mosses and liverworts, and in winter, when its entrance is barred with a palisade of thirty-foot icicles and its frozen water surface is studded with eerie ice stalagmites. The Surebridge mines (two great open pits in the woods south of Upper Cohasset Lake), the Pine Swamp mines on the south side of Fingerboard Mountain (the largest left as a slanting chamber), and the Hogencamp mines on the east side of the mountain of that name, north of Kanawauke Lake, are among the largest of these old workings. Others are scattered throughout the region. One of the largest, Bull Mine, east of Schunemunk, is described in chapter 5.

The Greenwood Ironworks, at Arden, consisted of the Greenwood charcoal furnace built in 1811 by James Cunningham, and the Clove anthracite furnace erected by Robert and Peter Parrott in 1854. The Greenwood furnace lies in ruins in the ravine at the outlet of Echo Lake, and the Clove furnace is about 200 yards east of the Arden railroad station and the New York Thruway. Tens of thousands of tons of magnetite ore from the Bradley, Surebridge, Hogencamp, Pine Swamp, Garfield, Boston, and other mines east and west of the Ramapo valley were smelted in these furnaces during the Civil War. The pigs were shipped by rail to Cornwall-on-Hudson where they were ferried across the river to the West Point foundry at Cold Spring to be made into the famous Parrott guns and shells. The two Parrott brothers were

Peter, who operated the mines and furnace, and Robert, who designed and made the guns and projectiles.

During the period 1861–65, Arden was a little Pittsburgh with a population of over two thousand engaged in the mining of ore, the production of charcoal fuel, and the smelting and shipping of pigs and blooms. The woods in the western part of the Highlands were filled with the homes and hamlets of the workers. There was a village of twenty houses and a school at the Hogencamp mines. Foundations of a considerable number of houses can still be traced near the Pine Swamp Mine by the side of the Dunning Trail.

Another center of the early iron industry that will interest walkers in the Highlands is the old Orange (or Queensboro) Furnace built about 1784, on the dirt road leading north from the Queensboro traffic circle on Seven Lakes Drive. About three quarters of a mile downstream from the furnace is the site of the Queensboro Forge. The furnace was last worked in 1800, whereas the forge was active as late as 1843. The Orange Furnace is the center of a remarkable network of old roads, which may still be traced. Ore and charcoal were conveyed to the furnace by ox team over considerable distances.

Smelting with coal replaced smelting with charcoal. The iron deposits of Pennsylvania and the Great Lakes region, so much more easily mined than those in the Highlands, although not so rich in high quality metal, were exploited. Thus the New York–New Jersey industry declined and by 1890 had almost completely

disappeared. The inhabitants drifted away from the region where there was no more work, leaving houses to fall into the cellar holes still visible along many old roads now overgrown. Apple trees, lilac bushes, and old-fashioned flowers remain as occasional mementoes of these homes. The orange-red day lily *(Hemerocallis fulva)* is one of the most common of these garden relics and has survived longest, although it was an importation from Europe that originated in Asia. It is strange to find the lily, perhaps a last survivor of this vanished horticulture, defiant after other adventitious species have been suffocated by the increasing density of the shade of the persistent native trees and shrubs that are recapturing the ground the pioneers cleared.

TRAILS IN THE BEAR MOUNTAIN–HARRIMAN STATE PARKS

Looping across the rugged landscape, draping upon the Highlands a network of infinite combinations, the two hundred miles of marked trails in the Bear Mountain–Harriman State Parks offer a variety unmatched in the area. The hiker may choose to scale the steep face of the Timp or to meander among rhododendron whose ancient forms arch above the Lost Road. To savor the dramatic views of the Hudson from high on Dunderberg or to ramble on old wood roads past sleepy swamps and abandoned mining villages are among the contrasts the parks offer hikers.

The Bicentennial Trails

The 1777 and 1779 trails were created in 1976 for the Bicentennial celebration to commemorate the strategically important military events occurring in the Hudson Highlands during the American Revolution. Under the direction of the Palisades Interstate Park Museum staff, these trails were drawn up following the routes used by the British and American armies two centuries before. Where private property restrictions interfered, portions were rerouted, while remaining faithful to the general routes. The maps consulted were the very ones made for Washington by his official mapmaker, Major Erskine. The Boy Scouts of America marked the trails with the respective numerals inside a white diamond, a unique blaze created for these special trails.

1777 Trail. Length: 1777E (Fort Clinton Branch) 2.5 miles
1777W (Fort Montgomery Branch) 7.0 miles
1777 Trail (common) 3.0 miles
Blazes: red numerals in white diamond.

HISTORY

The 1777 Trail generally follows the route taken by the British to capture Forts Clinton and Montgomery on October 6, 1777. The Hudson River had been an important transportation artery for both Americans and British, but the Americans had achieved control of shipping by means of fortifications and chains across the river. The first of these extended from Fort Montgomery to Anthonys Nose and was guarded by the batteries of both forts.

If the British could control the Hudson River, they would effectively separate the New England colonies from the others. To achieve this they had to remove the Fort Montgomery chain and capture the forts guarding it. As a diversionary tactic, British General Sir Henry Clinton landed his army at Verplanck Point on the east shore of the Hudson on October 5, 1777. As a consequence, General Israel Putnam, commander of the American forces in the Highlands, readied for an attack on his forces stationed at Peekskill and other nearby locations on the east shore of the river. On the following morning, under cover of a dense fog, most of the British force crossed the river undetected from Kings Ferry to Stony Point.

The British then marched north to attack Forts Clinton and Montgomery from the rear. After ascending the southern slope of Dunderberg Mountain to the east of Timp Pass, they descended into Doodletown valley. Here they encountered an American patrol sent out from Fort Clinton to scout the British troop movements. After a brief skirmish, the greatly outnumbered Americans retreated to Fort Clinton.

The British force divided a short distance south of the now-abandoned school in Doodletown. Nine hundred men headed northwest around the rear of Bear Mountain to attack Fort Montgomery (the 1777W Branch) while the remaining twelve hundred men proceeded northeast past the present Bear Mountain Inn to attack Fort Clinton (the 1777E Branch).

Because the militiamen were home harvesting their crops, the forts were undermanned, but the American forces put up a heroic struggle against a much larger British force. At dusk the forts fell, and the Americans escaped across the river or into the mountains.

The British removed the chain and the fleet continued up the Hudson as far as Kingston. After burning that city, they returned and completely destroyed Forts Clinton and Montgomery.

TRAIL DESCRIPTION

The 1777 Trail and the Timp-Torne Trail (blue blazes on white) have their common beginning at a parking area for about eight cars off Route 9W about 1 mile north of Tompkins Cove. The trails start about 200 feet north of the parking area and go west steadily uphill on the south slope of Dunderberg Mountain. The trails cross a brook on a good footbridge 0.4 mile from the start. Three quarters of a mile farther on, the 1777 Trail turns sharp right (north) and steeply ascends the south slope of Dunderberg, leaving the Timp-Torne Trail to continue in its westerly direction. It follows to a large extent the old Pleasant Valley Road, which is often overgrown in places. The trail reaches the crest 0.3 mile later, where it crosses the Ramapo-Dunderberg Trail (red circle on white) coming from the Timp on the left. The Ramapo-Dunderberg Trail continuing on the right goes past Cornell Mine 0.75 mile distant and to its terminus on the Hudson River.

The 1777 Trail goes steeply down the mountain's north side, crossing and recrossing the Timp Brook. The trail gradually levels as it reaches the abandoned village of Doodletown, 1.5 miles from the Ramapo-Dunderberg crossing. Here the thoughtful hiker pauses to look for evidence of past inhabitants. Foundations of former residences dot the trail on both sides, and discarded household objects are often found. In spring, flowering bushes from forgotten gardens splash color here and there. In what used to be the center of the village a road to the right leads to an ancient cemetery with graves of early settlers.

Shortly before the trail reaches the Doodletown Road (also known as Schoolhouse Road) coming in from the left, the trail divides into 1777E and 1777W. The 1777E branch turns slightly to the right on reaching Doodletown Road and continues past a reservoir on the right. The Cornell Trail (blue blazes) comes in from the right 0.3 mile from the reservoir. The two trails coincide for about a half mile to the administration building in the Bear Mountain Recreation Area where the Cornell Trail ends. The 1777E Trail skirts the parking lot, goes past the Bear Mountain Inn and along the east side of Hessian Lake, where it is joined by the Appalachian Trail (white blazes) coming down from the peak of Bear Mountain on the left. The two trails run together for a short distance, going through a tunnel under Route 9W and then following a nature trail. A short visit to the Nature Museum is worthwhile. The Appalachian Trail swings to the right, crossing the Bear Mountain Bridge across the Hudson River. The 1777E Trail continues to its terminus at the reconstructed Fort Clinton.

The 1777W Trail turns left a few hundred feet before the Doodletown Road comes in from the left. The trail crosses a brook, then travels over a meadow that lies along the brook. In early spring this meadow is a virtual swamp and it is advisable to take Doodletown Road past the old, crumbling schoolhouse instead. In 0.3 mile the road and trail come together. At this point the trail crosses the Suffern–Bear Mountain Trail (yellow blazes) coming from West Mountain's steep slope on the left, and continuing to the right and its terminus at the Bear Mountain Inn.

The 1777W Trail goes along the saddle between West and Bear mountains, and past a parking area off Seven Lakes Drive. The trail parallels the road and about 1.25 miles from the Suffern–Bear Mountain crossing it is rejoined by the Timp-Torne Trail coming down West Mountain. The two trails now traverse Highway 6 on a parkway bridge and go past Queensboro Lake and a water treatment facility. Here coming in from the left is the 1779 Trail (blue numerals on white). The three trails continue together for a short distance until the Popolopen Gorge Trail (red blazes), coming from the left down Long Mountain, joins them.

The four trails soon after cross Popolopen Gorge and continue together for about 1 mile. At a fireplace, the 1777W, 1779, and Timp-Torne trails recross Popolopen Brook on a footbridge, while the Popolopen Gorge Trail stays on the other side of Popolopen Brook. The three trails go steeply up the embankment to the Mine Road, once connecting the Forest of Dean Mine to the village of Fort Montgomery. Here the Timp-Torne Trail turns left and climbs steeply up the rocky wall to the top of the Popolopen Torne, with its superb views of the Hudson and the Hudson Highlands. The 1777W and 1779 trails continue on this road, which follows the contours of the gorge. After a short distance the 1777W and 1779 trails cross the Timp-Torne Trail coming down the northeast side of the Torne. One mile farther the trails leave Mine Road and, turning to the right, are rejoined by the Timp-Torne Trail. In another half mile the Timp-Torne Trail reaches its terminus on the west side of Route 9W slightly north of the Popolopen Gorge Bridge. The 1777W and 1779 trails cross the highway and follow the faint path to their common terminus, the ruins of Fort Montgomery, which lies a short distance off the highway.

1779 Trail. Length: 9.6 miles to park boundary. Blazes: blue numerals in white diamond.

HISTORY

The 1779 Trail follows the route taken by the Continental Army on their march from Sandy Beach on the Hudson just north of Fort Montgomery to the British works at Stony Point, about 12 miles south. Led by General "Mad" Anthony Wayne on the night of July 15, 1779, the American force of thirteen hundred men marched south over rough mountain trails under the cover of darkness to carry out successfully a daring surprise attack at midnight of the following night.

In May of 1779, the British Army captured American outposts at Verplanck and Stony points and the Kings Ferry connecting them. The British strategy was to disrupt the American communication and supply lines and to frustrate the movement of American troops between New England and the rest of the Colonies.

Shortly after the capture of Stony Point, a large portion of the British Army withdrew south to Yonkers. Washington then decided to stage a surprise raid to recapture Stony Point and devised a plan of attack entrusting the leadership to General Anthony Wayne. (Wayne received the nickname of "Mad Anthony" after the successful mission, for many thought he had to be "mad" to lead such a risky undertaking.) When Washington asked Wayne if he would lead the expedition, he replied: "I would storm hell if Washington would prepare the plan."

On the night of July 15, Wayne led his troops from Fort Montgomery southwest along the present Mine Road and then down the Fort Montgomery Road past the Queensboro Iron Furnace to Beechy Bottom. At Beechy Bottom, near the present Queensboro traffic circle, they headed south on a rough trail along the eastern side of Black Mountain. They passed through Owl Swamp and then headed east toward Stony Point. Around midnight of July 16, the Americans divided into three columns and advanced on the point over three different routes. The middle column opened fire on the British sentry as a diversion. Simultaneously, the real attacks were launched by the two outer columns, which captured the main works on the summit of the point. Although the British recaptured the fort a few days later, the victory was important as a great morale boost to the Americans and a humiliating defeat for the larger British Army.

TRAIL DESCRIPTION

Park at the Bear Mountain Inn and look for the trail which begins at the Bear Mountain Trailside Museum, the site of Fort Clinton. Leaving the museum area, it heads north through a service gate, coming out on Routes 6 and 202 by the Bear Mountain Bridge tollbooth. The trail heads west to the traffic circle and then north on Route 9W, crossing the Popolopen Gorge Bridge. At the north end of the bridge the trail turns left into the woods by a large stone blazed with the markings of the 1777, 1779, and Timp-Torne trails.

The trail soon emerges on Mine Road with the markers easily seen on telephone poles. At the side of the Popolopen Torne the trail follows a gravel road that turns to the left. (A steep climb up the Torne on the Timp-Torne Trail offers wonderful views in all directions.) Almost immediately the trail descends the hill and turns right, following an old road. After a short distance it turns left and descends to Popolopen Brook, which it crosses on a wooden bridge. Going uphill and to the right (west), the trail winds along the hillside following Popolopen Brook. After crossing the stream several times, the trail turns left on an old road. In this area, General Anthony Wayne and his forces paused to rest and eat at noon, July 15, 1779, on their way to storm Stony Point.

Traveling west, the 1779 Trail parts from the Timp-Torne Trail and skirts the north side of Queensboro Lake, separates from the Popolopen Gorge Trail, and continues through a park maintenance yard and down to Long Mountain Parkway a short distance west of the Queensboro traffic circle. The trail crosses the parkway and continues through a short stretch of woods to Seven Lakes Drive. Reentering the woods on a slight rise a short distance south of Queensboro traffic circle on the east side of Seven Lakes Drive, it soon crosses the Anthony Wayne Trail (white blazes). The trail gradually climbs through a small ravine until it levels out on a rise to cross the combined Appalachian (white) and Ramapo-Dunderberg (red and white) trails, which come down from Black Mountain to the right (west). A steep climb is rewarded by a wide view to the south with New York City visible on clear days.

After reaching an abrupt end to the rise, the 1777 Trail descends and turns slightly southwest. Soon it crosses a fire road that leads right around Owl Swamp to the abandoned dam at its outlet. The trail continues to descend and turns slightly to the east on an old wood road, passing a small swamp and then a stone wall and tall stand of evergreens. The remains of some old foundations can be seen along the trail as it approaches the Palisades Interstate Parkway, where, on a bridge, it crosses a small stream.

Crossing the parkway, the 1779 Trail heads southeast onto an old wood road for a short distance, bearing right over a small arch viaduct, paralleling the parkway. In a short distance the trail passes the intersections of the Suffern–Bear Mountain (yellow blazes) and Red Cross trails. The trail descends a hill and goes left, continuing downhill until it emerges from the forest onto a paved road.

Those interested in following this historic route to Stony Point may wish to continue on paved roads beyond the Harriman Park boundary to Stony Point Battlefield Park. The trail continues down the hill past several houses and turns left on Cedar Flats Road. The markers are easily observed on the telephone poles. After about a mile, the trail turns left on Franck Road downhill and bears right, following Franck Road for 0.8 mile to Wayne Avenue. It turns left on Wayne Avenue for another 0.8 mile to Route 9W and then right on Route 9W for about 0.5 mile. Turning left on Park Road, the trail descends a hill to tidal marshes and the entrance to the Stony Point Battlefield Park.

Anthony Wayne Trail. Length: 2.7 miles. Blazes: white.

This trail, a loop from the Popolopen Gorge Trail at Turkey Hill Lake to the Timp-Torne Trail on the west end of West Mountain, is named for "Mad Anthony" Wayne, a hero of the American Revolution. The trail does not follow the route over which Wayne and his troops marched to attack Stony Point in 1779, but it does cross it between the Seven Lakes Drive and the Palisades Interstate Parkway. Look for the "1779" signs coming in from the left (north) and leaving immediately to the right.

Hikers from Bear Mountain may walk this trail in a circular trip. Auto travelers can park at the small picnic area just south of Long Mountain traffic circle on Seven Lakes Drive, which the trail passes. The trail between Seven Lakes Drive and Turkey Hill Lake is fairly level. East of the drive the trail goes down and over the Palisades Parkway and then through the Anthony Wayne Recreation Area to an old road, which it follows to the left a short distance; it then turns off to the right over the shoulder of West Mountain. The Timp-Torne Trail (blue blazes) enters from the right and the two coincide to Seven Lakes Drive, where the Anthony Wayne Trail ends. The Timp-Torne Trail continues on.

Appalachian Trail. Length: From Bear Mountain Bridge to Route 17, approximately 21 miles. Blazes: white.

That colossus of trails, the Appalachian, its northern terminus the summit of Mount Katahdin in Maine, wends its way through Bear Mountain–Harriman State Parks for 21 of its 2100-mile length to its southern terminus at Springer Mountain in Georgia. Historically, the section of the trail in Harriman Park was the first to be built. The vertical, white, 2-by-6-inch blazes, and intermittent diamond-shaped metal markers, may be followed in the park between the Bear Mountain Bridge crossing the Hudson River and New York State Highway 17 at Arden. Parking near the bridge is convenient at the nearby Bear Mountain Inn. A nominal fee is charged for parking.

A pleasant diversion before climbing Bear Mountain is to retrace the trail a short distance from the inn to the bridge. The trail passes through the Nature Trail of the Trailside Museum with its zoological, geological, and historical exhibits. A heroic statue of Walt Whitman by Jo Davidson stands near the entrance to the Nature Trail with lines from Whitman's "Song of the Open Road" chiseled in granite. Farther along is the redoubt of Fort Clinton, built during the Revolution and vainly defended by Orange County militia in 1777. Along this section of the trail, hikers will also pass the lowest point of the entire Appalachian Trail.

Heading west past the inn, just beyond the ski jump, the Suffern–Bear Mountain Trail (yellow blazes) merges from the left. The two trails then ascend the flank of Bear Mountain, passing the ski jump. In approximately 0.75 mile the Appalachian Trail diverges right and climbs steeply to the 1305-foot summit of Bear Mountain, crossing an abandoned auto road about two thirds of the way up. The summit can also be reached by auto on the Perkins Memorial Drive and affords a splendid view of the Hudson River and the Ramapo hills. Picnic areas are provided. A memorial plaque honoring Joseph Bartha, trails chairman of the New York–New Jersey Trail Conference, 1940–55, is embedded in stone on the trail near the summit. Also on top is the impressive monolithic Perkins Tower, honoring George W. Perkins, the first president of the Palisades Interstate Park Commission, 1900–20.

At the summit the Appalachian Trail crosses the Major Welch

Trail (red blazes) as it begins its steep descent of Bear Mountain. Crossing Perkins Memorial Drive, Seven Lakes Drive, and the historic 1777 Trail, the AT climbs West Mountain, where it joins the Timp-Torne Trail (blue blazes) as both head south for the length of the West Mountain ridge. There are striking views on this ridge walk. The trail then diverges west for a scrambling descent to Beechy Bottom Road, now abandoned but used as a ski trail in winter. After a quarter mile on Beechy Bottom Road, the AT heads west, where it meets the Ramapo-Dunderberg Trail (red on white). The two trails continue together to cross the Palisades Interstate Parkway, the historic 1779 Trail, and then over the top of Black Mountain after a stiff climb. From this summit panoramic views can be enjoyed. West of Black Mountain the two trails cross a ski trail that climbs up from Silvermine Lake, pass the William Brien Memorial Shelter (formerly Letterrock Shelter), and then part at a small wooden bridge. The AT proceeds northwest, crossing Seven Lakes Drive toward Stevens Mountain to sweep in a southerly direction to Arden Valley Road. Nearby Lake Tiorati has a convenient parking lot for walkers in the park. Crossing Arden Valley Road, the trail rejoins the Ramapo-Dunderberg Trail and both continue on a wood road leading through open mixed deciduous woods, passing a water tank on the left, crossing a power line cut, and gradually ascending Fingerboard Mountain ridge (highest point 1328 feet). Occasional glimpses of Lake Tiorati may be seen to the left (east). At 1.1 miles from Arden Valley Road the Hurst Trail (blue blazes) branches off to the left. Not far down the Hurst Trail is a stone shelter accommodating eight.

About 500 feet after the Hurst Trail turnoff, the Ramapo-Dunderberg Trail continues south and the AT turns sharply right (west), dropping down through groves of mountain laurel and hemlock to Surebridge Brook and then south on Surebridge Mine Road (sometimes called Lost Road). On the left, water-filled Greenwood Mine may be seen.

Crossing the Surebridge Brook, the AT ascends the Surebridge Mountain ridge, shortly intersecting the Long Path (turquoise blazes) in the valley between Surebridge Mountain and Island Pond Mountain, near a small pond. At the top of Island Pond Mountain the trail crosses the Arden-Surebridge Trail (red blazes). The AT veers left (south) and descends the Island Pond Mountain ridge. Views of Island Pond may be seen to the right through open woods. Shortly, the trail passes through the Lemon Squeezer, a unique rock formation of tumbled boulders requiring a narrow, steep climb down. The less agile may prefer to bypass the formation by taking a more gradual path leading around to the right.

After the Lemon Squeezer the AT bears right, ascending a slight ridge, and turns left at the top. The trail generally follows a southerly route through stands of oak and mountain laurel, passing over several streams, then gradually turns westward past the Island Pond outlet. The white markers then follow a stony road west for a short distance and enter the woods as the road turns right. This road is a firebreak along the west side of Island Pond. Once in the woods, the AT climbs over Green Pond Mountain, reaching unpaved Old Arden Road, turns right, and heads north past the large parking area known as Elk Pen. The trail then comes out on the paved Arden Valley Road where it swings left, passes over the New York State Thruway and the Ramapo River, finally reaching Route 17. Beyond the road a strenuous climb awaits the hiker as the trail ascends Agony Grind, passing the park boundary and continuing west.

Arden-Surebridge Trail. Length: 5.4 miles. Blazes: red triangle on white.

This is one of the most varied and picturesque trails in Harriman Park. It extends from the junction of Route 17 and Arden Valley Road to the Seven Lakes Drive and the Red Cross Trail at Lake Skannatati, connecting with the Appalachian Trail, Long Path, Lichen, Dunning, Ramapo-Dunderberg, and Red Cross trails. A look at the map will show that a number of circular walks can be made on these trails.

The Arden-Surebridge Trail runs eastward with the Appalachian Trail on the Arden Valley Road, which is the Harriman entrance to the Bear Mountain–Harriman State Parks from Route 17. Buses from the Port Authority Bus Terminal, Manhattan, will discharge passengers at the Harriman entrance. Cars may be parked in a rough clearing south of the road and east of the bridge over the thruway.

After crossing above the railroad tracks, the Ramapo River, and the New York Thruway, the Appalachian Trail diverges to the right (southeast over Green Pond Mountain) and the A-SB continues along the paved road until, opposite a farm gate, it leaves the paved road and follows an old track to the right into the woods for about a half mile before it once again meets and crosses the Arden Valley Road. It then goes over a short stretch of rocky swamp, crosses the road once more, and, after crossing the rather obscure Crooked Road, begins the very steep ascent of

Island Pond Mountain. On the summit, which offers a fine view, the trail continues southeasterly over the mountain to a junction with the Appalachian Trail. Together the trails go through the curious rock formation known as the Lemon Squeezer. Sometime during the last great continental ice sheet, or after it melted approximately eleven thousand years ago, the rocks cracked and tumbled. One, coming to rest on the parent body, formed a triangular tunnel. Another, parting slightly from the bedrock, formed a narrow crevice. For the less adventurous, a bypass around the Lemon Squeezer has been blazed.

Once through the Lemon Squeezer, the A-SB turns left (east). It then goes over faint wood roads and in a short distance is joined by the Long Path, which comes in from the left. It passes the southern end of Dismal Swamp, a grassy clearing with dead trees here and there. After climbing the southern end of Surebridge Mountain, it passes the northern end of the Lichen Trail in a dense growth of rhododendron. It then continues through a picturesque arching tunnel of rhododendron and through a stand of hemlock to the Surebridge Mine Road. Over this road, iron ore was hauled during the Civil War by horses and oxen to the Greenwood Furnace at Arden, located opposite the railroad station at Arden, a half mile north of the A-SB at the Harriman entrance. Next the trail turns right and shortly crosses the Ramapo-Dunderberg Trail at "Times Square," identified by a stone fireplace beside a boulder. Care must be taken to follow the red triangles on white, since the Ramapo-Dunderberg is marked by red dots on white. The Long Path (turquoise blazes) leaves the A-SB here to the right heading southeast. About a half mile farther on, the trail meets the beginning of the Dunning Trail (yellow blazes).

After crossing a brook, the trail continues on for several hundred feet past a water-filled mine on the left and then makes a sharp right turn (southeast) off the road, continuing past the northeast corner of Pine Swamp in an area where the temperature can be twenty degrees cooler than the surrounding area. Stone foundations of an old mining village may be seen in this area. Following another old wood road, the trail makes another sharp right turn off the road and climbs gently up through a glen to the top of Pine Swamp Mountain. Here there are beautiful views to the south of Lake Kanawauke (Little Long Pond), Lake Sebago, and the Ramapo ridge. In a short distance the Red Cross Trail begins on the left. To continue on across the park, turn left (north) on the Red Cross Trail to the Timp-Torne Trail, which ends at Route 9W. After descending Pine Swamp Mountain, the

A-SB ends at the parking lot at Lake Skannatati on Seven Lakes Drive.

Beech Trail. Length: 3.6 miles. Blazes: blue.

The Beech Trail connects the Red Cross Trail with the Long Path in a section of Harriman Park that lies east of Seven Lakes Drive. First blazed in 1972, the trail incorporates wood roads once used by charcoal burners and workers at Hasenclever Mine and by rural settlers of Sandyfields, a hamlet inundated by the creation of Lake Welch in the 1940s.

From its terminus on the Red Cross Trail at a point approximately 1 mile northeast of Tiorati Brook Road, the Beech Trail heads south through deciduous woods, crossing a low shoulder of Flaggy Meadow Mountain. It crosses Tiorati Brook on a wood-plank footbridge and reaches Tiorati Brook Road at 0.7 mile. Here is a large parking area for hikers. Auto access in winter is from Tiorati traffic circle only, due to the seasonal closing of Lake Welch Drive and Tiorati Brook Road.

The trail crosses the road, turns into the woods, and, rising from Tiorati Brook valley, runs generally southwest, following a Tiorati tributary. It gently scales the east slope of Nat House Mountain. Arthurs Falls, a fine cascade, is passed. Much laurel and some venerable hemlocks are in evidence. At 1.5 miles the trail intersects Hasenclever Road (a wide fire lane, not an auto road). Northwest in less than 1 mile and at its junction with the Red Cross Trail, Hasenclever Road leads to the remains of Hasenclever Mine, active in Colonial times; southeast in about a half mile, Hasenclever Road leads to Lake Welch Drive and the beach area.

After crossing Hasenclever Road, the Beech Trail continues through level woods and reaches an area of stone walls, scraggly fruit trees, lilacs, wisteria, and barberry bushes—all traces of human habitation. A good-sized stone root cellar is just off the trail, and the remains of stone foundations are nearby. Though this land is overgrown with the ubiquitous blueberry, with sweet fern, birch, and wild cherry, the walker senses the openness of cleared land, and it is easy to visualize the farm dwellings and active life that were once here. A lone eighty-foot Norway spruce, not native to this area and undoubtedly planted by a human hand, stands sentinel. At about 2 miles and just before leaving this area of stone walls and cut overgrowth, the trail passes a small family burying ground. Among the laurel are two large, matching headstones, clearly chiseled—one for John R. Jones, 1817–1896, and one for Highlyann Babcock Jones who died in 1886 at the age of sixty-five years, nine months, fourteen days. A small stone for Hiram Jones, aged three years, ten months, twenty-five days, tells its story. Several other grave sites are indicated by small, rude, native stone slabs upended and set in the ground, their tips protruding. Beyond a stone wall separating it from the cluster of gravestones is a headstone for Timothy Youmans of Company K, 6th Heavy Artillery, who died April 7, 1865, just two days before Lee's surrender at Appomattox.

At 2.5 miles the trail joins a wood road, shown on old maps as Rockhouse Mountain Trail, and passes under the east flank of Rockhouse Mountain. At 3 miles the trail crosses Route 106 (Old Route 210). It follows a level wood road among laurel and oaks, passing on its left Green Swamp, one of two by that name in Harriman Park, and on its right an imposing hill of boulders. It reaches its terminus at the Long Path at 3.6 miles. From this point on the Long Path it is less than 1 mile south to Lake Welch Drive and from there a walk of about 1000 feet on Johnsontown Road to the hikers' parking area at the church of St. Johns in the Wilderness.

A circular hike of 9 miles can be made by linking the Beech Trail with parts of the Long Path and Red Cross trails. For this suggested circular the walker has a choice of four starting points, as auto access may be gained from the following four parking areas: Tiorati Brook Road at the Beech Trail, St. Johns Church for the Long Path, Lake Skannatati for the Long Path and Red Cross trails, and Tiorati Brook Road near the Red Cross Trail.

Blue Disc Trail. Length: 2.9 miles. Blazes: blue disc on white.

This trail begins at the turning circle at the end of old Johnsontown Road, where cars may be parked. It diverges left along a gas pipeline, which it follows to the Kakiat Trail crossing (white blazes). Here it makes a left turn, coinciding with the Kakiat to the base of Almost Perpendicular, which offers excellent views to the south and east. The trail then continues north along a ridge and descends gradually to Elbow Brush, where it squeezes between two boulders and under a small cliff to reach a stream. The trail follows the stream past a swamp and crosses the Tuxedo–Mount Ivy Trail (red dash on white) at Claudius Smith's Den. Next it continues north over Big Pine Hill, from which there is a fine all-around view, to its terminus at the place known as Tri-Trail Corners at the foot of Black Ash Mountain. It is so named because the southern terminus of the Victory Trail (blue V), the northern terminus of the Blue Disc Trail, and the Ramapo-Dunderberg Trail (red on white) meet here.

Breakneck Mountain Trail. Length: 1.5 miles. Blazes: white.

This trail connects the Tuxedo–Mount Ivy Trail south of Breakneck Pond with the Suffern–Bear Mountain Trail on the ridge east of the north end of the pond. The beginning of this trail is 0.1 mile east of Pine Meadow Road East on the Tuxedo–Mount Ivy Trail. It climbs and winds gradually over Breakneck Mountain and, in 0.2 mile, passes a large boulder called West Pointing Rock. A sharp projection on its west side accounts for its name. A short distance beyond is a fine view north. The radio relay tower on Jackie Jones Mountain also can be seen. Here, on the exposed bedrock, rests a boulder split in two, a reminder of the great ice sheet that once covered the land and left many such rocks in its wake as it melted back. From this point the trail descends steeply, then continues north to its terminus at the Suffern–Bear Mountain Trail. Big Hill Shelter is 0.8 mile north. There is no water at the shelter.

Conklins Crossing Trail. Length: 0.65 mile. Blazes: white.

This trail, a short cutoff from the Pine Meadow Trail to the Suffern–Bear Mountain Trail, shortens the distance from Pine Meadow Lake to Suffern for anyone using the Suffern–Bear Mountain Trail south to Suffern. From the Pine Meadow Trail near the eastern end of Pine Meadow Lake, turn right and cross a fairly level woods to the Suffern–Bear Mountain Trail on the crest of the rampart near a tremendous boulder. Left (north) on the Suffern–Bear Mountain 0.3 mile is the E. D. Stone Memorial Shelter. The Suffern–Bear Mountain right (south) leads to Suffern.

Cornell Trail. Length: 2.75 miles. Blazes: blue.

The Cornell Trail extends from the Bear Mountain Inn to the Ramapo-Dunderberg Trail near the summit of Bald Mountain. Its first section is fairly easy walking on wood roads and, when the trees are bare, offers pleasant views of the Hudson River. Beginning at a large signboard behind the Bear Mountain Inn, it travels south along the east side of the ice-skating rink, past the administration building to the parking lot, where it joins the 1777 Trail. Together they pass through a tunnel. After leaving the tunnel, the trail turns right immediately off the paved walk and onto an old wood road. Passing under another tunnel, the trail then starts to climb.

After passing along the west side of an open field, the Cornell Trail diverges left from the 1777 Trail, reaching the Old Doodletown Road with its broken asphalt surface. A right turn here leads to the abandoned village of Doodletown. The trail turns left onto the road and reaches Route 9W, where it turns right along the highway for a short distance. There is parking for a half dozen cars here on the east side of the road. Just after crossing a small bridge, the trail turns right and enters the woods. It climbs, at times steeply, along the top of a stream bank.

The final climb is steep and continuous for an approximate 500-foot change in elevation. The Cornell Trail ends when it reaches the Ramapo-Dunderberg Trail at the col between Dunderberg and Bald mountains. A short distance to the west (right) a moderate climb along the Ramapo-Dunderberg leads to the Cornell Mine and a good view across the Hudson River with the Bear Mountain Bridge to the left.

Dean Trail. Length: 0.9 mile. No blazes.

This is an unmarked trail connecting the Ramapo-Dunderberg and Red Cross trails, making possible a modest circular from Lake Tiorati. The trail begins at the Letterrock Shelter and heads southeast on an old, heavily eroded wood road. Going downhill gently, the trail meanders along, soon paralleling a brook that appears on the left. Another unmarked trail will intersect from the right. The trail meets the Red Cross Trail a short distance west of Burnt House. Depending upon the season, some spots may be wet.

Diamond Mountain Trail. Length: 0.25 mile. Blazes: white.

The Diamond Mountain Trail connects the Tower and Pine Meadow trails with the Seven Hills and Hillburn-Torne-Sebago trails. The start of the trail is on the Tower Trail (yellow blazes) near an old Civilian Conservation Corps building foundation and is visible from the nearby Pine Meadow Trail (red on white). The trail climbs steeply uphill, mostly over open ledges, with good views of Pine Meadow Lake and Lake Wanoksink to the east and of Raccoon Brook Hill to the south. It reaches its terminus on top of Diamond Mountain. From the top of the ridge parts of the skyline of New York City are visible to the south-southeast on clear days. Here the Diamond Mountain Trail meets the Seven Hills Trail (blue on white) and the Hillburn-Torne-Sebago Trail (white blazes). These trails run jointly along the ridge, to the left over Diamond and Halfway mountains to Pine Meadow Brook, and to the right to separate endings at the parking area and dam, respectively, on Lake Sebago.

Dunning Trail. Length: 3.8 miles. Blazes: yellow.

Extending from the Nurian Trail on High Peak to the Arden-Surebridge Trail at the crossing of Pine Swamp Brook, this trail connects with the White Bar, Ramapo-Dunderberg, and Long Path. It crosses no paved roads, nor does it begin or end at one, and is as uncommon and varied a trail as any in the park. The trail was opened and blazed by Dr. J. M. Dunning, a member of the New York Chapter of the Appalachian Mountain Club, and is shown as the "Dr. Dunning" Trail on Hoeferlin's maps. It gives access to several of the old mines and can also be used in combination with several other trails to form circuits.

From Southfields follow the Nurian Trail (white blazes) for 2 miles to the top of Green Pond Mountain. Here the Dunning Trail begins, its yellow markings going southeast from the summit to Green Pond, a small, swampy body of water with a rocky, precipitous north shore over which the trail winds. Most of the pond's shoreline is rimmed with thick vegetation. From Green Pond the trail runs east, and just before reaching Island Pond Road it crosses the Nurian Trail. It then follows Island Pond Road left (north) 100 yards, turns east 50 yards to Boston Mine, a water-filled cavern, and then goes to the right up over the hill behind the mine. It proceeds a half mile to the White Bar Trail, with which it coincides for 0.3 mile along the "Crooked Road." The two trails part when the Dunning turns right, leaving the White Bar on the old road, and a half mile farther on crosses the Ramapo-Dunderberg Trail on a ridge of Hogencamp Mountain. This point is a few hundred feet north of the Bald Rocks Shelter on the Ramapo-Dunderberg Trail, from which an unmarked trail shortcuts diagonally down the hill to the Dunning. The latter continues slightly downward and eastward, eventually crossing a broad plateau, much of which is bare rock. From here it follows old wood roads the rest of the way.

About 500 feet downhill from the plateau, the former route of the Dunning Trail comes in on the left. This path connects with the Long Path about a quarter mile distant and is distinguished by brown blazes painted over the old yellow ones. The Dunning Trail twists and turns for a third of a mile until it comes to a fire road on the right with a two-directional entrance. Running down through an abandoned camp, this road comes out on Route 106 (Old Route 210) opposite Little Long Pond.

The trail soon climbs over a slight rise and past a large swamp on the right. Many mounds of tailings may be seen at the edge of the swamp from the extensive Hogencamp Mine diggings on the left. The trail crosses a brook, and at the top of another small hill there is a huge rounded-off outcrop of rock on the right. Just this side of the outcrop a path leads off right from the Dunning Trail and follows an old wood road down to the fire road mentioned previously. A few steps farther to the left the Long Path comes in and follows the Dunning Trail north about 75 yards before turning downhill to the right toward Lake Skannatati and the parking area on Seven Lakes Drive. From here on, the Dunning becomes straighter, more level, and heads northward, passing the west side of Pine Swamp for about a half mile. The large open area offers a peaceful view to the far side of the swamp as the trail winds along below tall hemlocks.

Pine Swamp Mine is on the left, but the mine entrance cannot be seen from the trail. Look for a big pile of mine tailings to the left of the trail, from which it is a short climb to the entrance. (A more level approach is from the Arden-Surebridge Trail along a faint wood road that cuts back sharp left from the trail a few hundred feet past its junction with the Dunning.) The side trip is worthwhile. Water dripping down the side wall of the mine entrance has turned it into a mural of earth colors. The Dunning Trail continues to follow the old road past the mine for about 0.3 mile until it reaches its terminus at the Arden-Surebridge Trail (red triangle on white).

Hillburn-Torne-Sebago Trail. Length: 5.2 miles. Blazes: white.

The Hillburn-Torne-Sebago Trail extends from Seven Lakes Drive at the Lake Sebago dam south to the Ramapo Torne, connecting with the Tuxedo–Mount Ivy, Stony Brook, Seven Hills, Diamond Mountain, Kakiat, Pine Meadow, and Raccoon Brook Hills trails. The trail terminates at the Torne. At the north end, parking is available at the Lake Sebago parking area off Seven Lakes Drive, 0.7 mile past the start of the trail and 4.3 miles from Route 17.

The trail begins at the foot of the dam, on the north side of the brook. It follows Woodtown Road, turns off to the right (south) on a path, crosses the Tuxedo–Mount Ivy Trail (red on white) and continues on the unmarked Stony Brook Trail for a short distance. Turning off left, it climbs Diamond Mountain by a steep and rocky route. Near the top is a good lookout over Lake Sebago. At the top the Seven Hills Trail (blue on white) joins it from the left, from the Lake Sebago parking area. The two trails pass the start of the Diamond Mountain Trail (white blazes), which descends left to the Tower and Pine Meadow trails. The Hillburn-Torne-Sebago and Seven Hills trails continue over the summit, then take their separate ways to Pine Meadow Brook, the Seven Hills Trail straight ahead over Diamond Mountain, the HTS Trail turning off right over Halfway Mountain. At the base of the mountain, the trail turns left onto the Kakiat Trail (white blazes), coming from the right from Seven Lakes Drive. After a few feet, the HTS Trail turns off to the right and crosses the brook on a footbridge over the Cascade of Slid. It meets the Pine Meadow Trail (red on white), coming from the right from the Reeves Meadow parking area, joins it going left for a short distance, then turns off right up Chipmunk Mountain. Soon the Seven Hills Trail joins from the left, coincides briefly, and leaves to the right toward a junction with the Reeves Brook Trail. The HTS Trail next crosses the Raccoon Brook Hill Trail (black R on white), descending alongside the Russian Bear cliff to a hollow to cross a brook. On the opposite slope, the Seven Hills Trail joins again from the right, then leaves, going right toward Seven Lakes Drive. The HTS Trail continues to its terminus on the Ramapo Torne at a boulder near the southeast edge of the summit.

Hurst Trail. Length: 0.5 mile. Blazes: blue.

The Hurst Trail provides access to Fingerboard Shelter from Seven Lakes Drive, connecting with the Appalachian and Ramapo-Dunderberg trails on Fingerboard Mountain. The Hurst Trail starts on Seven Lakes Drive at a point about halfway between Tiorati traffic circle (parking available) and the Lake Skannatati parking area. The beginning, on the west side of the road, is marked by two metal posts with a bar across. The trail leads right, along the base of the mountain, then heads left and up. It goes to the left of the shelter and behind it. After a short additional climb, the trail ends at the joint Appalachian (white blazes) and Ramapo-Dunderberg (red on white) trails.

Jones Trail. Length: 1 mile. No blazes.

This trail across the east side of Dunderberg Mountain connects the Timp-Torne and Ramapo-Dunderberg trails, making possible an attractive circular hike starting from Route 9W. The trail also provides direct access to the long-abandoned Dunderberg Railway Tunnel.

Starting at the parking area for the Timp-Torne and 1777 trails, proceed west on the marked trail. After about ten minutes of steady walking, cross a small wood bridge where the trail bends left and uphill. Shortly thereafter, the trail makes a sharp left at the top of a rise, continuing straight ahead on the well-defined track that is the start of the Jones Trail. If this point is missed, a right turn on an old roadway about 30 yards farther on will lead downhill shortly to join the Jones Trail.

The trail bears north across the face of the mountain on old roadbeds once planned for the railway system. Glimpses of the Hudson River off to the right depend upon the season and foliage cover. On the left are some steep, rocky slopes. The trail continues to a brook, which may be dry in summer. There the trail forks, with the main trail veering left along the brook.

To find the Dunderberg Railway tunnel, cross the brook and a few yards beyond pass through a large cleft in the rock off to the right. Emerge onto a rocky roadway with a good river view. Keeping close to the cliffs, continue on the roadway about 100 yards to the mouth of the tunnel. It extends about 50 feet into the face of the cliff and could provide shelter from the elements in an emergency.

To resume following the Jones Trail, pick up the trail at the brook, which it crosses shortly to the right. Proceed directly across the brook and continue uphill. The trail then intersects another segment of the railway roadbed. A right turn leads to another good view of the Hudson River; a turn to the left takes one along a level section of the trail that is actually a mossy roadway. Passing a swampy pond on the right, the trail intercepts the Ramapo-Dunderberg Trail.

At the trail intersection, the Ramapo-Dunderberg goes uphill to the right, while to the left it slopes down with a sharp curve. Because there are several unmarked roadways intersecting the Ramapo-Dunderberg, look for a sharply defined roadbed with a steep, rocky shoulder on the downhill side to find the Jones Trail from the Ramapo-Dunderberg.

Kakiat Trail. Length: 8 miles. Blazes: white, sometimes black K on white.

Although this trail touches no high or open view points, it offers a considerable variety of terrain. Named after one of the oldest land grants on the east side of the Ramapos, Kakiat is a corruption or contraction of the Indian word "Kackyacktaweke," which appears on the land grant patent of 1696, referring to the land purchased from the Indians and confirmed by patent from King William III.

The trail crosses the park in a northwest to southeast direction, from the Ramapo-Dunderberg Trail near Tuxedo to Route 202 at the entrance to Kakiat Park in Rockland County. It crosses or connects with the Blue Disc, Stony Brook, Hillburn-Torne-Sebago, Seven Hills, Pine Meadow, Raccoon Brook Hills, and Suffern–Bear Mountain trails.

Leave the parking lot at the Tuxedo railroad station on the Ramapo-Dunderberg Trail (red on white), which heads south along the tracks, crosses the Ramapo River on a footbridge, passes under the thruway and turns left on Grove Drive. The Kakiat Trail starts at Grove Drive and continues jointly with the Ramapo-Dunderberg Trail to the edge of the woods, where it diverges right, up a wood road. The trail follows wood roads and a utility line around Daters Mountain and, at a point below Almost Perpendicular, joins the Blue Disc Trail (blue on white) coming in from the left from Claudius Smith's Den. After about 0.2 mile, at a gas pipeline, the Blue Disc Trail turns off right toward the Johnsontown Road parking circle. (Access to the Kakiat Trail by car is possible at this point. Park at the end of Johnsontown Road and walk east along the gas pipeline parallel to Seven Lakes Drive to the Kakiat Trail.)

At about 2.3 miles, the Kakiat Trail crosses Seven Lakes Drive and circles to the south around a ridge and down to a bridge across Stony Brook. It joins the unmarked Stony Brook Trail and both shortly cross Pine Meadow Brook on another bridge. The Stony Brook Trail continues ahead, while the Kakiat Trail makes a sharp right turn along the north bank of Pine Meadow Brook. The going here is quite rugged, over and around very large boulders along the ravine. The trail passes the Cascade of Slid, a spectacular sight during the spring runoff, and then crosses the Hillburn-Torne-Sebago Trail (white blazes), which goes left up Halfway Mountain and right toward Russian Bear.

Shortly after, the Seven Hills Trail (blue on white) comes in from the left from Diamond Mountain. The two trails meet the Pine Meadow Trail (red on white), coming in from the left from Pine Meadow Lake, and all three cross Pine Meadow Brook on a footbridge. The Seven Hills and Pine Meadow trails then head right, and the Kakiat Trail turns left along a tributary stream. It soon arrives at the terminus of the Raccoon Brook Hills Trail (black R on white), which goes left to make a long loop over Raccoon Brook Hill, coming down to cross the Kakiat Trail farther south. The Kakiat Trail now crosses several ridges and the deep ravine of Torne Brook, then crosses the Suffern–Bear Mountain Trail (yellow blazes) on Cobus Mountain. The Suffern–Bear Mountain Trail leads left to the Stone Memorial Shelter and right to Suffern, while the Kakiat Trail comes down the mountain, mostly on wood roads. Where it passes directly under the power line, it makes a sharp left turn that should be watched for. At the base of the mountain the Kakiat Trail follows along dirt roads (marked also with a green horizontal stripe on a large white blaze) in Rockland County's Kakiat Park, crossing the Mahwah River on a footbridge and then following the paved park road to its terminus at the entrance to the park on Route 202. Parking is available near the entrance or, lower down, at a loop in the park road.

Lichen Trail. Length: 0.5 mile. Blazes: blue L on white.

This trail connects the Arden-Surebridge and Ramapo-Dunderberg trails. Its southern end is 6.1 miles from Tuxedo on the Ramapo-Dunderberg Trail; the northern end is 3.1 miles from Arden on the Arden-Surebridge Trail. The trail was marked by Frank Place in 1933 and is named for the lichens found on the rocks along its route.

Starting from the north end at the Arden-Surebridge Trail, the Lichen climbs Hogencamp Mountain, through a hemlock grove, ascending about 100 feet in elevation before leveling off somewhat on the summit. It then follows the mountaintop, over ice-smoothed ledges and between clumps of pitch pine, dipping and climbing slightly until it meets the Ramapo-Dunderberg Trail on a flat area of exposed bedrock. Along the way are wide views over the country to the west, including Island Pond and the hills beyond the Ramapo Valley, toward Greenwood Lake. It is convenient as a shortcut between the Ramapo-Dunderberg and the Arden-Surebridge trails.

Long Mountain Trail. Length: 1.1 miles. Blazes: blue.

From the trail head of the Popolopen Gorge Trail on the Long Path east of Long Mountain Parkway, the Long Mountain Trail travels north up the slope of Long Mountain, with at least one good view southward. After attaining the ridge, it soon passes the Torrey Memorial, honoring Raymond Torrey, one of the authors of the original *New York Walk Book.* From here there is a fine view north, south, and east.

Continuing along the ridge, the trail dips into a saddle and then descends left into Deep Hollow to end, as it begins, on the Long Path. From the saddle, an unmarked trail continues 0.2 mile farther on the ridge to the park boundary. A dated permit is required to continue north of this point onto the grounds of the United States Military Academy.

The best parking spot for this whole area of trails is where the Long Path crosses Old Route 6. Drive up the present Route 6 from Long Mountain (Queensboro) traffic circle for about a mile. Old Route 6 leads off to the right, leading to the parking lot.

Long Path. Length: 22.8 miles. Blazes: turquoise.

This section of the Long Path runs from Mount Ivy on the park's eastern border north, west, and then north to Route 293 and the Long Mountain Parkway. In Mount Ivy, parking is available on nonbusiness days only in the commuter parking lot. Telephone the Haverstraw police, or visit the headquarters 2 miles to the east on the right (south) side of Route 202, and leave your car license number. Also have a decal of the New York–New Jersey Trail Conference or a hiking club in the car window. For those not planning to hike the LP from its entrance into Harriman Park, parking is also available at Lake Skannatati, where the LP crosses Seven Lakes Drive. In addition, the LP intersects thirteen of the park's trails and is easily accessible from many directions.

At the junction of Routes 45 and 202 head west under the Palisades Interstate Parkway and follow the entrance ramp on the right beyond Quaker Road to the triangle. Cross the ramp and enter the woods in a small pine grove. Continue north, paralleling the parkway for little more than a mile over a stony trail through pleasant woods to a grassy wood road. At this point the trail turns right for 0.1 mile and then turns left. The blazes are difficult to follow here and the tendency is to continue bearing right. The trail crosses over a small stream, and within several hundred feet turns right onto an old wood road. Soon the trail turns left uphill and after a short steep climb reaches a knob of Cheesecote Mountain. From here is an interesting view east to the Hudson River and the village of Haverstraw. To the southeast is the final dike of the Palisades, which the LP follows from High Tor to Mount Ivy.

Descending the far side, the trail turns right immediately on another wood road that soon intersects a fire road (the old Letchworth Road) and turns left. In a short distance picturesque Cheesecote Pond comes into view. This is 2.5 miles from Mount Ivy and the parking here is for the residents of Haverstraw only. Passing along the south and west shores of the pond, the LP takes the gravel road west, then north and west again, heading down off Cheesecote Mountain. It passes under power lines and along the western side of the Letchworth Village Cemetery to Calls Hollow Road at 3.25 miles. (Parking here is at your own risk.)

Continuing left on Calls Hollow Road for 0.1 mile, the LP enters the woods on the right (north) side of the road just before it makes a sharp turn left. In another 200 feet the trail crosses a small brook (a stream in the spring) and turns left uphill on a very old wood road (Turnpike Trail). Pay careful attention to the blazes. Within a mile the LP reaches the site of an old farmhouse. It passes the foundation of an old storage hut—the only remains of the farm.

After crossing several small crests strewn with rather large glacial erratics, the trail reaches a gravel road that runs above a buried cable. The trail follows it to the right (west). In 0.7 mile the Suffern–Bear Mountain Trail (yellow blazes) crosses the LP. It continues on for 0.3 mile to a white-blazed side trail leading in 0.1 mile to Big Hill Shelter, which offers a beautiful view across the valleys to the east. It was renovated in 1981 in a project sponsored by the DeWitt Wallace Foundation under the supervision of the park to provide meaningful work to underprivileged teenagers in the area.

The LP continues west for 0.5 mile where it passes on the right (north) a large clearing. This is where the ill-fated jet passenger plane that was to pick up the Baltimore Colts football team in Buffalo crashed in early December 1974.

Immediately after this clearing, the LP turns right (north) and crosses Beaver Pond Brook on stepping-stones. It then bears right and continues north, turns left up a low hill, crosses a boulder-strewn hollow, meanders through the woods for a few hundred yards, and then makes a sharp right turn along yet another wood road. Shortly it turns left, and straight ahead 1000 feet is St. Johns in the Wilderness, an Episcopal church. Shortly after, the trail crosses Lake Welch Drive at 7.75 miles from Mount Ivy.

Now the trail follows wood roads west and north to more old foundations. Heading down a short slope, it passes around several swampy areas and at 8.25 miles passes the terminus of the Beech Trail (blue blazes) on the right. Be careful here because the Beech Trail is also marked in blue. It goes off to the right (north) while the LP continues straight and slightly to the left. In .75 mile the trail crosses Route 106 (Old Route 210), makes a slight jog to the right, and enters the woods again, turning left along the shoulder of Rock House Mountain.

Heading north, the trail passes under a local (one-line) power line and soon comes to the south end of Lake Askoti, where it turns left to the Seven Lakes Drive, passing the parking lot at Lake Skannatati, 9.4 miles from Mount Ivy.

The trail now twists among the trees on the north shore of the lake, passing the terminus of the Arden-Surebridge Trail (red triangle on white) on the right. Continuing west, the trail crosses Pine Swamp Brook, and climbs uphill along a massive rock wall. In 2.2 miles, after going steeply uphill, it arrives at the Dunning Trail. Turning left, the LP coincides with the Dunning for 500 feet until turning right.

As it continues west, the trail passes foundations of buildings from the mining days. In a few hundred feet immediately to the left of the trail is one of the shafts of the Hogencamp Mine. Farther on, the LP winds its way through what was once beautiful hemlock groves until the gypsy moth devastation of 1981 destroyed them. A few more old foundations are passed and an old mine road.

At 3 miles from Seven Lakes Drive is "Times Square"—so-called because three major trails come together at this spot. Here the Ramapo-Dunderberg (red *dot* on white) and the Arden-Surebridge Trail (red *triangle* on white) cross the LP, which now joins the Arden-Surebridge for 1 mile. The LP passes the start of the Lichen Trail on the left in 0.6 mile. In another 0.4 mile, the White Bar Trail starts from the left, heading south, and the LP turns sharp right (north) while the Arden-Surebridge continues straight (west). The trail travels over more wood roads along the west side of beautiful swamps, which are actually natural reservoirs, with fine hemlock stands on the east side. In 4.8 miles from Seven Lakes Drive the trail crosses the Appalachian Trail, and from here, one can hike to Maine, Georgia, or any point in between, while the LP continues on its way to Lake Placid.

The LP now follows a pleasant winding course among maples and hemlocks, passing an area where tree stumps offer evidence of heavy beaver activity many years ago. After a few more climbs, several short and steep, the trail levels off to a view north. Slightly to the left Arden House can be seen. Formerly the Harriman estate, it is now owned by Columbia University.

Now heading east and downhill, the LP crosses Surebridge Mine Road, and heads toward Fingerboard Mountain. It stays on the gentle slope of the mountain and heads north, passing beautiful hemlock stands and deep valleys until in 6.8 miles it crosses Arden Valley Road. The trail then follows a wood road north around Bradley Mountain and along the ridge. Shortly before reaching Stockbridge Shelter, 2.7 miles north of Arden Valley Road, the curious Hippo Rock is passed. This is a large overhanging boulder that seems to be ready to topple over. The shelter commands a fine view south.

About 0.2 mile farther north are two small cave shelters located in a rocky hollow. From there the trail continues north, and in another 1.8 miles crosses the Long Mountain Parkway (parking available), a short distance beyond meeting the junction of the Long Mountain and Popolopen Gorge trails, both of which begin here. The LP travels to the site of the shelter, which was removed by the park because of vandalism, then crosses the brook and follows the military reservation boundary west up over the steep slope of Howell Mountain (named for William Thompson Howell, a pioneer trail walker of the Highlands). There is a fine view from the summit. After a descent into Brooks Hollow, the trail crosses the brook and a short way beyond that passes on the right a cave large enough to shelter one or two persons during a shower. The trail then climbs steeply up over Brooks Mountain and descends to Route 293 in the valley.

Major Welch Trail. Length: 3.3 miles, including loop. Blazes: red ring on white rectangle.

This trail, from Bear Mountain Inn to the summit of Bear Mountain, was named in honor of Major William A. Welch in 1947.

This trail ascends Bear Mountain's north slope. It starts behind the inn and follows the asphalt path along the western shore of Hessian Lake nearly to its north end before turning sharp left (west) into the woods. Climbing gently for a short distance, it then makes another sharp left turn and begins a steep, steady ascent of about 800 feet to the summit. There are several excellent vistas along this stretch. Before reaching the summit, the trail crosses Perkins Memorial Drive. At this point the trail divides: one branch follows the drive west, then turns back to the summit over a weathered bedrock ridge. The other branch leads straight across the road to the summit, a shorter, but less scenic, route.

Nurian Trail. Length: 3.4 miles. Blazes: white.

This trail goes from the old Southfields railroad station to the Ramapo-Dunderberg Trail. The junction with the latter is about 0.8 mile north of the crossing of Route 106 (Old Route 210), where there is parking. At Southfields, park on the east side of Route 17 just north of Railroad Avenue or at the Red Apple Rest away from the refreshment stand. Do not park at the post office at any time.

Although there is but one outlook point, and that with limited view, the climb up the ravine of the Island Pond outlet brook (Valley of the Boulders), past numerous falls, is one of the most attractive sections of trail in the park. The trail is named after Kerson Nurian, an indefatigable worker and walker and member of the New York Chapter of the Adirondack Mountain Club, who laid it out as a connection with the Ramapo-Dunderberg to make an interesting 8-mile walk, with considerable climbing, from the Southfields station to the Tuxedo station. The former is at the foot of Railroad Avenue, which is just a short distance north of the Red Apple Rest. Follow the railroad tracks north of the station for about 100 yards and then turn right down the hill and into the woods.

The trail will shortly cross the thruway on a pedestrian bridge that stands as a testament to the efforts of hiking clubs under the leadership of Robert P. Stephenson, who convinced state highway authorities that the park was being sealed off by the newly constructed highway and that for fullest use of park trails more access was needed than at only Arden and Tuxedo.

After crossing the thruway, make a left turn and follow the old road north for about 0.3 mile and then make a sharp right and start the ascent up the west side of Stahahe Mountain. After passing the summit, the trail enters a long hollow formed by faulting of the bedrock ages ago. After descending to the north end of Lake Stahahe and circling that end of the lake on an asphalt road, the trail makes a sharp left onto a road that passes some filter beds on the left. In about 200 yards, the trail continues straight ahead when the road makes a sharp right, going up the ravine of the Island Pond outlet brook and proceeding through an area covered with large rocks, called Valley of the Boulders. This ravine extends for approximately 0.2 mile, and a few spots are difficult to negotiate, especially in winter. The trail turns right (south) near the head of the ravine and goes up along a rock ridge, passing an outlook point. Shortly beyond, it meets the western terminus of the Dunning Trail (yellow blazes). The Nurian turns left and passes down and through a small valley, crossing the Dunning Trail again before meeting the Island Pond fire road.

To make a side trip to the Boston Mine, turn left and walk a short distance on the fire road. The trail goes right on the fire road, shortly makes a left turn, and in a few yards joins the White Bar Trail (horizontal white blazes), which comes in from the left. It turns right, joining the White Bar Trail, then turns left, leaving it after about 300 yards. The Nurian then goes downhill, crosses a brook, and climbs steeply up the west slope of Black Rock Mountain to meet the Ramapo-Dunderberg Trail. The last half of the trail passes through several areas of mountain laurel.

Pine Meadow Trail. Length: 6.5 miles. Blazes: red diamond on white.

The Pine Meadow Trail begins about 0.75 mile from Route 17, where Stony Brook goes under Seven Lakes Drive, and extends to the Suffern–Bear Mountain Trail near Catamount Mountain. Those who come by bus to Sloatsburg may walk to the start of the trail. The most convenient access by car is from the parking area at the Reeves Meadow Visitors Center on Seven Lakes Drive, 1.7 miles from Route 17.

From its western terminus, the trail enters a scrub-filled field on the south side of Seven Lakes Drive and Stony Brook, curves left, and follows Stony Brook. It travels to the right along a telephone cable route, and then left on a wood road, passing the terminus of the Seven Hills Trail on the right (blue on white). The trail soon arrives at the Reeves Meadow Visitors Center, where the Reeves Brook Trail (white blazes) begins, proceeding straight uphill on a narrow wood road. The Pine Meadow Trail parallels Stony Brook to a fork, where it swings to the right away from the brook and uphill. (The left fork is the start of the unmarked Stony Brook Trail.)

After about 0.3 mile, the trail runs parallel to Pine Meadow Brook, here 100 feet down in a ravine. Soon the Hillburn-Torne-Sebago Trail (white blazes) comes in from the left, coincides with the Pine Meadow Trail for about 100 yards, and then turns sharply right and uphill. The Pine Meadow Trail now levels off and meets the Seven Hills Trail (blue on white) coming in from the right at a fireplace, and both trails run together for a short distance to a log bridge across Pine Meadow Brook. The Kakiat Trail (white blazes) coming from the right joins them in crossing the brook, then turns left down the brook, while the Seven Hills Trail turns left and then climbs right steeply up Diamond Mountain. The Pine Meadow Trail turns sharp right along the brook to the large boulders called "Ga-nus-quah," or Stone Giants, by the Indians. In this rock gorge, melting snow waters provide a spectacular cascade in early spring.

A short distance later, Diamond Mountain Trail (white blazes) goes left, climbing Diamond Mountain. The Tower Trail (yellow blazes) starts and continues straight ahead, while the Pine Meadow Trail takes a sharp right turn onto a wood road to Pine Meadow Lake. Following the north shore of the lake, the trail passes the site of the Conklin cabin on the eastern end of Pine Meadow Lake. This structure, built in 1778, stood until 1935. Ramsey Conklin, the last of his family to live in it, died in 1952.

Beyond the cabin site, the trail turns away from the lake and slightly uphill. At the end of the lake the Conklins Crossing Trail (white blazes) starts and goes right, providing a shortcut to the Suffern–Bear Mountain Trail. (Turn left on the Suffern–Bear Mountain Trail for 0.3 mile to the Stone Memorial Shelter.) About a quarter mile farther on, the Pine Meadow Trail crosses a fire lane built by the CCC, and continues for another mile until it reaches its terminus on the Suffern–Bear Mountain Trail, which goes right (south) to Suffern, and left (north) to Bear Mountain.

Popolopen Gorge Trail. Length: 4.3 miles. Blazes: red square on white.

This trail provides a pleasant walk through the Popolopen Gorge to Turkey Hill Lake. Parking is available at the Bear Mountain Inn. The trail can be reached from the inn by walking north on the asphalt footpath along the east shore of Hessian Lake to the traffic circle. Proceed north on Route 9W past the traffic circle. The trail enters the woods to the left just before the Popolopen Gorge Bridge. For access to the western part of the trail, park at the Anthony Wayne Recreation Area and use the Anthony Wayne Trail.

From the bridge, the trail leads gently downhill along a wood road 0.4 mile to Roe Pond, where there is an old dam and the creek plunges in a thundering falls between the sheer rock walls of the gorge. Across the creek are the foundations of what was once a mill. The trail continues to follow the steep southern side of the gorge, passing the area called "Hell Hole," picturesque in early spring with water dashing over and around the boulders in the brook. Potholes and plunge basins show evidence of the erosional action of the creek.

The trail then climbs steeply for about 100 feet to the old Bear Mountain Aqueduct, which it follows for the next mile before joining the Timp-Torne, 1777W, and 1779 trails. This area is dominated by a hemlock forest. Often found in a rock ravine community, the hemlock is a shade-tolerant tree, which accounts for its growth in this east-west gorge.

The trail travels with the Timp-Torne, the 1777W, and the 1779 trails from 1.4 to 2.4 miles. The steepness of the gorge gradually diminishes and the trail crosses the brook on a footbridge, before entering a dirt road to the left. The Queensboro Furnace can be reached by turning right on this road, but permission to enter this area must first be obtained from the West Point Military Academy. The trail continues for 0.1 mile along the road, then turns right into the woods, while the Timp-Torne and 1777W trails continue straight. Continuing through the woods, the trail skirts the north shore of Queensboro Lake, and separates from the 1779 Trail after another 0.4 mile. Passing the dam of Turkey Hill Lake, it follows the south shore before joining the Anthony Wayne Trail and turning uphill away from the lake. After a short climb, it turns right on a small wood road, continuing through a small ravine to its terminus at the junction of Long Mountain Trail and the Long Path. The Popolopen Gorge Trail can be combined with a number of other connecting trails for a circular walk from the Bear Mountain Inn.

Raccoon Brook Hills Trail. Length: 2.3 miles. Blazes: white (or black R on white).

The Raccoon Brook Hills Trail connects the Kakiat Trail with the Hillburn-Torne-Sebago Trail and the Seven Hills Trail, offering fine views of the area around Pine Meadow Lake. The start of the trail is on the Kakiat Trail about 0.4 mile east of the footbridge spanning Pine Meadow Brook used by the Pine Meadow, Seven Hills, and Kakiat trails. The trail turns to the left and traverses rocky ledges to the top of a rise, then dips into a depression and rises again steeply up the rocky face of Raccoon Brook Hill with views of Halfway Mountain, Diamond Mountain with its fire tower to the north, and Pine Meadow Lake to the east.

Following the contour of Raccoon Brook Hill, the trail is first level, then gradually descends to the Kakiat Trail, crossing it at 0.3 mile. The trail at this point has described a semicircle of about 0.8 mile. After crossing the Kakiat Trail, it levels, goes slightly downhill, and then, turning left, goes steeply up a short, rocky incline. It levels again, crosses a gas line, and in a short distance meets the Hillburn-Torne-Sebago Trail (white blazes), which comes from the right off the Pine Meadow Trail and goes to the left to the Russian Bear and the Ramapo Torne.

After crossing the Hillburn-Torne-Sebago Trail, the Raccoon Brook Hills Trail goes down into a hollow and up another ridge. Near a rock formation called the Pulpit, the trail drops steeply down a rock wall, called a fault scarp, into another hollow, crossing a brook that flows along the fault line. It then climbs steadily up a ridge, where it terminates on the Seven Hills Trail (blue blazes on white), which comes from the right off the Pine Meadow Trail and goes to the left, joining the Hillburn-Torne-Sebago Trail.

Ramapo-Dunderberg Trail. Length: 20.8 miles. Blazes: red dot on white.

This trail, from Tuxedo to Jones Point, is the oldest of the park trails built by the walking clubs. Generally speaking, it is a ridge trail through different types of forest and offers many view points.

The trail starts from its western terminus at Tuxedo station, heads over the Ramapo River on a footbridge, follows the road left on the other side to an underpass of the thruway, and turns left on the road beyond. In a few hundred feet, it turns right into the woods in a northeasterly direction, climbing around a ridge and passing, in 0.1 mile from the road, the terminus of the Triangle Trail (yellow blazes). About 0.5 mile farther the Tuxedo–Mount Ivy Trail (red bar on white) begins, diverging to the right. The Ramapo-Dunderberg is the *left* branch. This must be emphasized, as both trails are blazed with red. The RD continues northeast to the crossing of Black Ash Swamp Brook. Here is a natural rock dam formed by the last glacier, which melted about eleven thousand years ago. Here also is Tri-Trail Corners, where three trails—the RD, the Blue Disc, and Victory—meet. The RD climbs northward to the summit of Black Ash Mountain, with a good view from near the top over the swamp to the south. The White Bar Trail crosses the RD in the dip between Black Ash and Parker Cabin mountains. Soon after, the terminus of the White Cross Trail is passed on the right.

The RD continues north up to the top of Parker Cabin Mountain, where, on the level summit, the Triangle Trail comes in from its western loop, coincides with the RD for about 150 feet, and then bears east (right). The RD descends the north side of Parker Cabin Mountain to a gap where it crosses the Victory Trail (blue V). From the gap, the trail ascends steeply up Tom

Jones Mountain. Near the stone shelter on the summit there is a fine view to the east and south. The trail descends steeply down the northeast slope to Tom Jones Gap, where it crosses a brook just before reaching Route 106 (Old Route 210). North of this road, the trail climbs gradually up Black Rock Mountain, named, it is said, for the many charcoal burners' pits that were once found there. At the top of the first ridge, between rock walls, the Nurian Trail (white blazes) begins at the left and the RD bears right over a rock ledge. From this point to its crossing of the Arden-Surebridge Trail it is easy walking, and easy to miss the trail. The Bald Rocks Shelter is a half mile from the junction with the Nurian Trail. The water supply is a small brook 100 yards downhill east of the shelter, but it is not reliable in dry weather.

Beyond the shelter the trail crosses the Dunning Trail (yellow blazes) and continues north over Ship Rock. The bright red leaves of the sour gum trees *(Nyssa sylvatica)* in the swamp below the west side of the rock give the park its earliest fall color. A tablet set in a rock beside the trail here is a memorial to George Goldthwaite, erected in 1964 by the Fresh Air Club. Goldthwaite was a pioneer trail walker who, although famous for his speed on the trail, is better remembered by his friends for his complete knowledge of park trails and old roads and for his skill and consideration as a walk leader.

A short distance northward the Lichen Trail (blue blaze) begins, meanders northwest over ledges, and offers a shortcut to the Arden-Surebridge Trail. The RD then winds through the woods and down to "Times Square," where it crosses the Long Path (turquoise blazes) and the Arden-Surebridge Trail (red triangle on white) at a stone fireplace beside a boulder. Remember, both the RD and the Arden-Surebridge have red markings, so take care not to choose the wrong path! From the crossing the RD begins the climb of Fingerboard Mountain around a low cliff and beneath a glacial pothole six or seven feet high on its face, geologically one of the most remarkable features of the route. As the mountain levels off at the top, the Appalachian Trail (white blazes), which coincides here, comes in from the left, and the two trails continue northward together, passing, about a tenth of a mile beyond the junction, the Fingerboard Shelter and the western end of the Hurst Trail (blue blazes). At Arden Valley Road the Appalachian Trail continues straight (north) and the RD turns east (right), following the road past the Tiorati traffic circle and lake to turn into the woods about 0.3 mile east of the circle.

The trail travels east over Goshen Mountain and, at 1.8 miles from the traffic circle, descends to join the Appalachian Trail again at a plank bridge. Continuing along Letterrock Mountain, the trail crosses an unmarked wood road in the saddle of the mountain by Letterrock Shelter before reaching a fine wood road, now a ski trail, which can be followed left to Silvermine Lake. The trail crosses a streambed and then climbs steeply on a switchback onto Black Mountain, which offers a good view toward the west that includes the lake. Soon the trail levels and winds along the top, then makes a short climb to travel along a rock ledge with views toward the south. On a clear day New York City can be seen in the distance. Reaching above the Palisades, the two towers of the George Washington Bridge come into view. Nearer, the unfinished dam at Owl Lake, abandoned since the 1930s, can be seen. From the summit the trails descend gradually down the east slope to Beechy Bottom, crossing the 1779 Trail, then a wood road, and finally the Palisades Parkway.

It was through this valley, along the 1779 Trail, that General Anthony Wayne and his soldiers marched on their way to storm Stony Point on the night of July 15, 1779. The valley and the road that they followed changed little until 1933–34, when three camps of the Civilian Conservation Corps, each with two hundred young men, were established here. Two were near the RD Trail where the old Wayne road crosses the Beechy Bottom Brook, and the third on the former site of the farm near the Mica Mine below the steep west face of West Mountain. The site of this camp is now covered by the Anthony Wayne Recreation Area. Under the direction of park foremen, the CCC boys living here, and those in eight other camps located in the park, accomplished an immense amount of work of permanent value in building new lakes, roads, fire lanes, etc. But even this activity did not disturb the character of Beechy Bottom itself, for until the construction of the Palisades Parkway in the 1950s, the grassy road along the west side of Beechy Bottom took the hiker past the foundations of farmhouses, clumps of lilac, and old apple trees remaining from the days when this valley was the route from Central Valley to the river. A segment of this road still exists in the gap between West Mountain and the Pines.

Beyond the parkway and the brook the Appalachian Trail diverges northeast (left) and the RD continues to cross Beechy Bottom Road, a fine wood road that is now a ski trail. The trail then ascends steeply to the southern crown of West Mountain, past the holes of an old iron mine, where a faint road diverges east. On the open ledges near the top, the trail meets the Suffern–Bear Mountain Trail (yellow blazes) just above the Cats Elbow.

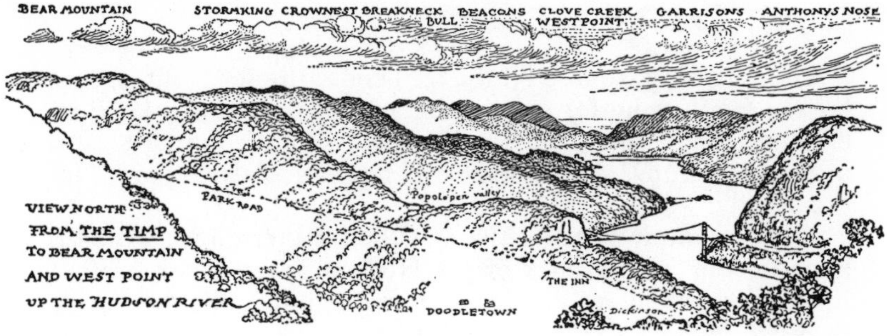

All of the view points enjoyed from here were once the posts of Continental, Tory, or British scouts.

After coinciding a short distance, the Suffern–Bear Mountain turns north (left) and the RD swings east across the summit and descends into Timp Pass, where it meets the Timp-Torne Trail (blue blazes). Here also is the eastern terminus of the Red Cross Trail. Rising above is the Timp, a striking cliff with a pronounced overhang at the west end of the Dunderberg massif, one of the most picturesque rock faces in the park. The overhang is there because the Timp is another of the southwest-facing uplifted ends of fault blocks, common in the Highlands, and weathering has split off the granite on its ancient joint planes. From Timp Pass the RD ascends by what was once known as Six Chins Trail, over a rough talus slope, up under the overhanging cliff. The RD turns right at the top, but the best overlook is from the open summit a few steps to the left.

The trail continues east, enters the saddle between the Timp and Bald Mountain, where it crosses the 1777 Trail, then climbs steeply up Bald Mountain to the summit, where there is a panoramic view west and north. A little farther east, and to the left of the trail, is the Cornell Mine, named for a family once numerous hereabouts. The mine is a small vertical hole, and should be approached with care. The trail continues east and soon passes the terminus of the Cornell Trail (blue blazes), which goes down to the left. At a "five corners" of wood roads and trails, the RD turns onto a wood road and then to a path. A few feet east of this junction it crosses part of the grade of the Dunderberg Scenic Railway. As the trail descends over ledges to Jones Point on the Hudson, it crosses several times the graded embankments of the uncompleted railway. The descent is broken by a number of climbs, some steep.

After crossing Route 9W, the trail ends at Jones Point, named for the family who for several generations owned this land, including Dunderberg. Captain Thomas Jones, the founder, came to America in 1692. Jones Beach on Long Island also is named for this family.

There is ample parking space at the trail terminus, which is opposite the former dock of the Hudson River Reserve Fleet. Buses from the Port Authority Bus Terminal, Manhattan, to Bear Mountain will stop to discharge or pick up passengers on Route 9W where the road to the Fleet dock turns off 2 miles north of Tompkins Cove.

Red Arrow Trail. Length: 0.3 mile. Blazes: red arrow (sometimes on white background).

This is a short connecting trail providing access to the Suffern–Bear Mountain Trail from Ladentown. It starts at the Tuxedo–Mount Ivy Trail approximately 1 mile northwest of the Ladentown Church on Old Route 202. It goes uphill and skirts Limekiln Mountain on the right, and 0.3 mile later ends at the Suffern–Bear Mountain Trail.

Red Cross Trail. Length: 8.3 miles. Blazes: red cross on white.

The Red Cross Trail goes through the middle of the park, generally northeast to southwest, from the intersection of the Ramapo-Dunderberg and Timp-Torne trails in Timp Pass to the Arden-Surebridge Trail, just north of the Lake Skannatati parking area. In addition, the trail crosses or connects with the 1779, Suffern–Bear Mountain, Dean, and Beech trails. To reach the trail, follow the directions for the Timp-Torne Trail from its southern terminus on Route 9W to Timp Pass. On the left, where the Ramapo-Dunderberg (red on white) leaves the Timp-Torne (blue blazes), near a large boulder, is the start of the Red Cross Trail.

The trail descends steeply and then goes up and down on several wood roads, crossing several brooks. Finally the trail turns right on the 1779 Trail (blue numerals on white), which follows the old Beechy Bottom Road used by General Anthony Wayne and his troops when they marched to attack Stony Point.

The Suffern–Bear Mountain Trail (yellow blazes), coming from the Pines, joins from the left and then leaves to the right toward West Mountain. Shortly after the 1779 Trail leaves to the right, the Red Cross Trail reaches the Palisades Parkway. It crosses the highway and jogs left to join an old road heading right. Next it goes through a swampy area and skirts a marsh to the left of the trail. About 1.5 miles beyond the parkway it passes the site of Burnt House on the right. Many years ago a woodcutter lived there until his house burned. The cellar hole is all that remains.

An unmarked wood road (the Dean Trail) leads right toward the William Brien Memorial Shelter on Letterrock Mountain. The Red Cross Trail continues west with more brook crossings and minor ups and downs. The terminus of the Beech Trail (blue blazes) is passed on the left. After going through another swampy section, the trail reaches Tiorati Brook, which it crosses on rocks. The trail then ascends to a grassy ball field, crosses it, and passes over the paved Tiorati Brook Road. This is the site of the old Orange Furnace. It is said that some of Washington's soldiers had a camp on the site of the present ball field. Parking is available off the north side of the road, just left (east) of the trail.

The Red Cross Trail continues south on a prominent wood road. This wood road and the present Tiorati Brook Road going west from this point to the lake are the remains of an old road of Revolutionary War days. Tiorati Brook Road, east of where the trail crosses, was not in existence then.

The trail passes the Hasenclever Mine, turns right on a cross road, and then ascends to near the top of Hasenclever Mountain, where it turns left and heads down. After crossing under a telephone line, the trail swings left and proceeds toward Lake Askoti. It goes up over a rock slab and continues down, with fine views of the lake. The trail continues south, then turns back north and finally heads west past the north end of the lake to Seven Lakes Drive. After crossing the highway, it climbs Pine Swamp Mountain, traverses the top, and terminates at its junction with the Arden-Surebridge Trail (red on white), which continues left down the mountain to its terminus at the Lake Skannatati parking area, just off Seven Lakes Drive.

Red Timp-Torne Trail. Length: 0.3 mile. Blazes: two red T's on a white background.

This trail is an unauthorized trail marked as a camp project by the Girl Scouts on Mott Farm Road. It can be used as a bypass on the Ramapo-Dunderberg Trail to avoid the steep exposed face of the Timp during wet or icy conditions.

It starts on the Ramapo-Dunderberg Trail about 325 yards east of the Timp overlook and drops off to the right on a moderately steep section. Leveling off, the trail meanders along zigzag fashion, then drops quickly through a sharply defined rock cleft over an old roadbed. After intersecting the Timp-Torne Trail, the Red TT swings right and then leaves the TT after about 300 yards with a sharp left turn. The trail then descends toward the park boundary and private property, where the public is not permitted.

Reeves Brook Trail. Length: 0.9 mile. Blazes: white.

This trail begins at the Pine Meadow Trail (red on white) near the Reeves Meadow Visitors Center (parking available), 1.7 miles from Route 17 on Seven Lakes Drive. Traveling southeast, it crosses the Seven Hills Trail (blue blazes) before ending at the Raccoon Brook Hills Trail (white blazes).

The trail starts behind the information center, about 20 yards to the right of the Pine Meadow Trail, where it enters the woods. The area over which the trail passes is rather uniform in forest cover but noteworthy geologically. Several fault lines are crossed as the Reeves Brook flows down over natural steps of rock. The trail makes a gradual ascent, crossing the brook at 0.4 mile, with the brook on the left a good part of the way. It terminates at its junction with the Raccoon Brook Hills Trail. The rock formation called the Pulpit is about 0.1 mile north of the eastern terminus of this trail on the Raccoon Brook Hills Trail.

The Reeves Brook Trail is a convenient trail to approach the Ramapo Torne. Until recently it was not a maintained trail and at one time was referred to as the "Frenchman's Trail." Supposedly a French businessman who made frequent trips to the United States hiked the area and jammed his empty wine bottles into the trees as blazes.

Seven Hills Trail. Length: 7.3 miles. Blazes: blue on white.

This trail runs mostly northeast-southwest, parallel to Seven Lakes Drive, from the old Lake Sebago Beach parking area to the Pine Meadow Trail near its western terminus. It crosses or connects with the Tuxedo–Mount Ivy, Tower, Hillburn-Torne-Sebago, Diamond Mountain, Kakiat, Pine Meadow, Reeves Brook, and Raccoon Brook Hills trails.

The trail starts on the east side of Seven Lakes Drive, 4.3 miles from Route 17, opposite the entrance to the Lake Sebago parking area. It ascends Conklin Mountain, joins Woodtown Road, and crosses Diamond Creek. Shortly thereafter, the white Monitor Rock comes into view, perched high on the left. A side trail (white) leads left to the rock, which supposedly was given its name by members of the Fresh Air Club who found a copy of the *Christian Science Monitor* under it.

At this point the Seven Hills Trail turns right, off Woodtown Road, and starts its traverse of Diamond Mountain. It soon crosses the Tuxedo–Mount Ivy Trail (red dash on white), coming from Lake Sebago dam on the right and heading left toward Breakneck Mountain. The trail briefly follows the fire tower service road and passes excellent views of Lake Sebago. Shortly, the Tower Trail (yellow) starts, leading left to the tower and down to the Pine Meadow Trail. Then the Hillburn-Torne-Sebago Trail (white) comes in from the right from Lake Sebago dam and joins the Seven Hills Trail over the summit of Diamond Mountain. Just before the top, the Diamond Mountain Trail (white) leads left down the mountain to the Tower and Pine Meadow trails.

Past the summit, the Hillburn-Torne-Sebago Trail diverges sharp right over Halfway Mountain to Pine Meadow Brook. The Seven Hills Trail continues ahead, making a steep descent to Pine Meadow Brook, where it turns left onto the Kakiat Trail (white), coming from the right from Seven Lakes Drive. The joint trails meet the Pine Meadow Trail (red on white) coming in from the left and all three cross Pine Meadow Brook on a footbridge. The Kakiat Trail turns off to the left and the joint Seven Hills and Pine Meadow trails turn right. Shortly, at a fireplace, the Seven Hills Trail turns off left up Chipmunk Mountain; the Pine Meadow Trail continues to the Reeves Meadow parking area. The Hillburn-Torne-Sebago Trail then joins from the right, coming up from Pine Meadow Brook, and soon leaves left toward Russian Bear.

After a steep descent of Chipmunk Mountain, the Seven Hills Trail crosses the Reeves Brook Trail (white), coming from the right from the Reeves Meadow parking area. The Seven Hills Trail then passes the start of the Raccoon Brook Hills Trail (black R on white) on the left. After another 0.4 mile the Hillburn-Torne-Sebago Trail joins once more, coming from the left from Russian Bear. The trails run together for 0.2 mile, the Seven Hills Trail then turning right down the mountain, the Hillburn-Torne-Sebago Trail continuing ahead to its terminus on top of Ramapo Torne.

The Seven Hills Trail now turns north, crosses Beaver Brook, skirts a large swamp and, in a short distance, reaches its terminus on the Pine Meadow Trail. The latter ends a short distance to the left on Seven Lakes Drive. To the right, the Pine Meadow Trail soon arrives at the Reeves Meadow parking area.

Stony Brook Trail. Length: 1.6 miles. No blazes.

The Stony Brook Trail connects the Pine Meadow Trail (red diamond on white) with the Tuxedo–Mount Ivy (red dash on white) and Hillburn-Torne-Sebago (white blazes) trails by the Lake Sebago dam at Seven Lakes Drive. It is a low-level trail with easy footing, much of the way being over an old wood road. Staying generally close to the brook, the trail gives good views of the waters cascading over and around large boulders, especially in early spring when it is flowing high and fast with meltwater from the winter's snow.

The trail starts on the Pine Meadow Trail at a point where that trail swings away from the brook and goes steeply uphill. The Stony Brook Trail follows the brook and in 0.3 mile joins the Kakiat Trail (white blazes) coming in from the left across a footbridge. The two trails coincide for 0.25 mile. At the confluence of Stony Brook and Pine Meadow Brook, the trails cross Pine Meadow Brook on another footbridge. The Kakiat turns right and uphill along Pine Meadow Brook, while the Stony Brook Trail, veering slightly left, follows Stony Brook. After crossing Diamond Brook, the trail ends at the Hillburn-Torne-Sebago Trail (white blazes) near the latter's northern terminus.

Suffern–Bear Mountain Trail. Length: 24.3 miles. Blazes: yellow.

This trail from Suffern to Bear Mountain is quite rugged in many places. One terminus is at the parking lot off Route 59 next to the police station in Suffern. Access to the southern portion of the Suffern–Bear Mountain Trail is also possible from the parking lot on Route 202 at the terminus of the Kakiat Trail.

A few hundred feet north of the Suffern parking lot the trail leaves the pavement, turns sharp right, and goes steeply up a ravine to a fine view point on the slope of Nordkop Mountain. Joining a wood road for a time, it follows north along the ridge of the Ramapo rampart. The wood road is soon left behind and the trail winds over the fairly level mountaintop, traversing several gas and power lines that permit long views through the woods on each side of the trail.

About 1.5 miles from Suffern, the trail climbs a rock formation known as the Kitchen Stairs. Beyond this the going becomes more rugged, until an area is reached at about 3 miles that is littered with giant boulders of all sizes and shapes. This area, located in a hollow through which flows the Ossec Brook, is called the Valley of Dry Bones. After climbing the next hill, the trail runs along the eastern edge of the rampart through the long-abandoned Sky-sail Farm, which, it is said, was the highest farm in the Ramapos. Swinging west around the stream heads, the trail crosses a gas line, and passes two big boulders called Grandpa and Grandma. Shortly beyond is the Kakiat Trail intersection (white blazes).

The trail continues north over Cobus Mountain or Cobusberg, named for Jacobus Smith, brother of Claudius (see Tuxedo–Mount Ivy Trail). On the next hill, the trail leads along a cliff overlooking the glacial cirque behind Horse Stable Mountain, and, over it, the valley to the east, then descends to Conklins Crossing Trail (white blazes). Farther along downhill, it crosses Many Swamp Brook and continues up the steep slope north of the brook to the Stone Memorial Shelter. About 100 feet east of the S-BM downhill on the Sherwood Path, a discontinued trail, is an excellent pipe spring.

The trail continues northward over Hawk Cliff, and soon bends sharply left, descending to its junction with the unmarked Pittsboro Hollow Trail, which comes up from the valley to the east. At this point stands a large white oak tree, on the north side of the path where the two trails meet. This is the Witness Oak, used as a surveyor's landmark in early days. The Pittsboro Hollow Trail is rarely used and easily overlooked. A short distance farther, the terminus of the Pine Meadow Trail is passed on the left.

The trail continues a bit eastward, bending north and descending to the Gyascutus Brook in the hollow. The trail then climbs steeply over Panther Mountain, where there is a fine view toward the Hudson and surrounding villages. Also to the northeast on the S-BM Trail, the towers on Jackie Jones Mountain can be seen. After descending over a field of boulders in the bed of a lost brook, which can be heard beneath the rocks, the trail again climbs steeply up to the crossing of the Tuxedo–Mount Ivy Trail (red blazes), where there is a stone fireplace. Farther along, atop Circle Mountain, the Ladentown benchmark gives the elevation as 1199 feet above sea level.

On the farther slope, the Red Arrow Trail comes in from the right, coming from the Tuxedo–Mount Ivy Trail. The S-BM Trail goes northwestward across File Factory Brook, crosses the old Woodtown Road just beyond the brook, and continues a half mile to Reservoir No. 3. Climbing Breakneck Mountain, the trail turns northeast, where it meets the beginning of the Breakneck Mountain Trail (white blazes). There are fine views as the trail follows the crest to Big Hill Shelter. Water from a brook to the east is uncertain. The trail then drops along some ledges, crosses a wood road, and enters another wood road going northeastward. This was the old Ramapo Turnpike, which is now a telephone line right-of-way. Crossing it, the trail reenters the woods, climbing gradually up the south side of Jackie Jones Mountain (1276 feet) to the radio relay tower and old fire tower. On the top the old trail (unmarked) branches off from behind the fire tower, and leads north down the hill to Lake Welch. Be sure to follow the yellow blazes.

The S-BM then goes down to a narrow asphalt road, which goes about a half mile to Route 106 (Old Route 210) where there is a small parking space, turns right to cross the brook via a highway bridge, and then left (north) into the woods along an old wood road. The trail shortly veers right off the wood road, climbs a ridge, and then passes a large boulder on the left known as the Irish Potato. Looking down to the right along this ridge one can see Upper Pound Swamp.

The trail goes down to Lake Welch Drive, which is soon joined by Tiorati Brook Road (parking a half mile west on this road, which is closed in winter). The trail turns right on the road and crosses the southbound lanes of the Palisades Interstate Parkway on a bridge.

After crossing the parkway, walk a short distance to the left looking for yellow blazes. The S-BM Trail now starts the steep ascent of the ledges on the south side of Pyngyp Mountain. Halfway up is a memorial tablet to Harold Scutt, erected by his friends in the walking clubs. Scutt found the route for the trail up these ledges and was killed in an airplane accident soon after.

The trail bears eastward near the summit, crosses the highest point (1016 feet), and then descends to a wood road in the notch beyond, and on down to Stillwater Brook at the old road from Bulsontown. It follows this road right 100 yards, then turns sharp left across the brook and up the elevation of the Pines (where there is not a single pine tree to be found). From the ledge on the west side of this summit there is a fine view north and northwest.

The trail drops off the Pines by faint wood roads to meet the Red Cross and 1779 trails, and then turns left with them about 200 yards. Leaving the road at a sharp right angle, the trail crosses a rough and broken area of small swamps and steep ledges, crosses a telephone line and then a brook, and meets the old road through Beechy Bottom. The trail climbs the steep slope beyond (with a detour to the left to a good view south from the top of a ledge) and through open oak woods to a stony road built by the CCC as a fire road, now a ski trail. This was formerly part of the old Horn Trail, a valley route to Tompkins Cove, and is now abandoned. The trail crosses this road and climbs over the knobs of the southern spur of West Mountain.

Just beyond a turn called the Cats Elbow, on the open ledges near the top, the S-BM meets the Ramapo-Dunderberg Trail. The two coincide for a short distance, then the Ramapo-Dunderberg swings east, while the S-BM takes the left fork northward, past fine views, into the hollow between West Mountain and the Timp. Here it follows an old wood road to the right for several hundred feet and then, at a curve, leaves it to climb the cliff to the north by a zigzag route called the Fire Escape. Near the top, the Timp-Torne Trail crosses. (On the latter trail, a little way to the east, is the West Mountain Shelter, from which there is a fine view south toward New York City. Water is available at the brook in the hollow.)

The trail heads northeast over a shoulder of West Mountain that rises above the now-abandoned hamlet of Doodletown. From the shoulder, the trail bends left down on a steep rock talus to a ravine, where, crossing the brook, it follows its left bank to a wood road. It goes left on the wood road and makes a loop around the western end of the Doodletown valley, crossing the 1777W Trail, and comes up the north side of the valley to cross Seven Lakes Drive. Beyond the drive the trail climbs over a low shoulder of Bear Mountain, at the top of which the Appalachian Trail joins from the left, coinciding with the S-BM to the terminus of the latter near the ski jump at Bear Mountain Inn.

Timp-Torne Trail. Length: 9.9 miles. Blazes: blue.

A trail of varied settings, the Timp-Torne follows deep, narrow gorges and open mountain ridges, offering many outstanding views of the park and the Hudson Valley.

The trail begins on Route 9W, 0.6 mile south of Jones Point Road. Parking is available 50 yards farther south on the opposite side of the road. In the first half mile the trail passes some of the grades of the Dunderberg Scenic Railway as it proceeds west around the Timp-Bald-Dunderberg massif. It coincides with the 1777W Trail until 1.1 miles, where the 1777W diverges right toward Doodletown. The trail gradually turns north to Timp Pass, where it crosses the Ramapo-Dunderberg Trail (red on white) and the Red Cross Trail (red blazes) at 2.2 miles. After a steep ascent, the trail reaches West Mountain Shelter at 2.9 miles with an excellent view of the Timp, High and Little Tor, and Haverstraw Bay. On a clear day the Manhattan skyline can be seen on the horizon.

Continuing along the southern ridge of West Mountain, the Timp-Torne is joined by the Suffern–Bear Mountain Trail (yellow blazes) at 3.2 miles, which coincides with the Timp-Torne for the next 100 yards. Turning north, the trail joins the Appalachian Trail (white blazes) after another 0.2 mile and, following the west ridge of West Mountain, offers a number of views of the park, Bear Mountain, and the Hudson River. At 4.1 miles it diverges left from the Appalachian Trail and gradually descends West Mountain, crossing a cross-country ski trail and the terminus of the Anthony Wayne Trail (white blazes) on the left. On Seven Lakes Drive the Timp-Torne joins the 1777W Trail, crosses a bridge, and turns right onto Old Fort Montgomery Road. The Popolopen Gorge (red on white) and 1779 trails join from the left a quarter mile after leaving the drive and the coinciding trails gradually descend into the Popolopen Gorge. Turning left off the Popolopen Gorge Trail, at 7 miles, the Timp-Torne, 1777W, and 1779 trails cross Popolopen Creek via a small footbridge and follow an old mine road a short distance. The Timp-Torne then leaves the 1777W and 1779 trails, turns left into the woods, crosses Mine Road, and climbs very steeply to the summit of Popolopen Torne (941 feet), which offers an outstanding 360-degree view.

The crescentic gouges that are convex toward the southeast and seen in the granite of the north side of Popolopen Torne are remnants of the last glacial period, when rocks embedded in the

glacier chipped the surface. The large rock slabs resembling eggshells that appear to be peeling off the surface are the result of a type of weathering called "exfoliation," caused by the expansion of the rock surface.

The trail climbs down the east shoulder of the Torne, crosses Mine Road, and rejoins the 1777W and 1779 trails on an old aqueduct along the Popolopen Creek for the next half mile. It joins Mine Road for a short distance, reenters the woods on the right, crosses a small paved road, and terminates on Route 9W just north of the Popolopen Gorge Bridge. Parking for this end of the trail is available on the east side of Route 9W north of the Popolopen Bridge, and at the Bear Mountain Inn.

Tower Trail. Length: 0.5 mile. Blazes: yellow or yellow T on black.

The Tower Trail connects the Pine Meadow Trail with the Seven Hills Trail providing access to the Diamond Mountain fire tower. Starting at the junction of the Pine Meadow and Diamond Mountain trails, the Tower Trail ascends diagonally to the open eastern ridge of Diamond Mountain, while the Diamond Mountain Trail goes uphill to the left.

The Tower Trail then goes uphill over open ledges for about 0.2 mile, with fine views of Lake Wanoksink and Pine Meadow Lake. The trail, almost level now, follows the ridge in a northerly direction to the tower, which was once used as a fire observatory but is now abandoned. Passing to the left of the tower, the trail ends in about 150 feet on the Seven Hills Trail (blue on white), which goes to the right to Lake Sebago and to the left over Diamond Mountain to Pine Meadow Brook.

Triangle Trail. Length: 4.9 miles. Blazes: yellow triangle.

The Triangle Trail makes an easy loop from the Ramapo-Dunderberg Trail near Tuxedo to the Tuxedo–Mount Ivy Trail near the Dutch Doctor Shelter. It crosses the White Bar, Ramapo-Dunderberg, and Victory trails.

Leave the parking lot at the Tuxedo railroad station on the Ramapo-Dunderberg Trail (red on white), which heads south along the tracks, crosses the Ramapo River on a footbridge, passes under the thruway, and turns left on Grove Drive. The Triangle Trail starts shortly after the Ramapo-Dunderberg Trail enters the woods, branching left on a wood road through Deep Hollow. After about 1.75 miles, on the slope of Parker Cabin Mountain, it joins the White Bar Trail (white) coming in on the left from Route 106 (Old Route 210) where parking is available.

The trails coincide for a short distance, until the Triangle Trail diverges left. The White Bar Trail continues right to its terminus on the Tuxedo–Mount Ivy Trail.

The Triangle Trail climbs steadily to the top of Parker Cabin Mountain by an easier route than does the Ramapo-Dunderberg Trail, which it joins at the summit. After about 100 feet, the Triangle Trail diverges right to the sharp eastern edge of the mountain, where there is an outstanding lookout over Lakes Skenonto and Sebago. The trail starts down steeply and then continues more easily over low ridges and level areas, crossing the Victory Trail (blue on white), which leads left to Route 106 and right to the junction of the Ramapo-Dunderberg and Blue Disc trails.

The Triangle Trail skirts Lake Skenonto and, farther on, Lake Sebago, ending at its junction with the White Bar Trail. To the right, the White Bar Trail heads back north. To the left, it leads in about 0.1 mile to the Dutch Doctor Shelter and, just beyond, terminates on the Tuxedo–Mount Ivy Trail (red on white), which goes left to Lake Sebago and Seven Lakes Drive. Following it sharply right 2.7 miles back to Tuxedo completes the "triangle."

Tuxedo–Mount Ivy Trail. Length: 8.15 miles. Blazes: red horizontal dash on white.

The Tuxedo–Mount Ivy Trail extends from the Ramapo-Dunderberg Trail near Tuxedo to Ladentown (near Mount Ivy), traversing the park in an east-west direction. It crosses or connects with the Blue Disc, White Cross, White Bar, Hillburn-Torne-Sebago, Seven Hills, Breakneck Mountain, and Suffern–Bear Mountain trails.

Leave the parking lot at the Tuxedo railroad station on the Ramapo-Dunderberg Trail (red dot on white), which heads south along the tracks, crosses the Ramapo River on a footbridge, passes under the thruway, and turns left on Grove Drive. At the edge of the woods, the Kakiat Trail (white) leads off right and shortly the Triangle Trail (yellow) diverges left. The Tuxedo–Mount Ivy Trail starts about a half mile farther on, going to the right up a rock slab.

In 0.4 mile is the overhanging rock formation known as Claudius Smith's Den, used by Smith and his band of outlaws as a hideout during the Revolutionary War. It is said that the fronts of the caves were covered with boulders for better concealment; small and secret entrances were left in the rocks. Smith and his men raided the farms in the valley to the west, stealing horses and

cattle, and spreading terror through the surrounding hills. He was eventually captured by Continental soldiers and was hanged at Goshen on January 22, 1779.

The trail climbs alongside the caves, crossing the Blue Disc Trail (blue on white), which to the right leads to the Johnsontown Road parking circle and to the left connects with the Ramapo-Dunderberg Trail. At the top of the hill, the White Cross Trail (white blazes) starts, heading left past the start of the Triangle Trail (yellow blazes), a short distance north. The Tuxedo–Mount Ivy Trail then goes over the shoulder of Blauvelt Mountain and down into the valley of Spring Brook, which it crosses. Shortly after, the trail passes the southern terminus of the White Bar Trail (white) on the left. Northeast of this point is the Dutch Doctor Shelter, located in an old farm clearing where a German herb doctor named Wagner once lived. A pipe spring near the brook provides water.

The trail continues down the road, then turns off left and goes over the ridge, crosses a camp service road and skirts the south shore of Lake Sebago, arriving at Seven Lakes Drive. The trail crosses the drive, turns left over the dam, and drops down the embankment on the right. Here is the start of the Hillburn-Torne-Sebago Trail (white), which takes a steep, rocky route up Diamond Mountain. The Tuxedo–Mount Ivy Trail veers right on a wide path (the unmarked Stony Brook Trail) and shortly crosses the Hillburn-Torne-Sebago Trail. The latter continues right, along the brook, and the Tuxedo–Mount Ivy Trail heads uphill to climb the north side of Diamond Mountain, angling left to the saddle. Here it crosses the Seven Hills Trail (blue on white), which goes left to the Lake Sebago parking area (4.3 miles from Route 17) and to the right over Diamond Mountain.

Soon Woodtown Road is crossed, then Pine Meadow Road West and Pine Meadow Road East. A few hundred feet farther the Breakneck Mountain Trail (white) begins, branching to the left. The Tuxedo–Mount Ivy Trail continues east and then follows a wood road to the Woodtown Road, on which it turns right for a short distance. It diverges left, goes through a swampy area, and, at a fireplace, crosses the Suffern–Bear Mountain Trail (yellow), which leads left to the Big Hill Shelter, and right to Suffern.

The trail continues down the Ramapo rampart on the old Two Bridges Road, passing the start of the Red Arrow Trail (red) on the left. This trail provides a shortcut to the northbound Suffern–Bear Mountain Trail for those ascending the Tuxedo–Mount Ivy Trail from Ladentown. The trail leaves the woods at a power line, turns left on a service road, crosses under the power line, and heads back right on another service road, finally turning left down a dirt road to a paved road where parking is available.

To reach this parking area from Route 202 (heading north), turn left onto Old Route 202 or turn left at the light just ahead at the junction of Routes 202 and 306. At the church, turn left onto Mountain Road, and then left again on the private road to the power station (marked "Dead End"). The parking area is on the left shoulder opposite the point where the trail turns right from the road.

Victory Trail. Length: 3.4 miles. Blazes: blue V on white.

This trail loops from the Ramapo-Dunderberg, having its southern terminus at the end of the Blue Disc Trail and northern terminus at Route 106 (Old Route 210). It also crosses the White Cross and Triangle trails and the Long Path.

The trail originates at the western end of Black Ash Swamp, at a spot called Tri-Trail Corners because of the three trails that intersect there: Ramapo-Dunderberg, Blue Disc, and Victory. The trail follows a wood road for most of its length and has some wet spots in the beginning. At the eastern end of Black Ash Swamp, the White Cross and White Bar trails cross. Farther on, near Lake Skenonto, the Triangle Trail crosses. After passing the lake, the trail follows a paved private camp road and soon makes a sharp left into the woods. From here there is a gradual but steady climb up through the pass between Parker Cabin and Tom Jones mountains where the Ramapo-Dunderberg Trail intersects. This last section is the remnant of Hemlock Hill Road of Revolutionary War days, which ran from Johnsontown to Southfields. There are a few more wet spots before the trail exits onto Route 106, a half mile west of the parking area where the Ramapo-Dunderberg Trail crosses the road. Note that the beginning of the trail going south from Route 106 is obscure and not easy to find.

White Bar Trail. Length: 6 miles. Blazes: white bar.

The unusual blazes of the White Bar Trail are not generally an approved marking. This trail was dormant for many years, having become part of the Long Path. With the recent relocation of the Long Path and the desire of many hikers to keep a trail along that route came a great opportunity to revive one of the oldest official trails in the park.

This trail connects the Arden-Surebridge Trail (red triangle on white), approximately 0.3 mile east of the Lemon Squeezer with the Tuxedo–Mount Ivy Trail (red dash on white) near the Dutch Doctor Shelter, in a fairly direct north-south line. It forms a good connecting link for a day's walk from Arden to Tuxedo; total length, 10.5 miles. It crosses other trails that lead to Southfields, by which the total walk can be shortened to 6.5 or 7 miles. Formerly, when the main Boy Scout Camp was on Lake Kanawauke, a system of trails was laid out as a wheel with numerous "spokes" from that center, all marked with the white bar. Occasionally these old markings can still be found on wood roads and overgrown trails, but the spoke described here is the only one now maintained as a park trail.

After leaving the Arden-Surebridge Trail, traveling south, the White Bar follows a wood road that crosses one of the brooks feeding Island Pond at a little waterfall, then meets and for a short distance coincides first with the Dunning Trail (yellow blazes) and then with the Nurian Trail (white blazes), either one of which can be followed out to Southfields. As it reaches Route 106 (Old Route 210), it runs close to a large brook. After crossing Route 106, the trail, now becoming less worn, goes over the top of Carr Pond Mountain and drops steeply down into the flat upper reaches of Parker Cabin Hollow. Here it again picks up a wood road, turns east, and starts up the slope of Parker Cabin Mountain. The Triangle Trail (yellow blazes) soon joins it from the right (south) and affords a quick way out to Tuxedo.

In a short distance, where the Triangle Trail turns left (north), the White Bar leaves the wood road, turning south, and crosses the Ramapo-Dunderberg Trail (red on white) in the saddle between Parker Cabin and Black Ash mountains. From this, its highest point, it runs south and then east over lower hills and through open woods, crossing the White Cross (white crosses) and the Victory (blue V on white) trails and joining the Triangle Trail 0.2 mile from its terminus at the Tuxedo–Mount Ivy (red dash on white) Trail near the Dutch Doctor Shelter. Follow the Tuxedo–Mount Ivy right (west) 2.5 miles to Tuxedo station.

White Cross Trail. Length: 2 miles. Blazes: white cross.

The White Cross Trail connects the Ramapo-Dunderberg Trail at the south side of Parker Cabin Mountain with the Tuxedo–Mount Ivy Trail at Claudius Smith's Den. It crosses the Victory and White Bar trails.

The trail follows a low-level route, passing several swamps, and its chief interest is the opportunity for observation of swamp growth and birds. It goes south from the Ramapo-Dunderberg Trail, 2.8 miles from Tuxedo, at the base of the steep slope of Parker Cabin Mountain. After descending to Parker Swamp, it goes along the west side of the swamp, crossing the White Bar and then the Victory trails. It then continues over level rocky ground covered with mountain laurel, around the south side of Black Ash Swamp, then southwest uphill to its terminus at the Tuxedo–Mount Ivy Trail, 1.5 miles east of Tuxedo.

Suggested Readings

Appalachian Mountain Club, New York Chapter
In the Hudson Highlands
Walking News, Lancaster Press, Lancaster, Pa., 1945.

Bear Mountain–Harriman Park
Palisades Interstate Park Commission, Bear Mountain, N.Y.

Bedell, Cornelia
Now and Then and Long Ago in Rockland County
The Historical Society of Rockland County, 1968

Boyle, Robert H.
The Hudson River
W. W. Norton & Company, New York, 1969

Carmer, Carl
The Hudson
Farrar & Rinehart, New York, 1939

HOWELL, W. T.
Hudson Highlands; Diaries of a Pioneer Hiker
Lenz & Rieckee, New York, 1933

Palisades Interstate Park Commission
Sixty Years of Park Cooperation: New York–New Jersey, 1900–1960
Palisades Interstate Park Commission, Bear Mountain, N.Y., 1960
(Available at the Commission Administration Building, Bear Mountain, N.Y. 10911)

SKLARSKY, I. W.
The Revolution's Boldest Venture—the Story of General Mad Anthony Wayne's Assault on Stony Point
Kennikat Press, Port Washington, N.Y., 1965

WARD, CHRISTOPHER L.
The War of the Revolution, Vol. 2: Stony Point and the Forts on the Popolopen, edited by John Richard Alden
The Macmillan Company, New York, 1952

3 · *STORM KING–BLACK ROCK FOREST*

(Map 7)

DOMINATING THE rugged Hudson River gorge on the west, Storm King Mountain looms above the Hudson River like a fortress. The northernmost part of the Highlands, the mountain is one of the most striking along the river, its glowering eastern end rising sheer from the river to well over thirteen hundred feet. Dropping sharply along the fault line that forms its steep northern side, the mountain offers some of the finest views of the river.

Much of this magnificent terrain was preserved for hikers by Dr. Ernest Stillman, a New York physician, who, in 1922, gave about seven hundred acres in Storm King Clove to the Palisades Interstate Park to ensure the preservation of the scenic surroundings of the old Storm King Highway. This tract now forms the foreground for the fine eastward view from the present Storm King Highway (9W) before it turns west for its descent to Cornwall.

Actually, this serene mountain only recently was the subject of a raging environmental conflict over plans by Con Edison to build a pumped-storage power plant at the base of the mountain. The outcome of the conflict proved to be a turning point in America's environmental movement.

In 1963 Con Edison announced plans to build a powerhouse at the base of the mountain, a two-hundred-acre reservoir within nearby Black Rock Forest, and transmission wires atop ten-story towers running from Nelsonville across Putnam County. Public interest groups such as Scenic Hudson Preservation, Natural Resources Defense Council, and the Hudson River Fishermen's

Association joined to contest the project, arguing that large numbers of fish eggs and larvae would be killed, an allegation the utility tried to refute through various studies.

The battle raged for nearly two decades until December 1980, when a negotiated settlement was worked out, calling for Con Ed to drop its plans for the project. The resolution of this conflict was hailed by the New York *Times* as a "peace treaty for the Hudson" and set a precedent for national environmental issues dealing with the question of whether commercial developers could carry out development to meet one need at the expense of others.

BLACK ROCK FOREST

Linked to Storm King by the Stillman Trail, Black Rock Forest lies to the southwest across Route 9W. Donated to Harvard University in 1949 by Dr. Stillman, Black Rock Forest is a preserve of unusual interest for hikers. Throughout the forest are many reservoirs supplying local communities with water and the hiker with refreshing vistas. It includes about four thousand acres of a high, rugged granite plateau, with a dozen summits over fourteen hundred feet. The forest is named for Black Rock, a prominent pitch-pine-clad summit south of Cornwall, which is one of the most conspicuous in the area, offering grand views to the north, east, and west.

This area includes the highest summits west of the river in the Highlands proper, that is, in the old Precambrian rocks. Schunemunk Mountain to the west is a somewhat higher ridge, but of a younger geologic age. The highest summit, Spy Rock, is 1464 feet above sea level, and gives a wide circle of views, including an outlook through clefts in the hills southward to the Hudson at Peekskill and Haverstraw. From this outlook sentinels from Washington's camp at Newburgh watched British vessels sailing up the Hudson to Haverstraw Bay.

In the south-central part of the forest, on the west side of Continental Road, stands a solitary stone house sheltered by tall spruces. Dating from the 1830s, the Chatfield Place is the only building on the property. A fire in 1912 gutted this stone building, but it was reconstructed in 1932 and has been used by the university for storage and for boarding summer employees from time to time.

Another nine residences are known to have existed within the present forest boundaries. The inhabitants of these widely scat-

Up the Hudson from West Point with snow on the Highland slopes

tered subsistence farms eked out a living by pasturing a few acres, cultivating a small garden, and cutting wood as a means of earning some cash. Hunting and trapping wild game also added food and revenue sorely needed by these isolated families. An observant hiker can locate these old homesteads by looking for old cellar holes, remnant lilac bushes, stone walls, or dense coniferous stands of trees. An occasional relic from these sites is unearthed by persistent explorers.

Access to the forest by bus is from the Port of New York Authority Terminal to Mountainville (on the west side), or to Cornwall-on-Hudson (on the east side). Parking on the west side for the major trails is noted in the trails descriptions in this chapter. To park on the east side, take the first right onto Mountain Road, 0.4 mile after passing the scenic overlook on Route 9W in Cornwall (coming from the south). A sharp right then leads through a tunnel under the highway and into the forest. After 0.3 mile at a T intersection, make a right turn to the Upper Reservoir, where there is parking for a small number of cars.

If the turnoff of Route 9W is missed, another approach is to take a U-turn at Angola Road (5.4 miles north of the junction of Route 9W and Route 293). The entrance to the forest is 1.6 miles south of Angola Road, accessible only from the southbound lanes.

FORESTRY

To the casual observer, the Black Rock Forest may give the impression of pristine wilderness. Except for its rough gravel roads and marked trails, signs of civilization are, for the most part, missing. Though it is dense and natural in appearance today, almost all of the woodland has been logged, not once, but at least two or three times since Colonial days.

Timber in Black Rock Forest supplied fuelwood for domestic heating for the numerous valley farms in the area during the eighteenth and nineteenth centuries, wood being the primary source of household fuel in those days. In addition, thousands of cords of wood cut in these mountains were used to fuel local brickyards, or were barged down the Hudson River to heat residences in New York City.

At the turn of the century, the drain on the timber resource alarmed the New York Fisheries Game and Forest Commission, now known as the New York State Department of Environmental Conservation (DEC). In its 15th Annual Report, dated 1909, F. F. Moon, forester, described past forest practices as follows: "For generations, it has been the custom to clearcut the woodland for brickyard fuel, and so blindly has this custom been followed that it is no uncommon sight to see areas which were clearcut at the age of fifteen years, the sprouts being no thicker at the stump than a man's wrist."

The forests of the Hudson Highlands fared much better during the years following this alarming appraisal. Of the long list of factors which relieved the drain on local timber, the advent of coal followed by fuel oil for heating were perhaps the most outstanding. In addition, forest fire control measures have allowed soils to become more efficient at retaining water.

In recent times, the science and art of forestry practice has been applied to increasingly larger acreages as this rather new profession grows in numbers and public recognition. Harvard University has conducted studies and experiments in forestry for many years in Black Rock Forest, and the reservation is still being used for research demonstrations and graduate instruction.

FLORA AND FAUNA

As a result of all the logging and farming, the woodlands of Black Rock Forest are comparatively young and contain few large, mature trees. Yet the area offers a lush terrain of tremendous diversity.

Several species of oak, including red, white, black, scarlet, and chestnut, make up the bulk of the tree population in the forest, especially in the higher and drier areas. Associated with these are many pignut and mockernut hickories, which also thrive in the dry, shallow soils, as well as a few stately white pines. The young sprouts of American chestnut are common in Black Rock Forest, indicating that this tree was once a dominant species before the blight of the early 1900s.

In the moist soils near streams and ponds, one can find sugar maple, red maple, tupelo, ash, black and yellow birch, basswood, beech, shagbark hickory, sycamore, and tulip poplar. Along some of the steeper stream valleys and shaded, north-facing ravines, dense groves of hemlock trees provide startling contrasts to the open, sunny oak forest. The hemlocks around Mineral Spring Falls are huge, ancient trees—at least two or three centuries old—and they give the forest here a truly primeval appearance. Pitch pine and red cedar, two hardy evergreen trees, are conspicuous at or near the mountaintops. These species persist on these exposed sites in association with several dwarf varieties of scrub oak. The latter rarely attain a height of more than eight or ten feet due to the harsh environment.

Beneath the oaks, maples, and birches, flowering dogwood, hop hornbeam, witch hazel, and the beautiful striped maple make up the bulk of the forest's understory. In the wetter areas, alder and smooth-barked ironwood are common smaller trees. The shrub layer is dominated by mapleleaf viburnum, mountain laurel, blueberry, huckleberry, sweet fern, and pink azalea, with swamp azalea, sweet pepperbush, spicebush, chokeberry, and elderberry in swamps and around ponds and streams. The forest floor contains a good variety of mosses and ferns, and is carpeted with choice wildflowers from early April to fall, including such rarities as trailing arbutus, wood betony, and several beautiful orchids, lilies, and buttercups.

Deer are common in the forest. Beavers inhabit several of the reservoirs, and they are so plentiful that their dams must periodically be destroyed by forest personnel to release water. Other common mammals include raccoons, opossums, red and gray foxes, woodchucks, gray, red, and flying squirrels, long-tailed weasels, cottontails, and several species of shrews, moles, bats, mice, and voles.

Both copperheads and timber rattlesnakes inhabit the forest, but they are seldom encountered. More often seen are black racers, pilot black snakes, garter snakes, and water snakes. Snapping and painted turtles inhabit the reservoirs, along with bull, green, and pickerel frogs and eastern or red-spotted newts. In shallower woodland pools and swamps, a variety of amphibians deposit their jelly-covered egg masses throughout the spring, beginning with the wood frog and spotted salamander in March, and followed by the spring peeper, American toad, and gray tree frog in April and May. These frogs are very vocal during the breeding season, each species producing a distinctly different call. Beneath moist logs and leaf litter are red-backed and slimy salamanders, while the streams are inhabited by two-lined salamanders and beautiful northern red salamanders.

Finally, the birdlife of the forest is diversified, especially during spring and fall migratory flights, when as many as eighty different species can be seen. The tops of several of the more exposed summits in Black Rock Forest, as well as Storm King Mountain itself, are excellent vantage points from which to observe the autumn migrations of thousands of hawks, including rare peregrine falcons, and of golden eagles and bald eagles. A lookout tower on Whitehorse Mountain on the southeast edge of Black Rock Forest has been used to study hawk migration since the early 1970s, and its owner consistently counts more than ten thousand hawks, falcons, eagles, and vultures each fall.

TRAILS AND WOOD ROADS

Black Rock Forest may be enjoyed from forest trails and wood roads. The former, with steep ups and downs, lead to spectacular lookout points, while the latter wind in and among the reservoirs.

There are two main forest trails, running approximately southwest to northeast: the Stillman (yellow blazes) and the Scenic (white blazes). The Sackett Trail (yellow circles) is a ridge trail with outlooks to the west and north. Crossing these trails—which are maintained by the New York–New Jersey Trail Conference—are a number of short trails running roughly north to south which can be combined in a variety of long and short walks. The latter are maintained by forest personnel and the Black Rock Fish and Game Club of Mountainville, New York. For over four decades the club has had exclusive hunting and fishing rights in the forest. Working in close coordination with the forest manager in patrolling and maintaining the forest and safeguarding the visitors, many Black Rock Club members have been in the front lines in fighting forest fires, mounting search parties, and repairing the roads after violent storms.

Along the floor of the forest meander scenic gravel roads from which the reservoirs may be enjoyed at closer range. Circular walks in different combinations are possible entirely on these wood roads, which survive from the days when this area was populated by families scattered on small farms, from pre-Revolutionary times to the beginning of this century. The Continental

Road was originally the only route across the mountains to West Point, Highland Falls, etc., and was used until the "New Road," leading past the Upper Reservoir, was built. The latter is now known as the "Old West Point Road," and is itself a hundred years old.

Public access to this unique private property has always been permitted by both Dr. Stillman and Harvard University. Because of its tax-exempt status, the university has felt a responsibility to allow local and nonresident visitors to enjoy hiking, cross-country skiing, and other recreation in the forest, providing such use does not interfere with research and other educational activities in progress. Fires, camping, and swimming (except in Sutherland Pond) are not permitted.

For maps, use the "West Point" and "Cornwall" quadrangles of the U.S. Geological Survey. For a current official trail map of Black Rock Forest write to the Harvard Black Rock Forest, Box 483, Cornwall, N.Y. 12518, and enclose a stamped self-addressed legal-size envelope.

MAJOR TRAILS

Stillman Trail. Length: 10.5 miles (eastern portion of Schunemunk–Storm King Trail), from Route 32 in Mountainville to Mountain Road in Cornwall-on-Hudson. Blazes: yellow.

This trail is a continuation of the Jessup Trail (yellow blazes) from Monroe over Schunemunk Mountain, connecting at Mountainville. At the junction of Route 32 with Angola Road there is a bus stop. (Parking is on Old Route 32, 0.8 mile south, where the Scenic Trail crosses.)

From this point, the Stillman Trail branches northeast. In just under 2 miles the trail leaves the road on the right and goes southeast uphill until it joins a wood road and follows that to the right for a short time. It then bears left, still uphill, following a ravine, climbing steeply to the top of the hill (994 feet). Here is a splendid view down the valley to Schunemunk, and, in the opposite direction, to the Hudson River, Breakneck Ridge, and Mount Beacon. In descending, the trail runs south, turns sharply right across a field to the west, and climbs a stone wall to an old wood road, where it turns left (south) and gradually descends. A gravel road passing through a field beside the trail is on private property and should not be used.

At a fork south of this point and within sound of a brook, the Stillman Trail bears right (while the old wood road bears left, uphill). The trail crosses the brook and shortly thereafter bears left at a point where a wood road comes in from the right. It soon ascends a ridge with spectacular views of Schunemunk (and an occasional hawk) and then swings east, entering the lands of Harvard Black Rock Forest. It continues through laurel woods, then climbs steeply, heading north as it slabs a long ridge. On the right a shortcut offers the opportunity to eliminate a loop in the Stillman Trail. Farther on, the trail reaches the western terminus of the Sackett Mountain Trail (yellow circles). At this junction, the Stillman Trail turns sharply right (east) and subsequently reaches Hall Road, a dirt road running north and south. Continuing south, the trail turns left into another wood road and climbs to a ridge above Sutherland Pond (1400 feet). Echo (or Split) Rock is an outlook over Sutherland Pond and the hills to the south, accessible from Split Rock Trail (white blazes), a short side trail at the edge of the ridge. Here also the Compartment Trail (blue blazes) intersects.

The Stillman Trail continues along the ridge, crosses the Continental Road, and climbs up to Black Rock (1410 feet), an open rocky summit with good views to the west, north, and east. Leading down to Aleck Meadow Reservoir, the trail passes the southern terminus of the Black Rock Hollow Trail (white blazes). Crossing Aleck Meadow Road, the trail continues east to the foot of Mount Misery, where the Scenic Trail (white blazes) comes in from the Hill of Pines. The Stillman then climbs steeply to the top of Mount Misery, with more fine views, and descends, crossing the brook which is the outflow of the Upper Reservoir. The Reservoir Trail (blue blazes) leaves at the brook crossing to continue north. Here the Stillman Trail briefly uses the Old West Point Road, which may be followed north to Route 9W and

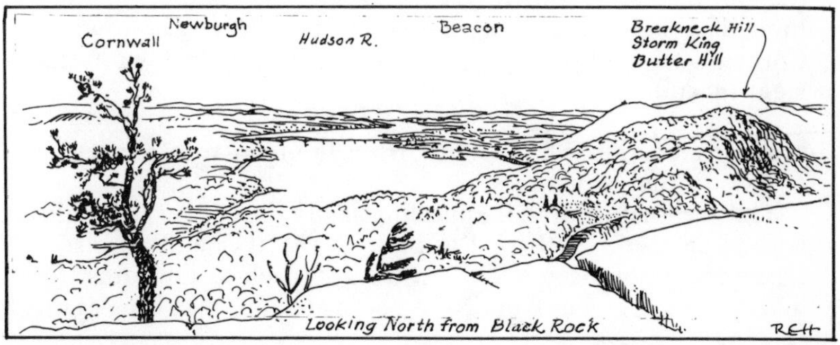

Mountain Road in Cornwall. A small parking area is located at the Upper Reservoir.

The trail continues east for about 200 yards and then turns left (north) into a wood road, leaving the Black Rock Forest, then cuts through the woods over the eastern slope of Whitehorse Mountain. The diamond-shaped lettered markers visible at some points on the trail are vestiges of a self-guided tour developed by the forest at one time to describe forestry experiments and historical data. The trail continues to Route 9W where it turns left (north) and, after a few hundred yards, crosses the highway into the northern end of a large parking lot and picnic area. Here are excellent views to the Hudson River through the clove between Butter Hill to the left and Crows Nest Mountain to the right. To gain access to the Stillman Trail at this point by car, park at the Scenic Overlook 3 miles north of the junction of Routes 9W and 293.

With views to the south and east, the trail then climbs steeply over the ramparts to the summit of Butter Hill, which offers a 360-degree view of the surrounding terrain. Continuing over the saddle between Butter Hill and Storm King (once part of Butter Hill but renamed around the turn of the century by a romantic journalist), the hiker is afforded views to the north and west from various ledges along the way. On reaching the brow of Storm King Mountain (1335 feet), the trail provides marvelous outlooks over the Hudson Valley from roughly southeast to northwest, including Mount Beacon, Breakneck Ridge, Mount Taurus, Schunemunk, the Shawangunks, and the Catskills. The trail then follows the contour of the mountain, with continual views north, descending on a fine sidehill trail cut into the steep slope of the mountain. This trail once carried pony-riding New Yorkers to the views at the top. There is one last look north up the Hudson before the trail turns west to a fire road which leads down (south and west) to its terminus at the two large stone pillars marking the entrance to Storm King Park on Mountain Road. There is limited parking here for two or three cars only. The town of Cornwall-on-Hudson is approximately 1 steep mile down to the right (north).

Scenic Trail. Length: 7.2 miles from Route 32 to Mount Misery. Blazes: white.

This well-named trail is appealing at any time of year. Popular both as an access to Black Rock Forest and as one of the major forest trails, the Scenic Trail is the approach to the forest for hikers coming by bus from New York City. The trail crosses the forest in a southwest to northeast direction, south of and generally parallel to the Stillman Trail (yellow blazes) until joining it and ending at Mount Misery.

The Scenic Trail is entered from Route 32 at 0.8 mile south of the bus stop in Mountainville, located at the junction of Route 32 and Angola Road. The trail is visible between a double row of maples on the east side of the road. Park along Old Route 32.

The trail proceeds uphill from Route 32 through timbered forests and down through pleasant woodlands to paved Mineral Spring Road. The trail uses the road for about 100 yards, then follows a stony dirt road diagonally southeast into the woods to Mineral Spring Falls (Green Falls), a triple cascade flowing over a series of ledges through a dark hemlock grove. Continuing straight ahead, the trail climbs up the ravine, paralleling the stream. After making a sharp left near the top of the grade, the trail winds through beautiful hemlock groves and over varied terrain to approach the slopes of Mount Rascal and enter Black Rock Forest.

After a few short diagonal rises, the trail parallels the ridge line and comes to Jupiters Boulder, the first of two outlooks to the northwest, which on a clear day afford distant views of the Shawangunks and Catskills. The trail continues generally northeastward, passing the western terminus of the Ryerson Trail (yellow blazes). After passing through a laurel lane, lovely in mid-June, the Scenic Trail joins Jims Pond Road. The trail continues south on the road until turning sharply east, coincides for a short distance with Arthurs Trail (yellow blazes), and then continues on. Less than 0.3 mile beyond, the Scenic Trail meets the Chatfield Trail (blue blazes) connecting across the forest with Chatfield Road. Shortly beyond, a blue-blazed side trail leads to Eagle Cliff, which overlooks Jims Pond and affords wonderful views to the south.

The next junction is with the Stropel Trail (yellow blazes), which leads down ledges to Jims Pond Road, then with the Ledge Trail (yellow blazes), leading to the Chatfield Trail.

A five-minute bushwhack, beginning about 190 paces north of the junction with the Ledge Trail, leads over rock outcroppings to the summit of Spy Rock (1461 feet), marked by one pitch pine. The views are especially fine north toward the Catskills and northwest to the Shawangunks. Across the Continental Road, the Scenic Trail continues northeast on Bog Meadow Road and in less than a half mile the trail abruptly turns right off the road to meander up Rattlesnake Hill. As the trail continues north over the hill, it crosses Carpenter Road, then goes up and over Hill of

Pines. Shortly after crossing the Swamp Trail (blue blazes), the Scenic Trail ends at its junction with the Stillman Trail (yellow blazes) on a slope at the southern base of Mount Misery.

Sackett Trail. Length: 1.5 miles. Blazes: yellow circles.

Winding along the crest of Sackett Mountain, this scenic trail offers two good view points for wide vistas to the northwest. Starting on the Stillman Trail near Mine Hill Road, the trail soon passes the Mine Hill Trail coming up on the left from a small parking lot on Mine Hill Road. To gain access by car, drive 2 miles east from Route 32 on Angola Road. Make a right on Mine Hill Road and drive to the hairpin turn with its small parking turnout.

From here, the trail continues north then east, and crosses two brooks before arriving at the crumbling walls and chimney of the old Beattie cabin. Dr. Beattie, visiting his patients, traveled up and down these mountain roads by horse and buggy. The cabin was built as a family camping retreat before Dr. Stillman owned the forest.

For about 150 feet the trail uses Hall Road, named for a family formerly living at the junction of the Continental Road and Route 9W. Here it passes the northern terminus of the Compartment Trail (blue blazes). After leaving Hall Road from the east side, the trail winds around a hill with rocky outcroppings and heads east and uphill to the Continental Road.

OTHER TRAILS IN BLACK ROCK FOREST

Arthurs Trail. Blazes: yellow.

This loop trail starts and ends on Jims Pond Road, named after Jim Babcock, woodsman, rattlesnake hunter, and first forester and caretaker of Black Rock Forest. Arthurs Trail was named for his son. Going north, the trail briefly coincides with the Scenic Trail, crosses the outlet of Sutherland Pond, and ends at the junction of Jims Pond Road and the Compartment Trail (blue blazes).

Black Rock Hollow Trail. Blazes: white.

The trail starts at the Stillman Trail and heads north following Black Rock Brook as it flows out of Aleck Meadow Reservoir. It terminates at the chlorinator building on a dirt road, closed to motor vehicles, which leads northwest to Route 9W.

Chatfield Trail. Blazes: blue.
This trail, named for a hamlet which is now a part of Cornwall, extends from the Scenic Trail northeast to connect the Secor Trail and Chatfield Road near Tamarack Pond.

Compartment Trail. Blazes: blue.
From the junction of Arthurs Trail and Jims Pond Road, this trail travels north, crosses the Stillman Trail (yellow blazes), and ends on Hall Road at its junction with Sackett Trail (yellow circles).

Hill of Pines Trail. Blazes: white.
The trail connects Carpenter Road with the Swamp Trail (blue blazes) shortly before the latter emerges on Old West Point Road.

Ledge Trail. Blazes: yellow.
This is a connecting link between the Scenic Trail and Chatfield Trail.

Mine Hill Trail. Blazes: yellow triangles.
This trail provides access to Black Rock Forest from the west. Parking is available for three or four cars only at the switchback on Mine Hill Road. The trail, beginning uphill and across the road, ascends to the Sackett Trail.

Reservoir Trail. Blazes: blue.
Starting at the Stillman Trail just west of the Upper Reservoir, the trail follows the reservoir outlet brook to the chlorinator building on a dirt road, closed to motor vehicles, which leads northwest to Route 9W.

Ryerson Trail. Blazes: yellow.
This trail branches right (southeast) from the Scenic Trail north of Mount Rascal and ends at Jims Pond Road.

Secor Trail. Blazes: yellow.
Named for a family residing in Cornwall, the Secor Trail acts as a shortcut from Chatfield Trail to Chatfield Road.

Split Rock Trail. Blazes: white.
This short spur trail leads from the Compartment Trail (blue blazes) to the lookout at Split (or Echo) Rock with views of Sutherland Pond and the hills to the south.

Stropel Trail. Blazes: yellow.

From the Black Rock Forest boundary corner, the Stropel Trail extends across Jims Pond Road. After climbing ledges, it ends at the Scenic Trail a short distance east of the blue-blazed side trail to the Eagle Cliff outlook.

Swamp Trail. Blazes: blue.

From Aleck Meadow Road the trail heads east between Mount Misery and Hill of Pines to the Old West Point Road, crossing the Scenic Trail (white blazes) about halfway. Shortly before ending, the trail passes the northern terminus of the Hill of Pines Trail (white blazes).

Tower Vue Trail. Blazes: yellow.

Connecting the east end of Arthurs Dam with Bog Meadow Road, the Tower Vue Trail parallels the east shoreline of Arthurs Pond.

White Oak Trail. Blazes: white.

The trail extends from the Stillman Trail northwest of Sphagnum Pond, across Continental Road, to White Oak Road south of Aleck Meadow Reservoir. it may serve as a pleasant shortcut which avoids the road walk from Continental Road around the north end of Arthurs Pond to White Oak Road.

4 · *SCHUNEMUNK MOUNTAIN*

(Map 8)

WEST OF the Black Rock Forest in the northern Hudson Highlands rises a land formation with several unique and striking features. Hikers on Schunemunk have much to marvel at, from the continuous views along the ridge to the unforgettable rock beneath their tramping feet.

Usually pronounced skun-uh-munk, the name means "excellent fireplace" in the Algonquin tongue. This name was given to the village that once existed on the northern spur of the mountain, in which lived the Indian tribe that originally owned the land. Today the northern half of the ridge is owned by the Star Expansion Company of Mountainville, New York, whose owner has permitted hikers to enjoy this region over the years.

An impressive ridge, nearly 1700 feet high, Schunemunk Mountain is double-crested on its north end. It extends more than 8 miles from Salisbury Mills on its northeastern end to Monroe on the southwest point. On a map it does not seem topographically different from the gneiss and granite Highlands eastward, but geologically it is much younger, composed of sandstone, shale, and conglomerate of Devonian time, with Silurian as well as Ordovician strata at its base. It is part of a long ridge of similar strata extending forty miles southwest into New Jersey, past Greenwood Lake and Green Pond, and ending near Lake Hopatcong. It was formed as sediments in a shallow sound of the ancient sea that vanished as the Taconic Highlands rose up.

The conglomerate ledges, composed of the highest and youngest of the Schunemunk strata, are conspicuous on the long level summit, with a reddish-purple matrix enclosing white quartz pebbles up to six inches in diameter—the remnants of erosion of

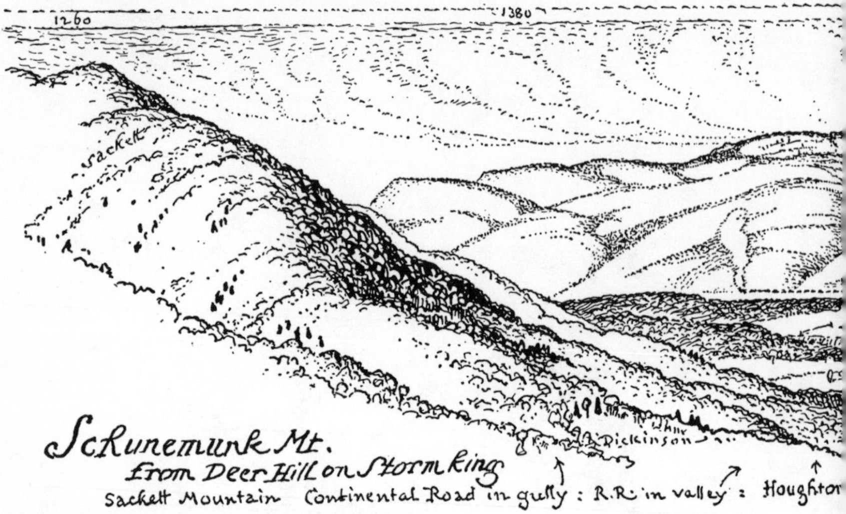

beaches and deltas from the Taconic Highlands to the east. Subsequent lateral pressure from the collision of Africa into North America deformed the formation into a series of folds, with the strata on the east limb of the ridge dipping to the west and those on the west limb dipping to the east. It has also undergone extensive longitudinal and cross faulting that has further confused the original sedimentary relations. A fault zone led to the cleft in the middle of the northern end, making double crests, with the densely wooded Barton Swamp in the depression between the crests.

On the other side of the valley to the west, and topographically associated with Schunemunk, is a line of wooded knobs of Precambrian gneiss extending from Woodcock Hill (over 1000 feet), west of the north end of Schunemunk, southwest to Sugarloaf. Their position, bounded on the east by Devonian and Silurian formations and on the west by Ordovician slates and limestones of the Wallkill Valley, has caused much geological speculation. Earlier interpretations held that these knobs were parts of a syncline, or a structural downfold, and were at the original western border of the Highlands, and that the Schunemunk strata had been laid down in this trough. Later studies suggest that these knobs are gigantic overthrust blocks, shoved from the western front of the Highlands during the great push of the Taconian Orogeny some 480 million years ago. Their relative hardness caused them to stand up as knobs, while softer formations around them wore down into the valleys. Woodcock Hill is made up of

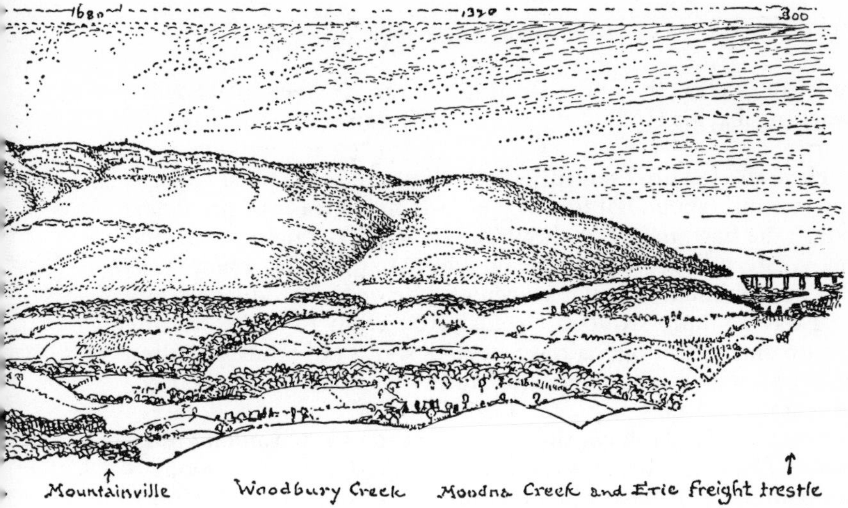

both Precambrian gneiss abutting the Ordovician formations on its west foot and Schunemunk strata on its eastern slopes.

Schunemunk Mountain is shown on four U.S. Geological Survey maps: "Popolopen Lake," "Monroe," "Maybrook," and "Cornwall." Car access is by Route 17, or the thruway to Exit 16 (Harriman), then north on Route 32 to Highland Mills, Woodbury, or Mountainville. Short Line buses from the Port Authority Bus Terminal, Manhattan, stop at these same towns.

A dirt parking area is maintained by the Star Factory at the north terminus of the Jessup Trail on Taylor Road, a half mile west of Route 32. Parking for the southern end of the Jessup is on Seven Springs Road, a few hundred feet east of the trail. Elsewhere, limited roadside parking can be found within reasonable distance of the trailheads.

Jessup Trail. Length: 8.1 miles. Blazes: yellow.

The main north-south trail, this trail traverses the full length of the mountain. Starting from Route 32 in Mountainville, walk or drive half a mile west on Taylor Road to the parking area on the right side of the road. Continuing on Taylor Road about 1 mile, enter a field on the left, following a faint dirt road west. The trail enters the woods and joins a clear dirt road in a hemlock grove, where it turns left. On the right side of the road, Baby Brook flows through still pools and cascades, and over a waterfall. The trail leaves the dirt road, veering right, and crosses the railroad tracks. It climbs steadily, about 700 feet in 0.8 mile, reaching Taylor Hollow at 2 miles, having risen 800 feet from the start.

Here the Jessup Trail turns left, climbing the central ridge to the summit, about 500 feet higher. Alternate trails begin at this point: the Barton Swamp Trail (red on white) straight ahead, and the Western Ridge Trail (blue on white) to the right. These trails can be combined to make a circular hike or to introduce variety to a day's hiking. A good circular hike from Route 32 via the Jessup and returning via the Sweet Clover Trail totals 4.6 miles, although it will seem longer because of the outstanding variety of terrain and views.

From Taylor Hollow, the Jessup ascends a ridge among pitch pines. The ridge displays the marvelous and unique conglomerate bedrock that makes Schunemunk so fascinating. This rock, sometimes called "puddingstone," has, because of the hematite present, a brownish gray or reddish-purple stained matrix of hard quartzite enclosing a kaleidoscopic assortment of pebbles up to six inches in diameter, many of them white quartz. It was originally a bed of mud, sand, and abrasion-rounded gravel on and near the shores of an ancient inland sea, material that was deposited about 350 million years ago, during the Devonian Period, by fast-flowing streams descending from the Taconic Highlands that existed farther to the east. Later, the mixture was gradually cemented together and compacted by pressure into solid, hard conglomerate. At the top surface of this rock the pebbles have been neatly ground flat by the massive layer of slowly moving ice of the last glacier.

Starting 0.1 mile after Taylor Hollow, and for 0.5 mile after that, is a continuous series of magnificent views of meadows, fields, and Beaver Dam Lake to the north, the Hudson River to the northeast, and Storm King Mountain and the hills of Black Rock Forest toward the east. There are also fine views of the western ridge of Schunemunk, parallel to the main ridge. The deep fold in the earth between the two ridges, through which runs the Barton Swamp Trail, is the result of intense horizontal pressure on the earth's crust toward the close of the Paleozoic Era, about 250 million years ago. Erosion and additional crustal uplift occurred later. The greater resistance to erosion of the hard conglomerate layer left the ridge standing high above the surrounding valley.

At 2.6 miles the Jessup intersects the Sweet Clover Trail (white blazes), the two trails turning together to the southwest. The cracks in the bedrock on the ridge here afford fine blueberry picking in season, usually from middle to late July. The pitch pines exposed on the ridge, stunted into rugged beauty by the winter winds, display their ability to survive the stringent conditions that nature provides. At 2.9 miles the trail drops into a forested cleft in the ridge, and the Sweet Clover Trail (white blazes) diverges to the left. The Jessup then climbs the ridge again, continuing south. At 3.5 miles the Dark Hollow Trail (white on black) goes off to the left. Both the Sweet Clover and the Dark Hollow trails are convenient for returning to a starting point at the north end of the trail.

The Jessup continues on the ridge, reaching at 3.8 miles a short spur to the Megaliths, a group of huge blocks that have split off from the bedrock. There is a good view here toward the western ridge, overlooking Barton Swamp.

At 3.9 miles, marked by a cairn, is the highest elevation in the area, 1664 feet, higher than any of the neighboring summits in Harriman State Park, Black Rock Forest, or the Hudson Highlands from Storm King to the Beacons. Excellent views of those summits can be had from this vantage point. There are views of at least four fire towers, and the Perkins Memorial Tower atop Bear Mountain to the southeast. On a clear day the higher peaks of the Catskill Mountains are identifiable across the horizon to the north: Slide, Cornell, Wittenberg, Plateau, Sugarloaf, and Indian Head. Toward the west are the Kittatinny Mountains with their monument atop High Point, the highest elevation in New Jersey at 1803 feet. The Shawangunks, part of the same ridge that forms the Kittatinnies, can be seen toward the northwest, stretching from Sams Point to Mohonk.

The Jessup continues southward, passing the end of the Western Ridge Trail at 4 miles, reaching one good lookout point after another. Hawks can often be seen circling in the updrafts from the cliffs, occasionally swooping down into the woods below for a meal.

At 4.6 miles, another high point, at 1662 feet, is reached, with more good views east and west. The trail continues, occasionally dropping down through gaps in the ridge, before reascending. At times, the ridge is as smooth as a sidewalk, ground down by the friction of moving glaciers. Occasionally large "foreign" boulders are found, carried from distant locations by the same glaciers that ground the bedrock smooth. Similarly, a huge boulder of Schunemunk conglomerate can be found on the grounds of Arden House, over 10 miles to the south. At 4.7 miles the Long Path, running northwest and southeast, crosses the Jessup at the widest part of the ridge.

At 6.1 miles the Jessup reaches the Forrest Trail (white blazes), which leaves to the left as the Jessup turns right. An extended area of bare rock provides an excellent view point looking northwest over Round Hill, one of a line of wooded knobs composed of Precambrian gneiss that march parallel to Schunemunk for most of its length. At 6.3 miles the trail passes a telephone line. Across ridges alternating with forested areas, the trail now gradually descends over a series of small rises. Views toward the east and west can occasionally be seen through the trees. The trail passes a strange white boulder. This is a glacial erratic of dolomitic limestone originating somewhere to the north and deposited on Schunemunk by the last glacier to grind south across the land. The last good lookout point is at 7.6 miles, where the elevation is 1320 feet. Farther down, the grade steepens, descending through forests near the end. At 8.1 miles the Jessup terminates at Seven Springs Road.

Western Ridge Trail. Length: 2.4 miles. Blazes: blue on white. This trail runs along the western ridge of Schunemunk, generally parallel to the Jessup Trail. Access is from Mountainville by the Jessup to Taylor Hollow, alongside Baby Brook. The trail ascends steep ledges to the western ridge and its splendid views of the Hudson River, North and South Beacon mountains, Storm King Mountain, and the central ridge of Schunemunk. It is said that somewhere here on the northern spur of the western ridge was the Indian village whose fireplace gave the mountain its name. The trail turns southwest along the relatively narrow ridge overlooking the Washingtonville valley. About 0.8 mile from Taylor Hollow is the terminus of the Sweet Clover Trail from the east. In another 0.8 mile the Western Ridge Trail reaches a bare ledge sloping eastward, where there is an excellent view of the central ridge and of Barton Swamp in the trough between the two ridges. Here the trail goes steeply downhill into Barton Swamp, where it turns right, joins the Barton Swamp Trail for a short distance, then turns left, climbing steeply southeast over ledges with views of the western ridge and the distant mountain ranges beyond. Continuing southeast, the trail ends at a cairn on the Jessup Trail.

Barton Swamp Trail. Length: 2.1 miles. Blazes: red on white. This trail follows the wooded trough that separates the central and western ridges of Schunemunk, providing a quick sheltered exit to Taylor Hollow. It extends north from the Long Path, a short distance west of Barton Swamp, to Taylor Hollow. The trail starts south for a short distance, then turns northeast where, after 0.2 mile, it is joined by the Western Ridge Trail (blue on white) coming in from the right. After another tenth of a mile, the Western Ridge Trail departs to the left, the Barton Swamp Trail continuing northeast through the forest, paralleling the headwaters of Baby Brook. At 1.6 miles, the Barton Swamp Trail crosses the Sweet Clover Trail (white blazes), then continues for a distance, crossing the brook occasionally, following one bank for a while, then the other. Large stands of white birch trees are evident, and mountain laurel proliferates at the drier spots. At 2.1 miles the trail terminates where it meets the Jessup (yellow blazes) and Western Ridge (blue on white) trails at Taylor Hollow. The Jessup Trail offers a direct exit route to Taylor Road in Mountainville.

Sweet Clover Trail. Length: 2.8 miles. Blazes: white.

This trail is a good east-west approach to the highest points. From the hiker's parking area on Taylor Road (see Jessup Trail) follow an asphalt private road south past a barn. Turning west into the meadow, the trail becomes a dirt road, turns south, then west into the woods. The trail leaves the dirt road to cross the railroad tracks about 1 mile from the start. A short detour south along the tracks leads to the start of Dark Hollow Trail (white on black).

The Sweet Clover Trail climbs steadily, crossing a slope of flaggy sandstone that plunges down to Dark Hollow Brook far below. The trail switchbacks up past the northernmost branch of Dark Hollow Brook, crosses a swampy stretch, and then heads uphill again.

At about 1450 feet the trail meets the Jessup Trail and runs north with it for about 0.3 mile on conglomerate rock, yielding splendid views. It then turns west and drops steeply into Barton Swamp and crosses the headwaters of Baby Brook. After reaching the Barton Swamp Trail (red on white), it climbs steeply to terminate at the Western Ridge Trail (blue on white).

The Long Path. Length: 5.2 miles. Blazes: turquoise.

Crossing Schunemunk at its widest part, the Long Path uses the old High Knob and Echo Glen trails. This section leaves Route 32 at the railroad trestle about 1.6 miles north of the Highland Mills bus station. From the west side of Route 32, follow the trestle to the top, walk north along the railroad tracks about 0.4 mile, and turn left on a dirt road. Follow this 0.2 mile to a gravel pit, turn right over a small stream, and enter the woods.

The trail climbs steadily west and north for over half a mile, then turns up a rocky defile to the top of Little Knob (1000 feet). The trail ascends a wooded incline, then to the right up a talus slope, up the rising edge of a cliff bordered with twisted pitch pines, then right again to the summit of High Knob (1383 feet). Here are excellent views to the east, north, and south.

From the western side of High Knob the Long Path descends north along the top edge of the high pine-bordered cliff above an impressive ravine. At the saddle of this ravine the trail turns left across a double notch, turns right and climbs steeply to the top of another rock wall. High Knob and its cliffs are visible from here.

The trail then goes northwest, ascending gradually about half a mile to a high point with a view to the north. It then drops a bit, bends left, then sharp right to cross the headwater of Dark Hollow Brook. From here it climbs steadily northwest for less than 0.3 mile where it joins the Jessup Trail at an elevation of 1600 feet. There are views east and west.

The Long Path continues northwest down a gentle slope, enters the woods, and descends a series of ledges overlooking Barton Swamp and the western ridge; the last ledge is steep. The trail plunges down a talus slope into Barton Swamp, crosses a brook, turns left onto a wood road for a short distance, then right again, leaving the road to the northwest. The trail then ascends a ridge, gradually turning right, following the ridge in a northerly direction. After descending into a saddle in the ridge, the trail passes the northern end of the Barton Swamp Trail (red on white). It then bears left, beginning a steep descent. Crossing under a telephone line and passing just left of a hidden pond, the trail continues downhill to the north for almost half a mile, joining Clove Road opposite a small lake about 1.8 miles south of Salisbury Mills. The Long Path continues 2 miles farther over Woodcock Hill to Route 94 west of Salisbury Mills.

Forrest Trail. Length: 2.3 miles. Blazes: white.

This trail is a short but steep approach to the southern half of the Jessup Trail from Route 32 north of Highland Mills. Access is at the beginning of Ridge Road, 0.7 mile north from Highland Mills bus station. The trail follows Ridge Road uphill to the northeast for 0.9 mile, then turns right into Schunemunk Road. Winding past a large red barn, a reservoir, and a horse-training stable, the trail continues on this road for 0.7 mile, then enters the woods to the right on a well-defined wood road. A car (or a taxi from Highland Mills) may be taken directly to this point, but note that parking is very limited here.

The wood road leads northwest 0.3 mile to the base of a steep slope of loose sandstone slabs that split into distinctively flat plates, commonly called "flagstone" but identified as graywacke. A 400-foot scramble up this slope leads to better footing near the top, where the trail meets the Jessup Trail at 1400 feet and ends.

Dark Hollow Trail. Length: 1.8 miles. Blazes: white on black.

This trail starts about 100 feet south of the Sweet Clover Trail on the west side of the railroad tracks. Meandering steeply up Schunemunk, it reaches the Jessup Trail 0.4 mile from the summit of the mountain.

5 · *THE SHAWANGUNK MOUNTAINS*

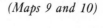

(Maps 9 and 10)

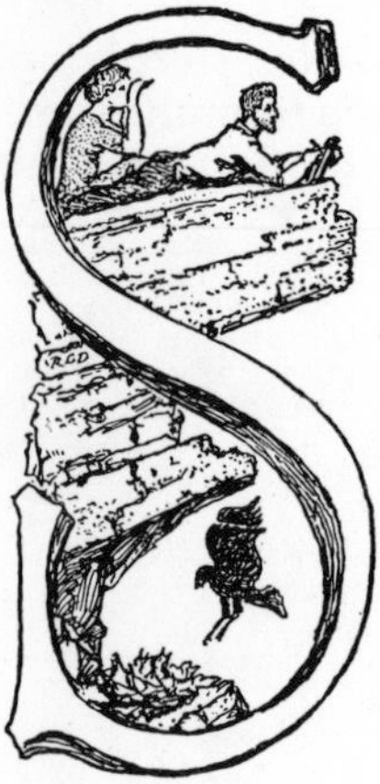

STANDING HIGH above the valleys on either side, the Shawangunk Mountain ridge (pronounced "shon gum") from the New York–New Jersey line northeast to Kingston is actually a section of the Blue Ridge range. Offering a hiking experience of great variety and beauty, the area supplies the veteran hiker with the challenge of rough trails and rock scrambles, while less-experienced hikers may enjoy spectacular views from gentle carriage roads. Dotting the cliffs, rustic ladders, benches, and Victorian gazebos surprise the hiker who approaches the sites of venerable hotels, while the lakes located near the summit afford plunging views into nearby valleys.

The Shawangunk Mountains are mapped on the U.S. Geological Survey's "Rosendale," "Mohonk Lake," "Gardiner," "Napanoch," "Ellenville," and "Wurtsboro" quadrangles (1:24,000). These maps are helpful in locating approach roads but are not useful for hiking because the trails are not shown; the scale does not permit an adequate representation of the cliff-riddled terrain. For walks on the Mohonk and Minnewaska estates, the detailed maps available from the hotels are essential; these may be obtained from Lake Mohonk Mountain House, Mohonk Lake, New Paltz, N.Y. 12561, and Lake Minnewaska Mountain Houses, Inc., Lake Minnewaska, New Paltz, N.Y. 12561, respectively.

Referred to affectionately by hikers as "the Gunks," this formation is actually a narrow mountain ridge, composed of extremely durable conglomerate—the Shawangunk Conglomerate of Late

Silurian age. This formed the basis of a substantial quarrying industry during the nineteenth century, providing millstones to mills around the country.

This formation stands as a striking example of the process described as differential erosion. The shale layers that lie both above and below the conglomerate are much softer and do not readily resist the forces of weathering and erosion; they are more rapidly reduced to lower elevations. The resulting linear Shawangunk ridge, with its striking talus slopes of downward-tumbled boulders, is different in character from the Catskills, the Adirondacks, or the Highlands, and, as a topographic feature, always comes as a surprise to those who see it for the first time.

At its northern end, the ridge rises gradually from the Hudson River Valley near Kingston as a series of low hills, suddenly dramatized by the "table rocks" and "ice caves" of High Falls and by the spectacular Mohonk escarpments of Bonticou Crag, Sky Top, and Eagle Cliff. The first of the five successively higher lakes, Mohonk (1250 feet), is cradled between the latter two cliffs. From this point southward, the ridge grows higher and broader, and at Gertrudes Nose it bends to the west toward Ellenville. The lakes, whose shores exhibit striking sculpture of cliff and fallen rock, in order are Minnewaska (1650 feet), Awosting (1875 feet), Haseco, known locally as Mud Pond (1850 feet), and Maratanza (2250 feet). Near the last is Sams Point, the highest elevation of the range (the widest point is near Haseco Lake). Beyond Sams Point, the ridge settles again into lower, less wild, and less spectacular hills until it reaches the Delaware Water Gap and New Jersey border at Port Jervis, where it is known as Kittatinny Mountain.

The shale layers that underlie the Shawangunk and Kittatinny mountains also make up the floor of the broad valley, the Great Valley, immediately to the east. Laid down originally as mud deposits in an extensive marginal sea during the Ordovician Period some 500 million years ago, they were subsequently folded, uplifted, and then eroded during a crustal upheaval near the end of the Ordovician. Submerged again beneath a warm, shallow sea during the succeeding Silurian Period about 450 million years ago, wave action laid down an almost beachlike layer of sand and fine gravel, the "white stone" of the Shawangunks. Another episode of crustal deformation about 280 million years ago tilted all these strata into their present position, but differential erosion alone is responsible for the present-day relief. Most recently, glaciers that crossed this region into New York City left their

SHAWANGUNK ESCARPMENT *from* MOHONK
FROM PHOTO BY MARY LOUISE WISE

marks too, as the north-south trending faint striae, seen most often along the ridge top. These should not be confused with the abundant slickensides, sections of highly polished and deeply grooved rock caused by friction between sliding masses subjected to the ancient crustal upheavals.

The Sams Point–Lake Maratanza–High Point section of the ridge is owned by the village of Ellenville. In 1967, part of this section, including an area containing one of the famous ice caves, was leased for a twenty-year period to a group which calls itself Ice Caves Mountain. These lessees have created a nature trail that points out various ecological, geological, and botanical items of interest.

Sams Point (2255 feet) is the most accessible and the most striking of the view points and consequently has suffered the most from vandals with paint cans. It is named for Sam Gonzalez, a hunter who was reputed to have jumped off the cliff to avoid being captured by Indians in hot pursuit. He survived by landing in a clump of hemlocks.

The ice caves consist of vertical crevices in the Silurian conglomerate in which melted snow and rain collect during the winter in sufficient quantity to freeze into ice three to ten feet deep, which lasts well into the summer. The resultant cool air creates a microclimate which encourages the growth of plants with northern affiliations and with different blooming dates from those outside the caves. Mountain laurel blooms four to six weeks later down in the caves than on top; dwarf dogwood has been observed blooming two months later at the bottom than at the top. In 1967 the ice caves on this part of the ridge were declared a national natural landmark, and fees are charged.

HISTORY

Arrowheads from 6200 B.C. testify to the long relationship between human beings and the Shawangunks. Indian hunting bands undoubtedly roamed the ridge in search of game to bring to their villages below.

In 1677 the New Paltz Patent brought French Huguenots to the area. Six of their original stone houses still remain on Huguenot Street in New Paltz. As the valleys became settled, and farming inched up the mountainside, the forest along the ridge began a steady decline. First felled for fuel and lumber, trees were used up for a variety of industries which peaked and passed during the nineteenth century. One important industry was charcoal production, which consumed trees voraciously, although the charcoal pits through which trails pass are scarcely recognizable now. Perhaps affecting the area more than any other was the tanning industry, which in the early 1800s began the systematic destruction of the hemlock forests, both here and in the Catskills. Today all that is left are two notable stands—the Palmaghatt on the Minnewaska estate, which received extensive damage during the 1950 hurricane, and Glen Anna at Mohonk. Using the saplings plentiful in the second growth, the barrel hoop industry followed and millions of hoops were manufactured in the Shawangunks.

The thin soil which lies atop the ridge is good for blueberries. Lasting into the 1930s, the berry picking industry flourished, particularly in the Sams Point area. The early commercial berry pickers spent the summer in shacks along the entrance road to Ice Caves Mountain. Some of their homes still exist as unattractive mementos of the past. Remains, too, may still be seen of a network of trails, marked by cairns, leading to favored picking areas.

As the West opened to settlers, many farms in this area were abandoned. Coal, and later oil and gas reduced the demand for wood fuel, allowing the forests gradually to make a comeback. Coinciding with the start of this trend was a romantic fascination for the picturesque, the mysterious, and the spiritual in Nature, found in the painting, literature, and landscape architecture of the time. "Wilderness" vacations became fashionable at luxurious resorts such as the Catskill Mountain House.

Enter the Smiley twins, Albert K. and Alfred H. In 1869 Albert acquired the original 300-acre parcel, comprising Mohonk Lake and the surrounding land, from John Stokes, who had run a tavern on the lake. To maintain the character of the property, adjoining farms and other private holdings were added to the estate as they became available, and the brothers entered the hotel business.

In 1879 Alfred H. Smiley opened his own hotel, the Lake Minnewaska House. The latter at one time consisted of two buildings: Cliff House east of the lake and Wildmere at the north.

Crevice
and
steps
Road
Sams Point
Dickinson

Both estates expanded until Mohonk reached 7500 acres, and Minnewaska more than 10,000 acres. Over the years, more than 200 miles of carriage roads, bridle paths and trails were created, all seeking out scenic view spots. The Smileys of Mohonk pioneered in road-building techniques, conservation, and land management practices, to the ultimate benefit of the hiking public.

FLORA AND FAUNA

Fires have changed the character of the Shawangunk forests as much as industry's need for timber. Stripped of their bark by the tanners, giant hemlocks were left to rot, providing fuel for frequent fires. Berry pickers periodically set fires rather than permit the berries to be shaded out by competing vegetation. The ashes served as fertilizer and the crop flourished. Besides blueberries, other species have benefited from the history of fires, notably pitch pine and mountain laurel, both characteristic of the Shawangunks.

The forests have returned, bringing red cedar, birch, white pine, chestnut oak, red oak, striped maple, and red maple. The second growth has also figured in the resurgence of whitetail deer, which feed on the low brush not present in a mature forest. Lacking the timber wolf and mountain lion, predators which once roamed the rocky cliffs, deer are more numerous now than ever. Preferring other low bushes to mountain laurel, the increased deer population has indirectly contributed to the flourishing of that beautiful shrub on the white cliffs of the Shawangunks.

In the absence of their natural enemy the fisher (a member of the weasel family), porcupines have so increased in number that they have become a problem. They delight in gnawing on wooden tool handles, signs, and even automobile tires. In 1976–77 the State Conservation Department reintroduced the fisher to the area in an effort to keep a natural balance between prey and predator.

Attempts to reintroduce the peregrine falcon to the area, one of the last nesting places in the eastern United States, have not borne fruit in the past five years. On the other hand, the pileated woodpecker and tufted titmouse are becoming more numerous. The black bear, the largest wild creature of the area, is rarely sighted. Rarer still is the bobcat.

MOHONK

The Mohonk estate extends for 8 miles, roughly from Bonticou Crag to Millbrook Mountain. Walking at Mohonk ranges from easy, scenic strolls on the 45 miles of carriage roads to rough scrambles over boulders, through crevices, and across open ledges, aided where absolutely necessary by strategically placed ladders. Only a brief indication of the possibilities can be made here; hikers must go, maps in hand, and make their own discoveries.

The traditional Mohonk estate, assembled by the many purchases of Albert K. Smiley and his descendants during the nineteenth and early twentieth centuries, is today divided into two property ownerships. Mohonk Mountain House, the resort hotel at Mohonk Lake, has grounds of 2500 acres, extending from Copes Lookout on the south to the Mountain Rest golf course on the north. The outlying forest lands, undeveloped except for carriage roads and hiking trails, now form the 5000-acre Mohonk Preserve, a nonprofit organization formed originally as the Mohonk Trust in the 1960s. A small fee is charged for a permit issued by either the Mohonk Lake Resort or by the Preserve entitling one to hike through the lands of both proprietors; permits should be shown to the rangers on request.

To walk in the Mohonk Preserve or Mohonk Lake Resort lands, one may choose to start at the Trapps, at Mountain Rest, or at the Mohonk Mountain House. Camping facilities are available at a number of points, and walks can also start from these areas. The three main areas may be reached by car from Exit 18 of the New York State Thruway via Route 299 West. To find the Trapps from 299 West, take Route 44 north to parking at two overlooks (one at and one after the switchback) and along the road near Trapps Bridge.

Mountain Rest is the gateway for entry by car or foot into the Mohonk Lake Resort grounds. Taking Route 299 west through New Paltz, turn right after crossing the Wallkill River, then left at the first intersection, marked by a Mohonk sign, and proceed up a winding hill to the Mountain Rest entrance to Mohonk. Parking, maps, and permits are available at the gate. Or, for the price of a lunch at the hotel, the hiker may opt to be a day guest. To do so, one may drive up the mountain to the Mountain House, and start the walk there, also earning the right to use the house facilities. For a luncheon reservation, phone (212) 233-2244 in the

New York metropolitan area, or (914) 255-1000 in the lower Hudson Valley area.

Hikes at Mohonk

Trapps Hike

A walk to the dramatic scarp of the Trapps from the Mountain House and back has the advantage of a relatively level hike high above surrounding terrain and at altitudes between 900 and 1200 feet. In three to four hours, one can traverse its 9.5 miles along carriage roads that pass through mature woods and by scenic valley panoramas. Trails are well marked by signs at intersections. Hikers parking at the Trapps Bridge may do a shorter circular of 4.5 miles on the lovely loop around the Trapps made by Undercliff and Overcliff roads.

From Mohonk Mountain House, take Lake Shore Road south, strolling along the eastern edge of pristine Mohonk Lake, a half mile long, sixty feet deep, and fed by cold springs. Rustic gazebos erected by Mohonk's Smiley family add to the picturesque setting. The path passes boulders, and crosses rough paths that climb through faults and crevices to Sky Top and its tower built in memory of Mohonk's founder, Albert K. Smiley. On the road, the hiker may have to make way for a carriage full of hotel guests pulled by a team of farm horses.

Lake Shore Road meets Old Woodland Drive on the right at 0.3 mile and Forest Drive on the left at 0.5 mile. Continuing on Lake Shore Road and shortly after Forest Drive, the walk goes by Partridgeberry Trail, then Woodland Drive, both on the right, after which point Lake Shore Road becomes Old Minnewaska Road. The trail continues south here through pines and maples, offering views eastward beyond pastures and a pond to the valley of the Wallkill.

At 1 mile, where Old Minnewaska Road bends westward, there is an opening in the woods on a hilltop to the left with a good vista across a ravine of the Trapps escarpment (created by the resistant Shawangunk conglomerate), which the hike will circle. The name may come from the Dutch "treppen," for steps. The western tack of the path continues 0.4 mile downhill and then angles south again at a junction with Rhododendron Path (unmarked) on the right.

At 1.5 miles the path crosses Rhododendron Bridge over a stream to where Undercliff, Overcliff, and Laurel Ledge roads meet. Proceed along the middle path, shown by a sign as Overcliff Road, which meanders at its start and then holds to a southerly direction until its end. Along its length are views across the Rondout Valley west to distant farms, houses, and roads. Farther west are the Catskills, often bluish with haze. In summer, blueberry bushes crowd along the way, and the leaf of a sweet fern may be crushed for a refreshing scent.

At 4.5 miles, the trail crosses the Trapps Bridge over Route 44, a state road north to Lake Minnewaska and Kerhonkson and south to New Paltz. The bridge carries the carriage road on which hotel guests of old visited back and forth between Mohonk and Minnewaska. Below the bridge and along the shoulders of the road are probably the parked cars of hikers and rock climbers. This marks the end of the outward leg of the journey. To return to the Mountain House, one should not cross the bridge but rather continue on Overcliff Road. It will become Undercliff Road, which heads back north along the east side of the scarp that Overcliff Road traversed on the west.

Along Undercliff is a panoramic view east across the Wallkill Valley to New Paltz and past the Hudson Valley to the Taconics and Berkshires. In the spring, juncos and ovenbirds nest near the road, and dogwoods bloom here and there. This spot is a favorite haunt of rock climbers. Climbing is strictly regulated and is not to be attempted by the uninitiated; fatalities have occurred here. Those who feel the urge should join one of the climbing groups for proper training.

At 7 miles the path returns to Rhododendron Bridge. Turn left before the bridge past the entrance to Overcliff Road and go on Laurel Ledge Road north and uphill past Rhododendron Path, Giants Path, and Laurel Ledge Path, with lookouts west to Clove Valley and the Rondout Valley. Continue past Zaidees Path and Clove Path; at about 8.2 miles, Laurel Ledge Road switches back south past more lookouts and then switches north again at 9 miles to a small traffic circle connecting Laurel Ledge, Copes Lookout, and Humpty Dumpty roads. Here there is a view south across the ravine to the Trapps and beyond, where, high on a ridge, are the water tower and buildings of the Lake Minnewaska Estate.

From the circle, Copes Lookout Road travels north to the Mountain House. For a change from carriage roads, one may take Copes Lookout Path instead, in the same direction. Either way, the walk ends at the Mountain House.

Hikes to Sky Top

One of the most popular objectives for hikers at Mohonk is Sky Top, a prominent cliff whose stone tower, the Albert K. Smiley Memorial Tower, is visible from as far away as the thruway. The easiest approach starts near the Mohonk Mountain House. Go east past the golf putting green to Sky Top Path, marked by a sign. Pass Council House and follow Sky Top Path as it climbs and crosses a loop of Sky Top Road at about 0.3 mile. Continue until another loop of the road is reached at the tower.

Here one may ascend a long, winding flight of stairs inside the tower to the observation deck and weather station. The views of the nearby valleys and distant mountain ranges are well worth the extra effort. Return the same way or via either the north or south loop of Sky Top Road. Both loops meet to form a single passage that meanders down the mountainside until it meets Huguenot Drive. Here, turn south and follow signs to the Mountain House past charming lookouts at Mohonk gardens and other places along the way.

A longer hike of about 2 miles ascends via Sky Top Path, as described above, but offers a more varied descent. At the tower and looking west from its entrance, turn right on Sky Top Road. Circle downhill past the Labyrinth Path to Pinnacle Path, about 0.2 mile from the tower. Go left on Pinnacle Path until it merges with Staircliff Path at Pinnacle Rock, and then continue on Pinnacle to Rock Spring Path, which is about 0.7 mile from the tower. Turn left here and proceed about 0.2 mile to Fox Path. Take a left on Fox Path, which is sometimes wet, past Sky Top Road to Huguenot Drive, and then another left to the Mountain House.

For a walk that is 3 miles long but more level, one can circle but not reach Sky Top. For this take Lake Shore Road south, past Old Woodland Drive, 0.5 mile to Forest Drive, where nearby is refreshing Mohonk Spring. Turn left on Forest Drive to Rock Spring Bridge at 1.4 miles. Then go left on Bridge Road, past Woodland Bridge, to Huguenot Drive at 1.8 miles. Follow Huguenot left back to the Mountain House.

The roughest way to Sky Top, a distance of 1.5 miles, is from the Mountain House south on Lake Shore Road about 0.1 mile to Labyrinth Path. Through narrow defiles, over rocks, and on rustic staircases with railings for handholds, the hiker reaches the Crevice at about 0.4 mile. Here is a narrow opening under a huge slab that fell from cliffs above and came to rest on giant boulder supports. Shortly afterward the trail meets a loop of Sky Top Road. Turn left for the tower and return via Pinnacle Path, Rock Spring Path, Fox Path, and Huguenot Drive.

Hikers preferring to start from the Mountain Rest Gate House to Sky Top will walk along gentle carriage roads with distant views across the wide valley to the Catskills. The route begins along Huguenot Drive, which serves in its beginning as a section of the auto road to the Mountain House. After Huguenot crosses Woodland Bridge at 0.9 mile, it veers right and briefly coincides with Garden Road. At 1.4 miles a left on Sky Top Road leads past a reservoir. Where Sky Top forks into its upper and lower loops, one should bear right on the upper loop to the tower, which is reached after 3.1 miles.

Bonticou Crag

From Mountain Rest Gate House, take Spring Hill Farm Road north past the golf course and past Guyot's Hill Road 0.6 mile to Bonticou Road. Turn right and pass Cedar Drive to a point about 1 mile from the start, where an opening provides a path that descends to the Bonticou Pass Trail. Here the trail goes right a short distance to markers leading up a rough scramble to Bonticou Crag, at 800 feet a lookout that dominates the surrounding area. Return to Bonticou Road, turn left, and walk back to Mountain Rest for a little over 2 miles total. A somewhat longer way back is possible by turning left on Bonticou Road and right on Guyot's Hill Road, which meanders picturesquely until Pine Water Circle and then branches left to Bonticou Road again or right to Spring Farm Road. Turn right on Bonticou or left on Spring Farm to get back to Mountain Rest.

Other Mohonk Hikes

More walks in the area are the Mossy Brook (one and a half hours), Rock Pass (one and a quarter hours), Eagle Cliff (easy way —one hour; rough paths—three hours), and Oakwood (three hours). These and still others are shown and described on a 22-by-34-inch map of Mohonk (scale: 1 inch = 0.1 mile) available at the Mountain House shop.

THE MINNEWASKA AREA

The lovely former Minnewaska estate, measuring ten thousand acres, has been divided into two parts. Seven thousand acres now form the Minnewaska State Park through which many miles of scenic trails and carriage roads wind their way to Lake Awosting and beyond. The three thousand acres which remained privately owned include Awosting Falls, as well as the sites of the two Minnewaska hotels atop the cliffs overlooking pristine Lake Minnewaska.

In 1979 the Marriott Corporation contracted to purchase about

five hundred acres, including the hotel sites, Lake Minnewaska, and the golf course, in order to construct a 450-room hotel, a conference center, 300 condominiums, an 18-hole championship golf course, and other amenities. This complex would occupy more than ten times the space of all previous development. As of this writing, suits are in court to block development and the future of this section is uncertain.

Minnewaska State Park

Minnewaska State Park extends north to Stony Kill Falls, west to Lake Haseco, and south to Millbrook Mountain, and includes a large tract on the northeast side of Route 44-55. Created in 1970 by the state of New York and the Nature Conservancy, the park contains a network of old carriage roads and a system of trails established by the New York–New Jersey Trail Conference.

To reach the Minnewaska State Park, take Exit 18 from the New York State Thruway to Route 299 and then west through New Paltz to Route 44-55. Turn right and continue up the mountain past the gatehouse of the Lake Minnewaska Resort on the left. About 0.3 mile farther on the left is a parking area.

Access to the park is also possible at the gap through the Trapps escarpment on Route 44-55. A small parking area is located near Trapps Bridge and a ranger is usually in the area to collect a small hiking fee. The Mohonk-Minnewaska Carriage Road crosses the bridge on its winding way southwest to Lake

Minnewaska with views to the right of the cliffs of Dickie Barre across Coxing Kill Valley. This is the region of the annual hawk watches. Great numbers of bird watchers gather each fall to see the huge variety of birds which funnel into the thermal currents of the ridge as they begin their southward migration. From the carriage road there is an unmarked trail which goes up over the huge rock slab to the observation point. A blue-blazed trail from the Trapps Bridge leads 2.5 miles through lands of the Mohonk Preserve to the boundary of Minnewaska State Park. Here it joins Millbrook Mountain Drive, an old carriage road which passes along the east side of the Palmaghatt Ravine and connects with the Hamilton Point Road (see "The Carriage Roads," page 138).

As of this writing, it is possible to drive cars to the old Wildmere Hotel at Lake Minnewaska by paying a fee at the Minnewaska Gatehouse. From here hikers have access to the lake with its network of roads and trails in the Lake Minnewaska Resort area. Hikers may choose one of three carriage roads, each of which takes a different scenic route to Lake Awosting. If the resort area is developed commercially this arrangement may be terminated.

Other possible routes to the interior of the park involve private roads or crossing private land. These should not be used unless the owner gives permission.

Lake Awosting is the center of greatest interest in the park and the area from which most other scenic attractions can be reached. At an elevation of 1875 feet, Lake Awosting is the largest of the five Shawangunk lakes, approximately a mile and a quarter long and a quarter of a mile wide at the widest point. Well known for the exceptional clarity of its water, which greatly exceeds that of other lakes in this part of the state, Lake Awosting is surrounded by fine stands of trees and has views of white cliffs nearby and in the distance.

The most direct route to Lake Awosting, a distance of approximately 3 miles, is the Peters Kill Road, which leaves from the rear of the state park entrance parking lot. The roadway, which provides access to both the Long Path and the Scenic Trail, is cleared to a considerable width, and the lack of shade makes for warm walking on hot, sunny days. Although closed to private vehicles, it is open to bicyclists and hikers.

Another route to the Lake Awosting area, about 3.5 miles in length, is the Long Path south from Jenny Lane. The Long Path also can be taken in the opposite direction north from Daschner Road to Lake Awosting (see "The Long Path"). The latter route is a little more than 3 miles, with the first mile a steep climb to the top of the escarpment.

Finally, the old Smiley Road from Ellenville may be taken to Lake Awosting. Only about half of this long road is inside the state park, but the entire right-of-way of the road is owned by the park. The road starts from the area of the old Ellenville town dump and climbs the mountain with switchbacks to Napanock Point. Continuing on to Fly Brook and then Lake Awosting, the road passes through a section which may be muddy in wet seasons.

At Fly Brook a side trip to Stony Kill Falls, a spectacular waterfall, is possible on an eroded road that branches off here. From the top the water makes a series of cascades followed by a sheer plunge of 90 feet, a drop of 135 feet in all. To go the short distance from the falls to the public Rock Haven Road it is necessary to cross private land and/or private roads, and permission should be obtained.

The Long Path—Jenny Lane to Daschner Road. Length: 8.6 miles. Blazes: turquoise.

The northeastern end of this section of the Long Path can be reached by taking Route 44-55 northwest. After passing the Minnewaska Resort gatehouse on the left, drive 1.2 miles and turn

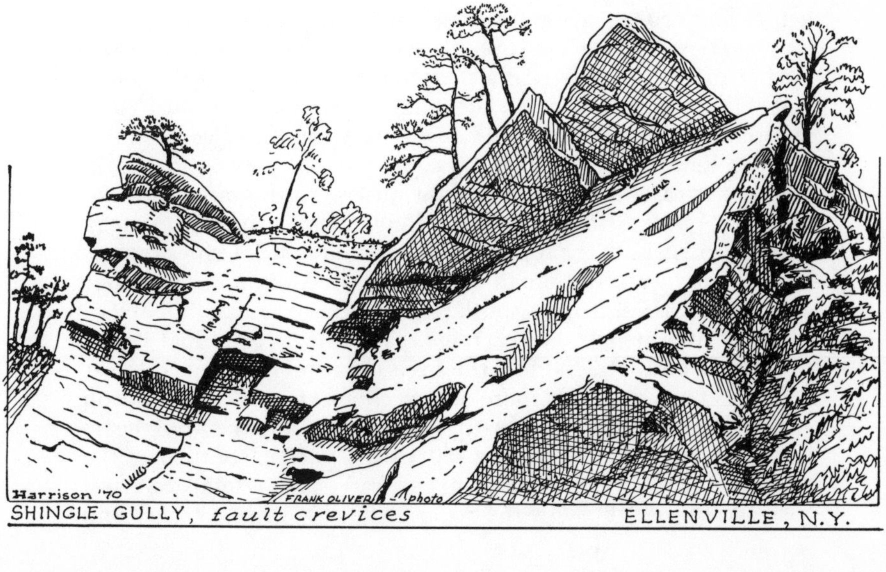

SHINGLE GULLY, *fault crevices* ELLENVILLE, N.Y.

right on Jenny Lane, an obscure dirt road, and then right again, to an unpaved parking area.

The Long Path, whose turquoise markers can be seen along the lane, turns west just before the parking area and passes Route 44-55. Entering the woods again, it soon crosses the Sanders Kill, which may be flooded or completely dry depending on the season. This portion of the trail was once known as the Jenny Lane Trail, and some of the original red plastic markers may still be visible.

The trail ascends gradually, shaded for the most part by rather stunted hardwoods whose roots encounter only a thin layer of soil, with solid rock ledges just beneath. In June an undercover of mountain laurel provides a spectacular display. On hot days this shady route should be the preferred approach to Lake Awosting.

There are several areas of bare ledges where topsoil was never able to accumulate, and some of these provide views to the south of Litchfield Ledge, the Huntington Ravine, and the Peters Kill. The Peters Kill Road, running roughly parallel to the Long Path, can also be seen.

At 2.5 miles, the trail comes to a power line where it makes a jog to the right and then again enters the woods. At 3 miles from Jenny Lane the trail turns onto the Peters Kill Road, crossing an earthen causeway over Fly Brook. A side trip to Lake Awosting is possible by continuing for a half mile on Peters Kill Road.

After entering the woods to the left, the Long Path ascends ledges and crosses a small brook, the outlet of Lake Awosting, before arriving at a view point of Peters Kill below. A little farther to the north there is a view to the east of Litchfield Ledge and Huntington Ravine. Descending through hemlock and mountain laurel, at 0.6 mile from its start, the Scenic Trail reaches Rainbow Falls with its cool mist. Ascending to an old carriage road, the trail turns right on the road, going approximately 0.4 mile before reentering the woods on the left. A steep climb over rocks to the top of Litchfield Ledge at 1.4 miles reveals views to the west and north of the Catskill Mountains and later of Lake Awosting to the south.

The trail bears left on a carriage road to begin a gradual ascent to Castle Point, at 2200 feet the high point on the trail. Here at 2.4 miles from the start there are excellent views of the Hudson Valley. Descending steeply to a carriage road, the trail bears right on the road for about 200 yards, before reentering the woods on the left. On the descent the trail passes a small cave and passable tunnel through the rocks. After crossing a brook and wood road, the trail ascends steeply to Margaret Cliff at 3 miles. Descending gradually over ledges with views to the south, the trail makes a sharp left turn from the ledges and reaches an old carriage road which it follows for a short distance before turning off to the left. The trail then ascends to the summit of Murray Hill with its spectacular 360-degree view. After traveling briefly on Lake Shore Drive, the Long Path turns left into the brush and continues in a southwest direction.

The trail enters a region of mostly open ledges, stunted pine trees, and frequent clumps of blueberry bushes mixed with sheep laurel. The ledges are not continuous; they end in one area only to form again, in places breaking up into jumbled rocks, or splitting to form deep crevices. The ledges terminate on the south as vertical cliffs that form a natural escarpment.

Three quarters of a mile from Lake Awosting, the Long Path bears to the right, going down from the ridge to circle the north side of Lake Haseco. This picturesque lake is actually shallow, with a mud bottom which earlier gave it the name of Mud Pond. The trail follows an old deer trail, using bare ledges wherever possible. Be sure to stay on the turquoise-marked trail in this area. The property owners have specifically asked that hikers *do not* follow the old trail around the south side of the lake. The Long Path then passes through an area of blueberry bushes and reaches a series of open, flat ledges that come down to the water's edge, affording a fine view. Bearing left through hemlock trees, the trail crosses the outlet of Lake Haseco, where an old beaver dam that contributes to the water level of the lake may be observed on the left.

At this point, the trail passes from park land to private land, on which it stays, through the generosity of the landowners, for the last 2.3 miles. After passing Lake Haseco, the Long Path climbs up onto high rock ledges that offer fine views of the lake and the countryside. At 7.3 miles it reaches Lookout Rock, an elevated platform that gives the best view up and down the valley of the Verkeeder Kill.

The trail steeply descends the mountain through a small wood to the stream above Verkeeder Kill Falls. A few feet farther down the stream, at 7.6 miles from Jenny Lane, the trail comes to Falls View Lookout, a small flat rock on the right, which should be approached with caution, since it is on the edge of a sheer vertical drop. From this point the entire falls can be seen as the water drops seventy-two feet into a natural amphitheater, with vertical rock walls on three sides and a large pool at the bottom. The volume of water over the falls varies greatly with the season. In times of drought the water trickles and cascades down the vertical headwall; during periods of rain or melting snow it becomes a miniature Niagara Falls with its own cloud of mist at the bottom.

From Falls View Lookout the trail descends for 0.1 mile till it makes a ninety-degree left turn. Do not continue on the straight trail which leads to a private road. The trail now begins its last mile with a series of flat ledges broken by deep crevices, with a few view spots. It soon reaches a place where one can clamber down the rocks and continues steeply down the mountain along a property boundary line. Upon reaching flat ground, the trail makes a ninety-degree turn to the left to avoid a swamp, and continues until terminating at a sandpit parking area just above Daschner Road.

Those wishing to hike this section of the Long Path in the opposite direction or to set up a shuttle hike can reach the southwestern end of the trail from Pine Bush, New York, by car as follows:

Proceed north on Route 52 from the Pine Bush traffic light 1 mile to the New Prospect Church. Turn right on New Prospect Road and continue 2 miles to the second left. At the Crawford sign, turn left on the Oregon Trail and continue 2.6 miles to a bridge over the Verkeeder Kill at Crawford. Turn right just before the bridge onto Church Road, and follow it 0.3 mile to Daschner Road (also called Upper Mountain Road) on the left. Turn left on this road and follow it 1.5 miles to the large stone house on the left where the owner will indicate where cars may be parked and where one may pick up the trail. By request of all the property owners, the trail markers do not show on the road.

The Carriage Roads

For those who never hike a woodland trail, the spectacular vistas unique to the Shawangunks are easily available along the old carriage roads which crisscross Minnewaska State Park. Desiring to provide their guests with access to the most scenic spots, whose romantic names survive today, the Minnewaska hotels built and maintained over fifty miles of roads on which only horse-drawn vehicles were permitted. In so doing, they left a rich legacy to today's hikers, who pause on Castle Point or along the Palmaghatt Ravine to imagine a Victorian kindred spirit stopping in the same spot.

Like the similar carriage roads at Mohonk, these are fairly level, having grades which horse-drawn vehicles could negotiate.

Pulled by matched pairs of horses, the early vehicles bumped along on iron-bound wooden wheels; later on, pneumatic tires on automobile wheels provided a quieter carriage ride.

Today the carriages are gone, but hiking, horseback riding, ski touring, and bicycling are permitted. Most of the roads are in the Minnewaska State Park; most of them fan out from the old hotel area. Partially overgrown in places today, they are all ideal for hiking and supplement the trails that cross, connect, and occasionally join them.

The Awosting Lake Road. Length: 4.5 miles.

The Awosting Lake Road extends from the South Lake Shore Drive 0.1 mile from the outlet of Lake Awosting to Lake Minnewaska by the site of the old Wildmere Hotel.

After winding around under the cliffs of Overlook Point on the right, the Awosting Lake Road crosses Huntington Ravine. Overhanging the road for some distance, a stand of trees unusually tall for this area provides heavy shade and cool air, even on hot days. Shortly after passing Overlook Cliffs, the Minnewaska Scenic Trail (yellow blazes) enters the road from the right, and follows along for about a quarter mile. Soon the cliffs of Litchfield Ledge appear on the right, looming above the road. As the cliffs terminate, the Scenic Trail turns off to the left to go down to Rainbow Falls. The road continues through sparse woods, finally entering the Lake Minnewaska Resort area, which requires a hiking fee, and ends near the site of the Wildmere Hotel on Lake Minnewaska.

The Hamilton Point and Palmaghatt Road. Length: 4 miles.

The Hamilton Point Road can be reached from Lake Awosting by following the South Lake Shore Drive a half mile from the lake outlet at Peters Kill to the second road on the left. One of the most scenic roads in the park, the Hamilton Point Road begins with views on the left of Overlook Cliffs and Litchfield Ledge, which face each other across Huntington Ravine. On the right, views of Margaret Cliff develop, while on the left the spectacular overhanging cliffs of Battlement Terrace come into view. Two roads branch off, Slate Bank Road on the right and Castle Point Drive on the left. Opposite the latter, the Scenic Trail (yellow blazes) comes in from the right, follows the Hamilton Point Road briefly, then goes off to the left to climb the steep cliff to Castle Point with its breathtaking view.

The road continues on in a southerly direction until, at an elevation of 2020 feet, it reaches Hamilton Point. Here the panoramic view is magnificent, with Gertrudes Nose visible to the southeast, the Wallkill Valley to the south, and Margaret Cliff and Murray Hill to the west. Here the road makes a sharp bend to the east, passes through a stand of small trees, and again comes to the open cliff with fine views.

The Hamilton Point Road now follows the north wall of Palmaghatt Ravine, an immense V-shaped ravine whose wide walls consist of a double row of high, vertical cliffs. On one side of the road towers a high rock wall, while on the other a huge precipice drops down to the floor of the Palmaghatt below. The ravine supports a growth of large virgin hemlock trees which survived the tanning industry's quest for hemlock bark. The lower, southwestern part of the Palmaghatt is private land and is closed to hikers. All of the cliffs and the portion northeast of the power line are in park land.

As the side walls of the Palmaghatt converge, one can see Pattersons Pellet, a large, white glacial erratic perched on the top of the opposite wall. By the side of the road a sliver of rock, known as Echo Rock, projects out over empty space. Shouts from here across the ravine are reflected back with great clarity.

The road turns left away from the cliff edge and into a stand of huge hemlock trees. Through the trees on the left are glimpses of Kempton Ledge, the cliff wall towering above, which approaches until it crowds the road.

A road coming in from the left connects with Castle Point Drive above and provides hikers with a circular return which avoids the Minnewaska Resort area. A short distance farther on, the Palmaghatt Ravine ends and Millbrook Drive, which follows the opposite Palmaghatt wall, comes in on the right. About a quarter mile farther the boundary of the Lake Minnewaska Resort is reached, which as of this writing can be hiked for a fee.

The Castle Point–Kempton Ledge Drive. Length: 4.5 miles.

To reach this road from the Lake Awosting outlet, follow the South Lake Shore Drive a half mile to Hamilton Point Road, the second road on the left. Take this a half mile to Castle Point–Kempton Ledge Drive, the first road on the left.

The road immediately starts to climb up across the face of the cliffs, affording one of the most impressive scenes in the Shawangunks. Here the hiker actually passes under huge blocks of rock high above that project out over the road. Battlement Terrace is one of the most spectacular examples of differential erosion, a phenomenon fairly common in the Shawangunks. Because the harder layers of rock are on the top with softer shale underneath, the latter tends to erode, leaving cantilevered overhangs above.

The road climbs until it makes a hairpin turn where the Scenic Trail (yellow blazes) joins. Together they climb along the top of the escarpment to Castle Point. Here, at an elevation of 2200 feet, is a beautiful area for having lunch or just enjoying the panorama. Extensive flat ledges offer commanding views of the immediate area over a range of nearly 360 degrees. On clear days Schunemunk, Black Rock Forest, and Storm King may be seen to the south, while the Catskills dominate the view to the north. Closer by are views of Lake Awosting, Margaret Cliff, Murray Hill, Sams Point, and the Wallkill Valley. The Scenic Trail goes over the edge here, and makes its way down the face of the cliff.

The drive continues in a northeast direction, twisting and turning between a series of miniature cliffs known as the Castles. There are frequent view spots similar to those seen on the Hamilton Point Road, but from a higher elevation. The drive gradually descends until it passes over Kempton Ledge at an elevation of 1640 feet.

Beyond Kempton Ledge, a cross road leads to the right and connects with the Hamilton Point Road, making possible a circular return to Lake Awosting without leaving park land. Continuing on the Castle Point Drive beyond Kempton Ledge, the hiker will reach the boundary of the Minnewaska Resort, where a fee is required.

Awosting Reserve

The Awosting Reserve, a private, nonprofit association, manages some three thousand acres of the Shawangunk Ridge. For the most part, this land is located along the southern escarpment, including the prominent cliff area known as Gertrudes Nose on the east, to and around Lake Haseco on the west and encompassing the wide flat area that includes the beaver pond; the pond and Lake Haseco are the main outlets to Fly Brook. Several waterfalls are included on the Reserve properties, of which the Upper and Lower Palmaghatt Falls along the Klinekill are the most prominent.

Maintained in a natural state, this area features a system of forest roads and footpaths that provide walks and access to special points of interest and complement a forest management plan for selective harvesting of mature timber. None of the facilities or lands is open to the public and the lands are patrolled by rangers under the Reserve's direction, but the Reserve does maintain a trail and hunting use program. Inquiries should be addressed to the Awosting Reserve Association, P.O. Box 57, Pine Bush, New York 12566.

Suggested Readings

Doughty, William E.
Lake Minnewaska
Dr. Doughty Book Fund, Herbert-Spencer, Inc., New York, 1960

Fried, Marc B.
Tales from the Shawangunk Mountains
Adirondack Mountain Club, Glens Falls, N.Y., 1981

Partington, Frederick C.
The Story of Mohonk
Turnpike Press, Annandale, Va., 1970

Smith, Philip H.
Legends of the Shawangunk and Its Environs
Syracuse University Press, Syracuse, N.Y., 1965

Snyder, Bradley, and Karl Beard
The Shawangunk Mountains
Mohonk Preserve, Inc., Mohonk Lake, New Paltz, N.Y., 1981

6 · *THE CATSKILLS*

(Maps 11, 12, and 13)

NORTH OF the more familiar metropolitan hiking areas are the Catskills, whose higher areas can provide especially rewarding hiking. The many paved roads through the mountains are well populated with hotels, boardinghouses, and homes, but the higher, more rugged and remote parts are unspoiled. From the summits and other vantage points the views are magnificent. To the east, below the escarpment, the Hudson Valley is spread out against a backdrop of the New England hills, and in other directions lie the fir-topped peaks with little or no sign of human intrusion.

There are at least thirty-four peaks and ridges with elevations of 3500 feet or more, about one third of which are trailless to the top; almost a hundred are over 3000 feet high. Hundreds of miles of trails of all degrees of difficulty invite the hiker to this varied and delightful area.

GEOLOGY

The Catskills encompass the highest topography in the Appalachian Plateau Province, with altitudes occasionally exceeding 4000 feet. The Catskills are mountainous only in the erosional sense: the region is structurally a plateau that has undergone a long cycle of stream erosion. Cutting deeply into the near-horizontal strata, the divides between adjacent valleys are often high and sharp-crested; thus the mountainous appearance.

The bedrock of the Catskills is almost entirely of sandstone, shale, and some conglomerate laid down during the Devonian Period some 380 million years ago in a complex delta-type environment. Elevated in a series of comparatively gentle uplifts to a height thousands of feet above the present highest elevations,

the land experienced a long period of extensive erosion. This long interval of erosion cut down the deep valleys and wore out the broad Hudson Valley, removing still younger Catskill rock formations that once extended east of the river. It also left the highest summits topped by more resistant late Devonian strata of hard conglomerate, a formation that can be seen on the top of Slide Mountain. The loose pebbles of milky quartz so generally distributed there and on other high summits resulted from the physical disintegration of the conglomerate. Variations in resistance of individual sedimentary layers are responsible for a series of cuestas, or unsymmetrical ridges with one slope long and gentle and the other a steeply sloping near-precipitous scarp. The boldest of these cuesta scarps forms the eastern margin of the Catskills and overlooks the Hudson Valley to the east, standing as much as 3000 feet above the valley.

This geological history of the Catskills can be read in the mountains' gentle curves, curves that are sharper on some slopes, notably on the eastern fronts of Overlook, Kaaterskill High Peak, and the Blackheads, and on Cornell and Balsam Cap. Here are terrace-like cliffs and shelves where the level strata have been cut back vertically, probably by ice erosion. But, unlike most mountains, there is relatively little bare rock in the form of flat ledges or high, exposed cliffs. The effects of the glaciation of the Pleistocene Ice Age are not as prominent as in the Adirondacks and Hudson Highlands. It is probable that the higher Catskills were not covered very deeply by the ice sheets, for foreign material is scarce above 3500 feet. Even where ice smoothing occurred, the softness of much of the sedimentary rock permitted postglacial weathering to roughen it and break it down into residual soil that

has been covered by dense vegetation. The dense forest cover often mantles cliffs fifty to a hundred feet high, unsuspected until they are reached.

The Catskills have no areas where there are typical above-timberline alpine flora, such as that found in the Taconics and the Hudson Highlands, which are lower and farther south. Above 3000 feet the Catskill flora is northern in associations but hardly as boreal as might be expected. The heavy residual soil from the soft sandstones has encouraged the invasion of southern or low-land species; "boreal islands" of subarctic plants are infrequent. Up to 3000 feet the vegetation is of the beech-birch-maple-hemlock zone, and above that of the northern spruce-fir. The Hudsonian or subarctic relicts are absent except for small stands of *Potentilla tridentata* on the ledges of Overlook Mountain at 3000 feet and on North Mountain east of Haines Falls.

HISTORY AND MYSTERY

The natural beauty of the Catskills is striking—the geology of the mountains, the variety of the forests, and the many wildflowers and birds. But it is also apparent that the land, now tree-covered, has been lived on and worked over. It is not unusual to come upon an old stone wall or the remains of a chimney or foundation, evidence that someone tried to farm a piece and raise a family. And here and there a cemetery will tell a story of sickness and death in its stones. Many old roads, faintly distinguishable, climb to overgrown clearings around vanished lumber camps. Above them there is no path to the fir-clad summits, where timber is so dwarfed and inaccessible that it has never been cut, and where the ledges are covered several feet deep with a humus made by centuries of decaying fir, spruce needles, and moss.

Much has been written about Indians, dwarfs, and Rip Van Winkle, making the Catskills a land of mystery and fancy—and beauty. The Hudson and Mohawk valleys were well traveled by Indians long before Henry Hudson sailed up the Hudson (which he named the North River). They lived in the Catskill valleys; they hunted in the mountains and went through them on war expeditions and, later, on forays against the Dutch settlers in the Hudson bottomlands. One of their routes was the valley of Esopus Creek, and they also attacked from the gulf of Peekamoose and Watson Hollow. But for the Indians as well as the colonists, the Catskills were not inviting. Until the end of the eighteenth century, these mountains remained mostly primeval hemlock wilderness. It was the need for this hemlock that finally brought men into the wilderness to destroy it.

Tanning of hides had been carried on in the United States to a limited extent prior to the Revolution. One tannery was established in Athens, New York, in 1750, but rapid growth came after the War of 1812, when Americans were free to engage in world trade without interference from the British. The two processes employed were based on the use of oak bark for sole leather and hemlock bark for uppers and other uses. Because one cord (128 cubic feet) of bark was required to tan ten hides, it was more economical for the tannery to be near the woods. With its ready supply of hemlock and water, the Catskills soon became a center for the industry. In 1817 Jonathan Palen established at the base of Kaaterskill Clove a tannery that processed hides from South America. Others followed in Prattsville, Edwardsville (now Hunter), Phoenicia, and later in Tannersville. Some of the present towns are named for the proprietors of these tanneries. By 1825, Greene County was producing more leather than any other county in the state, with Ulster not far behind.

The tannery itself was not a complicated setup—it usually was a series of tanks set on a flat stone foundation, with some sort of roof. The hides were spread out in layers, alternating with layers of ground bark, and covered with water. They were allowed to soak for weeks, then moved from one tank to the next until the process was complete.

Bark was cut only during May and June, when the sap was rising and peeling could be done readily. Using hemlock trees said to be seven to eleven feet in diameter, workers cut a gash around a tree as close to the ground as possible and then cut another gash four feet above this. Vertical cuts were then made twelve to sixteen inches apart and the sections stripped off. The tree was felled and additional strips removed up to the lower branches, above which the pieces were considered too broken up to handle economically. Most of the wood was left to rot. The tanning industry in the Catskills hit its peak during the Civil War and declined rapidly thereafter, when the supply of hemlock was exhausted. By 1867 most tanneries had closed, although the Simpson tannery in Phoenicia operated until 1870. Some idea of bark consumption may be gained from the report that, during its existence, the Pratt tannery turned out over two million hides, which would have required over 200,000 cords of bark.

Cutting down these tremendous trees opened the land to sunlight and conditions more favorable to growth of birch, maple, oak, and other hardwoods. As these took over, a new industry was born—the making of barrel hoops by cutting saplings with a drawknife. This industry began about 1848 and lasted until about 1890, when machine-sawed wooden hoops and steel hoops replaced hand-hewn hoops. Another wood industry that existed for a time was the making of furniture—the "chair factories," as they were known locally. This industry accounted for some of the buildings—now vacant—still seen in Catskill towns.

Still another industry that operated in the Catskills was the quarrying of bluestone—a hard, dense, fine-grained sandstone of gray-blue color. This industry flourished in the latter part of the nineteenth century, providing "curbstone" and "flagstone" for the sidewalks of New York until the development of Portland cement brought large-scale quarrying to an end. Piles of rejected stone may be found at many places where there were workings or exploratory openings, as in Shandaken or Phoenicia, and in the western Catskills there are still a few working quarries that supply bluestone for veneer and for walks and patios, but the demand is much smaller. The largest quarry still operating is near the eastern end of Ashokan Reservoir in West Hurley.

Evidence of farmhouses and cleared fields appears in the Catskills on land that looks impossible to work. To transport bark, lumber, and hides took many horses—thousands when the industry was at its peak—and horses require feed. So, as the land was cleared of hemlock, it was plowed where possible and sown to hay on the steep slopes, to corn and oats on more level areas, with some better space given to potatoes, wheat, and buckwheat for the men, women, and children. After tanning ceased, some farmers attempted general farming, but the soil was poor and the conditions too difficult. Left now are the fallen chimneys and sometimes an apple tree bearing misshapen, wormy fruit that is enjoyed only by bear and deer. The views from some of these old high-valley farms have prompted purchase by summer residents.

Railroad construction did not begin until 1866. Four years later the Ulster & Delaware Railroad began service from Weehawken to Phoenicia, to Stamford in 1879, and through Stony Clove to Tannersville in 1882. Passenger service has been discontinued on all lines, but bus service is available to many points.

Catering to summer visitors is a continuing business. It began when the Catskill Mountain House, built high on an overhanging ledge above Palenville between North and South mountains, opened with ten guest rooms in 1824. Patrons were transported by stage from Catskill up through Sleepy Hollow, which took the better part of a day. So popular was the view from its porch that the Mountain House grew to more than three hundred rooms. Among its frequent guests were Thomas Cole and other painters of the Hudson River School, many writers and educators, as well as society leaders and politicians, including President Ulysses S. Grant.

In 1878 the Overlook House was built on Overlook Mountain, then Mount Tremper House in Phoenicia, the Grand Hotel in Highmount, and the Laurel House at Kaaterskill Falls. In 1881 the Hotel Kaaterskill was built on South Mountain. This was said to have twelve hundred rooms and to be then the largest mountain hotel in the world. Not one of these large hotels has survived, although many smaller establishments serve guests in this area. The Hotel Kaaterskill burned in 1924, and the property was acquired by the state. The state later acquired the Laurel House and the Catskill Mountain House, the old structure of which was cleared away by burning in 1963. This whole area, including North and South lakes, and the network of trails built by these hotels to provide a series of panoramic views for their guests, is being managed for public use by the State Department of Environmental Conservation.

The political history of the Catskills is an almost unique and quite special story. In the late 1800s, there was concern over the vast lumbering operations in the Adirondacks. Leaders worried that this destruction of the great headwater area of the Hudson might even silt up New York Harbor. Thus in 1894 the State Constitution was amended, primarily to protect the Adirondacks, with the Catskills thrown in almost as an afterthought. Article XIV, Section 1 of the Constitution provides that *The lands of the state, now owned or hereafter acquired, constituting the forest preserve as now fixed by law, shall be forever kept as wild forest lands. They shall not be leased, sold or exchanged or be taken by any corporation, public or private, nor shall the timber thereon be sold, removed or destroyed.* This is the basis for present-day protection in the Catskills and has provided us with vast areas where the only human intrusion is by foot, ski, or snowshoe. Almost pure wilderness and only a few hours from our nation's largest metropolitan area, the Catskill Park covers more than 700,000 acres (1100 square miles), about thirty-five percent of it state land falling under the "forever wild" clause.

CLIMATE

A gentle spring day in New York City may be a day of snow flurries or freezing rain in the Catskills. The temperatures are generally lower in the mountains, and in the higher sections snow may accumulate in November and last well into May. In summer or winter, weather may change quickly; it is well to be prepared with extra clothing and suitable equipment. Also, although the main roads are plowed, many of the side roads on which there are no winter residents are not cleared.

The Catskills are beautiful in the snow, and people who hike are likely to enjoy snowshoeing and cross-country skiing here as well. Winter in the woods is exhilarating but exhausting, and daylight is shorter. Hikers and skiers should keep this in mind when planning winter trips. Recorded weather information can be obtained by calling (518) 476-1122 (Albany) or (914) 331-5555 (Kingston).

TRAILS AND BUSHWHACKING

Official trails in the Catskills are marked and maintained by the New York State Department of Environmental Conservation (DEC) with the cooperation of volunteers from the New York–New Jersey Trail Conference, the Catskill 3500 Club, and the Appalachian Mountain Club. These trails are designated with official markers—blue for trails that run generally north and south, red for trails running east and west, and yellow for connecting trails or trails running diagonally.

Camping is permitted at lean-tos and on state land below 3500 feet and at least 150 feet away from streams, water sources, and marked trails. Properly built and maintained fires, using only dead and down wood, are also permitted below 3500 feet. However, most experienced hikers find the safety and efficiency of backpacker stoves a real convenience. The topography above 3500 feet is subject to harsher weather conditions. Plants and soil do not recover well or rapidly from camping use (and abuse). This can still be clearly seen on the summit of Slide Mountain, which lacks the tree growth evident on most other summits. Camping was permitted on Slide until the late 1970s, and many trees were used to build campfires after all the dead and down wood was gone.

Some of the marked and maintained trails are described below. In addition, there are many usable wood roads and hunters' and fishermen's trails, some of which are blazed, usually with paint. Trails indicated on topographic maps, especially the earlier issues, are often so overgrown as to be difficult to follow. Although a great deal of the wilderness forest land in the Catskills can be explored by using the marked trails, it is only by getting off the beaten path that the hiker can really find out what the wilderness is like. Trailless travel, or bushwhacking, leads to many interesting discoveries—a little-known waterfall, a bear den, a balancing rock, or one of the remains of the mountain industries of the last century. Best of all, bushwhacking permits the hiker to be more keenly aware of the environment. However, the hiker should not blaze or otherwise mark his route. It is illegal, and it defaces the wilderness.

To provide incentive for visiting mountain peaks and areas not usually seen by the average hiker, the Catskill 3500 Club was founded in 1962. Current information on the 3500 Club can be obtained through the Trail Conference Office or at the Appalachian Mountain Club's Mountain Gate Lodge in Oliverea. This club has stimulated a great deal of interest in the Catskill summits over 3500 feet in elevation.

Roughly one third of these peaks have no trails to the top, so the hiker must use map and compass to make these ascents. Bushwhacking requires skill in the use of map and compass. Bushwhackers should use good topographic maps, such as the 7.5-minute quadrangles published by the U.S. Geological Survey (200 South Eads Avenue, Arlington, Va. 22202) and by New York State (Map Unit, New York Department of Transportation, State Campus, Albany, N.Y. 12232). The Trail Conference and the Appalachian Mountain Club have also jointly published a set of Catskill hiking maps, which can be ordered from either group.

Catskill trails may be considered in four groups, Central, Northern, Northeastern, and Western:

CENTRAL—south and west of Routes 28A and 28;

NORTHERN—north of Routes 212 and 28, east of Route 42, south of Route 23A;

NORTHEASTERN—north of Route 23A, south of Route 23;

WESTERN—west of Frost Valley and Fleischmanns, northwest of Shandaken.

CENTRAL CATSKILLS

Considered by many to be the hiking heart of the Catskills, this area contains the only known sections of virgin timber as well as some of the remotest peaks. The vast trailless area around Rocky and Lone mountains contains some very thick spruce, reminiscent of the Adirondacks. Since its establishment in the late 1970s, the Appalachian Mountain Club's Mountain Gate Lodge has become an information/rest center for hikers. Located in Oliverea, the lodge is a worthwhile stop for newcomers and old-timers alike.

Slide, Cornell, and Wittenberg. Length: 8.85 miles. Blazes: red.

The best-known trails in the Catskills are those that reach the summit of Slide Mountain (4180 feet), the highest point in the Catskills. These trails were originally blazed by private clubs and individuals but are now included in the Department of Environmental Conservation (DEC) system and are well marked and cleared. One approach to the Slide Mountain range is through Woodland Valley, one of the deepest valleys in the Catskills. The valley road leaves Route 28 at 1 mile west of Phoenicia. (This point can be reached by bus from New York via Kingston.) It follows Woodland Creek and is marked with yellow discs. At 5.4 miles, near the road's end, is the Woodland Valley State Campground. Cars can be parked here. (In season there is a small fee.) The red-marked trail for Wittenberg starts here. The yellow markers, now a foot trail, continue about 6 miles, over Forked Ridge and past the Panther–Fox Hollow Trail, to the Winnisook Lodge area and then to the other end of the red trail, as mentioned below.

From the campground, the red Wittenberg-Cornell-Slide trail crosses the creek and starts to climb Wittenberg (3780 feet), an ascent of 2400 feet in about 3.5 miles. It is steepest at the begin-

EAST from CORNELL MT. ASHOKAN RESERVOIR after photograph by Frank J. Oliver, 1962. R.E.H.

ning and again near the top. The trail was relocated onto state-owned land here in the mid 1970s after a spring flood took out the trail bridge 1.5 miles downstream. In 1981 the lower portion was rebuilt by the Appalachian Mountain Club trail crew under a program jointly funded by the Club's Catskill Trail Booster Fund and the DEC. At 2.3 miles a yellow trail leads left 0.9 mile to Terrace lean-to (no water). From the summit of Wittenberg there are splendid views east and south over Ashokan Reservoir. Views to the north are cut off by the growth in recent years of a good stand of evergreens. The dense growth of hardwoods on the Terrace and above has eliminated much of the azaleas, dogtooth violets, and Dutchman's-breeches that older hikers remember, a reminder that the woods are changing, constantly if not rapidly, as the cycle continues. A cave just off the summit has long been a refuge of climbers and porcupines alike. Remember that camping and fires are not permitted above 3500 feet.

From Wittenberg the trail goes south and, just before the low point of the next notch, reaches a junction with an unmaintained trail with faint red blazes (not recommended) that leads down steeply to Maltby Hollow above West Shokan. Continuing on the main trail there is a spur to the summit of Cornell Mountain (3865 feet) with views through the trees to the south. The trail then turns right and descends into the deep notch between Cornell and Slide through an isolated stand of virgin spruce and some wet areas. It then climbs steeply to the summit of Slide Mountain, passing a fine spring several hundred feet from the top. Just below the open rock top is a tablet in memory of John Burroughs, naturalist and poet.

In Memoriam
John Burroughs
Who in his early writings introduced Slide Mountain to the world. He made many visits to this peak and slept several nights beneath this rock. This region is the scene of many of his essays. Here the works of man dwindle in the heart of the southern Catskills.

Burroughs climbed from the end of Woodland Valley, following the west branch of Cornell Brook, then through brush and up the slide north of the summit. This slide, said to have occurred about 1820, is now covered with forest growth and seems stabilized.

From the top of Slide the red trail descends easily westward along the northern front of the mountain on what was a bridle path. In less than a mile the blue-marked Curtis-Ormsby Trail turns left to the East Branch of Neversink Creek. The nicest of the trails up Slide, it was cut and maintained for some years by the Fresh Air Club of New York in honor of "Father Bill" Curtis, a famous athlete, sportswriter, and club official who died with his companion Ormsby in a summer snowstorm on Mount Washington near what is now the site of the Appalachian Mountain Club "Lakes of the Clouds" Hut. At the lower end of this trail is a granite monument erected as a memorial to Curtis by former State Supreme Court Justice Harrington Putnam of Brooklyn, an ardent outdoorsman who had a farm at Denning.

The red trail continues ahead on the bridle path for 1.3 miles, where it ends at a junction with the yellow-marked Phoenicia–East Branch Trail, which to the left leads to Denning. Continue right, now on yellow markers, for the Slide Mountain parking area mentioned below.

An easier way to climb Slide Mountain is to drive to the state trailhead and parking area 0.6 mile west of Winnisook Lake on West Branch Road, from Big Indian on Route 28, or from Liberty via Route 55. The yellow trail from this lot gives easy access to either the Wittenberg-Cornell-Slide trail or the Curtis-Ormsby. The three mountains in the Slide range can be climbed starting from this point, with a car stationed at hike's end in Woodland Valley. For a circular hike, one could use the yellow Phoenicia–East Branch Trail, but its 1981 reroute includes many ups and downs and 2 miles of road walking.

Pine Hill–Eagle–West Branch Trail. Length: 14.6 miles. Blazes: blue.

This trail forms the backbone of a network of trails giving access to five major summits: Belleayre (3420 feet), Balsam (3600), Haynes (3420), Eagle (3600), and Big Indian (3700). While hikes can begin from either end or from trailheads in Big Indian, Oliverea (at Mountain Gate Lodge), Mapledale, or Seager, starting at the Pine Hill end is not recommended, as the trailhead is difficult to find and the markers spotty. The description starts at the southern end on the Big Indian–West Branch Road (County Route 47). This point is 12.8 miles south of Big Indian village and 8 miles northeast of Claryville. Cars can be parked near the trailhead. The trail stays fairly level along the Biscuit Brook Valley, reaching the lean-to at 1.85 miles, then begins a steady climb to a terrace on the shoulder of Big Indian Mountain, where it turns sharply north and climbs to the top. The trail skirts about a quarter mile from the summit (which is considered trailless) and then descends moderately into a col where, at 5.7 miles, there is a junction with a yellow trail that goes down southwest 1 mile to Shandaken Creek lean-to and the Seager–Dry Brook Road. Continuing north on blue markers, the trail reaches the summit of Eagle Mountain at 6.75 miles. This plain wooded summit is considered by many to be the least interesting of all the major peaks. Another easy 1.5 miles brings the hiker to Haynes Mountain (no views) and then 0.7 mile gently down to a col at 3000 feet and the red Oliverea-Mapledale Trail. To the right this trail goes steeply down to the Mountain Gate Lodge and Oliverea; left it goes down to the Rider Hollow lean-tos and Mapledale. The blue trail continues moderately up to the summit of Balsam Mountain in less than 1 mile, almost 10 miles from the start. Another mile of moderate downgrade brings one to the yellow Rider Hollow Trail, an alternate way down to the Rider Hollow lean-tos. The Pine Hill–Eagle–West Branch Trail continues another mile to the Belleayre Mountain lookout tower (closed). Here the red Belleayre Ridge Trail branches left to the top of the state-run downhill ski area and its summit buildings. The blue markers continue, reaching the Belleayre Mountain lean-to in a half mile, and the Lost Clove Trail junction in another 0.2 mile. This red-marked trail goes down 2.6 miles to Big Indian village.

The blue trail continues another 2.2 miles to its end in Pine Hill. As mentioned before, starting at this end is not recommended. It should also be noted that the trails in and around the Belleayre ski area are poorly marked and often confusing. They are not recommended, except for a hike to the summit ski house on a cold winter day. Who can resist a hot mug of soup in the middle of a winter's hike? This spot can be reached from the lookout tower via an easy 1-mile hike on the red Belleayre Ridge Trail.

South of Slide Mountain—Peekamoose and Vicinity. The area south of Slide-Cornell-Wittenberg is beautiful and largely trailless; it is unusual and remote, a large bowl drained by the East Branch of Neversink Creek. At its eastern rim are Friday and Balsam Cap mountains. Friday (3694 feet) comes off a shoulder of Cornell and is connected to Balsam Cap (3623) by a ridge. A slide on the eastern face of Cornell occurred in the spring of 1930 and another on Friday in the spring of 1968, both after heavy rains. These may be attractive to the venturesome; but be prepared for thick conifer tree growth. Swinging around to the southwest from Balsam Cap are Rocky (3508 feet), Lone (3721), and Table (3847), all of which are also of interest to bushwhackers.

Just south of Table Mountain lies Peekamoose (3843 feet), which together with Table and the lower Van Wyck Mountain (3206) close in the bowl of the East Branch. They also form the northern slope of the Rondout Creek watershed. Peekamoose Road—the road from West Shokan southwest to Sundown, Grahamsville, and Liberty—is called the Gulf Road because of the gulf between the headwaters of the Rondout and the head of Watson Hollow.

This is interesting geologically as the outlet of Esopus Creek during part of the last glacial period when the drainage was blocked by a heavy lobe of ice in the Hudson Valley. For a time the dammed waters flowed southwest and west through the gulf and down Rondout Creek. This accounts for large potholes, heavy glacial gravel beds, and the other glacial phenomena found there. Later, as some of the water escaped eastward under the melting ice, the creek cut a channel south across the eastern foot of High Point south of Olive Bridge Dam. This cut, known as Wagon Wheel Gap or Goblin Gulch, is conspicuous from Ashokan Reservoir. On its southern side there is evidence of a powerful cutting stream from the top of the gap down to the road from Ashokan Reservoir to Krumville, and even below the road. North of this road two distinct "fossil waterfalls" are evident, separated by waterworn brinks and a smoothed platform. The brink and plunge basin south of the road are larger and more striking.

Table Mountain may also be climbed by the Long Path from Denning lean-to or Peekamoose. The Long Path on its route from the George Washington Bridge comes around Samson Mountain (2812 feet) and east on Peekamoose Road. About 400 feet east of Buttermilk Falls it leaves the road and ascends through open woods to ledges and the fir- and spruce-covered summit of Peekamoose. There is no single vantage point, but good views are obtainable through the foliage. From the top of Peekamoose it is only a short distance on the Long Path to the top of Table Mountain, where a summit trail register is located in a metal box on a tree.

High Point (3060 feet), or Ashokan High Point, as it is often called to distinguish it from peaks with similar names, is worth a climb. It can be ascended easily by an old lumber road that takes off from Mountain Road in West Shokan just south of the junction with a blacktop road coming in from Route 28A just south of West Shokan. Permission to park in the field may be required. There is also a trail blazed in red paint farther south and one from the Old Kanape Trail between High Point and Mombaccus Mountain (3000 feet). The country between Mombaccus and the summit of Samson Mountain may repay a visit, and likewise the area south of Rondout Gulf.

Giant Ledge–Panther–Fox Hollow Trail. Length: 6.9 miles. Blazes: blue.

The north-south trail over Giant Ledge (3200 feet) and Panther Mountain (3720) offers a series of fine lookouts and a varied terrain. The complete traverse makes a good day trip if a shuttle can be arranged. Hikes can start from either of two parking areas on the yellow Phoenicia–East Branch Trail to reach the southern end of the blue trail over Giant Ledge and Panther. One parking area is located at Woodland Valley state campground, and from here one should follow the yellow markers over Forked Ridge to the blue trail junction (about 3 miles). A much easier way to reach the same junction is from the parking area at the hairpin turn on the Big Indian–West Branch Road (County Route 47). This area is about half a mile northeast of Winnisook Lake. The yellow trail from here reaches the junction with the blue trail in about a half mile. A third way in is from the northern trailhead of the Giant Ledge–Panther Trail on Fox Hollow Road about 2 miles up from its junction with Route 28 in Allaben.

Starting at the yellow trail junction the Giant Ledge–Panther–Fox Hollow Trail is level, with occasional moderate climbs to the Giant Ledge lean-to at a quarter mile. Except in very dry weather, there is water at a spring just west of the lean-to. The trail makes a steep, short climb, then stays along the east side of the ledge with fine views into Woodland Valley and beyond. An easy bushwhack over to the west side reveals other fine views. After a moderate descent into the col, the trail climbs steeply up Panther Mountain. The top has a fine view to the east, but it is becoming more restricted by tree growth each year. The descent is quite steep, in part through virgin spruce, to the Fox Hollow lean-to and the road to Allaben, 4.2 miles from Panther summit.

NORTHERN CATSKILLS

Although more populated and with few remote areas, this portion of the Catskills has many rewarding climbs. In addition to four trailless peaks, it includes the famous and rugged Devils

Path, a 24-mile backbone trail that touches five major summits, and skirts 4040-foot Hunter, the second highest in the Catskills. The entrance through Plattekill Clove from West Saugerties is spectacular, the eastern wall rising a half mile in a horizontal distance of about 1 mile. The road (closed in winter) requires caution, and the clove itself is extremely deep and steep with broken and falling rock. Climbing in it is definitely not recommended even with a hard hat. The Devils Kitchen, near the top, is accessible and scenic, especially in times of high water, but the rock is slippery. An easier route into this valley is via Route 23A to Tannersville and then on County Route 16 or Bloomer Road.

From the Devils Kitchen (1.5 miles from Pediger Road via the red-marked Devils Path) a blue trail leads south, running along the shoulder of Plattekill (3100 feet) and Overlook (3140) mountains. Overlook stands out as the Catskills are approached from the south. At 2.2 miles, a yellow spur heads west 0.6 mile to Echo Lake and a lean-to. This spur was part of a carriage road from Saugerties to Overlook House, one of the mountain hotels of the last century. At 3.6 miles, a red spur leads to the summit of Overlook, where the view from the fire tower is magnificent. To the east are the Hudson River and the hills of New England; and the peaks of the Devils Path stretch away to the north.

Just south of the summit is the site of Overlook House. The hotel burned in the 1920s, and concrete walls for a new building went up before the Depression closed it for good. The walls are still standing, with trees beginning to grow inside the shell. Stone pillars lie fallen in the weeds. It is possible to continue south on a red-marked trail 2 miles to Meads, where there is parking at the trailhead. Across the road is the former Meads Inn, built in 1863 and still in fine shape. The distance from the Devils Kitchen lean-to to Meads is 5.6 miles.

North of Plattekill Clove is Kaaterskill High Peak, the "High Peak" which, as late as 1870, was thought to be the highest of Catskill summits, even though it is only 3655 feet. The top is distinctive, with a cliff on the east side of the summit that marks it as seen from the thruway. There are various old trails on it starting at the Plattekill Road, all of which in part traverse private land on which permission to hike is necessary. There are several good lookouts on the way up and an excellent panorama of the Hudson Valley from an open area south of the top. Round Mountain or Roundtop (3440 feet), to the west of High Peak, is sufficiently open for bushwhacking.

The Devils Path. Length: 23.6 miles. Blazes: red.

So known because of the rugged country it traverses, the Devils Path is the backbone of the trail system in this area. It starts from Platte Clove Road a half mile west of the New York City Police Camp, topping Indian Head (3573 feet), Twin (3640), Sugarloaf (3800), and Plateau (3840) mountains, coming out at Devils Tombstone State Campground in Stony Clove. With these summits and the considerable drops into Jimmy Dolan Notch, Pecoy Notch, Mink Hollow, and Stony Clove, it is really a skyline trail with views aplenty. As there are trails out from each of these notches to the north, and in Mink Hollow one to the south as well, it is possible to do the entire length in sections. The distance from Platte Clove Road to Stony Clove is 12.4 miles.

To the west of Stony Clove lies Hunter Mountain (4040 feet), the second highest of the Catskill peaks. The summit, with its fire tower often open to the public, may be reached by many routes, some described later.

To reach Hunter, hikers can also use the Devils Path, which continues over a shoulder of the mountain from the Devils Tombstone campsite. At 2.1 miles the path reaches the Devils Acre lean-to and spring, where a yellow trail branches off, leading 1.4 miles to the summit.

Continuing from the lean-to on the Devils Path, a fine lookout is reached at a half mile, with Diamond Notch 1.5 miles farther. Here a blue-marked trail that comes up from Lanesville in the south (4 miles) can be walked northeast to the Spruceton parking area described below (1 mile).

The Devils Path continues over West Kill Mountain and its western second peak. This 7-mile section is indeed a rewarding climb. It starts through a fine stand of trees and, in season, wildflowers. Shortly before the summit (2.1 miles from Diamond Notch) is Buck Ridge lookout with rewarding views. The summit, however, is wooded and viewless. The trail continues into a col and over the second summit and then steeply down to the notch between West Kill and trailless North Dome Mountain. It ends at Spruceton Road (County Route 6), having covered 23.6 miles from Platte Clove Road.

Other Hunter Mountain Routes

Hunter Mountain, especially from the tower, gives an all-encompassing view of the Catskill peaks, though the cleared top is not inviting. Many routes ascend this lofty peak. From the east, the 2.4-mile Becker Trail (blue markers) starts from Stony Clove Road about 1 mile north of Devils Tombstone State Campground, near the old Becker farmhouse. The Becker family was associated with this mountain for many years. During the 1920s the oldest son was fire observer and lived with his family at the tower; the father ran the farm, and the daughter served good meals to boarders and hikers.

The Spruceton Trail (blue) starts at a state parking area 8 miles east of the village of West Kill on County Route 6. This is the easiest way up Hunter, much of the trail following a state jeep road used for the tower observer. At 2 miles there is a good spring with a lean-to less than a quarter mile beyond. At 2.4 miles a yellow-marked spur leads to the Colonels Chair and the top of a ski chair lift (1 mile). The fire tower and summit are reached at 3.3 miles.

Other Areas

Another popular climb in this area, because of its views, is Mount Tremper (2720 feet). It may be ascended from old Route 28 just over 1 mile south of Phoenicia or from the Willow Post Office to the east on Route 212. Neither climb is arduous.

In Spruceton Valley, to the west of Hunter, there are some excellent trailless climbs, but access to them is mostly over private lands and permission to cross should be obtained. On the north side of the valley is Rusk Mountain (3680 feet), with its dense conifer summit ridge, while on the south are North Dome (3610) and Sherrill (3540) mountains.

NORTHEASTERN CATSKILLS

This section is really two areas, the beautiful and historic North Lake area and the majestic Blackhead Range. The 24-mile Escarpment Trail connects the two.

North Lake Area

The state of New York now owns the entire area immediately to the north of Kaaterskill Clove and Route 23A. This was once the property of Laurel House, Hotel Kaaterskill, and Catskill Mountain House. All are now gone, but in their flourishing days these hostelries constructed many miles of trails so that their guests might see the falls, the lakes, and the vistas. It is said that

NORTH and SOUTH LAKES, NORTH MOUNTAIN THE CATSKILLS.

during the latter part of the last century these trails were more used than any others in the United States. The Department of Environment Conservation has wisely preserved and marked them.

The focal point is North Lake, a pretty lake where there is a state-owned campground with fireplaces, tent sites, and picnic spots, with road access from Haines Falls. To the east is the ledge with the view that brought thousands to Catskill Mountain House. Close by are the remains of the Otis Elevating Railway that once carried them up to that view. A loop trail from the lake leads to the many vantage points along the rim and then returns through Marys Glen.

The North Lake area is compact and filled with many trails. While it would be difficult to get lost, a hiking map should be carried for full enjoyment. In summer, these are available at the Hiker Information Booth maintained by the Appalachian Mountain Club near the entrance gate. They are also part of the Catskill Map set published by the Appalachian Mountain Club and the New York–New Jersey Trail Conference.

Escarpment Trail. Length: 24 miles. Blazes: blue.

The Escarpment Trail extends over varied terrain with considerable climbing. Its lower portion provides access to Kaaterskill Falls, with fine views down the clove. The trail starts from the north side of Route 23A in Kaaterskill Clove at a sharp bend in the road below Haines Falls. There is a parking place on the south side and a sign indicating the trail. Starting up past magnificent Kaaterskill Falls, the trail climbs about 500 feet onto the escarpment and makes a broad swing around the North Lake area, staying close to the cliff. Passing many points of interest, it reaches North Mountain (3180 feet) in 7.5 miles. From here to the Blackhead Range it follows the top of cliffs and ledges that show glaciation. Evidently the Hudson Valley lobe of the ice sheet, as it deepened and spread out of its confinement within the walls of the Catskills and Taconics, ground smooth the ledges around North Lake and north of Catskill Mountain House up to about 3000 feet.

The trail then runs along the ledges up to North Point, and, from there, climbs North Mountain (3180 feet) and Stoppel Point (3420), drops to Dutcher Notch, and then goes up the long ridge to Blackhead Mountain (3940).

It is a long 9.2 miles from North Lake to Blackhead, too much for a round trip for most hikers. However, there are many ways to hike in this fine horseshoe of mountains near the village of Maplecrest. Hikes can start from Elmer Barnum Road on the red-marked Blackhead Range Trail over the Camels Hump to Thomas Cole Mountain (3940 feet; named for the famous landscape painter of the Hudson River School), 3.2 miles, and the top of Black Dome (3980 feet), 4 miles. Going steeply down to the col between Black Dome and Blackhead, the trail turns left (north) down to the parking area in Big Hollow at the end of the road from Maplecrest, 2.2 miles, also a convenient starting point.

A yellow connecting trail starts in the col and climbs to the summit of Blackhead in 0.6 mile, where it joins the Escarpment Trail as it comes from North Lake. A little farther north on the blue markers of the Escarpment Trail, another yellow trail branches left to Batavia Kill lean-to (0.25 mile) and the parking lot at the end of Maplecrest Road (1.8 miles). The Escarpment Trail continues on the ridge and across to Acra Point (3085 feet), 3.7 miles from Blackhead. In another half mile, it intersects a red trail that also runs to the parking lot in Big Hollow (1.1 miles). After ascending Burnt Knob, the trail reaches Windham High Peak (3524 feet), the northernmost peak of the Catskills, with fine views north and east. Two more miles bring one to Elm Ridge lean-to and a trail junction: a left turn on yellow markers leads to a spring (200 yards), Peck Road, and Maplecrest. The Escarpment Trail continues to the right and ends 1 mile farther at a parking area on Route 23, 3 miles west of East Windham.

WESTERN CATSKILLS

Six of the Catskill peaks over 3500 feet are located in the Western Catskills. Five of these—Halcott (3520), Vly (3529), Bearpen (3600), Doubletop (3860), and Graham (3868)—are trailless. Access is by permission of private landowners and may be undertaken on hikes sponsored by the Catskill 3500 Club.

Much of the Western Catskills was originally part of the Hardenburg Patent, a two-million-acre tract granted by George III to a group of Catskill entrepreneurs. The area made up the northernmost reaches of the lands of the Lenape and the easternmost reaches of the Oneida and Tuscarora tribes. Dutch settlers reached the East Branch of the Delaware in 1763, but most evacuated during the Revolutionary War. Permanent white settlement dates from just before 1800, with Delaware County being organized in 1797.

Settlement spread from the valley of the East Branch along its tributaries and hillsides. In many cases a valley became associated with a particular family. The hillsides provided pasture and the proper climate for cool-weather crops such as cabbage. But the thin, rocky soil wore out quickly, and much once-farmed land has gone back to forest and to state ownership. Foundations, rock walls, and traces of old farm and lumber roads are seen everywhere.

The Pepacton Reservoir stores water of the East Branch of the Delaware River to supply New York City. Under the reservoir lie the sites of several towns and villages that once served the dairy, lumber, and quarrying industries of the region.

The villages along the East Branch and in the hills west of it were the site of the anti-rent wars of 1844–45, when tenant farmers rebelled against the foreclosure of farms and the collection, by federal landlords, of one quarter and more of proceeds from the sale of leases.

More recently the town of Hardenburg gained notoriety as the site of a taxpayers' revolt. In the 1970s all but a handful of its approximately 250 property owners became ministers of a mail-order church in order to receive tax exemptions. They were protesting the large amount of exempt land owned by religious, charitable, and educational groups, and by the state. By the 1980s, however, New York had placed some five thousand acres of state land back on the tax rolls, and the revolt ended.

Dry Brook Ridge Trail. Length: 14.1 miles. Blazes: blue.

This trail extends over Patatakan Mountain, Dry Brook Ridge, and Balsam Lake Mountain to Quaker Clearing and intersections with the Neversink-Hardenburg Trail and the Mongaup-Hardenburg Trail.

The northern terminus of the trail is located in Margaretville. Turn off Route 28 at the Agway store south of the village, and go east 0.2 mile to a road paralleling Route 28 and turn left again. The trailhead is another 0.2 mile from this intersection. The trail gains elevation rapidly and reaches the top of Patatakan Mountain in 1.9 miles. At 2.7 miles it reaches the yellow-blazed German Hollow Trail, which leads to the German Hollow lean-to, and from there to Drybrook Road.

The Ridge Trail continues nearly level for the next 3.5 miles, following ledges that offer striking views south across the Pepacton Reservoir. There is good blueberry picking here in July. Dry Brook Spring and lean-to are reached at 7.9 miles. Another 1.2 miles over a slight rise leads to Millbrook Road, which may be followed 2.2 miles to the left (north) to Dry Brook Road; to the right a yellow-blazed side trail leads a quarter mile to Millbrook lean-to.

The blue trail continues up and along the ridge as it starts to ascend toward Balsam Lake Mountain on a jeep road. At 1.7 miles from Millbrook Road, an unmarked wood road leads left to the top of Graham Mountain (3868 feet), with superb views north and east. Shortly, the steep red-blazed Balsam Lake Mountain Trail branches off to the right, climbing to the top of Balsam Lake Mountain (3720). There is a fire tower on the summit, and a half mile farther on is a lean-to. The blue-blazed Dry Brook Ridge Trail continues ahead and bypasses the top of Balsam Lake Mountain. A little more than 3 miles from Millbrook Road the Balsam Lake Mountain Trail rejoins the Ridge Trail. From here it is less than 1 mile downhill to the Balsam Lake Club road and another mile to Quaker Clearing and trail's end.

Neversink-Hardenburg Trail. Length: 11.9 miles. Blazes: yellow.

From Quaker Clearing an old road follows the headwaters of the Beaverkill River, where fishing is by permit only. At 1.5 miles the trail crosses the outlet of Vly Pond near a hunting shack. After crossing two more streams, the trail encounters an overgrown road on the left that leads in a quarter mile to Tunis Pond, a small beaver pond.

After crossing the Beaverkill, the Neversink-Hardenburg Trail ascends the ridge, reaching the top in less than 1 mile. Descending, it reaches Fall Brook lean-to, and then the trailhead and parking at 7.5 miles. From here it is 4 miles by road to the bridge over the east branch of the Neversink River in Claryville.

Long Pond Trail. Length: 7.6 miles. Blazes: red.
This trail connects the Neversink-Hardenburg Trail and the Mongaup-Hardenburg Trail at their southern ends. At the road intersection half a mile north of Round Pond, red markers lead 4.3 miles west to Long Pond and a lean-to. The trail ascends steeply at first, then levels off. Turn sharply to the left at a road junction; cars can be driven to this point. The trail leaves the road to the right and in 1.2 miles a yellow-blazed side trail leads to Long Pond and a lean-to. The outlet of Long Pond, at a beaver dam at the south end, offers a fine view of Fir and Doubletop mountains to the east. Soon afterward, the Long Pond Trail crosses the Willowemoc River on a footbridge, intersects a town road that leads left to Willowemoc, and then ascends to Beaverkill Ridge. After climbing sharply at first, the trail follows what appears to be an old lumber road on easy grades to a spring. From here it is a half mile to the top of the ridge, where there is a view of Sand Pond below on the left. At the top, the Long Pond Trail intersects the Mongaup-Hardenburg Trail, which leads right 3.6 miles back to Quaker Clearing, and left to Mongaup Pond and the state campground.

Mongaup-Hardenburg Trail. Length: 6 miles. Blazes: blue.
Follow the snowmobile trail to the north end of Mongaup Pond. From here the trail ascends 1.3 miles to the middle peak of Mongaup Mountain (2980 feet), where it turns east. The trail follows Beaverkill Ridge over an unnamed summit at 2.4 miles, and shortly afterward intersects Long Pond Trail (blazed red), which goes 3.1 miles to Long Pond. After passing a spring, the trail reaches the highest point on Beaverkill Ridge at 4.5 miles (elevation 3224 feet), before descending a ridge north off Beaverkill Ridge to intersect Hardenburg Road after crossing the Beaverkill River. At this point Quaker Clearing is 0.7 mile to the right.

Delaware Trails
The trails in this gentler area of the Western Catskills center around the towns of Colchester and Andes in Delaware County south of the Pepacton Reservoir. Many hiking trails in this area are also marked with large yellow snowmobile markers. Our

descriptions concern only trails with the smaller hiking-trail markers.

Going from east to west, the first trail in this network begins at Little Pond State Campground. The red-marked Touchmenot Trail heads northeast over Touchmenot Mountain and then swings west, passing a junction with the yellow Little Pond Trail that returns to the campground. After ascending a few hills, the trail descends steeply to Beech Hill Road at about 4 miles.

A quarter mile north on Beech Hill Road is the start of the Middle Mountain Trail, which also has red markers. This route runs about 2 miles west to Mary Smith Hill Road, via Middle Mount (2975 feet) and a nice lookout.

The Mary Smith Trail is next, running about 4.5 miles west, crossing Mary Smith Hill (2767 feet) and Holiday Brook Road before it ends at a junction with the Pelnor Hollow Trail. Now the trail network becomes blue-marked. Going south on Pelnor Hollow Trail leads to a lean-to at 2.3 miles and the end of the trail at 3.2 miles at the end of Pelnor Hollow Road. The blue markers continue northwest to the Campbell Mountain Trail, which starts at a junction with a yellow-marked trail that leads south 0.6 mile to Little Spring Brook Road. The blue trail continues to Cat Hollow Road at 1.7 miles and then the Campbell Mountain lean-to in another 2.3. Campbell Mountain Road and a parking area are 1.1 miles farther.

The last link in the network is the 5.4-mile Trout Pond Trail. Starting at Campbell Mountain Road, it ascends to 2461 feet and then descends, somewhat rapidly, to Campbell Brook Road at 2.1 miles. Less than 2 miles farther is Trout Pond, formerly Cables Lake, and its two lean-tos, a fine place for camping and swimming. Though its southern end is busy on summer weekends, few users camp out and get to enjoy the lake during quieter moments. Fishing is popular here but requires a permit, and there are some special regulations. Water is available from a spring just above the northeast inlet of the lake.

At the north end of the lake next to the lean-to, the blue trail forks. One fork continues south along the lakeshore and out to a large parking area at Russell Brook Road (1.4 miles). The other fork heads west and then south to Mud Pond. This fork ends in 1.75 miles at an old road. To the right, this road leads a quarter mile to Mud Pond. Left, it leads 1 mile to Russell Brook Road and a parking area.

A map of this trail system is available from the New York Department of Environmental Conservation, Albany, N.Y. 12226.

Suggested Readings

Adams, Arthur G., Roger Coco, Harriet Greenman, and Leon R. Greenman
Guide to the Catskills
Walking News, Inc., New York, 1975

Bennet, John, and Seth Masia
Walks in the Catskills
The East Woods Press, Fast & McMillan, Inc., Charlotte, N.C., 1977

Catskill Trails and Shelters
New York State Department of Environmental Conservation, Albany, N.Y.

Evers, Alf
The Catskills: From Wilderness to Woodstock
Doubleday & Company, Inc., Garden City, N.Y., 1972

Haring, Harry A.
Our Catskill Mountains
G. P. Putnam's Sons, New York, 1931

Longstreth, Thomas Morris
The Catskills
Century Company, New York, 1918

Mack, Arthur C.
Enjoying the Catskills
Funk & Wagnalls Company, New York, 1950

Van Zandt, Roland
The Catskill Mountain House
Rutgers University Press, New Brunswick, N.J., 1967

Part II

EAST OF THE HUDSON RIVER

7 · *WESTCHESTER COUNTY AND NEARBY CONNECTICUT*

NEWLY ESTABLISHED parkways in Westchester were praised in the 1934 edition of the *Walk Book* for setting "a new standard in highway construction" and providing "adequate highways in beautiful surroundings, with paths for the walker, as well as seats, gardens, and occasional camping spots with fireplaces." This concept of leisurely auto routes wedded to idyllic walkways has long since succumbed to the pace of modern traffic and the sprawl of residential and corporate complexes.

Yet the hiker will find that the parkways and their wider, straighter offspring still lead to as extensive a collection of parks and preserves as can be found anywhere this close to New York City. From smaller parks in the urbanized southern part of the county to more rugged ridges in the less populous highlands to the north, there remain quiet, open spaces steeped in geological and historical interest.

This was the "Neutral Ground" of mixed loyalties in the years after 1776. The restored manor houses of Frederick Philipse, who traded with the Indians at Tarrytown, and the Van Cortlandts of Croton-on-Hudson recall the age of the Dutch patroons. Sunnyside, Washington Irving's cozy retreat at Irvington, overlooks the Hudson, as does Jay Gould's Lyndhurst.

Quite complex geologically, the county belongs to the so-called Manhattan Prong of the New England Upland Province. In the southern part of the county the underlying rock consists of metamorphic schists and gneisses with minor limestone inclusions, while in the north intrusive granite and pegmatite as well as gneiss predominate. Evidence of glaciation abounds in the abrupt slopes and cliffs and the erratics found in the area. The marked relief of this landscape makes it pleasurable for excursions off the beaten track.

BLUE MOUNTAIN RESERVATION

The 1600-acre Blue Mountain Reservation south of Peekskill includes some 15 miles of bridle paths and walking trails. A half-day circuit over the two principal summits, Blue Mountain and Spitzenberg, offers panoramas of Tappan Zee and mountains to the north and west. An unusual feature of the reservation is the Blue Mountain Trail Lodge, which provides men's and women's dormitory accommodations, a central dining and living room, and a well-equipped kitchen for the use of groups of up to thirty people. Reservations may be made through the Westchester County Department of Parks, White Plains, New York. Applications must be submitted many months in advance.

The Welcher Avenue Exit from Route 9 in Peekskill leads east about a half mile directly to the reservation entrance. During the summer, a parking fee is collected from day visitors; after passing the guard post, bear left onto the road past the lodge and continue to the parking lot at the end. The "Peekskill" sheet of the U.S. Geological Survey shows Blue Mountain Reservation and several of its principal trails; a more detailed map may be obtained from attendants at the park.

OLD CROTON AQUEDUCT

From 1842 to 1955, the Old Croton Aqueduct supplied New York City with water from reservoirs formed by damming the Croton River. Although interrupted by major highways and urban congestion, certain sections of the aqueduct provide level, pleasant walks with some fine views of the Hudson between Ossining and North Yonkers. Suggested sections for walking include:

Scarborough-Tarrytown. Length: 5 miles.

This walk traverses storied Sleepy Hollow and ends about half a mile south of the Colonial Philipsburg Manor. From the Scarborough railroad station, walk south on the road along the Hudson, left on Creighton Lane, then take River Road almost to Broadway (Route 9). Turn south onto the aqueduct path at a small yellow marker. Part of the right-of-way appears to be on private property. Where the aqueduct crosses Broadway, walk a short distance south to cross near the IBM entrance; then walk up the hill through a field to rejoin the aqueduct, which also

serves as a bridle path at this point. After crossing the bridge over Route 117, turn sharply right to rejoin the aqueduct. In Tarrytown it may be necessary to walk behind the high school, which is on top of the aqueduct. Continue to Neperan Road in Tarrytown, then downhill to the railroad station. Cars may be parked near Scarborough or Tarrytown stations or at Tarrytown High School parking lot.

A detour of interest is the site of Rockwood Hall. It can be reached via the right (west) fork about half a mile south of the beginning of the aqueduct walk. Although the mansion was razed long ago, a tree-lined drive, an ivy-covered terrace, European beeches, and a creeping hemlock remain. The estate offers superb views of the Hudson and is open to the public by arrangement between the Rockefeller family and the Taconic State Park system. Another detour adjacent to the aqueduct is the Old Dutch Church, built by Frederick Philipse in 1697, and Sleepy Hollow Cemetery, where there are Colonial gravestones, some inscribed in Dutch; Washington Irving was buried here in 1859. The cemetery can be reached via a path leading southwest from a large square stone tower atop the aqueduct.

Yonkers-Tarrytown. Length: 9.5 miles.

From Greystone railroad station in Yonkers, walk uphill, cross Warburton Avenue, go a short distance on Odell Avenue, and north on the aqueduct. Since the path is difficult to follow after the intersection with Broadway in Tarrytown, it is better to walk north on Broadway and take a left on Franklin Street down to the railroad station. It is also possible to return to the railroad at Dobbs Ferry (Walnut Street), Irvington (Main Street), and Hastings. In Irvington, a colonnaded house built by Alexander Hamilton's son and a Victorian octagonal house, owned by historian Carl Carmer, may be seen to the west.

WARD POUND RIDGE RESERVATION

The 4500-acre Ward Pound Ridge Reservation, the largest area maintained by the Westchester County park system, is an agreeable mixture of rolling meadows, second-growth hardwood forest on abandoned farmlands, and hemlock-laurel forests in rocky ravines. Hills rise as high as 938 feet above sea level. There are about 35 miles of hiking trails in the reservation. The southern, undeveloped portion offers an attractive variety of wilderness trails. Circular hikes of 4 to 9 miles are easy to plan with the aid of the trail map available at the park office. Of particular interest is the fire tower from whose observation platform more than twenty-five bodies of water are visible, including reservoirs, lakes, ponds, and distant Long Island Sound. Also of interest are Raven Rocks, Wild Cat Hollow, Honey Hollow, and Stone Hill River. Pell Hill, Michigan Road, and Kimberly Bridge parking areas are good starting points for hikes in the southern portion.

The northern third of the reservation has been developed with several parking sites and picnic areas. There are also twenty-four lean-to shelters with fireplaces, with water and toilet facilities nearby, that may be reserved for day picnics or overnight camping. In winter, a ski slope and cross-country trails are available. A trailside nature museum with displays and programs suitable to the season is well worth a visit. An additional seventy-two acres north of headquarters, along the Cross River, was donated as a memorial, now known as the Meyer Arboretum.

The reservation may be reached by using the Saw Mill River Parkway or Route 684 north to Katonah, turning east on Route 35 for 4 miles to Cross River, and turning south on Route 121 about 100 yards to the entrance. Information on parking fees, use of shelters, and group picnics may be obtained by calling the office at (914) 763-3493.

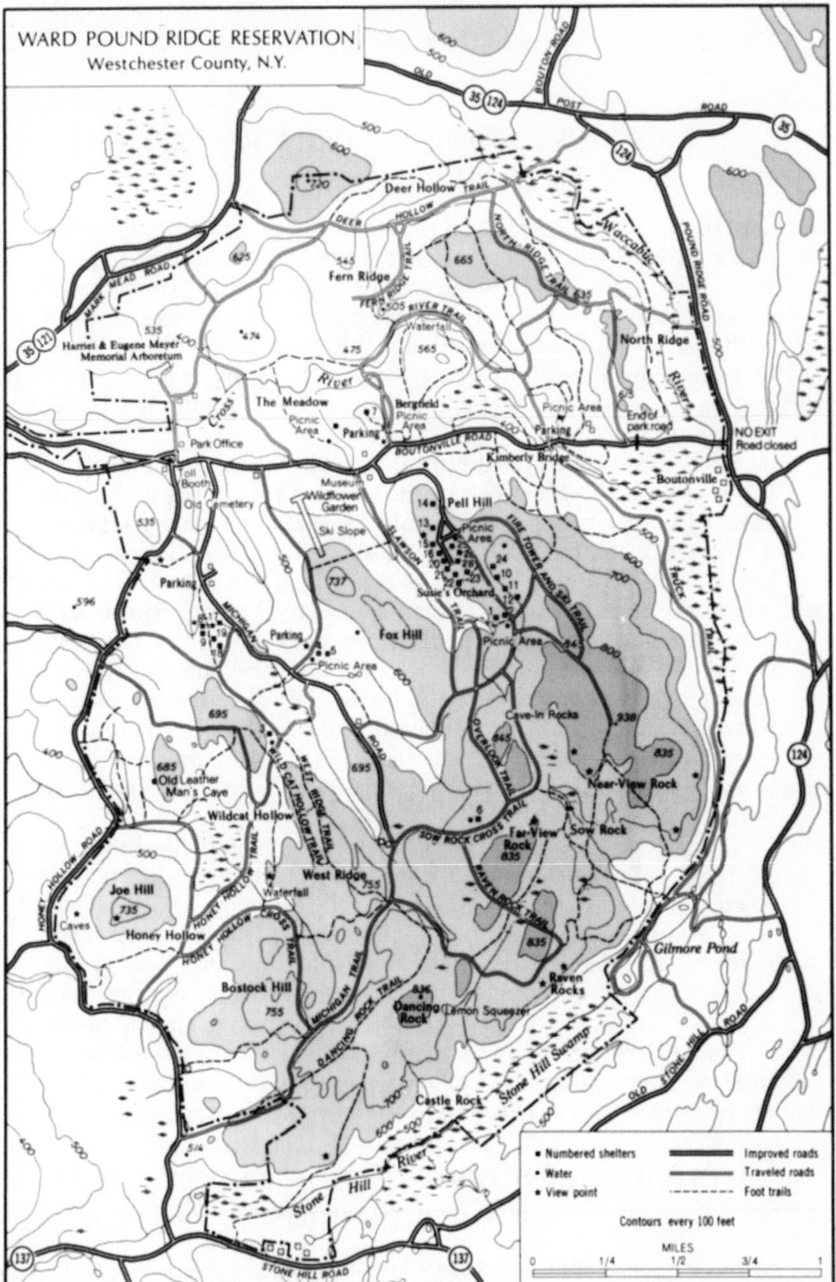
WARD POUND RIDGE RESERVATION
Westchester County, N.Y.
OLD POST ROAD
BOUTON ROAD
POUND RIDGE ROAD
MARK MEAD ROAD
Deer Hollow TRAIL
DEER HOLLOW
NORTH RIDGE TRAIL
Waccabuc
Fern Ridge
FERN RIDGE TRAIL
RIVER TRAIL
Waterfall
North Ridge
River
Harriet & Eugene Meyer Memorial Arboretum
Cross
River
The Meadow
Picnic Area
Parking
Bergfield
Picnic Area
End of park road
NO EXIT Road closed
Park Office
BOUTONVILLE ROAD
Kimberly Bridge
Boutonville
Toll Booth
Old Cemetery
Museum
Wildflower Garden
Ski Slope
Pell Hill
Picnic Area
SLAWSON TRAIL
FIRE TOWER AND SKI TRAIL
TRUCK TRAIL
Susie's Orchard
Parking
MICHIGAN
Parking
Fox Hill
Picnic Area
Picnic Area
Cave-in Rocks
OVERLOOK TRAIL
Near-View Rock
Old Leather Man's Cave
WILD CAT HOLLOW TRAIL
WEST RIDGE TRAIL
ROAD
Wildcat Hollow
SOW ROCK CROSS TRAIL
Far-View Rock
Sow Rock
HONEY HOLLOW ROAD
HONEY HOLLOW TRAIL
West Ridge
Waterfall
RAVEN ROCK TRAIL
Joe Hill
Caves
Honey Hollow
HONEY HOLLOW CROSS TRAIL
Gilmore Pond
Bostock Hill
MICHIGAN TRAIL
DANCING ROCK TRAIL
Dancing Rock
Lemon Squeezer
Raven Rocks
Stone Hill Swamp
OLD STONE HILL ROAD
Castle Rock
River
Hill
Stone
STONE HILL ROAD
Numbered shelters
Water
View point
Improved roads
Traveled roads
Foot trails
Contours every 100 feet
MILES
0
1/4
1/2
3/4
1

MIANUS RIVER GORGE WILDLIFE REFUGE AND BOTANICAL PRESERVE

Maintained since 1953 as a nature preserve under sponsorship of the Mianus River Gorge Conservation Committee of the Nature Conservancy, this 405-acre area extends approximately 1.5 miles along the gorge of the Mianus River in the townships of Bedford, North Castle, and Pound Ridge. A foot trail with several side loops runs south along the west bank of the gorge, from the visitors entrance to the upper end of the Greenwich Water Company Reservoir.

After 1 mile or so on the trail, the hiker reaches the heart of the preserve, the Hemlock Cathedral—twenty acres of hillside covered with virgin eastern hemlocks, some of which are giants dating back to the 1680s. The V-shaped gorge is rugged and spectacular, dropping sharply two hundred feet below the trail, where the roar of water can be heard. Much of the path is carpeted by needles from the giant hemlocks. Mineral outcrops occur, and over five hundred species of flora and fauna have been catalogued. A round trip on the main trail requires two hours, but considerable additional time can and should be devoted to the exploration of the various side trails, such as the one that leads to an abandoned mica and quartz mine. Detailed trail maps are available at the entrance.

Access is by car only. From Exit 34 of the Merritt Parkway, go north 7.7 miles on Long Ridge Road (Route 104) to Millers Mill Road. Turn left here for 0.1 mile over the bridge to Mianus River Road and then left again for 0.7 mile to the entrance. From the Bedford area, take Pound Ridge Road and Stamford Road (Long Ridge Road) to Millers Mill Road on the right. Cross the river and turn down Mianus River Road a half mile to the entrance.

The preserve is open 9:30 A.M. to 5:30 P.M. daily from April 1 to December 1. Bag lunches are permitted on the grassy banks of the parking area. Dogs are not allowed.

KITCHAWAN RESEARCH STATION AND TEATOWN LAKE RESERVATION

These scenic natural areas in Westchester County were developed by the Brooklyn Botanic Garden for research and education. Both are in the Ossining-Kitchawan area south of Croton Reservoir about 1 mile east and west, respectively, of the Taconic

State Parkway. The 226-acre Field Station property to the east, which houses the Kitchawan Research Laboratory, is open to hikers. In addition to a labeled nature trail, the property features streams, meadows, an area of mature hemlock, and 6 miles of trails that link up with the abandoned Putnam railroad bed, affording opportunities for an extended hike.

The western portion of the 400-acre Teatown Lake Reservation offers 15 miles of trails and provides the hiker with a wide variety of natural areas to explore, from old fields to climax forest. The 2-mile Hidden Valley circular is particularly rewarding. Included in the reservation are a thirty-three-acre lake, streams, a bird observation blind, a small menagerie of native animals, a nature museum, a maple sugar house (active in March), two self-guided nature trails, and a "Trail of Thoughts" featuring quotations by famous naturalists. Picnicking is permitted in designated areas, and guided tours can be arranged by calling the office at (914) 762-2912. There is a fee for group visits.

Access by car is via the Route 134 Exit of the Taconic State Parkway. Go east 1.5 miles to the Kitchawan Research Station or west a half mile to Teatown Lake Reservation on Spring Valley Road. Parking at each center is limited to fifteen to twenty-five cars, so car pools are advised. There is no bus transportation, but there is access by rail to Croton, Ossining, or Mount Kisco, where a cab can be hired for the 5-mile trip.

CRANBERRY LAKE PARK

Cranberry Lake Park, bordered by the Kensico watershed and private property, lies across Route 22 from Kensico Dam, which was constructed from stone quarried east of the lake. The principal geographic feature of the park is a ten-acre lake surrounded by bogs and wetlands. The land also rises to rocky outcroppings and wooded hillsides, furnishing a woodland trail, a lake trail, and a self-guided nature trail. A shelter and picnic tables are available. Follow Route 22 north past Kensico Dam, turn right on Orchard Street, then right into the park. By train, take the Metro-North to Valhalla, then walk across Kensico Dam to the park, or take the train to North White Plains and follow the bicycle path to the dam.

SILVER LAKE PARK

Within this park are the Heritage Trail (1.8 miles: red, white, and blue blazes) and the Silver Lake Trail (1 mile: white blazes).

The former is named for the route of the retreat of the Continental Army after the Battle of White Plains in 1776. Several graves beside the road mark some of the fallen Connecticut militia. Access is by car, with parking on Lake Street. The trail begins on Lake Street at Merritt Hill. Proceed downhill to lakeside and turn right (north) on the tricolor blazes to the end of the lake, then continue 1.5 miles to Buckout Road. This area is historically important in another context; Route 22 to Canada was the famous underground slave escape route, and parallels Buckout Road, where root cellars may have doubled as shelters. Follow Buckout Road left for a short distance to a sharp left bend, after which there is a gap in a privet hedge opposite an old cemetery on the right. Turn right, then quickly left to pick up the Silver Lake Trail. The Heritage Trail turns right at Buckout Road and ends 0.3 mile northwest at Old Orchard Street.

The Silver Lake white markers lead down across stone walls from early farms, with a steep descent crossing a brook. Turning sharply right (south) proceed for half a mile along a marsh. At the double marker go left (east) for 0.2 mile, then down a steep hill to the west side of Silver Lake. Follow the shore left to the north end to rejoin the Heritage Trail.

ARTHUR W. BUTLER MEMORIAL SANCTUARY

This 350-acre tract was donated to the Nature Conservancy in 1954 by Mrs. Arthur W. Butler in memory of her husband. With 6 miles of interconnecting well-marked trails and bridle paths, the relatively small area encompasses forest, marsh, meadow, ravine, ridge, and swampland. The highest point, 700 feet, is reached via the High Ridge Trail, where there is a hawk observation stand. The property has known many owners, who through the years have planted thousands of evergreens. Forty-eight species of trees and sixty species of shrubs have been counted. One hundred thirty species of birds have been sighted. The pileated woodpecker, red-tailed hawk, great horned owl, and screech owl are common to the area. Among numerous wildflowers the pink lady's-slipper has sanctuary here.

A walk at Butler may be combined with a visit to Westmoreland Sanctuary across Chestnut Ridge Road, or to the Eugene and Agnes Meyer Nature Preserve to the south. A half-mile continuation of the blue-blazed Long Trail provides a connecting link to the Meyer Preserve via Byram Lake Road, Oregon Road, and the private drive of Seven Springs Center.

A hike may be extended west from the sanctuary 2 miles via

a network of interconnecting trails to the village of Mount Kisco. As the red-marked Ridge Trail leaves the sanctuary, it becomes a bridle path through woods and across Sarles Street into the twenty-five-acre Cornelia V. R. Marsh Memorial Sanctuary. By keeping left at trail intersections, one reaches Leonard Park, a town park with parking restricted to Mount Kisco residents. Parking here is on local streets, or at the office buildings on Route 172 on weekends. To return to Butler Sanctuary from this point by car, take Route 172 east approximately 2 miles, turn right on Chestnut Ridge Road, and proceed 1.5 miles to the sanctuary entrance.

The Butler Sanctuary is open year round. A nature center and reference library may be used by appointment, and a resident naturalist is available for consultation. Trail maps and pertinent literature are placed at a trailside shelter a short distance into the woods from the parking area. Located directly west of Westmoreland Sanctuary, Butler is reached from Exit 3 of Route 684 at Armonk by driving north on Route 22 for 3.1 miles to the intersection of Chestnut Ridge Road on the left, then following Chestnut Ridge Road 1.5 miles to a bridge over Route 684 on the left, which leads to the parking area. The telephone number is (914) 666-4221.

WESTMORELAND SANCTUARY

The 625-acre Westmoreland Sanctuary with its 12 miles of interconnecting foot trails has open grassland, stands of hardwood and evergreen trees, a brook valley, a couple of modest rocky summits, and Bechtel Lake, named for one of the sanctuary's founders, Edwin Bechtel. The varied habitat produces an abundance of flowers and birds. Established in 1957, this private nonprofit organization sponsors wildlife and botanical research as well as educational programs for the public. Activity schedules and trail maps are available near the entrance. The paths, identified by signposts at junctions, are groomed for cross-country skiing in the winter. A walk in Westmoreland can be combined with a visit to Arthur W. Butler Memorial Sanctuary, directly across Chestnut Ridge Road via a bridge crossing Route 684.

The sanctuary is open daily and its museum Wednesday through Sunday, 9 A.M. to 5 P.M.; phone: (914) 666-8448. Westmoreland is reached from Exit 3 of Route 684 at Armonk by driving north on Route 22 for 3.1 miles, then going left on Chestnut Ridge Road 1.5 miles to the sanctuary entrance on the right.

BYRAM LAKE AND THE EUGENE AND AGNES MEYER NATURE PRESERVE

Byram Lake, 3 miles north of Armonk on Byram Lake Road, provides a scenic setting for fishing and walking. From the rocky west shore of this small gem of a lake rise the steep, wooded hills of the Eugene and Agnes Meyer Nature Preserve. Once the home of Eugene Meyer, editor and publisher of the Washington *Post* in the 1940s and '50s, this woodland tract of 350 acres has been administered by the Nature Conservancy since 1973. Hikes may be extended to the Arthur W. Butler Sanctuary to the north.

From Exit 3 of Route 684, follow Route 22 north a half mile, turn left at the flashing caution light onto Cox Avenue for 0.2 mile, then fork right onto Byram Lake Road. This reaches the south end of Byram Lake in another 1.5 miles, where there is parking alongside the road.

For a 4-mile circular, walk south, retracing Byram Lake Road for a half mile to Oregon Road. Follow Oregon Road uphill 0.2 mile to the preserve. There is room here for one or two cars, a convenience for those wishing to confine their walk to the nature preserve. A short distance from the road is a shelter containing trail maps. To continue the circular, there is a choice here of three parallel trails tending north through the preserve: the blue-marked Cliff Trail that overlooks Byram Lake, the red-marked Ridge Trail, and the green-marked Ravine Trail. All three, in approximately 1.25 miles, emerge from the woods at the private drive past Seven Springs Center, formerly the Meyer home, now a Yale University affiliate. In a half mile a more northerly intersection of Oregon and Byram Lake roads is reached. A right turn heads downhill, around the north end of the lake and back to the parked car in approximately 2 more miles.

For hiking solely in the nature preserve, there are two more parking areas at trailheads on Oregon Road, farther north than the one previously noted. The fact that the road has become a narrow dirt road, seldom used, makes it a pleasant trail link in circular hikes.

OTHER WALKS IN WESTCHESTER

Bronx River Parkway

Between Bronxville and Scarsdale a scenic 3.5-mile section provides a level, easy walk. You can park your car in the vicinity of the parkway on side streets and near the Scarsdale railroad station, or else take the Metro-North Harlem Division trains that run daily.

Byram River Trail

Located north of Greenwich, Connecticut, close to the New York state line, is a 3.6-mile, yellow-blazed trail mainly on bridle paths that follow the course of the narrow river. The southern end of the trail is reached by car from the Hutchinson River Parkway by driving north on King Street (Route 120A) 1.5 miles to the intersection of Sherwood Avenue and following the latter to its end at Riversville Road. Cars can be parked under the Merritt Parkway bridge.

Marshlands Conservancy

This 137-acre sanctuary offers walks of one or two hours on trails that wind through woods, brush, and open fields sloping to salt-marsh areas and tidewater land overlooking Milton Harbor on Long Island Sound. In spring, waterfowl nest along the quiet shore and herons may be seen high in the trees. John Jay, the first Chief Justice of the U.S. Supreme Court, is buried nearby in a private plot among the evergreens. For information on its active schedule of guided walks, lectures, and study sessions, call (914) 835-4466 Wednesday through Sunday. The Marshlands Conservancy is located on Route 1, the Boston Post Road, 2.5 miles south of the Metro-North station in Rye.

Mountain Lakes

This thousand-acre camping area, situated at North Salem, is one of Westchester's most beautiful parks, containing several ponds and the beginnings of Crook Brook. Take Route 684 to Exit 6 (Katonah/Cross River), go east on Route 35 to Routes 121 and 124; bear left to Grants Corner, then take a right onto Hawley Road and go 2 miles to the entrance.

Muscoot Park

Walkers may enjoy the 15 miles of well-marked trails through exceptionally beautiful fields and woodlands, or from May through October on weekends attend the Interpretive Farm Program, which displays farm life from 1880 through 1960. Located in Somers, the park may be reached by the Taconic State Parkway. Exit at Route 100, then go north to the entrance on the left.

Former New York Central Rights-of-Way

A pleasant level walk along the former railroad bed of the Putnam Division of the New York Central Railroad may be done in several portions. *Millwood to Croton Reservoir,* 3 miles, may be started at the former Millwood station on Route 133 half a mile east of the Millwood–Briarcliff Manor Exit of the Taconic Parkway. *Former Croton Lake Station to Lake Mahopac,* 10.5 miles, starts on Route 129, a short distance west of the Route 100 traffic circle. At the northern end of the walk, Mahopac station, now an American Legion hall, is located on the south side of Route 6 at the lower end of Lake Mahopac. *Goldens Bridge to Lake Mahopac,* 7.2 miles, begins at the commuter parking lot of the Harlem Division of Metro-North. Cross the parking lot and the adjacent north-south access road, where the overgrown Mahopac Branch right-of-way can be found down a wooded embankment, angling off to the northwest approximately 300 feet south of Green Street (Route 138).

Pans Altar Trail

This white-blazed trail runs 3.5 miles through woods from Dobbs Ferry to Irvington. Exit from Saw Mill River Parkway at Dobbs Ferry. Just west of the parkway is North Field Avenue. Four blocks north of Ashford Avenue, turn west on Gould Avenue, where there is ample street parking. The trail begins between 62 Gould Avenue and 3 Cyrus Place. It winds along the ridge above V. Everit Macy Park, crosses Cyrus Field Road, and continues to Pans Altar, the site of lectures by J. O. Swift, the famous nature writer. After returning to Cyrus Field Road the trail circles the reservoir.

Saxon Woods Park

Stretching for 2.5 miles through Scarsdale and Mamaroneck along the Mamaroneck River, this park offers especially fine birding in the spring, as well as an interpretive board describing the well-marked Boy Scout trails. Year-round parking is possible at the Saxon Woods Swimming Pool, on the west side of Mamaroneck Avenue just north of the Hutchinson River Parkway. Walk under the parkway, and follow the trail to the picnic parking area (open only from May through October with a parking fee).

Sprain Ridge Park

Grassy Sprain Reservoir, which supplies water to the city of Yonkers, is bounded on the west, beyond the Sprain Brook Parkway, by a ridge and an area of woods about half a mile wide and 3 miles long. This county park may be entered at the north end, on Jackson Avenue, half a mile west of the Sprain Brook Parkway.

Titicus Reservoir—Hammond Museum

Located on Deveau Road in North Salem, this former estate features an easy walk of about 4.5 miles with hilltop views, a

Japanese garden, and the atmosphere of a Currier & Ives print. The trail area is encircled by Titicus Road (Route 116) along the north side of the reservoir, June Road (Route 124), and Hardscrabble Road, all a few minutes from the Purdys Exit of Route 684. The territory immediately north of the reservoir offers a network of well-maintained bridle paths.

Turkey Mountain

The summit, about half a mile from the parking area if approached directly, has a splendid view of the Croton watershed. A hike hereabouts can be combined with one on the Old Putnam Division right-of-way. Exit from the Taconic Parkway at Millwood and follow Route 100 north to the traffic circle. Turn left onto Route 129 and then sharply right onto Route 118 for 0.8 mile. At the sign for Peter Pratt's Inn, turn left up the drive into Turkey Mountain Park.

Whippoorwill Ridge Park

Located west of the village of Armonk and east of Whippoorwill Road, this wooded area consists of approximately seventy acres of a ridge typical of those found in north-central Westchester. Outcroppings of schist in a beech-maple forest give it a special attractiveness. Access is from Old Route 22, 0.3 mile north of the Armonk Bowl.

Suggested Readings

Brooks, Van Wyck
The World of Washington Irving
E. P. Dutton & Co., New York, 1944

Irving, Washington
The Legend of Sleepy Hollow and Other Selections
Washington Square Press, New York, 1962

8 · *FAHNESTOCK STATE PARK AND ADJACENT CONNECTICUT*

(Map 3)

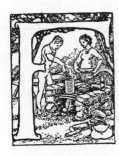

FAHNESTOCK PARK, situated in the heavily wooded, rolling countryside of northern Putnam County, lies about 8 miles east of Cold Spring. Now under the jurisdiction of the Taconic State Park Commission, the park originally consisted of about 3600 acres given to the state in 1929 by Dr. Alfred Fahnestock in memory of his father. Between 1960 and 1966 several additions were made so that the total is now nearly 6200 acres.

The park is shaped somewhat like a U, with the base at the junction of Taconic State Parkway and Route 301 and the sides running southeast and southwest along these highways.

Although most of the park is not rugged, there are two high ridges in its western portion—one culminating in Candlewood Hill in the south and the other in Mount Shenandoah (1282 feet), a little north of the park boundary—while to the southwest, Canopus Creek flows through a beautiful rugged ravine. With a few old hemlock groves and second-growth hardwood forests, the park's swamps and thick undergrowth of laurel make many sections of this area difficult to penetrate, except where there are trails. Canopus Lake—which along with Stillwater Pond, picnic and camping facilities and major horse trails, was built by the Civilian Conservation Corps during the 1930s—lies just west of Route 301, with Pelton Pond opposite it. Stillwater Pond is west of the parkway, and there are several small ponds elsewhere, which in summer mirror Queen Anne's lace and flowering water lilies.

Deer are numerous in the park, and beaver populate the swamps. All the usual woodland birds, including partridges, are abundant, and hawks often ride the updraft at the face of Candlewood Hill. Since it is much colder in the park than in neighboring districts, deep snow may linger until the end of March.

Throughout the park's younger forests are traces of early settlements, such as overgrown wood roads, cellar holes, stone fences, charcoal pits, and mine cuts, reminders that this area was once the site of considerable activity. Dennytown, once a hamlet of French settlers, is now abandoned, but the open fields around the former enclosure are ideal for a quiet rest, while its ruins are a poignant reminder of these early settlers and their life-style. Some of the park's wood roads lead past several flooded mines, which, during their heyday in the early and mid 1800s, supplied magnetic oxide of iron to the West Point Foundry. Much of the ore was shipped by train to Cold Spring Turnpike for transport to the foundry; the railbed for this route, built in 1862, now forms part of the recently relocated Appalachian Trail. Other early transportation routes include the Old Albany Post Road, authorized in 1703, which extended from Kings Bridge in Westchester

Clear Pond, north end. granite blocks & mountain laurel. XXIII June 14 1969 R.G.H.

to the ferry at Albany. Built during the reign of Queen Anne and originally known as one of the Queen's roads, it has since been mostly obliterated by Route 9, although several sections remain. The Old West Point Road, which ran from the Old Albany Post Road to the Hudson River, saw considerable activity during the Revolution, while the Cold Spring or Eastern Turnpike shown on old maps followed the route now taken by Route 301.

Access to the park, which is by car only, is via Route 301 and the Taconic State Parkway.

There is a ski area on the east side of the parkway a half mile north of Route 301, while picnic and camping grounds—which have drinking water in the summer—extend along the east side of Route 301 for 1 mile south of its junction with the parkway. Free parking is available on Route 301 opposite Canopus Lake, and on small turnouts on the gravel roads in the southwest section. For access to the southern section of the park (formerly known as Roaring Brook State Park), cars can be left under the bridge that carries the Taconic Parkway over Peekskill Hollow Road. Sunk Mine Road, used for access to trails in the park, is not maintained during the winter and may be closed to vehicular traffic due to ice or heavy snow.

Catfish Loop Trail. Length: 3.4 miles. Blazes: red.

The eastern trailhead of Catfish Loop, located in the southwest corner of the park, may be reached by taking Route 301 to Dennytown Road, then going south on Dennytown Road for about 1 mile to a large, grassy parking area on the east side, near a group of old stone buildings.

A short walk south on unpaved, blue-blazed Dennytown Road (which also serves as a side trail from the Appalachian Trail) leads to the trail, which enters woods on the right (west). The Appalachian Trail exits at this same point from woods on the left and continues south on the road. Catfish Loop gradually descends to the southwest, passing several stone walls and crossing two small brooks, then ascends gradually, reaching a trail register at a half mile and continuing for the next half mile or so on rolling terrain.

Passing a swamp on the left and crossing a yellow-blazed wood road and horse trail, the trail descends slightly and crosses a brook before reaching the blue-blazed Three Lakes Trail, with its southern trailhead appearing on the right (north). The red blazes then lead left and ascend to reach ledges at 1.5 miles, with an excellent view of the Hudson Highlands, including Storm King and Crows Nest.

The ledges continue, bringing thickets of mountain laurel, with a descent to a sign showing the direction to Catfish Pond, which is outside the southern boundary of the park. Having reversed its direction via a 180-degree loop, the trail descends gradually, crossing a brook and horse trail, before ascending over more ledges, with more views northwest at 2.5 miles. It then recrosses the same horse trail, following a stone wall on the left, which is the park boundary.

The last leg brings a descent to a brook crossing, and, continuing through mountain laurel (bear right to avoid a restricted area on the left), the trail gradually reverses direction again, and then descends to the western trailhead, 3.4 miles from the start, terminating at the blue-blazed Three Lakes Trail.

Return to the parking area by walking left (east) about 1 mile on the Three Lakes Trail, which crosses Dennytown Road at the parking area. The total length of this loop is 4.6 miles of fairly easy walking.

Three Lakes Trail. Length: 5.5 miles. Blazes: blue.

Three Lakes Trail begins just west of the Canopus Lake parking lot and travels generally southwest through the park. Access to various segments of the trail is available from Route 301, Sunk Mine Road, or Dennytown Road. The Appalachian Trail, used in conjunction with Three Lakes Trail, permits various loops or circulars.

To begin at Route 301, cars should be parked at the Canopus Lake parking lot. A walk west on the remnants of an old road just south of Route 301 leads, in approximately 500 feet, to the trailhead. Bear left (south), following a wood road to pass old mine pits, and then a swamp on the right. Leaving the wood road bearing southwest, the trail descends gradually, crosses Canopus Creek to pass a swamp on the right, with a moderate ascent to the Appalachian Trail crossing at 1.3 miles.

Some gentle rises offer a view of Hidden Lake to the south. Here a descent leads to the southern end of the lake and a short, unmarked side path to the lakeshore.

Approximately 300 feet south of this point, the Three Lakes Trail passes an unnamed white trail entering on the left, which reaches Sunk Mine Road in about a half mile. The blue-blazed trail continues over fairly level terrain through mountain laurel, then descends slightly to reach an old railbed, which leads off to the right to the shore of Sunk Mine Lake. Following the lakeshore, descending slightly, and crossing a brook below the lake's spillway, the Three Lakes Trail then ascends, reaching Sunk Mine Road at 2.8 miles.

At this point a white-blazed side trail to the left follows Sunk Mine Road to reach the Appalachian Trail crossing of the road in 0.6 mile.

Continuing, the Three Lakes Trail turns right (west) on Sunk Mine Road for a short distance, then reenters woods on the left. Ascending on a wood road, it passes the remnants of Denny Mine off the trail to the left after leaving the wood road. After a steep descent over rocks, the trail passes a swamp and pond on the left, swings right, and reaches Dennytown Road, with a large grassy parking area on the east side, 3.9 miles from the start. At this point a blue-blazed side trail starts left (south) on Dennytown Road, leading to the Catfish Loop Trail and the Appalachian Trail.

The Three Lakes Trail crosses Dennytown Road, enters woods to the west, and descends, crossing several stone walls and passing a group camping area on the right. A moderate ascent and a level walk that crosses a wood road brings a trail register at 4.4 miles. Avoiding a restricted area on the right, the trail descends, crosses a brook, and reaches Catfish Loop's western trailhead on the right at almost 5 miles. Bearing left (south) and following the brook, the trail terminates 5.5 miles from its beginning at its intersection with Catfish Loop Trail. About 1.25 miles east (left) on the red-blazed Catfish Loop Trail is the intersection of the Appalachian Trail and its side trail with Dennytown Road.

Candlewood Hill Trail. Length: 4 miles. Blazes: red.

This trail begins where the Appalachian Trail crosses Sunk Mine Road. There are several turnoffs near the trailhead where one or two cars may park.

The trail begins with easy walking on an unpaved, fairly level section of Sunk Mine Road. After crossing Canopus Creek, it continues for 0.8 mile before entering woods on the right.

After a moderate ascent of Candlewood Hill, it reaches ledges, ascending more steeply to the open summit, 1.4 miles from the start, with enjoyable views in all directions. Continuing south along ledges, the trail bears right and begins a moderate descent to Bell Hollow Road. Turning left on this dirt road, it crosses Canopus Creek again, about 3 miles from the start. In another mile, Bell Hollow Road joins Canopus Hollow Road, where the trail ends.

Return to the starting point by following the Appalachian Trail north on Canopus Hollow Road to Dennytown Road, then entering woods on the right and continuing to Sunk Mine Road. The total length of this loop is about 8 miles.

Appalachian Trail. Length: 8 miles. Blazes: white.

The Appalachian Trail enters Fahnestock proceeding north from Canopus Valley Crossroads on Canopus Hollow Road, the name of which changes at South Highland Road to Dennytown Road. At 2.5 miles the trail turns right (east) into woods, through a young hardwood forest, reaching Sunk Mine Road at 4 miles after passing a knoll with a swamp on the left.

At Sunk Mine Road, where red-blazed Candlewood Hill Trail goes right, a jog right, then left leads to a bridged stream and a hemlock grove. Some climbs and descents past abandoned mines and Hidden Lake on the left bring a right-angle crossing of the blue-blazed Three Lakes Trail at about 5 miles. After passing a trail register, the Appalachian Trail follows an abandoned mine railbed to Route 301 at 6 miles. The trail follows the road left, crossing it to enter woods at the southwest end of Canopus Lake. A climb through mountain laurel, across a rock-strewn creek, leads to a view of Canopus Lake, with more climbs and descents to the north end of the lake, with a good view point.

A short distance north of here the trail leaves Fahnestock State Park on its way north to the summit of Shenandoah Mountain and Long Hill Road, ultimately leading into Connecticut.

EASTWARD FROM FAHNESTOCK STATE PARK

East of the Hudson, and generally unnoticed by the hiker, are a number of wild tracts of forest administered by the New York State Department of Environmental Conservation (DEC). However, unlike the Forever Wild DEC lands in the Catskill and Adirondack preserves, these areas may be managed for a variety of purposes, including timber harvest. The management of these reforestation areas or state forests is similar to the multiple-use, sustained-yield policy of the National Forest System. Although not nearly the size of the great state parks such as Harriman and Fahnestock, and lacking marked trails and detailed hiking maps, these tracts are noteworthy and beautiful. A substantial relocation of the Appalachian Trail will cross the Depot Hill State Forest, while farther north, into Dutchess County, state lands have been acquired near Lafayetteville, on the southwest end of Stissing Mountain, and near Millbrook. In Putnam County there are tracts on Big Buck Mountain, California Hill, and, of the greatest interest to the hiker, Nimham Mountain near Carmel.

NIMHAM MOUNTAIN STATE FOREST

The 910-acre Nimham Mountain State Forest was created about 1962 on lands purchased from the Rohner Farm and Cornell Estate. Bordered on the south by a county park and on the north by private forests, it includes most of the southern end of a long and rugged mountain mass. The focal point of the park is the wild and beautiful Nimham Mountain. Once called Smalleys Hill, the name was changed late in the past century to that of Daniel Nimham, sachem of the Wappinger Indians, who was unsuccessful in his attempts to reclaim his tribal lands. He died bravely in 1778 serving Washington and Lafayette at Indian Field near Tibbets Brook. Surrounded by lakes and reservoirs and commanding a dramatic view of the vast lands once owned by Nimham and his people, Nimham Mountain is a fitting memorial.

On the lower valley fields the DEC planted red pine, Norway spruce, and European larch. To support a fire lookout tower already on the mountain, the DEC established the Field Headquarters, an office and a storehouse of forest fire control equipment for Westchester, Putnam, and Dutchess counties. At present, cutting in the forest is limited to fuelwood cuts by individuals, awarded by lottery because of heavy demand, a practice that increases both browse and cover for wildlife. The area is open to hiking, camping, hunting, and fishing; a permit from the ranger is required for camping more than three days. The best map available is the U.S. Geological Survey's "Lake Carmel" quadrangle, scale 1:24,000.

Nimham Forest lies some 7 miles east of Fahnestock via Route 301. A shorter southern approach from the Taconic Parkway is via Peekskill Hollow Road to Kent Cliffs. Turn right on Route 301 and drive about 3 miles to the point where it crosses West Branch Reservoir on a stone causeway. Do not cross the causeway but turn sharply left onto Gypsy Trail Road. The entrance to the Field Headquarters is 2.5 miles beyond.

Parking areas here and elsewhere in the forest, such as off the dirt road running northwest from Gypsy Trail Road to the fire tower, have a specified limit of cars, to regulate the number of hunters using the forest in season. The Nimham Forest ranger has requested hikers not to leave their cars in these areas and has kindly given permission to park in the large area behind the headquarters storehouse. The rules are simple but important: Do not block access by fire control trucks and other department vehicles; leave a note inside your windshield stating that you are a hiker; respect all boundaries and confine rambles to state land.

Three well-defined trails or wood roads, all of which run north and south, penetrate other portions of the forest. These woods, save for an occasional swamp or pocket of dense laurel and catbrier, are generally open. With a compass it is possible to fashion a loop of about 5 or 6 miles.

One recommended hike is to descend east from the Field Headquarters via a wide wood road to a beautiful pond created by a small dam across Pine Pond's south inlet. In autumn the massed effect of steepled golden larches rising to the eastern hill line is a magnificent sight. Near the dam, a narrow trail leads back to the east end of the headquarters road. From here the trail leads south through the red pine plantation to another forest of larches with excellent views of Nimham and the valley and hills to the north.

After reaching the county park boundary, the route turns west through the pines and descends, crossing Gypsy Trail Road, into the deep wooded gully of Pine Pond Brook, with its towering boles of tulip trees. The brook can be crossed in several places on boulders or fallen trees to follow the clearly marked forest boundary around the south end of an extensive marsh. Here begins the steep climb up the easternmost ridge of Nimham, a route that keeps always to the west with the blazed boundary in sight. Beyond the crest are several attractive hollows among low hills. Approximately a half mile from the brook the forest boundary turns sharply southeast, but one should continue northwest to skirt the thickest laurel. After a second hill, the route comes out on the well-defined north-south wood road that descends the southwest spur of the mountain. A rock spine, surmounted by hemlocks, rises just east of the trail, and it is not difficult to scramble to the top, where an opening in the trees offers a glimpse of the hills to the west. Continuing north, one descends to a wood road with better footing that leads to the fire tower. The road is lined by old stone walls and patches of farmland long returned to woods. The road passes an old root cellar, crosses two little brooks, and comes out at the locked gate on the gravel road to the tower, where there is parking for about six cars. In another 0.75 mile, the highest point on Nimham, 1270 feet, is reached, with its forest observer's cabin and the eighty-foot steel fire tower.

The view from here includes an arc one hundred miles across —a huge profile of the entire hiking region in southern New York State. Southwest, across the whole of Westchester County, rise the now-lilliputian towers of Manhattan, nearly sixty miles out, while an equal distance to the northwest lie the dark peaks of Slide Mountain and the highest Catskills. Between these points runs the colossal span of familiar highlands. Peekskill Hollow reveals a glimpse of the distant Hudson. Mount Beacon's fire tower, Mount Taurus, and the Fahnestock plateau stand clearly defined. And far below, in the triangle formed by Pine Pond, West Branch Reservoir, and Clear Pool, lies all of Nimham Forest. The two nearest fire towers still operated by the Department of Environmental Conservation are Clove Mountain, sixteen miles to the northeast, and Sterling Ridge, thirty-eight miles to the southwest.

Going down, a traverse southeast through an open young hardwood forest offers a pleasant alternative to the gravel road. A compass bearing of 135 degrees carries the hiker over a lower rocky summit out onto the gravel road at a parking spot for four cars. Larches edge this lovely field. A short trail begins here and leads south to a brook, which may be followed east to its confluence with Pine Pond Brook. The latter is best crossed by turning north and coming out at the bridge on Gypsy Trail Road a short distance beyond, although one may walk out on the gravel road, which leads to the paved highway, and, to the right, the Field Headquarters. By either route, the distance from the small parking area to headquarters is about 1 mile.

Housatonic Range Trail. Length: 8.1 miles. Blazes: blue.

The Housatonic Range Trail follows the route of an old Indian trail that roughly parallels the Housatonic River from Gaylordsville south to New Milford, Connecticut. The trail has a few short but challenging rock scrambles and several good views of the river valley, the lower end of Candlewood Lake, and the hills to the east.

The trail is more difficult than its maximum elevation of 1000 feet suggests, and 4.5 hours should be allowed. Add another half hour for two side loops.

Parking near the southern end of the trail is available at the Connecticut Light and Power Co. power station, 1.5 miles north of New Milford center. The trail starts at the west side of U.S. Route 7, almost half a mile north of the power station, at Rocky River Road. The northern end of the trail is on Gaylord Road, about 0.8 mile southwest of Route 7, past the old Gaylordsville Schoolhouse, which is worth a visit. Cars are usually parked on Cedar Hill Road, or along Route 7, where more space is available.

At its southern end, starting on Route 7, the trail follows

Rocky River Road, then turns onto an old wood road. Continuing southwest, it climbs Candlewood Mountain to a switchback at about 1 mile, where it changes direction to north. There are good views from this area to the east over New Milford, of the north end of Lake Candlewood, Connecticut's largest lake, and of the penstock that carries lake water to the hydro generators at the Connecticut Light and Power Co. power station.

The trail continues to rise as it goes north. At 1.5 miles it turns west, ascends, and then descends into a saddle, finally climbing to the summit of Candlewood Mountain (1007 feet) at almost 2 miles. After descending, it reaches a loop trail to the right, which leads to a rock cliff, a cave, and a trail link to Route 7. The main trail crosses a saddle between Candlewood Mountain and Pine Knob, the summit of which is at 2.5 miles, before descending through the Corkscrew, an area of steep ledges and tumbled boulders. Continuing through a hemlock grove, the Housatonic Range Trail crosses a brook at 3 miles, passing an overhanging rock and cave to descend to Route 37.

At Route 37, after crossing a bridge, the trail turns west, following the highway several hundred yards before turning into the woods to the right. Crossing a stream and climbing boulders to Suicide Ledge at 4.2 miles, it descends steeply to cross Squash Hollow Road. The trail turns left along this road, then right onto an old wood road at 5 miles. At 5.4 miles a short side trail leads to Tories Cave, whose several rooms should not be explored without lights and ropes. A trail from the cave connects to Route 7.

The main trail continues, passing another old wood road at 5.8 miles, before reaching another junction with Squash Hollow Road. Turn left on the road for about 200 yards, then right (north) into the woods; the trail climbs to reach the Pinnacle (Straits Rock), then descends steeply through a hemlock grove, around and down over large boulders.

Turning left at 7.5 miles, the trail ascends to take a sharp left, descending through hemlocks and a partially open meadow. The trail now reaches Naromiyocknowhusunkotankshunk Brook, at high water as difficult to cross as to pronounce. The northern trailhead is reached at Gaylord Road shortly after the brook, at 8.1 miles.

Suggested Reading

Connecticut Walk Book
Connecticut Forest and Park Association, P.O. Box 389, East Hartford, Conn. 06108

9 · *HUDSON HIGHLANDS EAST OF THE RIVER*

(Maps 1 and 2)

SELDOM DO large cities have anything to match the gorge of the Hudson through the Highlands. From Dunderberg north around Anthonys Nose to Storm King and Breakneck, the Hudson is narrow and winding, flanked by hills of a thousand feet or more. What we have now is merely the remnant of a gorge two, three, or more times that depth. Ice Age glaciers shaved off the tops of the mountains and filled the gorge with debris.

During the Revolution in 1777 a chain was stretched across the river from the foot of Anthonys Nose to Fort Montgomery. The remains of the fort are still visible on a knob overlooking the river, and just to the south across Popolopen Creek, one wall of Fort Clinton stands just below the museum at the western end of Bear Mountain Bridge. The site of one of the redoubts of Fort Clinton is marked by a plaque on a branch of the nature trail south of the bridge.

These log and stone ramparts were the scene of a brave defense by Orange County militia, on October 4, 1777, against an assault by British troops under Sir John Vaughan. The British finally took the posts and, with the aid of ships, broke the chain across the river. After the enemy had made a raid up the river in a vain attempt to save Burgoyne at Saratoga, the Americans fortified West Point and built outlying redoubts on several summits east of the river, on Fort Defiance Hill and Fort Hill, east of Garrison, and elsewhere. A new and heavier chain was stretched from West Point to Constitution Island, where the river is narrowest. This island, now under the administration of West Point, can be reached only by special launch from the Military Academy. The sites of the chain-fastening and the redoubts are marked by bronze tablets.

On the east end of the ridge of Anthonys Nose are the extensive dumps of the old Manitou Copper Mine. The ore was chiefly iron pyrite, with a small amount of copper. This mine was originally opened about 1767 for iron by the famous Peter Hasenclever, but it was not one of his successful operations because the ore, smelted in one of his furnaces at Cortlandt, south of Peekskill, proved too sulfurous. Years later, the mine was operated for the sulfur content of the ore rather than for its iron or copper.

The hills of the eastern Hudson Highlands are much like the highlands west of the Hudson; they are geologically similar, although the granites and gneisses include infolded limestones, slates, and quartzites not so much in evidence as on the other side of the river.

A striking feature of the topography of these eastern highlands is the bold escarpment running along the northwest front of the Fishkill Mountains. This abrupt rise, from sea level at the Hudson to 1200 to 1600 feet, is a part of the great fault that bounds the highlands on the north on both sides of the river. The southern boundary of the eastern highlands is not so well defined topographically, as several fault lines extend northeast into the hills along the valleys, the main one in Peekskill Hollow.

South Beacon, rising more than 1600 feet above the country to the north and dwarfing the other hills and mountains to the west and south, commands a superb view. One has to see that view to appreciate fully the significance of the following story of the first land purchase in the Fishkill region.

On February 8, 1682, a license was given to three New Yorkers—Francis Rombout, a distinguished merchant, Jacobus Kipp, and Gulian Ver Planck—to buy a tract of land from the Indians. Under this license they bought, on August 8, 1683, from Nimham, sachem of the Wappingers, all rights to a huge tract, afterward known as the Rombout Patent. In the preliminary bargaining, the Indians agreed to transfer to Rombout all "the land that he could see." Accordingly, Rombout led them to the summit of South Beacon Mountain. With a sweep of his arm northward and eastward, he laid claim to a vast expanse of land covering some 85,000 acres. The Indians held to their bargain for many years. However, in 1740, Chief Daniel Nimham of the Wappingers sought, in a celebrated but unsuccessful lawsuit, to recover the ancient lands of the tribe.

Gulian Ver Planck died before the English patent was issued. Stephanus Van Cortlandt then joined with Rombout in the deal,

while Jacobus Kipp married Ver Planck's widow, thereby neatly tying his share with that of his deceased partner. On October 17, 1685, letters of patent were granted by King James II to Rombout, Kipp, and Van Cortlandt.

The view from South Beacon is a beautiful combination of urban, rural, and mountain features. Beacon lies below, and Newburgh is to be seen across the widening of the river in Newburgh Bay. In the middle ground are the farms and fields, with interspersed woodlots, of Dutchess and Orange counties; beyond them, across the Wallkill Valley, is the long, level-topped line of the Shawangunk Mountains, and, on the far horizon, the sharper outlines of the Catskills. The night view, with the lights of Bear Mountain Bridge, and of cities, towns, and automobiles, is no less attractive. The view northeast is partly blocked by the extension of the ridge in Bald Hill.

The monument on the summit of North Beacon was erected by the Daughters of the American Revolution to mark a place where beacons were lighted during the Revolutionary War by the American troops camped below. It was badly damaged by lightning but was reconstructed in 1928. Coursing up the northwest face of the ridge is the path of the old Mount Beacon Incline Railway, which once ran from the city of Beacon below to a casino on top of the mountain.

Mount Taurus is situated north of the town of Cold Spring and opposite Crows Nest. Taurus, called Bull Hill on the U.S. Geological Survey "West Point" quadrangle, is one of the finest elevations at the northern end of the Hudson Gorge. On the southern face of Mount Taurus is an unsightly scar, the result of a quarrying operation that began in the early 1930s and ended several years afterward. For years, lovers of the scenery of the Hudson hoped that eventually the state of New York would acquire this property to protect it permanently.

HUDSON HIGHLANDS STATE PARK

The first efforts to preserve the scenic beauty of the Storm King–Breakneck section of the Hudson River Valley were made by the Hudson River Conservation Society, which worked to persuade landowners to donate property to the state of New York or to include restrictive clauses in their deeds regarding quarrying, mining, and other land uses detrimental to the natural beauty. In 1938 the society succeeded in having 177 acres on the northwest face of Breakneck Ridge deeded to the New York State Conservation Department as gifts of Rosalie Loew Whitney and the Thomas Nelson estate.

There had been no further additions to the protected areas by 1960, when the Hudson River Conservation Society was joined in its fight to save Storm King by the Nature Conservancy, the Appalachian Highlands Association, and the New York–New Jersey Trail Conference. But in 1965, as large corporate purchases began in the Highlands, the State Council of Parks began planning a program of scenic reservation, which was referred to the temporary Hudson River Valley Study Committee in 1965. By making the Highlands a high priority project in its recommendations to the newly formed Hudson River Valley Commission in 1966, and with continued enthusiasm among conservation groups, the hard work of the State Council of Parks and its supporters succeeded in saving Little Stony Point in 1967. A proposed industrial development for this unique area was halted, and the firm was persuaded to locate elsewhere. Little Stony Point was the first addition to the original acreage and launched the program of acquisition.

In the same year, Jackson Hole Preserve, Inc., a conservation foundation supported primarily by the Rockefeller family, presented a Deed of Trust to New York State for acquisition within the Highlands. This group negotiated agreements with many large landowners and began transferring the agreements to the state in 1968. Within a year the Jackson Hole Preserve grant and matching state funds resulted in the acquisition of more than

2500 acres, including Sugarloaf Mountain, Mount Taurus (Bull Hill), Bannermans Island, the south and west faces of Breakneck Ridge, and several riverfront properties. Even after the preserve money ran out, state acquisition continued, particularly along Route 9D.

Two other parcels are part of Hudson Highlands State Park even though they are separated from the main body of the park. Constitution Marsh, south of Cold Spring, was acquired in 1969 as a wildlife sanctuary and has been effectively operated as an educational facility by the National Audubon Society. And in 1974 William H. Osborn, past president of the Hudson River Conservation Society, donated 656 acres in Garrison for scenic preservation, hiking and riding trails. Including these properties, Hudson Highlands State Park now consists of approximately 3800 acres devoted primarily to scenic preservation.

The New York–New Jersey Trail Conference is responsible for planning, marking, and maintaining the hiking trails. Since 1970 the park has been operated by the Taconic State Park and Recreation Commission, which is planning to build structures on Little Stony Point for swimming, picnicking, fishing, and day-use docking.

TRAILS OF HUDSON HIGHLANDS STATE PARK AND VICINITY

Washburn Trail. Length: 2.3 miles. Blazes: white.

Starting from river level, the Washburn Trail climbs 1400 feet to the top of Mount Taurus. It ends just past the summit where it joins the Notch Trail.

The Washburn Trail starts 200 yards off the intersection of River Road and Route 9D, just north of Cold Spring. There is parking here along the road. The trail starts up an open grassy area below an abandoned quarry. The first views over the Hudson River to Storm King start immediately. They improve with each increase in elevation. From the quarry floor, the trail follows the south rim. It then goes into the woods for 0.3 mile before joining an old trail coming in from the south.

Continuing north, the trail rises steeply, with ever-increasing views of the river valley to the west and south. The trail meets an old carriage road at 1.8 miles. There is no view from the summit of Mount Taurus, but the trail continues on the carriage road to good views north and west to Surprise Lake Valley, Breakneck Ridge, the Shawangunks, and the Catskills. When the

DOWN THE HUDSON FROM COLD SPRING TO BEAR MOUNTAIN & WEST POINT

road swings to the east face of the ridge, there are more views. The trail descends into Bull Gap on a footway that crosses the carriage road twice. The Washburn Trail ends where it joins the Notch Trail, 2.3 miles from the start.

A circular trip is possible by taking the Notch Trail to the remains of Dairy Road, ending on Route 9D at a stone-pillared gate about a quarter mile north of the start.

Notch Trail. Length: 6 miles. Blazes: blue.

The southern trailhead, formerly in Cold Spring, is now the northern end of the Washburn Trail. It crosses through notches in the shoulders of Mount Taurus, Breakneck Ridge, and Sunset Hill. After passing through the valley of Lake Surprise between Taurus and Breakneck, it affords from Sunset Hill a panoramic view of the valley of Melzingah Reservoir, then swings around the reservoir to end at Dutchess Junction on Route 9D.

At its southern end, the trail turns and descends for about 1 mile into the valley of Lake Surprise. After crossing a tributary of Breakneck Brook and then the brook itself on a little wooden bridge, it turns sharply right (northeast) on old Lake Surprise Road, past the ruins of an old dairy farm, skirting the north side of a dammed pond. Near the end of the pond, the trail leaves the road, turning left and beginning its steep climb to the crest of Breakneck Ridge, with fine views in several directions.

Having now joined the Breakneck Ridge Trail (white) in the saddle of the notch, the Notch Trail runs with it, turning right for about 1 mile along the ridgeline, which includes a splendid view. Turning left off the Breakneck Ridge Trail, the Notch Trail comes out high on the north slope of Sunset Hill, into a lovely view of the valley of the Melzingah Reservoir after 0.3 mile.

The remaining distance of 2.7 miles is a long, mostly gentle downhill series of curves and loops, crossing Squirrel Hollow Brook on the hewn stringpieces of an old wooden bridge. Here the yellow-blazed Wilkinson Trail joins on the right, and in 0.2 mile leaves on the left. The Notch Trail now ascends slightly to a notch, and then descends to cross Gordons Brook on stepping-stones 0.5 mile later, immediately turning left on an old wood road to descend the ridge northwest of Melzingah Reservoir and emerge on Route 9D just north of the outlet brook from the reservoir, 1.9 miles north of the tunnel at Breakneck Point.

There is parking for several cars in pull-offs along Route 9D near the trailhead. Except for the climb up Breakneck Ridge and the walk along the ridgeline, the trail is almost entirely on old farm and wood roads.

Breakneck Ridge Trail. Length: 4.7 miles. Blazes: white.

One of the most rugged and scenic of the park trails, the Breakneck Ridge Trail follows an open ridge from the Hudson River to the top of South Beacon Mountain. Its southern end is at the north end of the tunnel on Route 9D about 2 miles north of Cold Spring, where Breakneck Point juts into the Hudson River. There is a small parking area just north of the tunnel and ample parking space a few hundred yards farther north.

The trail ascends the west embankment of the highway and crosses over the tunnel. The steep climb up the ridge is dangerous in slippery weather or in high winds. Each of the knobs which seems to be the top provides a more expansive view, the first 360-degree view being at an altitude of 1220 feet, about 1.2 miles from the highway. For more than 1 mile the trail runs along the ridge from knob to knob, with sags of varying depths between and several splendid views. At 1.5 miles the Breakneck Bypass, blazed in red, intersects on the left.

At 2 miles the blue-blazed Notch Trail enters on the right and travels with the Breakneck Ridge Trail for about 1.2 miles before leaving to the left, descending to cross the Wilkinson Trail and reach Route 9D at 2 miles north of the tunnel.

At 2.7 miles, after a steep, short descent, the trail runs with a wood road for about 20 yards before turning right from it. To the right the road leads to the Notch Trail, and to the left to the Wilkinson Trail north of Sugarloaf.

The Breakneck Ridge Trail climbs to a view at Sunset Point and soon descends steeply to cross Squirrel Hollow Brook and meet the southern end of the Casino Trail and the Wilkinson Trail. (Right, the yellow blazes lead to Hell Hollow, left to Route 9D just north of the tunnel.) The trails climb together for a short distance, then the Breakneck Ridge Trail diverges to the left more steeply uphill via the Devils Ladder to an excellent view. It continues to the fire tower on South Beacon, about 0.6 mile from the brook crossing. This is the highest point in the park. The trail descends to the right of the tower, ending at the Casino Trail.

Because of its steepness, this trail takes about three and a half hours in good weather, plus whatever time is needed to get to one of the highways on the north.

Breakneck Bypass Trail. Length: 0.8 mile. Blazes: red.

This trail provides access to Breakneck Ridge, but it avoids the difficult rocks at the southern end of the Breakneck Ridge Trail. The Bypass Trail begins just over half a mile from the southern end of the Wilkinson Trail. At 0.3 mile there is a view of Sugarloaf and the Hudson. At 0.5 mile the trail uses a much-gullied wood road. After reaching a view point at 0.8 mile, the bypass descends from a rock onto the Breakneck Ridge Trail 1.5 miles from its start.

Casino Trail. Length: 2 miles. Blazes: red.

This trail is important as a connecting trail to others in the area. The casino that gave this trail its name no longer stands, and the old Mount Beacon Incline Railway is no longer running. However, the railway route, still easily visible from Route 9D, climbs steeply up Mount Beacon to the site of the casino, where several communications towers now stand.

There is no direct car access to either end of the trail, the southern trailhead being at the junction of the Wilkinson and Breakneck Ridge trails, and the northern end in an open meadow atop North Beacon Mountain. The northern end can be reached by a combination of the Fishkill Ridge Trail up Dry Brook to the broad and well-traveled access roads to North Beacon Mountain.

At its northern end, the trail follows an old well-worn road, past ruins of summer cottages and side roads to various beacons and towers. At a half mile it forks right and continues uphill, passing the northern end of the Breakneck Ridge Trail at 0.9

mile. The fire tower on South Beacon is about 0.3 mile to the right on the Breakneck Ridge Trail. About 0.3 mile farther, the yellow-blazed Wilkinson Trail crosses the Casino Trail. At 1.6 miles a lookout to the east affords a beautiful view of Lake Valhalla, Cold Spring Reservoir, and the surrounding country.

A sharp right turn at 1.8 miles brings the trail westward through a valley to its end at 2 miles, at the junction of the Wilkinson and Breakneck Ridge trails.

Wilkinson Memorial Trail. Length: 8 miles. Blazes: yellow.

Named after Samuel N. Wilkinson, a tireless worker for trails, the Wilkinson begins on Route 9D, 2 miles above the town of Cold Spring and 0.3 mile above the Breakneck Tunnel. The trail runs generally north and east from its start, over Sugarloaf Mountain, down to Melzingah Reservoir, then gradually climbs through the notch formed by South Beacon Mountain and Sunset Rock to the top of Scofield Ridge. After traversing this ridge, it descends in a series of switchbacks into Hell Hollow, a rocky cleft in the mountain wall. However, it terminates for the present at the Fishkill Ridge Trail, since posted land bars its former path to Route 9 a few miles below Fishkill.

The trail begins by climbing a short access road into a small meadow, crossing it and entering woods along an old road. The trail crosses a small brook at a large oak at a half mile, where the red-blazed Breakneck Bypass Trail begins. This trail is widely used in a variety of circular hikes and as a way of returning from climbing the face of the ridge.

The Wilkinson continues straight ahead, soon turning left and crossing a second brook. From this point it ascends very steeply through woods, open areas and boulders, finally arriving at the summit of Sugarloaf Mountain (900 feet) at 1 mile. From here there are fine views to Mount Taurus to the south, Schunemunk to the west, the Shawangunks and Catskills to the northwest across the Hudson, and Bannermans Castle in ruins on Pollepel Island in the foreground.

Crossing the top of Sugarloaf, the trail descends to the east, skirting the edge of a former farm, with a chimney and the foundation of a burned house on the left. The trail turns left downhill along a rocky dirt road, passing a private house on the left at 2.2 miles. A right turn and an easy climb leads in 0.3 mile to Melzingah Reservoir, which supplies the city of Beacon.

The trail follows the reservoir to the upper end, then climbs gradually beside Squirrel Hollow Brook, crossing the Notch Trail, the Breakneck Ridge Trail in Squirrel Hollow, then the

VIEW NORTH *from* SUGARLOAF MOUNTAIN *through* STORM KING GAP GARRISON, N.Y.

Casino Trail at 4.5 miles. The Wilkinson emerges atop Scofield Ridge (1100 feet) with wide views in all directions, including the New York City skyline forty-five miles away. In this area, the trail may be difficult to follow, as in some places foliage is sparse, with cairns frequently used to mark the way. A yellow-blazed spur to the right leads to a view point. Other excellent views follow as the ridge is traversed.

Leaving the ridge at 6.2 miles, the trail descends fairly steeply to meet Overmountain Road, which leads out to the top of the Hell Hollow cleft. The end of the Fishkill Ridge Trail is reached at 7 miles, just before two long switchbacks descend to the foot of the Hollow, which is strewn with boulders that have been falling off the mountain for centuries. A steep descent of a half mile reaches the valley floor.

However, there is no point in making the descent at present, because posted private land to the east blocks the exit path to Route 9. Until alternate egress can be found, the Wilkinson should be considered to end at the Fishkill Ridge trailhead.

Fishkill Ridge Trail. Length: 5 miles. Blazes: white.

Fishkill Ridge is the northernmost of the Fishkill mountains, extending 3 miles between the Breakneck-Scofield ridge and Route 84. Access to the western terminus in Beacon is via East Main Street. Follow this road east uphill until it curves left (north); at this point follow the continuation of this road, as it branches off to the right past private homes, as far east as possible. Metal water tanks of the Beacon water supply are near the beginning of the trail. Parking may no longer be available on East Main. Local police suggest parking at the ski area at the foot of the old incline railway.

Following the south side of scenic Dry Brook, the trail steadily ascends, reaching falls after about 0.7 mile. This stretch formed the original north end of the Breakneck Ridge Trail. From the falls the trail turns north and climbs steeply to Reservoir Road (a dirt road), passing through a hemlock grove en route. To the left, Reservoir Road is an alternate easy return to Beacon, paralleling the trail; it is especially recommended in snowy or icy conditions, as the trail descent to the falls can be quite hazardous.

At this point the land has been posted by private owners but is open to hikers. After crossing another branch of Reservoir Road, a wood road leading to Hell Hollow, the trail ascends, gently at first, then steeply, to a ledge with fine views of the Hudson Valley. The view at the summit of this knob is more restricted.

After crossing another knob and descending to a hollow, the summit of Lambs Hill (1500 feet) is reached at about 1.5 miles, with further panoramic views. Descending gradually, the trail crosses a wood road, turns briefly south, and emerges at a panorama of Scofield Ridge. Descending east past a jumble of boulders, the trail skirts the southern edge of the ridge, soon emerging at a view point overlooking the Hudson far to the south threading its way between peaks, Hell Hollow, and an opposing summit on Scofield Ridge. Turning the corner, the trail circles past another view of Scofield Ridge before continuing north. After several ups and downs, a view south to Lake Valhalla is reached. The trail soon emerges at an open summit with good views of the valley to the right and Bald Hill ahead. Descending and turning west, the trail recrosses the wood road that it has paralleled, then

ascends Bald Hill. The trail continues on a more level grade, emerging just before the summit on a series of open ledges, with expanded views of the eastern summit and valley. Reentering the woods, the trail soon turns west on the summit of Bald Hill, the highest point on the ridge, marked by two U.S. Coast and Geodetic Survey markers. There is no view here. Descending, the trail reaches a wood road and follows it downhill to the north. Turning sharply east, the trail crosses to the east side of the ridge. From here an old wood road, a continuation of the one to Hell Hollow, is followed south, with little change in altitude or terrain, to the southern terminus at the Wilkinson Trail (yellow). It is no longer possible to reach Route 9 by heading left here, because private land has been posted.

To return to the original starting point, follow the Wilkinson Trail straight ahead (south) past Hell Hollow. Ignoring yellow blazes, stay on the wood road downhill until the white blazes are crossed. From this point either of the return routes mentioned above may be used.

ANTHONYS NOSE

The long, wooded ridges of Canada Hill, 840 feet, and White Rock, 885 feet, and the prominent cone of Sugarloaf, 765 feet, rise from the eastern shore of the Hudson River north of South Mountain Pass and Anthonys Nose. Cloaked in a forest of oaks, hemlocks, and laurel, and concealing several small ponds, these hills are interlaced with a network of unmarked, graded trails that have been used for decades by horsemen and hikers without objection by the property owners.

In recent years much of the private property has passed to public ownership. A corridor along the ridge of Canada Hill is being acquired by the National Park Service to ensure a perma-

nent route for the Appalachian Trail. This corridor will descend from the high point at White Rock to carry the trail east across the valley at the junction of Routes 9 and 403. Sugarloaf and adjoining acreage, including part of White Rock, have become a section of Hudson Highlands State Park. Fortunately, the area remains undeveloped.

Moderate hikes of 5 to 7 miles can be made in circular or figure-eight patterns. The wide wood roads are particularly fine for snowshoeing.

Access to the trails is from Route 9 across from Graymoor, from lay-bys near the Appalachian Trail in South Mountain Pass, and from Route 9D at the base of Sugarloaf.

Sugarloaf is encircled at its base by a 2.3-mile trail that connects with trails from White Rock. A bushwhack from the Sugarloaf Trail to the summit rewards the hiker with a panoramic view of the Hudson and the Highlands. To reach the trail one may park on Route 9D beside the picket fence of St. Francis Retreat House, or walk to this point from the Garrison station of Metro-North Commuter Railroad by following the blacktop road east a half mile and turning south for 1.5 miles on 9D. When the southern end of the long white fence is in sight and the partially open fields at the base of Sugarloaf meet thick woods at the roadside, leave the road, enter the woods, and walk uphill about 100 feet to the wide trail. Follow the trail to the right. Halfway around Sugarloaf, at 1 mile, and just before Osborn Pond, leave the trail and ascend left through brush to the wooded summit, where a faint footpath extends along the ridge to the southern outlook. Here one can appreciate how well Sugarloaf served during the American Revolution as a vantage point for patrolling the Hudson. Return to the trail at the foot of Sugarloaf; circle the hill by turning left onto the trail, passing the pond on the right. Bear left at a fork, and return to the starting point beside Route 9D.

It was here, in the open field at the foot of Sugarloaf, that the Beverly Robinson House stood. During the Revolution the house was used as headquarters by Benedict Arnold, then in command at West Point. On September 25, 1780, while at breakfast, General Arnold received word of the capture of Major John André, his liaison with the British. Arnold fled immediately, ordering his boatman to row him downriver to the safety of the British ship *Vulture,* which was lying in the Hudson near Croton Point. Within minutes General Washington arrived at the house, expecting to meet Arnold. Alexander Hamilton and Lafayette were with him. Here Washington faced the reality of Arnold's treason.

He read the dispatch that told of the detaining of one "John Anderson" at Salem, then the subsequent confession of Major André of his true identity. Before the day was over, Hamilton, sent to intercept Arnold, returned instead with Arnold's letter of explanation to Washington. The next day André was brought to the house under guard. Thus the ghosts of American history haunt this area.

Appalachian Trail. Length: 11 miles. Blazes: white.

This famous trail enters Putnam County near the eastern end of the Bear Mountain Bridge, offering a mixture of wilderness, heights with commanding views, and some road-walking. Traversing the county in a northeasterly direction, it enters Dutchess County after passing through Clarence Fahnestock Memorial State Park.

Leaving the bridge and turning left (north) on Route 9D, a walk of less than 1 mile brings a right turn uphill in woods over a contour of Anthonys Nose, the naming of which involves many conflicting legends. In a short distance, a walk on an unimproved road, part of Camp Smith, leads to woods containing oak, birch, and laurel, with views to the west. A descent through hemlocks opens onto Hemlock Spring campsite at 2.3 miles, with unpaved South Mountain Pass Road providing parking for two or three cars at the junction.

A corridor along the ridge of Canada Hill is being acquired by the National Park Service to ensure a permanent route for the trail. This corridor will descend from the high point at White Rock to carry the Appalachian Trail east across the valley at the junction of Routes 9 and 403.

From here, the trail is in woods and on secondary roads as it winds northeast across the Old West Point Road and Catskill Aqueduct, emerging on the Old Albany Post Road (unpaved) at 2.3 miles from the Route 9 crossing. Continuing left here, the trail passes to the left of Lake Celeste, a private development, reaching a right turn onto unpaved Chapman Road at 3.8 miles. At the dead end, the trail turns left into woods of beech and chestnut, with Canopus Hill to the west. Meeting Canopus Hill Road (unpaved) at 5.8 miles, a downhill jog to the right leads to paved Canopus Hollow Road, which becomes unpaved when followed north past Bell Hollow Road, with its red triple-blaze for Candlewood Hill Trail. Near Gilbert Corners the name of this road changes to Dennytown Road, and the Appalachian Trail enters Fahnestock State Park.

Suggested Reading

Howell, W. T.
Hudson Highlands: Diaries of a Pioneer Hiker
Lenz & Rieckee, New York, 1933

10 · *THE SOUTHERN TACONICS*

(Map 14)

EAST OF the Harlem Valley of New York and west of the Housatonic Valley of Connecticut and Massachusetts rises the Southern Taconic Highland. Seemingly remote from civilization, streams tumble down the highland's forested escarpments cutting scenic ravines and gorges. Much of the highland is protected as a relatively wild area, and its trail system features sweeping views over the highland and adjacent valleys, extending to Mount Greylock to the north, the Catskill Mountains to the west, and the Hudson Highlands to the southwest.

The forest of the Southern Taconics is second or third growth, much of it having been removed in the nineteenth century to provide charcoal for the local iron industry on Mount Riga and at Copake Falls. Large dense stands of mountain laurel *(Kalmia latifolia)* are a beautiful sight when in bloom in late June and early July, but, along with thickets of scrub oak *(Quercus ilicifolia)* found on the upper elevations, they encroach on trails and are a barrier to bushwhacking. Several attractive lakes and ponds bedeck the highland. Riga Lake and South Pond in Connecticut and Plantain Pond in Massachusetts have privately owned shorelines where public roads serve camps and cottages. Bingham Pond, highest in Connecticut at 1894 feet, is a botanically interesting bog.

The Southern Taconic Highland comprises the southernmost part of the main body of the Taconic Mountains and hills that extend north through western Massachusetts and eastern New York into southwestern Vermont, where they reach their highest elevations. The name "Taconic" is a modern rendering of an Indian name variously spelled Taghkannock and Taghkanic.

The area is particularly unusual geologically. About 440 million years ago, a chain of volcanic islands collided with what was then the North American continent, forcing slices of sediment and rock to glide westward from the impact. As a result, the Taconics are a "klippe," or displaced terrain sitting on top of rock originally many miles west of them. This represents one of the major mountain-building episodes in North America, appropriately called the Taconic Orogeny.

The highest and most prominent feature of the Southern Taconics is Massachusetts' Mount Everett, 2602 feet in elevation, formerly called the Dome of the Taconics. Also in the highland is the highest point in Connecticut (2380 feet), located at the Connecticut–Massachusetts line on the south slope of Mount Frissell, which rises from the tableland to a summit in Massachusetts. This is the only place in the United States where the highest point of a state is not the summit of a land feature. About a mile southeast of here is Bear Mountain, the highest summit in Connecticut at 2320 feet. The highest elevation of the western range is Brace Mountain in New York (2311 feet), which is also a takeoff point for hang gliders.

The trail system of the Southern Taconics features two parallel trails running north-south: the 15.5-mile South Taconic Trail following the western range and escarpment, and on the eastern range a 16.5-mile section of the Appalachian Trail. Other hiking routes consist mostly of side trails starting from the valleys on either side of the highland and making considerably greater ascents than those lying on the highland. This system provides for circuit hikes, some of which include stretches of unpaved road, but the system's real beauty lies in its route through the highland's many gorges.

Best known of the highland's scenic gorges is Bashbish Gorge in Massachusetts, with its towering walls and cascading brook ending in splendid Bashbish Falls. Indian legend has it that several Indians plunged to their deaths over the falls, notably a woman named Bash Bish, whose body was never found and who became the spirit of the falls. The gorge is reached by the South Taconic Trail and side trails. Another outstanding gorge is that of Sages Ravine on the eastern escarpment at the Connecticut–Massachusetts line. Although followed in part by the Appalachian Trail, its most scenic and precipitous section is below the trail on private land not open to public passage. Descending the eastern escarpment south of Mount Everett is Race Brook, a notable series of high cascades, paralleled by a blue-blazed trail. On the highland's west side in New York south of Copake Falls, the Robert Brook Trail and Alander Brook Trail lead up deep hemlock-clad ravines to join the South Taconic Trail.

A large part of the New York section of the highland, which lies along the western range and slope, is in Taconic State Park. The park has outdoor recreation and camping facilities at its Copake Falls area south of Hillsdale, and at its Rudd Pond area north of Millerton, both at the base of the highland. Cottages and cabins are also available for rent at the Copake Falls area. The season is from mid May until late October at Rudd Pond and until December at Copake Falls.

The Connecticut part of the highland is loosely called Mount Riga or the Riga plateau, named after a nineteenth-century community of ironworkers at South Pond (Forge Pond) on the highland, where a restored iron furnace can be seen. Most of this section is owned by Mount Riga, Inc., a private conservation-minded body, but the National Park Service has acquired 1175 acres from this group as a protective corridor for the Appalachian Trail. In addition, the state owns an area of woodland on the eastern slope above Route 41, called Mount Riga State Park (undeveloped), while the Appalachian Mountain Club owns 125 acres adjacent to the Massachusetts line.

The Massachusetts section is larger than that of New York or Connecticut and is occupied by the Town of Mount Washington, which has no post office or commercial establishments and a year-round population of less than a hundred. Here the hiking trails are mostly in Mount Washington State Forest, including the Mount Everett Reservation, and in the corridor for the Appalachian Trail being acquired by the state of Massachusetts and the National Park Service.

Road access to the highland from New York on the west starts as Route 344, which goes east from Route 22 through the village of Copake Falls, enters the scenic ravine of Bashbish Brook, and becomes Falls Road in Massachusetts. Climbing steeply past Bashbish Falls, it connects with West Street and East Street in Mount Washington. From East Street an unpaved state forest road climbs east in Mount Everett Reservation to a parking-picnic area at beautiful Guilder Pond, which at 2042 feet is one of Massachusetts' highest bodies of water. From here the road ascends steeply to a parking area with a splendid view, almost at the summit of Mount Everett.

The area is covered by the following topographic maps of both the U.S. Geological Survey and the New York State Department of Transportation, scale of 1:24,000: Sharon, Connecticut (USGS only); Bashbish Falls, Massachusetts; Copake, New York; Hillsdale, New York; and Egremont, Massachusetts.

South Taconic Trail. Length: 15.6 miles. Blazes: white.

Lying mostly in Taconic State Park and Mount Washington State Forest, this highly scenic trail along the western escarpment and range of the Southern Taconics may be divided into two sections. The longer southern section starts in New York's Harlem Valley about 5 miles north of Millerton and ends at Route 344 east of Copake Falls village, while the northern section continues northward to the place where Route 23 goes over a low point in the Taconic range just east of the New York–Massachusetts line. Plans to extend the trail farther south along the western edge of the highland and down to Rudd Pond of Taconic State Park have been delayed by private land problems.

Southern Section (Rudd Pond Farms to Route 344, 9.75 miles).

To reach the southern end of the trail, drive 5.5 miles north on Route 22 from the traffic light at Millerton, New York; go right on White House Crossing Road to its end; go left on Rudd Pond Road for a quarter mile; turn right (east) on a paved road into Rudd Pond Farms, a residential development, and follow it around to the east side of the development to a parking area on the left at the end of a field.

From the parking area at an elevation of 950 feet, the trail goes east along the edge of the field, enters the woods, and starts to ascend the western escarpment of the Southern Taconic Highland. A steep, rough section begins at 0.4 mile, the trail passing a high waterfall and ascending cliffs along switchbacks with open views westward. At 0.7 mile the trail turns left, crossing a short red-blazed side trail that passes an attractive pool in a brook before climbing along the escarpment to fine views over the Harlem Valley.

The South Taconic Trail continues north on the escarpment with more views west, then climbs South Brace Mountain with views southward. At 1.4 miles the trail turns left at a junction, where a turquoise trail of uncertain maintenance leads south to the northern tip of Riga Lake in Connecticut. Continuing, the South Taconic Trail reaches an open area on South Brace, which offers an excellent view southward over the Riga plateau section of the highland, featuring Riga Lake and South Pond beyond it.

Cross the open area with the summit of South Brace (2304 feet) to the right, descend to a saddle, and ascend along the attractive open crest of Brace Mountain to its summit (2311 feet) at 1.9 miles. The trail's highest point, this summit is marked by a large pile of stones that has given Brace Mountain the local name of Monument Mountain. There are splendid views, including Bear Mountain of Connecticut on the east and Mount Frissell in Massachusetts on the northeast.

Descend north on a wood road to a junction at 2.2 miles, where the Brace Mountain Trail, a wood road, leads right or southeast 1.6 miles to the Mount Washington Road on the highland in Connecticut. The Appalachian Trail on the east can be reached by side trails from this road. Continuing north 200 yards to another junction, the Southern Taconic goes left from the wood road, while the Mount Frissell Trail goes right.

Proceeding along an open crest with fine views, the trail enters Massachusetts. Regaining the wood road, it continues north on a route previously called the State Line Trail. At 3 miles a blue-blazed side trail goes northeast to the Ashley Hill Trail, which connects with the Mount Washington State Forest Headquarters on the north and with the Brace Mountain Trail on the south. At 4.5 miles the red-blazed Robert Brook Trail goes left.

The South Taconic Trail continues north and at 5 miles, where it curves left to descend, the Alander Loop Trail forks right. From this fork, the South Taconic Trail descends into New York from Massachusetts, and crosses Alander Brook on a bridge. At 5.2 miles it gradually climbs right from the wood road, and then ascends steeply up the southwest shoulder of Alander Mountain, reaching the open crest at 5.7 miles. The trail reenters Massachusetts at a boundary marker and goes northeast featuring fine views. At 6 miles the west summit of Alander Mountain (2240 feet) is reached, where there are foundations of a former fire tower. A few yards beyond, the blue-blazed Alander Loop Trail leads right.

The South Taconic Trail goes north along the remainder of Alander's open crest, a splendidly scenic section. Eastward is the Town of Mount Washington, with Mount Everett on the eastern escarpment the dominant feature. At 6.4 miles descend into the woods and continue north along the ridge. At 6.7 miles there is a view of a beautiful secluded valley on the west with Mount Washington beyond. Reach Bashbish Mountain, the high point of the northern section of the ridge, at 7.9 miles and descend to a lookout point with Cedar Mountain across Bashbish Gorge to the north. Descend steeply to a level stretch where, at 8.2 miles, the Bashbish Falls Bypass Trail goes left. The main trail goes right, descending through a hemlock forest to the edge of a high cliff over Bashbish Gorge at 8.5 miles, where there is a protective cable fence.

A rugged 0.2-mile shortcut can be taken by descending left by the fence steeply on a section of the blue-blazed Bashbish Gorge Trail. The Bashbish Gorge Trail descends by the fence to Bashbish Brook, then crosses the brook just above the gorge and climbs very steeply northward by the fence to a rocky pinnacle, which has views over the gorge and the Harlem Valley. From here one may descend east a short distance to the upper Bashbish parking area, or continue on the blue trail and descend steeply by the fence more directly to Bashbish Falls, regaining the South Taconic Trail by either route.

Continuing along the fence, the South Taconic Trail provides a spectacular glimpse into the gorge, and descends for a short, very steep pitch to Bashbish Brook above the gorge. Go a short way upstream and ford the brook, which is difficult in times of high water. From the other side the trail ascends a dirt road to the upper Bashbish parking area on Falls Road in Massachusetts at 8.7 miles. Falls Road goes to West Street in Mount Washington, and in the other direction it descends steeply westward into New York where it becomes Route 344.

The South Taconic Trail crosses the edge of the parking area and descends westward through a handsome hemlock stand, with state forest blue blazes supplementing the white blazes. At 9 miles reach the broad trail on the north side of Bashbish Brook, with splendid Bashbish Falls lying to the left. Go right on the broad trail, passing a service road on the right, entering New York, and following Bashbish Brook westward to the lower parking area on Route 344 at 9.75 miles. This road goes west to Copake Falls, New York, and Route 22, and eastward it becomes Falls Road.

One may walk to the nearby Copake Falls area of Taconic State Park, where camping is available, by crossing Cedar Brook on Route 344 next to the parking area, ascending a red trail on the right to a wood road, and going left (northwest) on it to the camping area. The entrance for cars is from Route 344 at Copake Falls.

Northern Section (Route 344 to Route 23, 5.9 miles).

From the entrance to the lower Bashbish parking area, at an elevation of 725 feet, cross Route 344 and hike north through hemlocks. The trail goes up the east side of Cedar Brook in a ravine, passes a flume of the brook with cascades, and crosses the brook five times. After the last crossing at 1 mile, the trail ascends a steep slope northward to a junction with the Sunset Rock Trail, whose red state park markers outnumber the white blazes of the South Taconic Trail along this stretch. Turn right and go north, ascending to an open summit at 1.7 miles, where a narrow side trail with red markers leads left a short distance to Sunset Rock, with a good view westward from an elevation of 1788 feet.

The trail continues northeast through thick scrub growth. Here it is also called the Gray Birch Trail and has yellow state park markers in addition to the white blazes. At 2.1 miles turn left at a junction and shortly reach Sunset Rock Road a few yards west of the Massachusetts–New York line.

Go left (northwest) on the road for 230 yards and at 2.25 miles turn right onto a footpath and cross a brook by an old springhouse. Climb Prospect Hill northeastward through dense scrub oak and mountain laurel, and at 2.6 miles reach the summit (1919 feet) in an open area with good views. Turn left at the Massachusetts–New York boundary monument and reach an open ledge with an outstanding view north, west, and south, including the Harlem Valley and the Town of Hillsdale, New York.

The trail enters Massachusetts, descends Prospect Hill gradually with a good view northward at 2.9 miles, and follows a lower crest line. Reenter New York and at 3.6 miles reach an open section along the edge of the escarpment with pleasant views of the valley on the southwest. The trail continues to Mount Fray, parallels its crest, and at 4 miles turns right and climbs a short distance to the crest, with a fine view from an open area. Go north along the broad summit of Mount Fray, reaching the 1900-foot level. Open areas in scrub growth offer distant views, including Mount Greylock on the northeast. From here on, the trail is on privately owned land, mostly Catamount Ski Area.

At 4.2 miles turn right on Ridge Run, a broad ski trail descending along the ridgeline. A short distance to the left is an area with splendid views, including two upper chairlift stations of the ski area. Follow Ridge Run eastward for 0.9 mile, reentering Massachusetts and, near the end, climbing right a few yards to a pleasant view of Jug End Valley and ridge. At the end of Ridge Run, at the top of the ski slope, is a view of the ski area.

The trail then climbs steeply eastward a short stretch and continues along the wooded crest, turning north and descending. Entering a driveway at 5.7 miles, the trail meets another dirt road coming in from the left, finally turning left for 65 yards to reach Route 23, where it crosses the height of land. This is the northern terminus of the South Taconic Trail at 5.9 miles (15.6 miles from its southern end).

A parking area is on the south side of Route 23, 150 yards to the left (southwest). Westward on Route 23 is Hillsdale, New York, and eastward is South Egremont, Massachusetts.

Following is a description of access trails to the South Taconic Trail.

Brace Mountain Trail. Length: 1.6 miles. No blazes.

Providing the easiest access to scenic Brace Mountain, this unmarked wood road on the highland extends from the Mount Washington Road in Connecticut northwest to the South Taconic Trail in New York. The trailhead, with space for parking, is on the west side of the road 2 miles north of the dam at South Pond, with a red gate barring access to the trail by vehicles. Proceed along the wood road through mountain laurel and cross Monument Brook at a half mile, the trail's lowest point at 1850 feet. At 1.3 miles an overgrown trail forks right to a nearby Connecticut–New York boundary monument and beyond. In a few yards the Brace Mountain Trail enters New York at a stream and climbs steeply west up Brace Mountain on a stony route, the

Ashley Hill Trail coming in on the right from Massachusetts. Continue climbing up to the crest, where the trail ends at the South Taconic Trail just north of Brace Mountain's peak. Turning left on the South Taconic Trail, one climbs 0.2 mile to the open summit of the mountain at 2311 feet.

Mount Frissell Trail. Length: 2.15 miles. Blazes: red-orange.

This is an especially rewarding trail, lying on the highland in three states, going over two summits, having fine views, and visiting the highest point in Connecticut, as well as the tri-state boundary point. It also takes the hiker through dense mountain laurel, scrub oak, and gray birch. The trail starts from Mount Washington Road–East Street at the Connecticut–Massachusetts line (1830 feet in elevation), where there is limited parking. Go northwest in Massachusetts along a wood road, turning left onto a footpath that leads into Connecticut. Ascend Round Mountain very steeply, with fine views from its open crest. Passing over the summit (2296 feet) at 0.7 mile, the trail descends northwest into Massachusetts, reaching the saddle between Round Mountain and Mount Frissell. The trail ascends Mount Frissell steeply to ledges with an easterly view, and then passes its summit (2453 feet) at 1.2 miles, marked by a cairn and a trail register off to the right. Descend the south slope of Mount Frissell, and just before the Massachusetts–Connecticut boundary is an especially fine view point over the highland. Turn right at the boundary and in 30 yards reach the highest point of Connecticut (2380 feet). The trail continues west along the state line, descending Mount Frissell with more good views. On level terrain the trail reaches the tri-state boundary point at 1.7 miles, where an 1898 granite monument bears the name of New York and Massachusetts but omits Connecticut on the southeast side. The trail continues westward in New York, crossing the Ashley Hill Trail, a wood road, ending at the South Taconic Trail by a scenic open section overlooking the Harlem Valley. Turning left on the latter trail, it is 0.3 mile to the summit of Brace Mountain.

Alander Brook Trail. Length: 1.4 miles. Blazes: blue.

Largely a wood road, this trail ascends to the South Taconic Trail from New York's Harlem Valley on the west, following a deep ravine. The trailhead, where cars may be parked, is on unpaved Under Mountain Road 0.8 mile east of its junction with Route 22, which is almost 4 miles south of Route 22's junction with Route 344 at Copake Falls. The trailhead lies a little north of Boston Corner, famed for having been a lawless no-man's-land in the 1850s when the area was being ceded by Massachusetts to New York. Just beyond the trailhead, Under Mountain Road turns right and goes to Rudd Pond Road.

The Alander Brook Trail starts north in woods next to a field, and in 150 yards the Robert Brook Trail goes right from it. The Alander Brook Trail continues north along the base of the highland, and in 0.75 mile crosses Alander Brook and turns right from the wood road. Ascending through mountain laurel, it turns right onto another wood road at 1 mile and climbs along the hemlock-clad ravine of Alander Brook. The trail ends where its blue blazes meet the white blazes of the South Taconic Trail, which comes from the opposite direction and turns north from here off the wood road.

A scenic loop hike would be to turn left here on the South Taconic Trail and ascend to Alander Mountain's west summit, then go right on the blue-blazed Alander Loop Trail, left on the South Taconic Trail, and right on the Robert Brook Trail to descend to the starting point. Total distance is 5 miles, with a 1500-foot ascent of Alander, and one should add another 1.4 miles north along the splendid crest of Alander and return, before taking the Alander Loop Trail.

Robert Brook Trail. Length: 1.1 miles. Blazes: red.

The Robert Brook Trail begins at the Alander Brook Trail, 150 yards from its western trailhead. The Robert Brook Trail ascends eastward along the ravine of Robert Brook on a rocky route of an eighteenth-century road; it turns north to an 1898 state boundary monument and follows the Massachusetts–New York line up to a second monument. It continues as a narrow trail in Massachusetts to the South Taconic Trail, having made an ascent of 1050 feet.

Bashbish Falls Bypass Trail. Length: 1.1 miles. Blazes: red-orange.

This trail climbs 950 feet southeastward from the lower Bashbish parking area on Route 344 in New York to the South Taconic Trail on Bashbish ridge. Bypassing 1.6 miles of the South Taconic Trail, it avoids fording Bashbish Brook, but misses Bashbish Falls and Gorge, though offering a fine lookout from a short spur.

From the brook side of the parking area, the trail descends the embankment to an unpaved state park road, which it follows for 175 yards, initially crossing Bashbish Brook on a bridge. Turning right from the road, it passes a shower house on the left before ascending by a brook. The trail curves left on a wood road from the brook at a point where another trail continues ahead upstream toward an old dam and a series of falls above it. The Bypass Trail climbs gradually and then more steeply as it swings east and north. At a junction on a western spur of Bashbish ridge, turn right. Here a side path goes left 150 yards to a precipitous rock outcropping with a beautiful 180-degree view westward. The trail ascends east another 0.15 mile into Massachusetts to the South Taconic Trail.

Sunset Rock Trail. Length: 1.75 miles. Markers: red.

The Sunset Rock Trail starts from an unpaved road at the southeast end of the campground and ascends as a wood road east and north through conifers, an access trail coming in from the left from the northern part of the campground. The broad trail climbs along a crest line in a beautiful section of white pines, and reaches a fork where the yellow-marked Gray Birch Trail goes left. Continue northeast on the red trail, which narrows and levels out, with the white-blazed South Taconic Trail joining it from the right. Ascend an eroded route to an open summit with views at 1.75 miles. Take a short spur left to Sunset Rock, where at the edge of the escarpment there is a good view west over the Harlem Valley.

Gray Birch Trail. Length: 1.9 miles. Markers: yellow.

The route above continues as both the Gray Birch and South Taconic trails, and in conjunction with the Sunset Rock route forms a loop of more than 4.5 miles. Continue northeast through thick scrub growth and turn left to a junction with unpaved Sunset Rock Road. Go left (northwest) on the road. In 230 yards the South Taconic Trail goes right, reaching the top of Prospect Hill in 0.4 mile with a splendid view from the top of Prospect Hill. The Gray Birch continues along the road and after a steep descent diverges left. It proceeds southwest and south along level terrain, then climbs to a junction at the fork mentioned in the Sunset Rock description. Retrace on Sunset Rock Trail to the campground.

Trails from Mount Washington State Forest Headquarters

A trail network on the highland in Massachusetts, connecting with the South Taconic Trail, starts from the Mount Washington State Forest Headquarters on East Street in the Town of Mount Washington. The two main components are the Alander Mountain Trail, which ascends to its summit, and the Ashley Hill

Trail, which goes south to Connecticut. Both trails are wood roads, except the upper part of the former. There are three side trails, two between the two main trails and one connecting the Ashley Brook Trail with the South Taconic Trail. Attractive hemlock groves are a feature of this area.

The state forest headquarters can be reached from New York on the west by following Route 344 through Copake Falls and its continuation (Falls Road) onto the highland in Massachusetts. At the end of Falls Road turn right (south) on West Street and drive to its end at East Street. The headquarters is on East Street just south of this junction. Hikers park by the trailhead beyond the office.

Alander Mountain Trail. Length: 2.75 miles. Blazes: blue.

The Alander Mountain Trail goes from here westward across a field and through woods. It descends another field and crosses a brook near a vacant house on the right. A little beyond, the Charcoal Pit Trail goes left, ascending southwestward almost a mile to the Ashley Hill Trail. The Alander Mountain Trail continues to a fork at 0.75 mile, where it goes right, the left fork being the start of the Ashley Hill Trail. The trail descends a steep pitch to cross Ashley Hill Brook at 1450 feet, the trail's lowest point, and then climbs gradually westward. At 1.5 miles a side trail climbs left to a state forest primitive camping area, going through the camping area to the Ashley Hill Trail. The Alander Mountain Trail continues westward, becomes narrower and steeper, and climbs to a small notch just below the top of the mountain. It passes a state forest cabin and ends in the notch at the Alander Loop Trail at 2.75 miles. The latter trail climbs right a short distance to the South Taconic Trail and the west summit of Alander, and to the left it goes to the east summit and beyond. Both summits at 2240 feet are in a highly scenic area.

Ashley Hill Trail. Length: 3.5 miles. Blazes: blue.

The Ashley Hill Trail, from its start at the Alander Mountain Trail, climbs southwest along the picturesque, steep ravine of Ashley Hill Brook. In 0.6 mile the side trail from the Alander Mountain Trail and the primitive camping area comes in acutely from the right; at 0.9 mile the Charcoal Pit Trail comes in from the left. The Ashley Hill Trail continues southward on relatively level terrain and at 2.1 miles it turns left at a junction. Continuing generally southwest, it crosses Ashley Hill Brook, climbing 200 feet and descending a short way at the end to reach the South Taconic Trail. The Ashley Hill Trail reaches the state line at 3.5

miles at a boundary monument. It continues south a short distance into Connecticut without blazes, where it is crossed by the red-blazed Mount Frissell Trail, and descends to end at the Brace Mountain Trail.

The Appalachian Trail. Length: 16.5 miles. Blazes: white.

The Southern Taconic section of the Appalachian Trail extends along the eastern range of the highland in Connecticut and Massachusetts. It has rough sections, especially in Massachusetts, but has splendid views from Lions Head and Bear Mountain in Connecticut, and from Race Mountain, Mount Everett, and Jug End ridge in Massachusetts.

The trail is divided into the Connecticut and Massachusetts sections, managed respectively by the Connecticut and Berkshire chapters of the Appalachian Mountain Club. Backpackers hiking the Connecticut section should camp within the designated camping zones, one of which has a shelter (Brassie Brook). In the Massachusetts section one may camp in the trail corridor until specific camping zones are designated.

Connecticut Section.

The trail starts from a relocated site on the west side of Route 41 (Under Mountain Road) 0.8 mile north of the junction of Routes 41 and 44 in Salisbury village. Parking for hikers is available here. The trail goes west in woods and then ascends a wood road on a switchback, with a camping zone on the left at 0.2 mile. The trail climbs northwest along the wooded slope, turning southwest before climbing steeply up the ridge of Lions Head. At 2 miles the trail goes right at a junction.

At 2.2 miles the blue-blazed Lions Head Bypass goes straight ahead while the Appalachian Trail turns right and climbs a steep pitch to the south lookout of Lions Head at 2.25 miles. Here is a splendid view south and east over the Housatonic Valley. Continuing north along Lions Head summit (1738 feet, an ascent of 1000 feet from Route 41), it passes the Bypass Trail on the left before reaching the north lookout at 2.4 miles. Here is a view featuring Bear Mountain and Mount Everett on the north. The trail descends, and at 2.7 miles the blue-blazed Bald Peak Trail goes left 1.1 miles over Bald Peak to the Mount Washington Road.

The Appalachian Trail continues north on relatively level terrain, crossing Ball Brook at 3.6 miles, where there is a designated camping zone. The Bond shelter is reached at 4.2 miles, nicely situated to the right of the trail above the south branch of Brassie

Brook. At 4.7 miles the blue-blazed Under Mountain Trail goes right and descends 1.9 miles to Route 41. In another 0.2 mile the Appalachian Trail turns right from a wood road. This road, called Bear Mountain Road, goes 0.9 mile northwest from here on level terrain to the Mount Washington Road at a point 0.3 mile south of the Connecticut–Massachusetts line.

The trail makes a steady 430-foot ascent of Bear Mountain through stunted growth, with views southward from ledges. At 5.6 miles is a collapsed stone monument near the summit. Erected in 1885, it was unfortunately vandalized in the 1970s and is to be stabilized as a permanent relic. From here is a good view east over the Housatonic Valley, including Connecticut's Twin Lakes. A short distance west of the trail is the open-summit Bear Mountain at 2320 feet, the highest summit in Connecticut, with broad views over the highland.

The trail descends the north slope of the mountain very steeply. At 6.2 miles it goes right from a wood road, the Northwest Road, which goes three quarters of a mile west from here to the Mount Washington Road just south of the Connecticut–Massachusetts line. The trail enters Massachusetts, the Paradise Lane Trail coming in from the right from the Under Mountain Trail, and descends through hemlocks to Sages Ravine Brook. One follows the cascading brook eastward downstream for two thirds of a mile through the upper part of Sages Ravine, an attractive area that is a designated camping zone. Cross the brook at 7 miles, the end of the Connecticut section.

Massachusetts Section.

From the Sages Ravine Brook crossing, the Appalachian Trail ascends eastward, levels off, and turns north from Sages Ravine. At 0.7 mile a side route goes right, descending as a wood road and driveway to Route 41 a little north of the Massachusetts–Connecticut line, a hiking route only for emergencies, as it is partly private. The trail ascends an eroded stretch and crosses Bear Rock Brook at 1.25 miles. To the right of the trail the brook goes through an attractive area with hemlocks, where hikers have camped, and then drops down the escarpment as Bear Rock Falls, with a good view from the top.

The trail ascends along the edge of the escarpment with occasional lookouts on the right. At 2 miles it emerges onto the open cliffs of Race Mountain, which it follows for a quarter mile, with sweeping views eastward over the Housatonic Valley. The trail then ascends to the summit of Mount Race (2365 feet) at 2.5 miles, a bare rock with a 360-degree panoramic view. The trail descends

Mount Race steadily to the notch between it and Mount Everett where, at 3.7 miles, the blue-blazed Race Brook Trail goes right. The latter passes a camping area by the headwaters of Race Brook, descending 1.5 miles to Route 41 to pass a series of beautiful waterfalls and cascades of Race Brook.

The Appalachian Trail ascends steeply 700 feet, with good views southward, to the summit of Mount Everett at 4.6 miles. An open area with scrub growth, it has a fire tower that is closed to the public, and broad, distant views, including New York's Catskill Mountains on the western horizon. The trail turns right here and goes along the east slope of Everett with fine views eastward, descending past the upper parking area of the Mount Everett Reservation road, which has an excellent view and a stone shelter not authorized for camping. The trail descends to cross the road at an angle and reaches the reservation's picnic area at 5.2 miles. Beyond, a red-blazed trail goes left, following a beautiful route around Guilder Pond.

The trail proceeds northeast and north, descending a rough route through dense mountain laurel. At 6.4 miles the blue-blazed Elbow Trail goes right and descends 1.2 miles to Berkshire School west of Route 41. The Appalachian Trail reaches the beginning of Jug End ridge and follows its narrow crest with peaks or knolls of descending elevation, starting with Mount Bushnell at 7 miles. This is an especially attractive stretch of trail with nice views. At the north end of the ridge crest, at 8.7 miles, a prominent rock outcropping offers a beautiful view, including Jug End Valley on the west. An unmarked trail leads left here and descends southwest to a wood road going along that valley. Turning right on it one goes north to Jug End Road at a point just east of the Jug End resort.

The trail swings abruptly right, passes another open view from a cliff, and descends roughly and steeply southeastward over rock ledges, moderating somewhat to reach unpaved Jug End Road in the Housatonic Valley at 9.5 miles. From this north end of the Southern Taconic section of the trail, it is 0.8 mile left on Jug End Road and the Avenue to the Mount Washington Road west of South Egremont village, and 1.6 miles right to Route 41.

Lions Head Trail. Length: 0.5 mile. Blazes: blue.

The shortest access to Lions Head, this is the former route of the Appalachian Trail. One drives up almost to the end of Bunker Hill Road northwest of Salisbury village, Connecticut, and parks on the right below the sign. At the road's end, turn left and go through a pasture, descending moderately to cross a brook.

Ascending through woods and fields of ferns northwestward, the trail reaches the Appalachian Trail on the ridge, which comes in from the right and proceeds ahead 0.2 mile to the top of Lions Head, an ascent of 600 feet from Bunker Hill Road.

Bald Peak Trail. Length: 1.1 miles. Blazes: blue.

The trail starts from a parking area on the west side of Mount Washington Road on the highland in Connecticut, a half mile north of Mount Riga Road and South Pond dam. The trail climbs eastward 120 feet in 0.15 mile to the top of 2010-foot Bald Peak, an open rocky knoll with a fine wide view over the highland. Continuing another mile eastward over some rough terrain with a net descent of 400 feet, the trail reaches the Appalachian Trail a half mile northwest of Lions Head.

Under Mountain Trail. Length: 1.9 miles. Blazes: blue.

This popular feeder trail climbs more than 1000 feet to the Appalachian Trail, providing the shortest access from the Housatonic Valley to Bear Mountain and the adjacent highland. The trail is wet in the spring.

The prominent trailhead is on Route 41 (Under Mountain Road), 3.4 miles north of Salisbury, Connecticut, and a short distance south of Beaver Dam Road. From the parking area on the west side of the road, the trail goes west across partly open terrain, enters the woods, and ascends. At 1.1 miles the blue-blazed Paradise Lane Trail goes right. The Under Mountain Trail reaches the Appalachian Trail at a point a half mile north of the Bond shelter and 0.9 mile south of the summit of Bear Mountain.

Paradise Lane Trail. Length: 2.1 miles. Blazes: blue.

The Paradise Lane Trail begins from the Under Mountain Trail 1.1 miles from its trailhead on Route 41. The Paradise Lane Trail turns left near its start, heading north along the highland. It passes the east side of Bear Mountain in a swampy area, joining the Appalachian Trail in Massachusetts just north of the state line, where the latter descends to Sages Ravine.

Race Brook Trail. Length: 1.5 miles. Blazes: blue.

This popular but steep trail starts at the parking turnout on the west side of Route 41 a few yards north of Salisbury Road, which goes east to Sheffield, Massachusetts. From the parking area, cross the brook and pasture, then enter the woods westward. After a moderate ascent, cross Race Brook and start a very steep ascent of the escarpment, paralleling a series of beautiful, high falls and cascades of the brook. Above the falls the trail follows the brook along gradual or level terrain, passing a camping area just before reaching the Appalachian Trail in the saddle between Mounts Race and Everett. The ascent to here is 1150 feet, and continuing north on the Appalachian Trail to the summit of Everett it totals 1850 feet, the highest ascent in the Southern Taconics.

Elbow Trail. Length: 1.2 miles. Blazes: blue.

This trail is reached by driving west from Route 41, at a point 3.5 miles south of its junction with Route 23 at South Egremont, into the grounds of Berkshire School at the base of the highland. Hikers may park during the day behind the school's Stanley Hall. Ascend a driveway northwestward and continue on a wood road that angles up the escarpment with a long switchback (the "Elbow"), a route that was an eighteenth-century wagon road. A newer trail parallels the first part of this route. After passing a camping area, reach the Appalachian Trail at a point 1.2 miles north of the Mount Everett Reservation road and picnic area. Jug End ridge lies to the right.

Part III

NEW YORK CITY AND LONG ISLAND

11 · PERIMETER PARKS AND STATEN ISLAND

SOLITUDE AND open space are in short supply within the New York City limits, yet a number of places along its perimeter still offer a respite from the bustle of the metropolis. Most of these walks are doubly rewarding for their geological or historical significance.

Walkers can choose among sites of Revolutionary skirmishes, the famous Jamaica Bay Wildlife Refuge and other valuable wetlands, and the parklands and hills of Staten Island.

FORT TRYON AND INWOOD HILL PARKS

Take the No. 1 subway to Dyckman Street or the "A" train to 190th Street and walk west toward the Hudson. At any time of year the broad views of the river are a reasonable substitute for open spaces. Several paths run through Fort Tryon Park to The Cloisters, a branch of the Metropolitan Museum, with its magnificent collection of medieval art. Other paths descend to the river and run south toward the George Washington Bridge. The little red lighthouse beneath the bridge marks the spot where sunken ships and chained logs were anchored during the Revolution in an attempt to prevent the passage of British ships.

Inwood Hill Park occupies the northwest corner of Manhattan Island, from Dyckman Street up to Spuyten Duyvil, once one of the main centers of Indian population in the area. Here there was shelter from the icy winds that made Manhattan's rocky ridge inhospitable, a good freshwater spring, and level planting fields. There was an ample supply of fish, especially shad, and the surrounding forests provided bear, deer, and beaver.

To reach the Indian rock shelters from the top of Inwood Hill,

THE
INDIAN
CAVES
ON
MAN:
:HAT:
:TAN
SHORAKAPKOK
·INWOOD·
Dickinson
1923
NECK
ORNAMENT
(STONE)
ARROW
HEAD
(FLINT)
PIPE
BOWL
HARPOON
POINT; BONE
PIPE STEM WITH TOOTHMARKS

follow the ravine down the east side of the ridge, past the great glacial potholes in the exposed rock, and through the grove of spicebush. Quantities of oyster shells found here were the most obvious evidence of Indian habitation. The village was called Shorakapkok, "as far as the Sitting-Down Place." Artifacts found here may be seen at the Museum of the American Indian, Broadway and 155th Street.

The bedrock visible in the heights of Fort Tryon and Inwood Hill is primarily Ordovician-age Manhattan schist. On the Bronx side of Spuyten Duyvil, Inwood marble appears in the cliff faces.

PELHAM BAY PARK

Most of this park lies between the Hutchinson River and Long Island Sound, and is accessible from the Hutchinson River Parkway or Pelham Parkway. The last stop of the No. 6 train of the Lexington Avenue subway is 2 miles southwest of the Hunters Island section of the park.

Hunters Island, the area north of Orchard Beach, is of interest for its great trees and jutting rocks, as well as its tide pools, salt marshes, and glacial boulders. Actually a peninsula, the area was a favorite place of the Indians. Their conference rock, "Mishow," located near a cove at the eastern end of the beach boardwalk, is now almost buried. "Gray Mare," an unusually formed erratic, lies off the northwestern part of the "island." In addition to waterfowl, the park harbors great horned, long-eared, and barred owls.

Another sanctuary in this two-thousand-acre park is the Thomas Pell Wildlife Refuge, located along the Hutchinson River and west of the golf courses. From the Split Rock clubhouse, walk toward the river on paved paths and a bridle path, which traverse much of the area. The tract includes woodland, salt marsh, and a tidal estuary.

The refuge is notable as the site of the Battle of Pells Point (1776), in which Colonel Glover and 750 men held off the British under Lord Howe long enough for Washington to lead his troops north to White Plains. Near Split Rock—a huge cracked boulder —was the home of the early religious dissenter Anne Hutchinson, who was murdered here by Indians in 1643.

ALLEY POND PARK

Located in eastern Queens amid some of the busiest highways in New York, this area contains fresh and salt water marshes, oak uplands, and glacial kettles. One kettle, Oakland Lake, is stocked with black bass. Near the Winchester Boulevard parking lot at the south end of the park is a pedestrian path that is a remnant of the original Vanderbilt Motor Parkway. A guide for a number of very short trails is available at the Alley Pond Environmental Center, 228-06 Northern Boulevard, Douglaston, N.Y. 11363. Located just east of the Cross Island Parkway intersection, the center maintains trails and conducts educational programs that are a good way to introduce young walkers to a variety of habitats.

Among the species that survive in the park are muskrat, flying squirrel, opossum, and raccoon. Migratory waterfowl frequent the wetlands. North of Northern Boulevard, a paved pedestrian path along the Cross Island Parkway provides a pleasant walk of 3 miles along Little Neck Bay to Fort Totten. About halfway, an overpass leads to Crocheron Park, with a small pond just off the parkway.

JAMAICA BAY WILDLIFE REFUGE

A part of the Gateway National Recreation Area, created in 1972, the refuge dates to 1953, when the New York City Parks Department set aside 9170 of the bay's 14,000 acres and impounded ponds on either side of Cross Bay Boulevard. The west pond has walks around it and is adjacent to the Gateway Visitors Center, where walkers must obtain a permit. The larger east pond has no path but is more popular with the birds.

Hundreds of thousands of birds come to the sanctuary. The breeding water birds include great egret, snowy egret, glossy ibis, and colonies of terns and skimmers. Birds are attracted to the sanctuary partly because of its location at the junction of the Hudson River and Atlantic Coast flyways and partly because the management's skillful clearing and planting made food and cover available. Visitors will marvel at the chance to spot some of the more than three hundred species that have been seen here, with the shadow of Kennedy Airport to the east and the Manhattan skyline in the distance to the west.

The visitors center may be reached by driving south from the Belt Parkway on Cross Bay Boulevard, or by taking the Rockaway subway to the Broad Channel station and walking a half mile west.

STATEN ISLAND

Long the "forgotten" borough of New York City, Richmond County (Staten Island) developed rapidly after the Verrazano-Narrows Bridge opened in the 1960s. Nevertheless, its woods, wetlands, and hilly terrain remain rewarding walking territory. Along the Harbor Hill Moraine, which forms the southwest-northeast ridge of the island, lie Clove Lakes, La Tourette and Willowbrook parks, and the High Rock Conservation Center. This central spine of open space is generally known as the Staten Island Greenbelt. Together with Great Kills Park on the outwash plain below, these parks comprise over four thousand acres linked together by the Olmsted Trail network.

Frederick Law Olmsted, the great architect of Central Park and close to eighty others, was never able to develop a park in the hills near his Staten Island farm. In more recent times, efforts to preserve the Greenbelt ran afoul of the State Transportation Department's plans to push the Richmond and Willowbrook parkways through the area. Finally, between 1973 and 1979, the City Parks Department worked with a conservation group, Conservation and the Outdoors, to establish not the ten miles of trail that Olmsted visualized, but thirty-five miles divided into the five paths described below.

Greenbelt Circular Trail. Length: 13.1 miles. Blazes: blue.

This trail covers scenic and mostly hilly terrain located entirely on public land. Take the 107 bus from the St. George ferry terminal along Forest Avenue to Clove Road. Fifty yards past the intersection, the path begins to the left.

The trail runs 1.3 miles through Clove Lakes Park, following an old glacial valley that was dammed to create four lakes and a number of waterfalls. Side paths lead to wooded hillsides and an oak-beech climax forest on the western slope of the park. Just outside the park, at Clove Road and Martling Avenue, is the Staten Island Zoo (Barrett Park), with its fine reptile collection. The trail climbs to scenic heights before leaving the park at Victory Boulevard. Walkers wishing to skip Clove Lakes may take the No. 6 bus from the ferry to this point.

The trail follows Little Clove Road and the Staten Island Expressway grounds, taking an underpass to the Staten Island College campus. Beyond the school grounds, it enters woods and climbs Todt Hill from the northwest. The Precambrian bedrock of serpentinite, identifiable by its greenish color, appears in outcrops here, as it does in a number of places in the first nine miles of this trail. Continue climbing through a forest of birch, beech, oak, and sweetgum; patches of catbrier denote areas that have been burned.

At the corner of Todt Hill Road and Ocean Terrace is the top of 410-foot Todt Hill, the highest tidewater elevation on the Atlantic seaboard south of Mount Desert in Maine. Fifty feet beyond the corner, on private property, is a never-dry kettle, one of a dozen or so such ponds left behind by the retreating Wisconsin Glacier.

The trail enters woods bearing west and then south. It runs along a dirt road, turns left through woods behind a seminary, and passes a campground and the Richmond County Golf Course. Hikers here spend a mile or so on the glacial Richmond Escarpment, with views east to the Atlantic.

Beyond the golf links lies the Moravian Cemetery, the burial place of Commodore Cornelius Vanderbilt and his family. Many rare and unusual plants have been introduced here, and it is frequented by migrating birds. However, a visit would involve leaving the trail and using the main entrance on Richmond Road.

Once past the cemetery, enter the grounds of High Rock Conservation Center, which offers short nature trails, a visitors center, and rest rooms. The trail runs 0.5 mile to Rockland Avenue; the No. 111 bus from the foot of nearby Nevada Avenue returns to the ferry, for walkers who wish to stop near what is the halfway point of the trail. If you continue, the terrain will be hillier, with a corresponding reward in terms of scenery. The trail goes through a pine, oak, and beech forest, comes out on Meisner Avenue, and reenters woods at London Road. After 0.75 mile it descends past La Tourette Golf Course and crosses the restored Colonial village of Richmondtown. Before heading down, you may wish to visit the old Coast Guard lighthouse high above the trail, or the exquisite Jacques Marchais Center of Tibetan Art at 338 Lighthouse Avenue.

Once in Richmondtown, the visitor could spend considerable time enjoying the surroundings and learning the history of the island. Staten Island was discovered by Giovanni da Verrazano in 1524. Henry Hudson came less than a hundred years later and named the place Staaten Eylandt, in honor of the States General of the Netherlands. At that time it was inhabited by Delaware tribes: Hackensacks on the north shore, Raritans on the south, and Tappans on the east. The nearby Fresh Kills were used extensively as a canoe route to link the tribes with others living in Manhattan, Long Island, and New Jersey. Fresh Kills is the only river to begin and end within the city limits.

Richmondtown was originally called Cocklestown because of the mounds of shells left by the Indians. It became the county seat in 1730 and remained so for two centuries until it was eclipsed by the development of St. George and faded into obscurity. In the 1960s the Staten Island Historical Society undertook its restoration, and today it makes a fine stop on a walking tour of the island.

From here, cross Richmond Hill Road and climb the bluffs for a view west over the Fresh Kills. After 0.5 mile on the undulating crest, descend and turn right to the woods of La Tourette Park. After 0.25 mile the trail opens into a big loop inside La Tourette Golf Course, following Golf Brook and Golf Lake, and turns left along Richmond Hill Road. At the intersection with Forest Hill Road, the trail measures 10.5 miles. Turn right for 0.5 mile along the edge of the golf course, then pass through woods for 0.75 mile before crossing Rockland Avenue and entering the grounds of Seaview Hospital.

In its remaining 1.75 miles, the trail passes through a burned-out area, descends through a stand of sweet gum to a crossing of Manor Creek, and parallels a deep ravine known locally as Bloodroot Valley for the white-petaled flower found in the area. The ravine contains maidenhair fern, sweet cicely, and other plants common in the South but rare here.

LIGHTHOUSE & SASSAFRASS from golfhouse Latourette Park. Staten I. (in path of Richmond X pressw'y) Jan. 27 1968 REH.

At the end of the walk, turn right on Brielle Avenue to Bradley Avenue, where the No. 111 bus stops on its way to the ferry. On weekends, a transfer to the No. 6 bus at Jewett Avenue is necessary.

La Tourette Trail. Length: 7.1 miles. Blazes: yellow.

The La Tourette Trail is the oldest in the Greenbelt, dating to the 1930s. However, only three miles of the original path remain, the rest having been rerouted around encroaching developments. The trail starts at Spring and Targee streets, opposite Doctors Hospital. Bus No. 113 stops nearby at Richmond Road and Spring Street.

The trail runs for a half mile along a quiet residential section before entering woods and climbing Todt Hill. Before the hill, walk left behind some new houses to see one of the largest outcrops of serpentinite on the island. This rather unglamorous spot also contains two rare minerals: artinite, which occurs in white radiating crystals, and pyroaurite, which occurs as brown hexagonal plates along cracks and joints in the rocks.

Climb steeply and go through the Reed Basket Willow Swamp area. The swamp itself, originally a glacial pond, is some 200 yards to the right on an unmarked trail. These thirty acres of woodland harbor scores of species of trees, shrubs, vines, and ferns.

Cross Todt Hill Road, continue straight ahead on a dirt road, and to the left enter woods behind the seminary. Pass the Kaufman campgrounds and walk for about a mile along the Richmond Escarpment. Descend and pass around the figure-eight Orbach Lake, past Moravian Cemetery, and right toward Manor Road. Turning right, enter woods from Meisner Avenue and join the white trail for 0.2 mile; at this point, the trail measures 4 miles. Follow an old bridle path to a left turn across a stream. Eventually the trail makes a loop inside La Tourette Golf Course before exiting on Independence Avenue, where the No. 4 bus takes you to the No. 107 (ask for a transfer), which goes to the ferry.

Richmondtown Circular. Length: 5.2 miles. Blazes: red and white.

The Richmondtown Circular is the latest addition to the Olmsted Trail system, having been inaugurated in 1979. It starts and ends in Richmondtown across from the Church of St. Andrew. From there it climbs the bluffs overlooking Fresh Kills and heads generally north through La Tourette Park and west on an old bridle path. From there turn right through

Bucks Hollow, which occupies the northeastern end of La Tourette and consists of beech and oak woodland with some brushy areas of birch and sumac. This rises to an elevation of 238 feet and bears the name of its former owners, Heyedahl Hill. Remnants of grapevines and the foundations of an old house are still here, as are outcrops of serpentinite and erratics deposited during the Ice Age.

At 3.5 miles, the trail briefly joins the white and yellow paths, follows a bridle path, and climbs Lighthouse Hill from the north. Once there it follows the blue trail back to Richmondtown, avoiding only the last hill and following instead the banks of Mill Pond.

Willowbrook Trail. Length: 4.4 miles. Blazes: white.

This is the shortest trail in the network. It starts at the entrance to Willowbrook Park on Victory Boulevard, which is accessible on the No. 112 bus. The park consists of oak and sweet gum woodland and, especially in its undeveloped parts, is excellent territory for birders.

After passing the lake near the entrance, the trail enters woods and loops toward the grounds of Willowbrook School. From a dirt road on the edge of the school, it enters a brushy area that provides good cover for catbirds, cardinals, and thrushes. Then it skirts an open meadow for about a mile. Meadowlarks, chickadees, jays, and song sparrows thrive here.

Beyond, follow Forest Hill Road south to Rockland Avenue, where the trail measures 2.7 miles. Enter Bucks Hollow and cross the blue and the red trails, join the yellow trail for 0.2 mile, and continue along Richmond Creek. The trail ends at Rockland and Nevada avenues, where the No. 111 bus returns to the ferry.

Great Kills Trail. Length: 5.5 miles. Blazes: white and blue.

This trail is an ideal companion to a walk on the Willowbrook Trail, whose end at Nevada Avenue is the start of this path. It follows the right-of-way of the Willowbrook Parkway to Great Kills Park on the Atlantic, a fine spot for observing ducks, killdeer, plover, teal, and other shorebirds. Visitors may wish to skip the very northern end of the trail for the convenience of using the Oakwood Heights station of the Staten Island Rapid Transit line, which is a five-minute walk from the path.

On the south side of the railroad underpass at Willowbrook, a marker on a boulder to the right points out the trail. Follow the blazes to Great Kills Park; from here the trail still has 3.5 miles to run, in a loop that returns to Hylan Boulevard and the No. 103

bus back to the ferry. Once inside the park, visitors have the choice of fishing, birding, swimming, or plain loafing.

Walkers will find dense shrubbery composed of bayberry, blackberry, wing-rib sumac, and lance-leaved goldenrod. The circular Great Kills Harbor and the sandspit of Crookes Point offer good seaside walking.

Great Kills Park is now part of the Gateway National Recreation Area, P.O. Box 37, Staten Island, N.Y. 10306; phone: (212) 351-8700. Additional information may be obtained by contacting the Staten Island unit or by stopping at the ranger station in the park.

Additional information, trail maps, and updates for any of the Greenbelt walks may be obtained by contacting Conservation and the Outdoors, Box 284, New York, N.Y. 10031.

OTHER STATEN ISLAND PARKS

Clay Pit Pond State Park

Inaugurated in the summer of 1980, Clay Pit Pond State Park, which resembles in many respects the Pine Barrens of New Jersey, forms an important part of New York State's coastal ecology. Within the bounds of its more than two hundred acres are ponds, bogs, swamps, and mature woodland. Take the No. 113 bus from the ferry to Arthur Kill and Clay Pit roads. Contact the State Park Commission for information on scheduled guided tours.

Wolfe's Pond Park

South of the Princess Bay station of the Staten Island Rapid Transit and bisected by Hylan Boulevard, the 224 acres of Wolfe's Pond Park offer birding, boating, and walks in basically undeveloped wetlands.

William T. Davis Wildlife Refuge

Named for one of the founders of the Staten Island Institute of Arts and Sciences, this 260-acre refuge in the New Springville section offers short self-guided trails keyed to a brochure available from the institute at 75 Stuyvesant Place, Staten Island, N.Y.

10301. The Davis Refuge stands in a transition zone between the mixed hardwood forests on the glacial moraine and the now severely stressed salt marshes, some of which are occupied by oil company operations. In the center of the preserve is Main Creek, which runs into Fresh Kills.

Suggested Readings

Staten Island Walk Book
Staten Island Institute of Arts and Sciences, New York, 1962

Barlow, Elizabeth
The Forests and Wetlands of New York City
Little, Brown & Company, Boston, 1971

12 · LONG ISLAND

WHILE THE Long Island of the 1980s bears little resemblance to the pastoral landscape preserved in the paintings of William Sidney Mount, it still offers surprisingly diverse and rewarding opportunities for hiking. Visitors can walk the barrier beaches of Fire Island National Seashore, make a north-south traverse on a National Recreation Trail, explore large tracts of pine barrens, and enjoy a number of individual preserves dotting what Walt Whitman called "fish-shape Paumanok."

In recent years the area's hikers have begun to look more closely to their own backyards for interesting walks. This renewed consciousness has already fostered a system of marked trails, with the possibility of more to come in eastern Suffolk County. The next decade will prove critical in the fight to preserve the area's remaining open spaces, which not only have esthetic value but protect a vast aquifer of pure water.

Lacking high peaks and unbroken wilderness, Long Island yields its treasures more subtly to the observant walker. There is delight in finding deer or fox just minutes from a suburban tract, or in walking some of the same paths once used by Indians and Colonial settlers. Birders, botanists, and biologists can revel in the richness of the island's species. Photographers can work in the same pure, unique daylight that has attracted generations of artists to Long Island's East End. Geologists can marvel at the abundant evidence of the last Ice Age.

The most obvious features of the island's topography are the glacial moraines deposited in the Pleistocene Epoch by the Wisconsin Glaciation, though earlier periods of the three major glaciations during the last two million years are present, less spectacularly, along the south coast of Long Island. About seventy-five thousand years ago, the glacier reached as far south as the middle of Long Island. There, like a giant conveyor belt, it dumped debris plucked from New England as it advanced southward, forming the Ronkonkoma Moraine. This band of low hills runs from Lake Success, on the Queens-Nassau border, to Montauk Point. At Montauk, the moraine juts like the prow of a ship into the prevailing ocean currents, which have gradually scoured the bluffs and carried them westward, grain by grain, to the barrier beaches along the Atlantic shore. Eventually the glacier retreated and advanced again, at a slightly different angle and not quite as far in the eastern areas, to form the Harbor Hill Moraine, which stretches from beyond Staten Island to Orient Point and crosses the older formation near Westbury.

The ice's handiwork manifests itself today in a number of ways. Kettles, depressions left by stranded ice blocks after they melted, are common—the largest in the area being Lake Ronkonkoma. Erratics, large boulders carried great distances by the glacier, dot Long Island from Queens to Montauk. Rows of hills resembling ripples in a pond mark areas where the glacier pushed the earth before it. One startling example is Adirondack Drive, a residential street in Selden running south from Route 25.

South of the moraines lies a flat outwash plain, deposits of sand and silt left by ancient glacial streams. Many of the outwash channels are still visible, appearing to be dry streambeds. A few, notably in the pine barrens, are still mistakenly shown on local maps as active watercourses. The major features of the plains are the wetlands and beaches for which Long Island is justly famed, and which offer much pleasure for the walker.

Knowing when to walk on Long Island is as important as knowing where. Large crowds at major parks, stifling heat in upland woods, and the presence of wood ticks carrying Rocky Mountain spotted fever can all discourage the summer visitor.

From late May to mid September, it is wise to walk early in the morning and finish by noon. The great bird migrations in spring and fall make the wetlands a feast for the eye. In May the spring flowers brighten morainal woodlands; in June the bogs have orchids; in September the cranberries, blueberries, and bayberries ripen; in October the deciduous forests present their colorful valedictory to warm, lazy days. Leaf-fall may linger into mid November, and then begin perhaps the most satisfying times for hikers. Salmon-hued sunsets glow behind traceries of bare branches, the moorlands of the South Fork offer rugged solitude, and snow dusts the woods. Most winter days on Long Island are temperate enough for the average hiker, who can cap a day of reddened cheeks and sharpened appetite with a visit to any of the many restaurants convenient to parks and trails. There one can reflect on the essence of hiking Long Island: enjoying the contrast of finding exquisite, undeveloped places nestled amid populous suburbs.

THE LONG ISLAND GREENBELT TRAIL

The Long Island Greenbelt Trail was officially established in 1978 through the cooperative efforts of the Greenbelt Trail Conference, Suffolk County, New York State, and the Towns of Islip and Smithtown. Stretching almost 34 miles from Heckscher State Park on Great South Bay to Sunken Meadow State Park on the Sound, the path encompasses the drainages of the Connetquot and Nissequogue rivers, which virtually bisect the Island. Along the way, one finds bay beaches, pine barrens, deciduous forests, and tidal marshes. Parts of the trail follow old Indian paths and farm-to-market roads. The southern section traverses a flat outwash plain, while the northern portion passes through gently rolling morainal hills under two hundred feet in elevation. The trail shelters populations of deer, fox, raccoon, opossum, egret, kingfisher, and many other species. In 1982, the Department of the Interior recognized the significance of the Greenbelt by granting it status as a National Recreation Trail.

A Seashore Trail due to open in 1985 will extend from the Greenbelt at Montauk Highway via a road walk through the parks and historic areas of Sayville south to the Fire Island ferries. On Fire Island it will proceed east along the National Seashore, then turn north to Smith Point on Long Island and go through the Wertheim National Wildlife Refuge along Carmans River. As an alternative to the road walk, the Babylon-Patchogue county bus passes near the Sayville and Patchogue ferries.

Hiking the Greenbelt is like walking in an hourglass. Large tracts of relatively undeveloped land are linked by narrow corridors within sight of suburbia; shorter sections of road walking remain, though some may be eliminated in the future. Though hikers seeking stretches of rugged wilderness may not find this generally flat trail to their liking, it does offer intriguing beauty and variety. Much in the fashion of Japanese gardens set in bustling urban areas, the Greenbelt's sharp contrast with its surroundings makes it memorable.

Because of the jumble of jurisdictions and easements along the trail, and as a means of protecting the land from abuse, free permits are necessary for all sections of the Greenbelt except Sunken Meadow Park and the five-mile section below Sunrise Highway. Hikers should call ahead, though this may be done even on the day of the hike. Permits for the south (Town of Islip) section may be obtained at Connetquot River State Park by calling (516) 581-1005. Permits for the north (Town of Smithtown) section may be obtained at Caleb Smith River State Park by calling (516) 265-1054. When picking up a permit here, be sure to obtain the combinations for gate locks on either end of this restricted-use park. The two parks are *closed on Mondays.*

Trail maps, updates, and Greenbelt Conference information are available by sending a stamped, self-addressed envelope to: L.I. Greenbelt Trail Conference, Inc., 23 Deer Path Road, Central Islip, N.Y. 11722.

Heckscher State Park to Great River. Length: 4 miles. Blazes: white for the entire trail.

Beginning at the east end of Parking Field 8 with views of Great South Bay and Fire Island, the trail swings north through an area noteworthy for its transition from tidelands to oak and pine woods. Nearly 2 miles up the trail is a state-operated campground, open in the summer season only. Deer, fox, and pheasant inhabit this 1657-acre park, whose picnic facilities and beaches make it a good place to end a summer hike. The trail continues north through a wooded corridor along the Heckscher Spur of Southern State Parkway to Montauk Highway. Here you can detour a few hundred yards east to the entrance of *Bayard Cutting Arboretum,* a 690-acre preserve notable for its conifers, spring flowers, and paths along the Connetquot River. The arboretum, closed on Mondays and Tuesdays, contains several miles of well-marked nature walks. The Greenbelt itself continues north into woods east of Connetquot Avenue. One block west is the Great River station of the Long Island Railroad.

Great River to Lakeland County Park. Length: 7 miles.

Park free at the LIRR station in Great River. Walk south one block and find the trail just east of the Union Boulevard intersection. The trail crosses the tracks on a highway bridge and soon passes through a small meadow near Westbrook Farms, a defunct dairy. Here a large barn designed by Stanford White was destroyed by fire in 1981. West Brook, dammed into a small lake, harbors migratory waterfowl and is a popular spot for local fishermen. Follow the east side of the lake to a pedestrian underpass of Sunrise Highway.

At this point the hiker enters Connetquot River State Park, one of the cornerstones of the Greenbelt system. From here on, the hiker should have a permit, obtainable at the park headquarters. Formerly the Southside Sportsmen's Preserve, this lightly used area of 3473 acres is a fine example of a pine barrens system. The Connetquot River flows gently through the center of the park, affording opportunities to observe herons, egrets, kingfishers, and a host of other species. Near the entrance is a grist mill from the early 1700s and the large Sportsmen's Club, parts of which were built in the early 1800s. Proceeding north, look for deer in the woods, and huckleberry and wintergreen underfoot. Near the north gate, a raised, moss-covered section denotes the remains of a hundred-year-old carriage road.

Crossing Veterans Memorial Highway, the trail reenters woods to Lakeland County Park. Here Honeysuckle Pond marks the source of the Connetquot and provides an example of freshwater pond life. Free, primitive camping is available here; call ahead on weekdays at (516) 567-1700.

Lakeland County Park to Route 111. Length: 7 miles.

This section is interesting principally for its passage from the headwaters of the Connetquot to those of the Nissequogue. From the moraine near Colonie Hill convention center, there are views south to the Bay and north to the Sound. However, there are a few sections of unappealing road-walking, some of which may eventually be rerouted.

From Lakeland Park, cross Johnson Avenue and walk north alongside the very end of the Connetquot drainage to the Long Island Expressway. Go right to the Terry Road underpass and then left to a power line right-of-way, a total of 0.4 mile. Turn left and follow the white blazes to an incline that marks the foot of the moraine. From here the trail ascends about 120 feet to Motor Parkway, a local road that follows the route of one of the nation's original toll auto roads, the site of the Vanderbilt Cup races before World War I. Just to the left is Colonie Hill. A good bet for day hikers would be to bypass the walk from Lakeland, park here and walk north.

The trail passes through wooded Hidden Pond Park to a walk, now in the process of being eliminated, on Terry and Town Line roads. (Check with the Greenbelt Conference.) North of a horse stable on Town Line Road is a small swamp, best examined in drier months, that is the source of the Nissequogue. The trail then skirts a farm on Route 347; at busy times of day, cross at a light 0.2 mile to the left. Here a large farm stand is a refreshing summer stop. Continue north 1.5 miles to Route 111. A shopping center to the north just below Route 25 provides a handy parking place.

Route 111 to Sweetbriar Farm. Length: 7 miles.

Two adjoining parks totaling over 1100 acres of beautiful terrain along the Nissequogue make this section a delight. Walk south on Route 111 for 0.2 mile to a point just north of Darling Avenue; turn right along a wooded corridor below Miller Pond, a portion of the river dammed about a century ago to provide a source of ice. Beyond, a short walk on residential Wildwood Lane leads to the Brooksite Drive entrance of Blydenburgh County Park. From this entrance, a blue-blazed trail diverges 1 mile to a primitive campground.

With its 120-acre, L-shaped Stump Pond, early-1700s grist mill, miller's house, and quiet woods, this former estate provides a quiet refuge amid one of Suffolk County's busiest areas. Especially in the fall and winter, detour west from the small dam near the mill, and follow paths to the top of a small bluff overlooking the lake. From here the landscape seems to resemble the upper Midwest more than it does Long Island.

The trail itself turns north from the dam a few yards to a locked gate leading to Caleb Smith State Park, formerly Nissequogue River State Park. (The combination can be obtained with a permit from park headquarters.) Here the trail moves away from the river into rolling wooded uplands formed by the Harbor Hill Moraine. In less than 1 mile, a steep descent leads to a second locked gate and a crossing of busy Route 25. Upon reentering the park, continue through forested terrain to Willow Pond, an arm of the river, and the park headquarters building, which houses a small nature museum. Inside this former rod-and-gun club is an impressive carving of Wyandanch, an Indian chief.

The trail levels off as it continues through woods east toward

Smithtown. From a pedestrian entrance on Meadow Road, turn right one half block to a railroad underpass. On the other side is a famous statue of a bull, commemorating Richard Smith's purchase from the Indians of as much land as he could ride around with his bull in one day. Cross Route 25A and enter gently rolling woodland laced with several small streams. Parts of this area may be swampy in springtime. Look for cedars, skunk cabbage, and marsh marigolds. The trail leaves the woods on an easement between two houses; just to the right is a cul-de-sac on Summerset Drive, an excellent spot for parking and car-ferrying. Summerset exits on Route 25A one block north of the bull.

Sweetbriar Farm to Sunken Meadow. Length: 8 miles.

This section of the Greenbelt currently involves considerable but pleasant road-walking, much of which may be eliminated by pending acquisitions of property. There are fine views of the Nissequogue in its tidal zone, and of Long Island Sound from the bluffs in Sunken Meadow State Park. From the cul-de-sac on Summerset Drive, proceed through Sweetbriar Farm, now owned by the Town of Smithtown, about a half mile to Landing Avenue. Turn left to Landing Meadow Road, and follow this quiet, heavily wooded street 1.2 miles until it reenters Landing Avenue. A planned rerouting will allow hikers to bypass this road and follow the bank of the Nissequogue. Walk north to the entrance of Smithtown Landing Golf Club (town-owned), then descend on the club's road a half mile to the shore. Hikers wishing to skip the road walk may park here.

From here, the trail follows the banks of the Nissequogue north for over 2 miles, part of the way on Riviera Drive, which parallels the shore. It is possible to avoid virtually all of the road walk and spend considerable time exploring the water's edge. The views here are always a pleasure, though the spring and fall waterfowl migrations may be the most spectacular times.

The trail then runs for two blocks along St. Johnland Road, long enough to pass pretty Harrison Pond Park, and just north of the circa-1700 Obadiah Smith House, before turning back to the shore. Follow the blazes through the grounds of Kings Park Psychiatric Center and tiny Old Dock Road Park before entering Sunken Meadow State Park. This developed facility has ample parking and picnic areas. Its beaches and breezy bluffs along the Sound are a refreshing place to end a summer hike, but it won't be as quiet as in the colder months.

A note on backpacking: The Long Island Greenbelt is better suited for day hikes than for backpacking. However, ambitious walkers may wish to attempt two- or three-day traverses of the trail by making use of the campsites at Blydenburgh and Lakeland. City residents who want to leave their cars at home can take the LIRR to Smithtown and the bus from the station to Caleb Smith Park headquarters on Jericho Turnpike (Route 25). Obtain a permit here, then hike south 4 miles to the camp at Blydenburgh. From there, it is another 9 miles to Lakeland, and 7 more to the LIRR station in Great River.

NASSAU GREENBELT TRAIL

In decades past, the *New York Walk Book* contained descriptions of walks in eastern Nassau County, a now heavily suburban area. Surprisingly, a narrow belt of open land still exists from Cold Spring Harbor south to Massapequa, and it is possible to walk most of this route today without resorting to roads. It includes picturesque ponds, morainal ridges, open fields, and a long watershed. At this writing, efforts are underway to preserve this corridor as a Nassau Greenbelt Trail. No blazed path yet exists, but hikers armed with a Hagstrom map of the county should be able to explore much of the route.

Generally, the trail parallels the ponds south of Route 25A and west of Route 108, with parking available at St. Johns Church and the old fish hatchery. Nearby is the historic old whaling village of Cold Spring Harbor. The two lower ponds are on Nature Conservancy property; seek permission to enter or choose a course along Route 108. Below Stillwell Lane, the trail enters Nassau County–owned Stillwell Woods, beautiful wooded uplands perched on the Harbor Hill Moraine and frequented by red-tailed hawks. South of here, it follows the right-of-way for a never-built extension of the Bethpage State Parkway. This section can be difficult to negotiate in summer because of dense underbrush and catbrier.

To cross Northern State Parkway, use the Exit 38 overpass a quarter mile west of the right-of-way. More woods on the south side of the parkway lead to an unpaved underpass of the Long Island Expressway. Below here the corridor narrows somewhat, wedging between suburban tracts, and the terrain flattens into the outwash plain that characterizes the south shore of Long Island. Patches of open fields and cultivated land recall a time when a unique treeless plain stretched from Queens Village to Plainview, and a more recent era when Nassau was the breadbasket of New York City. A worthwhile side trip takes in Old

Bethpage Village Restoration, an assemblage of historic buildings culled from their original sites on the island.

Next, the trail traverses the picnic grounds and woods to the north and west of Bethpage State Park's five golf courses; here observant hikers will find the remnants of an overpass for the pioneer Vanderbilt Motor Parkway. Heading south, it follows the parkway and, below Southern State Parkway, the Massapequa watershed to Merrick Road. Though a paved bicycle path parallels the east bank, walkers should explore the band of woods on the opposite side of the creek, a good area for birding.

In England, travelers on foot may cross private land to reach their destinations, provided they close any gates as they go. Though the proposed Nassau Greenbelt would be virtually all on public land, the route would offer some of this same sense of wandering through the margins of developed areas. The mere existence of such a route in one of the nation's most populous suburban counties is an asset in itself. Add to this the chance to see foxes, hawks, kingfishers, and a number of unusual plant species, and this slender thread offers great potential as a diversion for the area's hikers.

For further information on the status of the trail, write to the Long Island Greenbelt Trail Conference.

ATLANTIC BARRIER BEACHES AND FIRE ISLAND NATIONAL SEASHORE

The barrier islands along the South Shore of Long Island are justly famed as some of the finest bathing beaches in the world. Consequently, they are often filled to overflowing on hot summer days. In the off-season, however, they become excellent territory for walks of almost unlimited length and surpassing beauty. Any walk along the ocean in the nearly hundred-mile stretch from Atlantic Beach to Montauk will be a rewarding experience; the walks noted below may offer the best combinations of accessibility and attractiveness.

Short Beach

At the west end of 2400-acre Jones Beach State Park there is a good winter walk from the West End Parking Field to the jetty at Short Beach. Snowy owls, short-eared owls, and snow buntings frequent the dunes, and large flocks of brant come to the inlet.

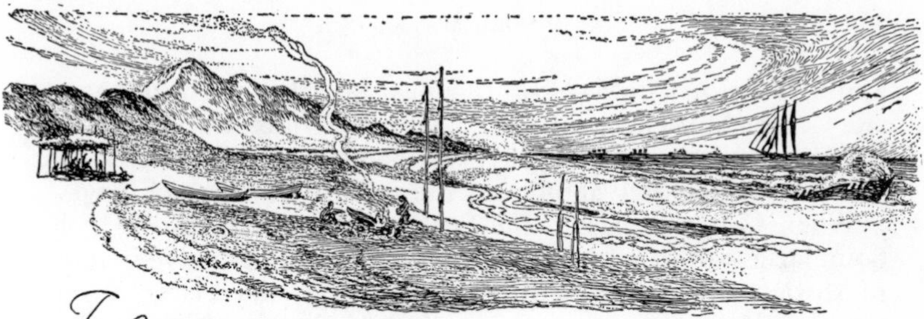

The South Shore of Long Island : dunes, beech grass : arbor : dories : drift-wood fire
wave markings : beech pools : wreck : coal barges : sunshine.

John F. Kennedy (Tobay) Bird Sanctuary

In 1959 this former hunting preserve became the first area in the state to fall under the protection of the Long Island Wetlands Act. Managed jointly by the Town of Oyster Bay and the State Department of Environmental Conservation, its five hundred acres contain several miles of trails through one of the finest sanctuaries on the Atlantic coast. Walkers can see a large, brackish pond, maritime forest, salt marsh, and dunes. Obtain a free permit from the Town of Oyster Bay and park in the small field just east of the wooden lookout tower.

Cedar Beach

Operated by the Town of Babylon, this beach is open to all in the off-season, and affords excellent beach-walking toward Gilgo Beach or Captree.

Robert Moses State Park

The western gateway to Fire Island National Seashore, this park offers visual proof of the power of the littoral drift—the inexorable scouring of the barrier beaches by ocean currents that carry the sand westward. To the east of Robert Moses Causeway lies the Fire Island Lighthouse, built in 1858 on what was then the tip of the island; since that time, the island has "grown" almost five miles westward to the present tip, Democrat Point.

Fire Island National Seashore

Until 1931, Great South Beach stretched from Fire Island Inlet eastward for more than fifty-five miles without a break to Southampton. A storm in March of that year breached the dunes opposite Center Moriches and carved Moriches Inlet, through which the ocean now pours swiftly and dangerously. Similarly, the great hurricane of 1938 opened the inlet to Shinnecock Bay.

When Congress passed the Seashore legislation in 1964, the boundaries ran from the community of Kismet twenty-six miles to Moriches Inlet; the Lighthouse Area was added later. Seventeen beach communities occupy parts of the island, but several magnificent sections of untouched beach remain. In 1980, the seven miles from Watch Hill to Smith Point earned designation as a Wilderness Area, the only one in New York State.

Access by car is limited to Robert Moses State Park on the western end and Smith Point County Park on the eastern end. Both are toll facilities during the busy summer season. Ferries operate from May to November from Bay Shore, Sayville (to Sailors Haven Visitors Center), and Patchogue (to Watch Hill Visitors Center). Park headquarters is 120 Laurel Street, Patchogue, N.Y. 11772; phone: (516) 289-4810.

Noted below are some of the primary attractions for walkers on the National Seashore.

Lighthouse Area

Accessible from Robert Moses Field No. 3, this area of about two hundred acres contains a freshwater pond, pine forests, and diverse plant communities. The great lighthouse, no longer functioning, stands 167 feet high. A short distance west, one may see the crumbling base of the original 1825 light. A natural interpretive area and museum depicting the maritime history of Fire Island have been proposed for this area.

Sailors Haven and Sunken Forest

A ferry from Sayville leads to Sailors Haven Visitors Center, including a small museum of the maps and equipment used by the old Life Saving Service and Coast Guard. A loop trail leads west to the famous Sunken Forest, so called because of its location down behind the dunes. Holly, sassafras, tupelo, and shadbush envelop the walker in a cool, dark environment. Here, as it is almost everywhere on the island, poison ivy is common. Before walking on Fire Island, be sure that you can identify this shiny plant with its "leaves of three."

High Dunes Wilderness Area

Take the ferry from Patchogue to Watch Hill and walk east, or drive to Smith Point and walk west. Either way, this 7-mile segment attains a primitive, wild beauty that will leave an indelible impression on any visitor. Here lie thick groves of pitch pine and some of the finest salt marsh in the Northeast. The signs of deer, fox, and rabbit are everywhere, though hikers are more likely to hear the animals in the dense undergrowth than to see them. Here the shifting dunes rise hauntingly to an elevation of forty feet or more. In the swale behind the primary dunes, the abundant plant life includes reindeer lichen, bayberry, beach plum, and—of course—poison ivy.

Near Old Inlet, about 2 miles west of Smith Point, the first transatlantic steamship, S.S. *Savannah*, sank on November 5, 1821. Earlier editions of this book mention Halfway Huts in this area. These were built by the Life Saving Service as shelters for shipwreck victims, and contained oil lamps and stores of dried beans. For modern hikers, the only overnight refuge is a limited primitive camping area near Old Inlet. Contact park headquarters for information.

Everywhere along this barrier, the primary dunes offer the only coastal protection against violent storms. They have taken years to form, are extremely fragile, and can be destroyed by careless tramping. Do not climb the dunes or cross them except at designated spots.

Smith Point to Moriches Inlet

Adjacent to the Smith Point West Visitors Center is a mile-long boardwalk trail designed for the handicapped. This self-guided walk is a good introduction to the intricacies of the dune systems.

Heading east, walkers can trek 4.2 miles along lonely, undeveloped beaches to the raging maw of Moriches Inlet. Harbor seal frequent the area in winter. In cold weather, be forewarned that a brisk walk east along any of these beaches can turn into a chilling experience when it comes time to turn back to the west in the face of the prevailing winds. Dress accordingly.

THE SOUTH FORK

East of the Shinnecock Canal lies a wide triangular expanse of rolling moraines generally called the South Fork. The history of the towns in the area parallels that of some of the earliest New England settlements. The forests were all cut down by 1676. Indeed, trees were so scarce by the time of the Revolution that settlers were obliged to drive their cattle into glacial kettles to hide them from lookouts high on the masts of British ships. Wooded once again, the Hamptons and Sag Harbor bustle in the summer as world-famous resort areas. After Labor Day, the population dwindles, allowing the walker easy access to a number of beautiful parklands.

Beyond the narrows at Amagansett, where the Ronkonkoma Moraine was probably once cut by the sea, the eastern end of the South Fork rises to a magnificent topography which more closely resembles Cape Cod than anything else for a hundred miles up or down the coast. These hills end in the spearhead of Montauk Point, tapering from three miles in width to the headland where the tall light station juts into the sea.

Elizabeth Morton National Wildlife Refuge

This long sandspit on Jessup Neck, west of Sag Harbor on Peconic Bay, remains relatively undiscovered despite its beauty and variety. Due east from the parking area off Noyack Road, hidden in the woods, is a wood duck pond. The trail itself goes north through cedar woods, then drops to a pristine beach facing westward. Side trails on the east side lead through the undergrowth to rich marshlands complete with short boardwalks over some of the wetter areas. Farther north lies a forested bluff which eventually drops down to a sand bar jutting into the currents of Noyack and Little Peconic bays.

Total distance from the parking area to the tip is 2 miles; side trips can—and should—stretch a visit into an all-day affair. When walking from your car to the beach, keep a few seeds handy for chickadees, which will perch on your palm to snack.

Cedar Point County Park

This 608-acre park on Gardiners Bay contains numerous lanes through oak woods, several ponds, and quiet beaches. It is wise to avoid the area during the summer camping and fall hunting seasons. When visiting, be sure to walk the beaches for a view of picturesque old Cedar Island Lighthouse. The park entrance is on Alewive Brook Road, off Old Northwest Road in East Hampton.

Napeague State Park

Once the site of the Gilbert P. Smith fish-rendering factory at Promised Land, this 1362-acre tract of several separate parcels was transferred to the Park Commission in 1978 by The Nature Conservancy. It is largely a level area, a fragile one of salt marsh, cranberry bogs, low dunes, pitch pine woods, and a few ponds (the largest of which is called the Pond of Pines, or Napeague Pond). It includes most of the peninsula west of Napeague Harbor and runs from the tip of Hicks Island to the ocean, fronting the sea with nearly three miles of undeveloped beach. On that side, little more than a mile of motels and other buildings separates it from Hither Hills State Park. The northern section is composed primarily of dunes, pines, and salt marsh; the central of salt marsh and cranberry bogs; the southern of extensive primary dunes and beach vegetation, including hudsonia, reindeer moss, and varieties of mushrooms and orchids.

Along with the fine outer beach, good walking territory includes an east-west jeep trail behind the primary dunes, with several approaches to it from Montauk Highway. An overgrown and rusting railroad spur runs north from the LIRR Montauk Branch to the old Smith factory. Beyond this point, a tote road runs northeast through pine woods to fishing cabins, which are on private property. Another route, fragile and wet much of the time, is the original road to Montauk, now overgrown and running east-west some distance to the north of the present highway. Hikers are discouraged from using this path.

Hither Hills State Park

This 1800-acre tract is largely in virgin wilderness condition and is contiguous to another larger wild area extending nearly to Montauk village. It contains no marked trails and few roads. A U.S. Geological Survey's Gardiners Island East quadrangle will help greatly in gaining an appreciation of the rugged terrain. One way of staying oriented while walking here is to remember that an old blacktop road, and the railroad track parallel to it, cross the area in a northeast-southwest direction.

For a basic loop of about 7 miles, first park in the main field at the state park camping area. Head west along the swale 0.8 mile, until a hundred-foot-high dune is visible just to the north. Cross Montauk Highway and enter the old blacktop road. A few hundred feet in, leave the road and walk northwest along the line of high dunes, with their rich growths of hudsonia, cranberry, and bayberry. Far to the northwest is the curving spit of Goff Point.

To the east lies an amazing world of shifting sands, the so-called "Walking Dunes." Here the oak forest is slowly being buried; the tops of fifty-foot trees rise from the sand like young saplings. Work north through a grove of large hollies and along another dune line with a constant, spectacular shifting of contours and hues. You may wish to climb to an excellent prospect of Fresh Pond lying to the east amid a forest broken by smaller ponds and marshes.

Continue north to Napeague Bay, then east 0.6 mile to its southernmost point. Here a wood road runs south 0.1 mile to a good view of Fresh Pond. Retracing, continue along the bay another mile to Quincetree Landing, identified by a view of the railroad track, a small marsh beneath it, and some large boulders. Cross the tracks and road, and head southeast 0.1 mile on a wood road, then south 1.6 miles to Montauk Highway. The paved road down to the camping area is nearly opposite.

This loop may be greatly expanded by hiking to Goff Point, then over the high forested hills east of Fresh Pond, then south to the ocean and back to the camping area.

Montauk Point

With the state park of 724 acres contiguous to a new county park of 1059 acres, much of the land east of Lake Montauk is now protected. It is a country of lonely, rolling moors, some forested, reaching elevations of a hundred feet or more. Cattle once grazed this range. Today it is renowned for its bird life. One may find sea ducks and many offshore species such as gannets, kittiwakes, dovekies, and razor-billed auks. Harbor seal visit in winter, and deer and fox are abundant.

Atop the cliff of Turtle Hill stands the octagonal sandstone tower of the Montauk Point Light Station, commissioned by George Washington in 1795. At that time, the edge of the bluff lay some three hundred feet to the east; the unrelenting sea has eroded the cliff to within a few feet of the Light.

Head west on foot from this point. Two miles along the shore of Block Island Sound lies the beautiful, land-locked Oyster

Pond, its east bank lined with a thick holly forest. To the northwest stands Shagwong Point, with a view of the entire Montauk headland. From here a dirt road leads southwest to Big Reed Pond, the easternmost body of fresh water on Long Island, now designated a National Natural Landmark.

Montauk Light and the two forms of cliff
DICKINSON

THE PINE BARRENS

From the Towns of Smithtown and Islip east to Hampton Bays, a distance of nearly fifty miles, lies the region of *Pinus rigida*, the pitch pine. Once encompassing over a quarter of a million acres, the pine barrens have been decimated by development in the last half century. Yet over eighty thousand acres remain in a fairly natural state, about one quarter of the total in the hands of various government agencies and the rest still vulnerable to development. Beneath the sandy soil of the region (the glacial outwash of the Ronkonkoma Moraine) lies a huge aquifer of pure water, rising to the surface occasionally in isolated bogs. From these barrens are born the four major rivers of Long Island: the Connetquot, Nissequogue, Carmans, and Peconic. In the more remote sections, the gnarled pines stretch unbroken for miles. Beneath is an understory of scrub oak and ground cover rich in bearberry, wintergreen, and a myriad of other species.

Deer, foxes, flying squirrels, grouse, and pheasants frequent the area. Rare lichens and such endangered creatures as the tiger salamander greet the observant walker.

When Walt Whitman traveled here, he commented on the "wide central tracts of pine and scrub-oak . . . monotonous and sterile. But many a good day or half day did I have, wandering through those solitary cross-roads, inhaling the peculiar and wild aroma." Modern-day hikers who sample several sections of the barrens should find them neither monotonous nor sterile, and they still have a chance at finding solitude. Some representative walks are described below; visitors who wish to explore further should arm themselves with topographical maps or, more convenient and just as valuable in this land of low relief, a Hagstrom Street Atlas for Suffolk County.

Manorville Hills

This 5.5-mile hike includes old carriage roads, morainal hills, and a sweeping view westward from a quiet hilltop. It is best attempted in the winter or early spring, when the soft, sandy soil is still frozen. Look for wintergreen, as well as the uncommon closed-cone pine. Flying squirrels abound here.

Drive south 1.5 miles from Long Island Expressway Exit 70 to Hot Water Street, named for an old warm-water pond which has been ruined by road construction. Turn left onto a dirt road and park. Continue on foot about a half mile to a spot 100 yards before the crest of a small hill. From here, an arrow-straight trail, originally a carriage road and property boundary, runs north 1.2 miles, up and over a steep hill. From the top is a startling view to the west and south, almost unbroken by the development one associates with Long Island. The odd piles of moss-covered dirt appearing irregularly along the trail were left decades ago by the builders of the road.

Continue until the trail ends, just south of the Long Island Expressway, then turn right for 1.1 miles to Topping's Path, a wide dirt road running south 1.5 miles to Hot Water Street's unpaved portion. Many side trips are possible here; glacial kettles dot the area, and the low hills on the east side of Topping's Path contain several erratics, boulders carried from New England by the last great glaciers. Rock tripe and British redcoat, lichens uncommon to Long Island, are found here.

Turn right onto Hot Water Street and return to the parking area. (For an alternate route, go north on Topping's Path to the vicinity of Exit 71 of the Long Island Expressway.)

Peconic River County Park

This undeveloped area of 2010 acres surrounding the headwaters of the Peconic includes a number of ponds and wetlands. There are two dirt roads and some unmarked trails. From Long Island Expressway Exit 69, drive north to the first left (North Street); proceed 0.8 mile to a sharp bend to the left. Park here and walk north 0.8 mile on a dirt road to Zeeks Pond. North of here is a chain of ponds: Grassy, Sandy, Duck, and Peasys. A corridor of parkland protects the river drainage for almost 5 miles east of here. It is possible to follow the river and then diverge into pine barrens north of the expressway and east of the hamlet of Manorville.

As an alternate, park at the intersection of Schultz Road and Wading River–Manorville Road, and walk directly west to Grassy Pond. It is wise to avoid the entire area during hunting season.

Dwarf Pine Plains

This is a highly unusual area of fully grown pines standing from three to six feet tall, products of infertile soil. The walk is flat and easily accessible. From Sunrise Highway Exit 63, drive south on Route 31 about a half mile to a dirt road on the right; take this to a wide parking area. Unmarked trails and fire-access roads line the plains. Heading south and making a counterclockwise loop back to the parking area covers about 2 miles and offers a representative sampling of this unique area.

For a fine companion walk, return to Route 31 and drive south to Westhampton. Go east to . . .

Quogue National Wildlife Refuge

The refuge is on the north side of South Old Country Road, 1.4 miles east of an intersection with Montauk Highway. A nature exhibit, including live animals, greets visitors at the entrance. Just beyond lie Old Ice Pond and North Pond, good sites for birding. The sanctuary is rarely crowded, and few visitors venture into the quiet pine woods north of the ponds. A walk to the north end and back covers about 3 miles. With vacant land on one side and little-used Suffolk County Airport on the other, the narrow preserve seems much larger than it actually is.

Riverhead Area

Hilly terrain, with elevations to 180 feet, and wood roads lacing pitch pine forests characterizes the area southwest of Riverhead. County Route 51 runs through the area, offering easy access to a number of good walks. East of Wildwood Lake is the old RCA transmitter property, some two thousand acres now managed by the Department of Environmental Conservation. Obtain a free permit from the DEC Office, Building 40, State University at Stony Brook. The permit is good for a year and covers other DEC areas as well.

Other large stretches of pine barrens run north and south from the campus of Suffolk County Community College on Route 51. North of Wildwood Lake is Cranberry Bog County Preserve, which may soon become the sole habitat of its type remaining on Long Island. Originally a commercial operation, this 211-acre bog contains fine nature walks and rich small-animal life.

Hubbard and Sears-Bellows County Parks

Comprising over thirteen hundred acres on either side of State Route 24, southeast of Riverhead, these parks offer fields, wetlands, and woods to entertain the hiker. Hubbard, situated on Flanders Bay, is undeveloped and provides hours of exploration through wetlands. Sears-Bellows is a popular, multi-use park. Walkers should avoid the freshwater beach at Bellows Pond and head instead to Sears Pond, near the western end of the park. Maps are available at the park.

Toward the North Shore, the pine barrens come under state protection in two large tracts:

Rocky Point DEC Area

(Obtain a permit from Building 40 at SUNY Stony Brook.) Used as a base for broadcasting towers for decades, this land was acquired from RCA in 1978. It occupies an unbroken parcel east of Rocky Point Road and south of Route 25A; a good parking spot is located 1.3 miles north of Whiskey Road on Rocky Point Road. This dry tract is somewhat hilly in its northern sections and more level farther south. A network of paths, jeep trails, and firebreaks traverses the area. Among the ground-cover plants are yellow cinquefoil, violet, hay-scented fern, and bearberry. A map, the same one provided for hunters, is issued with the permit.

Brookhaven State Park

Similar in character to the RCA tract, this area was originally the northern section of the U.S. Army's Camp Upton, and more recently of the Brookhaven National Laboratory. Its 2590 acres are bounded on the west by William Floyd Parkway and on the north by Route 25A. An old dirt road bisects the park in a southwest-northeast direction. Hikers can find paths leading south from the parking lot on the east side of Shoreham–Wading River High School on Route 25A.

OTHER PARKS AND PRESERVES

Long Island is rich in individual parklands varying greatly in size and character, ranging from converted private estates or narrow strip parks along streams to larger wooded preserves. Some are crowded, some are quiet; all offer worthwhile day walks.

Garvies Point Preserve

This preserve consists of sixty-two acres of glacial moraine covered by forests, thickets, and meadows. There are about 5 miles of trails. Small animals and over 140 species of birds have been spotted here. High cliffs along the shore of Hempstead Harbor exhibit such erosional features as alluvial fans, talus slopes, and slumping caused by ancient clays oozing from the beach. Follow signs from the Glen Cove Bypass to the preserve.

Muttontown Preserve

With a visitors center and 10 miles of trails, this fifty-acre tract of uplands is one of the more beautiful open areas left in populous Nassau County. The entrance is at the south end of Muttontown Lane, one block west of the intersection of Routes 106 and 25A.

Mill Neck

One of the most delightful preserves on Long Island is the North Shore Bird and Game Sanctuary in Mill Neck. Park on the south side of the track at the Mill Neck train station; a short distance to the northwest, lovely Beaver Lake is worth a visit. Return to the station parking area, opposite which is the sanctuary gate. Wander around in the sanctuary and the woods to the south of Shu Swamp Road. Also close by, to the south, on Planting Field Road, is Planting Fields Arboretum, with greenhouses, the former Coe Estate house, and shady paths on its 415 acres.

Tackapausha Preserve

Operated by Nassau County, this extremely narrow preserve protects the Seaford Creek watershed. Though walkers are rarely out of sight of neighboring houses, the preserve is worthwhile for its wet-woods walks and spring wildflowers. A good nature museum is at the south end of the property, on Washington Avenue at Merrick Road.

Caumsett State Park

The former Marshall Field estate at Lloyd Neck in the Town of Huntington is located on a beautiful peninsula. It contains 1475 acres of woodland, meadows, rocky shoreline, salt marsh, and former farm and garden areas. Elevations vary from sea level to 120 feet. A number of permanent buildings on the property are used for environmental education programs and other activities. There are paved and unpaved roads as well as some narrow foot trails. A freshwater pond 1.5 miles from the gatehouse can be viewed from a hill in the northeastern section of the park, with the expanse of Long Island Sound in the background. The northwestern section projects 2 miles into a marshy, sandy, open site from which an old boardwalk directs the visitor to the very tip, known as Lloyd Point.

From Main Street in Huntington, take West Neck Road (4 blocks west of Route 110) north to the park entrance. There is an entrance fee for autos from Memorial Day through Labor Day. Maps are available at the gate.

West Hills County Park

The old trails and bridle paths in this heavily wooded tract afford several hours of good walking. One notable feature of the park is that it contains the highest point on Long Island, Jaynes Hill, with an elevation of 401 feet. This spot is accessible from Walt Whitman Road by driving west on West Hills Road and then taking Reservoir Road to its end at the park entrance. Jaynes Hill is just ahead; in winter, when there is no foliage, it is possible to see all the way to the ocean.

Belmont Lake State Park

Easily accessible from Southern State Parkway, Belmont has paths on either side of the lake, extending north to a feeder brook. In the other direction, follow a pedestrian underpass of the parkway to a trail paralleling the narrow Carlls River. Though hemmed in by suburbs, this 2.5-mile walk to the village of Babylon is a good example of a Long Island stream system, one which may be adversely affected by sewer construction, which will lower the water table in the area.

Gardiner County Park

A relatively new park, this area has a long past. Originally owned by the Gardiner family, Suffolk County's first non-Indian landowners, and later part of Sagtikos Manor estate, it contains a transition zone between inland woods and bayside salt marshes within its 231 acres. The entrance is on Montauk Highway in West Bay Shore, a half mile east of Robert Moses Causeway.

Southaven County Park

The first, and one of the largest, parks opened by Suffolk County, Southaven protects the beautiful Carmans River. Wander north from the picnic areas and other developed facilities and you will find rewarding, wild country along one of the major streams on Long Island. It is possible to walk for miles in the area between Sunrise Highway and the Long Island Expressway far to the north. The park entrance is on the north side of Sunrise, between the Yaphank Avenue and William Floyd Parkway exits. Farther south along the east bank of the Carmans, west of William Floyd Parkway, is the Wertheim National Wildlife Refuge, a large area of pines and marshland at the end of Great South Bay. To the east in Mastic Beach is the newly opened William Floyd Homestead, with still more woodland and marsh, as well as peat bogs, fronting Moriches Bay.

Wildwood State Park

For walkers, this park is worth noting primarily because it offers access to the North Shore beaches, with spectacular high bluffs overlooking the Sound. These beaches are much different in character from those along the Atlantic. Since wave action is much less intense, the beaches are not as well developed. Pebbles and boulders from many of the rock formations—sedimentary, igneous, and metamorphic—as far north as the Berkshires and Green Mountains were carried hundreds of miles in the continental glacier and deposited on this shore. From Wildwood to Orient Point, the beach is the resting place of large boulders from the gneisses, granites, and schists of eastern Connecticut and central Massachusetts.

Orient Point

Almost at the tip of the North Fork lies 363-acre Orient Beach State Park. Park at the New London ferry and take the long walk along the beach, or drive into the park to take a shorter walk west to Long Beach Point. There find the wreckage of the old lighthouse. In spring the prickly-pear cactus and beach plum bloom; in summer there are roseate terns and porpoises; in fall tremendous numbers of migrating monarch butterflies hang from the cedars; in the winter there are sea birds and snowy owls. At all times of the year the park is an outstanding bird sanctuary and a favorite place for beachcombers. Getting there—driving through the rural and historical North Fork—adds to the enjoyment of Orient Point.

Suggested Readings

Albright, R. & P.
Short Walks on Long Island
Walking News, Inc., New York, 1974

Casey, Tom
Journey on the Long Island Greenbelt Trail
Long Island Greenbelt Trail Conference, Central Islip, N.Y., 1982

Murphy, Robert Cushman
Fish-Shape Paumanok—Nature and Man on Long Island
American Philosophical Society, Philadelphia, 1964

Paul, Lawrence G.
The Pine Barrens of Ronkonkoma
New York–New Jersey Trail Conference, New York, 1983

Part IV

NEW JERSEY

13 · *THE RAMAPOS OF NEW JERSEY*

(Map 22)

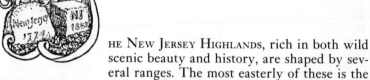

THE NEW JERSEY HIGHLANDS, rich in both wild scenic beauty and history, are shaped by several ranges. The most easterly of these is the Ramapo Mountain Range, which anchors its northeastern section at Tompkins Cove, New York, on the Hudson and crosses into New Jersey at Mahwah, just below Suffern.

As it heads southwest, the range defines a distinctly different geologic province from the Newark Basin farther east. The Ramapo River channels along the Great Border Fault (Ramapo Canopus) which separates the metamorphic rock complex of the Ramapos from the Triassic sandstone and shale of the lowlands, out of which rise the diabase intrusions that form the Palisades and the basalt extrusions that form the Watchungs. In general, the Precambrian crystalline rocks of the Ramapos are sharply distinguishable, both by topography and by composition, from those in the Newark Basin.

Glaciation of the peaks and lake sediments in the eroded sedimentary blocks have created a terrain in the Ramapos of rugged ridges and gentle valleys. From here, one may gaze west over the Wyanokies, whose smoky blue-green color on a late summer afternoon reminds one that the great Appalachian mountain chain is not too far away. The growth of public lands in recent years, and the resulting trail networks that have sprung up, provide greater access to a region long treasured by hikers and not yet discovered by the summer crowds which haunt hiking areas in New York's Ramapos.

HISTORY

Strategically placed among the thirteen colonies, New Jersey was the focal point of considerable activity during the American Revolution. Located both on the coast and in a direct line between Boston and Philadelphia, New Jersey offered something else besides its strategic location—the iron-laden Highlands.

The abandoned shafts, pits, and dumps of old iron mines are familiar to hikers in Harriman State Park; for example, the Hasenclever Mine, south of Lake Tiorati, is well known. Not so well known is that iron baron Peter Hasenclever's main work in the late 1700s was centered at Ringwood in what is now Passaic County, New Jersey. This business served as the heart of a thriving iron industry in the region, coloring the history of the area. Even today, families connected with the Ringwood ironworks and subsequent landowners are remembered as place names in state forests.

Iron mining and smelting began in the Ringwood area around 1740 with the formation of the Ringwood Company, named after a town in the New Forest of England. The company was organized by colonists of New York City and Newark, who subsequently sold their interests to an English group, the American Iron Company. It was this group that in 1765 brought over Peter Hasenclever, a man of German birth but of English iron mining and smelting experience. Hasenclever became the first real ironmaster in America and is credited with being the founder of the original Forges and Manor of Ringwood. He brought hundreds

Waterwheels of the Long Pond Ironworks

of iron miners, charcoal burners, and other specialists from abroad. His operations were extended to Charlottesburg and to Long Pond, as well as into the Hudson Highlands and the Mohawk Valley.

Hasenclever introduced the newest English and German methods and greatly improved output at Ringwood. He built a dam on Long Pond to form Greenwood Lake in order to supply blast power for operating the furnaces in that area. He also dammed Tuxedo Lake to permit its outlet, Summit Brook, to flow into Ringwood River to increase the supply of water power for the Manor furnaces.

Difficulties caused by overextension of his business, failure to receive payment from England for his iron, and the general disturbance of international trade as unrest grew in the colonies led Hasenclever to suffer one of the biggest "crashes" of his time.

In 1771, Robert Erskine, a Scottish civil engineer, was brought over by Hasenclever's creditors to straighten out the iron business at Ringwood. Operating the mines there, Erskine sided with his adopted country when the colonies revolted, and Ringwood became one of the chief munitions works for the Americans. In fact, much of Washington's maneuvering in northern New Jersey after the fall of New York was designed to defend Ringwood and keep it hidden in the forests. The second of the great iron chains across the Hudson, that at West Point, was made of metal from the Long Mine near Sterling Lake.

In 1777 Erskine was appointed Surveyor General to the American Army by General Washington and made the first good maps of the Highlands of northern New Jersey and southern New York. He died in 1780, and his remains were placed in a stone vault on the Manor property in a graveyard where more than 150 soldiers of the Revolution are reported to have been buried. George Washington, who was present at the Manor the day Erskine died, returned in 1782 to plant a tree at Erskine's grave. The grave may still be seen on the west shore of Sally's Pond, but the tree was destroyed by lightning in 1912.

Following the Revolution, activity at Ringwood declined, until its purchase several owners later by Peter Cooper, inventor, philanthropist, and guiding spirit behind the laying of the first Atlantic cable. Cooper, who was also founder of Cooper Union for the Advancement of Science in New York City, became one of the largest single landowners in New Jersey, with the Ringwood properties consisting of nearly 100,000 acres.

During the Civil War years, the works were extremely active. Upon the death of Cooper in 1884, title to Ringwood Manor passed to his son-in-law, Abram Stevens Hewitt, America's foremost ironmaster of the nineteenth century. He was associated with the New Jersey Steel & Iron Company, the Trenton Iron Company and Cooper & Hewitt, all of which were absorbed into United States Steel when it was formed by J. P. Morgan in 1911. What survived was the Ringwood Company, which was re-formed in 1905 by Mrs. Abram Hewitt following her husband's death. It was this firm that worked the Ringwood Mines during World War I.

In 1936, Hewitt's son, Erskine, deeded the Ringwood Manor House and 95 surrounding acres to the state of New Jersey in order to preserve this historic property for posterity. His nephew, Norvin Hewitt Green, gave additional property, bringing the total to 579 acres. He also donated 1000 acres in the Wyanokies, the Norvin Green State Forest. The Abram S. Hewitt State Forest, another gift, is west of Greenwood Lake and south of the New York State line.

NATURAL HISTORY

The forests of the Ramapos are regarded by many naturalists as an intermediate zone between the central hardwood forests, as exemplified by the mixed oak forests of the nearby Palisades to the south and west, and the northern hardwood forests of upstate New York and New England.

The Ramapos contain elements of both. On dry, sunny hillsides and ridges, the mixed oak forest predominates, characterized by five species of oak (red, white, black, scarlet, and chestnut) and two hickories (mockernut and pignut). Flowering dogwood flourishes in the understory, and the shrub layer is composed of maple-leaf viburnum, blueberry, huckleberry, mountain laurel, and pink azalea. On the most open, exposed summits, red cedar and pitch pine grow from the cracks in the granite and gneiss.

However, in the valleys and cooler, more shaded slopes of the Ramapos, a more northern forest takes over. Sugar maple, beech, hemlock, both yellow and black birch, and some white pine form the climax forest here. Yellow birch and white pine are rare on the Palisades, as is the small, beautiful striped maple, the green-and-white-striped trunks of which are so common in the understory of the Ramapo valleys. On the other hand, the huge, straight tulip trees which are so magnificent on the slopes below the Palisades are not nearly as common in the Ramapos, and the sweet gum, one of the dominant trees in Palisades wet woods, is absent altogether, since it reaches its northern limit on the Palisades. Ramapo lowland swamps and stream banks have red maple as the most common tree, with shagbark hickory, elm, ash, tupelo, and big sycamores. Spicebush, sweet pepperbush, swamp azalea, highbush blueberry, and elderberry make up the dense shrub layer in Ramapo wetlands.

Since the forests of the Ramapos are much more extensive and less disturbed than those of the Palisades, the hiker can expect to see a greater diversity of animal life. Deer are much more common, beaver occasionally are seen in the ponds (or at least their lodges and dams are), and occasionally a porcupine or mink is reported. Copperhead and black snakes (both racers and rat snakes) are sometimes encountered, and the rocky, more rugged sections represent one of the last strongholds of the timber rattlesnake in New Jersey. However, they are very rarely encountered by hikers, and need not be feared if left alone. Ruffed grouse, broad-winged hawks, great horned owls, pileated woodpeckers, brown creepers, hooded warblers, ovenbirds, scarlet tanagers, and towhees are just a few of the more unusual birds which nest in the forests of the Ramapos, and over two hundred other species use these woods throughout the year.

TRAILS DEVELOPMENT

Formerly much of the wild land in the Highlands was privately owned, and where the public could hike, the persistent encroachment of the real estate developer often led to frequent trail relocations.

Fortunately, hikers are now able to enjoy much of this area, thanks to the efforts of state and local officials and members of the hiking community who have worked to open land throughout New Jersey to the public. This began with the acquisition of open space for conservation and recreation, spurred by a series of Green Acres bond issues created by the New Jersey State Legislature, beginning in 1961 and followed by others in 1971, 1974, and 1978. On a fifty/fifty basis, state money was supplemented by federal grants from the Land and Water Conservation Fund, allowing both the state and counties to acquire acreage in many areas of New Jersey, particularly in the Ramapos.

Another critical step in the effort to protect land for public enjoyment was the signing into law in 1976 of the Natural Areas System Act, for which the League for Conservation Legislation, the Sierra Club's New Jersey Chapter, and then Assemblyman Thomas Kean can take credit. Following the lead of the New York state constitution, the act banned the sale or leasing of lands or the cutting of trees in areas designated as "forever wild." Since then, some 24,500 acres in the state, including sections of Wawayanda, Allamuchy, High Point, Ramapo Mountain, Wharton, and Worthington state parks and forests, as well as the Dunfield Natural Area near the Delaware Water Gap, through which the Appalachian Trail passes, have been designated Natural Areas.

The third important step in trails development came with the New Jersey Trails System Act, passed into law in November 1974. It ordered the state's Department of Environmental Protection to set up a statewide system of recreation and scenic trails, designating the Appalachian Trail as the initial component of that system. A Trails Council of volunteers was set up by the Department of Environmental Protection that included representatives of a wide range of trail users, including hikers. In addition to giving the green light to park and forest superintendents to further trail work, especially through the help of volunteers, this act led to the New Jersey Trails Plan approved in 1982, which sets in motion development of the statewide system of trails to include each of the six major trail-use categories: foot, water, horse, bicycle, snow, and motor.

The effect of these changes is already evident in the state, but nowhere more so than in the Ramapos, where a trail network has blossomed in the past several years. Most of the land here is contained within the Ramapo Mountain State Forest and Ringwood State Park, where volunteers, in cooperation with the state, have blazed miles of trails. In 1981, the purchase of 540 acres of a section of land called the Muscarelle Tract closed the gap separating the state forest from the state park and brought about the completion of a connecting trail, the Ringwood-Ramapo Trail, thus assuring the hiker of an unimpeded walk from the state line to Pompton Lakes.

Public enjoyment of the Ramapos has also been broadened thanks to recent state- and county-funded expansion of the Ramapo Valley County Reservation, whose trails provide access to state land bordering its western flank. Four Boy Scout properties in the northern Ramapos, all bordering on state land, are also helping to retain open space. On the initiative of trail volunteers of Camp Yaw Paw (Ridgewood–Glen Rock Council), a regional Ramapo Trails Council was formed in 1978 "to bring order out of trail building and maintenance" and to allow certain trails through Scout property to be open to hikers.

RINGWOOD STATE PARK

Featuring both wild and "cultivated" land, Ringwood State Park contains miles of trails suitable for hiking and cross-country skiing. Bordering New York State, the park was begun with Erskine Hewitt's donation of the Hasenclever Manor (now Ringwood Manor) and the surrounding land. A major historical shrine, the rambling old mansion contains a priceless collection of relics of the iron-making days, as well as the furnishings of the Ryersons, Coopers, and Hewitts from about 1810 to 1930.

Also contained in the park are Sheppard Pond—which, as part of a 541-acre tract, was added in 1964, thanks to Green Acre funds—and Skylands Manor, located on a 1000-acre parcel purchased in 1966 from Shelton College. This manor had been built in 1924 by Clarence McKenzie Lewis, who purchased the land from one of J. P. Morgan's top aides. Its interior is furnished with woodwork and fireplaces obtained from castles abroad; outside, it is surrounded by huge gardens with trees and shrubs from all over the world, a constant source of delight to visitors.

What captured the interest of hikers in the Ringwood area was a series of switchback carriage roads built by Lewis, extending east to Pierson Ridge, as well as a bridle path up Mount Defiance overlooking the gardens. Following the acquisition of the Bear Swamp Lake section from a vacation home club in 1972, volunteer trailblazers worked with Ringwood State Park superintendent Richard Riker to add a connecting trail from Pierson Ridge to the lake, the first bona fide trail in the area. Next, in 1978, came the purchase of the Green Engineering Camp of Cooper Union, a narrow belt that had bisected the park, and which contained several trails laid out by the former Cooper Union Hiking Club.

Access to this area by car from the northeast is from Route 17 just south of Sloatsburg, New York, on a new road beginning with a jug-end left turn "to Ringwood." While still in New York State, a left turnoff leads to Sheppard Pond, which has become a major picnic, fishing, and swimming area, as well as a trail crossing. Farther along in New Jersey, two other major parking areas can be reached—Ringwood Manor and Skylands Manor, via Morris Avenue. These two areas can also be approached from the south via Skyline Drive and Greenwood Lake Road, with a turnoff on Sloatsburg Road.

Hikers can also reach the area via the New Jersey Transit bus line from New York City. There is a designated stop at the Cupsaw Lake entrance at Skyland Road off Greenwood Lake

Road (N.J. Route 511), where hikers can either walk in or be picked up by car. Another bus pickup point is on Route 17 in Sloatsburg. Hikers should be prepared to pay fees to enter the parklands, particularly during the summer months. Another access is:

Bus Stop Trail. Length: 1 mile. Blazes: red.

Starting on Margaret King Avenue at the town hall, this small trail leads to Ringwood Manor. New Jersey Transit buses stop here twice a day.

Ringwood-Ramapo Trail. Length: 10.5 miles. Blazes: red.

This trail is a new addition to the park, taking over an existing section of trail from Ringwood Manor to Sheppard Pond and Mount Defiance, and extending it south to Ramapo Mountain State Forest.

From the Ringwood Manor picnic area, the Ringwood-Ramapo Trail crosses Ringwood River on a sturdy bridge, going over Sloatsburg Road before heading uphill over Cupsaw Mountain. Near the summit, the Cooper Union Trail (yellow) is crossed. The trail drops down and joins the Blue Trail (blue) for a short distance before crossing Cupsaw Brook and following it for a way. From the brook valley there is an easy climb to Sheppard Pond. The trail picks up an estate road through a large hemlock grove along the south shore of the lake, then makes a right turn uphill over an unnamed summit. Dropping down, the trail crosses a gas pipeline before beginning a steep ascent up the northern point of Mount Defiance (1100 feet). Heading south and partway down the ridge, the Ringwood-Ramapo Trail crosses the Halifax Trail (green), with a lookout 250 yards to the right over Skylands Manor. The trail continues south, picking up an estate carriage road before crossing the Crossover Trail (white) at the top of the shoulder. A right turn will take one back to Ringwood Manor via Skylands Manor.

Directly ahead, the Ringwood-Ramapo Trail continues south to a rock ledge lookout called Warm Puppy, then drops down the ridge to cross a road leading north to Glasmere Ponds. Descending to a brook, which it crosses on a stone slab, the trail then travels through a bamboo garden to a fire truck road. Making a left turn, it follows the road south before taking to the woods. A wood road is met and followed uphill and through a low pass to a broader wood road. A left turn brings one to the south end of Catnest Swamp.

The trail turns right and heads south a quarter mile on the road before making a left turn into the woods. Shortly it crosses the Blue Trail (left), leading to the Hoeferlin Memorial Trail (yellow) on the ridge. The Ringwood-Ramapo Trail soon reaches High Mountain Brook, which it parallels for three quarters of a mile. After crossing the brook, it ascends some 250 feet on an old trail and makes a right turn past a spring. There is a short pitch through a rock pile before the trail levels off and follows the state property line in a southwesterly direction. The trail ends as a trail marked red where it joins the Hoeferlin Memorial Trail (yellow), some 500 feet north of Hill 1082 on the U.S. Geological Survey's "Ramsey" map. From this point to the upper parking lot on Skyline Drive in Ramapo Mountain State Forest, it is an estimated 2.6 miles.

Cooper Union Trail. Length: 5 miles. Blazes: yellow.

A north-south trail, Cooper Union features Suicide Ledge, which affords fine views over the Wanaque Reservoir. It begins at Ringwood Manor parking lot and, after crossing the Ringwood River on a sturdy bridge, turns left and parallels Sloatsburg Road on the west side. Just short of the New York State line, the trail crosses the highway and heads due south over Cupsaw Mountain, meeting Ringwood-Ramapo Trail (red) near the summit. Descending the mountain, the trail meets the Blue Trail (blue) and then the Crossover Trail (white), which it follows for the next quarter mile.

After both cross Morris Avenue, the Crossover diverts left to Cupsaw Brook Valley, while the Cooper Union heads right, soon joining a gas pipeline, which it follows west before turning left into the woods. Presently a well-worn wood road is met and followed due south. Swinging around to the east, the trail soon crosses Carltondale Road and shortly becomes an established wood road starting up Governor Mountain. In 200 yards, a return loop trail comes in at the left. At the bare summit, there are views to the west, but the spectacular view south and west over Wanaque Reservoir is actually 40 feet lower at Suicide Ledge.

To complete the loop, the hiker should take the trail left from the ledge over a shoulder, dropping down to a wet spot and then picking up a rocky ridge heading north. Swinging west, the trail joins its original section just south of a hemlock grove. The visit to Suicide Ledge can be shortened by starting from Skylands Manor and using the Crossover Trail to its intersection with the Cooper Union Trail. To return to Ringwood Manor by the Crossover Trail adds 2.5 miles to the trip.

Blue Trail. Length: 0.5 mile. Blazes: blue.

This is a lowland connecting trail between the Cooper Union Trail and the Ringwood-Ramapo Trail, to avoid the climb over Cupsaw Mountain.

Crossover Trail. Length: 6 miles. Blazes: white.

Connecting Ringwood Manor with Bear Swamp Lake, this trail leaves from the mansion's northern parking area, crossing the Ringwood River and Sloatsburg Road before turning right to contour Cupsaw Mountain. In three quarters of a mile, the trail joins the Cooper Union Trail (yellow), crosses Morris Avenue, and then turns left to head downhill to Cupsaw Brook. The trail uses the Morris Avenue auto bridge for a crossing, then turns right into the woods. A pipeline is crossed and a sewage plant is skirted. The trail leads through an open meadow before turning uphill to the parking lot at Skylands Manor. A stroll around the Manor House and its spectacular gardens is well worth the time.

Picking up the trail again, the hiker heads southeast past some houses and gardens before reaching deep woods. On the left, the Halifax Trail (green) starts up a shoulder of Mount Defiance on a switchback trail. For the next several miles, the Crossover Trail makes use of estate carriage roads. At the top of the southern shoulder of Mount Defiance, it meets the Ringwood-Ramapo Trail (red).

Continuing east, the Crossover Trail crosses the Glasmere Ponds Road, skirts Gatum Pond, and reaches an open area that is often used for model airplane flights. Ascending Pierson Ridge, the trail leaves the carriage road about 100 yards past a hairpin turn and heads uphill in a southeasterly direction. On the ridge, it meets the Pierson Ridge Trail (blue), and then joins the Hoeferlin Memorial Trail (yellow), making a right turn south. At Ilgenstein Rock overlooking Bear Swamp Lake, the Crossover Trail leaves the Hoeferlin and descends sharply to end at the Cannonball Trail, which heads north to Bear Swamp Lake.

Halifax Trail. Length: 6 miles. Blazes: green.

Featuring switchback trails and views of the surrounding land, this east-west trail starts in Ringwood State Park at Skylands Manor using a combination of old carriage trails, wood roads, and fire roads to reach Ramapo Valley County Reservation.

To reach the trail, hikers should take the Crossover Trail (white) from the main parking lot at Skylands Manor. After about a half mile partly on blacktop through the main grounds of the estate, the hiker can pick up the trail on the left. It ascends the mountain by a series of switchbacks, at least a hundred years old, to a fine view point looking northwest over Ringwood, West Milford, and Sterling Forest. From the lookout, the trail continues east, passing the Ringwood-Ramapo Trail, before descending on switchbacks to pass Glasmere Ponds.

After crossing Pierson Ridge, the trail leaves state park land and crosses onto privately held land. Paralleling a gas pipeline, the trail passes several unmarked trails, intersecting the yellow Hoeferlin Memorial Trail. After the intersection, it is a moderate descent on private lands along several streams through Havemeyer Hollow, named after a onetime owner of the valley. Unfortunately, this stretch is a dump for abandoned auto wrecks. A highlight from the hollow is an unmarked side trail on the left which will take the hiker to Dancing Rock, which, as legend would have it, Indians danced upon. Passing Havemeyer Reservoir on the left, the trail descends further to the flood plain of the Ramapo River. Bearing south, the trail enters the county reservation in about a half mile. Here, a lava butte, a northern remnant of the Second Watchung Range at the edge of the Ramapo Fault, can be seen. The trail ends shortly thereafter at the Silver Trail by Scarlet Oak Pond, which leads to a parking lot on Route 202 in Mahwah.

Havemeyer Trail. Length: 1 mile. Blazes: blue.

This little trail, which features old beech and tulip trees, connects the Halifax Trail with the Ridge Trail (blue) in Ramapo Valley County Reservation, to provide the hiker with an alternative route. Highlights include the ruins of several old farms.

Orange Trail. Length: 0.25 mile. Blazes: orange.

This restricted Scout trail connects the Hoeferlin Trail with the Green Trail.

Green Trail. Length: 0.5 mile. Blazes: green.

This Scout trail connects the Hoeferlin Memorial Trail with the Cannonball Trail, providing access to Camp Yaw Paw. The trail is restricted.

Pierson Ridge Trail. Length: 1 mile. Blazes: blue.

Traversing the ridge for which it is named, the trail begins on the Halifax Trail (green) just before it leaves state land. It follows a carriage road for a little more than a half mile before reaching its southern terminus at the white Crossover Trail.

West Shore Trail. Length: 1 mile. Blazes: blue.

Following the scenic west shore of Bear Swamp Lake, this trail begins at the Cannonball Trail at the south end of the lake before the dam. After passing by a few abandoned dwellings, the trail hugs the lake before ending at the Hoeferlin Memorial Trail beyond the north end of the lake.

RAMAPO MOUNTAIN STATE FOREST

A rugged 2340-acre area, Ramapo Mountain State Forest has elevations ranging from 200 to 1100 feet. Including the wild lands of Mahwah, Oakland, Pompton Lakes, Wanaque, and Ringwood, it was added to New Jersey's public lands in 1976 using Green Acres and federal funds for conservation and recreation. It had been the estate of the late Clifford F. MacEvoy, a wealthy contractor for large public works, including the Wanaque Reservoir.

Centerpiece of the park is Ramapo Lake, formerly called Rotten Pond (or Lake LeGrande), a name more than likely derived from Dutch settlers who called it Rote (Rat) Pond for the muskrats they trapped there. Fishing is permitted, but no swimming. In the southern end of the state forest, there are eight private holdings, served by one-lane access roads not open to the public. Public access is by foot only. Other estate roads have been allowed to deteriorate, and some are marked in places as hiking trails. Many also serve as ski touring trails. Trail bikes are prohibited. One patrol road encircles the lake and passes a ranger station on the west shore. The northern part of the forest is wild and open to hunters as well as hikers. No fires or camping are permitted.

More than 20 miles of trails have been laid out since the purchase to provide gradual ascents to rock-ledge view points from which the land may drop off sharply. Three are through trails. One, the old Suffern-Midvale Trail, has been renamed the Hoeferlin Memorial Trail to honor William Hoeferlin, a noted trailblazer and mapmaker. Another through trail beginning in the state forest is the rediscovered historical Cannonball Road, which originated at Pompton Lakes where there was an iron furnace. Trail routes were laid out by Frank Oliver, as a member of the New York–New Jersey Trail Conference, and were cleared primarily by the Youth Conservation Corps in 1977 and 1978.

Hikers going by car have four access points. Two can be reached by taking West Oakland Avenue, at the end of Route 208, right to Skyline Drive. The lower parking lot is about 0.3

mile on the left, signed Ramapo Mountain State Forest; the upper lot is about 1.1 miles farther on the left. Drivers may also take West Oakland Avenue left from the Skyline Drive corner. About 1.1 miles from this intersection, turn right onto Pool Hollow Road and park on the right, just short of the railroad tracks. A fourth parking area can be used by turning right onto Schuyler Avenue, some 2.1 miles from the Skyline Drive corner, and then right onto Barbara Drive. There is parking for three or more cars at the end of the road. This area can also be reached by a short walk from public transportation to Pompton Lakes. The New Jersey Transit buses from New York City stop at the former railroad station in town, as do those from Paterson and Newark.

Cannonball Trail. Length: 8.5 miles. Blazes: white C on red.

In his book *Vanishing Ironworks of the Ramapos* (Rutgers University Press, 1966), James M. Ransom defines the Cannonball Road, after which this trail is named, as part historic, part legendary. His historical evidence about the Pompton Furnace reveals that cannonballs were cast here in great quantity during the American Revolution. The furnace was located adjacent to the northern end of the natural basalt rock dam of Pompton Lakes. A portion of the support for the charging bridge from the hillside to the top of the furnace is all that remains. From here, the obvious valley route to the Hudson would have followed the Ramapo River to Smiths Clove on what is now U.S. 202. Because the Loyalists might tip off the British, it seems reasonable to believe that a hidden route was laid out through the Ramapos. The criterion had to be easy grades over the ridge for heavily laden oxen-drawn wagons.

With the aid of old maps and the help of Ransom, the route has been rediscovered and marked as the Cannonball Trail. To pick up the trail, hikers should begin at the parking area at the end of Barbara Drive in Pompton Lakes. Here, the first trail marker is found at the entrance to a town minipark. The trail skirts a ballfield to pick up a left turn into the woods at the western edge, the beginning of Ramapo Mountain State Forest. The trail keeps left at a fork, climbs steeply, and runs above and parallel to the Du Pont fence. Shortly thereafter, it picks up a wood road, the historic Cannonball Road, which is followed 0.9 mile to a fork on the right, marked yellow. This is the crossover route to the Hoeferlin Memorial Trail (yellow), which may be used on an alternate return loop.

The Cannonball Trail bears left and soon picks up large boulders, bordering a depressed roadway, evidence of the original route. The road follows minor ups and downs, crosses a small stream, and ascends at a moderate grade. The wood road becomes gravel as a MacEvoy estate road is picked up, followed right, then left at a fork.

The marked trail keeps on the gravel road along Ramapo Lake, passes Ranger Headquarters (map available here), and shortly makes a left turn on a grass-covered road. In 400 feet, the Cannonball Trail turns right and joins the MacEvoy Trail (blue) and follows it to a gravel estate road leading uphill. At the elbow is the start of the Castle Point Trail (white), leading to a former mansion. At the top of the hill, the road bears sharp left, while the trail keeps straight ahead into the woods. A stream is crossed and the trail, mostly a wood road, begins its ascent to the height of the ridge. An estate road is crossed and the trail parallels it through woods and fields, skirts around a private holding, and reaches Skyline Drive, 3.5 miles from Pompton Lakes.

North of the highway, on a wide wood road, the trail is joined by the Hoeferlin Memorial Trail (yellow) coming in from the right and remains with it for the next 1.75 miles. At a pipeline crossing beside the highway, there is limited parking. At a Y fork, the Hoeferlin Memorial Trail goes left to Matapan Rock view point, but soon rejoins the Cannonball, heading north. At the hollow beyond the next hill, the trail leaves the Hoeferlin and heads northeast downhill.

The trail skirts a large swamp, crosses its outlet, and with minor ups and downs reaches the original Cannonball Road that passes through Camp Glen Gray. The wood road proceeds through Camp Yaw Paw on a high line and enters Ringwood State Park land, passing the terminus of the white Crossover Trail before dipping down to Bear Swamp Lake. It crosses the dam and follows along the east shore through a former cottage area.

Shortly after leaving the last house on the lakeshore, a wood road on the right brings in the Silver-Red Trail from Ramapo Valley County Reservation. Halfway down the lake, the gravel road goes uphill, while the Cannonball diverts left to the lakeshore. In 0.3 mile the blazed trail ends at the junction with the Hoeferlin Memorial Trail, 8.5 miles from Pompton Lakes. Northeast, the Hoeferlin Memorial Trail reaches Suffern in 4.5 miles. Using the trail through the reservation cuts the distance to 2.5 miles to the parking lot on Route 202 in Mahwah.

Hoeferlin Memorial Trail. Length: 14 miles. Blazes: yellow.

Featuring views of the Wyanokies, this trail is a modification of the long-established Suffern-Midvale Trail. The trail begins at the three-car parking area on the right side of Pool Hollow Road immediately off West Oakland Avenue. After crossing the railroad tracks, it goes around a small pond in sight of houses. A horse corral is passed before the trail reaches a washed-out MacEvoy Estate road leading to Ramapo Lake. Beyond a rise on the left is a small upper pond, a possible lunch spot. In a half mile from the parking lot, a short crossover trail to the Cannonball Trail is met on the left.

The Hoeferlin Memorial Trail continues on the gravel road up a series of S-turns and crosses the planned route of Interstate 287 from Montville to Suffern, which bisects the lower part of the state forest. Continuing north, the gravel road swings left at the top of the ridge, while the trail enters the woods straight ahead and descends steeply to a brook crossing before rising to a rock-ledge view point on the border of private land. To the southeast, High Mountain and Beech Mountain can be seen in the Watchung Range. The trail then begins to climb up the ridge partly over rock ledges, with a view back toward Pompton Lakes. At the top of the ridge, another rock ledge amid scrub pines offers a view west to the Wyanokies.

Here the Lookout Trail (red) is met as it diverts to the right, but it is combined with the Hoeferlin Memorial Trail for the next 0.7 mile north along the ridge. Before descending from the ridge, both trails pass a rocky ledge with a view of Ramapo Lake and Windbeam's hump to the northwest. The combined trails reach the lakeshore road and follow it around to the dam, where the Lookout Trail starts its loop down the outlet brook. The Hoeferlin Memorial Trail crosses the dam and follows a blacktop road uphill 100 yards before entering the woods. The general route is uphill, picking up a wood road and a gravel road before reaching the blacktop again just short of the entrance gate on Skyline Drive (upper parking lot).

After crossing the highway, the Hoeferlin Memorial Trail requires hand pulls to gain a rock ledge with views to the east. Paralleling the road, it merges into the Cannonball Trail, and the two become one for the next 1.75 miles. The trail touches the drive at a pipeline crossing and ascends the ridge. At a fork, the Cannonball goes right, while the Hoeferlin turns left to Matapan Rock, where there is a fine view of the Wyanokies. Turning east, the trail shortly rejoins the Cannonball at a left turn. In the dip beyond the next hill, the Cannonball branches right. Ahead on the western rim of the next hill, the Ringwood-Ramapo Trail (red) starts left downhill. Shortly thereafter, the Hoeferlin leaves the state forest and enters Scout property, part of Camp Glen Gray's North Quad and of Camp Yaw Paw. Erskine Lookout to the west is encountered on High Mountain.

From here, the trail borders state land and crosses the Blue Trail from Camp Yaw Paw down to High Mountain Brook. It now enters Ringwood State Park and climbs to Ilgenstein Rock with a view east over Bear Swamp Lake. The white Crossover Trail is met as it comes up from the lake and is joined for the next 0.6 mile before turning off left for Skylands Manor.

The Hoeferlin continues north past Butler Mine diggings, then descends the ridge to a tricky brook crossing before joining a wood road around a hill and crossing the feeder brook of Bear Swamp Lake. The northern terminus of the Cannonball Trail is met on the right. For a short distance, the trail follows a pipeline service road before becoming a wood road. The Halifax Trail (green) is crossed.

The Hoeferlin Memorial Trail continues northeast to a road that goes through a settlement on Stag Hill, after passing tiny Silver Lake. It leaves the road, drops down to another settlement, and ascends to Split Rock on Houvenkopf Mountain. Descending steeply to cross high-speed Route 17, the trail passes a row of houses and crosses the Ramapo River on an unused railroad bridge. It skirts a ballfield and reaches the Suffern railroad station, where the Hoeferlin Memorial Trail ends. There are connections to and from Hoboken Terminal. A bus stop is a quarter mile north on Orange Turnpike.

MacEvoy Trail. Length: 2.2 miles. Blazes: blue.

From the lower parking lot on Skyline Drive, the MacEvoy Trail climbs to the lake in 0.6 mile, passing the Todd Trail on the right 500 feet short of the dam. The blue trail follows the gravel road along the north shore, going right at a fork uphill through gateposts. At the second curve, the trail joins the Cannonball Trail and turns left into the woods. Upon reaching a grass-covered road, the MacEvoy Trail turns right, the Cannonball, left. There is a right and left jog of the MacEvoy along a pipeline before the trail proceeds almost on the level on a wood road. Near the end, the trail goes downhill to Wolff Drive at its dead end in a housing development in Wanaque.

Lookout Trail. Length: 2.3 miles. Blazes: red.

From the south end of Ramapo Lake dam, this trail starts down the outlet brook and picks up a wood road on the edge of a wetland before becoming a footpath leading up to the top of the ridge. At a reverse fork, the trail keeps ahead a short distance to a wide lookout east to Oakland and Route 208. A descent to the right leads to a rock ledge with views south to Pompton Lakes and Potash Pond. From these view points, steps are retraced to the fork and followed left around the rim of a wide cirque. There are a few short pitches, one around a knob, another around a cliff to join the Hoeferlin Memorial Trail (yellow) at the top. From the view point at an open rock ledge, the two trails go north, passing a second rocky view point amid scrub pine, which gives views across Ramapo Lake and the mountains of Norvin Green State Forest. From the lookout, the combined trails drop down to the gravel road at the lakeshore, where the Lookout Trail ends. From the lower parking lot the round trip is 3.5 miles.

Castle Point Trail. Length: 1 mile. Blazes: white.

Highlight of this trail is a burned-out fieldstone mansion, which looks out over a stunning panorama of lake and mountain. To reach it, one should walk north on Skyline Drive from the upper parking lot about a quarter mile, to a blacktop road on the left which leads into private holdings in the state forest. The Castle Point Trail starts shortly thereafter on the right. A rock ledge is met with views west. The trail zigzags down the steep slope to a logging road, then breaks out to a grass-covered pipeline, which it follows left around a wide bend. At the foot of the

LAKE LAGRANDE, or ROTTEN POND

steep slope, the trail goes left, picks up a wood road, then heads south uphill to a wide view point, west to Wanaque Reservoir. The trail passes a stone tower on the way to the burned-out shell of the mansion. Below the ruin is a parapet with a gorgeous view of Ramapo Lake. The trail climbs over the rock wall and drops down the point to the Cannonball Trail at a bend in the gravel access road to a private holding.

Todd Trail. Length: 2.2 miles. Blazes: white.

The trail traverses land east of Skyline Drive, taking in a wide view point. From the upper parking lot, the Todd Trail heads downhill east with some ups and downs around ravines. It reaches a gravel road joining Camp Tamarack with Camp Todd, both Scout camps. In sight of the Todd ranger's cabin, the trail diverts right uphill to wide views east from grassy Todd Hill, before traversing a side slope. It then drops down, using pieces of an abandoned camp road, before turning left off the road and crossing a hill to Skyline Drive. On the far side, it traverses between private lands before ascending a ridge and dropping down to a stream valley, wet at times. A short ascent brings the Todd Trail out to its junction with the MacEvoy Trail, 500 feet east of Ramapo Lake.

Yellow Trail. Length: 2 miles. Blazes: yellow.

This trail takes off from the Todd Trail heading north through Camp Todd private lands and Camp Glen Gray, where it reaches the Silver-Yellow Trail in the Ramapo Valley County Reservation. It then continues north to its terminus at Cannonball Lake.

RAMAPO VALLEY COUNTY RESERVATION

Providing the opportunity for both rugged day-long hiking and pleasant afternoon strolling—as well as access to state lands on its western flank—the 1400-acre reservation was created in 1972 with land purchased through the Green Acres program and federal monies. Left in its natural wild state by the Bergen County Park Commission, which administers the area, the reservation is mostly hilly, forming the eastern tier of the Ramapos. A wildlife sanctuary, it includes among its features the Ramapo River, Scarlet Oak Pond, MacMillan Reservoir, Ramapo Fault, Hawk Rocks, and an Indian fish weir.

Purchased from the Indians, the land was settled around 1720. The boundaries of the farms that spring up are still present, and the reservation once boasted grist and saw mills, as well as a bronze foundry. The land was ultimately purchased by A. R. Darling, whose country estate gave the name Darlington to the area. The foundation of his manor house, situated near the entrance to the park, is still visible.

Access to the area is from a parking area on Ramapo Valley Road (Route 202) in Mahwah. Access from the south will eventually be available.

No open fires are allowed in the park without a permit, and tent camping is allowed only in designated areas near Scarlet Oak Pond. For further information, call the reservation office at (201) 825-1388, or the Bergen County Park Commission at (201) 646-2680.

Silver Trail. Length: 2 miles. Blazes: silver.

Of the reservation's many trails, the Silver is the primary feeder trail. Starting at the parking area, the trail crosses the Ramapo River and follows the northwest shore of Scarlet Oak Pond. Immediately diverting to the right along the Ramapo River is the unmarked start of the Halifax Trail which eventually leads into Ringwood State Park after traversing miles of private lands. Before the Silver Trail reaches the end of the pond, the Waterfall Trail branches off on the left. A little farther, a shore path loops around the pond in open fields. At a fork, the Northern Ridge Trail loop diverts to the right, while the Yellow follows the Reservation Service Road uphill to MacMillan Reservoir. Across the dam is the stub of the Reservoir Trail.

Above the reservoir, the Silver-Yellow starts on the left. After the Silver Trail swings right at the top of the grade, in a short distance the Northern Ridge Trail (blue) diverts right. Later, at not too obvious a turn, the Yellow goes left, and ends at the Bear Swamp Brook Road, leading into Camp Yaw Paw. Straight ahead is the Silver-Red Trail.

Silver-Red Trail. Length: 1 mile. Blazes: red and silver.

Skirting Rocky Mountain, this trail connects the Silver Trail with the Cannonball Trail at Bear Swamp Lake.

Silver-Yellow Trail. Length: 2.3 miles. Blazes: silver and yellow.

Picking up from the Silver Trail, this path passes through the southern reaches of the reservation, skirting Matty Price Hill and crossing Bear Swamp Brook on the road bridge. It continues southwest to a switchback wood road leading into Camp Glen

Gray. At that point a Yellow Trail continues ahead to Camp Todd and the Todd Trail in Ramapo Mountain State Forest, on the way crossing the auto road into Glen Gray.

Northern Ridge Trail. Length: 2 miles. Blazes: blue.

With the Silver Trail, this trail forms the only loop trail wholly within the reservation. Taking off from the Silver, it follows a stream up to Monroe Ridge. As it diverts from the ridge, a turnoff (right) leads to a rock-ledge lookout over the Ramapo Valley. The Ridge Trail terminates at the Silver in sight of Scarlet Oak Pond.

CAMPGAW COUNTY RESERVATION

Also located in Mahwah and coming under the jurisdiction of the Bergen County Park Commission, this reservation contains 5 miles of marked trails on its western and undeveloped ridge, as well as some 5 miles of unmarked trails. The 1300-acre reservation also has skiing, picnicking, and camping (by permit only) facilities. The reservation is bounded on the east by Campgaw Road, where there is access, and on the west by Route 202.

Further information is available from the reservation office (closed during the ski season), phone: (201) 327-7800, and from the Bergen County Park Commission, phone: (201) 646-2680.

Suggested Readings

Cohen, David S.
The Ramapo Mountain People
Rutgers University Press, New Brunswick, N.J., 1974

Cottrell, Alden T.
The Story of Ringwood Manor
Trenton Printing Company (pamphlet available at Manor House), Ringwood, N.J., 1954

Heusser, Albert H.
George Washington's Map Maker: A Biography of Robert Erskine, edited by Hubert G. Schmidt
Rutgers University Press, New Brunswick, N.J., new edition, 1966

Pierson, E. F.
The Ramapo Pass
(Privately printed) Free Library, Suffern, N.Y., 1915

Ransom, James M.
Vanishing Ironworks of the Ramapos
Rutgers University Press, New Brunswick, N.J., 1966

14 · *THE NEW JERSEY HIGHLANDS*

(Maps 20 and 21)

MOST OF the area known as the New Jersey Highlands lies beyond the Wanaque River's western shore. Although the Ramapo Mountains to the east are also considered part of the Highlands, the two sections differ as much from one another as the Ramapos do from the Newark Basin.

Consisting of Paleozoic sandstone-and-quartz conglomerate ridges and shale-and-limestone valleys—which form Bearfort Ridge and Greenwood Lake respectively—this downfaulted wedge is sandwiched between the Wawayanda and Wyanokie plateaus. Most of the area is on public land. Dotted with reservoirs, this region seems to have no shortage of flowering bushes. From the giant violet rhododendron in Wawayanda to the pink and white stars of mountain laurel shimmering on the Wyanokies' sunlit slopes, the region is a particular joy in early summer, as well as early spring when the patient photographer can discover tiny wildflowers growing in among shards of iron, remnants of the area's once-thriving iron industry. And for those who delight in more subdued palettes, winter snows cling to the hemlocks, firs, and unadorned laurel to create fairy-tale-like forests.

THE WYANOKIES

The 34-square-mile Wyanokie wild area, which includes the 2260-acre Norvin Green State Forest, has one of the largest concentrations of trails in the state. Elevations here range from 400 to 1300 feet and, although within sight of the New York skyline, the hiker can find peace and beauty aplenty in the area's streams, waterfalls, and scenic vistas. Also featured are several abandoned iron mines, one of which is still open to the public.

The original trails in this area were laid out in the early 1920s by Dr. Will S. Monroe of Montclair and his co-workers in the Green Mountain Club. When he retired, the property and trail maintenance were taken over by the Nature Friends, who named the area Camp Midvale. This camp is now known as the Weis Ecology Center.

Primary access to the area is at the ecology center, located on Snake Den Road, uphill from West Brook Road. A fee may be charged to park in the center's lot, and groups planning to park a number of cars should call the camp in advance. This central starting point is approached from Route 511, north of Midvale, over a causeway across Wanaque Reservoir. Other entrance points where parking is available are at the eastern end of Hewitt at the junction of the East Shore Road with Greenwood Lake Turnpike, and at the beginning of Doty Road in Haskell for the trail up Post Brook. There is also a parking spot on West Brook Road, north of Saddle Mountain, in the middle of the Wyanokie area, and on Glen Wild Road in the Otter Hole area.

Hikers in the Wyanokie region should also know that the reservoir environs, which the Wyanokie area borders, are patrolled by uniformed guards of the North Jersey District Water Supply Commission. The Green Mountain Club open shelter at Blue Mine is within an eighth of a mile of a guard station, and walkers are warned not to cross the line.

Burnt Meadow Trail. Length: 1.5 miles. Blazes: yellow.

The Burnt Meadow Trail begins on top of Horse Pond Mountain on the Horse Pond Mountain Trail (white). After descending to Burnt Meadow Road, which it follows for about 50 feet, the trail regains the woods to ascend Long Mountain and its terminus with the Hewitt-Butler Trail (blue).

Carris Hill Trail. Length: 1 mile. Blazes: yellow.

The Carris Hill Trail begins on the Lower Trail (white) and ascends steeply to an impressive view of the Wanaque Reservoir and the surrounding mountains. Continuing, it reaches Carris Hill and the Hewitt-Butler Trail (blue).

Hewitt-Butler Trail. Length: 18 miles. Blazes: blue.

Featuring impressive views, the Hewitt-Butler Trail extends the entire length of the Wyanokie region, from Hewitt, at the junction of Route 511 with East Shore Road, to Cold Spring Lake on Macopin Road in Bloomingdale.

In Hewitt, the trail starts on an old railroad route cut through a rocky hill. Follow the blue blazes up the hill to the left. At approximately .4 mile, the trail turns west on a pipeline. Ascending into the woods, the trail passes the Horse Pond Mountain Trail on the left before descending to cross two brooks and Burnt Meadow Road. Continuing, the trail passes under a power line and ascends a ridge which offers an excellent view of Long Hill ahead and another view, southeast, of the Ramapos and Garrett Mountain in the Watchungs. The trail descends from the ridge to the former Huyler Farm before ascending to follow the top of Long Hill, with two westward view points of the valley and Bearfort Range. It now descends to Kitchell Lake Trail and, after many ups and downs, crosses a brook to an excellent view of Burnt Meadow, passes West Brook Trail (also yellow), and ascends to Tip-Top Point. Here the Mine Trail (yellow on white) joins, and they descend together to Manaticut Point with superb views eastward.

Descending, sometimes steeply, to a brook and beautiful hemlock grove, the trail crosses West Brook and West Brook Road (6.5 miles), then ascends to an easterly view which includes the New York City skyline. Descending past Wolf Den, a jumble of rocks, the trail has several ups and downs before crossing a brook and joining the Wyanokie Circular Trail (red on white). Together, they cross two brooks before traversing the three Pine Paddies. Of these, No. 3 offers a north-to-east panorama of the Wyanokies and beyond, and No. 1 a view of Wanaque Reservoir and Wyanokie High Point. The trails separate after crossing a brook west of the Weis Ecology Center (9.5 miles). Following Snake Den Road west about a quarter mile, the Hewitt-Butler Trail joins the Mine Trail (yellow on white) a short distance before ascending to views of the Wyanokie region. Passing the Macopin Trail (white) and just below the top of Wyanokie High Point, it joins the Wyanokie Circular Trail again for 0.4 mile. The trail ascends past Yoo-Hoo Point to Carris Hill Trail (yellow) and Carris Hill with a view in many directions. Descending to a pipeline and the end of Post Brook Trail (white), it crosses a brook and parallels Post Brook northwest, crossing Wyanokie Crest Trail (yellow), to Otter Hole Trail (green on white). Crossing Post Brook, it ascends to Glen Wild Road (13.5 miles), which it follows west before entering woods to pick up Torne Trail (red on white) and make a steep ascent of Torne Mountain. The summit offers many excellent views of the surrounding valley and mountains. Continuing past the upper end of Torne Trail, the Hewitt-Butler Trail comes to South Torne and Osio Rock, both with impressive views. Descending steeply, it then follows an old road through the valley, crosses a brook, and traverses a hill before arriving at Star Lake.

Approximately a half mile before reaching Star Lake and an unpaved camp road, the trail is on Salvation Army property. Follow the camp road to the gate and Macopin Road. The Salvation Army does not object to hikers passing through; however, the grounds and facilities should be respected as strictly private. Hikers starting at this end of the trail should check in at the administration building, whose entrance is on the west side. Parking may be allowed if space is available.

Horse Pond Mountain Trail. Length: 2 miles. Blazes: white.

The Horse Pond Mountain Trail starts from the Stonetown Circular Trail (red triangle on white) on Harrison Mountain. It descends steeply to a brook before ascending sharply to traverse the entire length of Horse Pond Mountain. While descending, watch for a spectacular view of the Wanaque River and Ringwood State Park. The trail then passes a power line and meets the Hewitt-Butler Trail south of the gas pipeline.

Lower Trail. Length: 1.7 miles. Blazes: white.

The Lower Trail extends between the Wyanokie Circular Trail east of High Point and the Post Brook Trail east of Chikahoki Falls. At the southern end, it borders the Wanaque Reservoir property line and passes the Carris Hill Trail.

Macopin Trail. Length: 2.5 miles. Blazes: white.

The Macopin Trail begins at the junction of Larsen Road with Otter Hole Road, a short distance south of Mountain Glen Lakes. It crosses two brooks before ascending to intersect the Wyanokie Circular Trail (red on white). Continuing on, it crosses Wyanokie Crest Trail (yellow) to meet the Otter Hole Trail. The trail then jogs right and left after crossing a brook, ascending to meet the Hewitt-Butler Trail (blue) west of Wyanokie High Point.

Mine Trail. Length: 5.4 miles. Blazes: yellow on white.

The Mine Trail, which takes the hiker to a mine that can be entered, begins approximately 150 yards east of the Weis Ecology Center parking lot on Snake Den Road. Passing through private land, the trail picks up with the Wyanokie Circular (red on white) for a while, and then branches off to the right. Descending steeply, it crosses a brook before reaching Wyanokie Falls (0.5 mile) and Wyanokie Circular Trail. The trail then ascends Ball Mountain at 0.8 mile, named for two large boulders shaped like giant balls. From here, there is an excellent view of Wyanokie High Point and its surrounding mountains.

The trail continues along the ridge to another view point before descending to Roomy Mine (1.1 miles), which can be entered. It shortly joins the Wyanokie Circular Trail to pass the flooded Blue Mine (1.5 miles) and the Green Mountain Club open shelter. It leaves the Wyanokie Circular Trail east of High Point and follows a low route to the Hewitt-Butler Trail (blue on white) and Snake Den Road (2.3 miles). Continuing on, it passes the abandoned Winfield Farm, Otter Hole Trail (green on white), Wyanokie Crest Trail (yellow), and Boy Scout Lake, where it crosses the Wyanokie Circular Trail again. The trail follows the lake overflow to West Brook Road (4.8 miles). After crossing the road, it ascends, sometimes steeply, to view points and Tip-Top Point on the Hewitt-Butler Trail, which it follows to Manaticut Point.

Otter Hole Trail. Length: 2 miles. Blazes: green on white.

The Otter Hole Trail connects the Mine Trail at old Winfield Farm with the Hewitt-Butler Trail at the Otter Hole. Following an old road from the farm site, it crosses a brook as it intersects the Macopin Trail (0.4 mile). The Wyanokie Circular Trail (red on white) enters from the left (0.8 mile) and joins the Otter Hole Trail for 0.3 mile. At 2 miles the trail ends at the Hewitt-Butler Trail (blue).

Post Brook Trail. Length: 3 miles. Blazes: white.

The Post Brook Trail begins at the junction of Route 511 and Doty Road in Haskell. It follows Doty Road 1 mile west before entering the woods (right) and passing between hills to a rhododendron grove. After crossing two more roads, it zigzags around boulders through a ravine of hemlocks. Crossing Post Brook twice, then paralleling it, the trail passes the Lower Trail and Chikahoki Falls, and ends at the Hewitt-Butler Trail (blue on white).

Stonetown Circular Trail. Length: 9.5 miles. Blazes: red triangle on white.

The Stonetown Circular goes over a number of peaks, which classifies it as strenuous, since it totals about the equivalent of a 2500-foot climb. If a car must be parked, a good starting place is at the Ringwood Fire Station on Stonetown Road at Magee Road, 1 mile north of the reservoir police booth located at the junction of West Brook Road and Stonetown Road.

Going counterclockwise from the fire station, the trail follows Stonetown Road south and turns left into the woods (0.5 mile). From here it leads up Windbeam Mountain, a climb of about 600 feet. At a lookout point on the way up (1.2 miles) is a good view. At 1026 feet, Windbeam Mountain is a landmark not only for its height, but also for its isolation from other high points. Miss M. M. Monk's book *Windbeam,* published in 1930, has much material on this mountain and the locale in the days before motor and reservoir brought their changes.

The trail descends through woods, crosses a wood road, which leads left to a gate at Windbeam Lane, and ascends 400 feet to the precipitously craggy peak of Bear Mountain (2.7 miles). The trail then drops down again before its easy ascent of Board Mountain. A broad view toward Sterling Ridge is just below the summit. From here, the trail descends steeply and crosses three brooks, then leads up to White Road, where there is parking. Next, it follows White Road to Stonetown Road at a point 2 miles north of the firehouse. Here it turns south and follows Stonetown Road 0.3 mile, then turns right on Riconda Drive. At the end of the road, the trail enters the woods and ascends Harrison Mountain with a beautiful panorama of the Wyanokies. At the top of the mountain, the trail passes the southern terminus of Horse Pond Mountain Trail (white).

The trail then descends, crossing a power line and then Harrison Mountain Lake on the left before turning right to cross

Sawmill Brook on a bridge on Burnt Meadow Road (6.2 miles). At the end of the bridge it turns left into the woods for a short distance, and then follows Burnt Meadow Road; again enters the woods (6.5 miles) and leads up to Tory Rocks, so named because they were used as a hideout by some Tories during the Revolution. These are 40-foot cliffs, with a view of Windbeam Mountain. From here the trail descends, crosses a brook, and ascends to Signal Rock (8.2 miles), with a view of the Ramapos framed by Windbeam and Bear mountains. Descending, it parallels Stonetown Brook to Magee Road (9.2 miles) and turns left to the fire station on Stonetown Road.

Torne Trail. Length: 1 mile. Blazes: red on white.

Beginning on the Hewitt-Butler Trail (blue) south of Otter Hole and Glen Wild Road, this trail shortcuts the Hewitt-Butler's ascent to the peak of Torne Mountain, regaining the trail at a point southeast of the mountain.

West Brook Trail. Length: 1 mile. Blazes: yellow.

The West Brook Trail begins on West Brook Road 0.7 mile east of Kitchell Lake. Ascending on several old roads, it reaches a shoulder of West Brook Mountain and meets the Hewitt-Butler Trail (blue) west of Tip-Top Point.

Wyanokie Circular Trail. Length: 7.5 miles. Blazes: red on white.

The Wyanokie Circular Trail begins at the Weis Ecology Center on Snake Den Road. Starting east of the Center from the road, the trail passes between houses, enters the woods, and intersects the Mine Trail (yellow on white), which it later joins to pass Blue Mine and the Green Mountain Club open shelter. Leaving the Mine Trail, it ascends steeply to Wyanokie High Point, where there is an excellent panorama of the surrounding countryside, with the New York City skyline on the horizon.

Descending steeply over rocks, the trail joins the Hewitt-Butler Trail (blue) for 0.4 mile. Climbing to 1100 feet, it then descends, crossing an old pipeline to the Otter Hole Trail (green on white), which it joins for 0.3 mile. Continuing on, the trail intersects the Macopin Trail (white), before joining a wood right for a quarter mile. The trail turns right to avoid a wet area, then regains the wood road to join the end of Snake Den Road, before continuing on to Boy Scout Lake (owned by the Borough of West Caldwell (6.2 miles), where it crosses a dam, again intersects Mine Trail, and traverses Saddle Mountain to a brook and the

Hewitt-Butler Trail. From here, it follows the Hewitt-Butler Trail over two brooks, the three Pine Paddies, each with varying views of the Wyanokies, crosses a brook, and turns left from the Hewitt-Butler Trail. Shortly, it reaches Snake Den Road, which it follows left 0.6 mile past the Weis Ecology Center to the beginning of the trail.

Wyanokie Crest Trail. Length: 7 miles. Blazes: yellow.

The newest trail in the area, the Wyanokie Crest Trail traverses the two highest summits in the Wyanokies—Buck and Assiniwikam mountains—extending from the Pine Paddies south to Glen Wild Road.

The trail begins on Glen Wild Road just north of Lake Kampfe and 0.7 mile south of Otter Hole, at which point a pullout on the east side will accommodate five to six cars. From Glen Wild, the trail follows a fire road in a northeast direction, crossing Post Brook and briefly joining the Hewitt-Butler Trail (blue) after about 0.7 mile. Leaving the latter, the Wyanokie Crest Trail swings north, descending gently to a "feeder" of Post Brook after about 0.3 mile.

The next mile or so, largely following this stream, is perhaps one of the wildest areas in all of Norvin Green State Forest. The stream, with its many roaring cascades, is followed closely, gradually uphill, with occasional rough footing. It is recommended that this section be experienced during high water.

Leaving the stream, the trail skirts a swampy area before ascending steeply to an open outcropping (view in winter). Meandering up and down and through a family of boulders, the trail rises west to its high point on the ridge. Continuing on this ridge, the trail emerges in about 0.3 mile at a view point overlooking Buck Mountain with its steep ledges. The trail descends, tunneling through laurel and crossing a brook and the Otter Hole Trail. After descending to a hollow, the trail makes an abrupt climb of 200 feet to the ledges of Buck Mountain, with its panoramic view. The trail soon reaches a second view, this time of the Otter Hole area, Torne Mountain, and hills to the west and south. Continuing north through laurel, the trail ascends to a rockface; this, at 1290 feet, is the highest point in the Wyanokies, but has no view. Descending, the trail attains a secondary summit before reaching another view point, which offers its best vistas in winter. From here, the rounded summit of Assiniwikam Mountain may be seen.

Descending gradually from Buck Mountain, the trail reaches a series of brooks, which it follows closely before ascending to cross the Wyanokie Circular Trail (red on white). After further ups and downs, the Macopin Trail (white) is crossed. The Wyanokie Crest Trail then ascends the slopes of Assiniwikam Mountain, with several false summits and occasional rough footing. There are good views west just off the trail in winter atop the first main summit.

Meandering ahead, the trail emerges at an open view point. Here, Bearfort Mountain and the Greenwood Lake areas can be seen. After several ledge traverses, passing the true summit at 1210 feet, the trail eventually emerges at another panorama, this time of Wyanokie High Point, with Windbeam Mountain and Wanaque Reservoir in the background. Continuing its ups and downs on ledges, the trail descends to another view point before dropping down to the Mine Trail (yellow on white) at about the northernmost boundary of the state forest.

Crossing the Mine Trail, the Wyanokie Crest Trail wanders through open forest before ascending and joining the Hewitt-Butler/Wyanokie Circular trails (blue and red on white) amid the Pine Paddies. From here it is a short climb to a view of Assiniwikam Mountain and about 1 mile to the end of the trails at Snake Den Road.

SOUTH OF THE WYANOKIES

South of the Wyanokie wild area, a venerable trail system struggles for existence against suburban sprawl. Due to the efforts of local hiking clubs, however, the trails have been rerouted in some sections to avoid encroaching development and preserve the joys of this area for the hiker.

Butler-Montville Trail. Length: 7.5 miles. Blazes: blue.

Bear and Tripod rocks are landmarks on this delightful trail which passes through stands of dogwood, ironwood, tulip, and red cedar, filled with such wildflowers as Solomon's seal, goldenrod, striped wintergreen, aster, and star moss growing in season. The periodic intersections with blacktop allow parking and permit the hiker to complete specific sections.

The trail begins on Bubbling Brook Road at the gate just north of Butler Reservoir. To reach it from the intersection of Route 23 and Kiel Avenue, go south on Kiel 0.1 mile to the first left, Kakeout Road. Go southeast on Kakeout 0.5 mile looking for brick waterworks on the left, called Cascade Way. Turn right onto Bubbling Brook Road 0.2 mile to the gate, where there is parking for three or four cars.

From the gate, which has three blue blazes, follow the paved road 0.5 mile, continue on the path along the reservoir, and cross the footbridge over Stony Brook inlet to Fayson Lakes Road. A mile beyond the road the trail crosses another stream and passes through a meadow to Miller Road. After a short distance on the road, the trail enters the woods on the left to a gentler path at a well-marked rock and meanders southeast along the valley floor to Bear Rock, an unusual landmark with an uncanny resemblance to a giant bear.

Here the trail turns to the left, crosses the brook, and makes a steep 200-foot ascent through a stand of laurel to a ridge where it turns south. A side trip of 200 yards to the left, following the white blazes of the Kinnelon-Boonton Trail leads to nature's engineering work, Tripod Rock, balanced for eons on three small boulders.

After a gradual ascent of 100 feet to the summit of Pyramid Mountain, which features good views east toward New York City and points south, the trail descends steeply to a power line, which it follows east for 1 mile to cross Boonton Avenue. Still following the power line, the trail passes through a meadow, then rises 300 feet before turning right and descending through pleasant woods. After a half mile, the trail crosses a logging road, which exits west on Boonton Avenue and east at the north end of Lake Valhalla. A pleasant woodland walk of 1 mile south leads to a sharp descent to the right onto a wood road running south to Taylortown Road, where the trail terminates 1 mile from Route 202. There is parking for three cars at the trailhead.

Kinnelon-Boonton Trail. Length: 6 miles. Blazes: white.

This trail is on the east side of Butler Reservoir and crosses the Butler-Montville Trail (blue blazes) farther south. It affords more level valley-walking, but has enough climbs and descents to make it interesting and pleasant.

The trail begins on Birch Road, a private, unpaved section at the end of the road, owned by Messrs. Fehr and Pettersen. To reach it, take Kiel Avenue in Butler south from the shopping center at the intersection with Route 23 to the first left (Kakeout Road). Kakeout Road may also be entered from Butler by crossing Route 23 south on Kinnelon Road, immediately jogging left, then right onto Kiel Avenue. Go southeast on Kakeout Road 0.7 mile, looking for Birch Road on the right. Turn here, bending left 0.3 miles to "Private Property" sign. Continue 0.1 mile to turnoff on left (room for two cars here) or U-turn at Pettersen's barn, parking two cars on the left side. Parking and the start of the trail on the Pettersen property is by permission, so leave a note on your windshield and park off the road.

Walk south from the triple-blazed start on a wide path, which shortly leads onto Butler Reservoir property. One mile south, with views of a reservoir on the right, and a causeway at a right oblique, the trail turns left and 0.3 mile later emerges onto Toboggan Trail on a narrow right-of-way between two houses. Continuing south to Fayson Lakes Road, the trail takes a left turn past a bus shelter, crossing the road and entering a 0.3-mile wood trail south, which then turns left onto Lakeview Drive. A hundred feet to the right, a left turn at the next corner (Brentwood Drive) leads to a bit more road-walking: the trail jogs left, then right, then left again onto Glenrock Drive East, which ends by intersecting Reality Drive after 0.2 mile.

On the opposite side of Reality Drive, one will see an open area between the houses, which funnels down to the trail on the right. The path rises and falls through fairly rugged terrain, with rocks on the right concealing most of the houses on Reality Drive. After 0.3 mile, the trail descends south to the first water crossing in a gully. Continuing south, a fair climb brings a pleasant wood walk for 0.7 mile, to a rendezvous with a well-known and popular landmark, Tripod Rock.

Two hundred yards farther south, the trail joins the Butler-Montville Trail for a sharp 200-foot descent through a stand of laurel to a water crossing near Bear Rock. Here, the trails separate, the white trail turning south 1 mile to a power line where it turns left around a pylon and descends to a water crossing. Beyond this crossing the trail turns right from the wood road, going right into the third section, a fairly level wood road. Shortly thereafter, the trail turns left, widening, before meandering southeast. During the spring thaw, this area may be under several inches of water, requiring walking on the shoulder.

Emerging onto a logging road, a right turn brings the hiker to a somewhat shaky pedestrian bridge over the fourth water crossing. A walk downstream leads in a few hundred yards to an active beaver dam and colony. Continuing from the bridge, the trail shortly leaves the logging road, turning right for a narrow, bush walk which then encounters an east-west wood road. A left turn here reduces it to a hiking trail, gradually bending left and paralleling Boonton Avenue to the right. The trail reaches the end after 0.3 mile, emerging onto a bend of Boonton Avenue opposite a large swimming pool. There is parking here for two cars, off the road.

Butler Connecting Trail

This trail skirts the north end of the Butler Reservoir to connect the Butler-Montville Trail (blue blazes) on the west side of the reservoir to the Kinnelon-Boonton Trail (white blazes) on the east side. It connects with the blue trail a half mile south of the blue trailhead at the point where the paved reservoir road turns east to cross the dam/causeway. Shortly after daybreak or at twilight the peaceful scene is reminiscent of a small hidden lake in the Adirondacks. No human habitation is in sight, nor is the noise of an outboard heard. The paved and lighted dam/causeway should not be confused with a narrow, crumbling, concrete reservoir spillway 0.2 mile downstream, on which no attempt to cross should be made.

After crossing the dam the connecting trail leads up to the turnaround at the end of paved Seabert Lane, which it follows to Birch Lane and turns right on Birch a quarter mile to the trailhead of the white trail. The "No Trespassing" sign at the end of the pavement may be disregarded by legitimate hikers, by permission of the owner of the property.

Towaco-Riverdale Trail. Length: 6 miles. Blazes: yellow.

Formerly known as the Towaco-Pompton Trail, this path at one time ran south to north between two railroad stations. With the near demise of rail passenger service, the shortened trail now starts and ends where cars can be conveniently parked. However, there is still rail service to Towaco, where drivers can meet passengers for car hospitality to the trailhead.

The southern trailhead is located on Indian Lane, Towaco, 1 mile north of Route 202, and 500 feet east of Waughaw Road, where there is parking for several cars. The trail starts north along a gas pipeline right-of-way; after 0.3 mile, it veers left onto a wooded path which leads upward past an archery range in the woods. After another 0.3 mile, it emerges onto a cleared right-of-way marked by wooden utility poles and proceeds north on this right-of-way to the top of Waughaw Mountain. From its 887-foot summit, there are excellent views to the south.

Continuing, the trail skirts a horse corral blocking the right-of-way, dropping steadily down a wooded slope to a right turn onto an unused wood road. The wood road gradually bends right to rejoin the power line after 0.3 mile, then continues a little farther to where the trail leaves the power line at a 30-degree angle to the right onto a wood road, which descends to paved Brook Valley Road.

Going east, the trail turns onto a sometimes muddy road, with a closed summer camp on the right. A left-hand jog opens onto the path which, after 1.3 miles of rolling terrain, ascends Mine Hill (elevation 930 feet), with magnificent views to the southeast of Pompton Plains and the New York City skyline. Descending north, there are views of the Wyanokies and two small brooks to cross before reaching well-known Sawmill Pond.

At the large rock, the trail takes a sharp right, then crosses a wood road, which furnishes the opportunity for an unblazed side trip to the right down Pompton Gorge. Returning to the yellow blazes, the hiker makes a gradual ascent to the north, bringing a pleasant walk across a small brook. Skirting a swamp, the trail opens onto a somewhat confusing network of roads and bridle paths before encountering the aqueduct for the city of Newark.

After a short walk, the trail leaves the aqueduct, turning left up an embankment, and proceeds north for its final mile up and down Pequannock Knob, through some of the most attractive woods on the trail. Toward the northern end, blazes will be difficult to find due to extensive logging; at this point, the trail begins to parallel a paved road to the right through a small stand of laurel, before emerging onto the gas pipeline. A right turn down the pipeline leads to the triple blazes marking the northern terminus on Route 23, where there is parking for two cars on the shoulder just west of the pipeline. Parking east of the pipeline is not advisable due to logging. Additional parking is available at an office building 0.4 mile east on Route 23.

NEW YORK–NEW JERSEY BOUNDARY WALKS

A way to exercise one's skill in woodcraft is to trace portions of the New York–New Jersey boundary, the southern boundary of Rockland and Orange counties. The dot-and-dash line, which, on the map, separates New Jersey and New York, runs for many miles through the deep woods of the Highlands. At the end of every mile, measured from the Hudson River, there is a small and inconspicuous stone marker. It takes some skill in the use of the topographic map, the compass, and the pace counter to find these markers—in fact, to find even the position of the boundary itself. Unlike Mason and Dixon's Line between Pennsylvania and the South, the New Jersey–New York boundary is not marked by a wide swath in the woods. To the public, the only sure evidence of its existence is an occasional and inconspicuous stone marker, unnoticed by most travelers, at the place where the boundary crosses a public road or a railroad.

All the other boundaries of New Jersey are natural shorelines or river courses. Its northeastern boundary was first defined in 1664, when James, Duke of York, sold the province of New Jersey to Berkeley and Carteret. The terminal points were defined as the mouth of "the northernmost branch of the said bay or river Delaware, which is 41° 40′ of latitude [there is no such point], and the intersection of latitude 41° with Hudson's River." The actual positions of the terminal points were not agreed upon until 1769. In 1770 a joint Colonial boundary commission tried to locate the line, but was discomfited by a show of weapons and other evidence of unfriendliness on the part of residents of the coastal plain section and consequently took to the woods to do what it could toward defining the boundary there. The cause of all this, one may surmise, was local satisfaction with a state of affairs that made taxes difficult for either colony to collect. The job was finally completed, however, and mile markers were set in 1774. Most of them can still be found down among the leaves and bushes, with their antiquated and amateurishly carved lettering.

A survey with more modern precision was made just one hundred years later, in 1874, and was followed by a joint state resurvey in 1882, when new markers were set alongside the old stones. The new ones are of granite, with dressed tops six inches square projecting six inches out of the ground. Even these are a little difficult to find, particularly under a heavy snow.

The 1874 and 1882 surveys, made with reference to astronomically fixed positions, revealed that the boundary of 1774 had the general shape of a dog's hind leg, for a reason unsuspected by the pioneers. The 1774 survey was done with the magnetic compass and, since the Highlands are full of magnetic iron ore, the compass line rambles accordingly. At Greenwood Lake the marker was 2415 feet, or nearly half a mile, southwest of the "straight line" (great circle) between the termini. Since the land in the Highlands was of little value, the commissioners, being practical men, left well enough alone and did not disturb the mileposts of 1774. New York State thus retained, through magnetic attraction, a good many acres which the Duke of York intended to convey to the proprietors of New Jersey.

The most interesting walks begin with Stone No. 15 in the town of Suffern, and continue approximately north 60° west for 33.5 miles to Stone No. 49, near Port Jervis. No. 21 is about 0.1 mile east of the old unused road leading north from Ringwood

Manor to the Snyder iron mine. No. 23 is about 0.1 mile northwest of the wood road that leads southwest from the vicinity of Sterling Furnace. No. 26 is on the northwest shore of Greenwood Lake. The distance between Nos. 22 and 23 is just under 0.9 mile; evidently someone accidentally dropped ten chains (660 feet) from his count in 1774. In some sections the boundary is hazily indicated by dim dark-red blazes on the trees, deviating from the true course as if marking surveyors' gores.

The best time to follow the boundary is in the beginning of winter after the lakes and swamps are frozen, but before the snow has become too deep to permit finding the markers.

GREENWOOD LAKE REGION

North of the Wyanokies lies Greenwood Lake, the long sliver of water created by Peter Hasenclever when he built a dam at Long Pond to provide power for his ironworks downstream. The site is still in evidence, and hikers on the Sterling Ridge Trail can still see the old furnace and giant waterwheels just south of a hemlock-laced section of the Wanaque River. Plans are underway to construct a seven-billion-gallon reservoir in West Milford and Ringwood by damming the river north of the Wanaque Reservoir. The ironworks site is to be protected, although much beautiful land will be submerged.

Most of the area east of the lake lies within Greenwood Lake

GREENWOOD LAKE *seen from near* TERRACE POND

State Park, and the privately owned Sterling Forest. Once famous for its gardens, Sterling Forest was also known for its role in the history of early mining and smelting industry. Long-abandoned and overgrown roads cross it. The remains of over twenty old mines and several furnaces are on the Sterling property. Several of the mine shafts have been filled in and closed. Sterling Mine, one of those that can no longer be seen, was opened in 1750 and closed shortly after 1900; its shaft sloped nearly a thousand feet under Sterling Lake. Just to the north of it can still be seen the water-filled opening of the lake mine shaft which goes down a distance of thirty-eight hundred feet on the slope, far out under the lake. This was the principal producer from 1900 to 1921 when it closed down along with the other Sterling workings. The concrete headframe still stands at Scott Mine. Near the Red Back Mine, whose ore was high in sulfur, may still be seen the ruins of the huge cast-iron roaster, twenty feet high, in which the sulfur was burned out. Still farther north near Route 17A lie the extensive workings of the Alice Mine. Southwest ridges are faced on their west sides by steep rugged cliffs, hidden in dense forest and invisible from any outside point but striking to come upon in this little-visited region.

Immediately west of Greenwood Lake lies the Bearfort Mountain area, almost wholly within the A. S. Hewitt State Park. It includes Surprise Lake and is separated by Warwick Turnpike from land to the south. With some minor road-walking, it is possible to make a 22-mile loop from this park through Wawayanda State Park, using the Bearfort Ridge, Appalachian, Old Coal, Terrace Pond, and other trails.

Sterling Ridge Trail. Length: 8.4 miles. Blazes: blue on white.

The Sterling Ridge Trail traverses the Tuxedo Mountains between Hewitt and its terminus north and east of Greenwood Lake Village. The New York section is on the property of Sterling Forest (privately owned), and the New Jersey portions are within wild lands of Ringwood Manor State Park. "No trespassing" signs are at both ends of the trail, but it is open to bona fide hikers, particularly those of member clubs of the New York–New Jersey Trail Conference.

One of the highlights of a walk on the Sterling Ridge Trail is the ruins of Peter Hasenclever's Long Pond Ironworks, which encompassed at its height a thriving community devoted to the ironworks.

To reach the ruins, and the start of the trail, one may either park at the junction of East Shore Road and Route 511 in Hewitt, and hike in on the trail, or drive west through Hewitt on the highway to Greenwood Lake, turn off to the right on the dirt road that lies a few yards past "Ye Olde Country Store" building. The trail comes in from the left just after a stream, at which point the road turns right.

At the dead end of this dirt road is the location of the old Long Pond iron furnace, first developed by Hasenclever and continued by Erskine, and those of two later furnaces erected by Abram Hewitt just prior to and during the Civil War. The ruins of the latter two furnaces have been standing for years plainly visible, as have the two 25-foot waterwheels, burned by vandals in June 1957 and now mere skeletons compared to their original appearance. The ruins of the Hasenclever furnace were discovered in a mound covered with leaves in 1956 and were excavated in 1967. The site is worth exploring.

From here, the trail crosses the river and shortly joins an old road, which veers away from the river. The trail then passes the Jennings Hollow Trail (yellow) before ascending Big Beech Mountain, which offers a view of Bearfort Mountain. Continuing on, it arrives at a view, to the southwest, of Big Beech Mountain, Bearfort Mountain, and the Wyanokies. In a hemlock forest, it crosses Cedar Pond wood road and ascends to the Sterling fire tower. From the tower there are views in all directions. After many ups and downs, the trail reaches an excellent view of Sterling Lake with the mountains beyond. From here, it descends and follows a ridge past a power line before reaching Route 210 near the summit of Tuxedo Mountain.

Parking is located at a wide spot on the south side of Route 210 that will accommodate a few cars.

Allis Trail. Length: approximately 2 miles. Blazes: blue on white.

Connecting the Appalachian Trail with the Sterling Ridge Trail, the Allis Trail begins at a sharp left bend on Route 210, about 2 miles west of Sterling Forest. Cars may be parked at the trailhead.

From here, the trail almost immediately crosses a pipeline and a power line before reaching Cedar Mountain, where there is a view northeast. From here, it descends to the Appalachian Trail west of Mombasha High Point. This trail is named for J. Ashton Allis, a pioneer hiker and trail builder in the metropolitan area, and for many years president of the Fresh Air Club.

Bearfort Ridge Trail. Length: 2.5 miles. Blazes: white.

The Bearfort Ridge Trail begins on the north side of Warwick Turnpike about 1 mile west of the intersection of Lakeside Road (Route 511). There is parking for three or four cars near a concrete bridge where a stream passes under the road. The trail begins at one end of the bridge, ascending through a hemlock grove to a wood road, but soon turns left, passes two small streams, and then climbs steeply to the top of the ridge, where there are excellent views to the south and west. The trail now continues at basically the same elevation, about 1300 feet, except for short descents into stream channels. For over a mile the trail follows conglomerate rock ridges in a summit forest of pitch pine and scrub oak. Just before its junction with the Ernest Walter Trail several view points are found, including a view of Surprise Lake to the north.

State Line Trail. Length: 1.15 miles. Blazes: blue dot on white square.

The State Line Trail begins on Lakeside Road (Route 511) about 70 feet south of the New York–New Jersey State Line. Parking is recommended off 511 on a side street about 100 feet north of the Greenwood Lake Marina to avoid blocking private property. The trail starts a short distance in on the north side of a stream which passes under the road. From here, the trail soon crosses a brook and after about a quarter mile begins a climb through an oak forest following a rocky streambed. Near the top of the ridge it passes the yellow Ernest Walter Trail on the left and later a "red triangle" trail which follows a low route to Surprise Lake. The State Line Trail terminates at its junction with the Appalachian Trail on the main ridge.

Ernest Walter Trail. Length: 1.4 miles. Blazes: yellow.

The Ernest Walter Trail, named for a dedicated hiker and trail worker, encircles Surprise Lake and West Pond, connecting to the State Line Trail at one end and to the Appalachian Trail at the other. The trail maintains basically the same elevation with a few short but steep ascents and descents. Just before its connection with the State Line Trail are excellent views to the east from a large glacially smoothed projection of conglomerate.

WAWAYANDA STATE PARK

Wawayanda State Park embraces almost ten thousand acres of forests and waters in the rough hilly country of the New Jersey

Highlands. The name "Wa-wa-yanda" is the phonetic rendition of the Lenape Indian name said to mean "water on the mountain."

Wawayanda Lake, one of the focal points of the park, is 1.5 miles long, has 5.5 miles of wooded shoreline, and covers 255 acres. This lake was once called Double Pond and was two bodies of water separated by a narrow strip of land which still shows, in part, on the west side of Barker Island in the center of the present lake. In the middle of the last century the Thomas Iron Company built the earthen dam at the northeastern end of the lake. A wing dam also was constructed on the eastern shore over which the waters spill to help feed Laurel Pond. These dams raised the lake level about seven and a half feet.

Three hundred feet beyond the northeast end of Wawayanda Lake, along the Wawayanda Road, are the remains of a charcoal blast furnace where iron was produced. Oliver Ames and his sons William, Oakes, and Oliver, Jr., constructed it in 1845–46. William supervised the work. His initials "W.L.A." and the date 1846 are still visible on a lintel in the main arch of the old furnace. Shovels and wheels for railroad cars were produced here. During the Civil War, the Ames factories filled government orders for shovels and swords.

The Wawayanda iron mine is 2.5 miles northeast of the iron furnace along the east side of the Wawayanda Road and consists of five openings or shafts. The largest was a hundred feet in depth, and traveled along a vein of ore twelve to fifteen feet wide. Mules worked in shifts in the mines, hauling the ore and tailings to the surface. The "Mule Barn" was directly opposite the most southeasterly shaft, across a small creek on the west side of Wawayanda Road. The foundation of the barn still exists. A story told by old-timers in the area claims that several men and one or more mules were buried in a tunnel cave-in.

Laurel Pond, east of Wawayanda Lake, is about ten acres in extent, and is mostly spring-fed. It is a fairly deep lake and is free from contamination. At the southeast end of the pond, on a steep slope, is a stand of hemlock which is probably the only virgin timber on the mountain. Bear signs have been found in this wild area.

Toward the eastern part of the Wawayanda "Plateau" (it is not a plateau in the geological sense), on which the park is situated, various old wood roads and paths lead southward and penetrate one of the finest jungles of this kind in New Jersey. The cedar swamp and rhododendron, whose great glossy leaves present a tropical display at any season, are glorified in July by the handsome flowers. The extensive stand of southern white cedar *(Chamaecyparis thyoides)*, here far away from and above its usual stands along the seacoast marshes, is interesting to students of plant distribution.

The park's offering to the hiker has been enhanced in recent years by the addition of the Terrace Pond area, one of the most attractive parts, and designated in 1978 as a natural area. This wild gem of water lies at an altitude of 1380 feet, surrounded by high cliffs of pudding-stone conglomerate, massive rhododendron, and blueberry swamps.

The main entrance to the park is off Warwick Turnpike, about 3 miles north of Upper Greenwood Lake. There is also parking on Clinton Road 1.8 miles from its northern terminus on Warwick Turnpike and 7.5 miles from its southern terminus on Route 23, as well as on Banker Road, about a half mile south of Warwick Turnpike.

Trails in Wawayanda State Park

The trail system in this park has become quite extensive in recent years. Today thirteen marked trails, not including the Appalachian Trail, are indicated on the park trail map available from the ranger's office. In general, these trails are former roads and have been blazed with colored tags and designated by signs or posts at each end. Most of these trails are fairly level and are

excellent for cross-country skiing when conditions are favorable. Snow cover accumulates and lasts longer here than in other areas because of the heavy foliage and numerous evergreens. Among the most scenic trails are:

The Appalachian Trail. Length: 7 miles. Blazes: white.

From Warwick Turnpike to Route 94, the Appalachian Trail is almost completely within the state park. There is a variety of scenery in this section, ranging from hemlock forests to picturesque dairy farms to bare rock outcrops. Although the trail can be picked up just beyond the eastern edge of the park on Warwick Turnpike, about 0.75 mile south of the state line, it is advisable to leave cars in the park at Wawayanda Lake and hike up Wawayanda Road or the Iron Mountain Trail (blue blazes) to the trail.

From Warwick Turnpike, the trail passes west through a pasture to a small ridge. After crossing a swampy area, the trail then ascends steeply to Wawayanda Road, where a short distance down the road the blue-blazed Hoeferlin Trail can be picked up heading south. Campsites are about a quarter mile down on the Hoeferlin Trail.

Continuing on, the Appalachian Trail heads north on the road for about a quarter mile before reentering the woods and ascending over a knob to reach Iron Mountain Road. After traveling on the road for about a half mile, the trail crosses a brook, bearing

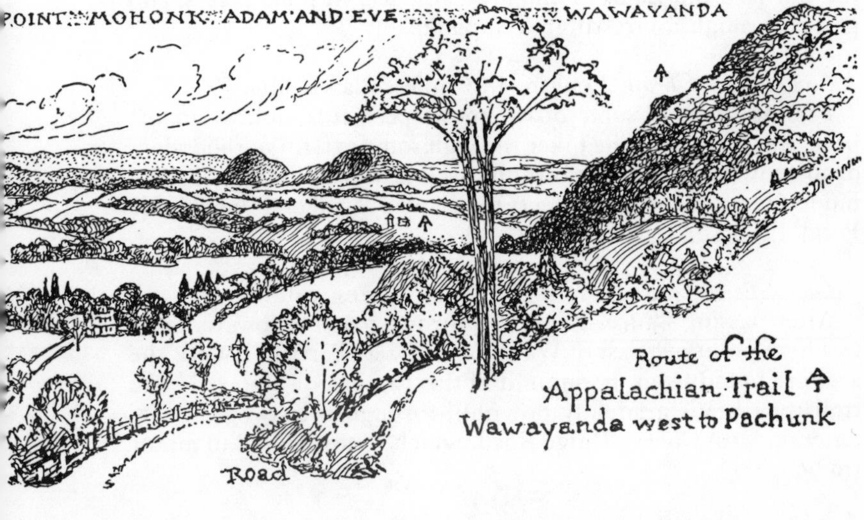

right to continue west across open fields on a grassy track, with views north to Adam and Eve mountains and the distant Shawangunks.

The trail then opens onto Barrett Road, and from here to Route 94 the hiker will encounter perhaps the most spectacular scenery on this section of the trail. From Barrett Road, the trail follows a deep hemlock ravine and climbs gradually before emerging on the 1422-foot summit of Wawayanda Mountain, with extensive views to the west. Turning southwest, the trail drops down to a good view across Wallkill Valley and over Pochuck Mountain to the Kittatinnies before continuing on to Route 94.

Hoeferlin Trail. Length: 5 miles. Blazes: blue.

From its connection with the Appalachian Trail at its northern end, this trail loops around to Iron Mountain Road, providing the hiker with a circular walk of pleasant, easy hiking. Starting at the Appalachian Trail, the Hoeferlin Trail passes the park's campsites and the office area to connect with the Double Pond Trail. Along the way the trail also passes Wawayanda Lake and the Wawayanda Furnace. It has no connection with the yellow Hoeferlin Memorial Trail in the Ramapos.

Double Pond Trail. Length: 2 miles. No blazes.

Formerly Double Pond Road, this trail starts east of Wawayanda Lake and connects the Hoeferlin and Banker trails with the Furnace and Laurel Pond area. It is wet in some places, and passes through interesting swampland.

Cedar Swamp Trail. Length: 1.25 miles. Blazes: blue.

Passing through some of the most spectacular foliage in the park, this trail takes the hiker through some extensive rhododendron growth. The Cedar Swamp itself is worth risking wet and muddy feet. The trail connects the Banker Trail and the Double Pond Trail.

Laurel Pond Trail. Length: 1.5 miles. Blazes: yellow.

After passing Laurel Pond, this former road climbs gradually to a high point just east of Wawayanda Lake. Partial views of the area are found from the summit of this rise just off the trail. The trail then heads gradually downhill through deep woods to its junction with Cherry Ridge Road, which is now closed to motor traffic.

Terrace Pond South Trail. Length: 2.5 miles. Blazes: yellow.
From the parking lot on Clinton Road, this trail leads circuitously eastward, partly over watershed land. As the trail swings northward toward Terrace Pond, fine views of the nearby Bearfort Mountain to the east can be seen. The Terrace Pond Red Trail, originating in watershed property comes in from the right just south of Terrace Pond. Terrace Pond South Trail ends at the white-blazed trail circling the pond.

Terrace Pond North. Length: 4.5 miles. Blazes: blue.
Starting about a quarter mile east of the parking lot on Clinton Road, at a point where a pipeline clearing extends southward, this trail leads toward Terrace Pond. Climbing the hill leading to the pond, this trail features outstanding lookouts to the west. At Terrace Pond, it intersects with the White Trail encircling the pond and continues northeast along high ridges with fine views to end on Warwick Turnpike at telephone pole No. 25, 1 mile west of the junction of Routes 210 and 511.

Terrace Pond Red Trail. Length: 3 miles. Blazes: red.
This trail takes off in a southerly direction from the pond and travels to Stephens Road where a slight jog to the left leads to the jeep road to the Bearfort fire tower. Here are fine views in all directions. The easiest approach to the Bearfort fire tower for the casual walker is from Stephens Road, which runs for 2 miles between Clinton Road (at 6.5 miles north of Route 23) and Union Valley Road (at 4.5 miles north of Route 23). Stephens Road is not passable by car. Walk in 0.8 mile from the eastern terminus or 1.3 miles from the western terminus and then south 0.6 mile to the fire tower.

White Trail. Length: 0.75 mile. Blazes: white.
This short scenic trail leads around Terrace Pond, and is accessible via the Terrace Pond North Trail, the Terrace Pond South Trail, and the Terrace Pond Red Trail. Hikers to the pond will find good lunch spots overlooking the pond on the trail's western side, although the proximity of the area to Clinton Road sometimes makes these spots a bit too populated for the hiker seeking solitude.

Yellow Dot Trail. Length: 0.75 mile. Blazes: yellow.
This trail leaves the Terrace Pond South Trail at a Y intersection. The Yellow Dot picks up a wood road, which it follows

approximately a half mile before the road ends. The trail turns left, goes uphill, and then levels off to join the White Trail midway on the east side of the lake.

Red Bar Trail. Length: 0.5 mile. Blazes: red.

This trail, which connects the Terrace Pond Red Trail to the west side of Terrace Pond, follows a ridge that provides many fine views of the surrounding terrain.

NEWARK WATERSHED

The city of Newark's Pequannock watershed property adjoins the southern boundary of Wawayanda State Park. Encompassing thirty-five thousand acres in portions of Morris, Passaic, and Sussex counties, it is traversed east to west by Route 23.

The watershed contains five major reservoirs providing a substantial portion of the water supply for Newark. The clear lakes, streams, and ponds, the mountains and the dramatic rock outcroppings, the forests and the varied vegetation of the watershed combine to make it one of the most scenic areas in New Jersey.

In 1974 the Newark Watershed Conservation and Development Corporation (NWCDC), a nonprofit organization, was assigned responsibility for managing the property on behalf of the city of Newark. As part of a major policy shift in land use, the NWCDC opened the property for recreational use by the general public and, at the same time, invited an all-volunteer trails development group to create and maintain a first-class hiking trail system for the Clinton, Buckabear, Bearfort section. Since its inception, the trails group has completed and maintained, measured and mapped approximately thirty miles of superb hiking trails in this area. The group is now in the process of developing, clearing, and mapping new interconnections between that system and the system in Wawayanda State Park to afford additional hiking opportunities.

Hiking in this area is by permit only. To obtain further information, call (201) 697-2850, or write: NWCDC, Box 319, Newfoundland, N.J. 07435.

Suggested Reading

M. M. Monk
Windbeam
Knickerbocker Press, New York, 1930

15 · *THE KITTATINNY MOUNTAIN RIDGE*

(Maps 15, 16, 17 and 18)

PARALLELING THE forty-mile stretch of the Delaware River from Port Jervis to Delaware Water Gap is the long, wooded ridge of the Kittatinnies, the Indian name for "Big Mountain." The ridge continues on the Pennsylvania side of the Water Gap southwest to Wind Gap and beyond; northeast, the ridge continues into New York State as the Shawangunk Mountains. With elevations of 1400 to 1800 feet, the Kittatinnies offer spectacular panoramas from High Point, Sunrise Mountain, and innumerable other overlooks. In addition, much of the New Jersey section of the Appalachian Trail runs along the ridge.

The Kittatinny ridge is divided into four administrative areas. Beginning at the northwest corner of the state and running southwest, they are High Point State Park, Stokes State Forest, the Delaware Water Gap National Recreation Area, and Worthington State Forest, which is within the boundary of the recreation area.

HIGH POINT STATE PARK

High Point State Park, extending from the New York State line southward for ten miles, was given to the state in 1923 by the late Colonel Anthony R. Kuser of Bernardsville, New Jersey. Within the park is the highest elevation in the state, at 1803 feet. Here in 1930 a memorial modeled after the Bunker Hill tower was erected to honor the men of New Jersey who served in the nation's wars. Also included in the park is Lake Marcia, the highest in the state at 1570 feet, and Colonel Kuser's former residence.

There are nine named and marked trails in High Point, plus a stretch of the Appalachian Trail. Though the trails range from only 0.5 mile to 4 miles in length, it is possible, by using park roads in conjunction with these paths, to walk a number of more extended circular routes.

During the winter when conditions are suitable, the Parker, Mashipacong, and Iris trails, all west of Route 23, are reserved for snowmobile use; east of Route 23, the trails and unplowed roads are open for snowshoeing and cross-country skiing.

Naturalists will enjoy a visit to a swampland area about 1 mile north of the old Kuser lodge. Southern white cedar, common to the Pine Barrens of southern New Jersey, and red spruce, usually found farther north and at higher elevations, grow side by side in a unique combination that has few counterparts in the East. The area is easily accessible by a road that encircles the swamp and is banked high with great masses of rhododendron, hemlock, and pine.

Campsites and group camping are available in the park. Contact the Park Superintendent, R.R. 4, Box 287, Sussex, N.J. 07461; phone: (201) 875-4800. Hikers making overnight trips on the Appalachian Trail may use a parking area after obtaining a permit from the superintendent's office.

STOKES STATE FOREST

Below High Point is Stokes State Forest, which is bisected by Culvers Gap and borders Culvers and Kittatinny lakes. There are eighteen marked trails here, most of them northeast of Route 206, ranging in length from less than 0.5 mile to a 9-mile section of the Appalachian Trail. As in High Point, trails and park roads can be combined for interesting circular routes. In winter, the Lackner, Coursen, Swenson, and Tinsley trails are snowmobile routes; the area southwest of Route 206 is set aside for snowshoeing and cross-country skiing.

One outstanding feature of Stokes Forest is Tillman Ravine, at the southern end and easily accessible by a well-used path leading off Brink Road. The steep banks of the ravine are covered with hemlock and rhododendron and there are, in seasons of high water, fine cascades near its upper end.

The 4-mile Swenson Trail parallels the Appalachian Trail; to reach it, walk west 0.8 mile from the Appalachian Trail at Crigger Road. It is a level walk until Crigger Brook crossing, where it begins to ascend. Portions of the area were logged sixty to eighty-five years ago, and oak forests have supplanted the once-dominant chestnut.

The Tinsley Trail connects the Swenson with the Appalachian Trail 1.5 miles south of Crigger Road. It passes through oak, maple, hickory, and birch forests, and stands of mountain laurel. A mile farther south is another connecting link, the Stony Brook Trail, a moderately steep descent but interesting for its fungi and lichen.

DELAWARE WATER GAP NATIONAL RECREATION AREA

On September 1, 1965, President Lyndon B. Johnson signed into law the act authorizing establishment of the Delaware Water Gap National Recreation Area. Intended to be developed as a part of the now-dormant Tocks Island Dam project, the area includes the Kittatinny Mountains from the southern end of Stokes State Forest southward across the Water Gap to Totts Gap, and on both sides of the Delaware for thirty-five miles between the Kittatinny ridge and the Pocono Mountain Plateau. The gap itself is a popular natural landmark composed of Mount Minsi on the Pennsylvania side and Mount Tammany in New Jersey.

Archeological evidence indicates that the Indians came to the valley almost ten thousand years ago, and early written records reveal that Dutch explorers began building here even before William Penn founded Philadelphia. By 1664 the Dutch were transporting copper from the Pahaquarry Mines some 104 miles to Esopus (now Kingston, New York). Still evident are portions of the Old Mine Road, possibly the first road in America over a hundred miles long. Descendants of these early settlers participated in the Indian Wars of the eighteenth century, and during the Revolution their valley was a vital communication link between New York and Philadelphia.

The many cultural, educational, and recreational facilities within the recreation area include Dingmans Falls, Peters Valley Crafts Village, the Pocono Environmental Education Center, and Thunder Mountain Vocational-Environmental Center. Canoeing on the Delaware is popular, with rentals available outside the park. Private campgrounds are located nearby, as are facilities in Worthington State Forest.

Trails on the Pennsylvania side of the river include the 0.75-mile, circular Dingmans Falls Trail, in Dingmans Ferry, which

provides views of two waterfalls; the Tumbling Waters Trail, a 4-mile loop at the Pocono Environmental Education Center; Hidden Lake Trail, 1.5 miles on moderate terrain encircling Hidden Lake, below Bushkill; and the Mount Minsi Trail, 1.2 miles, with an excellent view of the gap.

Further information can be obtained at the Kittatinny Point Information Station or by contacting the Delaware Water Gap National Recreation Area, Bushkill, Pa. 18324; phone: (717) 588-6637.

WORTHINGTON STATE FOREST

Located within the national recreation area, Worthington contains some of the most rugged terrain in the state. Comprising the bottom part of the Kittatinny ridge in New Jersey, it extends approximately seven miles along the ridge and includes about five thousand acres. Among the forest's features is the beautiful glacial lake, Sunfish Pond, which was restored to the state after a long fight by conservationists defeated a planned pumped-storage utility project there.

At the southern end of the forest is Dunnfield Creek Natural Area. The creek falls over a thousand feet from Mount Tammany to the Delaware, and is one of the few in the state to support native brook trout. Overlooking this rocky stream are stands of hemlock, maple, and birch. Mountain laurel adds color to the area when in bloom.

The 2-mile William O. Douglas Trail, named by the New Jersey Department of Environmental Protection to honor the late U.S. Supreme Court Justice for his conservation efforts, is a pleasant route to the crest of Kittatinny Mountain. It links up with the Appalachian Trail about a half mile from Sunfish Pond, where a 1.5-mile route encircles the water. Two other trails to the summit of Mount Tammany can be combined into a 3.6-mile loop.

The main entrance to the forest is on Old Mine Road or River Road, about 4 miles north of Route 80 on the western boundary of the preserve; the Douglas Trail begins here. Parking is available here and at the Dunnfield Creek Natural Area. For further information, contact the Worthington State Forest, Old Mine Road, Columbia, N.J. 07632; phone: (201) 841-9575. Since boundaries between Worthington State Park and the Delaware National Recreation Area are not well defined, it is advisable to obtain maps and information at the National Park Service Visitors Center just off Route 80 or at their headquarters in Bushkill, Pennsylvania; phone: (717) 588-6637. The Park Service maintains the two trails to the summit of Mount Tammany and Millbrook Village, well worth a visit.

THE APPALACHIAN TRAIL IN THE KITTATINNIES

Coming from Wawayanda State Park through a state-owned corridor, over woods, fields, and farms, the Appalachian Trail crosses Route 519 about a quarter mile south of the New York–New Jersey border and enters High Point State Park. Parking is available just north of the trail.

After a short, steep ascent, the trail crosses a wide field to climb to the first ridge, which offers a fine view over Sussex County. Following this ridge for about a mile, the trail encounters a short blue trail, which leads to High Point shelter, and, climbing to a notch, reaches another blue side trail that turns off to the monument. The trail now climbs to the top of the ridge before descending to Route 23, which it crosses just east of the park headquarters, where maps and information are available.

From Route 23, the trail continues partly on wood roads until it climbs to the ridge, which is reached in about 0.75 mile. There are frequent overlooks to the valley land east and west, with Lake Rutherford a prominent feature to the east. About 3 miles south of Route 23, a quarter-mile side trail leads east to the Rutherford shelter. Beyond here the main trail follows a rough roadway through the woods for its final half mile before crossing Deckertown Turnpike. Here there is a parking area. To visit the Mashipacong shelter, continue on the trail beyond the turnpike for a few hundred feet, near the southern boundary of High Point. The Appalachian Trail now enters Stokes State Forest.

The Stokes State Forest portion of the trail can easily be walked in a day by setting up a car ferry to return to the starting point at the end of the trip. From Route 206 near Culvers Gap, drive north on Sunrise Mountain Road to a parking area at the end of a spur road to Sunrise Mountain, or south past Kittatinny Lake on Woods Road to Brink Road, where there is a trail shelter. For a longer walk, begin at Deckertown Turnpike, reached by a circuitous continuation of Sunrise Mountain Road; there is another parking area just north of Route 206, where Sunrise Mountain Road begins its ascent. For the latter route, turn north opposite Worthington's Bakery onto County Road 636.

A large stone rain shelter on Sunrise Mountain, heavily used by picnic parties, offers a panoramic overlook, with High Point Monument prominent to the north. No camping or fires are permitted here.

To the south the Appalachian Trail parallels Sunrise Mountain Road, passing through woods and scrub growth with occasional views. The Glen Anderson shelter and a spring (not reliable in exceptionally dry seasons) are on a short side trail leading to the road, about 2 miles from Sunrise Mountain. After 1 mile, the trail passes a fire tower and descends steadily for the better part of a mile. Turning sharply to the right, it crosses a meadow, with good views, and descends in a long switchback to Sunrise Mountain Road, north of the parking area, following the road to reach Route 206 opposite the bakery.

On the other side of the highway, the trail continues slightly to the left and ascends sharply to the summit of a ridge; it follows the crest for 3 miles to Brink Road, where a shelter is located about 0.2 mile to the west. To reach the boundary of Stokes State Forest, enter the Delaware Water Gap National Recreation Area, cross Brink Road and continue for another mile, climbing 300 feet to a ridge with fine views of the Delaware Valley. Retrace your steps to Brink Road, from which the Appalachian Trail continues southward to the Delaware Water Gap.

After crossing the river on Route 80, the trail continues south through the recreation area. It is about 2.7 miles from the gap to the summit of Mount Minsi.

16 · WESTERN NEW JERSEY

USUALLY THE area extending southwest from the Wawayanda Plateau is similar to the New Jersey Highlands, but more open. Where rough topography has preserved forested valleys and summits, there are worthwhile walks, and there are a number of parks in the western part of the state which have these characteristics and which are worth exploring. Because of their scattered locations, however, access can be only by automobile.

JENNY JUMP STATE FOREST

This forest of 1118 acres is situated in Warren County, along the Jenny Jump Mountain, between Hope and Great Meadows and lies to the north of the Pequest River at Buttzville. Lying about 12 miles southeast of the Delaware Water Gap, it is typical of the mountain country in northern New Jersey, with elevations ranging from 399 to 1108 feet.

To the hiker, the main features of Jenny Jump State Forest are the spectacular views from forest roads and trails. Toward the west, on clear days, there is an unbroken view of Kittatinny Valley and of the Kittatinny Mountains, from Wind Gap, Pennsylvania, to the west, to the highest peak in High Point State Park far to the north. This also includes an unusually fine view of Delaware Water Gap. To the east, the views include Old Silver Mine Valley and the Great Meadows, six thousand acres of rich, black muck soil used for intensive truck farming. The contrast of black soil with rows of green vegetables between the hillsides sprinkled with farms and woodlands provides a striking and pleasing panoramic view.

A self-guiding trail has been laid out near the Notch picnic area. Along this trail grow five kinds of oak, three kinds of maple, including the striped maple *(Acer pennsylvanicum)*, three kinds of pine, three kinds of birch, wild cherry, the slippery elm *(Ulmus rubra)*, hornbeam, red cedar, aspen, beech, hemlock, ash, sumac, tulip tree, spruce, walnut, and sassafras. Other species of trees grow nearby as well as a large number of shrubs such as arrow-wood, witch hazel, silky camel, and fox grape. Wildflowers and ferns are abundant in season, and the bird life is plentiful and easily observed.

Several picnic areas with sites for family-size groups have been provided. Near the forest headquarters two camp shelters may be rented between April 1 and October 31. The shelters are completely enclosed buildings, each with a fireplace-type stove for heating, an out-of-doors fireplace for cooking, and bunk facilities for four people. Twenty campsites are available for tents or small camp trailers. For further information write to: Forest Officer, Jenny Jump State Park, P.O. Box 150, Hope, N.J. 07844.

To get to Jenny Jump, take Route 80 to the Hope-Blairstown Exit. Turn left on Route 521 to the old Moravian village of Hope, 1 mile from Route 80. Turn left at the traffic light onto Route 519. One mile ahead, on the right, a small sign points the way to the forest.

ALLAMUCHY MOUNTAIN STATE PARK

Embracing most of the Allamuchy Mountain upland between Route 517 and the Musconetcong River, and bisected by Interstate 80, this 15,000-acre park provides miles of hiking. Having been declared a natural area, thus remaining in an undeveloped condition, Allamuchy Mountain Park is particularly appealing to hikers. At present, the region around Deer Park Pond, south of Route 80, is the most accessible section and the trails here (unmarked wood roads) are shown on the map provided by the park. To the hiker the park presents an uncommon blend of forest and overgrown pasture, a combination which supports an abundance of wildlife.

From Route 80 (Exit 19) take Route 517 south for 2 miles and turn left on a rough road. After about 1 mile on this road the state land is reached and there is a main parking area. Three other parking areas are located farther along this unpaved road at approximately 1-mile intervals. By parking at the second of these three areas, which is near a sharp bend in the road, one can hike due north on a wood road for about 1.5 miles to the overlook on

Route 80. This is the feature of the park that most people see, it being the rest area on Route 80 eastbound. From the trail this overlook is to the left and can be reached by following a short path. Bearing right from this point, and swinging around to a southerly direction, one can return to the parking area via a different trail which leads to Deer Park Pond, a beautiful, calm body of water used for fishing and boating. Follow the park access road to return to your car.

The Stephens section of Allamuchy Mountain Park is located on the Musconetcong River and contains fifty camping sites. Also within the park is the restored village of Andover Forge, now called Waterloo Village, once a busy port along the Morris Canal. Earlier, it was part of the Andover iron forge, which produced cannonballs for the Colonists. For half a century, beginning in 1832, the Morris Canal was the chief means of conveying coal, iron, and zinc across New Jersey. It was ninety miles long, and the trip from Newark to Phillipsburg required five days.

Other reminders of the canal can be seen at Hopatcong State Park and at Saxton Falls, 1 mile north of the Stephens section. At the falls are the remains of one of the twenty-eight locks of the canal.

For further information write to Allamuchy Mountain State Park, Hackettstown, N.J. 07840.

MAHLON DICKERSON RESERVATION

This tract is administered by the Morris County Park Commission which believes that no more than fifteen percent of a county park should be developed for intensive recreational use; the remaining eighty-five percent must be left untouched except for trails. A result of this philosophy is that many of the Morris County parks, particularly Hedden Park in Dover and Torne Park in Denville, offer interesting walking possibilities.

Mahlon Dickerson Reservation, named after a former state governor and U.S. senator active during the early nineteenth century, is the largest of the Park Commission's holdings (over 1500 acres) and offers excellent hiking opportunities. The reservation, which also offers year-round trailer, tent, and Adirondack shelter camping, is located on Weldon Road in Jefferson Township, east from Route 15 near Lake Hopatcong.

Trails in the reservation follow old logging roads and as such are especially suited to large groups and cross-country skiing. Coming from Route 15 on Weldon Road, park at the third reservation entrance (second on left) for access to the trails. From the parking area a short trail leads back across the road to the Headley Overlook from which an arm of Lake Hopatcong may be seen.

Also from this parking area is access to the white-blazed Pine Swamp Trail, a 3.5-mile loop trail which takes one to the edge of the Great Pine Swamp, a wet area densely covered with spruce, rhododendron, and native azalea. The Pine Swamp area is very remote; a plane crashed here in May some years ago and was not found until November of that year. The trail also climbs to the highest point in Morris County, 1388 feet, from which there are no views. A map of the reservation showing the trails is available from the Morris County Park Commission, 53 East Hanover Avenue, Box 1295R, Morristown, N.J. 07960.

HACKLEBARNEY STATE PARK

Lying about 3 miles southwest of Chester and the intersection of Routes 24 and 206, this park contains 574 acres. Situated along the deep gorge of the Black River, the park is traversed by a system of winding footpaths. Its topography, with its ridges of gneiss, is rugged. An elevation of 804 feet is attained on the west side of Black River.

One story about the origins of the park's name states that a quick-tempered iron ore foreman in the vicinity was persistently heckled and soon "Heckle" Barney, as he was called, became Hacklebarney. Another theory is that the name is of Lenni-Lenape derivation, meaning "to put wood on a fire on the ground," a bonfire. A feature worth noting in the park is "Indian Mill"—a pothole in the river.

Across the Black River from the main day-use area of the park is the Lamington Natural Area, a transition forest.

To get to Hacklebarney, take Route 24 west from Chester. Go for 1.25 miles, then turn left at the bridge for 3 miles.

ROUND VALLEY STATE PARK

Annandale, reached by either Route 78 or Route 22, is the center for a number of pleasant jaunts. A couple of miles to the north, off Route 31, is the town of High Bridge, named for the railroad trestle, and still the site of an operating ironworks which made cannonballs for Washington's army. Just to the east, along the south branch of the Raritan River, is Ken Lockwood Gorge, an area owned by the state but not yet developed. The river cascades down for about 2 miles through many interesting "rock gardens" and into quiet pools, and the high banks on both sides contribute to a sense of isolation. The unpaved road which runs through the gorge makes for a pleasant walk.

Southeast from Annandale is the Round Valley State Park (Cushetunk Mountain), a curious horseshoe-shaped ridge encircling a reservoir. The traprock is similar to the diabase of the Palisades of the Hudson and is part of the same outflows of Triassic time. The rocks of this curving ridge had their origin in an intrusion of diabase between strata of the Brunswick shales and sandstones of the Triassic period. They were eventually exposed by erosion, which wore down the softer shales above and around and left the harder igneous material standing 800 feet above sea level and 400 feet above the surrounding Hunterdon countryside.

The Cushetunk ridge, never having been glaciated as were the Palisades, has more residual soil than the latter. A good second growth of hardwood covers most of its upper portion. The region is particularly attractive in spring, at the time of the blossoming dogwood, which is plentiful on the slopes of the ridge. There are good views eastward over the plain of the valley of the Raritan, bordered on the south by similar trap ridges, which are also a southwestward extension of the Palisades intrusion. Half a mile west of the south limb of the Cushetunk horseshoe, in abandoned limestone quarries, are the remains of the kilns where the rock was burned. The rock has a peculiar blue color, possibly due to its manganese content. Four miles north of Round Valley Reservoir a smaller horseshoe of diabase shows a curious topography. The Brunswick shales of the interior valley are open, while the contact with the traprock and border conglomerates is generally indicated by the forest which covers the ridge.

In recent years, the state has developed a comprehensive recreation area here, with hiking, swimming, camping, picnicking, boating, and other facilities. With its three-mile-long, two-mile-wide reservoir and four-hundred-foot hills, the area provides an outdoor experience increasingly hard to find in urbanized New Jersey. To reach Round Valley, take Route 22 to the marked turnoff south about 4 miles east of Clinton. The headquarters is around the reservoir to the southwest.

Round Valley Trail. Length: 9 miles.

A combination hiking/bridle trail with fine views nearly encircles the reservoir on the Cushetunk ridge and passes the back-country camping area. The trail begins at the main parking lot at the west end of the reservoir on Lebanon-Stanton Road and was originally planned to encircle the reservoir. The restricted areas at the dam have prevented this and, for now, hikers must return to the parking area over the same trail.

The trail itself is marked only by an occasional footprint or horseshoe sign, but it is generally easy to follow. It starts from the southwest corner of the parking area and climbs a small rise to give a view of the deep-blue and sparklingly pure reservoir surrounded by the nearby hills. Continuing on through open fields into a patch of woods, the trail climbs a hill after a short walk on paved road, to reveal good views south.

Entering the woods to follow the ridgeline, the trail dips down to near lake level at the camping area, and then climbs Cushetunk Mountain with its magnificent views. View points have been cleared and have small log benches that make ideal lunch spots.

The trail continues on the ridge through dense forests with some steep ups and downs and rough places for 3 miles past the camping area, before terminating at 9 miles.

Round Valley also has 116 wilderness campsites spread over some 3 miles of the south and east shores of the reservoirs. This backcountry camping area, accessible only by walking or boating, represents a unique experiment in camping in New Jersey. These wooded sites, many of them near the water, are available year round with a permit from headquarters.

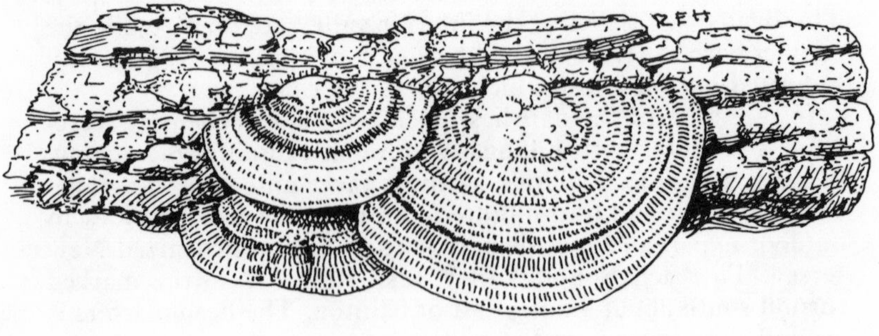

17 · *THE WATCHUNGS AND CENTRAL NEW JERSEY*

No hills of any height appear in northern New Jersey west of the Hudson River until the Watchungs are reached. A double line of ridges from one to two miles apart running from Paterson southwest into Somerset County, the Watchungs formed from outflows onto the Newark Basin nearly 200 million years ago. The fifty-mile ridges, primarily of basalt (known commercially as traprock), show cross faulting at Paterson, Great Notch, Summit, Plainfield, and Bound Brook. Although no elevations exceed 900 feet, the Watchungs are still of interest as outlook points. In fact, the views obtainable from the First Mountain are their chief attraction.

The northern end of the First Watchung is Garrett Rock overlooking the city of Paterson. From here the ridge runs southwest to Eagle Rock Reservation and then to South Mountain Reservation, both of which are in Essex County. The First Watchung continues southwest into Union County, where the Watchung Reservation runs between Summit and Scotch Plains. At Bound Brook the ridge swings northwest, its tip having an elevation of 589 feet.

At the northern end of the Second Watchung are High Mountain (879 feet) and Beech Mountain (866 feet), the latter at the northern end of the Preakness Hills. From here southwest the only public areas along the Second Watchung are in South Mountain and Watchung reservations, both of which straddle the two ridges.

The Watchungs run through a densely populated area, so the principal areas available for hiking are those in the various county parks and reservations. Suburban developments have inundated all but isolated sections just as a rising tide submerges all but the highest points of a rocky reef running into the sea.

Because of their height, the Watchungs played an important part in the American Revolution. These outstanding walls form natural ramparts that could not have been better designed by a military engineer for General Washington's needs. The fronts of the ridges were steep and easy to protect and afforded many places from which to observe the movements of the British in the lowlands to the east. The double line of the Watchungs was further engineered by nature in that its flanks curve, from Bound Brook back to Bernardsville on the south and from Paterson around to Oakland on the north, right up to the older, solid mass of the Precambrian granites and gneisses of the Ramapos.

The British never passed the great double line of the Watchungs in force. They marched along the foot of the columned cliffs of the First Watchung on their way to Trenton in December 1776, but, when Washington turned and captured the Hessian garrison and fought the British at Princeton, he eluded the superior forces that soon gathered, and escaped into his hill fortress around Morristown via the north branch of the Raritan, where the enemy feared to pursue him. The only occasion when the British penetrated the Watchung barrier was in December 1776, when a small cavalry patrol surprised General Charles Lee and his aides in a tavern at Basking Ridge. Never afterward did any British or Hessians pass these ridges. Every month, Washington strengthened his main camp at Morristown and its outposts, which served as a rallying place and source of supplies for the rest of the war.

Three of the locations around Morristown that were of most importance during the Revolution now make up the Morristown National Historical Park. One is the (Jacob) Ford Mansion, open to the public, which served as Washington's headquarters during the bitter winter of 1779–80. A good historical museum is located at the same site, just off Route 287 in Morristown.

The second section of the park is a 1937 reconstruction of Fort Nonsense, about 1 mile southeast of Morristown off Route 202. Most of the army supplies for the 1777 spring campaign were concentrated in Morristown and their protection became essential. On May 28, therefore, Washington issued orders for one detachment to remain in the town "to Strengthen the Works already begun upon the Hill near this place, and erect such other as are necessary for the better defending it, that it may be a safe retreat in case of Necessity." How the works came to be called Fort Nonsense is not known, but there is some evidence that the name is of Revolutionary War origin.

The third section of Morristown National Historical Park is Jockey Hollow, the site of the main encampment of the Continental Army during the winters of 1776–77 and 1779–80.

JOCKEY HOLLOW

Jockey Hollow, located in the rugged hills 3 miles south of Morristown, is a beautiful area of about a thousand acres, including all but three units of the campsite of the Revolutionary Army. In its generally wooded and rural appearance, abounding with huge oak and tulip trees, Jockey Hollow today closely resembles the conditions existing when the Continental troops arrived there in the 1770s. Many of the campgrounds have remained relatively undisturbed, and observant visitors can still see physical evidence of army occupation. Jockey Hollow also features structures of the Revolutionary era, including several log huts, typical of hundreds once used as quarters for officers and men, that were reconstructed by the National Park Service after careful historical and archeological research.

Jockey Hollow can be reached by car from Route 202 or Route 287. Trains from Hoboken and buses from New York City also run to Morristown, from which a taxi can be taken 3 miles to Jockey Hollow. Maps and brochures are available at the visitors center.

Jockey Hollow has miles of trails, some being fire trails and others simply footpaths. At trail intersections, maps of the park are displayed, each with an arrow indicating the hiker's current location. All of the parking areas give access to the trails, though the parking area on Jockey Hollow Road, between the comfort station and the visitors center, is located on several trails, and as such makes a good place to start any number of circular hikes.

A branch of Primrose Brook runs past this central parking area and is followed by trails on both sides, one being the Wildflower Trail. The Patriot's Path, marked with metal discs, also passes through this parking area. A view point to the east and toward the Watchungs is found on the slope of Mount Kemble and can be reached easily from this parking area. To reach it, take the Patriot's Path east (across the road); where it turns south, continue east up the hill. After passing a ranger's residence, turn left and follow this trail to the view point. This is also the site of John Stark's New Hampshire brigade encampment.

Other attractions in the park easily hiked to from this parking area include the Wick House and the soldiers' huts. The Wick

House was built about 1750 and has been restored and furnished. It served as military quarters for Major General Arthur St. Clair during the encampment of 1779–80.

Patriot's Path.

The Patriot's Path is a linear park in Morris County that comprises several trails. A multi-use trail, the path was created as a common effort by several groups, including the Morris County Park Commission and the New Jersey Conservation Foundation (which initiated the project), to prevent the degradation of the Whippany River and to provide ecologically sound recreational opportunities. In 1980, completed sections of the path were designated as a National Recreation Trail.

Today parts of the main artery—which follows the Whippany River from Mendham Township to East Hanover Township—have been paved for bicycles, while other sections have been cleared for walking. The section of the Patriot's Path that passes through Jockey Hollow and the adjoining Lewis Morris County Park is specifically for walkers and is complete. Future plans include connections with the Great Swamp and also the Lenape Trail in Essex County. For further information write to: Friends of the Patriot's Path, 300 Mendham Road, Morristown, N.J. 07960.

Patriot's Path Hiking Trail. Length: 9 miles. Blazes: brown and white.

Not to be confused with the multi-use trail of which it is a branch, this trail follows a varied route through rolling, wooded hills. Marked with metal discs displaying the Patriot's Path symbol of tree and river, it begins in Jockey Hollow on Hardscrabble Road near the New Jersey Brigade hut sites, which are of archeological interest. Here there is parking for only a few cars. Parking for larger groups can be found off Old Jockey Hollow Road near the Cross Estate, which has an extraordinary display of flowers and trees. The Patriot's Path can be picked up here with a loss of about a half mile and the hut sites.

The trail runs through the woods to the Passaic River, which at this point is a beautiful rocky brook. After crossing the river, it is about 1 mile to Tempe Wick Road, which is crossed east of the main entrance to the park. The trail now meets with many other trails, and it becomes more important to keep track of the blazes at intersections. After following Primrose Brook, the trail comes to the soldiers' huts clearing. Just past this area the trail enters Lewis Morris County Park, passing through to its junction with the main artery of the Patriot's Path near Route 24. Parking at this end of the trail is found at Sunrise Lake, which is very close to both the end of the trail and Route 24.

GREAT SWAMP NATIONAL WILDLIFE REFUGE

The 6700-acre Great Swamp occupies most of a basin that is a vestige of prehistoric Lake Passaic. Most of it is in marshland, meadows, and dry woodlands, and its 10 miles of hiking trails bring the hiker in contact with an unusual variety of plant life produced by the area's converging climatic zones.

Here one will find some three hundred species of birds, mammals, reptiles, amphibians, and fish, including not only common species such as beaver, raccoon, and skunk, but also rare creatures such as the bog turtle and the blue-spotted salmon. The yellow marsh marigold in early April, blue iris in May, and the magnificent display of pink and white mountain laurel in June are great attractions, and the observant hiker will find three varieties of ground pine *(Lycopodium)* in the woods.

Located in Morris and Somerset counties thirty miles west of Manhattan, the Great Swamp is unique because of the scope of its ecology in the most populous area of the United States. In order to preserve the natural environment, the U.S. Department of the Interior established a National Wildlife Refuge in the Great Swamp. Subsequently, under the Wilderness Act of 1964, the department designated a larger portion to be included in the Wilderness System. Yet, in the past decade, the area has come perilously close to destruction. Heavy development around the area has damaged the ecology of the preserve, with Route 287 and expanding townships taking a particularly heavy toll. However, biologists and environmentalists, supported by state and international environmental organizations, are studying the area to determine the extent of damage done and find ways of rectifying it.

The U.S. Refuge Headquarters and Information Booth is located on Pleasant Plains Road, which can be reached from Meyersville, east of Basking Ridge, off Route 287. Also near Meyersville is the Wildlife Observation Center and the Ground Pine Trail in the wilderness area. Rambles and hikes of up to 6 miles can be made over established trails or boardwalks. Maps are available at Refuge Headquarters; phone: (201) 647-1222.

The Morris County Park Commission also uses the land for nature walks, operating an education center off Southern Boulevard in Chatham Township. A boardwalk and series of paths enter the swamp at this point and penetrate into it for a short distance. To reach this area, drive from the center of Chatham over Fairmount Avenue, and take a right on Southern Boulevard. Drive about 1 mile to the sign that marks the dirt road that leads to the Outdoor Education Center. A map and description of the whole area are available at the center; phone: (201) 635-6629.

The Somerset County Park Commission's Lord Stirling Park is located on the western border of the refuge. It contains about 5.5 miles of hiking trails, as well as guided field trips and educational courses. Until further facilities are developed, however, the park is open to groups only by appointment. Further information is available from the commission; phone: (201) 766-2489.

WATCHUNG RESERVATION

The Watchung Reservation, maintained by the Union County Department of Parks and Recreation, is a two-thousand-acre wooded tract in the Watchungs where animal and plant life are protected. Although Route 78 is now under construction along its northwestern flank, most of the reservation remains in a natural wild state, affording many delights to the hiker.

Highlights of the park include Surprise Lake, Glenside Village, Trailside Nature and Science Center, the plant nursery, Seeley's Pond, and the Watchung Stables. In May and early June, the dogwood and rhododendron displays near Surprise Lake are outstanding.

Drive, or take the Somerset bus from the Port Authority Bus Terminal, Manhattan, along Route 22 to the traffic light at New Providence Road in the borough of Mountainside. If one goes by bus, there is a 1.5-mile walk up New Providence Road and W. R. Tracy Drive to the Surprise Lake parking area and refreshment stand.

From this point, it is a quarter-mile stroll south through an arboretum to the Trailside Nature and Science Center, where a map showing the reservation's hiking trails can be had. The new building has nature displays and an auditorium, and every weekend there are programs for young and old alike. Nearby is a small planetarium and the old Trailside center, which is now a small nature museum.

Passing near the new building is an interesting 10-mile circular, the Sierra Trail, which takes one through most of the park. The trail, blazed with white X's, heads northeast, following the ridge of First Mountain about 1 mile, where it rounds a water tower now officially closed to the public, then heads back south-

east. It crosses a road near a traffic circle, then heads down into the valley separating the two Watchung ridges. It follows dirt roads southwest, passing near Surprise Lake before plunging back into the woods. The trail soon passes an old graveyard, then moves onto a blacktop road through Glenside Village. Also known as the Deserted Village and Feltville, it contains the remnants of a small community that flourished in the mid 1800s, including ruins of old mill structures. Several of the houses have been refurbished and are rented to county employees.

After the trail passes through the village, it continues southwest to the boundary of the reservation, where it runs along a rock face used by rock climbers. After descending to a route along Green Brook, where it passes the ruins of a millrace, the trail turns back along First Mountain. It runs generally northeast, with some detours up and down the ridge, sometimes on dirt roads and sometimes through the woods, and comes out at Trailside. A small network of much shorter trails is laid out in this area, just southeast of Trailside.

SOUTH MOUNTAIN RESERVATION

South Mountain Reservation, the largest open space managed by the Essex County Department of Parks, Recreation, and Cultural Affairs, is a beautifully wooded area of more than two thousand acres north of Millburn. There are many footpaths and bridle trails throughout, with the reservation the starting point of the Lenape Trail. In the northeastern section, Turtle Back Rock is an interesting formation, and the Turtle Back Zoo displays animals from many parts of the world. There are numerous picnic areas, with fine views from several spots along Crest Drive.

The reservation can be reached by car, bus, or train to Millburn or by car on Route 280 to Exit 7 and then south on Pleasant Valley Way into the park.

Lenape Trail. Proposed length: 36 miles (partially complete). Blazes: yellow.

A joint undertaking of the Sierra Club and the county parks department, the Lenape Trail will, when complete, link dozens of county and municipal parks, the Patriot's Path, historical

POND IN SOUTH MOUNTAIN RESERVATION NEAR MILLBURN

areas, and other landmarks along a 36-mile route. The entire path, closed to motorized vehicles, will be suitable for hiking and walking, with various portions lending themselves to cross-country skiing, cycling, and jogging—a trail in the true spirit of New Jersey's trails development plan. Already a 5-mile section through South Mountain and a 12-mile section from Cedar Grove to Newark have been completed.

The trail starts in South Mountain Reservation's Locust Grove picnic area, just north of the Millburn station, running 5 miles north to Mayapple Hill. From the picnic area, the trail follows a long path to the top of First Mountain, where it turns back to Washington Rock, from which George Washington surveyed the countryside during the Revolution.

Continuing west, then north, the trail passes Maple Falls, Beechbrook Cascades, and Balls Bluff before dropping down to a small natural amphitheater at Hemlock Falls. Crossing the footbridge over South Orange Avenue—where there is parking available immediately east of the bridge—it turns left through a pine grove and bends back to cross Brookside Drive at the traffic light. Running west and then north again along Second Mountain, the trail continues past a lookout at the Crag, crosses Northfield Avenue on a footbridge, and reaches the Mayapple Hill parking area.

The Lenape Trail continues across the playing field and into the woods another half mile to the park boundary, where a blue trail leads back along a bridle path to the Lenape Trail near Northfield Avenue. A variety of return routes to Locust Grove can be taken from many points along the trail by way of various foot and bridle paths. Maps are available at the park police station on South Orange Avenue.

From here, the Lenape Trail is planned to continue north to O'Conner Park in West Orange to connect with a recently completed 5-mile section of the trail that runs along the public service right-of-way to Becker Park. At Becker Park, the hiker may take a short detour to the connecting Riker Hill Park. The trail then goes a little farther to the County Environmental Center in Roseland, where it connects to the Morris County Patriot's Path. Ultimately, the trail will go northeast to the Caldwells and Cedar Grove.

From here, the last 12-mile section of the trail, which is completed, starts in Cedar Grove Community Park off Bowden Road. Taking the trail along the abandoned Caldwell Branch Railway, the hiker passes through woods to cross Ridge Road, which leads around the Cedar Grove Reservoir. Proceeding through Mills

Reservation on a blue loop path, the Lenape Trail runs east past several scenic lookouts onto First Mountain.

After a short, steep descent into Mountainside Park, site of noted iris gardens, it passes through Yantacaw Brook and Brookdale parks before crossing the Garden State Parkway on a footbridge. Following the Newark Aqueduct, the trail soon reaches Belleville, running along quiet streets before passing through Belleville Park to enter Branch Brook Park, a turn-of-the-century Olmstead design now being restored.

Here, a festival every April at the Japanese cherry blossom area celebrates the flowering of hundreds of trees and draws thousands of visitors. After wending its way south past Sacred Heart Cathedral, the trail leaves the park, crossing Clifton Avenue to follow Nesbit and James streets. In this historic area, nineteenth-century brownstones struggle against urban blight on the west and downtown commerce on the east.

Passing the restored Ballantine House and Newark Museum—both of which are open to the public—the Lenape Trail crosses Washington Park before reaching Trinity Episcopal Cathedral, which served as a hospital during the Revolution. The trail ends at the south end of Military Park near the Wars of America Monument by Gutzon Borglum.

For more information on the Lenape Trail, contact the Sierra Club's Lenape Trail Committee, 39 Crystal Avenue, West Orange, N.J. 07052; phone: (201) 731-1765.

PREAKNESS RANGE AND HIGH MOUNTAIN

The Preakness Range north of Paterson is a continuation of the Second Watchung Mountain, although the Passaic River flows through a considerable gap between them. Geologically similar to the Palisades far to the east and Packanack Mountain to the west, Preakness is the middle of a three-layer basalt series lying roughly parallel to one another.

Although much of the range is occupied by William Paterson State College, a golf course, Urban Farms Development, and private estates, its northern end contains some twelve thousand acres of wild wooded country, including a wonderfully unobstructed and extensive view from High Mountain. At 879 feet, it is one of the highest points on the East Coast. Also accessible from this area are the geologically interesting Franklin Clove and Lake, part of a glaciated lowland. The clove is a fault zone, or area of crustal displacement, in the traprock ridge through which a considerable stream of ice must have flowed eons ago during the retreat of a glacier. This deep, shady pass is similar to many seen along the trap ridges but is by far the deepest and longest. It has counterparts in Long Clove and Short Clove below Haverstraw in New York.

Franklin Lake is the largest of a series of ponds occupying depressions along the irregular knolls, called kames, left by the glacial ice as it retreated northward. Stratified sand and gravel deposited along the ice front is also typical of this area.

Hikers may also wish to take a side trip to the Van Riper Ellis House, which is open to the public, and the 1706 House, which is closed. These houses, north of the Point View Reservoir on the west side of Berdan Avenue, are two of the oldest in the area.

Hiking is primarily on wood roads, which are also used by motorized vehicles such as trail bikes. Since the perimeter of the area is becoming developed, parking is often a problem, and it is suggested that hikers driving to the area park in Lot 6 at the college or at the Ramapo Mall shopping center. Bus service to the western area is via Warwick Bus Lines from the Port Authority Bus Terminal, Manhattan, and hikers can alight at Hamburg Turnpike and Valley Road. Public transportation to the eastern area is available from Paterson via Beaumont Avenue on a New Jersey Transit bus, which leaves hikers off at Overlook Avenue near the college's east entrance.

Yellow Trail. Length: 8 miles. Blazes: yellow.

Featuring both High Mountain and the geological formations, this is the longest trail in this area. There is free public parking on Belmont Avenue, about 100 yards south of West Overlook Avenue. To reach the trail, follow West Overlook Avenue uphill, where the road turns into Buttermilk Falls Road, to entrance No. 6 of William Paterson College, where there is also parking. The trailhead can be picked up on the north side. After a right turn at the brook crossing, the path reaches the top of Bridal Falls (also known as Quarry Falls or Buttermilk Falls).

The falls are the result of quarrying that supplied stone for many of the homes in the area. Bridal Falls has a free drop of about twenty feet and is most spectacular in the winter when ice cones develop. On the face of the cliff, the contrast between the sandstone below and the traprock above is visible.

Blazes for the Yellow Trail start at the brook crossing and go north for about 2 miles to the top of High Mountain. High Mountain is barren at its summit and provides a spectacular 360-degree view. Northwest and north lie the Ramapos, with Suffern and the gap of the Ramapo River slightly east of the north point. To the east the horizon is bounded by the Palisades with Hook Mountain at the northeast. Southeast the skyscrapers of Manhattan are visible, with the towers of the George Washington Bridge north of them. Nearer are the towns of Wyckoff and Ridgewood (northeast), and Fair Lawn (east), with Paterson lying in the bowl of the valley. Directly opposite is the long slope of the "Goffle," or ridge of the First Watchung Mountain. The eastern cliff is almost vertical, but it cannot be seen from here. To the south is the abrupt drop of Garrett Mountain.

Continuing north and then west, the trail comes upon a pretty cascading brook before turning south to a well-traveled dirt road. Turning west at a medium-sized boulder, it meets the terminus of the Red Trail. The Yellow Trail then descends a rocky outcrop and turns north on a well-traveled woodland road, where it meets the terminus of the White Trail. Turning west, the Yellow Trail ascends steeply up Beech Mountain and wanders along the ridge to a sweeping panorama of Point View Reservoir, Wayne, and the Pompton Hills. About a mile farther, the trail goes by Buttermilk Falls, a pleasant rest spot where water cascades down the fractured basalt rock. The trail here is next to Scioto Drive in Urban Farms and can be a starting point or an exit.

The trail then goes southwest through Franklin Clove, where the rock formation should be observed. About a quarter mile farther, the slant rock formation can be seen before the trail turns southeast. It exits into a bank parking lot. One can continue across the lot to Valley Road Extension and south to Hamburg Turnpike, where it is approximately 1.3 miles back to the college parking lot.

White Trail. Length: 2 miles. Blazes: white.

The White Trail meets the Yellow Trail, as noted above, and continues southward past the reservoir and fairways of the North Jersey Country Club, exiting on Hamburg Turnpike, about a half mile east of the Valley Road Extension. If one follows the White Trail about a half mile south, it meets a side trail on the east, which, after going up a long rise, meets the Red Trail. Proceed south for a half mile to the college parking lot.

Red Trail. Length: 1.5 miles. Blazes: red.

The third principal trail is the Red Trail, which starts a quarter mile west of the Yellow Trail on the North College Road. It is accessible directly north of parking lot 6, starting at the brook and east/west fence. It climbs a fair grade and bypasses Pennyroyal Hill, ending at the Yellow Trail as noted above. The White and Red trails provide shortcuts for the Yellow Trail.

MILLSTONE VALLEY

Few of North America's rivers flow northward. One of the exceptions is the little Millstone, the axis of a charming valley of modest hills and green prairies. The river, from Carnegie Lake at Princeton to its junction with the Raritan near Bound Brook, provides a delightful canoe trip when the rains have been adequate and if one is willing to portage occasionally.

Parallel to the river is the Delaware and Raritan Canal, which extends all the way from the Delaware River at Trenton to New Brunswick on the Raritan River. This was a functioning canal from 1834 to 1933, but now it is a state park, used for recreational purposes only. Fishing is a common pursuit, and canoeing, again with portages, can be enjoyed, combining a southward stretch along the canal with a downstream paddle on the river to make a round trip. Ordinary road maps or the Hagstrom Somerset County map will furnish adequate guidance for access to the towpath.

Most of the towpath provides excellent walking. At Princeton the path follows the shore of Carnegie Lake. Three miles from here, a huge red mill and abundant water at Kingston form an impressive picture. In another 2 miles is Rocky Hill; here, at the Berrien House, off Route 518 overlooking the canal, General Washington drafted his farewell address. A small parking lot next to the canal is provided for public use in this area. The locks, the little swing bridges, and the canal tenders' shacks are characteristic of the route. From Griggstown on, the scenic beauty is especially notable. One caution: watch for poison ivy.

From Blackwells Mills north, the east side of the canal heading toward the village of East Millstone is moderately traveled and provides an attractive alternate route to the towpath to Millstone. Between Millstone and Bound Brook, the religious community of Zarephath is of interest. The path continues along the Raritan Valley another 7 miles beyond Bound Brook to New Brunswick.

Another attraction in the Millstone Valley is a 136-acre forest tract, of which 65 acres are virgin forest, long known as Metlars Woods. Widespread contributions, capped by a major one from the Carpenters Union, have preserved this as the William L. Hutcheson Memorial Forest. It is used for teaching and research by Rutgers University. The forest, located on Amwell Road

(Route 514) about 2 miles east of East Millstone, is open to the public only on guided tours. Information is available from the Forest Director at Rutgers University, New Brunswick, New Jersey.

Suggested Readings

Brydon, Norman F.
The Passaic River—Past, Present and Future
Rutgers University Press, New Brunswick, N.J., 1974

Cavanaugh, Cam
Saving the Great Swamp
Columbia Publishing Co., Frenchtown, N.J., 1978

Davison, Betty B.
The Delaware and Raritan Canal: A User's Guide
Delaware and Raritan Canal Coalition, Princeton, N.J., 1976

Lee, James
The Morris Canal—A Photo History
Canal Press, York, Pa., 1973

Menzies, Elizabeth G. C.
Millstone Valley
Rutgers University Press, New Brunswick, N.J., 1969

Miers, Earl Schenck
Crossroads of Freedom
Rutgers University Press, New Brunswick, N.J., 1971

Scherzer, Carl B.
Washington's Forgotten Encampment
Washington Association of New Jersey, Morristown, N.J., 1975

18 · *THE PINE BARRENS OF NEW JERSEY*

(Map 19)

NEW JERSEY'S Pine Barrens have a strange wild beauty that is both fascinating and forbidding. A unique block of wilderness close to the urban areas of New York and Philadelphia, the region is a broad expanse of relatively level land covering approximately 1.65 million acres. Roughly eighty miles long and thirty miles wide, it lies on the coastal plain and extends into nine counties in southern New Jersey. The region is entirely unglaciated, with few hills and no rock outcroppings.

A person flying over this area or driving its long straight highways is likely to think of the Pine Barrens as wasteland. Pine forests, sometimes scorched or scrubby, cover vast sandy stretches with little signs of habitation, crops, or livestock. But this remarkable physiographic and biologic province is far from being botanically barren. Temperature maps for the winter and spring months show that it has a climate nearly as mild as that of Virginia and the Carolinas, two hundred to four hundred miles farther south.

Wild and primitive, the region claimed the attention of early naturalists and became especially well known for unusual plants. To botanists, the Pinelands are a natural wilderness recovered from its early clear-cutting by lumbermen and charcoal burners. A number of areas have become major botanical meccas and many have historical and sentimental value as well. The combination of natural history and human interest associated with those places gives them an intellectual aura and educational value that many would preserve.

There are places in the Pine Barrens—for instance, the fire tower on Apple Pie Hill—where the outlook to the four horizons

N.J. PINE BARRENS
Mullica River w. of Batsto *looking downstream.* Dec. 13 1970

is an apparently unbroken carpet of forest with a glimmer here and there of small ponds and only a distant hint or two of human intrusion. Attractive at all seasons—spring and summer with the beauty of countless bog flowers and the fragrance of sun-warmed pines and cedars, autumn with a colorful palette on a background of green, and winter with its stark snow-streaked loneliness—the region has a continuing appeal the more striking because of its geographic setting.

The principal streams that drain the Pine Barrens are the several branches of Rancocas Creek at the west; Great Egg Harbor River at the southeast; Westecunck, Oyster, and Cedar creeks, and the Toms and Metedeconk rivers at the east and north; and the Mullica River and its tributaries (Wading, Bass, and Batsto rivers, and Nescochague and Landing creeks) easterly. Oswego River and Tulpehocken Creek flow into Wading River.

Under the mats of vegetation and layers of sand are great aquifers, which underlie the whole region. It was this tremendous water resource, now estimated at more than seventeen trillion gallons, that influenced the late Joseph Wharton to acquire nearly a hundred thousand acres in the last century. Wharton estimated that the water from his holdings would furnish nearby cities with up to three hundred million gallons daily. In 1905, however, New Jersey passed a law that gave the state control of the export of its waters, and Wharton could not carry out his plan. Subsequent laws have replaced the 1905 law, but the state retains control over its waters; and a 1981 law specifically restricts removal of water from the Pinelands. Today, the Wharton tract is part of Wharton State Forest.

Other state holdings in the Pine Barrens include state forests and parks, wildlife management areas, natural areas, and wild river areas. The state forests are among the areas of most interest to hikers. Bass River State Forest, a tract of more than thirteen thousand acres, is located immediately east of Wharton State Forest. To the northeast of the latter is Penn State Forest, covered mostly with young pine, and with young cedar along the streams. About eight miles to the north is Lebanon State Forest, consisting of about thirty thousand acres of interesting bog and upland. The Lebanon Glass Works, which were located here, gave the area its name.

Human activities in the Pinelands at present are generally in keeping with their natural aspect and condition. Hikers, canoeists, campers, hunters, fishermen, nature students, history buffs, solitude seekers—all find a rewarding place to pursue their interests. Forest management practices, such as selective harvesting of timber in special plots, experimental planting, and controlled burning to combat wildfire and maintain the dominance of the pines, have little effect on the Pine Barrens as a whole. The culture of cranberries and blueberries contributes to the appeal of the area; these are basic earthy occupations that fit the environment and add a human touch.

The trend in recent years has been for slow but continuous development to eat away at the edge of the Pines. Uncontrolled development could have a negative effect not only on the surface environment, but also on the quality and yield of the tremendous aquifer beneath the Pinelands, the largest potential source of fresh water in the state. The disturbance that would be caused by industry, housing developments, and more access highways is incalculable.

Fortunately, a recent body of legislation has recognized the tremendous value of the Pine Barrens and attempted to control development there. In 1978, the Federal Government established the Pinelands National Reserve and called for the state of New Jersey to adopt a comprehensive plan for the region. In 1979 New Jersey adopted the Pinelands Protection Act, which specified a framework for the plan. The Pines are divided into seven management areas, each accommodating a particular class of land use: Preservation Area, Protection Area, Agricultural Production

Area, Rural Development Area, Regional Growth Area, Pinelands Towns, and Military and Federal Installations.

The two largest management areas, which are also the ones of most interest to hikers, are the Preservation Area and the Protection Area. The Preservation Area, covering about 370,000 acres centered around the Wharton tract in the heart of the Pines, is to preserve a large, contiguous tract of land in its natural state, and to promote compatible agricultural, horticultural, and recreational uses. The Protection Area, covering about 790,000 acres extending through much of the state east and south of the Preservation Area, is to preserve the essential character of the existing Pinelands environment while accommodating needed development in an orderly way. The other areas are to be managed in accord with the uses designated for them.

Other statutes, such as the 1981 law that protects the water of the Pines, continues to move through the state and federal legislatures. But not all of the new laws are favorable. It is too much to hope that the Pines are safe from all unwise exploitation. Yet a new awareness of their great value offers hope that the essential character of the Pine Barrens can be preserved and protected.

HISTORY

The first whites to enter the Pinelands of southern New Jersey undoubtedly followed the trails of the Lenni-Lenape that led to the shell fisheries on the coast. The peculiar wildness of the region, empty of human life, must have impressed these early explorers, accustomed as they were to the massive deciduous forest trees and the grass meadows of the uplands, and the river valleys and the coastal marshes where an occasional Indian village could be found. Although these trails through the Pines represented a long day's journey, there is no evidence of any permanent Indian camp or village within the area. Native Americans apparently held the deep Pinelands in certain awe and shunned them as much as possible.

Long before Wharton saw water sale possibilities in the massive aquifers of the Pinelands, the people of New Jersey were using the region for whatever profitable ventures it afforded. First to move in were the loggers, who cut clean. Pine and cedar lumber moved steadily to shipyards and nearby towns for years before, during, and after the Revolution. Roads to the coastal communities followed the loggers and charcoal burners, and hostelries were established at a number of places along the sand roads. Bog iron was discovered in the Pines, and forges and furnaces were built on the major streams and branches. Iron proved a fairly profitable venture for a generation or so, but the bog ironworks were forced to rely on the uncertain qualities and limited availability of charcoal for fueling their forges. Shortly after the mid nineteenth century, the Jersey iron industry practically disappeared, overwhelmed by competition from the Pennsylvania furnaces with their superior ore and coal fuel.

One of the principal communities of the iron days was Batsto, established in 1765 in Burlington County a few miles from the salt reaches of the lower Mullica River. Although fire and neglect have left their destructive marks, the core of the village has remained. Protection and restoration by the state have resulted in an attractive and authentic early Pine Barrens village. Open to visitors now are the "big house" where the master lived, several workers' cottages, the general store and post office, sawmill, gristmill, and a number of other old buildings. Restoration is continuing.

Glassmaking, using the fine silica sands of certain areas, followed the iron era and flourished for a time; a few large glassworks still prosper on the southern edge of the Pines, around Glassboro. Paper mills were built on several of the streams, with salt hay used for fiber, but they, too, were short-lived. The ruins of a paper mill and its community can be seen at Harrisville.

An interesting industry that has disappeared in many sections is the gathering and drying of sphagnum moss for sale to nurseries and for packing and insulating. In former days, local inhabitants augmented the family income by gathering laurel, mistletoe, arbutus, and medicinal herbs for sale in Philadelphia and other cities. In a few sections, as in the vicinity of Tabernacle and Indian Mills, considerable truck farming is carried on today.

By the turn of the twentieth century, extensive acreage of cutover white cedar swamps had been cleared for cranberry growing, while large tracts of drier ground were used for blueberry production, continuing to the present day. Although cranberrying has declined to some extent, these are the only substantial and profitable industries now active in the Pinelands.

Aside from the berry growing, the Pine Barrens have been put to little productive or consumptive use in recent times. Over the years there have been many attempts by individuals and land promoters to settle the area with homes and farms. Most were complete failures, resulting in property abandonment, tax sales, removal of names from assessment lists, selling and reselling, subdividing, and a general confusion of ownership. Clear titles were often difficult to obtain; the land appeared worthless to many hopeful owners, and the attempt to populate the uninhabited Pinelands slowed to a halt.

Where the ironworks once stood, nature has practically obliterated all traces of once-busy communities. Ghost towns now dot the Pines with only the remains of a structure or two, or none at all, as vague reminders of the places where people once lived and worked. A number of the ponds that were built to power sawmills and gristmills and to furnish water for other purposes still remain. The shores of these ponds, such as the ones at Harrisville and Martha, provide fertile grounds for typical Pine Barrens flora. Likewise, the abandoned cranberry bogs and the old clearings have become ideal propagation grounds for the characteristic growth of the Pinelands.

FLORA AND FAUNA

The unusual soil and water acidity and great areas of sand have truly made the New Jersey Pine Barrens an "island" habitat for several species of plant and animal life not found in other parts of the state. As an outdoor laboratory and museum for biologists and ecologists, the Pinelands has no equal in the state.

The vegetation in general is an old and relict flora that has occupied this area since prehistoric days. Existing essentially as in its original state, it provides rare opportunities for plant research. There are areas here that are visited regularly by students from Eastern schools and colleges for teaching and special projects. Many of these special areas are in the protected state lands within the Pines, but there are other sites of equal ecological significance presently outside of state ownership that should be protected from disturbance.

The multiacred pine and oak natural areas of southern New Jersey are among the last of these biologically important types. Much basic information is available here in the study of the structure, function, and development of mankind's natural environment. Ecologists look to the Pine Barrens with its oak interludes as a significant segment of a continent-wide biological reserve.

The white sandy soil of the Pines, developed on what is known to geologists as the Cohansey formation, is largely infertile. With the exception of blueberry and cranberry culture and isolated truck farms, it is not suited to commercial agriculture. The natural forest covering the bulk of the region is predominantly pitch pine *(Pinus rigida)* with scattered stands of shortleaf pine *(Pinus echinata).* In no other region in North America is the pitch pine the dominant tree over such an extended area. Oaks of several species are common where the pines have been removed, and oak becomes the climax type where firmly established. In the swamps and along the streams, southern white cedar, sweet and swamp magnolia are very common, with sour gum, red maple, and gray birch on somewhat drier soils nearby.

The forest understory and thicket consist of a variety of woody shrubs and subshrubs such as blueberry, huckleberry, sweet pepperbush, buttonbush, winterberry, chokeberry, poison sumac, shadbush, staggerbush, greenbrier, and Virginia creeper. There is also an abundance of sweet fern, sand myrtle, sheep laurel, hudsonia, bearberry, viburnum, and azalea. Well over a hundred species of herbaceous plants, some exceedingly rare, are found in the bogs, wooded swamps, and dry woods, and along the roadsides. In areas of fire-ravaged woodland, the underbrush is often very dense and furnishes protection for the young pitch pines that sprout profusely from the burned stumps of the parent trees.

The cranberry lands were established in cutover cedar swamps. Where cranberry growing has been abandoned, the bogs have gradually changed to savanna types with grasses, other herbaceous plants, and seedling deciduous trees and shrubs moving in. Where conditions have been favorable, a few pines will also enter the bog edges. Students of natural phenomena find here an excellent example of plant succession and the attempt by nature to vegetate an exposed area.

The white cedar swamps still in existence approach their primeval condition and appearance in every way except in size of trees. The straight trunks of the southern, or Atlantic, white cedar *(Chamaecyparis thyoides)* grow in thick stands, rising from the soggy ground where their buttress roots are matted with sphagnum mosses. Shade-tolerant ferns, vines, and shrubs thrive in the dark and humid surroundings, and a few moisture-loving flowers find a home in the brandy-colored cedar water. The mossy hummocks and fallen logs also carry their little colorful gardens of interesting plant life. There is little animal life in these gloomy but intriguing morasses. A few birds call, and the occasional track of a raccoon or fox may be found.

Some of the more extensive and typical white cedar swamps within or bordering the Pine Barrens include the excellent forest at Double Trouble on the upper reaches of Cedar Creek, the exceptionally photogenic stand on Route 539 near Warren Grove, and the swamp downstream from Lake Oswego in Penn State Forest. Other cedar swamps of note and worth visiting are found along the streams in the northern part of Lebanon State

Forest, and in the Batsto River drainage in Wharton State Forest, particularly a couple of miles northeast of Atsion. A small white cedar bog (as well as a cross section of typical Pine Barrens pine and oak woods) is traversed by the Lake Absegami Nature Trail at Bass River State Forest.

The special wildness of a white cedar swamp is unequaled in this part of the Northeast. It is an attractive remnant of original New Jersey that will continue to flourish and generate its own wilderness atmosphere, provided it is not drained, cut, or opened to the often questionable designs of certain types of planners and developers.

In the east-central part of the region, north and northeast of Bass River State Forest and Penn State Forest, there is a tract of about fifteen thousand acres popularly known as the Plains. This tract supports a growth of unusually scrubby oak and pine that scarcely reaches an average height of four feet. Scientists have published several theories accounting for this stunted forest, the consensus pointing to a combination of factors: fires, infertility, exposure, and aridity. But under the trees grows a fairly heavy ground cover, mostly heath types, with a generous mixture of herbaceous plants. Typical of Plains flora are carpets of the Conrad crowberry *(Corema conradii)* and the bearberry *(Arctostaphylos uva-ursi)*, both reminiscent of the cold barrens of the North. In spite of repeated fires that have swept the Plains since before white settlement, an interesting variety of plant life continues to thrive there.

Forms of wildlife are present in the Pines in addition to the much-publicized plant life. Where underbrush furnishes browse and protection and the savannas support desirable grasses, white-tailed deer are plentiful. The local herds do not seem to have been reduced to any appreciable extent by the heavy hunting in this intermetropolitan area; deer may be seen on almost any excursion into the woods. Throughout the region where once black bears, panthers, timber wolves, and bobcats were found, there are now only deer, gray foxes, skunks, raccoons, rabbits, and opossums. Muskrats thrive on many of the creeks and rivers; minks are found here and there; otters are known to be present in a few places; and beavers are increasing to the point of being a nuisance in some areas on the edge of the Pines. Smaller mammals such as mice, red squirrels, gray squirrels, common moles, shrews, little brown bats, and weasels are more or less common.

The last of the big mammals to disappear was the black bear. Not wholly carnivorous, the bear subsisted in season on the abundant blueberries and acorns. Bruin was said to be so common that he would sometimes be seen sharing a blueberry patch with a lone human berry picker.

More than eighty species of birds are known to breed in the Pines, some regularly and others occasionally, including those kinds that follow the clearing of the woods and the establishment of homes and farms. Little concentrated study of the bird life of the Pines has been made, although ornithological research is much needed in such an unusual environment.

Reptile and amphibian species in the Pine Barrens are represented by thirteen frogs and toads, nine salamanders, three lizards, eighteen snakes, and ten turtles. Two of the frogs are rare: the Pine Barrens tree frog *(Hyla andersoni)* and the carpenter or sphagnum frog *(Rana virgatipes).* The former has its principal habitat here and is known elsewhere only in isolated colonies in the South. The carpenter frog lives in cool, mossy bogs elsewhere than in New Jersey, but nowhere is it a common species. It is undoubtedly the peculiarly acid waters of the habitat that have localized these two amphibians.

WALKS IN THE PINE BARRENS

Trails and old sand roads used by hikers interlace the pines and cedar swamps. Every now and then along these roads, one sees ghost towns of one or two structures—vague reminders of a flourishing past. The Batona Trail is the only real hiking trail in the Pines, running 40 miles through Lebanon and Wharton State forests. Except for a few short nature walks in the state forests, there are no other marked trails. Several canoe routes are popular on the bigger streams. The most frequent routes follow stretches of the Oswego, Wading, Batsto, and Mullica rivers. Lengths vary from 1 mile or so to 12 miles. Some courses are easy paddling; others, especially on the less-traveled branches, require carrying, poling, or dragging, and forcing the canoe through overhanging underbrush. There are no white-water stretches, however, nor dangerous sweepers to upset the canoeist. A number of campsites are available to canoeists and hikers on the major streams and hiking trails.

Given the near absence of trails, it is not surprising that there are no good hiking maps of the area. Yet the Pines, with hundreds of thousands of acres of public land crisscrossed with sand roads, offer fascinating and rewarding hiking for those who know how to use maps and compass. The U.S. Geological Survey maps of the region are sold at the visitors center at Batsto, the ranger station at Atsion, and the headquarters of Lebanon State Forest.

The Pine Barrens' bewildering web of sand roads and the dearth of marked trails make it hard to describe any but the simplest of routes, a few of which are outlined below. In addition, several suggestions are made for areas to explore with map and compass.

Batona Trail. Length: 40 miles. Blazes: pink.

This longest of blazed hiking trails in southern New Jersey extends 40 miles through the heart of the Pine Barrens, from Ongs Hat in Lebanon State Forest down to Batsto Village in Wharton State Forest, then east on a new section of trail to Evans Bridge on Route 563. The trail was established in 1961 by the Batona (Back to Nature) Hiking Club of Philadelphia and is still maintained by that group. To pierce the genuine wilderness of this unique area, the Batona avoids the sand roads as much as possible. About twenty percent of the trail is soft sand, however, and this makes for slower-than-expected progress in parts of this generally level trail.

Good starting points for trips on the trail are the Batsto Visitors Center or the Lebanon State Forest Headquarters, where trail maps and information may be obtained and where one may register for the use of campsites along the trail. Camping without a permit is illegal in the state forests. The campsites are nicely placed—6 to 9 miles apart—to make for flexible trip-planning if one wishes to hike the entire trail. A shuttle to the trailhead at Evans Bridge is also convenient. The northern portion of the trail, though less interesting than the southern, is crossed by a number of paved roads, which also make possible a variety of trips.

Starting from the southern end at the Evans Bridge parking lot, which is also a takeout for canoe trips on the Wading River, the Batona runs generally west for 9 miles to Batsto Historic Village, the restored iron town where the headquarters of Wharton State Forest is located. Camping is possible at nearby Buttonwood Hill, which is not directly on the trail but is accessible by car. From Batsto the trail proceeds north, generally following the Batsto River and playing tag with a sand road that also parallels the eastern bank of the stream. The trail passes Quaker Bridge about 6 miles from Batsto, at a point where several sand roads converge to cross the river. From here the trail follows the sand road for 1 mile, then veers northeast through the woods. A short spur heads north along the river to the Lower Forge Camp, 7 miles from Batsto. This camp is also used on canoe trips on the Batsto; it is not accessible by car.

Twelve miles from Batsto, the Batona crosses railroad tracks to reach the Carranza Memorial, a monument to the Mexican pilot Emilio Carranza, whose plane crashed here in 1928 while he was returning to Mexico City after a goodwill flight to New York. A half mile to the north is the Batona Camp, which can be crowded and noisy, since it is accessible by paved road. The blazes are confusing as they leave the camp and cross Skit Branch stream, which is followed for about 1 mile. The trail runs up and down over several hummocks, then reaches the fire tower on Apple Pie Hill, which is the highest point on the trail and provides an interesting view over the Pine Barrens. The hill area suffers a great deal of abuse and is often badly littered.

For the next 6 miles, the trail continues on a northeasterly course generally on sand roads, crossing a couple of paved roads before reaching Route 72 and Lebanon State Forest. Butler Place Camp is located just before Route 72, some 22 miles from Batsto. The Batona turns northwest through the forest, generally paralleling Route 72, past Pakim Pond and the site of the Lebanon Glass Works. The trail reaches forest headquarters, which has a fire tower, about 27 miles from Batsto. A mile later, Deep Hollow Pond is reached on the way to the trail's northernmost point at Carpenter Spring. The trail turns southwesterly, passing through some oak-pine forests where shoots have sprouted from the stumps of harvested trees. The Batona ends at Ongs Hat on Route 72, about 30 miles from Batsto and 40 miles from the terminus at Evans Bridge.

WHARTON STATE FOREST

Wharton State Forest, having grown even larger than the original Wharton tract, now covers more than a hundred thousand acres in the heart of the Pines. The Batsto Visitors Center, on Route 542 on the southern edge of the Wharton tract, is a good place to begin hikes in the central Pine Barrens. The Batona Trail, which passes nearby, can be combined with sand roads for a variety of circular hikes from Batsto. There is also a nature area in the Batsto–Pleasant Mills vicinity that has been set aside for those who wish to know more of the flora of the region. Tours of the area are available. The visitors center has maps and books for sale, including books on the history of Batsto and the other iron towns in the area. To reach Batsto, follow the signs from Exit 52 of the Garden State Parkway.

A 12-mile circular from Batsto Village begins by following village trails up the east side of Batsto Lake. The route is unmarked but easy to follow. There are a few short spurs that dead-end at the lake with nice views. The lake becomes shallower toward the north, more filled with grasses and trees, grading off at the sides into cedar swamp. Along here are dozens of tree stumps left by the beavers that live around the lake.

The path runs generally along the shore of the lake, following in part a fire cut and in part a sand road. After skirting the lake for its full length of about 1 mile, the path meets the Batona Trail, which comes up from the south, having crossed Route 542 at the fire tower a few hundred yards northeast of Batsto.

Continue on the Batona Trail about 6 miles to a spot where four sand roads converge from the east into a single sand road that crosses the Batsto River on Quaker Bridge. This was the site of a tavern on the stage route from Philadelphia to Tuckerton. Cross the bridge and turn left on the first sand road on the west side of the Batsto River, heading back south to Batsto. This road runs between the Batsto and Mullica rivers, two of the popular canoeing routes through the Pines. The road comes out in the village of Batsto, which can be explored for a leisurely finish.

Another hike from Batsto is to Atsion, about 10 miles northwest. Atsion is the site of another Pine Barrens iron town, with a manor house and several other buildings still standing, though none of the buildings is now open to the public. Several routes over sand roads connect Atsion and Batsto, and the section of the Batona between Batsto and Quaker Bridge may also be used. In addition, the Mullica and the Batsto rivers, which run between

Atsion and Batsto, make for fine canoeing routes as well. The entire area between Batsto and Atsion is shown on the U.S. Geological Survey "Atsion" quadrangle. Atsion, which includes a ranger station and a state recreation area at Atsion Lake, can be reached by car on Route 206.

Another interesting part of Wharton State Forest is the southeastern section around Evans Bridge, the terminus of the Batona Trail. West of Evans Bridge, sand roads lead 2 miles to Washington, the site of one of the vanished Pine Barrens towns, where a stone ruin stands in the middle of the woods. Southeast of Evans Bridge are the ruins of Harrisville on the Oswego River, where a paper mill once stood, and a little farther upriver is the site of Martha, another iron town, of which almost no traces remain. The ponds at Harrisville and Martha are well known for the beauty and variety of the plants that grow there. This entire area, shown on the "Jenkins" quadrangle, can be explored on sand roads and on unmarked trails that generally follow the streams and ponds. Access by car is from Route 563, where there is parking at Evans Bridge at the Batona trailhead, or from Route 679, where there is room for several cars along the side of the road at Harrisville.

LEBANON STATE FOREST

Lebanon State Forest covers nearly thirty thousand acres in the northern Pinelands. The forest headquarters, on Route 72 less than 1 mile east of its intersection with Route 70, offers a number of free maps and brochures, and also sells the U.S. Geological Survey quadrangle maps of the area. A fire tower here offers a panoramic view of the woods.

The headquarters is a good place to begin a couple of circular hikes that use the Batona Trail. Pick up the trail just a few yards up the sand road that leads past the office. Hiking northwest leads in about 4 miles to the terminus of the Batona Trail at Ongs Hat on Route 72. This section of the trail passes stands of pine, oak, and cedar, including some sections of harvested oaks that are now profusely sprouting from their stumps. Continue across the highway, bearing left along the sand road that parallels Route 72 back southeast. The road stops at the State Colony at New Lisbon, from which Route 72 and the headquarters building are a few hundred yards to the left along another sand road. The distance from Ongs Hat is 2 miles, for a total of about 6 miles.

Another circular from state forest headquarters can be made by taking the Batona southeast. The trail leads in about 3 miles to Pakim Pond, a beautiful spot with picnic tables, camping facilities, swimming, and guided nature walks. There is a fine cedar swamp just on the other side of the dam. Follow the Batona around Pakim Pond, continuing another mile or so to cross Route 72 onto a sand road. Shortly the pink blazes veer left onto another sand road; for the circular, however, stay on the first road for almost a mile, then take the first big sand road heading to the right (northwest). Stay on this road for 2 miles to reach Route 72 a few hundred yards southeast of headquarters. Finish the walk along Route 72, or follow the sand road on the other side to the Batona Trail, and return via the starting section.

Other interesting hikes start at Pakim Pond, which can be reached by car from Route 72. They are too complicated to be described in detail here or to be attempted without map and compass. With the U.S. Geological Survey "Browns Mill" quadrangle map, however, it is not hard to follow Coopers Road northeast to explore the cranberry and blueberry bogs around McDonald. The round trip is about 5 miles.

A hike from Pakim Pond can be extended several miles north to view the excellent cedar bogs near and north of the railroad tracks. An even longer walk, about 14 miles round trip, is to Whitesbog, an important early center in the development of cultivated blueberries. Whitesbog today is still the site of berry farming, with a handful of houses, some abandoned workers' huts, and an office of the New Jersey Conservation Foundation. Whitesbog may also be reached by car from Route 530.

BASS RIVER STATE FOREST

Bass River State Forest covers about fourteen thousand acres to the southeast of the Wharton tract. Forest headquarters is at Lake Absegami, where there are also camping areas, a beach, cabins for rent, and a short nature trail that traverses a fine cedar swamp. To reach Lake Absegami, follow the signs from Exit 52 of the Garden State Parkway. With map and compass it is possible to hike any number of circular routes over the sand roads in the area. A circular hike of about 10 miles to Munion Field and back leads through typical Pine Barrens forests, with stands of oak and cedar as well as pine, and passes through private lands where timber has been heavily harvested.

In the Bass River Forest, as in other areas in the Pines, the state maintains a program of controlled burning. Strictly controlled fire clears away forest underbrush that, if it were allowed to accumulate, could make wild fires much more dangerous and harder to control. As part of its forest management program, the state maintains a network of fire cuts—paths bulldozed through the underbrush every few hundred feet. On days that are cool and not too dry, fires are set along roads and fire cuts on the side the wind is coming from. With these downwind barriers keeping it from running with the wind, the fire backs slowly into the wind, with flames only a few inches high, clearing out the debris on the forest floor but doing no damage to trees or larger shrubs. Winter is the best time to see these burns. Even when it is controlled, fire in the Pines is an eerie sight.

PENN STATE FOREST

The smallest of the state forests in the Pines, Penn covers about thirty-four hundred acres near the northeastern section of the Wharton Forest. The Penn State Forest has no headquarters or other public buildings. The primary attraction is Oswego Lake, one of the beautiful Pine Barrens lakes, where there is a beach and parking. The lake offers wonderful swimming in cool, clean water that, because of the iron and the cedar in the Pines, is the color of tea. Stretching out northeast from the lake, the forest is interlaced with the usual Pine Barrens sand roads that can be hiked in many combinations. In the center of the forest is Bear Swamp Hill, where there is parking and the foundation of a fire tower that was knocked down in an airplane crash several years ago.

In the forest, as in other sections in the Pines, activity by military aircraft is quite noticeable. Fort Dix, McGuire Air Force Base, and Lakehurst Naval Air Station form a huge presence in the northern part of the Pines. About 4 miles east of Oswego Lake is the U.S. Navy Target Area at Warren Grove, and it is common in the Pines to see fighters and bombers in practice here. In fact, the area around the target installation, just west of Route 539, is one of the best places to see the Plains, the bizarre pygmy forests where full-grown trees are less than four feet tall.

OTHER AREAS

Many other areas in the Pines offer rewarding hiking. Belleplain State Forest, which covers nearly twelve thousand acres in the southern Pinelands, offers a number of nature walks and circular routes on sand roads. Other public lands include several wildlife management areas and the Double Trouble State Park a few miles south of Toms River. All the public lands in the Pinelands are shown on brochures and maps available from the New Jersey Department of Environmental Protection.

Suggested Readings

Bisbee, Henry H., and Colesar, R. B.
Martha—1808–1815: The Complete Furnace Diary and Journal
Published by the authors, Burlington, N.J., 1976

Forman, Richard T. T., ed.
Pine Barrens: Ecosystem and Landscape
Academic Press, New York, 1979

McPhee, John A.
The Pine Barrens
Farrar, Straus & Giroux, New York, 1968

Pierce, Arthur D.
Family Empire in Jersey Iron—The Richards Enterprises in the Pine Barrens
Rutgers University Press, New Brunswick, N.J., 1965

Pierce, Arthur D.
Iron in the Pines—The Story of New Jersey's Ghost Towns and Bog Iron
Rutgers University Press, New Brunswick, N.J., 1957

19 · *THE JERSEY SHORE*

THE JERSEY SHORE evokes images of Atlantic City, hordes of summer sunbathers, and traffic crawling on the Garden State Parkway. When the summer crowds recede, however, walkers have a chance to enjoy brisk autumn and winter treks on miles of empty beaches. Just behind these strands are teeming marshes and patches of forest that offer many enjoyable strolls.

CHEESEQUAKE STATE PARK

Enter Cheesequake from Exit 120 of the Garden State Parkway or from Route 34 on the southwest side. Salt marsh and cedar swamp dominate here, so avoid the park during the summer's mosquito season. At other times, follow a marked trail from the parking area for a glimpse of chestnut oaks, pitch pines, ferns, and a series of small creeks. Scattered spoil banks remind the visitor that the area was once mined for clay for a thriving pottery industry in New Jersey.

Perrines Pond, visible to the left, hosts kestrels and ospreys on occasion. Boardwalks carry hikers over swampy sections where impatiens, sweet pepperbush, and red maple color the trail. A spur from the loop trail leads to an old dock on Cheesequake Creek where farmers of a hundred years ago brought produce for shipment to market. Adding this segment makes for a walk of 3.5 miles total.

SANDY HOOK
(GATEWAY NATIONAL RECREATION AREA)

The rich history and varied habitat of this 7-mile sandspit make it well worth a stroll. The oldest lighthouse in the United States, built in 1762, now lies 1.5 miles south of Sandy Hook's growing tip, the result of two centuries of littoral drift. As late as 1919, the beach was a proving ground for military weapons, and the Nike missile was tested here in the 1950s. Vegetation typical of barrier beaches thrives here: bayberry, beach plum, wild cherry, prickly pear, and poison ivy. A fine stand of American holly, some of which is over three hundred years old, is accessible through conducted tours. Sandy Hook is also on the migratory flyway for songbirds and monarch butterflies.

From the visitors center at Spermaceti Cove, the Old Dune Trail meanders in the direction of the lighthouse through heather and bayberry to a small holly grove. Beyond an old dirt road, near the site of the old proving ground, is a freshwater pond that harbors marsh hawks, turtles, and frogs. Farther along is Fort Hancock, a now-deserted battery built in the 1890s to protect New York Harbor. The trail loops back toward Spermaceti Cove, completing a circuit of some 5 miles.

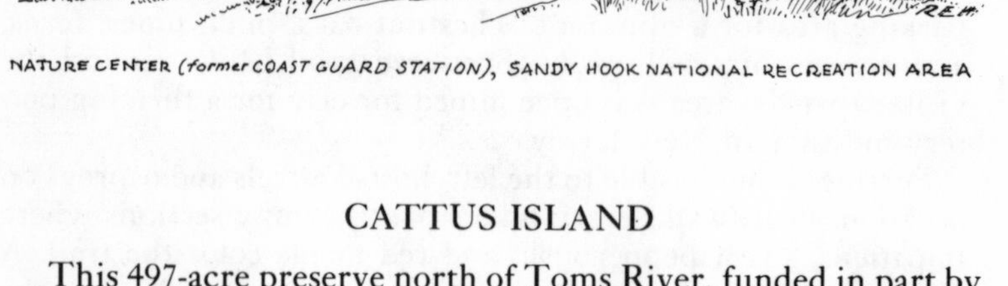

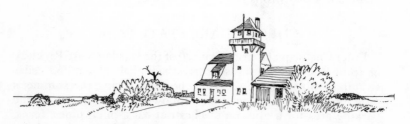

NATURE CENTER *(former COAST GUARD STATION)*, SANDY HOOK NATIONAL RECREATION AREA

CATTUS ISLAND

This 497-acre preserve north of Toms River, funded in part by New Jersey's Green Acres Program, contains salt marshes, lowland and upland forests, and a stand of the once-common Atlantic white cedar. Central to the park is the Cooper Environmental

Center, where visitors may register for a wide variety of nature programs or obtain a trail map and wander on their own. A boardwalk threads through the marshes, allowing walkers a close look at the complex life here. Look for maple, gum, magnolia, and holly.

For information contact Ocean County Parks and Recreation, 659 Ocean Avenue, Lakewood, N.J. 08701; phone: (201) 270-6960.

ISLAND BEACH STATE PARK

An undeveloped stretch of barrier beach and salt marsh on the north side of Barnegat Inlet, this 2694-acre, 10-mile strip of unspoiled dune land has an almost impenetrable barrier of brier, holly, bayberry, and other shrubs between the foredunes and the bay. Little grows above the height of the dunes, which shelter the vegetation from killing salt spray. A good walk is the dune buggy road extending to the tip of the park, with a return along the beach for a total of 5 miles.

To reach the park, take Route 37 east from Exit 81 of the Garden State Parkway and follow the signs.

Across the Barnegat Inlet is beautiful Barnegat Lighthouse (172 feet), whose spiral staircase leads to fine views of the bay and ocean. The light is accessible via Route 72 across Manahawkin Bay.

HOLGATE

A unit of the Brigantine National Wildlife Refuge, Holgate is a low, ever-shifting barrier with a large expanse of beach grass. Endangered black skimmers and least terns breed here, in areas off-limits to walkers in the summer months. It is 2 miles from the refuge entrance to the end of the spit. Take Route 72 east to Ship Bottom, then drive south 9 miles to Holgate.

The main unit of Brigantine, a twenty-thousand-acre Eden for wildlife, is more suited for car touring than walking. Even so, it is well worth a visit for its variety of habitat and the spectacular array of shorebirds and raptors, including the peregrine falcon. The refuge is located in Oceanville, off Route 9.

PORICY PARK

An ancient fossil bed and a Colonial house dating to 1704 attract visitors to this 250-acre park in suburban Middletown. In addition to a Nature Center staffed by naturalists, Poricy offers 4 miles of trails encompassing fields, forest, and marsh. The park is located on Oak Hill Road.

MONMOUTH BATTLEFIELD STATE PARK

On a hot day in June 1778, Molly Pitcher drew water from a spring to wet the swab of her husband's cannon as he fought the British. One mile west, Tennent Church was a field hospital littered with dying men from both sides. Some of these soldiers were buried under oaks in the courtyard. All of these sites are preserved in this thousand-acre park off Route 9 in Freehold. Its orchards, woodlands, and fields offer a quiet walk steeped in history.

Suggested Readings

Bennett, D. W.
New Jersey Coastwalks
American Littoral Society, Sandy Hook, Highlands, N.J., 1981
Wilson, Harold F.
The Story of the Jersey Shore
D. Van Nostrand Co., Princeton, N.J., 1964

TRAILS

Trails were the first paths in America, the routes of the Indians, following streams and crossing mountain ranges through the notches and divides, leading from villages and campsites to hunting and fishing grounds. The white settlers adopted them for hunting, trading, and military expeditions, often blazing or spotting trees along the way with axes, thus starting the tradition of blazed trails, so unlike the footpaths of Europe. However, because these early paths often followed the lines of easiest grades, they were natural routes of highways and railroads. As the population grew, these trails were slowly erased, and by the early part of this century few remained, most of them simply old trail names surviving on some highway.

Those who sought exercise and a chance to study nature followed the rural roads, which, up to about 1900, provided pleasant walking with only an occasional, slow-going, horse-drawn vehicle to share them with the pedestrian. But in the first decade of the twentieth century came the invasion of the automobile. Highway surfaces were improved to meet the demands of auto traffic, and soon secondary routes were asphalted to extend state and county road systems.

In search of safer, more pleasurable routes, walkers retreated to long-abandoned Colonial paths and eighteenth-century wood roads which offered delightful strolls through second-growth forest. However, because these routes were meant to take people someplace, they often missed the scenic charm walkers sought. So hiking clubs and individuals began making their own trails over routes which the Indians and settlers would never have thought of using, routes selected because they offered a vista, a stroll through a stand of silver beech, or access to a place that had previously been inaccessible or unknown. Deer paths often proved useful because they followed natural terrain and were often the easiest routes up a mountain or across a valley.

TRAILS DEVELOPMENT

As trails began to spread throughout the Hudson Highlands and the Wyanokies, it became evident that planned trail systems would be necessary if hiking areas were to be properly utilized. In 1920, Major William A. Welch, general manager of the Palisades Interstate Park, called together representatives of hiking organizations in New York to plan with him a network of marked trails that would make the Bear Mountain–Harriman State Parks more accessible to the public. The meeting resulted in an informal federation known as the Palisades Interstate Park Conference, named after the first tract acquired for this system of parks. These pioneers—including Raymond Torrey, Professor Will Monroe, Meade Dobson, Frank Place, and J. Ashton Allis—and their friends planned, cut, and marked what are now the major park trails. The first to be completed was the Ramapo-Dunderberg Trail from Jones Point on the Hudson to Tuxedo, 20 miles west. In 1923, the first section of the Appalachian Trail to be finished was constructed through the park. In that year, the organization changed its name to the New York–New Jersey Trail Conference, uniting under one banner a number of hiking organizations throughout the metropolitan area.

In the ensuing years, volunteers from the Trail Conference's member clubs worked hard to extend hiking opportunities to the public, building trails to open new areas, locating routes to permit access by public transportation, and then, as now, maintaining trails. Although much of the land upon which they built trails was publicly owned, much of it was not, and hikers enjoyed some areas only through the kindness of landowners whose property the trails traversed.

Unfortunately, acquisition of public land progressed slowly. As the population grew, commercial developers, and landowners who closed trails due to occasional abuses, limited public access. By the time the second edition of the *New York Walk Book* was published, in the mid 1930s, the editors felt constrained to point out that "it looks as though it will be only a few years before the tramper will be largely confined to national, state, and county parks, reservations, and forests. For that reason, lovers of the outdoors should lend all possible support to the conservationists who are fighting the continual efforts of commercial interest to encroach upon our public lands."

Spurred by the environmental movement of the 1960s, a new

chapter in trails development opened as national and state laws preserved thousands of acres of land for public use. The creation of state parks in New York culminated in new trail networks in the Minnewaska section of the Shawangunks and in the Hudson Highlands. In New Jersey, a series of legislative steps to protect public land led to the establishment of sizable state parks throughout the state, opening up such areas as the New Jersey Ramapos to trails development. At the same time, counties in both states, in an effort to create more recreational opportunities for their communities, acquired land and in many cases developed their own systems of trails.

Today the hiker in the metropolitan New York area has over seven hundred miles of trails from which to choose, each representing a different hiking experience. While many of the trails built in the last twenty years have been constructed to afford access to scenic areas, some capitalized on the revival of interest in early American history sparked by the 1976 Bicentennial: hikers can now walk in the footsteps of Revolutionary armies on the 1777 and 1779 trails in Bear Mountain–Harriman State Parks, or follow the Cannonball Trail in New Jersey, along which Americans are said to have hauled iron from furnaces hidden in the New Jersey Highlands. With many trailheads relocated to provide circular routes to which hikers can drive, trail systems have truly been modernized.

Some of the trails in the region, such as the Long Island Greenbelt or the Pine Barrens Batona Trail, are single paths that lead the hiker through an ecologically interesting area. Most, however, are organized into trail systems to permit the hiker to experience the wide diversity of a particular area. In addition to the smaller systems of county parks, extensive trail systems exist in the Bear Mountain–Harriman State Parks, the Taconics, the New Jersey Ramapos, the Hudson Highlands, the Kittatinnies, Schunemunk Mountain, Black Rock Forest, the Shawangunks, the New Jersey Highlands, and the Catskills.

Connecting these networks are the Appalachian Trail and the Long Path. The Appalachian Trail, which extends more than two thousand miles between Maine and Georgia, links the Taconics, Hudson Highlands, New Jersey Highlands, and the Kittatinnies. The Long Path, which intersects the Appalachian Trail in Harriman State Park, begins on the New Jersey Palisades and extends two hundred miles northward to the Catskills. These two trails predate many of the trails they cross, and their development is worth singular mention.

APPALACHIAN TRAIL

The longest continuous footpath in the world, the Appalachian Trail was proposed by Benton McKay in an article entitled "The Appalachian Trail, a Project in Regional Planning," published in the *Journal of the American Institute of Architects* in 1921. Wishing to save green space for recreation and make it accessible to the metropolitan regions on the eastern seaboard, he envisioned a continuous corridor along the ridge of the great Appalachians, connecting already existing trails, such as the Long Trail in Vermont.

The Palisades Interstate Park Trail Conference undertook the task of building the first sections of the trail. In 1923, the first portion, from the Bear Mountain Bridge to the Ramapo River south of Arden, was completed, followed in 1924 by the section from Arden to Greenwood Lake. The entire trail, built by hiking clubs and coordinated by the Appalachian Trail Conference, formed in 1925, was finally completed in 1957.

While the original intent and basic premise of the Appalachian Trail has survived intact, the route has remained fluid over the years. Private lands, and bridges, dams, and other construction, have forced many relocations of the trail.

To prevent encroaching civilization from obliterating the trail corridor, hiking organizations working through the Appalachian Trail Conference asked Congress for help in protecting and preserving it. In 1968, Congress passed the National Trails Systems Act, designating the Appalachian Trail as a National Scenic Trail. In 1978, the act was amended, authorizing funds for the National Park Service to acquire the land needed for the trail corridor not already in the public domain, thus inaugurating a massive trail relocation project.

Since then, the volunteer hiking community, through the Appalachian Trail Conference—the principal manager of the trail—has entered into cooperative agreements with national and state agencies responsible for the areas through which the trail passes and has drawn up local management plans. Federal funds have been used to purchase land in New York, while in New Jersey, acquisitions have been made with funds from the state's Green Acres bond issue.

In 1982, New Jersey became the first state to place its section of the Appalachian Trail entirely on protected lands. Elsewhere, acquisition and relocation continue, changes being clearly marked with the familiar white blazes of the Appalachian Trail.

A detailed trail description, as well as other information about the trail, can be found in the *Guide to the Appalachian Trail in New York and New Jersey.*

THE LONG PATH

The history of the Long Path stretches back several decades. It was originally proposed in 1931 by Vincent J. Schaefer of the Mohawk Valley Hiking Club of Schenectady, who thought that, like Vermont, New York should have a "long trail," which would connect New York City and Lake Placid in the Adirondacks.

Some work began on the project south of the Catskills, through which the trail would pass en route to a hookup with the Northville–Lake Placid Trail, forming the northern section of the Long Path. However, despite the acquisition of property along the Hudson River for the Palisades Interstate Park system, the momentum was lost after several years, and the project lay dormant.

In the early 1950s, acquisition of property on top of the cliffs for the Palisades Interstate Parkway increased accessibility to the fine views afforded by the Palisades, sparking interest once again in the Long Path. Then in 1960, Robert Jessen of the Ramapo Ramblers urged revival of the project and began fieldwork from New York City to the Catskills. In 1981, the New York–New Jersey Trail Conference received a grant from the Archbold Trust to further develop and define the route of the Long Path, relocating it where necessary.

The turquoise-blazed Long Path generally seeks mountain ridges but occasionally crosses valleys and lowlands. Hikers can now enjoy its scenic beauty from the Palisades to Windham Peak in the Catskills; arrangements for completing the remainder of the route from here across the Mohawk Valley and up to the Adirondacks are in various stages of planning and development. A detailed trail description can be found in the *Guide to the Long Path.*

THE NEW YORK–NEW JERSEY TRAIL CONFERENCE

The New York–New Jersey Trail Conference is a nonprofit federation of over sixty hiking and outdoor clubs and nearly three thousand individuals working together to build and maintain trails and promote conservation.

In 1920 the New York–New Jersey Trail Conference was formed when local hiking clubs gathered to plan a system of marked trails to make Bear Mountain–Harriman State Parks more accessible to the public. In this same area, Trail Conference founders constructed and opened the first section of the Appalachian Trail in 1923. During the 1930s more trails were built and a system of trail maintenance was developed, giving each hiking club a share of responsibility. Today this maintenance network covers over seven hundred miles of marked trails from the Connecticut border to the Delaware Water Gap.

The activities of the Conference are carried out almost entirely by volunteers who work together to advance these common goals:

- building and maintaining trails and trail shelters in the metropolitan area of New York
- promoting public interest in hiking and conservation
- aiding in the protection of wildlands, wildlife, and places of natural beauty

Volunteers of the Trail Conference, in addition to trail building and maintenance, have devoted many hours to current projects and issues affecting the trails. Every fall and spring the Conference sponsors "Litter Day," a massive effort to clean the trash out of our woods. Nearly a thousand people participate in this event, carrying out tons of litter from the trails. The Conference has also worked on solutions to the problem of throwaway beverage containers through support of "bottle bills" in New York and New Jersey. Special recent projects of Trail Conference members include defining routes and relocations for the Long Path in New York and local planning for the Appalachian Trail in New York and New Jersey, as well as relocating segments of the Appalachian Trail away from roads and threatened trailways, onto more appropriate protected woodlands. The Conference has also worked with other environmental groups to save Lake Minnewaska in the Shawangunk Mountains of New York from major construction that would draw thousands of gallons of water a day from the lake.

Besides the *New York Walk Book*, Trail Conference publications include the *Day Walker*, the *Appalachian Trail Guide for New York–New Jersey, Guide to the Long Path, Guide to Ski-Touring in New York and New Jersey,* maps for Bear Mountain–Harriman State Parks, New Jersey Highlands, Putnam County, and the Catskills, as well as *Trail Walker*, a bimonthly newspaper for members. For further information about the Trail Conference, write:

New York–New Jersey Trail Conference
P.O. Box 2250
New York, N.Y. 10001

SUGGESTIONS FOR NEW HIKERS

If you can walk, you can hike. You will need little or no training, and age is no obstacle. A good way to become familiar with hiking trails and learn from experienced hikers is to hike with a club or organized group. For a list of such clubs, write to the New York–New Jersey Trail Conference, P.O. Box 2250, New York, N.Y. 10001. Whether you walk with an organized group or with friends, some knowledge of the area to be hiked is necessary for safety and valuable for enjoyment. Such knowledge can be obtained from highway maps, topographic maps, and trail maps. From these one can learn the nature of the terrain, and where to find the trails. Highway maps are available at gas stations, and the "Yellow Pages" phone books list stores which sell topographic and trail maps. In addition, organizations like the New York–New Jersey Trail Conference publish hiker's maps; you will also find a list of trail guides and other books under "Suggested Readings" at the end of each chapter and at the end of this book.

HIKING ALONE

If you haven't had trail experience, you should not hike alone—and even an experienced hiker always lets someone know the area he or she will be hiking in.

EQUIPMENT

Use what you now have, as far as possible. Avoid investing in expensive equipment until you have seen what other hikers use, have heard their opinions, and have decided what will suit you best. You might also wish to rent equipment to better help you determine what you should buy.

Clothes

1. Sturdy, comfortable, waterproofed shoes with nonskid soles. Shoes should preferably be ankle high and large enough to accommodate one or two pairs of wool socks. In hot weather, many hikers prefer athletic shoes.
2. Slacks or jeans, or in winter wool pants. On hot days, shorts can be worn on clear trails.
3. Extra wool shirt or sweater.
4. Rainproof parka or poncho.
5. Gloves, hood, etc., according to the weather.
6. Hat or bandanna.
7. In winter, start "cold," with warm clothes in your pack. You may feel chilly, but you'll soon be warm and won't perspire. Put on the extra sweater or other heavy clothing at the lunch stop. It is best to wear or bring several layers rather than one heavy coat or jacket.

Pack (Knapsack)

Lightweight, but large enough to carry: the extra garments; lunch and beverage; extra socks if desired; small first-aid kit; a flashlight; compass; map; matches in a waterproof case; a sturdy jackknife; waterbottle or canteen; and insect repellent.

Food

Compact, nonperishable, lightweight food to supply protein and extra energy.

Water

In the areas covered by this book, do not drink from springs, streams, or ponds, as they may be polluted. There is no dependable water supply at the shelters along the trails. Always carry water, in either a plastic waterbottle or a canteen. Dehydration can occur in cold weather as well as hot weather.

You want to travel light, but not at the cost of being hungry or uncomfortable. Remember, you're supposed to be enjoying yourself!

SAFETY AND COMFORT

Hike Plan

Before leaving your home, consult your map and the *Walk Book* to determine the time and effort involved. If you are not going with an organized group, tell someone of your plan. On smooth level ground your pace may be three to four miles an hour; on trails, two to three. The pace will be slowed by rough terrain, snow, rain, heat, and the effort of ascents and descents. Consider available hours of daylight so that you won't have to finish your hike in darkness. If you are not an experienced trail hiker, it might be wise to limit yourself, at first, to distances of five miles or less if the ground is level. On hilly terrain, three miles would be a safe upper limit for an over-twenty-five neophyte hiker.

Escape Routes

Before starting, note routes that may be used to shorten the hike in case of storm, illness, accident, or an overambitious hike plan.

Blazes and Cairns

The clubs belonging to the New York–New Jersey Trail Conference mark and clear over seven hundred miles of trails in the metropolitan area. A system of painted "blazes" placed on trees and sometimes on rocks makes these trails understandable to any hiker. A double blaze indicates a change in direction. The trail descriptions explain the colors used on each trail. Where a paint blaze is not practical, watch for a pile of stones, purposely placed to indicate the direction. This is a "cairn."

Lost—You or the Trail?

1. Stop, look around, then go back to the last blaze or cairn seen.
2. If no blaze or cairn is in sight, look at the ground for a trace of the path. Perhaps a turn in the trail was missed.
3. If no trail is in sight, sit down and relax. Think about where you have been. Look at your map.

4. If you are with a group, wait a reasonable time for your absence to be noted, and for someone to come back. Three of anything—shout, whistle, flash of light—is a call for help.

5. If alone, consult your map and compass, and decide on the most direct route out to the nearest road. Remember that the top of the map is North. Use the compass to follow the route decided upon. In the Catskills follow any stream downhill.

6. If darkness falls, stay put and keep warm with those extra garments in the pack and with a fire. Build the fire in front of a rock, because its heat will be increased by reflection. But be careful not to let the fire spread.

First Aid

For a one-day hike, carry Band-Aids and an antiseptic for cuts and scratches, and moleskin for blisters. Put the moleskin on irritated spots before the blisters form. Other items useful and certainly necessary on longer trips are: Ace bandage with clips, for sprains; gauze pads; eye cup and ointment; adhesive tape; safety pins; aspirin; ammonia inhalants; snakebite kit; and change for a telephone. These items, plus a pencil and paper, should be carried in a metal box or waterproof case, in the knapsack. Training in first aid is recommended; contact your local Red Cross chapter for information on courses.

NATURAL HAZARDS

A good outdoors person knows the possible hazards of the trail, and what to do about them. But he or she doesn't worry about them.

Thunderstorms

A thunderstorm is dangerous only because of lightning. If you are on an exposed ledge or on a mountain peak, get off quickly. If you are on the trail, among trees, avoid taking shelter under a tall tree.

Wild Fruits and Mushrooms

Do not eat any without positive identification.

Poison Ivy

The sap of this plant is probably the principal trail hazard, for it can cause intense itching and a weeping rash. Poison ivy, easily identified by its groups of three shiny green leaves (red, in the fall), is prevalent along fences and stone walls, on tree trunks, and along stream banks. It bears white or green berries, which also should not be touched. Even in late fall, the bare vines exude enough sap to be dangerous if the hiker comes in direct contact with them.

Poison Sumac

This shrub, found mostly in the swampy areas, has thirteen pointed leaflets, six or more inches in length. Although not considered as virulent as the sap of poison ivy, the sap of the poison sumac is capable of provoking a rash.

Insects

Long sleeves, long pants, and insect repellent are the best guards against insects. Most maps indicate swampy areas which are best avoided during the mosquito season. Ticks, sometimes prevalent on Long Island, are among the more insidious insects hikers will encounter. Care should be taken in removing them so that their feelers do not remain embedded in the skin; their grip can be loosened by touching them with a lighted match.

Snakes

The careful hiker soon learns to identify the small and harmless garter snake. This snake, quite common in our region, is beneficial to humans and should be left alone. Rarely encountered are the region's two poisonous snakes, the rattlesnake and the copperhead. A rattlesnake is most quickly recognized by the rattle on its tail; its markings are not uniform, varying in coloration from yellow or tan to nearly black. When suddenly disturbed, a rattlesnake will rattle, and as a rule will try to get away rather than attack. The copperhead is pale brown with reddish blotches on its body and a coppery tinge on its head. It is not an especially vicious snake, preferring to escape rather than to attack. But it is a slow-moving reptile, and this sluggishness increases the chance of an unexpected encounter.

These two poisonous snakes are not found on Long Island. When walking trails in other parts of our region during the "snake season" (May to October), the best protection is always to be alert when climbing rock ledges and over logs. Look before placing your hand on an overhead ledge for support. If you are bitten, don't panic. Get out your snakebite kit, follow directions, stay quiet, keep warm, and send a companion for help.

TAKE CARE OF THE TRAILS AND WOODLANDS

Smoking

Never smoke when hiking—smoke only when sitting down. Carry a plastic bag or metal container (such as Band-Aids or lozenges come in) to carry out used matches and cigarette butts, and always make sure they are completely out.

Fires

On day trips use a fire only for warmth, if needed, and build it in stone fireplaces provided at shelters and campsites. If necessary, in a real emergency, build a small fire and only on rock or sandy soil, never near trees or on dry leaves, pine needles, or roots. Brush away leaves, twigs, etc., for an area of five feet around the fire, and beware of overhanging branches. For best results in building a fire, use standing dead wood such as branches from dead trees, or bare twigs from evergreens. Do not cut green wood; it won't burn. Before you leave, put out the fire completely, then douse with water or cover with earth; in fireplaces, do not use water because it cracks the heated rock. Make sure it is cool to the touch before leaving.

Litter

Whatever you have not used up, carry home. Do not attempt to burn or bury refuse; there is no space for this in our heavily used woodlands. Leave the trail and lunch stop and campsite as if no one had been there. "Leave nothing but footprints." Plan ahead for carrying out your refuse by bringing along an extra plastic bag. Help keep the trails the way you'd like to find them by picking up litter left by inconsiderate trail users.

Property

Many of the trails cross private land, with the owner's permission. Respect this privilege and build no fires, leave no litter, and stay on the trail. Leave plants, animals, and other property alone for others to enjoy.

Closing of the Woods

When the woods are dangerously dry from lack of rain, parks and other public areas may be closed to hikers. The New York–New Jersey Trail Conference urges complete cooperation with park commissions and others who must make these decisions. Stay out of the woods, and request others to do the same.

Overnight Backpacking Trips

Overnight backpacking is permitted in some of the parks mentioned in this book. However, before you go, it's advisable to check with park officials concerning their regulations.

NOTE ON THE MAPS

One of the functions of the *Walk Book* is to allow the hiker to roam in imagination over the land during the week and select and plan a forthcoming weekend outing. Sitting at home in an armchair, maps and guides in hand, the hiker can select at leisure the view points or other features of interest and the routes going and coming.

Planning a walk includes not only selecting a route but also estimating its length and the time it will take to walk over it. A trail can be measured readily on a map. However, a walk of 10 miles on a smooth path in level country and one of the same distance over rough trails through mountainous terrain require much different amounts of exertion and time. How much the speed of walking falls off on a steep gradient can be estimated roughly by looking at the contour lines, each one connecting all points of the same elevation. The interval between lines, equaling 100 feet on most of the following maps, depends on the roughness of the terrain and the scale of the map (Maps 11, 12, and 13, interval equals 500 feet; Map 19, 10 feet). The closer the contour lines, the steeper the terrain.

The topographic maps in this book were compiled chiefly from the quadrangles on scales 1:24,000 (2½ inches to 1 mile) and 1:31,680 (2 inches to 1 mile) produced by the Corps of Engineers, U.S. Army, and from the quadrangles on scale of 1:62,500 (a little larger than 1 inch to the mile) produced by the U.S. Geological Survey.

In earlier editions of the *Walk Book*, similar maps were reproduced on scales of 1:125,000 (about 1 inch to 2 miles) and approximately 1:75,000. The scales of these maps varied somewhat as they received slightly different amounts of reductions. In the present edition, maps are reproduced on uniform scales: Maps 11, 12, 13, and 19 are on the scale of 1:125,000; all other maps are on the scale of 1:62,500.

The smaller scale was found to be satisfactory for areas in which there are large mountain masses and no complicated trail pattern. The larger scale is used for southern New York and northern New Jersey where the country is more broken and many of the more popular walking areas carry a close network of trails. On all of these maps, both marked and unmarked trails or wood roads have been plotted, and as much detail has been retained from the quadrangles as the scale would permit. In addition, symbols and colors of the marked trails are indicated, and hypsometric tints are used to enhance readability.

These maps cover those areas in southern New York and northern New Jersey most easily accessible from the metropolitan area and consequently the most popular for walkers. No maps have been provided for Long Island since the walk directions there are so simple that a detailed map is not called for. To supplement the maps in this book, and for the more distant sections covered by the text, the New York–New Jersey Trail Conference publishes maps of a larger scale which show more detail: Bear Mountain–Harriman State Parks (two-map set), the New Jersey Highlands (two-map set), Putman County (three-map set) and the Catskill Mountain State Park (five-map set). The U.S. Geological Survey quadrangles are available and can be obtained from any large commercial map dealer or by writing to the Branch of Distribution, U.S. Geological Survey, 1200 South Eads Street, Arlington, Va. 22202. New York State Department of Transportation quadrangles are available from: New York State Department of Transportation, Map Information Unit, State Campus Building 4, Room 105, Albany, N.Y. 12232. A list of New Jersey maps and publications is available by writing: Map Sales Office, New Jersey Geological Survey, CN402, Trenton, N.J. 08625.

Hagstrom's Atlases of the counties of New Jersey and southern New York published by Hagstrom Co., Inc., 311 Broadway, New York, N.Y. 10007, are also useful since they not only show roads but also name them so that they can be identified. For most state and county parks, reservations, and forests there are maps issued by the authorities in charge. Other good sources of maps are the Hammond Map Store in New York City and Geographics in Montclair, New Jersey.

EDITOR'S NOTE: With the exception of Map 23, all maps in this book appeared in the fourth edition of the *New York Walk Book* and were purchased by the New York–New Jersey Trail Conference from the American Geographical Society. Revision of the maps for the fifth edition was coordinated by Miklos Pinther, under the supervision of the New York–New Jersey Trail Conference.

SUGGESTED READINGS: NUCLEUS OF A TRAMPER'S LIBRARY

Geology

The American Geological Institute
Dictionary of Geological Terms
Anchor Press/Doubleday, Garden City, N.Y., revised ed., 1976

CALDER, NIGEL
The Restless Earth
The Viking Press, New York, 1972

Geological Highway Map of Northeastern Region (Map No. 10, United States Geological Highway Map Series, Bicentennial Edition)
The American Association of Petroleum Geologists, P.O. Box 979, Tulsa, Okla. 74101

HOBBS, WARFIELD G., ed.
Field Guide to the Geology of the Paleozoic, Mesozoic, and Tertiary Rocks of New Jersey and the Central Hudson Valley
Petroleum Exploration Society of New York, New York, 1981

ISACHSEN, YNGVAR W.
Continental Collisions and Ancient Volcanoes, Education Leaflet 24, 1980
The State Education Department, N.Y. State Geological Survey, N.Y. State Museum Science Center, Cultural Education Center, Albany, N.Y. 12230

MCPHEE, JOHN A.
Basin and Range
Farrar, Straus & Giroux, New York, 1981

MCPHEE, JOHN A.
In Suspect Terrain
Farrar, Straus & Giroux, New York, 1983

SCHUBERTH, CHRISTOPHER J.
The Geology of New York City and Environs
The Natural History Press, New York, 1968

SUBITZKY, SEYMOUR, ed.
Geology of Selected Areas in New Jersey and Eastern Pennsylvania and Guide Book
Rutgers University Press, New Brunswick, N.J., 1969

WILSON, J. TUZO, ed.
Continents Adrift and Continents Aground, Readings from Scientific American
W. H. Freeman & Co., San Francisco, 1976

WOLFE, PETER E.
The Geology and Landscapes of New Jersey
Crane, Russak & Co., New York, 1977

WYCKOFF, JEROME
Rock Scenery of the Hudson Highlands and Palisades
Adirondack Mountain Club, Glens Falls, N.Y., 1971

Natural History

ARBIB, ROBERT
Enjoying Birds Around New York
Houghton Mifflin Co., Boston, 1966

BULL, JOHN L.
Birds of the New York Area
Harper & Row, New York, 1964

COBB, BOUGHTON
A Field Guide to the Ferns
Houghton Mifflin Co., Boston, 1956

CONANT, ROGER
A Field Guide to Reptiles and Amphibians of the United States and Canada East of the 100th Meridian
Houghton Mifflin Co., Boston, 1958

CONRAD, HENRY S.
How to Know Mosses and Liverworts
W. C. Brown Co., Dubuque, Iowa, 1956

DUNHAM, ELIZABETH MARIE
How to Know the Mosses
The Mosher Press, Boston, 1951

GLEASON, H. A.
Plants of the Vicinity of New York
New York Botanical Garden, Hafner Publishing Co., New York, 1962

GOLDRING, WINIFRED
The Oldest Known Petrified Forest
New York State Museum, Albany, N.Y., 1927

KIERAN, JOHN
A Natural History of New York City
The Natural History Press, New York, 1971

KRIEGER, LOUIS C. C.
The Mushroom Handbook
Dover Publications, New York, 1967

MURIE, OLAUS J.
A Field Guide to Animal Tracks
Houghton Mifflin Co., Boston, 1954

PETERSON, ROGER TORY
A Field Guide to the Birds
Houghton Mifflin Co., Boston, 1981

PETRIDES, GEORGE A.
A Field Guide to Trees and Shrubs
Houghton Mifflin Co., Boston, 1972

RICKETT, HAROLD W.
Flowers of the United States: The Northeastern States
New York Botanical Garden, McGraw Hill Book Co., New York, 1965

RICKETT, HAROLD W.
The New Field Book of American Wildflowers
New York Botanical Garden, G. P. Putnam's Sons, New York, 1963

ROBICHAUD, BERYL and BUELL, MURRAY F.
Vegetation of New Jersey
Rutgers University Press, New Brunswick, N.J., 1973

TEALE, EDWIN WAY
The Strange Lives of Familiar Insects
Dodd, Mead & Co., New York, 1962

Others

DANN, KEVEN
25 Hikes in New Jersey
Rutgers University Press, New Brunswick, N.J., 1982

GARVEY, ED
Appalachian Hiker II
Appalachian Books, Oakton, Va., 1978

HOWAT, JOHN K.
The Hudson River and Its Painters
The Viking Press, New York, 1972

KJELLSTROM, BJORN
Be Expert with Map and Compass. The Orienteering Handbook
American Orienteering Service, c/o Bjorn Kjellstrom, Honey Hollow Road, Pound Ridge, N.Y. 10576, 1967

New York–New Jersey Trail Conference
Day Walker
Anchor Press/Doubleday, Garden City, N.Y., 1983

New York–New Jersey Trail Conference
Guide to the Long Path
New York–New Jersey Trail Conference, New York, 1982

New York–New Jersey Trail Conference
Official Guide to the Appalachian Trail in New York and New Jersey
The Appalachian Trail Conference, Harpers Ferry, W. Va., 1972

NIXDORF, BERT
Hikes and Bike Rides for the Delaware Valley and South Jersey
American Youth Hostels, Delaware Valley Council, Philadelphia, 1981

O'BRIEN, RAYMOND J.
American Sublime
Columbia University Press, New York, 1981

PIERCE, ARTHUR D.
Smugglers' Woods—Jaunts and Journeys in Colonial Revolutionary New Jersey
Rutgers University Press, New Brunswick, N.J., 1960

PRICE, LYNDA
Lenni-Lenape—New Jersey's Native People
Paterson, N.J., Museum, 1979

SCHELLER, WILLIAM B.
Country Walks Near New York
Appalachian Mountain Club, Boston, 1980

SIMPSON, JEFFREY
The Hudson River 1850–1918: A Photographic Portrait
Sleepy Hollow Press, Tarrytown, N.Y., 1981

SUTTON, ANN and MYRON
The Appalachian Trail: Wilderness on the Doorstep
J. B. Lippincott Co., Philadelphia, 1967

THOMAS, BILL and PHYLLIS
Natural New York
Holt, Rinehart & Winston, New York, 1983

INDEX

Page numbers in *italics* refer to illustrations.

LEGEND

Boundary, state
Boundary, county
Railroad
Super highway (9W)
Main road (17)
Secondary road
Marked Trail (R) red (B) blue (W) white (Y) yellow
Unmarked Trail or wood road
P Parking
Shelter
View point
Mine
Quarry or pit
Airfield
Power line
Telephone line
Tower
Town or village
Church
Cemetery
School
Spring or well
Aqueduct
Canal
Dam
Marsh
Contours, every 100 feet (500)
Spot height, in feet (.1029)

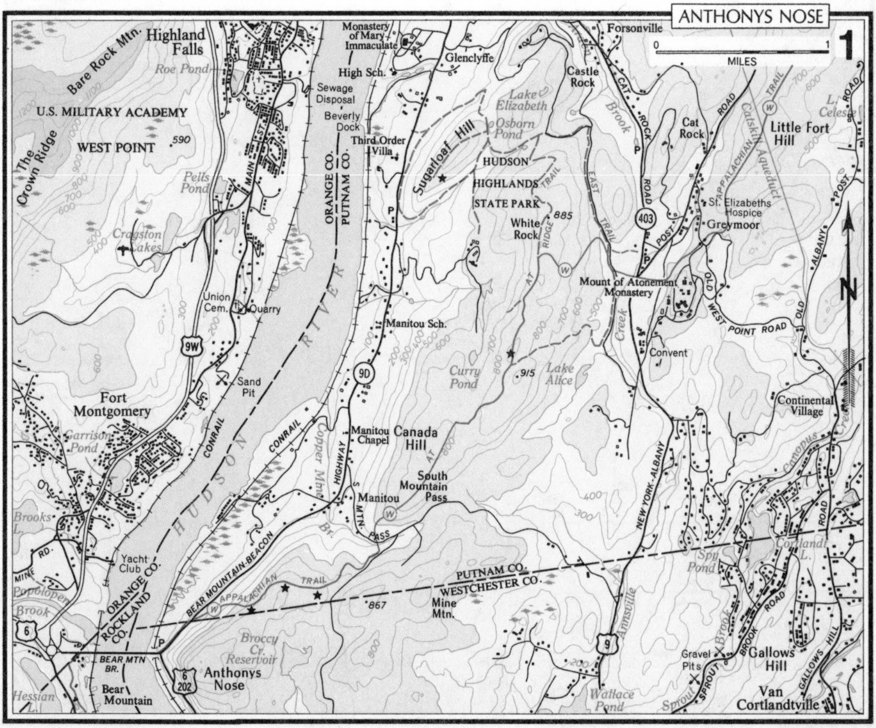

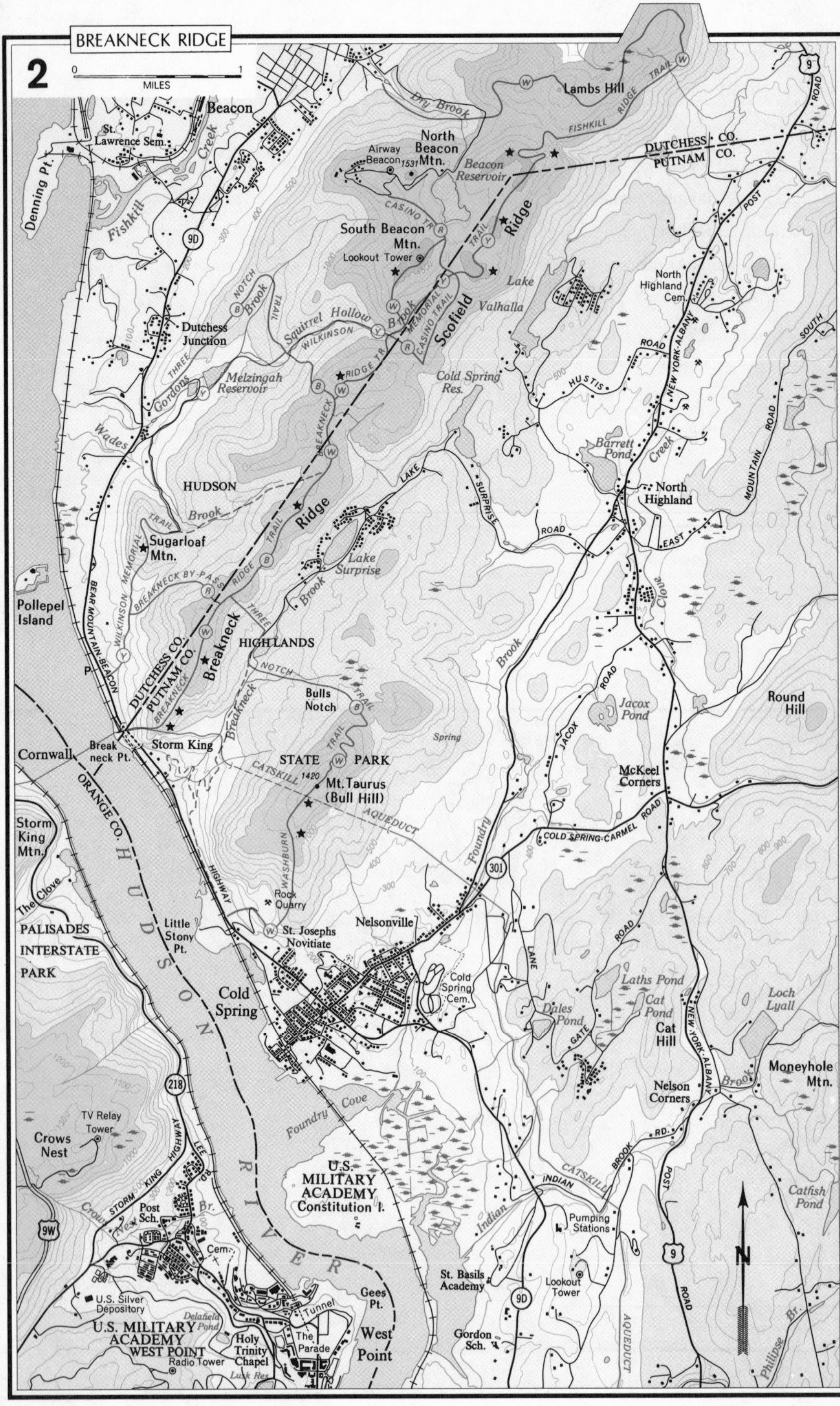

BREAKNECK RIDGE
2
0
1
MILES
Beacon
St. Lawrence Sem.
Denning Pt.
Fishkill
Creek
Dry Brook
Lambs Hill
FISHKILL RIDGE TRAIL
North Beacon Mtn.
Airway Beacon
1531
Beacon Reservoir
DUTCHESS CO.
PUTNAM CO.
CASINO TR.
South Beacon Mtn.
Lookout Tower
Ridge
Scofield
Lake Valhalla
MEMORIAL
CASINO TRAIL
NOTCH
Brook
TRAIL
Squirrel Hollow
WILKINSON
Dutchess Junction
THREE
Gordons
Melzingah Reservoir
RIDGE TR.
BREAKNECK
Cold Spring Res.
North Highland Cem.
HUSTIS
ROAD
NEW YORK-ALBANY
POST
SOUTH
MOUNTAIN
Barrett Pond
Creek
North Highland
Wades
HUDSON
Brook
MEMORIAL TRAIL
Sugarloaf Mtn.
LAKE
SURPRISE
RIDGE TRAIL
Ridge
Lake Surprise
ROAD
EAST
BREAKNECK BY-PASS
WILKINSON
Pollepel Island
BEAR MOUNTAIN-BEACON
Breakneck
THREE
Brook
HIGHLANDS
Clove
Brook
NOTCH
DUTCHESS CO.
PUTNAM CO.
BREAKNECK
Breakneck
Bulls Notch
TRAIL
Jacox Pond
JACOX
ROAD
Round Hill
Spring
Cornwall
Break neck Pt.
Storm King
STATE
PARK
CATSKILL
1420
Mt. Taurus (Bull Hill)
AQUEDUCT
McKeel Corners
COLD SPRING-CARMEL
ROAD
ORANGE CO.
Storm King Mtn.
HUDSON
WASHBURN
HIGHWAY
Foundry
301
The Clove
Rock Quarry
PALISADES INTERSTATE PARK
Little Stony Pt.
St. Josephs Novitiate
Nelsonville
LANE
ROAD
Cold Spring
Cold Spring Cem.
Laths Pond
Cat Pond
Dales Pond
GATE
Cat Hill
Loch Lyall
218
Moneyhole Mtn.
Nelson Corners
Brook
Foundry Cove
TV Relay Tower
Crows Nest
HIGHWAY
LEE RD.
STORM KING
RIVER
U.S. MILITARY ACADEMY Constitution I.
BROOK RD.
CATSKILL
INDIAN
Indian
POST
Catfish Pond
9W
Post Sch.
Br.
Cem.
Pumping Stations
9
N
U.S. Silver Depository
Tunnel
Gees Pt.
St. Basils Academy
9D
Lookout Tower
AQUEDUCT
ROAD
U.S. MILITARY ACADEMY WEST POINT
Delafield Pond
Holy Trinity Chapel
The Parade
West Point
Gordon Sch.
Radio Tower
Lusk Res.
Philipse Br.
9D

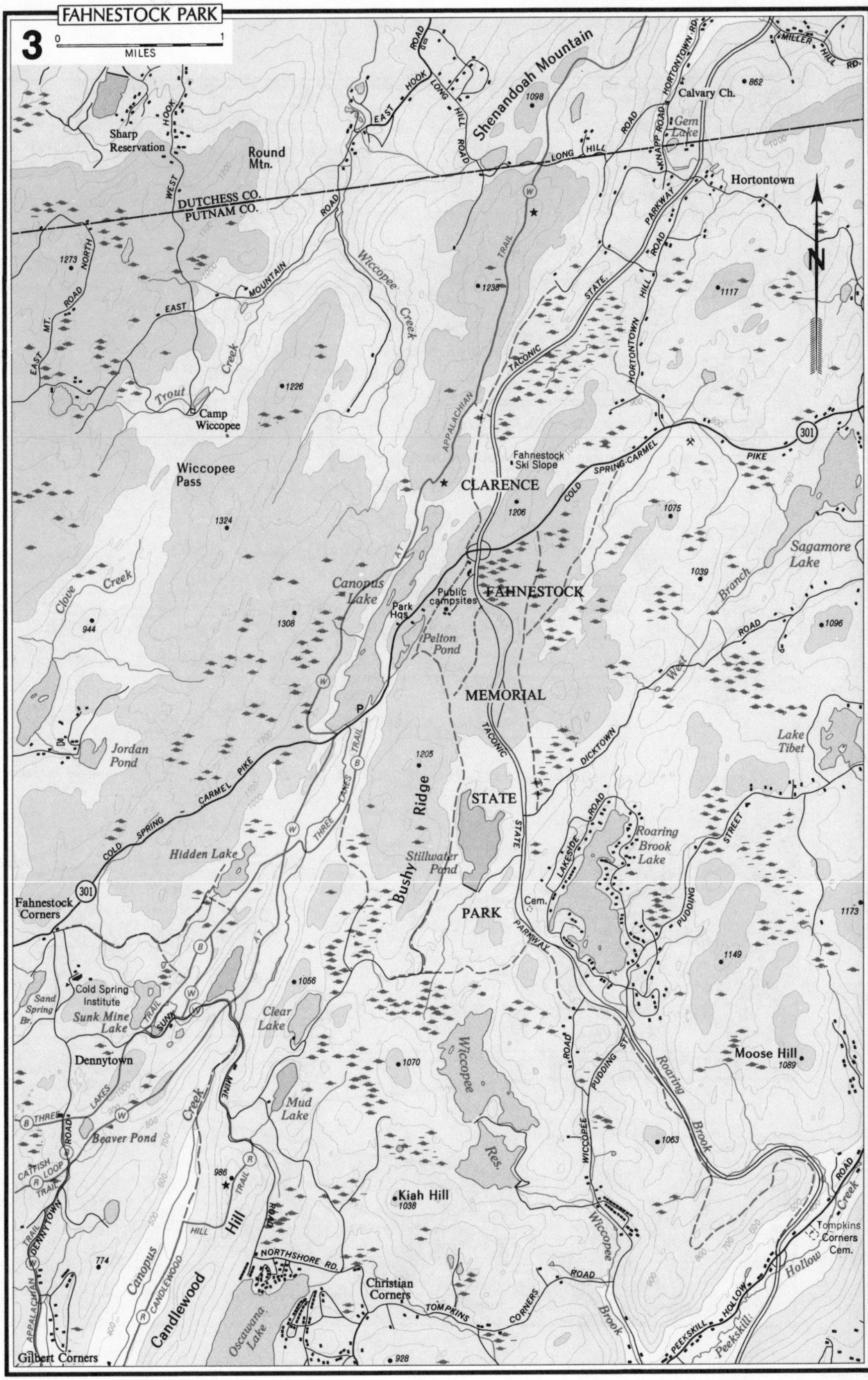

FAHNESTOCK PARK
3
0
1
MILES
Sharp Reservation
Round Mtn.
Shenandoah Mountain
Calvary Ch.
Gem Lake
Hortontown
DUTCHESS CO.
PUTNAM CO.
WEST HOOK
EAST HOOK ROAD
LONG HILL ROAD
KNAPP ROAD
HORTONTOWN RD.
MILLER HILL RD.
EAST MT. ROAD NORTH
EAST MOUNTAIN ROAD
Wiccopee Creek
Trout Creek
Camp Wiccopee
Wiccopee Pass
APPALACHIAN TRAIL
TACONIC STATE PARKWAY
HORTONTOWN HILL ROAD
Fahnestock Ski Slope
CLARENCE
FAHNESTOCK
MEMORIAL
STATE
PARK
COLD SPRING-CARMEL PIKE
301
Sagamore Lake
West Branch
ROAD
Clove Creek
Canopus Lake
Park Hqs
Public campsites
Pelton Pond
Jordan Pond
Bushy Ridge
THREE LAKES TRAIL
DICKTOWN
Lake Tibet
LAKESIDE ROAD
Roaring Brook Lake
PUDDING STREET
Hidden Lake
Stillwater Pond
Fahnestock Corners
Cem.
Cold Spring Institute
Sand Spring Br.
Sunk Mine Lake
SUNK MINE
Clear Lake
Dennytown
Wiccopee Res.
PUDDING ST.
Roaring Brook
Moose Hill
Mud Lake
Beaver Pond
Canopus Creek
CATFISH LOOP TRAIL
DENNYTOWN ROAD
Hill
Kiah Hill
NORTHSHORE RD.
Christian Corners
TOMPKINS CORNERS ROAD
Wiccopee Brook
Tompkins Corners Cem.
Hollow Creek
PEEKSKILL HOLLOW ROAD
Peekskill
Candlewood Hill
CANDLEWOOD HILL
Oscawana Lake
Gilbert Corners
1273
1226
1098
862
1238
1117
1324
1206
1075
1039
1096
944
1308
1205
1173
1056
1149
1070
1089
1063
986
1038
774
928

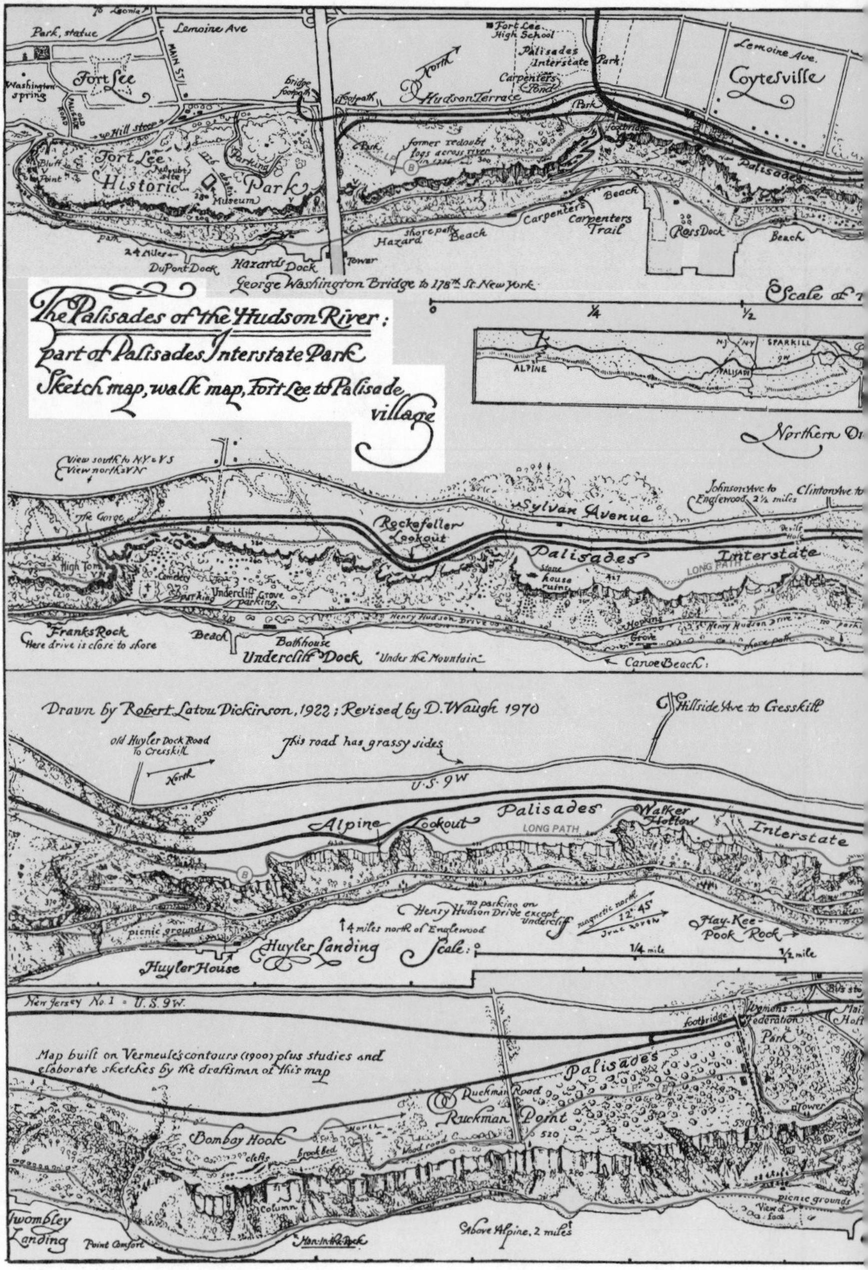
The Palisades of the Hudson River:
part of Palisades Interstate Park
Sketch map, walk map, Fort Lee to Palisade village
Drawn by Robert Latou Dickinson, 1922; Revised by D. Waugh 1970
Map built on Vermeule's contours (1900) plus studies and elaborate sketches by the draftsman of this map
George Washington Bridge to 178th St. New York
Lemoine Ave
Fort Lee
Washington spring
Fort Lee Historic Park
Museum
Bluff Point
Fort Lee High School
Palisades Interstate Park
Carpenters Pond
Hudson Terrace
North
bridge footpath
footbridge
Coytesville
Lemoine Ave.
former redoubt
Hazard Beach
Carpenters Beach
Carpenters Trail
Ross Dock
Beach
Du Pont Dock
Hazards Dock
Tower
Scale
1/4
1/2
ALPINE
SPARKILL
PALISADE
Northern
Sylvan Avenue
Rockefeller Lookout
Palisades Interstate
LONG PATH
Johnson Ave to Englewood 2½ miles
Clinton Ave
The Gorge
High Tom
Undercliff Grove parking
Henry Hudson Drive
Franks Rock
Here drive is close to shore
Beach
Bathhouse
Undercliff Dock
"Under the Mountain"
Canoe Beach
Hopkins Grove
shore path
Hillside Ave to Cresskill
old Huyler Dock Road to Cresskill
This road has grassy sides
U.S. 9W
Alpine Lookout
Palisades
Walker Hollow
Interstate
Henry Hudson Drive
no parking on Henry Hudson Drive except Undercliff
magnetic north
12° 45'
true north
4 miles north of Englewood
Huyler Landing
Huyler House
picnic grounds
Hay-Kee-Pook Rock
Scale: 0
1/4 mile
1/2 mile
New Jersey No. 1 = U.S. 9W.
footbridge
Women's Federation Park
Palisades
Ruckman Road
Ruckman Point
Bombay Hook
brook bed
wood road
cliffs
Column
Twombley Landing
Point Comfort
Man-in-the-Rock
Above Alpine, 2 miles
picnic grounds
Tower

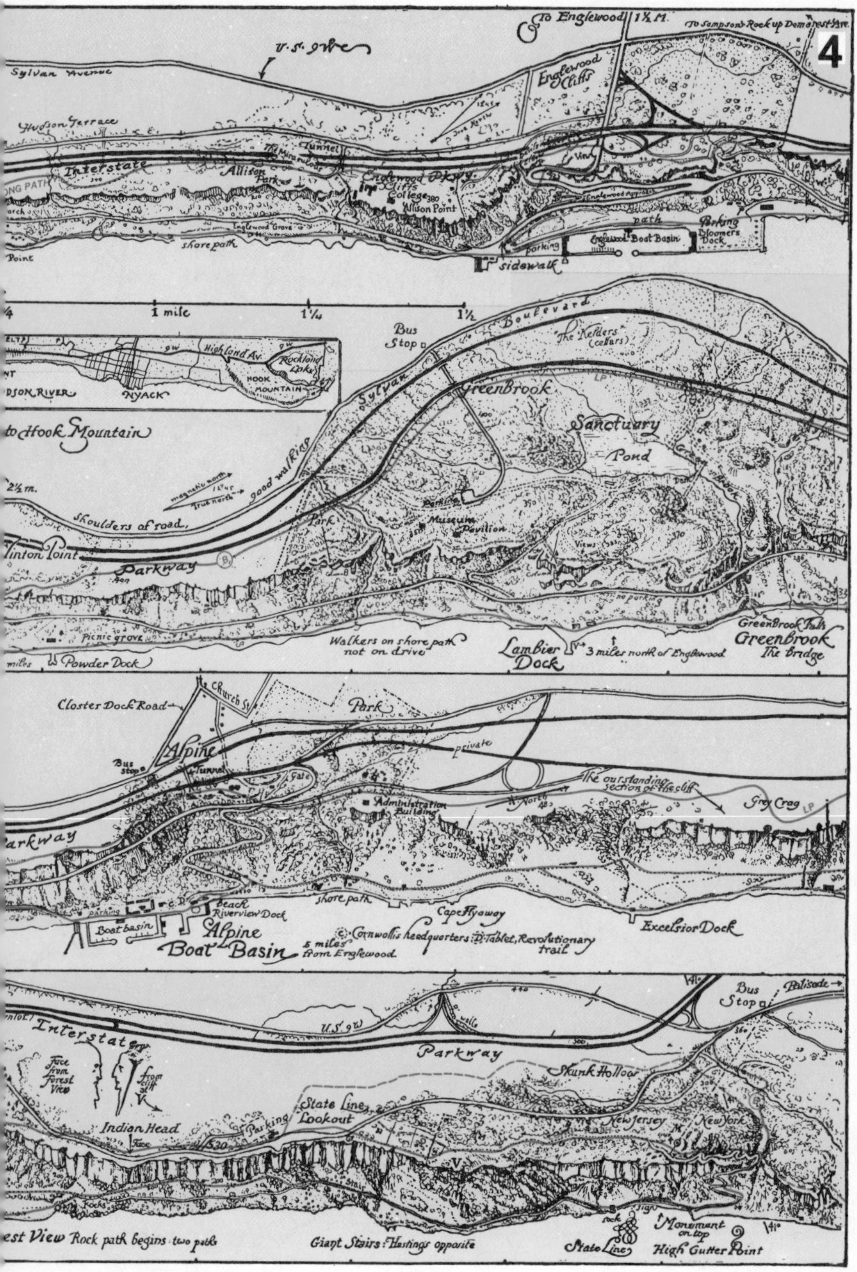
4
To Englewood 1¼ M.
To Sampson's Rock up Demorest Ave.
Sylvan Avenue
Hudson Terrace
Tunnel
Interstate
Allison Park
Englewood Cliffs
Englewood P'k'y
College
Allison Point
Englewood Boat Basin
Parking
Bloomers Dock
path
shore path
Englewood Grove
parking
sidewalk
Point
1 mile
1¼
1½
Highland Av.
Rockland Lake
HOOK MOUNTAIN
NYACK
to Hook Mountain
2½ m.
magnetic north
true north
good walking
Shoulders of road
Bus Stop
Sylvan Boulevard
The Kelders (cellars)
Greenbrook
Sanctuary
Pond
Parking
Park
Museum
Pavilion
Parkway
Clinton Point
Picnic grove
Powder Dock
Walkers on shore path not on drive
Lambier Dock
3 miles north of Englewood
no parking
Greenbrook Falls
Greenbrook
The bridge
Closter Dock Road
Church St.
Park
Alpine
Bus stop
Tunnel
Gate
private
Administration Building
North
The outstanding section of the cliff
Grey Crag
Parkway
shore path
Beach
Riverview Dock
Boat basin
Alpine Boat Basin
5 miles from Englewood
Cape Flyaway
Cornwallis headquarters: Tablet, Revolutionary trail
Excelsior Dock
Interstate
U.S. 9W
Parkway
Bus Stop
Palisade
Face from Forest View
from cliff
Skunk Hollow
State Line Lookout
Parking
Indian Head
New Jersey
New York
Rocks
Stairs
Forest View
Rock path begins: two paths
Giant Stairs: Hastings opposite
Monument on top
State Line
High Gutter Point

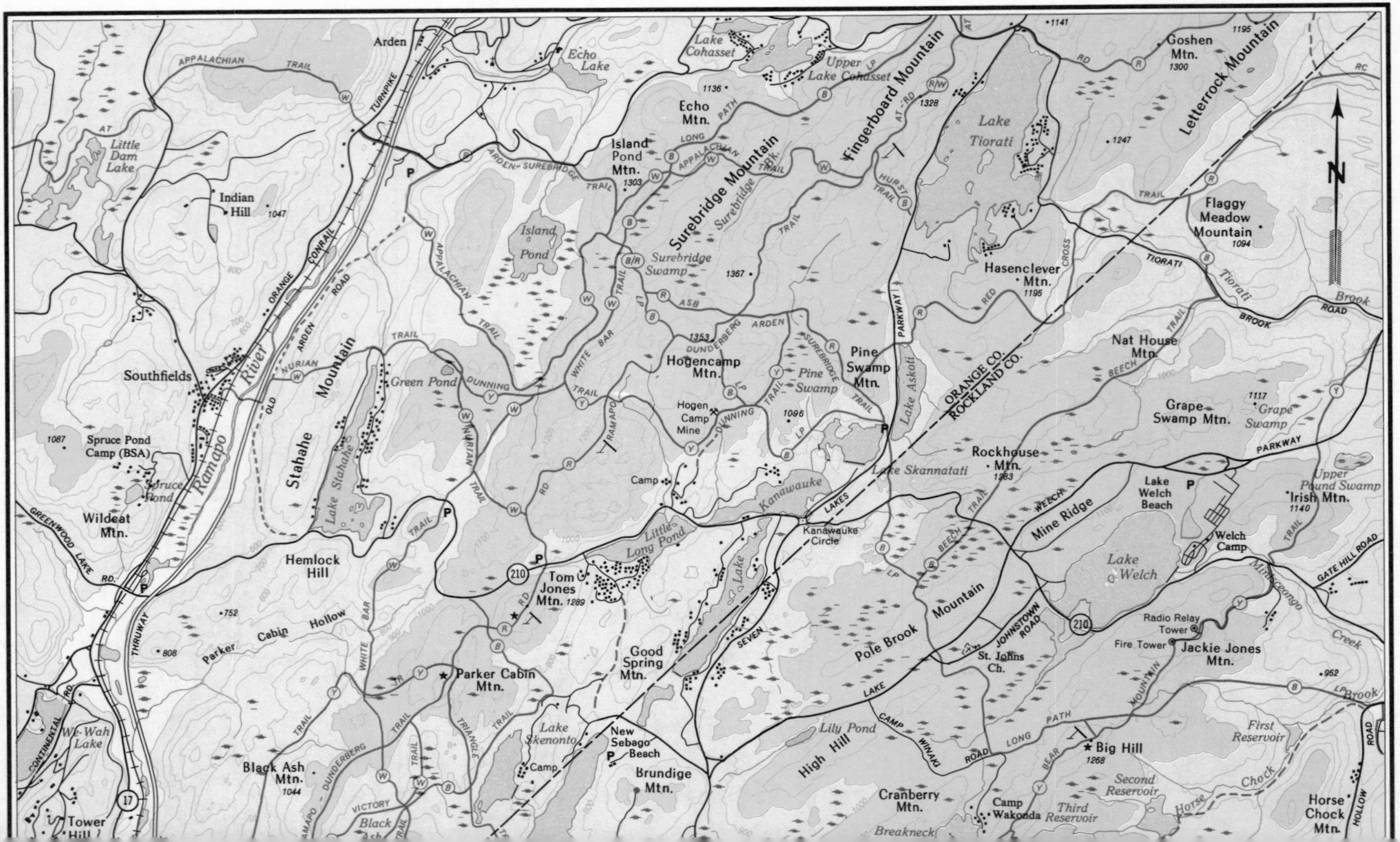

Arden
Appalachian Trail
Turnpike
Echo Lake
Lake Cohasset
Upper Lake Cohasset
Fingerboard Mountain
Goshen Mtn.
1300
1195
1141
Letterrock Mountain
Little Dam Lake
Indian Hill
1047
Echo Mtn.
1136
Island Pond Mtn.
1303
Surebridge Mountain
Surebridge Swamp
1367
Lake Tiorati
1328
1247
Flaggy Meadow Mountain
1094
Hasenclever Mtn.
1195
Tiorati Brook
Arden-Surebridge Trail
Island Pond
Long Path
Hurst Trail
Cross
Red
Orange Conrail
Arden Road
Nurian
Old
Ramapo River
Southfields
Stahahe Mountain
Green Pond
Dunning
White Bar Trail
1353
Dunderberg
Hogencamp Mtn.
Hogen Camp Mine
Pine Swamp
Pine Swamp Mtn.
Lake Askoti
Parkway
Orange Co.
Rockland Co.
Nat House Mtn.
Beech Trail
Grape Swamp Mtn.
1117
Grape Swamp
1096
Spruce Pond Camp (BSA)
1087
Spruce Pond
Lake Stahahe
Camp
Lake Skannatati
Kanawauke
Rockhouse Mtn.
1283
Lake Welch Beach
Upper Pound Swamp
Irish Mtn.
1140
Wildcat Mtn.
Greenwood Lake Rd.
Hemlock Hill
Little Long Pond
Lakes
Kanawauke Circle
Mine Ridge
Welch
Welch Camp
Gate Hill Road
Lake Welch
Minisceongo Creek
Tom Jones Mtn.
1289
210
Thruway
752
Parker Cabin Hollow
808
Good Spring Mtn.
Seven Lakes
Mountain
Pole Brook
Johnstown Road
St. Johns Ch.
Radio Relay Tower
Fire Tower
Jackie Jones Mtn.
952
Parker Cabin Mtn.
Triangle
Lake Skenonto
New Sebago Beach
Lily Pond
Camp Winaki Road
Long Path
Big Hill
1268
First Reservoir
Continental Rd.
We-Wah Lake
Black Ash Mtn.
1044
Victory Trail
Brundige Mtn.
High Hill
Cranberry Mtn.
Camp Wakonda
Bear
Second Reservoir
Third Reservoir
Horse Chock
Horse Chock Mtn.
Hollow Road
17
Tower Hill
Black Ash
Breakneck
Ramapo-Dunderberg

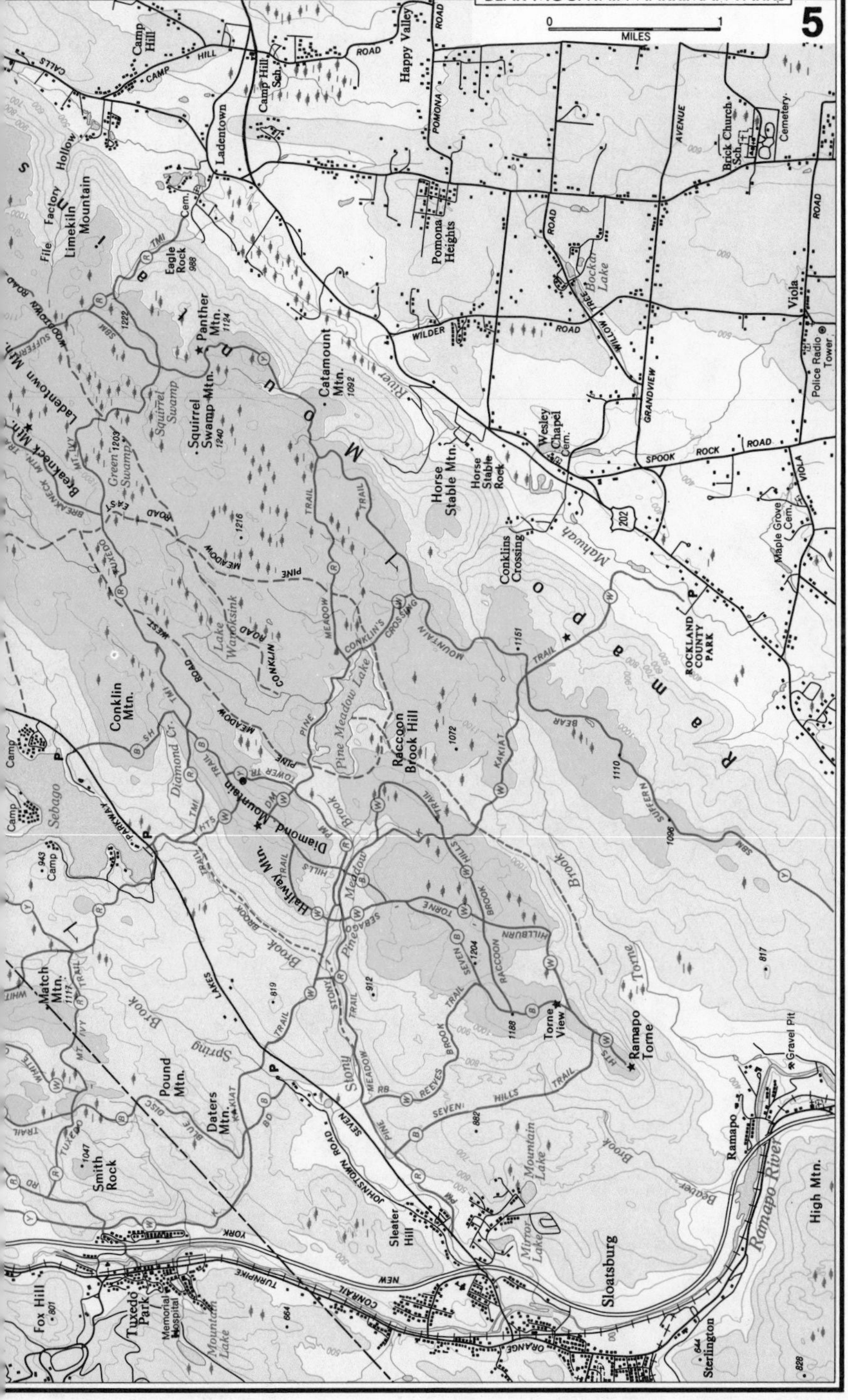
0
1
MILES
Camp Hill
Camp Hill Sch.
Ladentown
Happy Valley
Pomona
Pomona Heights
Brick Church Sch.
Cemetery
Viola
Police Radio Tower
Wilder Road
Willow Tree Road
Grandview Avenue
Spook Rock Road
Bockar Lake
Catamount Mtn.
1092
Horse Stable Mtn.
Horse Stable Rock
Wesley Chapel Cem.
Conklins Crossing
Mahwah River
202
Maple Grove Cem.
Rockland County Park
Ramapo Mountains
Limekiln Mountain
File Factory Hollow
Eagle Rock
988
Panther Mtn.
1124
Squirrel Swamp Mtn.
1240
Squirrel Swamp
Green Swamp
1203
1222
Ladentown Mtn.
Breakneck Mtn.
Sufferin Bear Mountain Trail
Lake Wanoksink
Conklin Road
Pine Meadow Road
Pine Meadow Lake
Raccoon Brook Hill
1072
1151
1110
1096
Kakiat Trail
Conklin's Crossing
Diamond Mountain
Halfway Mtn.
Tower Tr.
Diamond Cr.
Conklin Mtn.
Sebago
Camp
943
Match Mtn.
1117
Pound Mtn.
Daters Mtn.
Smith Rock
1047
Spring Brook
Stony Brook
Seven Hills Trail
Hillburn Torne Brook
Raccoon Brook Hills
Torne View
Ramapo Torne
Torne Brook
1204
1188
912
819
882
817
Reeves Brook
Mountain Lake
Mirror Lake
Sleater Hill
Sloatsburg
Seven Lakes Drive
Johnstown Road
Palisades Interstate Parkway
Tuxedo Park
Memorial Hospital
Mountain Lake
Fox Hill
801
664
New York Turnpike
Conrail
Orange
Ramapo
Ramapo River
Beaver Brook
Gravel Pit
High Mtn.
Sterlington
644
828

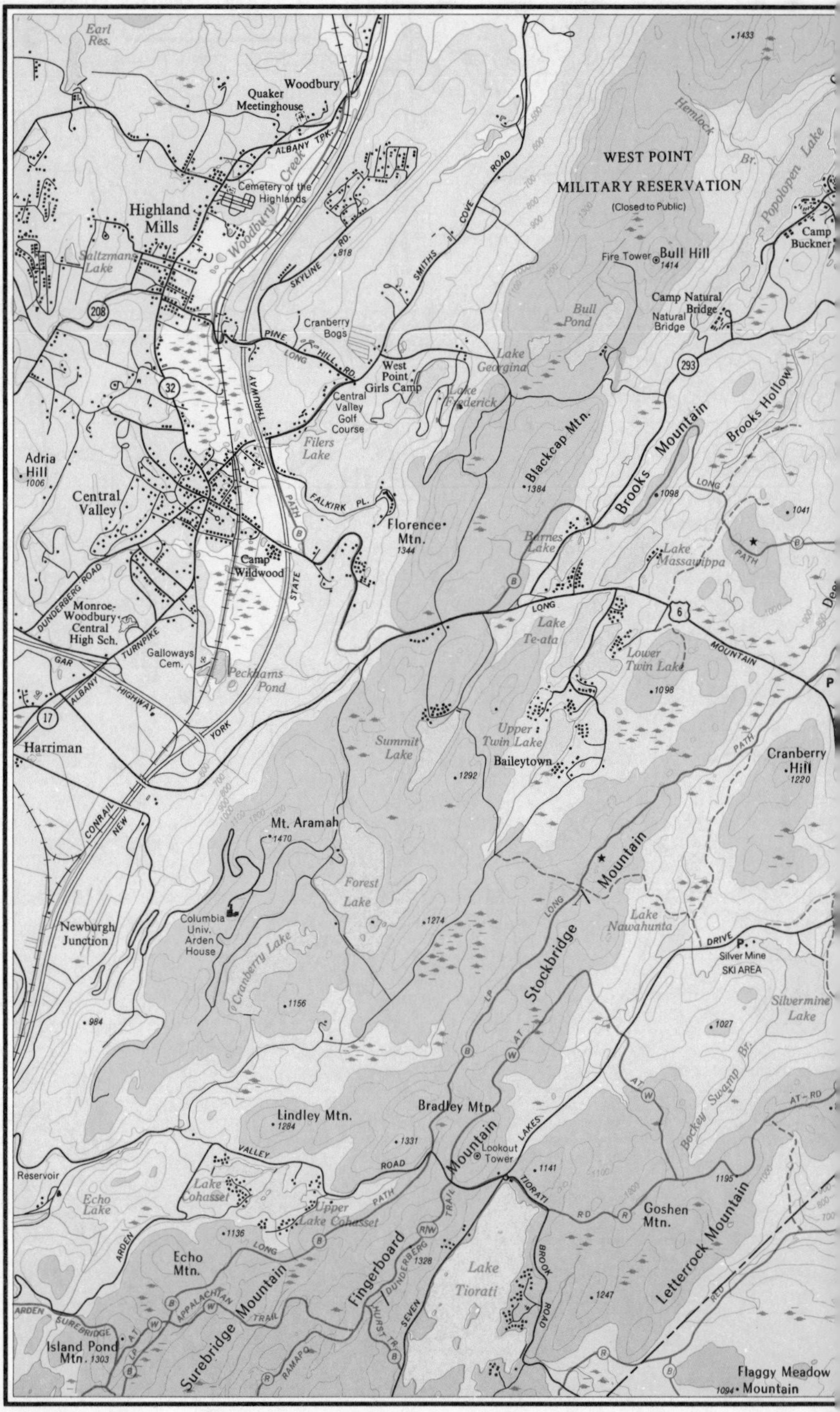

Earl Res.
Woodbury
Quaker Meetinghouse
ALBANY TPK.
Cemetery of the Highlands
Woodbury Creek
Highland Mills
Saltzmans Lake
208
SKYLINE RD.
818
SMITHS COVE ROAD
WEST POINT MILITARY RESERVATION
(Closed to Public)
Hemlock Br.
Popolopen Lake
Camp Buckner
Fire Tower
Bull Hill
1414
1433
Bull Pond
Camp Natural Bridge
Natural Bridge
Cranberry Bogs
PINE HILL RD.
LONG
West Point Girls Camp
Lake Georgina
Lake Frederick
293
32
THRUWAY
Central Valley Golf Course
Filers Lake
Blackcap Mtn.
1384
Brooks Mountain
Brooks Hollow
1098
LONG PATH
1041
Adria Hill
1006
Central Valley
FALKIRK PL.
Florence Mtn.
1344
Barnes Lake
Lake Massawippa
Camp Wildwood
STATE
DUNDERBERG ROAD
Monroe-Woodbury Central High Sch.
LONG
Lake Te-ata
6
MOUNTAIN
GAR
TURNPIKE
Galloways Cem.
Peckhams Pond
Lower Twin Lake
ALBANY HIGHWAY
17
YORK
Harriman
Summit Lake
Upper Twin Lake
Baileytown
PATH
Cranberry Hill
1220
1292
CONRAIL NEW
Mt. Aramah
1470
Stockbridge Mountain
Forest Lake
Lake Nawahunta
DRIVE
Silver Mine SKI AREA
Columbia Univ. Arden House
Newburgh Junction
Cranberry Lake
1274
1156
Silvermine Lake
1027
984
AT
Bockey Swamp Br.
AT-RD
Lindley Mtn.
1284
Bradley Mtn.
1331
VALLEY ROAD
Lookout Tower
LAKES
Mountain
1141
TIORATI RD
1195
Reservoir
Echo Lake
Lake Cohasset
Upper Lake Cohasset
PATH
Goshen Mtn.
Letterrock Mountain
1136
LONG
ARDEN
R/W
TRAIL
Echo Mtn.
Fingerboard
DUNDERBERG
1328
Lake Tiorati
BROOK ROAD
1247
RED
ARDEN SUREBRIDGE
APPALACHIAN TRAIL
Surebridge Mountain
HURST TR.
SEVEN
Island Pond Mtn.
1303
RAMAPO
Flaggy Meadow Mountain
1094

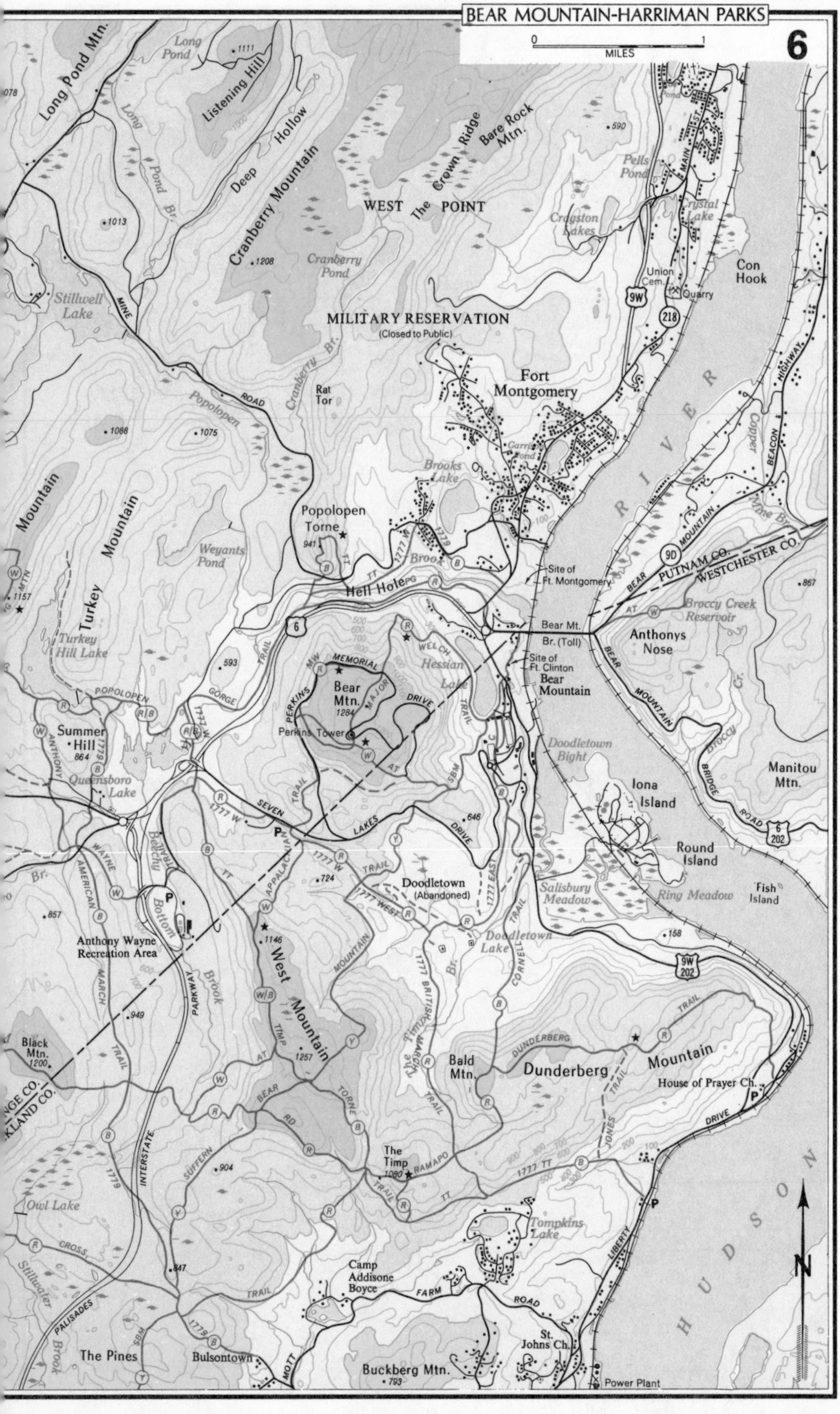
BEAR MOUNTAIN-HARRIMAN PARKS
6
0
1
MILES
Long Pond Mtn.
Long Pond
Listening Hill
Long Pond Br.
Deep Hollow
Cranberry Mountain
The Crown Ridge
Bare Rock Mtn.
WEST POINT
Pells Pond
Crystal Lake
Cragston Lakes
Cranberry Pond
Stillwell Lake
MINE ROAD
Union Cem.
Quarry
Con Hook
MILITARY RESERVATION
(Closed to Public)
Fort Montgomery
Rat Tor
Popolopen
Cranberry Br.
Brooks Lake
Garrison Pond
Popolopen Torne
Weyants Pond
Turkey Mountain
Mountain
Turkey Hill Lake
Hell Hole
Site of Ft. Montgomery
PUTNAM CO.
WESTCHESTER CO.
Broccy Creek Reservoir
Anthonys Nose
Bear Mt. Br. (Toll)
Site of Ft. Clinton
Bear Mountain
Hessian Lake
Bear Mtn.
Perkins Tower
MEMORIAL
MAJOR
DRIVE
WELCH
PERKINS
POPOLOPEN
GORGE
TRAIL
Summer Hill
Queensboro Lake
Doodletown Bight
Iona Island
Manitou Mtn.
Round Island
Fish Island
SEVEN LAKES DRIVE
Belchy Bottom
Doodletown (Abandoned)
Salisbury Meadow
Ring Meadow
Anthony Wayne Recreation Area
West Mountain
Doodletown Lake
Black Mtn.
ORANGE CO.
ROCKLAND CO.
Bald Mtn.
Dunderberg Mountain
House of Prayer Ch.
BEAR RD
TIMP
TORNE
The Timp
RAMAPO
INTERSTATE
PARKWAY
PALISADES
SUFFERN
Owl Lake
Tompkins Lake
Stillwater Brook
CROSS
Camp Addisone Boyce
FARM ROAD
LIBERTY DRIVE
The Pines
Bulsontown
MOTT
St. Johns Ch.
Buckberg Mtn.
Power Plant
HUDSON RIVER
N

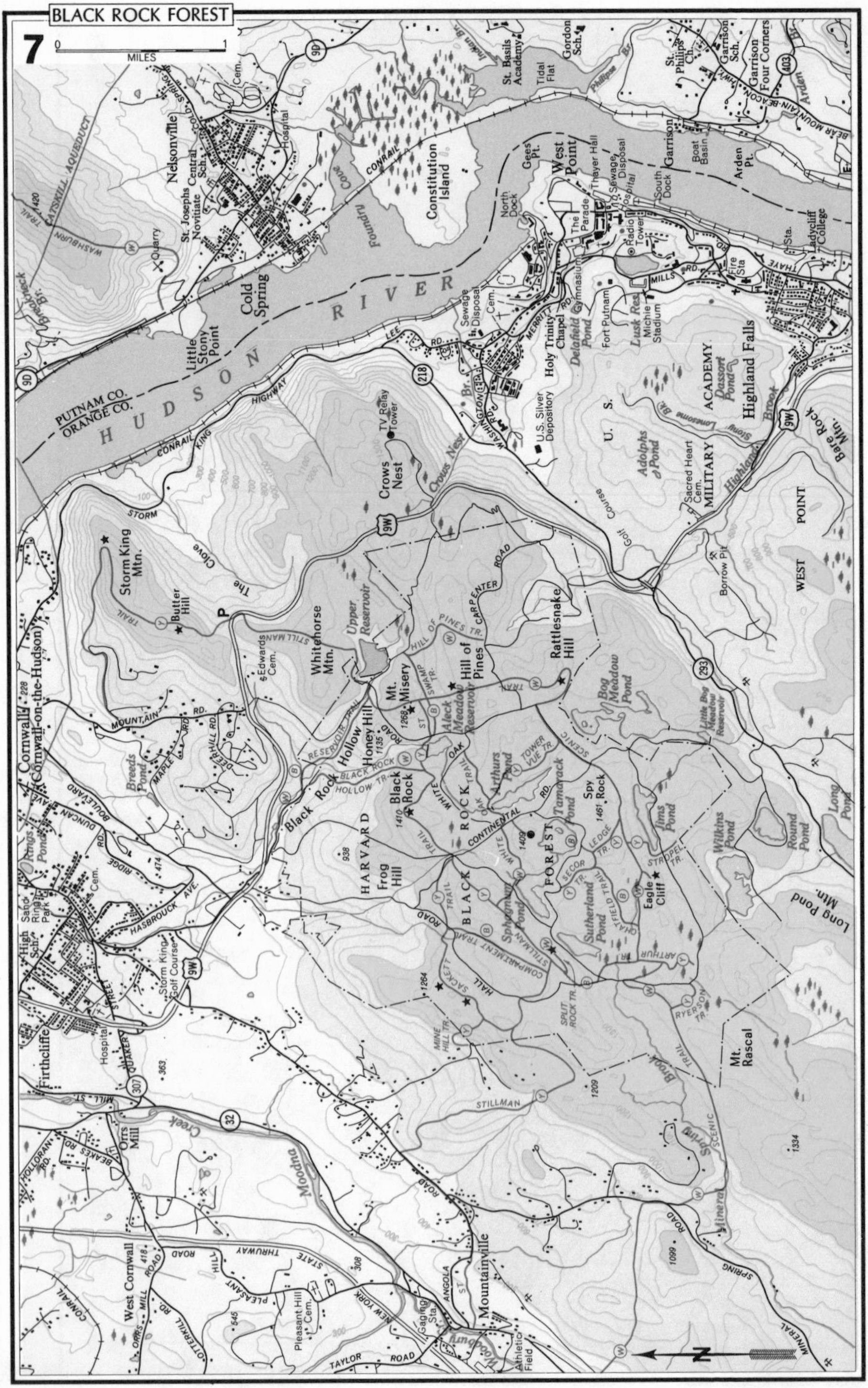
BLACK ROCK FOREST
7
0
1
MILES
HUDSON RIVER
PUTNAM CO.
ORANGE CO.
Nelsonville
Cold Spring
Little Stony Point
Constitution Island
Foundry Cove
West Point
Gees Pt.
North Dock
South Dock
Garrison
Arden Pt.
Boat Basin
Tidal Flat
St. Basils Academy
Gordon Sch.
St. Philips Ch.
Garrison Sch.
Garrison Four Corners
Ladycliff College
Highland Falls
Fort Putnam
Michie Stadium
Lusk Res.
Delafield Pond
Holy Trinity Chapel
Thayer Hall
The Parade
Gymnasium
Radio Tower
U.S. Silver Depository
Dassori Pond
Adolphs Pond
U. S. MILITARY ACADEMY
WEST POINT
Sacred Heart Cem.
Borrow Pit
Golf Course
Bare Rock Mtn.
Crows Nest
TV Relay Tower
Storm King Mtn.
Butter Hill
The Clove
Whitehorse Mtn.
Upper Reservoir
Mt. Misery
Hill of Pines
Aleck Meadow Reservoir
Rattlesnake Hill
Bog Meadow Pond
Little Bog Meadow Reservoir
Honey Hill
Black Rock Hollow
Black Rock
Arthurs Pond
Tamarack Pond
Spy Rock
HARVARD BLACK ROCK FOREST
Frog Hill
Sphagnum Pond
Sutherland Pond
Eagle Cliff
Jims Pond
Wilkins Pond
Round Pond
Long Pond
Long Pond Mtn.
Mt. Rascal
Cornwall (Cornwall-on-the-Hudson)
Breeds Pond
Rings Pond
Sand Ring Park
High Sch.
Storm King Golf Course
Firthcliffe
Hospital
Orrs Mill
Moodna Creek
West Cornwall
Pleasant Hill Cem.
Mountainville
Athletic Field
Taylor Road
Mineral Spring Road
CATSKILL AQUEDUCT
Quarry
Hospital
St. Josephs Novitiate
Central Sch.
9D
9W
218
293
307
32
403
N

SCHUNEMUNK MOUNTAIN

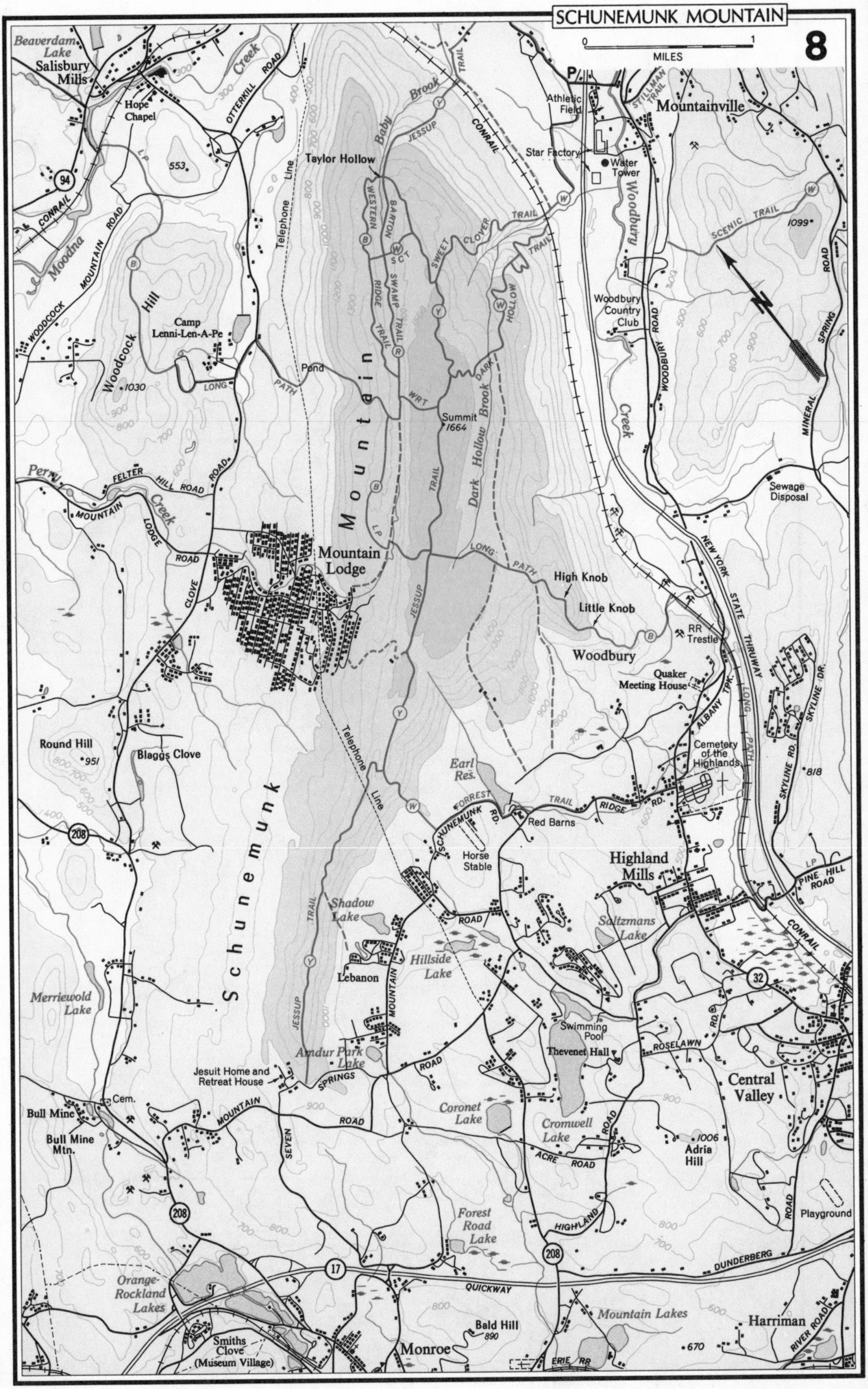

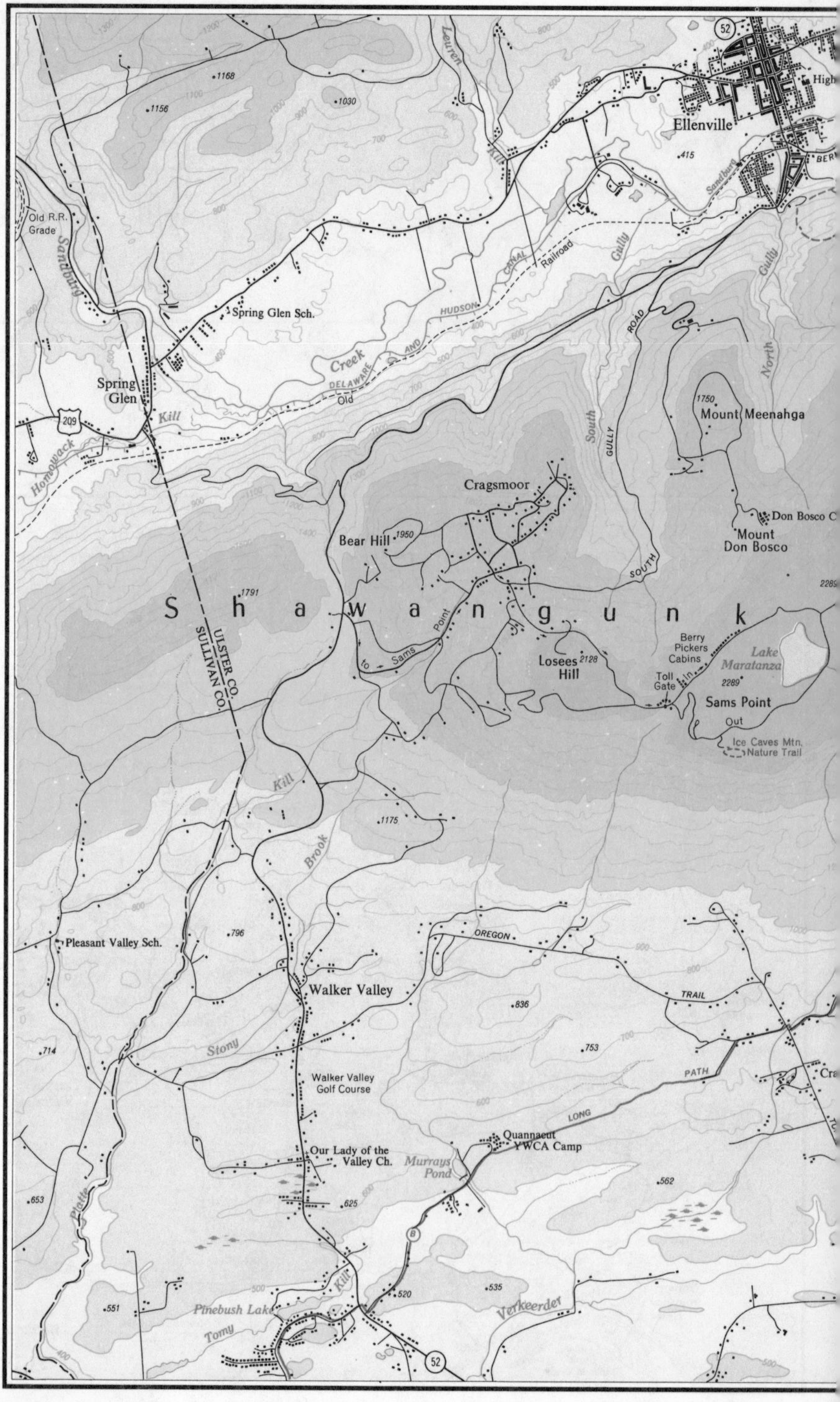

Ellenville
Spring Glen
Spring Glen Sch.
Old R.R. Grade
Sandburg
Homowack
Kill
Creek
Delaware and Hudson Canal
Old Railroad
Leuren Kill
Gully
South Gully Road
North Gully
Mount Meenahga
1750
Cragsmoor
Bear Hill
1950
Don Bosco
Mount Don Bosco
S h a w a n g u n k
1791
ULSTER CO.
SULLIVAN CO.
to Sams Point
Losees Hill
2128
Berry Pickers Cabins
Toll Gate
In
Out
Lake Maratanza
2289
Sams Point
Ice Caves Mtn. Nature Trail
Kill
Brook
1175
1168
1156
1030
415
209
52
Pleasant Valley Sch.
796
Walker Valley
Oregon Trail
836
753
714
Stony
Walker Valley Golf Course
Long Path
Quannacut YWCA Camp
Our Lady of the Valley Ch.
Murrays Pond
562
625
653
Platte
Pinebush Lake
Tomy
Kill
520
535
551
Verkeerder

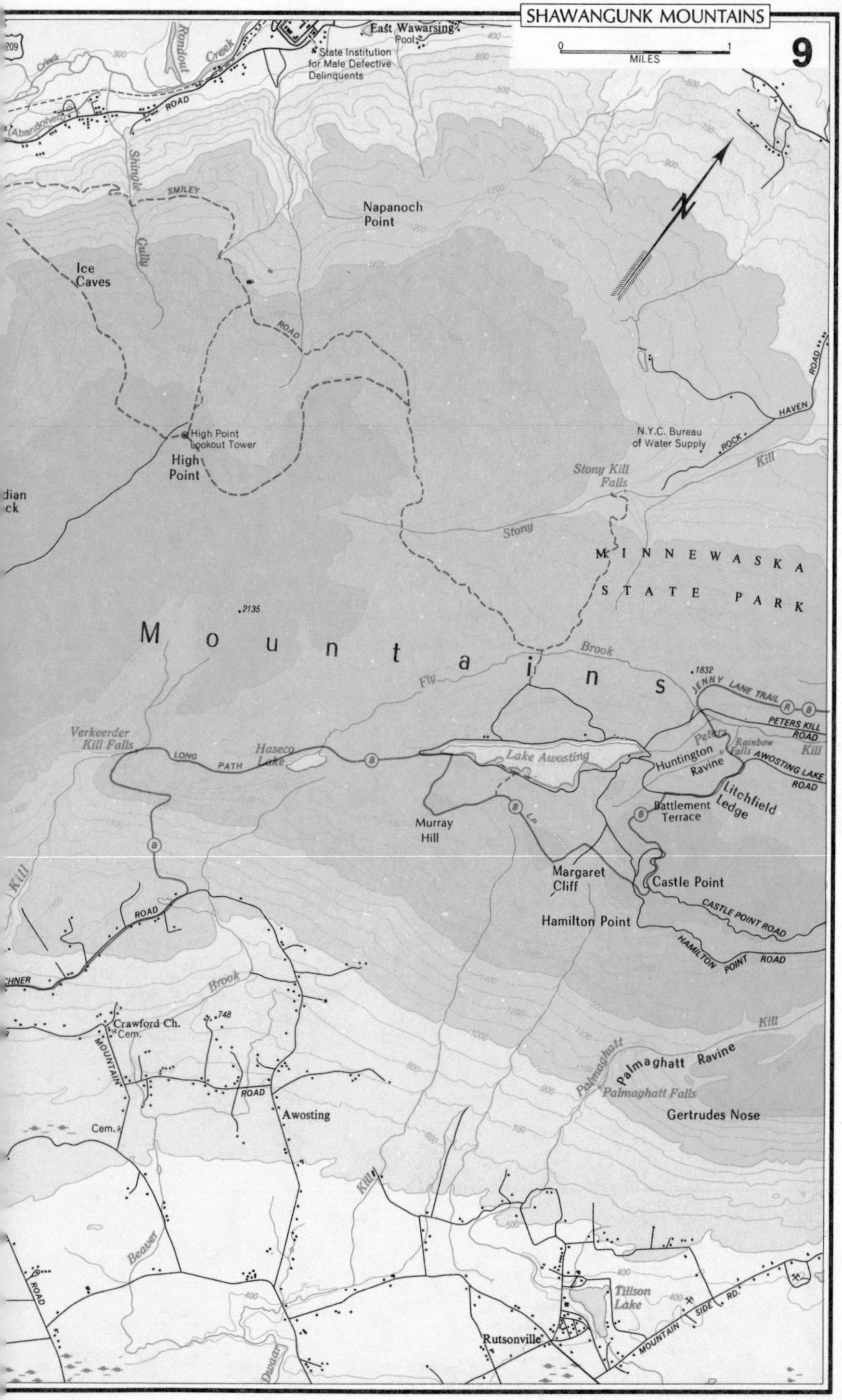
SHAWANGUNK MOUNTAINS
9
0
MILES
1
East Wawarsing
Pool
State Institution
for Male Defective
Delinquents
Rondout
Creek
ROAD
Shingle
Gully
SMILEY
ROAD
Napanoch
Point
Ice
Caves
High Point
Lookout Tower
High
Point
N.Y.C. Bureau
of Water Supply
ROCK
HAVEN
ROAD
Kill
Stony Kill
Falls
Stony
MINNEWASKA
STATE PARK
2135
Mountains
Brook
Fly
1832
JENNY LANE TRAIL
PETERS KILL
ROAD
Peters
Kill
Verkeerder
Kill Falls
LONG PATH
Haseco
Lake
Lake Awosting
Huntington
Ravine
Rainbow
Falls
AWOSTING LAKE
ROAD
Litchfield
Ledge
Battlement
Terrace
Murray
Hill
Margaret
Cliff
Castle Point
CASTLE POINT ROAD
Hamilton Point
HAMILTON POINT ROAD
ROAD
Brook
748
Crawford Ch.
Cem.
MOUNTAIN
ROAD
Awosting
Cem.
Palmaghatt Ravine
Palmaghatt
Palmaghatt Falls
Kill
Gertrudes Nose
Kill
Beaver
ROAD
Tillson
Lake
MOUNTAIN SIDE RD.
Rutsonville
Dwaar

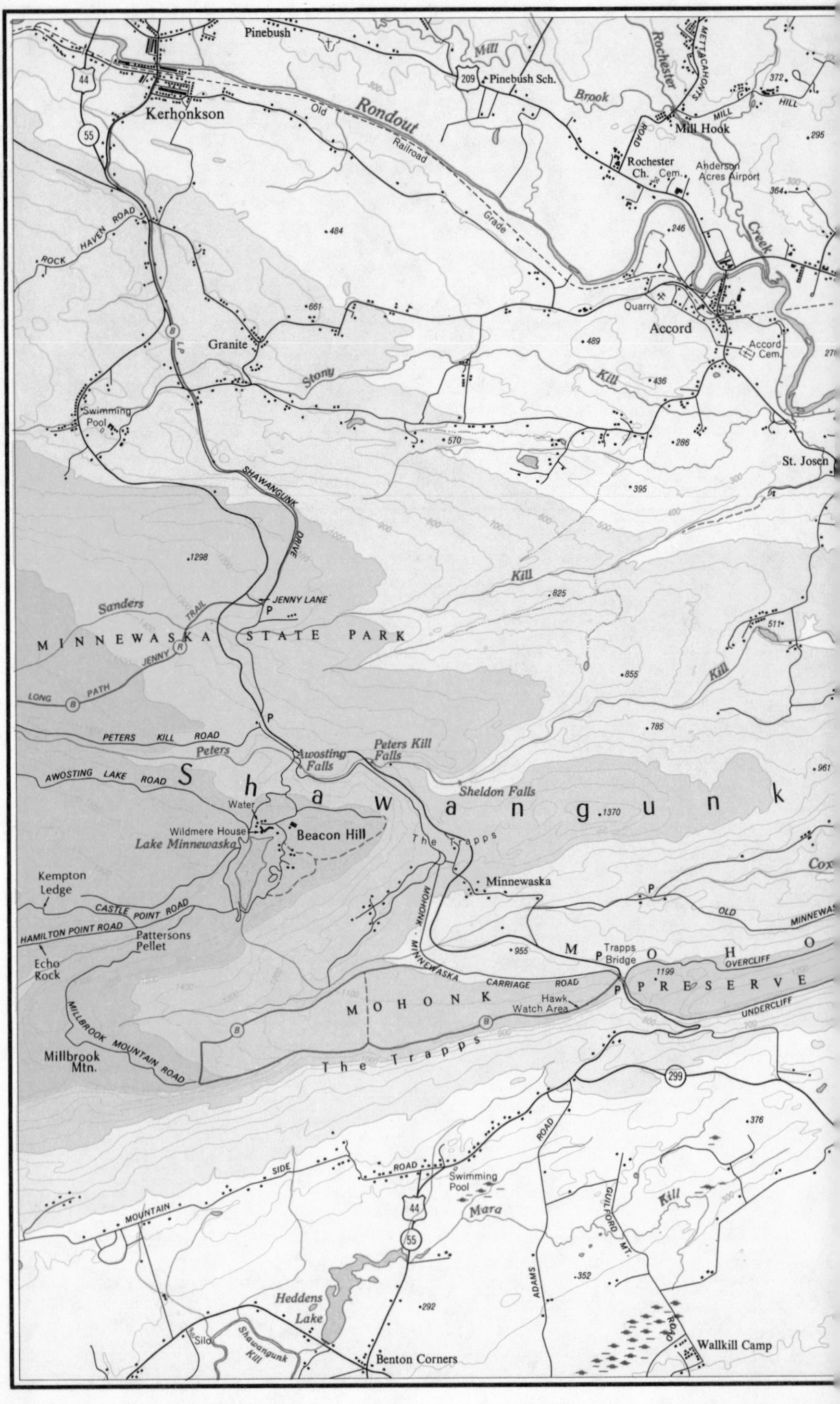

Pinebush
Mill
Brook
Rochester
METTACAHONTS
209
Pinebush Sch.
372
HILL
MILL
Mill Hook
295
44
Kerhonkson
55
Old
Rondout
Railroad
Grade
ROAD
Rochester Ch.
Cem.
Anderson Acres Airport
300
364
Creek
246
ROCK
HAVEN
ROAD
484
661
Quarry
Accord
489
Accord Cem.
Granite
B
LP
Stony
Kill
436
Swimming Pool
570
286
St. Josen
SHAWANGUNK
DRIVE
395
1298
Kill
825
JENNY LANE
P
Sanders
TRAIL
MINNEWASKA STATE PARK
JENNY
R
511
LONG
PATH
855
Kill
PETERS
KILL
ROAD
785
Peters
Awosting Falls
Peters Kill Falls
AWOSTING
LAKE
ROAD
Shawangunk
961
Sheldon Falls
Water
1370
Wildmere House
Beacon Hill
Lake Minnewaska
The Trapps
Kempton Ledge
Minnewaska
Cox
CASTLE
POINT
ROAD
MOHONK
OLD
MINNEWASKA
HAMILTON POINT ROAD
Pattersons Pellet
MINNEWASKA
CARRIAGE
ROAD
955
M
Trapps Bridge
MOHONK PRESERVE
1199
OVERCLIFF
Echo Rock
MILLBROOK
MOUNTAIN
ROAD
MOHONK
Hawk Watch Area
UNDERCLIFF
Millbrook Mtn.
The Trapps
299
376
ROAD
SIDE
ROAD
Swimming Pool
MOUNTAIN
Mara
Kill
GUILFORD
MT.
ROAD
ADAMS
352
Heddens Lake
292
Silo
Shawangunk Kill
Benton Corners
Wallkill Camp

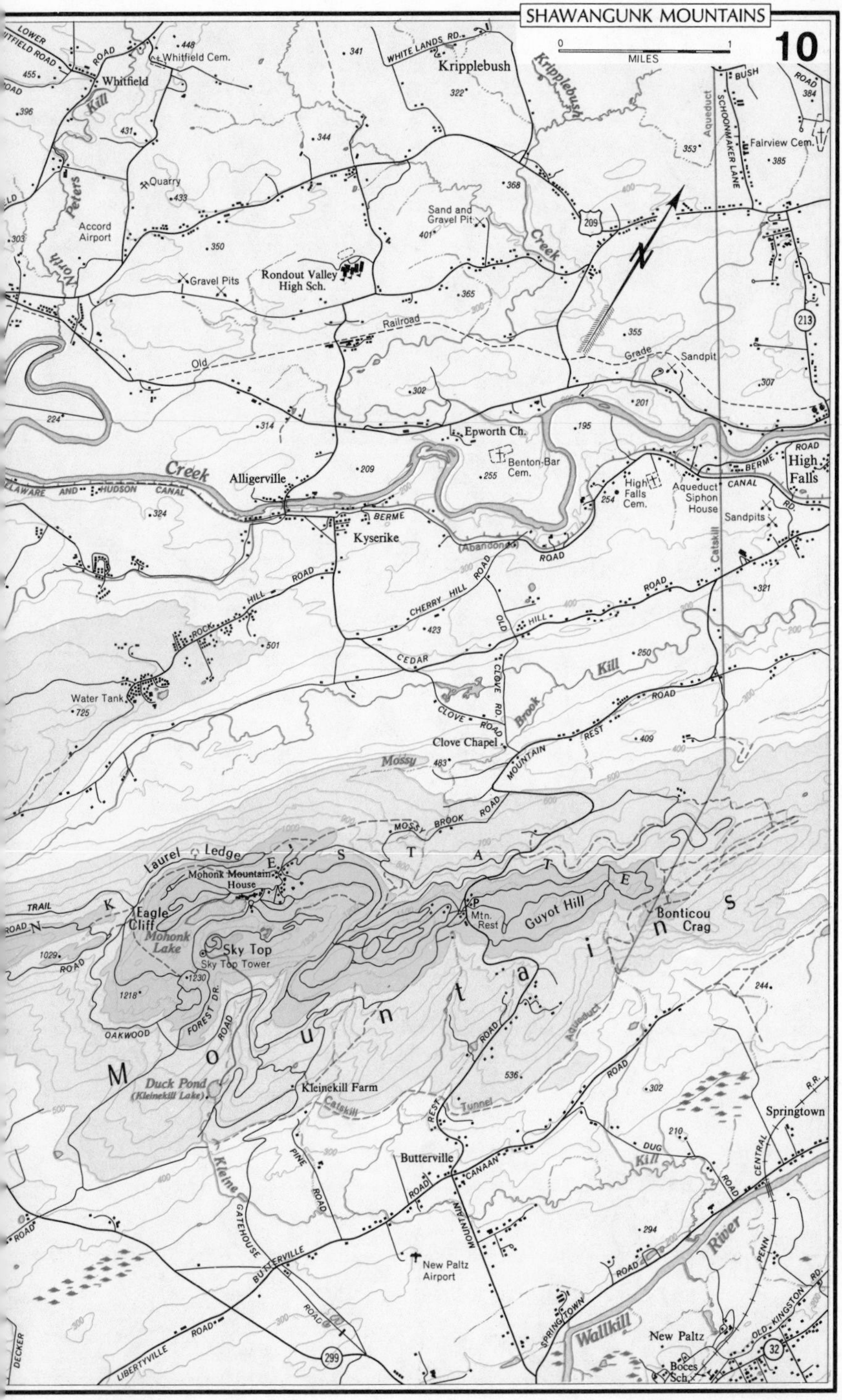
0
1
MILES
Whitfield
Whitfield Cem.
Kripplebush
WHITE LANDS RD.
Kripplebush
Peters Kill
Quarry
Accord Airport
North
Gravel Pits
Rondout Valley High Sch.
Sand and Gravel Pit
Creek
209
Aqueduct
SCHOONMAKER LANE
BUSH
Fairview Cem.
213
Old Railroad Grade
Sandpit
Epworth Ch.
Benton-Bar Cem.
Creek
Alligerville
DELAWARE AND HUDSON CANAL
BERME
Kyserike
(Abandoned)
High Falls Cem.
Aqueduct Siphon House
High Falls
BERME ROAD
CANAL
Sandpits
Catskill
ROCK HILL ROAD
CHERRY HILL ROAD
OLD HILL ROAD
CEDAR
CLOVE RD.
CLOVE ROAD
Brook
Kill
Water Tank
Clove Chapel
Mossy
MOUNTAIN REST ROAD
MOSSY BROOK ROAD
Laurel Ledge
Mohonk Mountain House
E S T A T E
TRAIL
Eagle Cliff
Mohonk Lake
Sky Top
Sky Top Tower
Mtn. Rest
Guyot Hill
Bonticou Crag
M o u n t a i n s
OAKWOOD
FOREST DR.
ROAD
Aqueduct
Duck Pond (Kleinekill Lake)
Kleinekill Farm
Catskill
Tunnel
REST
Springtown
R.R.
CENTRAL
DUG Kill
Butterville
CANAAN
ROAD
PINE ROAD
Kleine
GATEHOUSE
MOUNTAIN
BUTTERVILLE
New Paltz Airport
River
PENN
OLD KINGSTON RD.
SPRINGTOWN ROAD
Wallkill
New Paltz
32
Boces Sch.
299
LIBERTYVILLE ROAD
DECKER

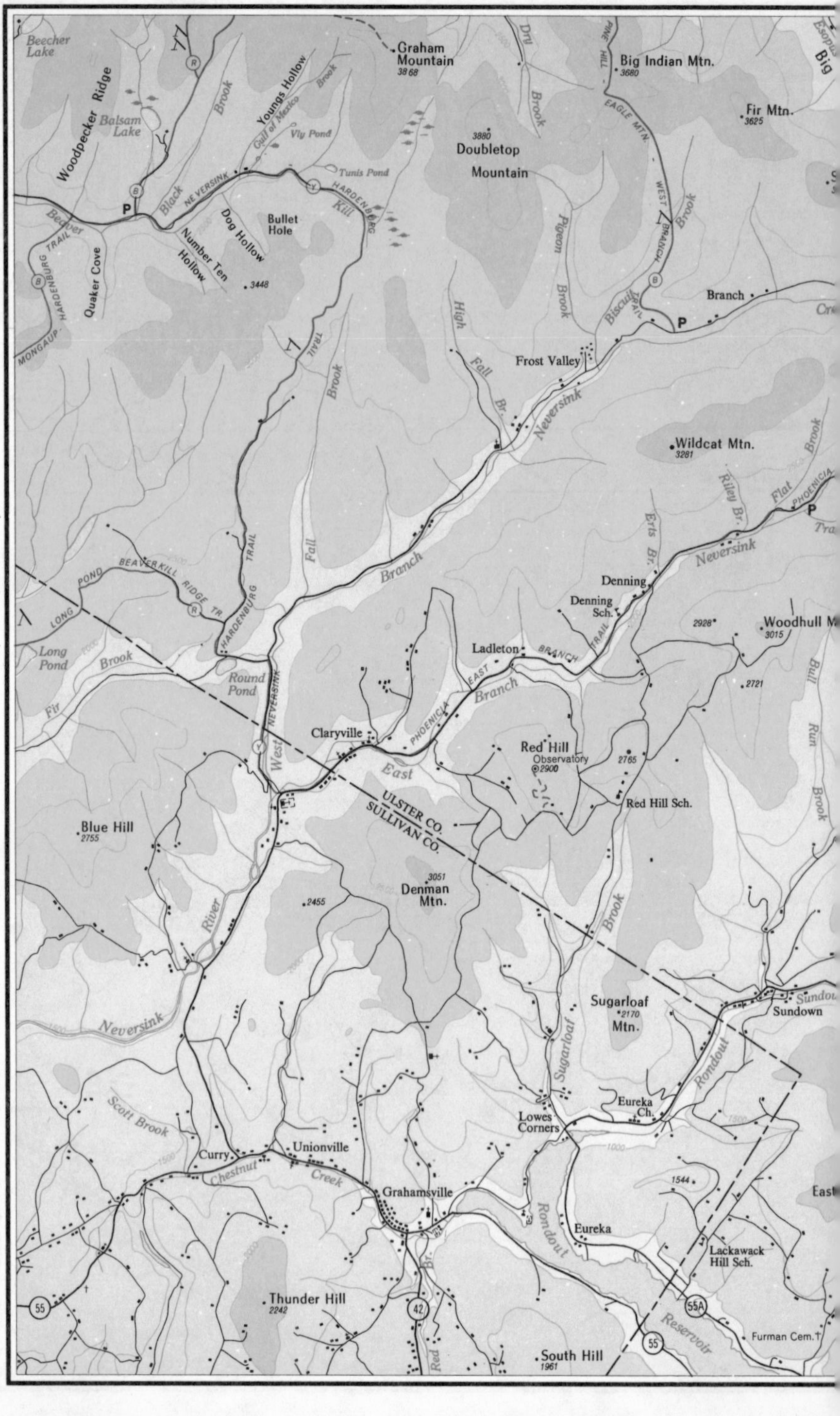

Beecher Lake
Woodpecker Ridge
Balsam Lake
Black Brook
Youngs Hollow
Gulf of Mexico Brook
Vly Pond
Graham Mountain
3868
Tunis Pond
Hardenburg Kill
Neversink
Dog Hollow
Bullet Hole
Number Ten Hollow
Beaver
Mongaup Hardenburg Trail
Quaker Cove
3448
Dry Brook
3880
Doubletop Mountain
Pine Hill
Eagle Mtn.
West Branch
Big Indian Mtn.
3680
Fir Mtn.
3625
Brook
Pigeon Brook
Biscuit Trail
Branch
High Fall Br.
Frost Valley
Neversink
Wildcat Mtn.
3281
Hardenburg Trail
Brook
Fall Brook
Riley Br.
Flat Brook
Phoenicia
Erts Br.
Neversink
Denning
Denning Sch.
Trail
2928
Woodhull M
3015
2721
Bull Run Brook
Long Pond Beaverkill Ridge Tr
Long Pond
Brook
Fir
Round Pond
Hardenburg Trail
Branch
Ladleton
East Branch
Phoenicia East Branch
Neversink West
Claryville
East
Red Hill
Observatory
2900
2765
Red Hill Sch.
Ulster Co.
Sullivan Co.
Blue Hill
2755
River
3051
Denman Mtn.
2455
Brook
Sugarloaf
2170
Mtn.
Sugarloaf
Sundown
Sundown
Neversink
Rondout
Scott Brook
Eureka Ch.
Lowes Corners
Curry
Unionville
Chestnut Creek
Grahamsville
1544
Rondout
Eureka
Lackawack Hill Sch.
55
Thunder Hill
2242
42
Red Br.
55A
Reservoir
55
South Hill
1961
Furman Cem.
East

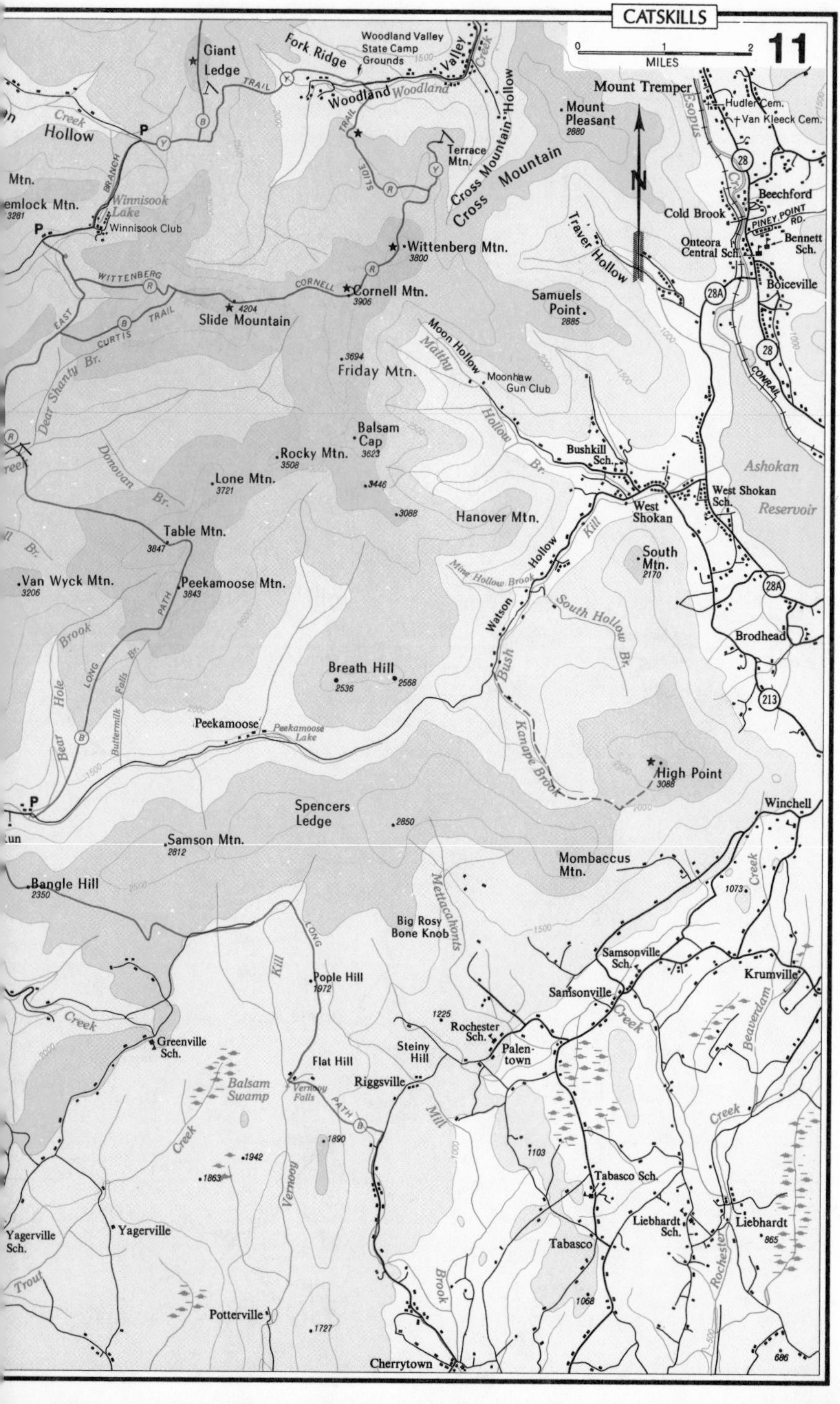

CATSKILLS
11
0 1 2
MILES
Giant Ledge
Fork Ridge
Woodland Valley State Camp Grounds
Woodland Valley Creek
Woodland
Mount Tremper
Esopus
Hudler Cem.
Van Kleeck Cem.
Mount Pleasant
2880
Hollow
Creek
Winnisook Lake
Winnisook Club
Hemlock Mtn.
3281
Mtn.
BRANCH
TRAIL
SLIDE
Terrace Mtn.
Cross Mountain Hollow
Cross Mountain
Beechford
Cold Brook
PINEY POINT RD.
Onteora Central Sch.
Bennett Sch.
Boiceville
Traver Hollow
Wittenberg Mtn.
3800
WITTENBERG
CORNELL
Cornell Mtn.
3906
Slide Mountain
4204
EAST
CURTIS
Samuels Point
2885
Dear Shanty Br.
Moon Hollow
Maltby
Moonhaw Gun Club
3694
Friday Mtn.
CONRAIL
Balsam Cap
3623
Rocky Mtn.
3508
Lone Mtn.
3721
Donovan Br.
Hollow Br.
Bushkill Sch.
Ashokan Reservoir
West Shokan
West Shokan Sch.
3446
3088
Hanover Mtn.
Table Mtn.
3847
Kill
South Mtn.
2170
Mine Hollow Brook
Watson Hollow
Van Wyck Mtn.
3206
Peekamoose Mtn.
3843
PATH
South Hollow Br.
Brodhead
Bear Hole Brook
LONG
Buttermilk Falls Br.
Breath Hill
2536
2568
Bush Kill
Kanape Brook
Peekamoose
Peekamoose Lake
High Point
3088
Winchell
Spencers Ledge
2850
Samson Mtn.
2812
Mombaccus Mtn.
Bangle Hill
2350
1073
Creek
Mettacahonts
Big Rosy Bone Knob
Samsonville Sch.
Samsonville
Krumville
Beaverdam
Pople Hill
1972
1225
Rochester Sch.
Palentown
Steiny Hill
Flat Hill
Greenville Sch.
Balsam Swamp
Vernooy Falls
Riggsville
Mill
Creek
1890
1942
1863
1103
Vernooy
Tabasco Sch.
Yagerville Sch.
Yagerville
Liebhardt Sch.
Liebhardt
865
Tabasco
Rochester
Trout
Brook
1068
Potterville
1727
Cherrytown
686

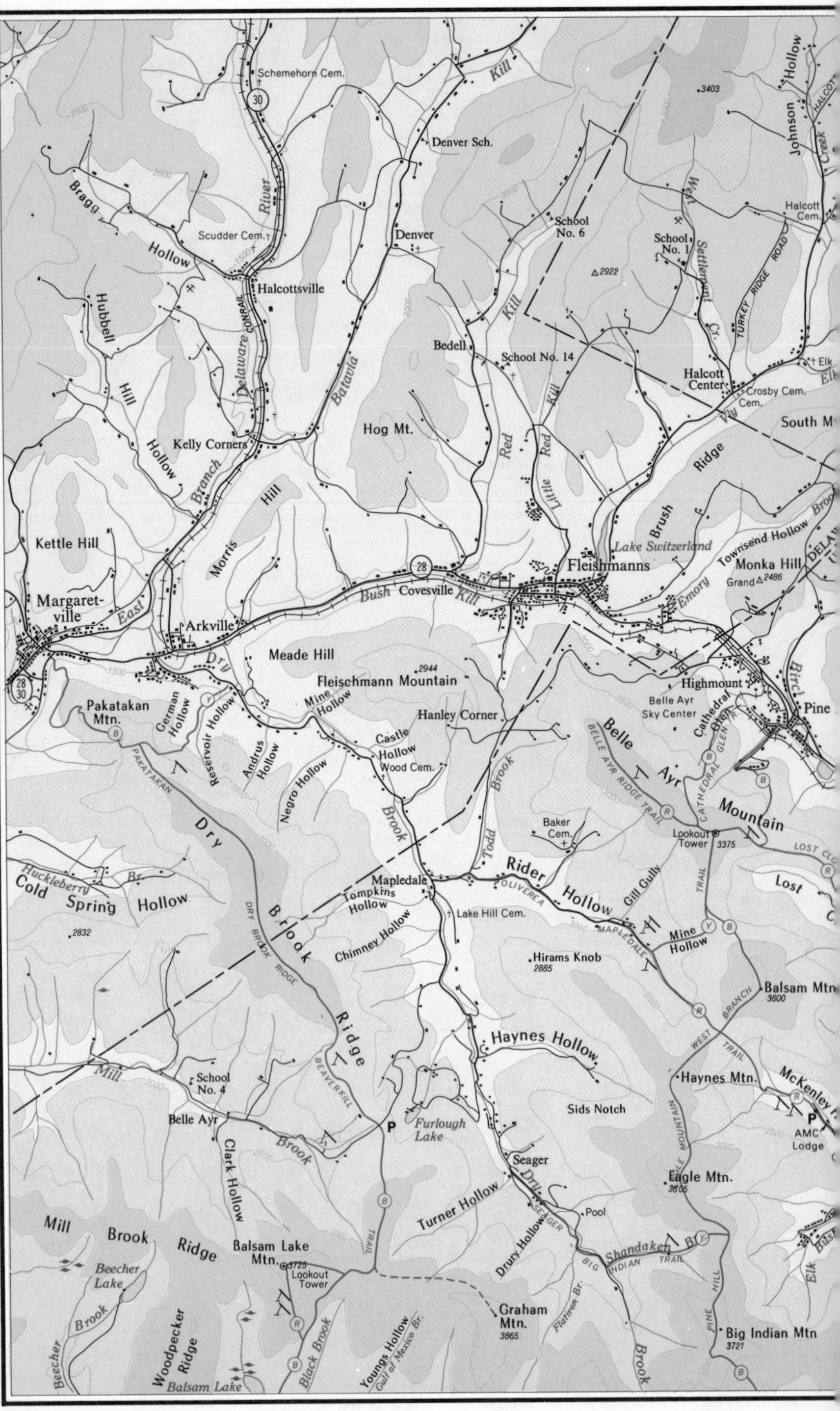
Schemehorn Cem.
30
Denver Sch.
Kill
3403
Johnson Hollow
Halcott Creek
Bragg Hollow
River
Scudder Cem.
Denver
School No. 6
West Settlement Cr.
School No. 1
Halcott Cem.
Halcottsville
2922
Turkey Ridge Road
Hubbell Hill Hollow
Delaware
Conrail
Batavia
Kill
Bedell
School No. 14
Halcott Center
Crosby Cem.
Elk
Red Kill
Little Red Kill
Hog Mt.
Vly
South M
Kelly Corners
Branch
Morris Hill
Brush Ridge
Kettle Hill
Lake Switzerland
Townsend Hollow
28
Fleishmanns
Monka Hill
Grand 2486
Margaretville
East
Bush
Covesville
Kill
Emory
Arkville
Meade Hill
Dry
2944
Fleischmann Mountain
Highmount
Birch
28
30
Pakatakan Mtn.
German Hollow
Reservoir Hollow
Mine Hollow
Hanley Corner
Belle Ayr Sky Center
Cathedral Glen
Pine
Castle Hollow
Wood Cem.
Andrus Hollow
Negro Hollow
Pakatakan
Belle Ayr Mountain
Belle Ayr Ridge Trail
Cathedral Glen Tr.
Dry
Brook
Todd Brook
Baker Cem.
Lookout Tower 3375
Lost Clove
Huckleberry Br.
Cold Spring Hollow
Mapledale
Rider Hollow
Oliverea
Lost
Tompkins Hollow
Lake Hill Cem.
Gill Gully
Trail
2832
Brook
Dry Brook Ridge
Chimney Hollow
Mapledale
Mine Hollow
Hirams Knob 2885
Balsam Mtn. 3600
West Branch Trail
Ridge
Haynes Hollow
Mill
School No. 4
Beaverkill
Haynes Mtn.
McKenley
Belle Ayr
Sids Notch
P
AMC Lodge
Brook
Furlough Lake
Clark Hollow
Seager
Eagle Mtn. 3605
Belle Mountain
Turner Hollow
Dry
Trail
Pool
Mill Brook Ridge
Balsam Lake Mtn. 3725
Lookout Tower
Seager
Drury Hollow
Shandaken Br.
Big Indian Trail
Pine Hill
Beecher Lake
Elk Bush
Brook
Graham Mtn. 3865
Flatiron Br.
Woodpecker Ridge
Black Brook
Youngs Hollow
Gulf of Mexico Br.
Big Indian Mtn 3721
Beecher
Balsam Lake
Brook

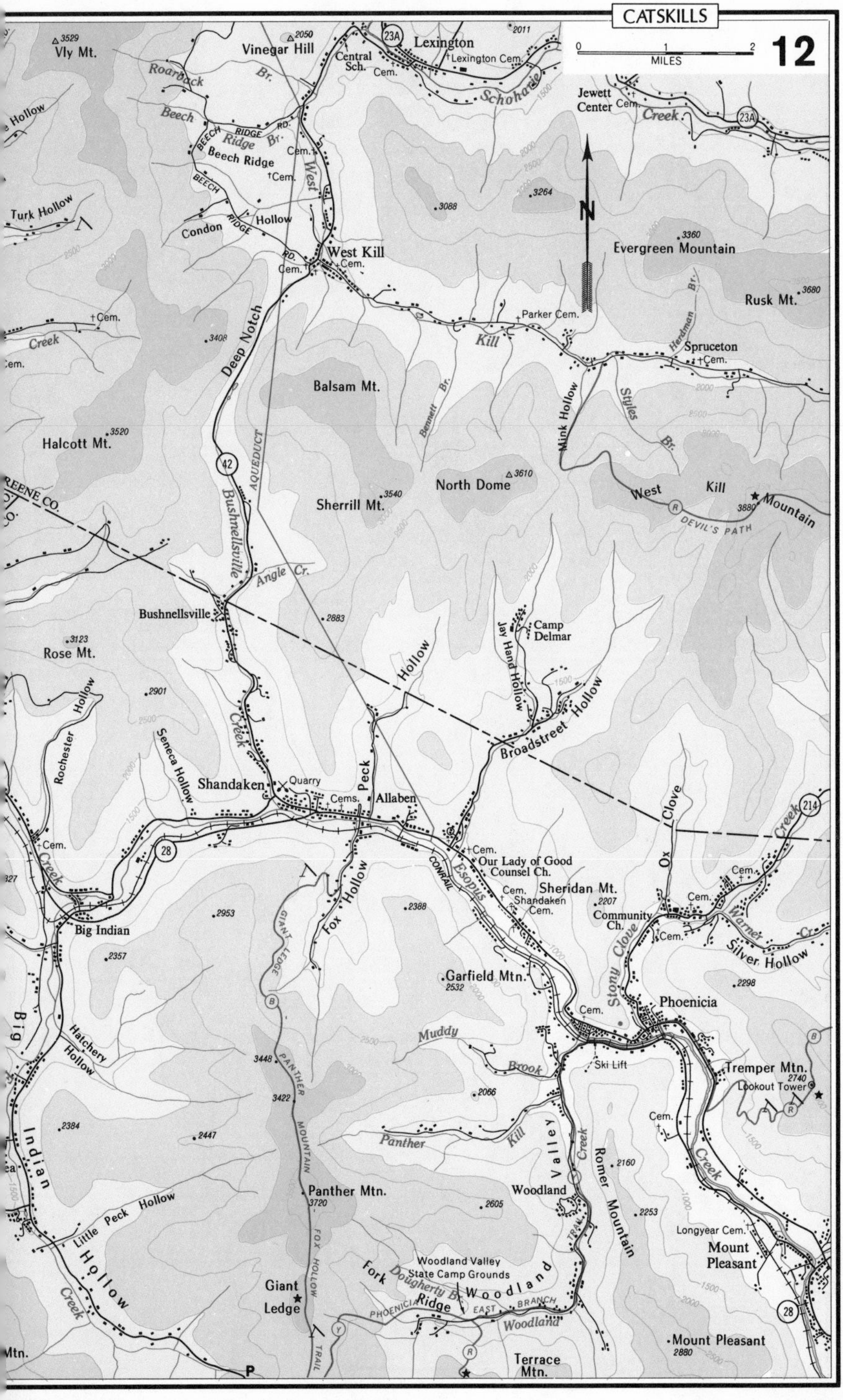

0 1 2 MILES
Vly Mt. 3529
Vinegar Hill 2050
Lexington
23A
Central Sch.
Cem.
Lexington Cem.
2011
Roarback Br.
Schoharie
Jewett Center
Cem.
Creek
Hollow
Beech Ridge Br.
BEECH RIDGE RD.
Beech Ridge
Cem.
West
Turk Hollow
Condon Hollow
3088
3264
N
3360
Evergreen Mountain
West Kill
Cem.
Deep Notch
Parker Cem.
Kill
Herdman Br.
Rusk Mt. 3680
Spruceton
Cem.
Creek
3408
Balsam Mt.
Bennett Br.
Mink Hollow
Styles Br.
Halcott Mt. 3520
AQUEDUCT
42
Bushnellsville
North Dome 3610
Sherrill Mt. 3540
West Kill Mountain 3880
DEVIL'S PATH
GREENE CO.
Angle Cr.
Bushnellsville
2883
Camp Delmar
Jay Hand Hollow
Rose Mt. 3123
Hollow
Broadstreet Hollow
Rochester Hollow
2901
Seneca Hollow
Creek
Shandaken
Quarry
Cems.
Peck
Allaben
Ox Clove
214
Creek
28
Cem.
Our Lady of Good Counsel Ch.
CONRAIL
Esopus
Fox Hollow
Sheridan Mt. 2207
Cem. Shandaken Cem.
Community Ch.
Cem.
Warner Cr.
Silver Hollow
Big Indian
2953
2388
GIANT LEDGE
2357
Garfield Mtn. 2532
Stony Clove
Phoenicia
2298
Cem.
Muddy Brook
Hatchery Hollow
Big Indian Hollow
PANTHER MOUNTAIN
3448
Ski Lift
Tremper Mtn. 2740
Lookout Tower
3422
2066
Cem.
2384
2447
Panther Kill
Valley Creek
Romer Mountain
2160
Creek
Panther Mtn. 3720
Woodland
2605
2253
Little Peck Hollow
FOX HOLLOW
Longyear Cem.
Mount Pleasant
Woodland Valley State Camp Grounds
Fork Ridge
Dougherty Br.
Woodland
Giant Ledge
PHOENICIA
EAST BRANCH
Woodland
28
TRAIL
Mount Pleasant 2880
Terrace Mtn.
Mtn.

Windham
Mitchell Hollow
Nauvo Road
Reservoir
Ashland Cem.
Batavia
Cem.
Brooksburg
Silver Lake
Bowery
South Durham
Windham High Peak
3524
Escarpment
Trail
Elm Ridge
Elm Ridge Tr.
Burnt Knob
Acra Point
Long Path
Range Trail
St. Edmunds Chapel
Acra
Woodstock
Catskill Cr.
Cairo
Hensonville
Cave Mountain
3025
Black Dome Valley
Kill
Maplecrest
Round Hill
2585
Van Loan Hill
Round Hill Road
Blackhead Range
Blackhead Mountains
Thomas Cole Mtn.
3945
Black Dome
3990
Blackhead
3940
Yellow Jacket Lookout
Trout
Purling
Brook
Shingle
Round Top
Kiskatom Br.
Glen Falls
Jewett
Hollow
Mill
Roaring
Brook
Beecher Corners
East Kill
Lower East Jewett Ch.
Camp Beecher
Dutcher Notch Trail
Countryman Kill
Escarpment
East Jewett Range
East Jewett
Halsey Br.
Colgate Lake
Stoppel Point
3422
Winter Clove
Maplewood Cem.
South Jewett
Schoharie
Camp Schoharie
Onteora Mt.
Onteora Pond
Parker Mtn.
Star Rock
Onteora Park
Newmans Ledge
Rip Van Winkle Hollow
Sunrise Rock
North Lake Public Campgrounds
North Mtn.
3140
Spruce Creek
North Lake Bypass
Marys Glen
North Lake
Artists Rock
Hunter
Central Sch.
Cem.
St. Marys Ch.
Red Kill
Saw mill
Allen Brook
Haines Falls
Rusk Mtn.
3680
Colonels Chair
Colonels Chair Tr.
Shanty Hollow
Ox Hollow
Spruceton Cem.
Spruceton Hunter
Camp Mayfair
Central Sch.
Tannersville
South Lake
Kaaterskill Falls
Site of Catskill Mountain House
Escarpment
Road

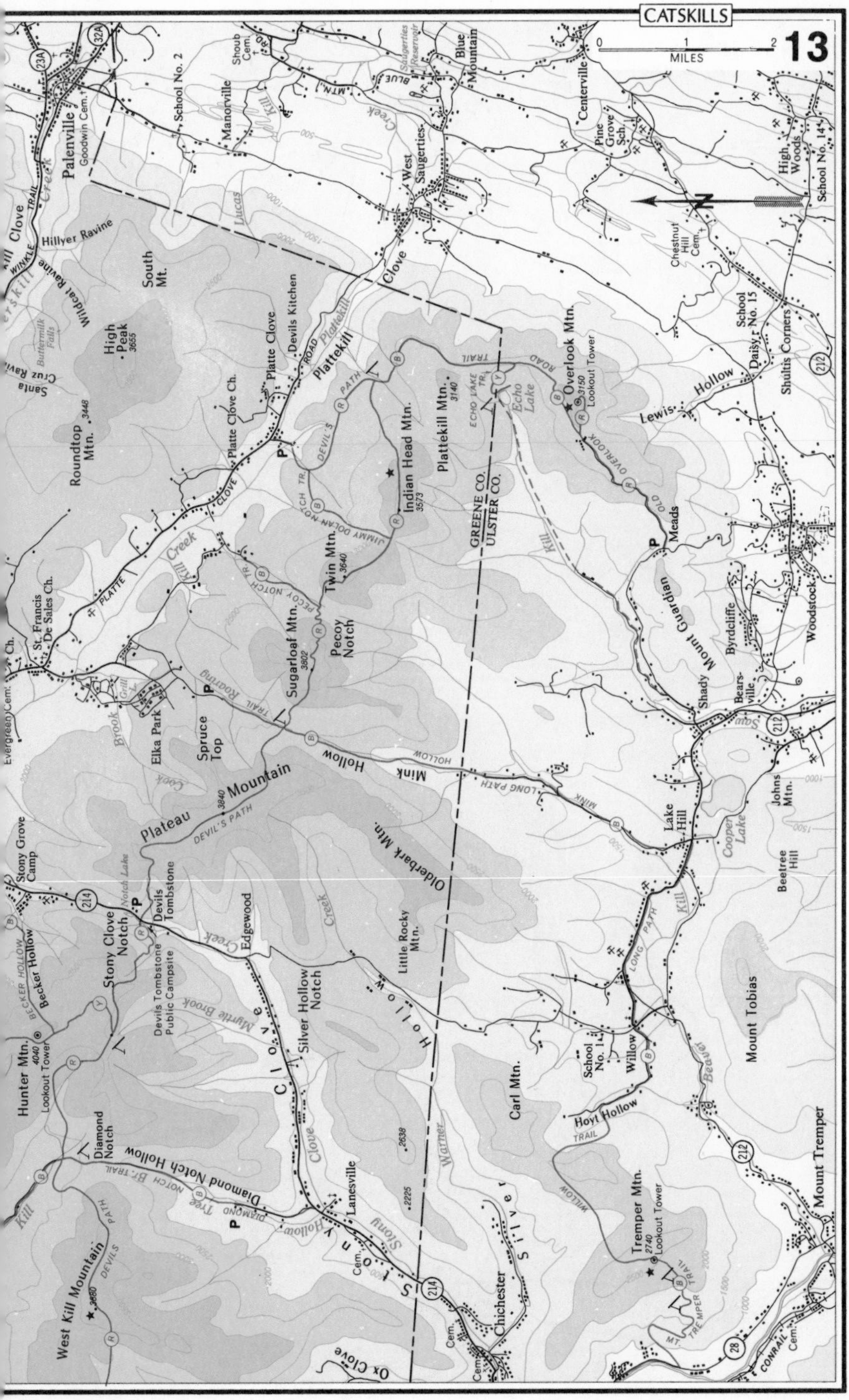
0 1 2 MILES
Palenville
Goodwin Cem.
School No. 2
Manorville
Shoub Cem.
Saugerties Reservoir
Blue Mountain
West Saugerties
Centerville
Pine Grove Sch.
High Woods
School No. 14
Chestnut Hill Cem.
School No. 15
Daisy
Shultis Corners
Lewis Hollow
Overlook Mtn.
3150
Lookout Tower
Echo Lake
Meads
Woodstock
Byrdcliffe
Bearsville
Shady
Mount Guardian
Lake Hill
Cooper Lake
Johns Mtn.
Beetree Hill
Mount Tobias
Willow
School No. 14
Hoyt Hollow
Carl Mtn.
Mount Tremper
Tremper Mtn.
2740
Lookout Tower
CONRAIL
GREENE CO.
ULSTER CO.
Plattekill Mtn.
3140
Indian Head Mtn.
3573
Twin Mtn.
3640
Sugarloaf Mtn.
3802
Pecoy Notch
Mink Hollow
Olderbark Mtn.
Little Rocky Mtn.
Plateau Mountain
3840
Devils Tombstone
Notch Lake
Stony Clove Notch
Devils Tombstone Public Campsite
Edgewood
Silver Hollow Notch
Hunter Mtn.
4040
Lookout Tower
Diamond Notch
Diamond Notch Hollow
Lanesville
Stony Clove
West Kill Mountain
3880
Chichester
Ox Clove
Becker Hollow
Stony Grove Camp
Spruce Top
Elka Park
Evergreen Cem.
St. Francis De Sales Ch.
Roundtop Mtn.
3448
High Peak
3655
South Mt.
Platte Clove
Platte Clove Ch.
Devils Kitchen
Plattekill Clove
Hillyer Ravine
Wildcat Ravine
Santa Cruz Ravine
Buttermilk Falls
Kaaterskill Clove

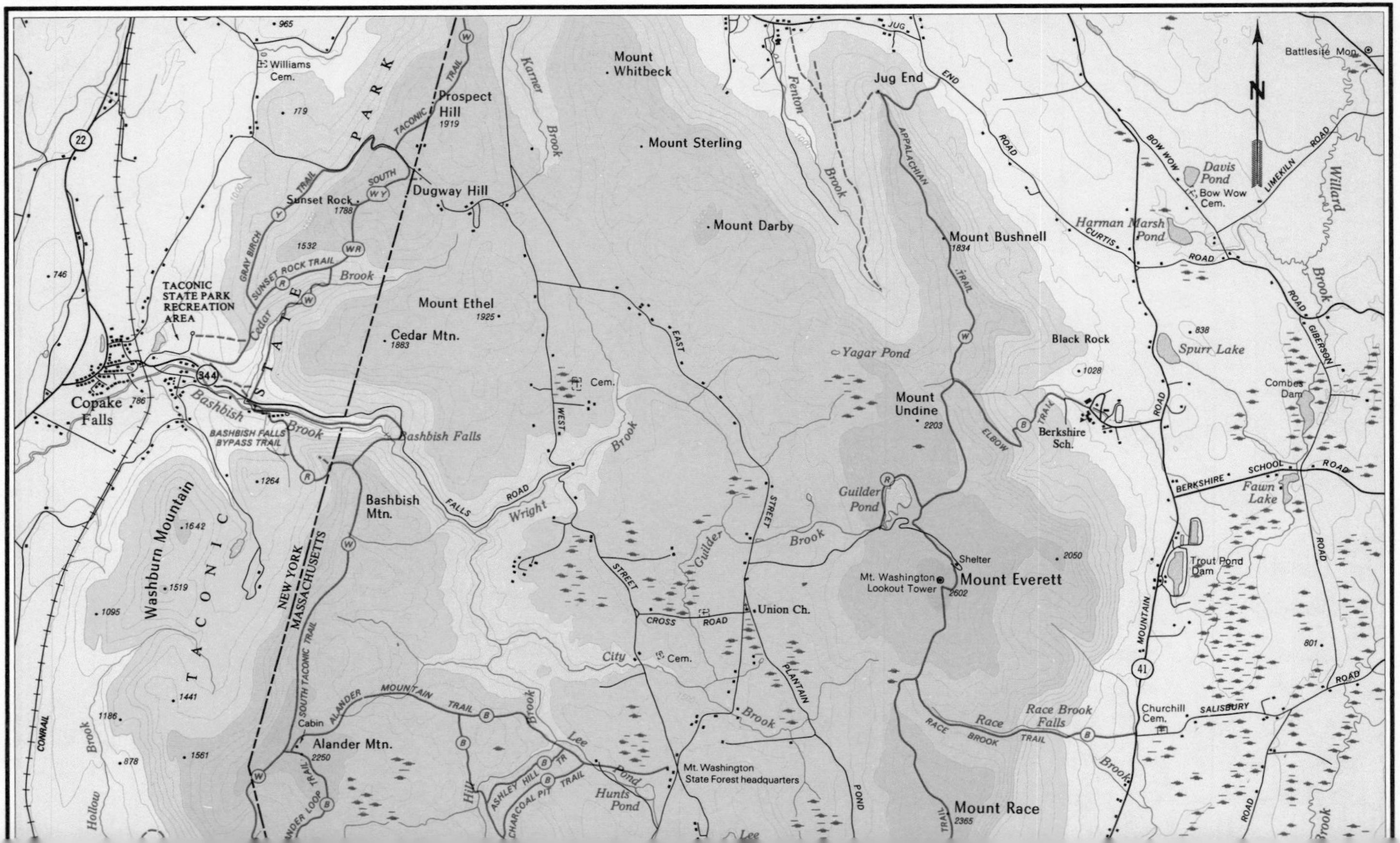

Mount Whitbeck
Mount Sterling
Mount Darby
Jug End
Mount Bushnell
1834
Black Rock
1028
Berkshire Sch.
Mount Undine
2203
Yagar Pond
Guilder Pond
Mount Everett
2602
2050
Shelter
Mt. Washington Lookout Tower
Mount Race
2365
Race Brook Falls
Prospect Hill
1919
Dugway Hill
Sunset Rock
1788
Mount Ethel
1925
Cedar Mtn.
1883
Bashbish Falls
Bashbish Mtn.
Alander Mtn.
2250
Cabin
Washburn Mountain
TACONIC
STATE PARK
TACONIC STATE PARK RECREATION AREA
Copake Falls
Williams Cem.
NEW YORK
MASSACHUSETTS
SOUTH TACONIC TRAIL
APPALACHIAN TRAIL
BASHBISH FALLS BYPASS TRAIL
SUNSET ROCK TRAIL
GRAY BIRCH TRAIL
ALANDER MOUNTAIN TRAIL
ASHLEY HILL TR
CHARCOAL PIT TRAIL
RACE BROOK TRAIL
ELBOW TRAIL
Union Ch.
Cem.
Mt. Washington State Forest headquarters
Hunts Pond
EAST STREET
WEST STREET
CROSS ROAD
PLANTAIN POND
FALLS ROAD
Karner Brook
Fenton Brook
Wright Brook
Guilder Brook
Lee Pond Brook
City Brook
Cedar Brook
Bashbish Brook
Race Brook
Willard Brook
Hollow Brook
JUG END ROAD
BOW WOW ROAD
LIMEKILN ROAD
CURTIS ROAD
GIBERSON ROAD
BERKSHIRE SCHOOL ROAD
MOUNTAIN ROAD
SALISBURY ROAD
Davis Pond
Bow Wow Cem.
Harman Marsh Pond
Spurr Lake
Combes Dam
Fawn Lake
Trout Pond Dam
Churchill Cem.
Battlesite Mon.
N
22
344
41
CONRAIL
965
179
1532
746
786
1264
1642
1519
1095
1441
1186
878
1561
838
801

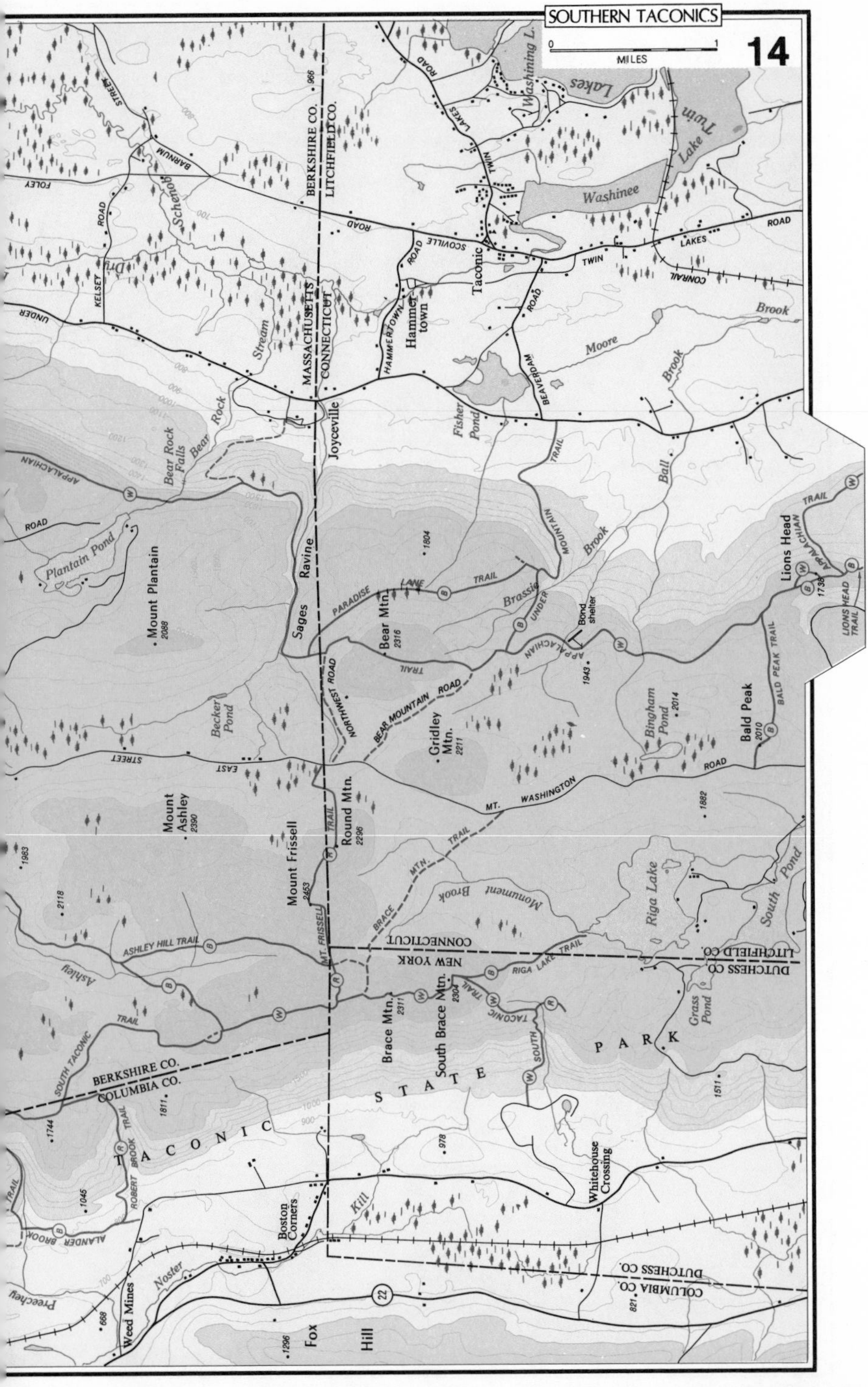

0
1
MILES
Twin Lakes
Washining L.
Lake Washinee
Twin Lakes Road
Conrail
Taconic
Hammertown
Hammertown Road
Scoville Road
Beaverdam Road
Moore Brook
Fisher Pond
Joyceville
Massachusetts
Connecticut
Berkshire Co.
Litchfield Co.
Barnum Street
Foley Road
Kelsey Road
Under Mountain Road
Schenob Brook
Stream
Bear Rock
Bear Rock Falls
Appalachian Trail
Road
Plantain Pond
Mount Plantain 2088
Sages Ravine
Paradise Lane Trail
Bear Mtn. 2316
Brassie Brook
Under Mountain Trail
Bond shelter
1943
Ball Brook
Lions Head 1738
Lions Head Trail
Bald Peak Trail
Bald Peak 2010
Bingham Pond 2014
Northwest Road
Bear Mountain Road
Gridley Mtn. 2211
Becker Pond
East Street
Mt. Washington Road
1882
Mount Ashley 2390
Mount Frissell 2453
Round Mtn. 2296
Mt. Frissell Trail
Brace Mtn. Trail
Monument Brook
Riga Lake
South Pond
1983
2118
Ashley Hill Trail
Ashley Hill Brook
Connecticut
New York
Litchfield Co.
Dutchess Co.
Riga Lake Trail
Brace Mtn. 2311
South Brace Mtn. 2304
Taconic Trail
South Taconic Trail
Grass Pond
Berkshire Co.
Columbia Co.
Taconic State Park
1811
1744
1511
Robert Brook Trail
978
Whitehouse Crossing
1045
Alander Brook Trail
Fox Kill
Boston Corners
Weed Mines
Noster Kill
Preechey
668
22
Dutchess Co.
Columbia Co.
821
1296
Fox Hill

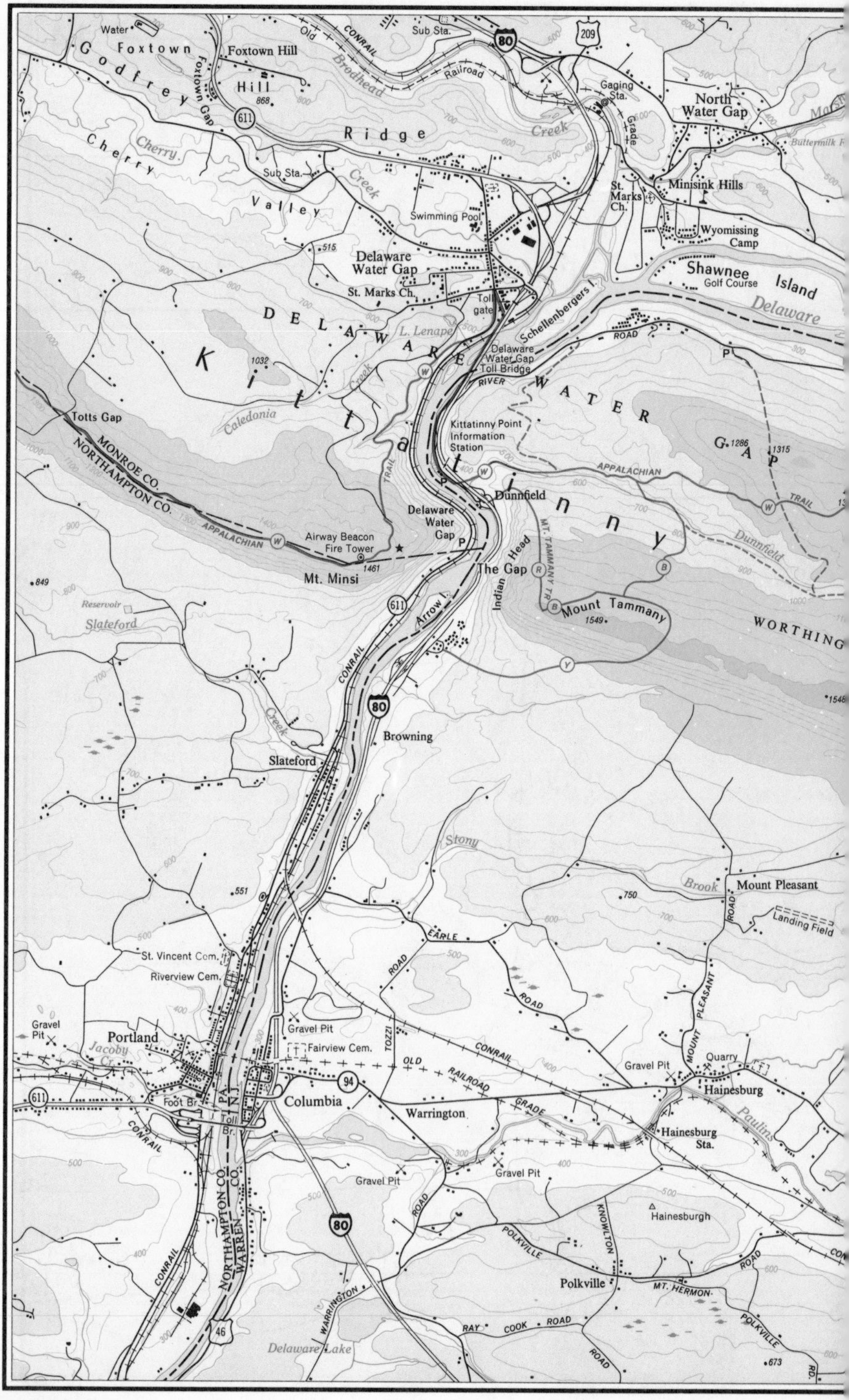

Water
Foxtown
Godfrey
Foxtown Hill
Hill
868
Foxtown Gap
611
Ridge
Cherry
Cherry
Valley
Sub Sta.
Creek
Old
CONRAIL
Brodhead
Railroad
Sub Sta.
80
209
Gaging Sta.
Grade
Creek
North Water Gap
Buttermilk F
St. Marks Ch.
Minisink Hills
Wyomissing Camp
Shawnee Island
Golf Course
Delaware
Swimming Pool
515
Delaware Water Gap
St. Marks Ch.
Toll gate
Schellenbergers I.
ROAD
DELAWARE WATER GAP
L. Lenape
Kittatinny
1032
Delaware Water Gap Toll Bridge
RIVER
Caledonia
Creek
Totts Gap
MONROE CO.
NORTHAMPTON CO.
Kittatinny Point Information Station
1286
1315
APPALACHIAN
TRAIL
Dunnfield
Delaware Water Gap
APPALACHIAN
Airway Beacon
Fire Tower
1461
Mt. Minsi
The Gap
Indian Head
MT. TAMMANY TR.
Dunnfield
Mount Tammany
1549
WORTHING
849
Reservoir
Slateford
611
Arrow I.
CONRAIL
80
1548
Creek
Browning
Slateford
Stony
Brook
Mount Pleasant
750
551
ROAD
Landing Field
EARLE
ROAD
St. Vincent Cem.
Riverview Cem.
ROAD
ROAD
PLEASANT
MOUNT
Gravel Pit
Portland
Jacoby Cr.
Gravel Pit
Fairview Cem.
TOZZI
OLD RAILROAD
CONRAIL
Gravel Pit
Quarry
94
Hainesburg
611
Foot Br.
PA.
N.J.
Toll Br.
Columbia
Warrington
GRADE
Hainesburg Sta.
Paulins
CONRAIL
Gravel Pit
Gravel Pit
NORTHAMPTON CO.
WARREN CO.
ROAD
KNOWLTON
Hainesburgh
80
CONRAIL
POLKVILLE
ROAD
Polkville
MT. HERMON
WARRINGTON
RAY
COOK
ROAD
ROAD
POLKVILLE
46
Delaware Lake
673
RD.

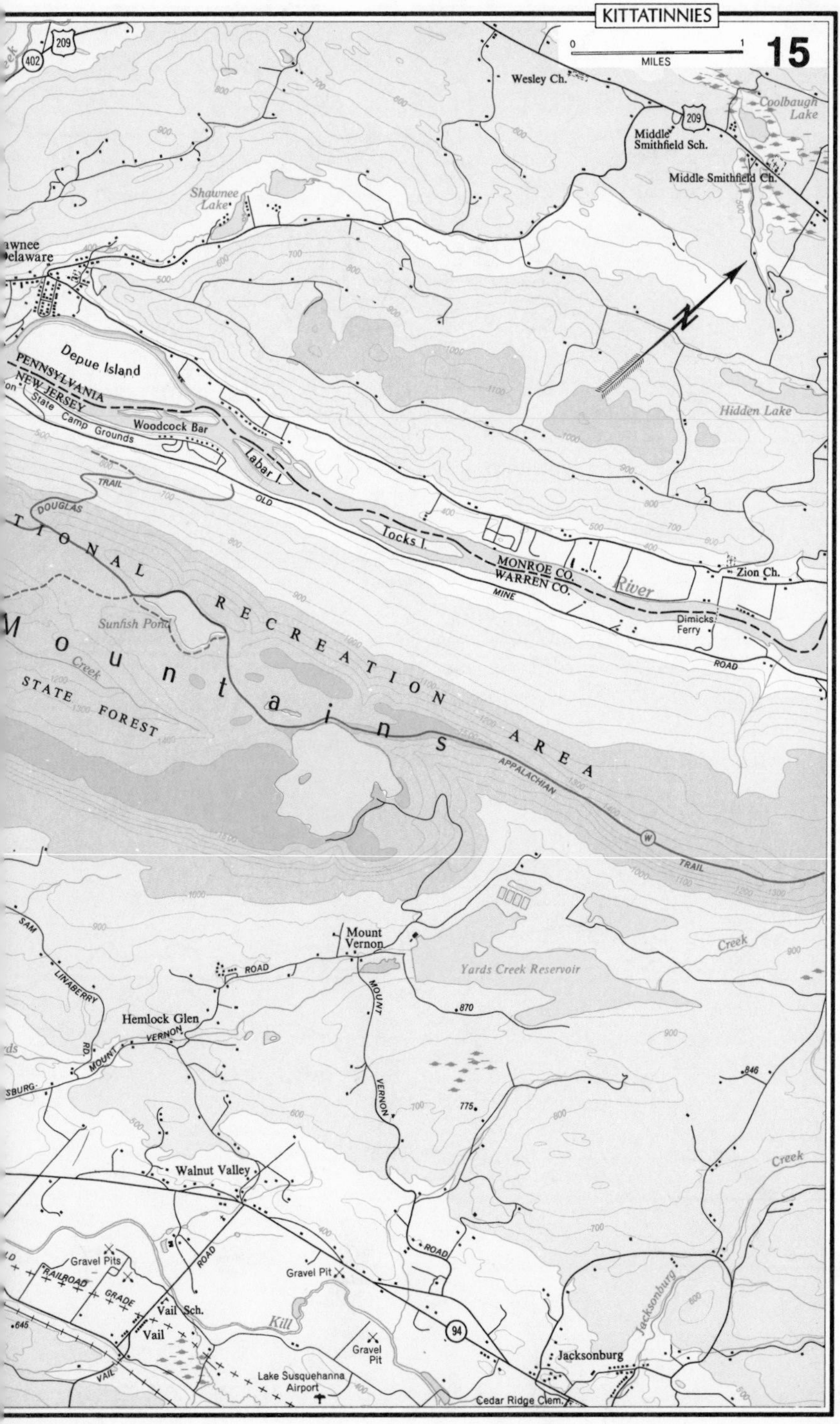
0
1
MILES
209
402
Wesley Ch.
Coolbaugh Lake
Middle Smithfield Sch.
Middle Smithfield Ch.
Shawnee Lake
Delaware
Depue Island
PENNSYLVANIA
NEW JERSEY
State Camp Grounds
Woodcock Bar
Labar I.
Hidden Lake
TRAIL
DOUGLAS
OLD
Tocks I.
MONROE CO.
WARREN CO.
River
Zion Ch.
MINE
Dimicks Ferry
ROAD
NATIONAL RECREATION AREA
Mountains
Sunfish Pond
Creek
STATE FOREST
APPALACHIAN
TRAIL
Mount Vernon
Creek
Yards Creek Reservoir
SAM
LINABERRY
RD.
ROAD
MOUNT
VERNON
870
Hemlock Glen
846
775
Walnut Valley
Creek
ROAD
Gravel Pits
RAILROAD
GRADE
Gravel Pit
Jacksonburg
Vail Sch.
Vail
Kill
645
94
Gravel Pit
Jacksonburg
Lake Susquehanna Airport
Cedar Ridge Cem.
VAIL

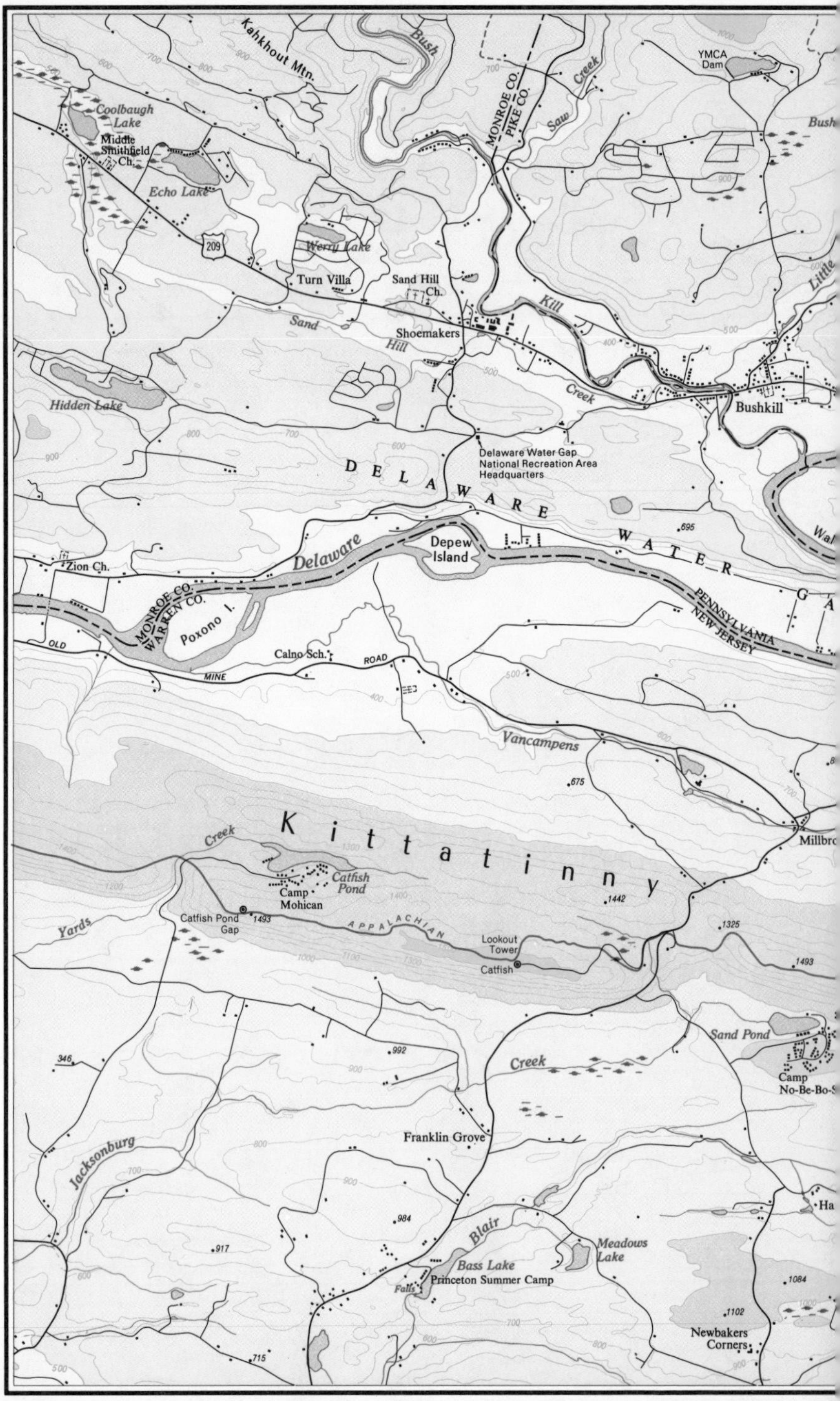

Kahkhout Mtn.
Bush
Coolbaugh Lake
Middle Smithfield Ch.
Echo Lake
209
Werry Lake
Turn Villa
Sand Hill Ch.
Sand Hill
Shoemakers
Hidden Lake
MONROE CO.
PIKE CO.
Saw Creek
YMCA Dam
Kill
Creek
Bushkill
Delaware Water Gap National Recreation Area Headquarters
DELAWARE WATER GAP
Depew Island
Delaware
Zion Ch.
MONROE CO.
WARREN CO.
Poxono I.
OLD MINE ROAD
Calno Sch.
PENNSYLVANIA
NEW JERSEY
Vancampens
Kittatinny
Creek
Catfish Pond
Camp Mohican
Catfish Pond Gap
APPALACHIAN
Lookout Tower
Catfish
Yards
Sand Pond
Creek
Franklin Grove
Jacksonburg
Blair
Meadows Lake
Bass Lake
Princeton Summer Camp
Falls
Newbakers Corners

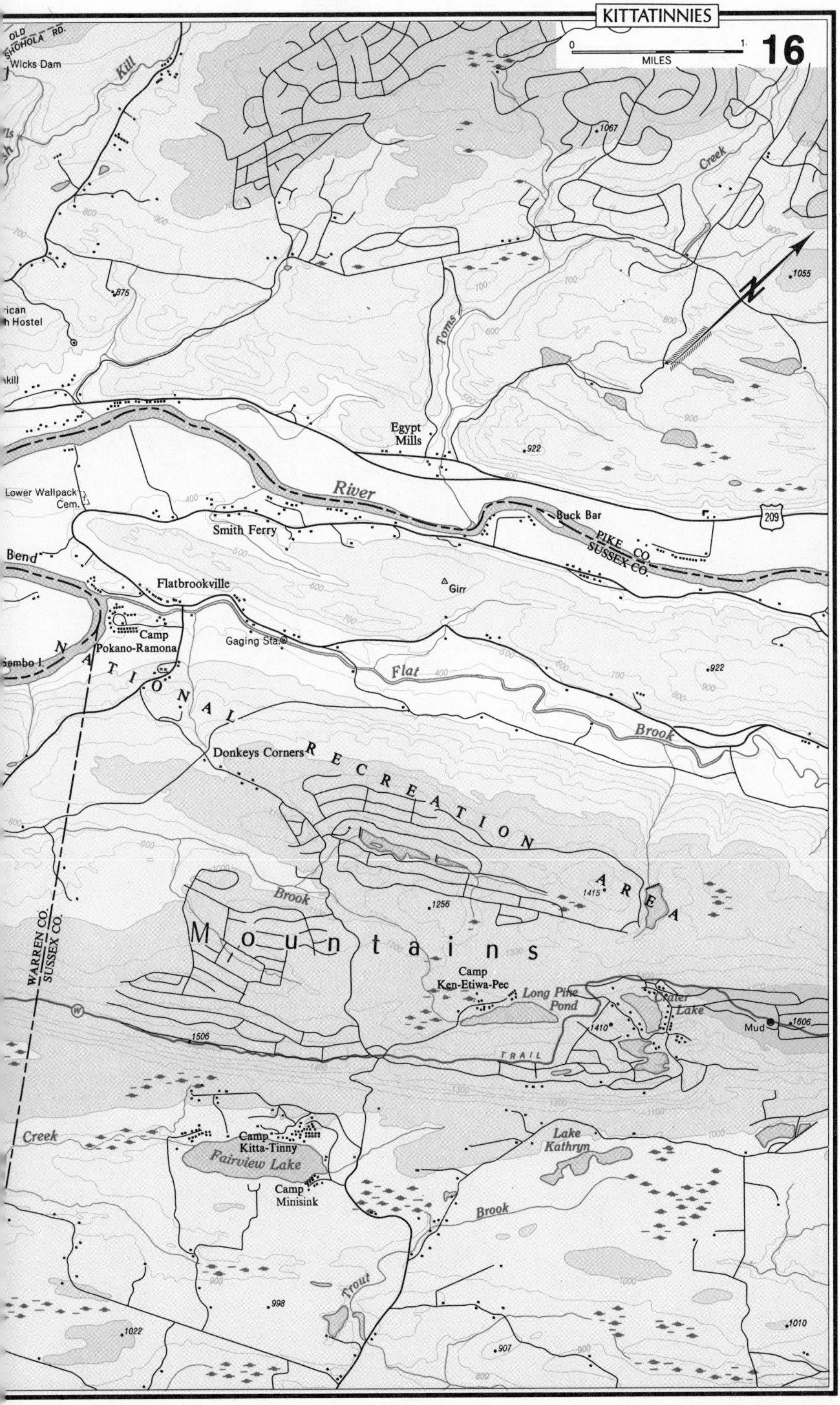

0 MILES 1
OLD SHOHOLA RD.
Wicks Dam
Kill
Creek
Toms
Egypt Mills
River
Lower Wallpack Cem.
Smith Ferry
Buck Bar
209
PIKE CO.
SUSSEX CO.
Bend
Flatbrookville
Girr
Camp Pokano-Ramona
Gaging Sta.
Flat
Brook
NATIONAL RECREATION AREA
Donkeys Corners
Brook
Mountains
WARREN CO.
SUSSEX CO.
Camp Ken-Etiwa-Pec
Long Pine Pond
Crater Lake
Mud
TRAIL
Camp Kitta-Tinny
Fairview Lake
Camp Minisink
Creek
Lake Kathryn
Brook
Trout
1067
1055
875
922
922
1415
1256
1410
1606
1506
998
1022
907
1010

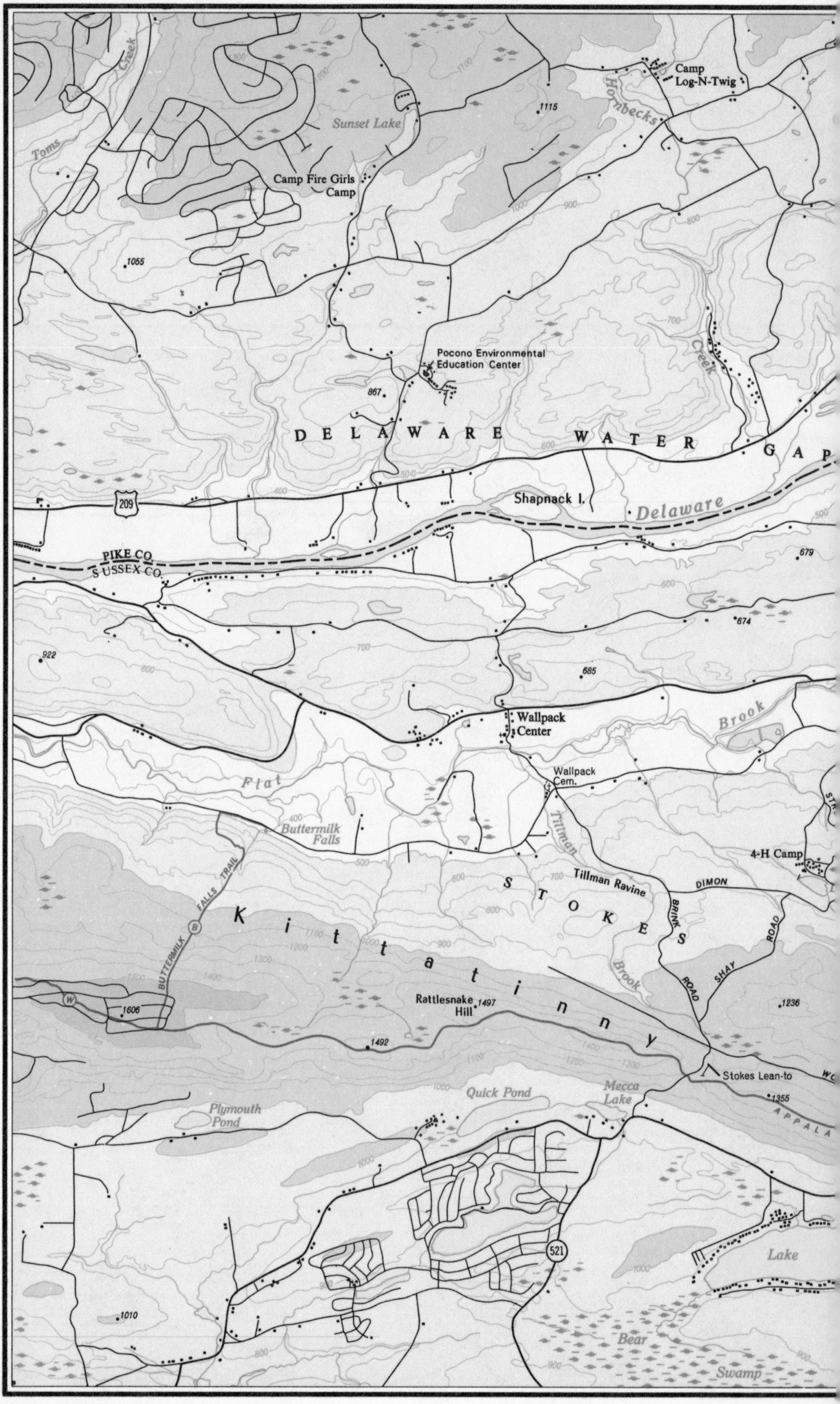

Toms Creek
Sunset Lake
Camp Fire Girls Camp
1115
Camp Log-N-Twig
Hornbecks Creek
1055
Pocono Environmental Education Center
867
DELAWARE WATER GAP
209
Shapnack I.
Delaware
PIKE CO.
SUSSEX CO.
679
674
922
685
Wallpack Center
Brook
Flat
Wallpack Cem.
Tillman
Buttermilk Falls
BUTTERMILK FALLS TRAIL
B
4-H Camp
Tillman Ravine
DIMON
BRINK ROAD
SHAY ROAD
STOKES
Kittatinny
Brook
W
1606
Rattlesnake Hill 1497
1236
1492
Stokes Lean-to
Quick Pond
Mecca Lake
1355
APPALA
Plymouth Pond
521
Lake
1010
Bear Swamp

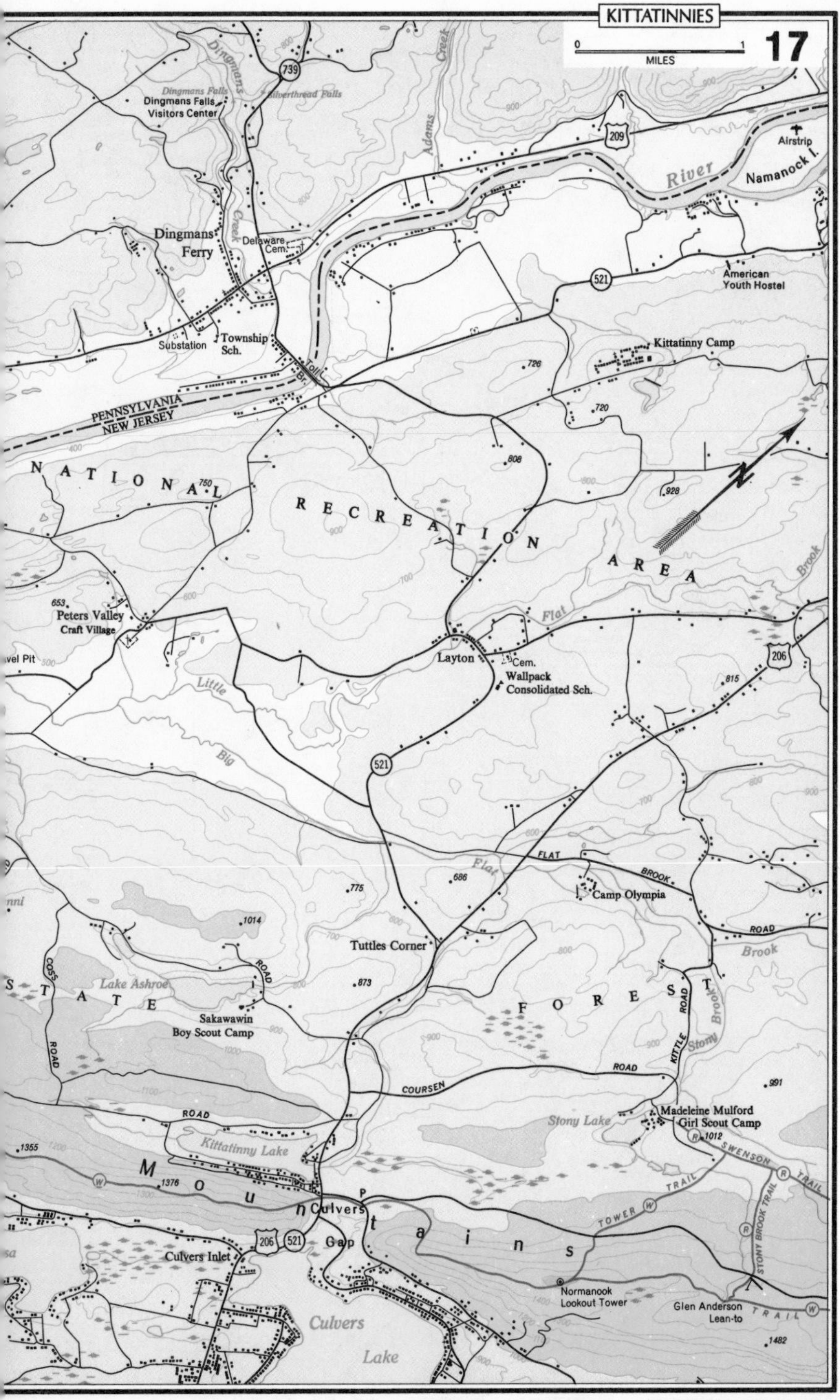
0
1
MILES
Dingmans Falls
Dingmans Falls
Visitors Center
Silverthread Falls
Dingmans Creek
Adams Creek
739
209
Airstrip
Namanock I.
River
Dingmans
Ferry
Delaware
Cem.
521
American
Youth Hostel
Substation
Township
Sch.
Toll
Br.
Kittatinny Camp
726
720
PENNSYLVANIA
NEW JERSEY
NATIONAL
RECREATION
AREA
808
750
928
653
Peters Valley
Craft Village
Flat
Brook
Layton
Cem.
Wallpack
Consolidated Sch.
206
815
Little
Big
FLAT
BROOK
ROAD
686
775
Camp Olympia
1014
Tuttles Corner
873
Brook
Lake Ashroe
COSS
ROAD
STATE
FOREST
KITTLE
ROAD
Stony Brook
Sakawawin
Boy Scout Camp
COURSEN
ROAD
991
Madeleine Mulford
Girl Scout Camp
Stony Lake
1012
SWENSON
TRAIL
Kittatinny Lake
1355
1376
Mountains
Culvers
Gap
TOWER
STONY BROOK TRAIL
Culvers Inlet
Normanook
Lookout Tower
Glen Anderson
Lean-to
Culvers
Lake
1482

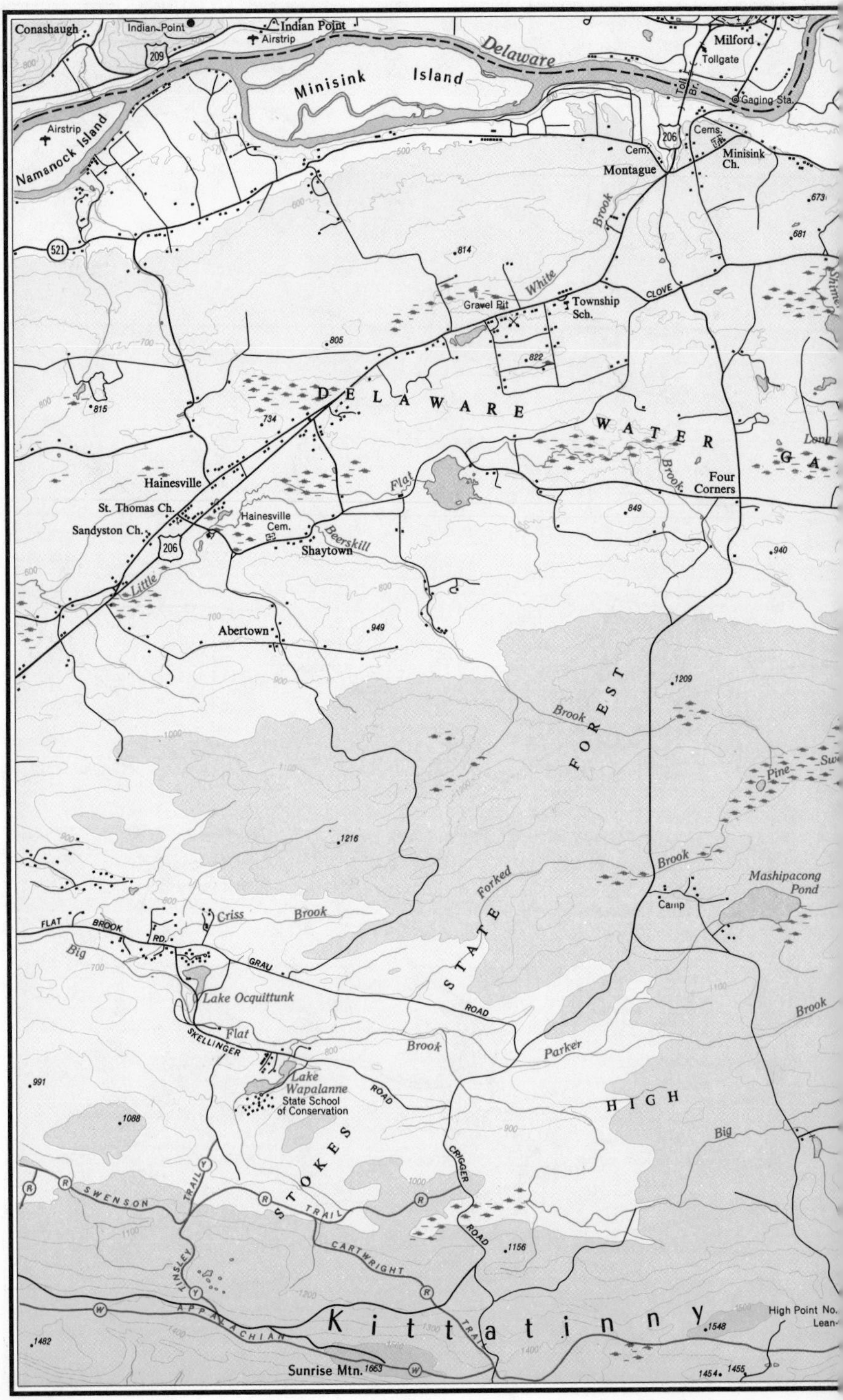

Conashaugh
Indian Point
Indian Point
Airstrip
209
Delaware
Minisink
Island
Milford
Tollgate
Toll Br.
Gaging Sta.
Airstrip
Namanock Island
206
Cems.
Cem.
Minisink Ch.
Montague
Brook
521
White
Gravel Pit
Township Sch.
CLOVE
D E L A W A R E
W A T E R
G A
Hainesville
St. Thomas Ch.
Sandyston Ch.
Hainesville Cem.
Beerskill
Shaytown
Flat
Brook
Four Corners
Little
Abertown
Brook
F O R E S T
Pine
Brook
Forked
Mashipacong Pond
Camp
FLAT BROOK RD.
Criss
Brook
Big
GRAU
S T A T E
Lake Ocquittunk
ROAD
SKELLINGER
Flat
Brook
Parker
Brook
Lake Wapalanne
State School of Conservation
ROAD
H I G H
S T O K E S
CRIGGER
ROAD
Big
SWENSON
TRAIL
TRAIL
CARTWRIGHT
TINSLEY
APPALACHIAN
TRAIL
Kittatinny
High Point No.
Lean-
Sunrise Mtn.

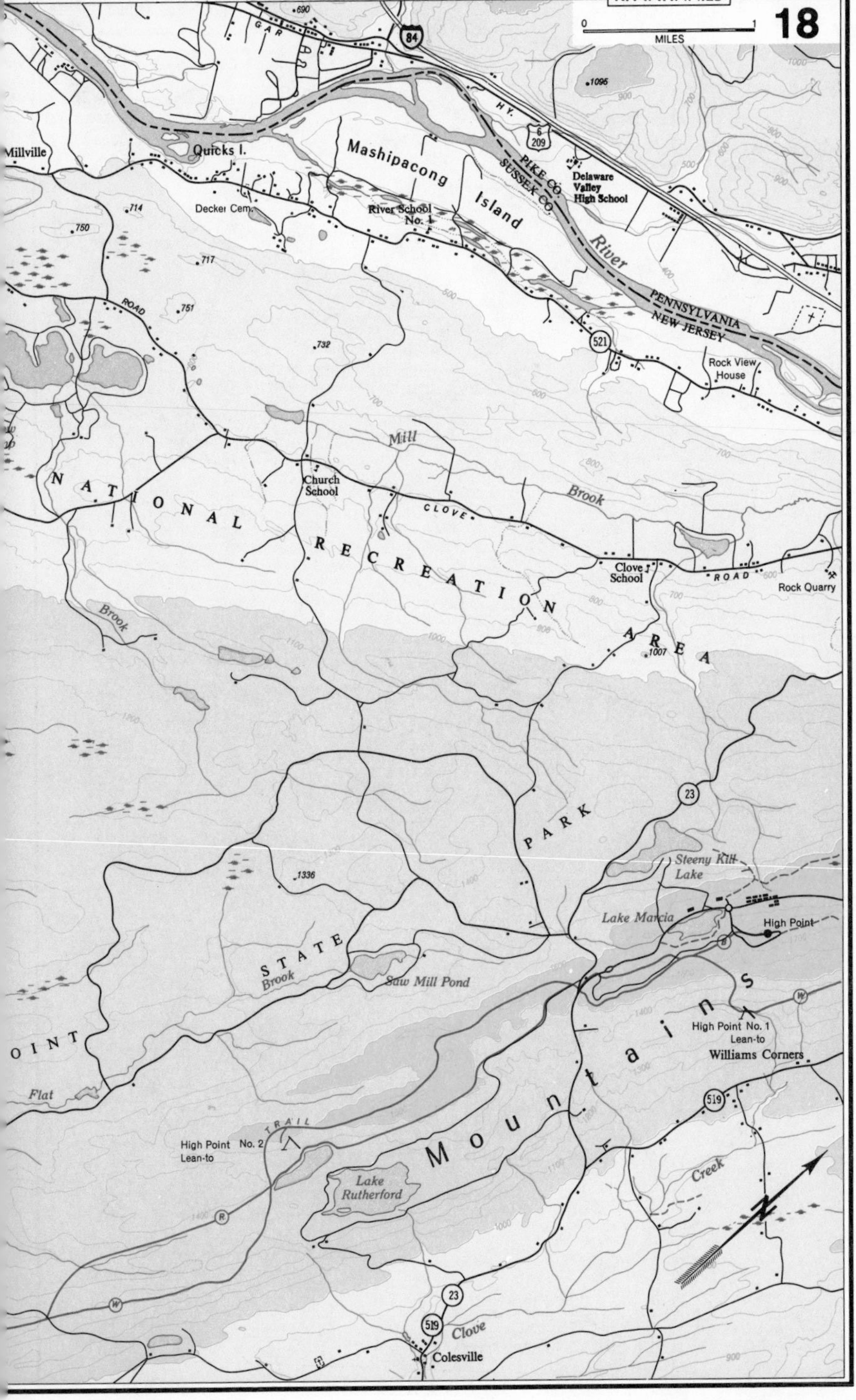
0
1
MILES
84
GAR
HY.
6
209
PIKE CO.
SUSSEX CO.
Millville
Quicks I.
Mashipacong
Island
Delaware
Valley
High School
River
Decker Cem.
River School
No. 1
PENNSYLVANIA
NEW JERSEY
521
ROAD
Rock View
House
Mill
Brook
Church
School
CLOVE
ROAD
Clove
School
Rock Quarry
N A T I O N A L
R E C R E A T I O N
A R E A
Brook
P A R K
23
Steeny Kill
Lake
Lake Marcia
High Point
S T A T E
Brook
Saw Mill Pond
High Point No. 1
Lean-to
Williams Corners
OINT
Flat
TRAIL
High Point No. 2
Lean-to
Mountains
Lake
Rutherford
519
Creek
23
519
Clove
Colesville
.690
.1095
.714
.750
.717
.751
.732
.1007
.1336

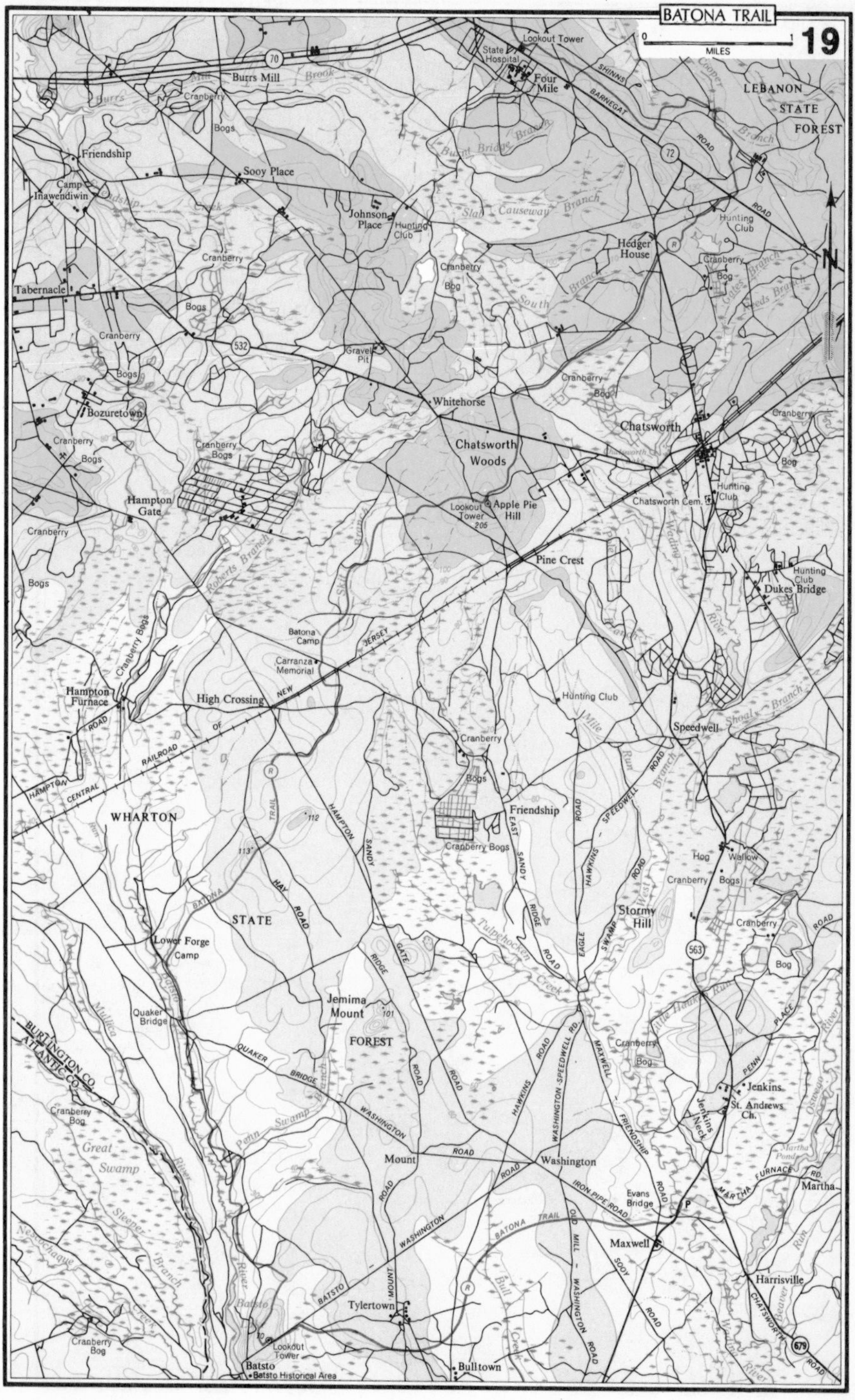
0
1
MILES
Lookout Tower
State Hospital
Four Mile
70
Burrs Mill
Burrs Mill Brook
Cranberry
Bogs
SHINNS
BARNEGAT
ROAD
72
LEBANON STATE FOREST
Cooper Branch
Friendship
Sooy Place
Camp Inawendiwin
Friendship Creek
Burnt Bridge Branch
Slab Causeway Branch
Johnson Place
Hunting Club
Hedger House
Cranberry Bog
Gates Branch
Reeds Branch
Tabernacle
South Branch
532
Gravel Pit
Whitehorse
Bozuretown
Chatsworth
Chatsworth Woods
Chatsworth Lake
Chatsworth Cem.
Hampton Gate
Lookout Tower
205
Apple Pie Hill
Roberts Branch
Skit Branch
Pine Crest
Wading River
Dukes Bridge
Batona Camp
Carranza Memorial
JERSEY
NEW
OF
RAILROAD
CENTRAL
HAMPTON
Cranberry Bogs
Hampton Furnace
ROAD
High Crossing
Hunting Club
Mile Run
Speedwell
Shoal Branch
TRAIL
112
113
WHARTON
STATE
FOREST
HAMPTON
SANDY
HAY
ROAD
Friendship
EAST
SANDY
RIDGE
ROAD
HAWKINS
SPEEDWELL
Hog Wallow
Stormy Hill
West Branch
SWAMP
EAGLE
563
Tulpehocken Creek
BATONA
Lower Forge Camp
Batsto River
Mullica
Quaker Bridge
Jemima Mount
101
GATE
RIDGE
QUAKER
BRIDGE
ROAD
BURLINGTON CO.
ATLANTIC CO.
WASHINGTON-SPEEDWELL RD.
MAXWELL
FRIENDSHIP
Little Hauken Run
PENN
PLACE
Jenkins
Jenkins Neck
St. Andrews Ch.
Oswego River
Penn Swamp Branch
WASHINGTON
Mount
Washington
IRON PIPE ROAD
Evans Bridge
Martha Pond
MARTHA FURNACE RD.
Martha
Great Swamp
Sleeper Branch
Nescochaque Creek
BATONA TRAIL
OLD MILL - WASHINGTON ROAD
SOOY
Maxwell
Bull Creek
Beaver Run
Harrisville
CHATSWORTH
679
BATSTO
Tylertown
Lookout Tower
Batsto
Batsto Historical Area
Bulltown

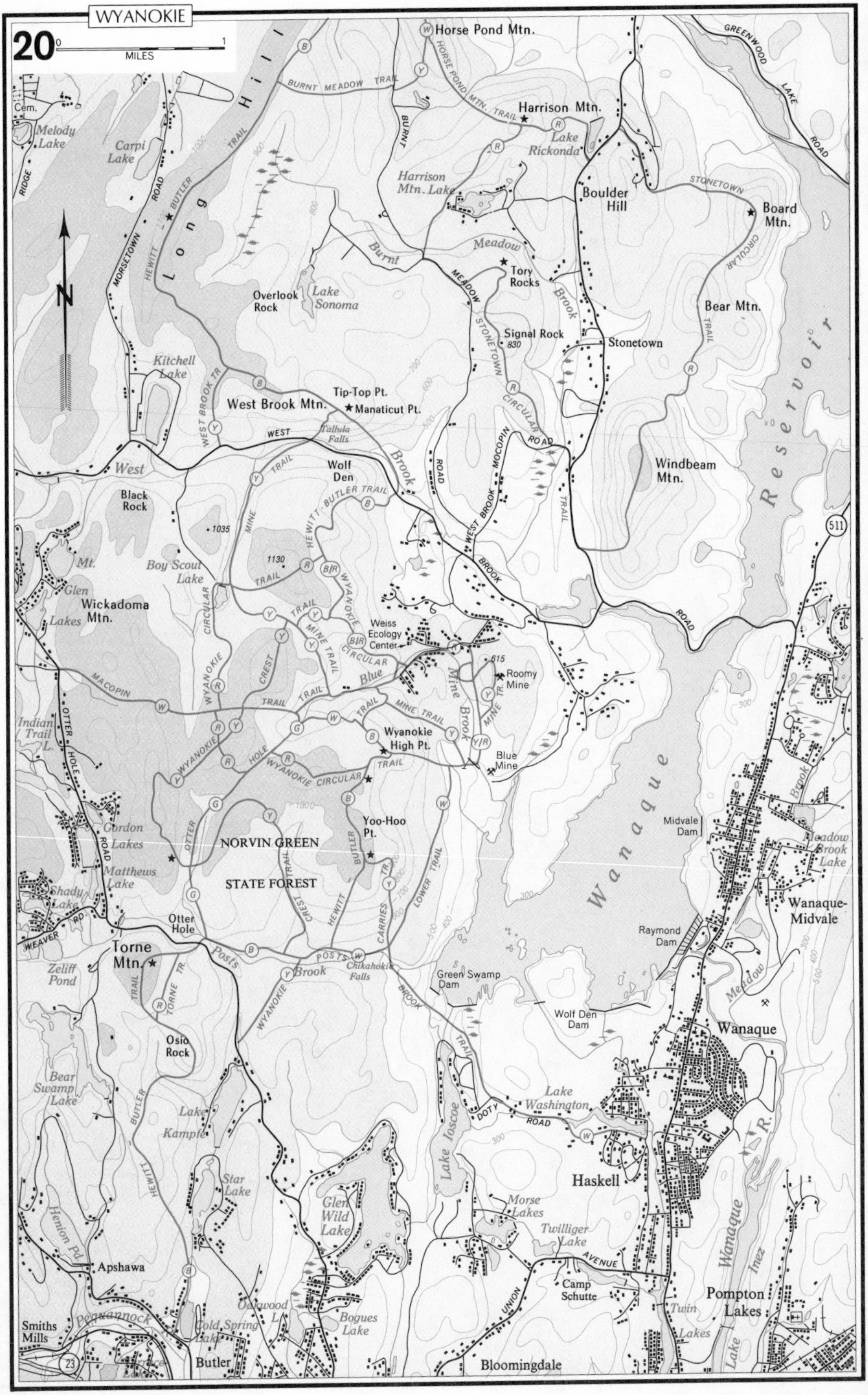
WYANOKIE
20
0
1
MILES
Horse Pond Mtn.
Harrison Mtn.
Lake Rickonda
Boulder Hill
Board Mtn.
Harrison Mtn. Lake
Burnt Meadow Trail
Horse Pond Mtn. Trail
Greenwood Lake Road
Stonetown Circular Trail
Tory Rocks
Meadow Brook
Burnt
Overlook Rock
Lake Sonoma
Signal Rock
830
Stonetown
Bear Mtn.
Melody Lake
Carpi Lake
Cem.
Ridge
Morsetown Road
Hewitt Butler
Long Hill Trail
Kitchell Lake
West Brook Tr
Tip-Top Pt.
West Brook Mtn.
Manaticut Pt.
Tallula Falls
West Brook Road
Wolf Den
Black Rock
Hewitt-Butler Trail
Mocopin
Stonetown Circular Road
Windbeam Mtn.
Reservoir
511
1035
1130
Mine Trail
Boy Scout Lake
Mt.
Glen Wickadoma Mtn.
Lakes
Wyanokie Circular
Crest Trail
Weiss Ecology Center
Macopin Trail
Blue Trail
615
Roomy Mine
Mine Brook
Indian Trail L.
Otter Hole Road
Wyanokie High Pt.
Blue Mine
Wanaque
Yoo-Hoo Pt.
Gordon Lakes
Matthews Lake
NORVIN GREEN
STATE FOREST
Lower Trail
Carries Tr.
Midvale Dam
Meadow Brook Lake
Wanaque-Midvale
Shady Lake
Weaver Rd.
Otter Hole
Torne Mtn.
Zeliff Pond
Posts Brook
Chikahoki Falls
Raymond Dam
Green Swamp Dam
Wolf Den Dam
Torne Tr.
Osio Rock
Bear Swamp Lake
Lake Kampfe
Lake Ioscoe
Lake Washington
Doty Road
Wanaque
Haskell
Star Lake
Glen Wild Lake
Morse Lakes
Twilliger Lake
Avenue
Union
Camp Schutte
Wanaque R.
Inez
Henion Pd.
Apshawa
Pequannock
Oakwood L.
Bogues Lake
Cold Spring Lake
Smiths Mills
23
Butler
Bloomingdale
Twin Lakes
Pompton Lakes
Lake

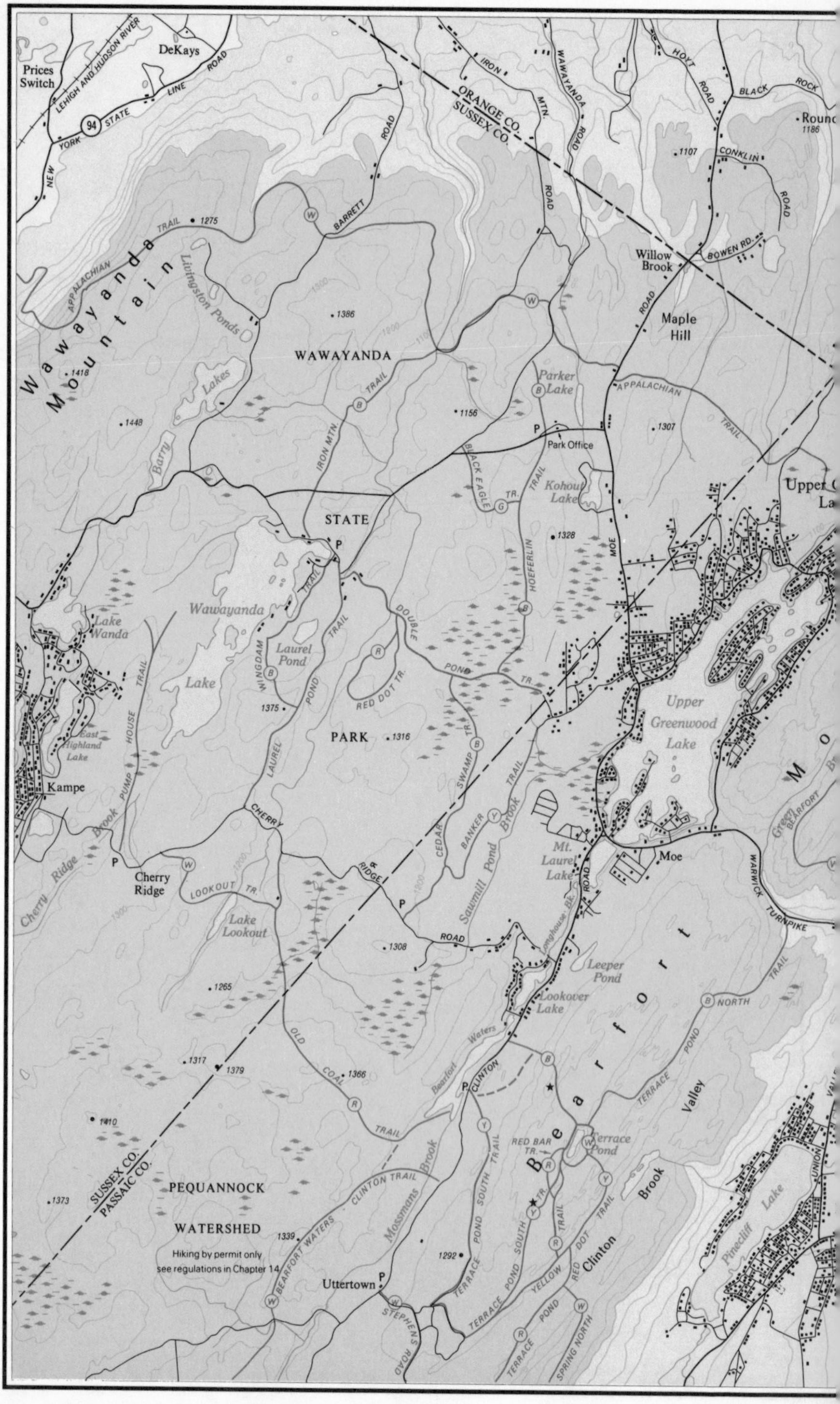

Prices Switch
LEHIGH AND HUDSON RIVER
DeKays
NEW YORK STATE LINE ROAD
94
IRON MTN. ROAD
ORANGE CO.
SUSSEX CO.
WAWAYANDA ROAD
HOYT ROAD
BLACK ROCK
Round
1186
1107
CONKLIN ROAD
BOWEN RD.
Willow Brook
ROAD
Maple Hill
BARRETT ROAD
APPALACHIAN TRAIL
1275
Wawayanda Mountain
Livingston Ponds
1386
WAWAYANDA
1418
1448
Lakes
Barry
IRON MTN. TRAIL
1156
Parker Lake
Park Office
APPALACHIAN TRAIL
1307
BLACK EAGLE TR.
HOEFERLIN TRAIL
Kohout Lake
Upper
STATE
1328
MOE
Lake Wanda
Wawayanda Lake
WINGDAM TRAIL
Laurel Pond
DOUBLE POND TR.
RED DOT TR.
East Highland Lake
Kampe
PUMP HOUSE TRAIL
1375
LAUREL POND TRAIL
PARK
1316
SWAMP TR.
Upper Greenwood Lake
Cherry Ridge Brook
CHERRY RIDGE ROAD
CEDAR
BANKER TR.
Sawmill Pond Brook
Mt. Laurel Lake
Moe
WARWICK TURNPIKE
BEARFORT
Cherry Ridge
LOOKOUT TR.
Lake Lookout
1308
Longhouse Bk.
Leeper Pond
1265
Lookover Lake
NORTH TERRACE POND TRAIL
Bearfort Mountain
Bearfort Waters
OLD COAL TRAIL
1317
1379
1366
CLINTON
Valley
1410
RED BAR TR.
Terrace Pond
SUSSEX CO.
PASSAIC CO.
PEQUANNOCK WATERSHED
Hiking by permit only
see regulations in Chapter 14
1373
CLINTON TRAIL
BEARFORT WATERS
Mossmans Brook
1339
TERRACE POND SOUTH TRAIL
1292
YELLOW
RED DOT TRAIL
Clinton Brook
Pinecliff Lake
UNION
Uttertown
STEPHENS ROAD
TERRACE POND
SPRING NORTH

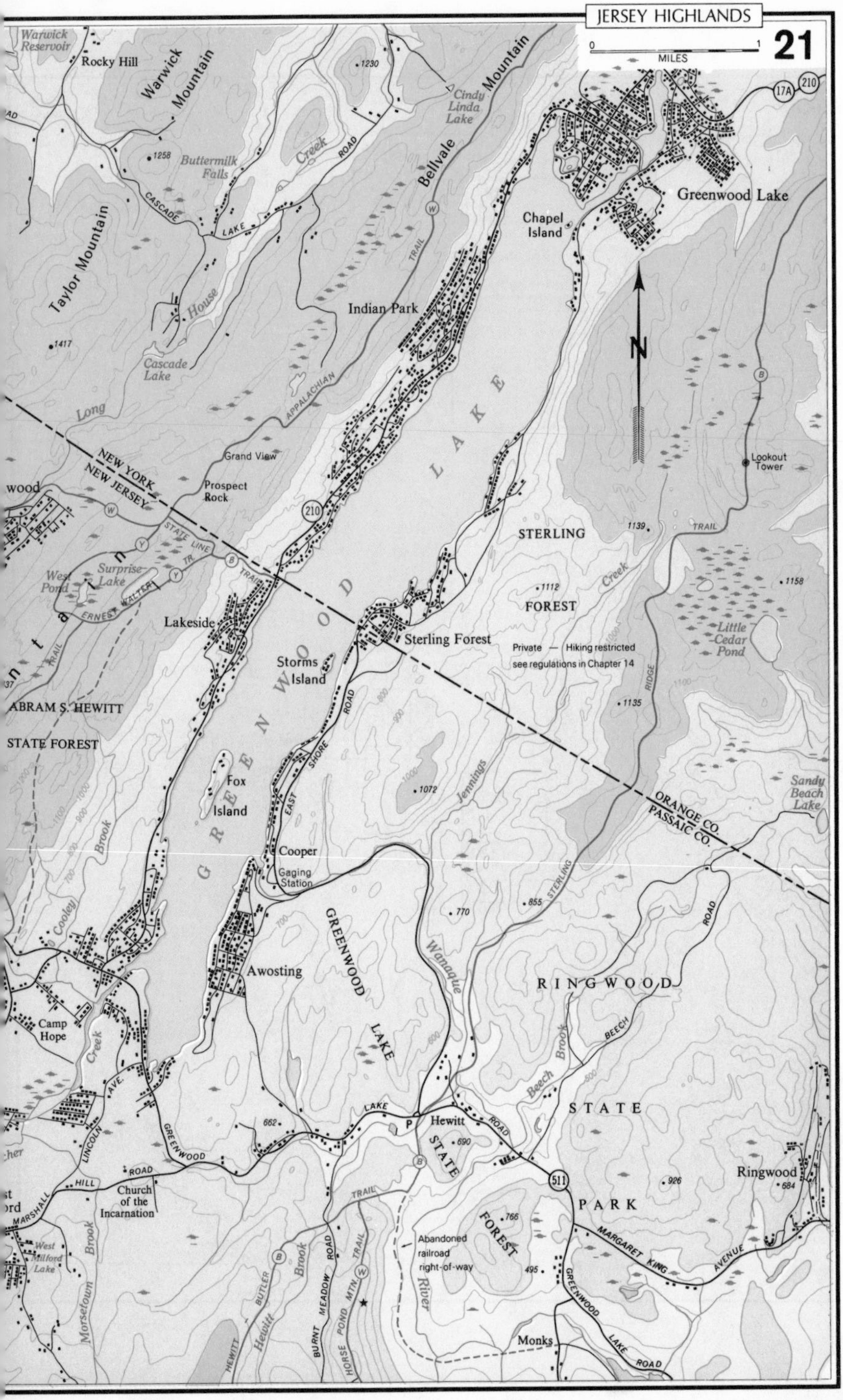
0
1
MILES
Warwick Reservoir
Rocky Hill
Warwick Mountain
1230
Cindy Linda Lake
Bellvale Mountain
17A
210
1258
Buttermilk Falls
Creek
ROAD
CASCADE
LAKE
Greenwood Lake
Chapel Island
Taylor Mountain
House
TRAIL
Indian Park
1417
Cascade Lake
N
APPALACHIAN
LAKE
Long
Grand View
NEW YORK
NEW JERSEY
Prospect Rock
Lookout Tower
210
STATE LINE
TR
1139
TRAIL
STERLING
Surprise Lake
West Pond
ERNEST WALTER
TRAIL
1112
FOREST
1158
Creek
Lakeside
Sterling Forest
Little Cedar Pond
Private — Hiking restricted
see regulations in Chapter 14
Storms Island
RIDGE
1135
ABRAM S. HEWITT
STATE FOREST
ROAD
GREENWOOD
EAST SHORE
Fox Island
1072
Jennings
Sandy Beach Lake
ORANGE CO.
PASSAIC CO.
Brook
Cooper
Gaging Station
GREENWOOD LAKE
STERLING
855
770
ROAD
Cooley
Awosting
Wanaque
RINGWOOD
Camp Hope
Creek
BEECH
Brook
Beech
AVE.
LINCOLN
LAKE
Hewitt
ROAD
STATE
662
690
STATE
GREENWOOD
ROAD
HILL
Church of the Incarnation
511
926
Ringwood
684
PARK
MARSHALL
TRAIL
766
FOREST
MARGARET KING
AVENUE
West Milford Lake
Brook
Abandoned railroad right-of-way
BUTLER
Brook
ROAD
MEADOW
BURNT
MTN.
TRAIL
POND
HORSE
River
495
GREENWOOD
Morsetown
Hewitt
HEWITT
Monks
LAKE
ROAD

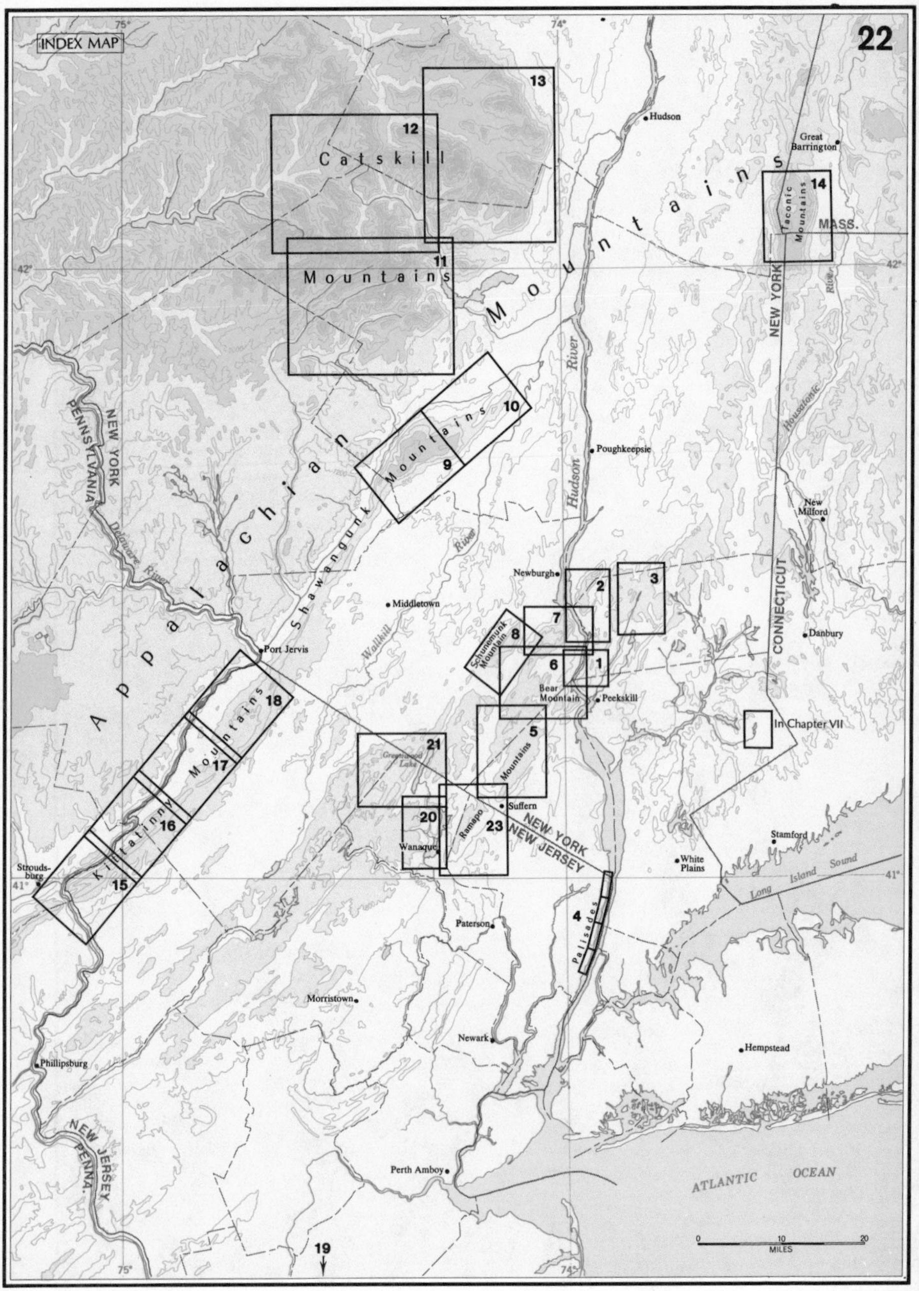

INDEX MAP
22
Catskill
Mountains
Appalachian
Mountains
Shawangunk
Mountains
Kittatinny
Mountains
Taconic Mountains
Ramapo Mountains
Schunemunk Mountain
Palisades
Hudson
Great Barrington
MASS.
NEW YORK
CONNECTICUT
PENNSYLVANIA
NEW YORK
NEW JERSEY
NEW JERSEY
PENNA.
Hudson River
Delaware River
Wallkill River
Housatonic River
Poughkeepsie
New Milford
Newburgh
Middletown
Danbury
Port Jervis
Bear Mountain
Peekskill
In Chapter VII
Greenwood Lake
Suffern
Wanaque
White Plains
Stamford
Long Island Sound
Stroudsburg
Paterson
Morristown
Newark
Hempstead
Phillipsburg
Perth Amboy
ATLANTIC OCEAN
MILES

23 Jersey Ramapos *(overleaf)*

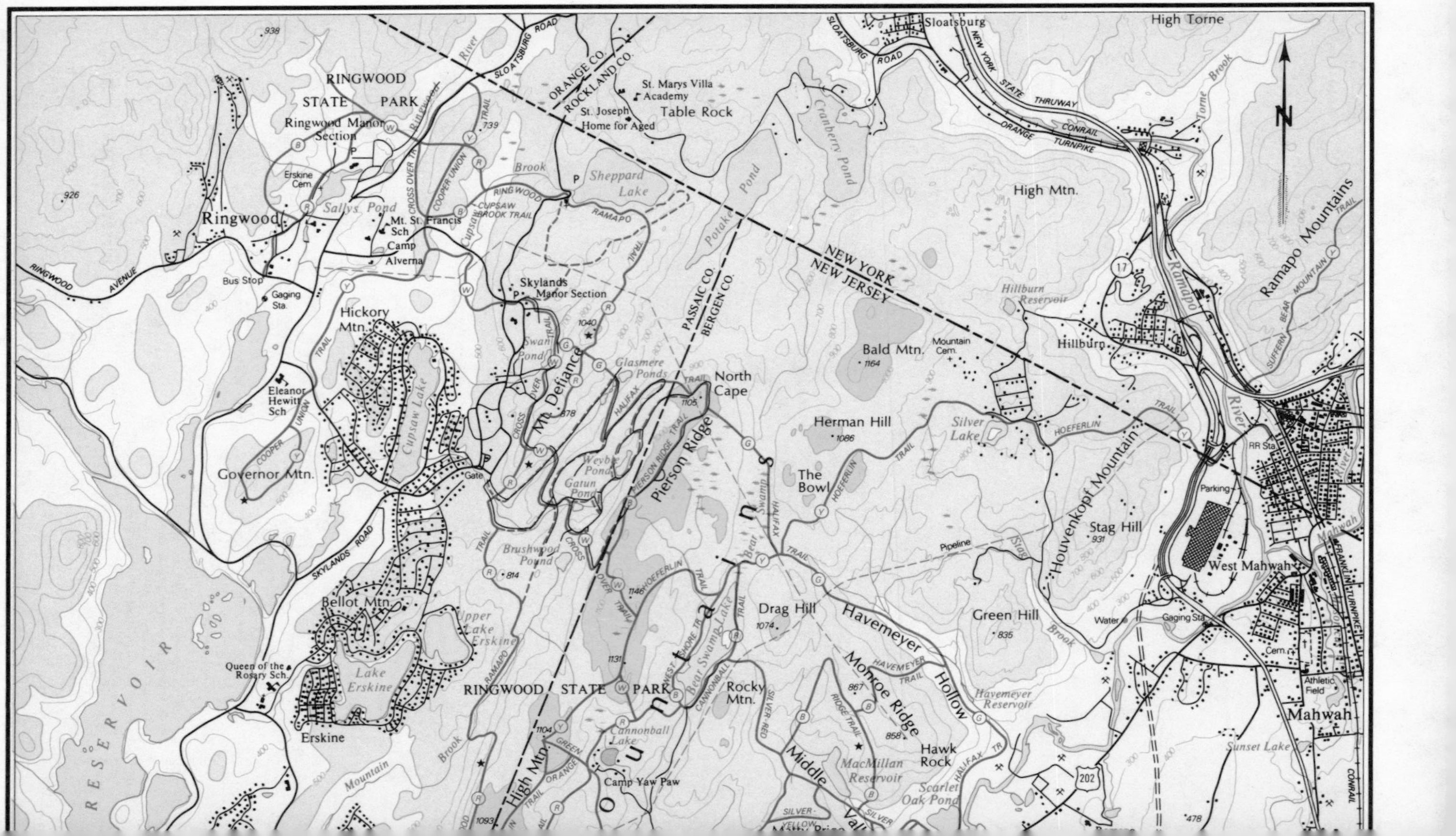

High Torne
Sloatsburg
SLOATSBURG ROAD
NEW YORK STATE THRUWAY
CONRAIL
ORANGE TURNPIKE
Torne Brook
Ramapo Mountains
SUFFERN BEAR MOUNTAIN TRAIL
High Mtn.
Cranberry Pond
Potake Pond
ORANGE CO.
ROCKLAND CO.
St. Marys Villa Academy
St. Joseph Home for Aged
Table Rock
RINGWOOD STATE PARK
Ringwood Manor Section
Erskine Cem.
Sallys Pond
Ringwood
RINGWOOD AVENUE
Bus Stop
Gaging Sta.
Mt. St. Francis Sch
Camp Alverna
CROSS OVER TR
COOPER UNION
CUPSAW BROOK TRAIL
RINGWOOD RAMAPO TRAIL
Sheppard Lake
Skylands Manor Section
NEW YORK
NEW JERSEY
PASSAIC CO.
BERGEN CO.
Hillburn Reservoir
Hillburn
Ramapo River
Mountain Cem.
Bald Mtn.
Hickory Mtn.
Swan Pond
Mt. Defiance
Glasmere Ponds
North Cape
Herman Hill
The Bowl
Silver Lake
HOEFERLIN TRAIL
Houvenkopf Mountain
RR Sta.
Parking
Stag Hill
Pipeline
West Mahwah
Eleanor Hewitt Sch
Cupsaw Lake
Governor Mtn.
Gate
Weyble Pond
Gatun Pond
Pierson Ridge
Bear Swamp
Brushwood Pond
SKYLANDS ROAD
Bellot Mtn.
Upper Lake Erskine
Lake Erskine
Queen of the Rosary Sch.
Erskine
RINGWOOD STATE PARK
Drag Hill
Havemeyer Hollow
Green Hill
Water
Gaging Sta.
Cem.
Athletic Field
Mahwah
Bear Swamp Lake
WEST SHORE TR
Rocky Mtn.
Monroe Ridge
Hawk Rock
Havemeyer Reservoir
Sunset Lake
Cannonball Lake
Camp Yaw Paw
High Mtn.
Mountain
RESERVOIR
MacMillan Reservoir
Scarlet Oak Pond
Middle Vall
FRANKLIN TURNPIKE

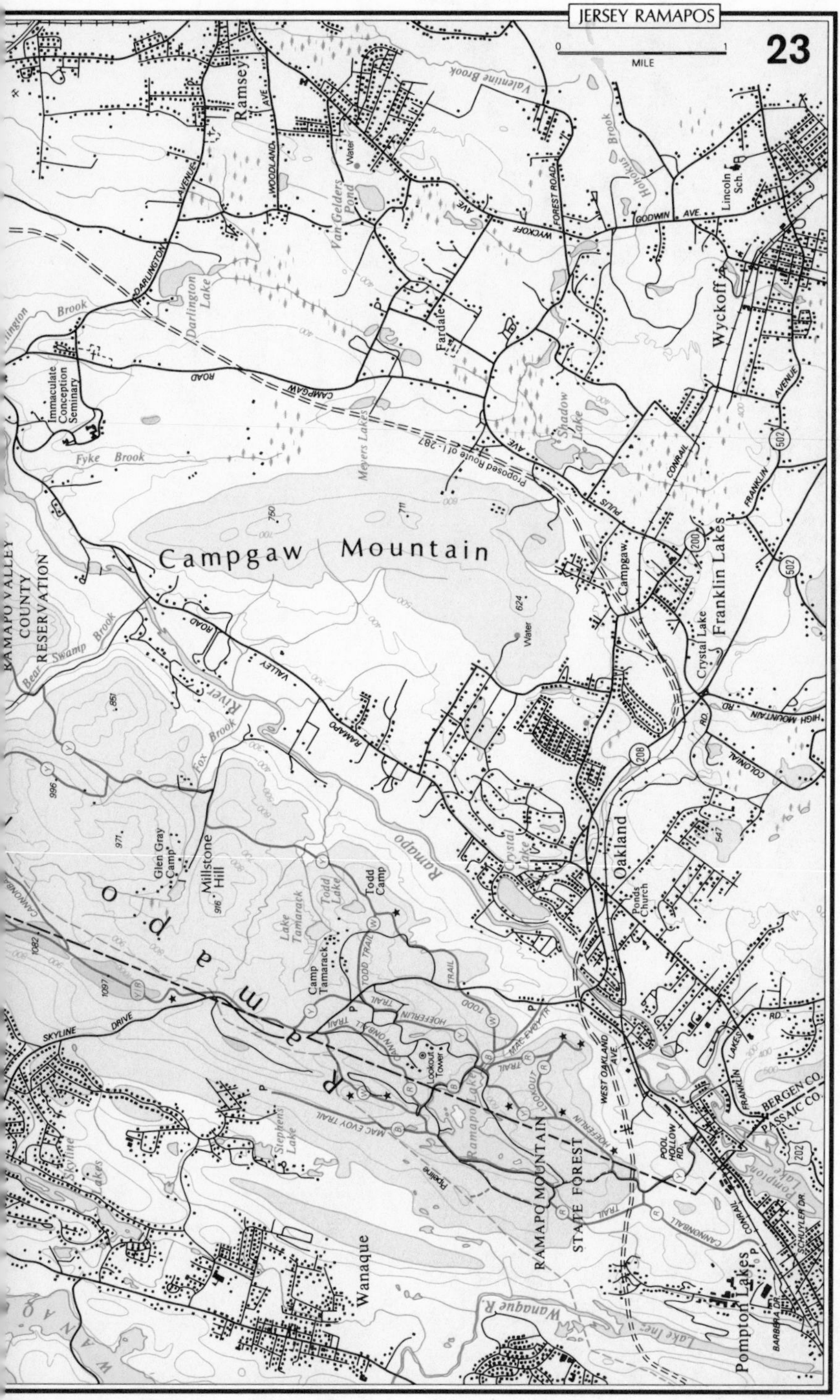
0
MILE
1
Ramsey
Valentine Brook
WOODLAND AVE.
Water
Van Gelders Pond
AVENUE
DARLINGTON
Darlington Lake
Brook
Immaculate Conception Seminary
ROAD
CAMPGAW
Fardale
WYCKOFF AVE
FOREST ROAD
Hohokus Brook
GODWIN AVE.
Lincoln Sch.
Wyckoff
AVENUE
502
Shadow Lake
Meyers Lakes
Proposed Route of I-287
Fyke Brook
AVE
PULIS
CONRAIL
FRANKLIN
750
Campgaw Mountain
Campgaw
200
Franklin Lakes
502
RAMAPO VALLEY COUNTY RESERVATION
Bear Swamp Brook
ROAD
VALLEY
RAMAPO
624
Water
Crystal Lake
HIGH MOUNTAIN RD
RD.
COLONIAL
851
River
Fox Brook
208
996
971
Glen Gray Camp
Millstone Hill
Ramapo
Oakland
Crystal Lake
547
916
Todd Lake
Todd Camp
Ponds Church
Lake Tamarack
Camp Tamarack
TODD TRAIL
TRAIL
1082
1097
SKYLINE DRIVE
HOEFFERLIN TRAIL
CANNONBALL TRAIL
TODD
MAC EVOY TR.
RD.
Lookout Tower
LOOKOUT TRAIL
WEST OAKLAND AVE.
FRANKLIN LAKES
BERGEN CO.
PASSAIC CO.
Stephens Lake
MAC EVOY TRAIL
Ramapo Lake
HOEFFERLIN
Pipeline
RAMAPO MOUNTAIN STATE FOREST
POOL HOLLOW RD.
202
Pompton Lake
Skyline Lakes
TRAIL
CANNONBALL
CONRAIL
SCHUYLER DR.
Wanaque
Wanaque R.
Lake Inez
Pompton Lakes
BARBARA DR.
WANAQUE